Praise for The Good Retreat Guide

'*The Good Retreat Guide* is indispensable.' *Traveller*

'To find peaceful retreats read this guide.' *Top Santé*

'An excellent publication that will give you dozens of ideas immediately.' *London*

'Europe's best-selling book on retreats.' *The Softback Review*

'Whether you fancy a music or yoga retreat, meditation workshop or simple solitude, this guide will help you choose your sanctuary.'
Zest

'I feel rested and refreshed after reading this calm, come-hither compendium.'
Christina Hardyman, *Telegraph Magazine*

'An inexpensive way of finding peace.' *Guardian*

'Spiritual sustenance without being force-fed.' *The Sunday Times*

'This fascinating book is not just a guide to the idyllic retreats of northern Europe, it's a guide to living.'
Daily Express

'The definitive guide.' *Marie Claire Health and Beauty*

'If you are on a quest for inner harmony, the guide might have the answer.'
Woman's Journal

'A flip through its pages is an eye-opening experience.'
Sunday Telegraph

'Deservedly popular and a very helpful book.' *Yoga and Health*

'Stafford Whiteaker encourages us to step off the world at least occasionally.'
The Universe

'Vital breaks from the pace of work.' *Time Out*

'Explains the differences and details the facilities and changes.' *Daily Express*

'Most notable is the inner-faith emphasis.' *The Tablet*

'Choose from Anglican, Buddhist, Roman Catholic or non-denominational with retreats in complete silence or interactive.'
Sunday Mirror

'Describes what you are likely to encounter at New Age centres, healing retreats or prayer retreats'.
Daily Telegraph

'The Good Re[...]iliated

Praise for *Tips* and *Retreats Guide*

The Good Retreat Guide details hundreds of Christian, Buddhist and non-affiliated retreats both here and on the Continent.
Tatler

THE GOOD RETREAT GUIDE

6TH EDITION

THE GOOD RETREAT GUIDE

6TH EDITION

STAFFORD WHITEAKER

HAY HOUSE

Australia • Canada • Hong Kong • India
South Africa • United Kingdom • United States

First published and distributed in the United Kingdom by:
Hay House UK Ltd, 292B Kensal Rd, London W10 5BE. Tel: (44) 20 8962 1230
Fax: (44) 20 8962 1239. www.hayhouse.co.uk

Please note: While every effort has been made to ensure that the information in this guide is accurate at the time of going to press, readers are advised that details and prices may be subject to change. We therefore strongly recommend that readers contact retreat centres directly in order to confirm the details of their stay and discuss their requirements, especially with respect to the availability of facilities for the disabled. *The Good Retreat Guide* is not a medical text and does not recommend using any practices or practitioners mentioned in this book as a substitute for orthodox medical treatment. Please be certain to consult your doctor or a licensed therapist before making any decisions that affect your physical and emotional health if you suffer from any diagnosed medical condition or have symptoms serious enough to interfere with your ordinary functioning. We do not recommend fasting for anyone under 21 years nor over 65 years nor for anyone suffering a pre-existing medical condition or who is in a post-operative state. We draw your attention to the established fact that ointments and oils rubbed onto the skin are absorbed into the bloodstream and this includes what are known as essential oils and that ingested herbal preparations and tisanes can act medicinally in the body. We do not recommend meditation or yoga or other spirituality practices for children unless conducted by teachers professionally qualified to work specifically with children in these areas. We do not believe children under 16 years should receive healing therapies or treatments of any kind at any retreat centres. We strongly urge all parents to be satisfied that those giving children's and young people's retreats, classes, courses or group camps have been suitably vetted under national child safety procedures. *The Good Retreat Guide* contains addresses to external websites where we believe that such links are relevant and add to the information supplied by us. These links are provided in good faith, and we cannot be held accountable for their content or any changes to their content or if the location (URL) changes.

A catalogue record for this book is available from the British Library.

ISBN 978-1-84850-187-4

Printed in the UK by CPI William Clowes Ltd, Beccles, NR34 7TL.

All of the papers used in this product are recyclable, and made from wood grown in managed, sustainable forests and manufactured at mills certified to ISO 14001 and/or EMAS.

ACKNOWLEDGEMENTS

Kimberley Didden, Associate Editor of *The Good Retreat Guide, 6th Edition*.

With thanks for assistance, reports on places, research and support to Annie Sachs-Marie, Dianne Davies, Michael Brisbane, Jo Wood, Lionel Lefevre, Anna Howard, Sue Frogg, Urs Mattmann, Ann Barlow Carr, David Gadsby, Ingrid Palairet, Ros Frecker, Emma Badley and to the many readers who sent in opinions and information. Guide website design by Stuart Skelton. Website programming and IT assistance by Terry Pugh.

For my daughter, Victoria

CONTENTS

RETREAT CENTRES BY REGION

PREFACE

Today we are witnessing a vast breakdown in every society's traditional cultures and customs, and even in its languages. Some of this may be for the good, but a lot of it is bad for us. It has resulted in a loss of faith in political, scientific and religious institutions. Disorientation, loneliness and fear continue to grow even as the world is drawn into a single global community through technology and communications. On top of that, we behold a planet being destroyed by our all-consuming greed. In such a situation, we must have time to reflect and to reassess our values. It is not just being able to think about it but to *feel* it at a deep level. This has to take place in our inner spiritual realm.

We need time, space and peace to be able to do this and that is what retreats are offering today. Moreover, they can serve to inspire us to hope and to act on that hope. Such profound changes to the way we are have a foundation made from spiritual matter. It is like a commitment in a relationship. We don't make it just by our mind and body; it is our heart that signs the deal and says, *Yes, this is right!*

Some would say that giving such a place of honour to retreats, in shaping the future of ourselves and our world, is unreal. However, it is not just the millions who go on retreat that bear witness to the importance of retreating in modern life. It is the growing millions who are going on retreat who do *not* belong to any one faith, any one religion or spiritual way. These are pilgrim seekers – asking questions, finding answers and reclaiming spiritual traditions and practices as their own heritage. Most retreat houses have had to choose either to create programmes that preach to the converted or to rethink and offer events and courses for retreats that meet this contemporary searching for spiritual values and practices.

This leads, of course, to consider whether this proliferation of retreats with such wide varieties of themes and types of programmes is not simply making retreats into yet another consumer choice. Have retreats, then, just become a cherry bowl for picking and choosing? Many religious leaders think this is the case. We disagree. We think the bigger the bowl, the more choice, the better. We are long past the time when the average person in the Western hemisphere spoke of sin and felt being spiritual necessitated some kind of self-inflicted punishment or was a matter of someone's else's authority. The journey to the oneness of the universe is different for each person. There are no rules. Some, like the mystics in all the religions, do arrive at a spiritual destination, but most of us dawdle along the way and are happy just to keep going. God and the common ground of universal being are uniquely hidden and mysteriously revealed to each of us as individuals. People today want the liberty to choose what most opens their hearts to peace and compassion. We believe this is why having a wide choice in spiritual matters, including the kind of retreats you choose, is likely to make more saints than spoiled sinners.

Regardless of what brought you to a retreat or whatever its form, type or spiritual practice, your ultimate goal remains love – for love is the real liberty of self. Love is the crown jewel of human life. Seek it.

Stafford Whiteaker

Visit the *Guide*'s website at www.thegoodretreatguide.com or email Stafford on whiteaker@wanadoo.fr for more information or to tell him about a retreat you have been on. Both positive and negative reports are welcomed.

INTRODUCTION

The Good Retreat Guide is for everyone. It does not matter whether you are just beginning your spiritual journey or you are an experienced pilgrim on the spiritual path. It is for seekers of faith, explorers of the heart, tasters of truth, church-goers, chasers of dreams, and those who believe in no gods. Everyone in fact who hears an inner voice that calls them to peace and respite from this busy and too often cruel world. It is for all who still yearn for that elusive feeling of being one with the universe.

The choice of retreats is huge today. Some are traditional and some are new developments. The most popular retreats are all forms of meditation and yoga, silent ones, Buddhist teachings and practices, and those like *Lectio Divina* which introduce new approaches to deepening faith for non-monastic Christians. Others like spa and healing therapies help us listen to mind, body and soul.

WHAT IS A RETREAT?

A retreat is an inward exploration that lets our feelings open out and gives us access to both the light and dark corners of our deepest feelings and relationships. For most it will be a movement away from the ego and towards peace. For many it will be an awakening to the presence of God in their lives.

Retreats are not a new phenomenon. All the world's great religions have found that men and women need at times to withdraw temporarily from daily living in order to nourish their spiritual life. Moses retreated to Mount Sinai. Jesus went into the desert. Buddhists annually make a retreat. Muslims go for a day of prayer and fasting within the mosque. The Hindu withdraws to the temple or wanders alone across the land.

A retreat is not just an escape from reality, because personal stillness is a very great challenge in this age of noise, diversion and aggression. Most of us have lives that are rushed, confusing, too challenging and with too many responsibilities and relationships to balance. Time has become an enemy to conquer. Going on a retreat gives you a break from all that. Suddenly, there are no radios, televisions, friends, children, pets and the constant background of human activity. There is no gossip, no grumbling, no meetings, no decisions, no interference with where you are inside yourself. You are faced with you alone. At last you have some space. You begin to slip into a slower physical, mental and emotional gear and start to think differently. In these moments your retreat truly begins, for this new consciousness starts a meditation on self that is the giving of undivided attention to your spirit. Some have said that it is opening the door to God. But going on retreat is not necessarily about having spiritual experiences. You might have one, but most people don't. It is about refreshing yourself, relaxing and taking an interior journey. Reassessment about your life and relationships and values can happen. And why not? What other time have you ever had to do it?

DO YOU NEED A RETREAT?

So what happens when one day you wake up and – in spite of the good job, the right relationship, even the children you always wanted, and all those many signs of a successful lifestyle – you start asking yourself: 'Is this all there is to life?'

Such a question usually brings a sense of discomfort and unease. Some people cope by ignoring it or finding new roles or activities to boost their confidence, but many more today are accepting the challenge and discovering that increasing the awareness of self can be an exciting and rewarding one. The self is always with you, like an irritating little jingle that you cannot get out of your head. It spins around and around and is always there. Everything you feel and do is filtered through this sense of self. Even sleep offers no escape. Call it self-awareness, self-identity or consciousness but the sense of self is intrinsic to being human. Most people take little time to look deeper inside themselves to discover what the nature is of this inner self who so dominates their lives. If you find yourself in such a position, you have already begun to be in touch with the search for something more in life. You need a retreat.

You will be joining millions of others in the search for the spirit of themselves and the world around them. After decades of catering for the demands of our minds and bodies, the spiritual has truly risen to restake its claim in our well-being. Drawn by inner needs that we only partially understand, we want to comprehend the universal in our lives. Here alone may lie the answer to that question: 'Is this all there is to life?' This quest for the sacred for most people is inspired by the simple need to connect their lives to something larger – that invisible and mysterious dimension which some call the universe and others simply 'God'.

WHO GOES ON A RETREAT?

At a retreat centre you will meet people of all ages and from every kind of background – students, housewives, grandparents, businessmen and women, the millionaire celebrity and the unknown poor. It is a kind of spiritual club with membership open to all. A group retreat can be fun and a time of making new friends. Even on a private retreat you are likely to meet interesting people.

DO YOU HAVE TO BE RELIGIOUS?

Men and women of all faiths and those of none go on retreat. You do not have to believe in God. You do not have to be a Christian or Buddhist to go on a retreat in a monastery. The important factor is your positive decision to take this time for the nourishment and enrichment of your spiritual life. Access to places of the Islamic faith is a different matter and you must enquire first as to the position.

PEOPLE YOU MAY MEET ON A RETREAT

Having placed yourself among strangers at a retreat, you may meet people you like at once, those you do not want to know better and those who may make a nuisance of themselves – the kind of person who has some problem and cannot help talking about it to everyone they meet. You may also encounter another kind of person: someone who persists in hammering away about God and salvation or the greening of the planet or why vegetarianism or raw juicing is the key to happiness. This is apt to annoy even the most virtuous and polite. If cornered by this sort of person, don't be embarrassed about cutting it short. You are there for another purpose, so excuse yourself without hesitation and go away at once to your room or for a walk. On the other hand, you may find it both charitable and instructive to *really listen* to what the person is saying – even if you do not believe a word of it.

GOING ON RETREAT FOR THE FIRST TIME

Nothing is obligatory on a retreat unless the organisers state it in their programme. You do not have to discuss any of your beliefs or feelings unless *you* want to. When you arrive, you can expect to be welcomed and made to feel at home. Don't worry about what to do next – someone will tell you what the arrangements are for all the basics like meal times, etc. You are not obliged to attend any activities if you choose not to. A typical Buddhist day retreat may have more silence and certainly more formal meditation times. At a Mind Body Spirit centre, the day may well include active practice sessions and involve treatment or therapy options. When you book, get all the details if it is a course or group retreat.

OBTAINING SPIRITUAL HELP AND SPIRITUAL DIRECTION

If you need to talk to someone about your life or your personal problems, many retreat places offer time for personal interviews of this nature. However, such talks should lead to some spiritual benefit. A spiritual director or guide is someone who helps you in your spiritual journey by being a good listener and by making suggestions for meditation, reading, study or prayer. They are often religious men and women, clergy or lay people who have had special training and experience in helping people with spiritual matters. Those with overriding emotional and psychological problems should seek help elsewhere unless this kind of counselling by professionally trained and qualified people is specifically offered at the retreat centre.

TALKING ON RETREAT

Since guests come on retreat to seek peace in order to restore a healthy balance in mind and spirit, a guest house should be a place of quiet and recollection. Guests should not engage members of the resident community or other guests in unnecessary chatter.

MEALS

Most retreat houses offer home-cooked meals that are traditional for their country. Some have their own restaurants. Retreat houses that offer Mind Body Spirit, yoga, Tai Chi and other such practices are often vegetarian. They almost always can do special diets. Buddhist retreats are vegetarian. There are more meat and fish dishes in Spain and much more meat served in Eastern European countries. Conversely, you will find a wider selection of vegetarian-type cuisine in Asia. If you go on retreat in France, most retreat places do not cater for vegetarians – unless it is run by British people. Britain leads Europe in vegetarian, vegan, dairy-free, wheat-free, fruitarian and other various special diets. For some people these are diets based on a medical diagnosis. For many they are a matter of personal choice. Many retreat places simply do not have the time, money or know-how to cater for such personal diets.

TAKING YOUR PET ON RETREAT

There are excellent reasons why most retreat places do not accept pets. A guest house is for a diverse collection of people, and some may not like domestic animals while others may be allergic to them. Retreat houses normally allow guide dogs.

SMOKING AND DRINKING

'No smoking' is sometimes listed and sometimes not by retreat houses. Buddhist places do not usually allow it. It is better to assume no smoking is permitted and, if you do still smoke, to ask where you can do it. Alcohol is forbidden if you are a Muslim. Buddhists do not permit alcohol on the premises. Most Christian places are not concerned one way or the other as long as you do not get drunk.

GENDER AND GUEST HOUSES

If you have accommodation inside a monastery rather than in the guest house, then a female community usually receives women only and a male community only men. A guest house may welcome everyone or just be for one gender. Some nuns do not receive men unless they are clergy, monks or in a family. This is for the protection of the women. Buddhist monasteries have separate sleeping accommodation for men and women – even when they are a married couple.

GOING ON RETREAT FOR PEOPLE WITH
DISABILITIES

Many retreat accommodations have not yet been updated to the national standard set for the disabled. Increasingly, retreat houses are including high-standard access for the disabled. However, these facilities rarely provide for those who need to be accompanied by a carer. If you are disabled, always double-check when booking so that you are certain of exactly what is on offer.

SPIRITUALITY AND HEALTH

Scientific studies suggest that the stress reduction produced by meditation could effect changes in the brain that cut stress hormones and could also help to lessen the risk factors of atherosclerosis. This is just one of the over 100,000 medical and health studies coming from non-religious affiliated research institutes which have appeared to establish a positive link between regular spiritual practices, such as meditation, prayer and regular church attendance, and health benefits. Today, a number of universities, including the University of Manchester, have a designated chair in spirituality and health within their medical schools. Many of the findings of such studies have been used as the basis of reformulating medical and nursing schools' best patient practices. In addition, some neurologists claim evidence for physical changes in the brain as outcomes of some meditation practices. Believe what you will about cause and effect, but healing and transformation through spiritual practices do take place.

THE APPEAL OF SILENCE

Finding silence in ordinary life today is nearly impossible. So it has become a much-desired commodity and is paying dividends to many retreat houses who can offer it. It has been said that silence is our first language and so it is not surprising that we long for it. Meditation, contemplation and interior prayer are just a few of the ways into an inner silence that can be maintained. We can also try for greater outward silence at home – turn off the radio, television and music, put away the MP3 player, turn off the mobile and learn to work in a more peaceful environment. This is hard stuff, but if you found the silence on your retreat rewarding, then why not try it at home?

STAYING IN A MONASTERY

Many people who have never stayed in a convent or monastery fear they will feel awkward and out of place. Once you understand the daily routine and discover that the monks or nuns are also ordinary folk, then you will relax. As a guest, you may expect to be received with warmth and affection. Buddhist monasteries are not much different from Christian ones. Some Christian monasteries belong to *enclosed* orders, like that of the Carmel sisters. This means that the community members remain in their part of the monastery, separate from the world. There will be a Guest Sister or Brother who will see you. Within a monastery, the basics of life are in most ways like those of the outside world. Monks and nuns must eat and sleep. They have emotional ups and downs like all of us. There are health complaints and moans about changes that take place. The religious life is supposed to make you more human, not less, and even saints have been assailed with doubts. In a monastic guest house, you get up when you want to, and if you do not feel like attending any parts of a retreat programme, no one is likely to demand that you do so. Most Christian monasteries do not ask or expect you to attend their religious services. Yet why not do it anyway? You do not have to be religious to experience the inspiring feelings that a group chanting the Psalms can bring. Your presence at at least one daily office in a monastery is a sign of the spiritual activity you have undertaken by going on retreat there. Most Buddhist monasteries require you to participate in the meditation periods even if you do not take part in the devotional practices.

HEALTH AND HOLIDAY SPA RETREATS

Spas and their treatments and well-being programmes are in much fashion these days. You can breeze up the M1 to a luxury weekend of Ayurvedic massage and Reiki, or buy a special to Bali and relax with Ananda yoga, a nature walk and some rejuvenation cuisine. All these and dozens more types of treatments, therapies and relaxing situations are on offer and we say, 'Great!' Their aim of greater inner awareness and peace is the same one as in a monastery. Okay, you probably will take a dip in a pool instead of singing the Psalms, yet you will begin to relax and unwind, and to forget about the illusions and cares of a confusing world. From such a point, thinking about your life, your values and what it all means can be just a short step away. These health and holiday spa retreats are not holidays as most people understand them. They are places with staff, facilities and programmes deliberately designed to enhance your well-being. With such greater peacefulness, the heart can begin to unfold. It is a moment in time, a pause, a reflection, a space and place just to be. So when you next see a photo of a woman blissfully being massaged, don't think she is just there for more a beautiful body, because she may be seeking some soul time. In any case, whoever said you had to be in a church to find God?

CHRISTIAN SPIRITUALITY

While there is a shared basic content in all Western Christian spirituality, the approaches to it may differ. There are many Christian paths, including the traditions of Anglican, English, Franciscan, Augustinian, Dominican and Benedictine spirituality, to name but a few. Some, such as Black spirituality and those from the Orthodox tradition, may be less familiar. Most people find, after a while, a particular way that seems to suit them. But for a Christian, Jesus Christ and Holy Scripture must be at the heart of the retreat.

BUDDHIST SPIRITUALITY

Buddhism is often called 'a way of harmony', for the Buddha's teachings offer a set of tools to find inner peace by working with your own feelings and experiences of life. This inner examination and insight is a direct method of transforming consciousness and is termed *meditation.*

MIND BODY SPIRIT SPIRITUALITY

This spirituality movement is a collection of practices aimed at personal growth. The majority of the ideas, techniques and approaches spring from well-established traditions of healing and self-discovery. Many of the approaches to health, healing and self-discovery that this form of spirituality has to offer are now part of everyday living in Western Europe.

WHAT IS PRAYER?

Each faith has its own tradition of prayer, which is a way of offering to a mysterious and unknown universal power your innermost and deepest feelings. These may be prayers for help or for the benefit of others or simply gratitude for your life. The Christian prayer, the 'Our Father', and the opening prayer of the Koran, when Allah, most glorious, most merciful, is praised and His guidance sought, are examples of outstanding and important single prayers to which all may turn.

WHAT IS MEDITATION?

Meditation is a stillness of body and a stillness of mind. There are many different meditation techniques to help you attain this state of being. Meditation methods are mainly drawn from Buddhist, Christian and Hindu sources, although some teachers have developed their own systems. Others are non-religious based. Meditation begins by relaxing the body into a state of stillness, then the mind into inner silence.

YOGA TODAY

One of the most significant developments in European spirituality over the last 20 years has been the widespread popularity and appeal of yoga. This ancient way to stillness, spiritual openness and better health is now practised by millions of people of all ages and from all walks of life. In addition to yoga centres, you will find that many retreat places offer yoga in their programmes.

BUDDHIST MINDFULNESS AND 'LIVING IN THE PRESENT' RETREATS

These two spiritual aspects have much in common. They both return us to the reality of the moment in which we are living. Most people worry all the time about yesterday, today and what might happen tomorrow. This causes great distress and makes us want to do something about it. This pressure to act makes us even more stressed. Becoming mindful and living in the present turns us towards a cultivation of contentment. It also increases awareness of our physical body and its messages.

BEREAVEMENT AND RETREATS

We are often asked to recommend a retreat for someone in the early stages of loss and grief. We do not feel that this is usually the right time to go on a retreat, because you would be changing surroundings, people and all your ordinary habits when you are already in an unsettled state. While prayer groups, meditation, group and personal sharing and much else that happens on a retreat are appropriate in themselves, we feel it is far better to find these locally, perhaps through your local church, synagogue, temple or mosque (even if you are not a member). There are also national organisations in most countries that will offer advice and help. It is better to wait until you are feeling better and less emotional and then go on a weekend group retreat which has a theme that really takes your interest. You will get more out of it then and also give more of your usual self to others.

IS GOD FEMALE?

It is no longer rare and, indeed, it never seems to have been formally forbidden for Christians sometimes to change the gender of God in reading scripture or in their devotions. Even if you are not a Christian, it can be a bit of shock to hear God called *Mother*. While the historical Jesus was male, in God there is neither male nor female. With women's liberation and the movement towards equality for all, it is helpful to many women *and* men to recognize this and deliberately to leave behind the traditional male hierarchical structure of their religion at least once in a while. It brings a new perspective and often liberates how we might perceive the nature of the universal force of life.

DIFFERENT KINDS OF RETREATS

The choice of spirituality retreats, courses and workshops is now so wide that, hopefully, there is a retreat available for everyone, whether they are a person of faith or none, just a pilgrim on the journey of life, or a seeker of better self-awareness and development – and not forgetting the millions who simply need some peace and quiet in which to relax and refresh themselves. Here are just a few of the kinds of retreats you may find on offer.

Beginners' retreats Beginners' retreats are for those who starting off for the first time with spiritual practices such as meditation or yoga.

Bereavement retreats Bereavement retreats are usually only for a weekend and are about living with loss.

Celtic spirituality retreats Rich in poems and songs, Celtic spirituality can bring an understanding of the depth of God's presence in his own creation. It is an ancient inheritance of Christian spirituality that has become newly appropriate in a time when we are concerned for the environment and the future of our planet.

Contemplative retreats Contemplative retreats have the aim of being still and, through silence and intuitive prayer, to hold yourself open to God.

Dance retreats Dance retreats help to release physical and emotional tensions and bring to the surface deep feelings and increased self-aware-ness. Sacred dancing is common to most spiritualities and the Sufis remind us *to dance with joy*! The Christian Psalms tell us the same thing.

Day retreats Day retreats are very flexible. It might be a day for si-lence, a theme- or activity-centred day, a time for group discussion or talks, or for lessons in meditation technique. The day retreat is rather like a mini retreat. It allows you to explore a number of different types of retreat during the year without taking a great deal of time away from your ordinary life.

Drop-in retreats Drop-in retreats are non-residential. The idea is that you live at home or stay elsewhere and 'drop in' to take part in the resident community's regular pattern of worship or for a series of talks and other activities planned around a programme.

Eco-spirituality, nature and permaculture retreats Eco-spirituality, nature and permaculture retreats link caring for the environment to your life and they help you gain an increased awareness of the unity of all things in creation. These are active retreats, but ones in which stillness, meditation or prayer can also play their part. They include adventure, farm, fishing, hiking, nature, outdoor activity and wilder-ness retreats.

Embroidery, calligraphy and painting retreats Embroidery, callig-raphy and painting retreats are theme retreats that focus on awaken-ing personal creativity through a craft or other art form. There can be many other subjects as themes, such as pottery, poetry, music, garden-ing – the list is extensive.

Enneagram retreats The Enneagram is a method intended to help you see yourself in the mirror of your mind, especially images of your personality that have become distorted by your basic attitudes to yourself. Representing a journey into self, the purpose of the Enneagram is self-enlightenment.

Family retreats Family retreats, which are held at places that have suitable facilities, give a family the experience of going on retreat together. These retreats need to be well planned and worked out so that each member of the family, from the youngest to the oldest, has a real chance to benefit from the experience. Buddhist centres and monasteries often have children's *Dahampasala*, which is a school study-session held each Sunday. Otherwise family retreats are often organised by larger Christian retreat and holiday centres who specialise in this type of event.

Gardening and prayer retreats Most retreat houses have good gardens, and this form of eco-spirituality retreat combines some practical work with various spiritual practices.

Gay and lesbian retreats Gay and lesbian retreats can address and be supportive of the problems gay and lesbian people may have in gaining access to established church life and to various spirituality groups. Such retreats often have themes that bear directly on living as a gay or lesbian person within society and which link into spiritual matters.

Group retreats Group retreats are usually led by someone who acts as a facilitator. Group retreats often have a theme or cover a particular topic or approach to spirituality.

Healing retreats Healing retreats may use prayer, meditation, chanting, the laying-on of hands, treatments or therapies. Healing may be concerned with a physical complaint but is more likely in retreat terms to focus on the healing of the whole person in order to eliminate obstacles to personal and spiritual growth. Such centres may offer detox, fasting, stress management and weight loss retreats.

Hermitage and Poustinia retreats Hermitage and Poustinia retreats are solitary, usually self-catering retreats in separate accommodation in situations of solitude. They are a Buddhist and Christian tradition, and retreat places are offering more such experiences.

Holistic retreats Holistic retreats make use of one or more of the many healing therapies and techniques now available. Some may be ancient practices like Ayurveda or herbal medicine or more contemporary concepts such as Aromatherapy. All are designed to relax the person and to bring about whole-person healing.

Icon retreats Icon retreats are about creating and/or using a religious work of art as a form of prayer. It is an established Christian spiritual tradition, particularly in the Orthodox Church. You do not have to be an artist to enjoy and benefit from such an experience. Similar to this, but in the Hindu tradition, is *yantra* painting, offered by a number of yoga centres.

Ignatian retreats Ignatian retreats are based on the spiritual exercises originated in the sixteenth century by the founder of the Jesuits, Saint Ignatius of Loyola. A selected retreat director works with you on a one-to-one basis and provides different material from the Gospels for your daily contemplative meditation. You then discuss what this has provoked within you. It is a way of spiritual practice that is designed for anyone, whether Christian or not.

Individually guided retreats Individually guided retreats are often structured around a particular system of spiritual exercises, such as those of Saint Ignatius, or based upon a defined form of meditation such as Vipassana, one of India's most ancient forms of meditation. Buddhists do such retreats regularly.

Inner child retreats Inner child retreats seek to bring you into contact with the most real and innocent part of yourself to renew and bring to life a greater sense of your true nature and inner being.

Insight retreats Insight retreats are especially good for people who have had no contact with a church or religion. It introduces them to a new vocabulary of spirituality and helps demystify religion. It is especially suitable for young men and women who are seeking access to forms of spirituality and the possible spiritual or religious paths they might take.

Journalling retreats Journalling retreats introduce you to the concept and practice of keeping a journal as a spiritual exercise. The aim is to become more sensitive to the content of your life and to see the continuity of your spirituality.

Lectio Divina retreats *Lectio Divina* is an ancient Christian tradition in which a slow meditative reading, usually of Holy Scripture, results in a state of inner prayer and contemplation. Part of the daily devotional practices of Christian monasteries, it is being done today by an increasing number of lay people. There is also a form of this contemplative study in the Buddhist tradition.

Meditation retreats While all retreats usually allow some time for individual meditation, there is a demand for retreats specifically aimed at the study and practice of meditation. The Buddhist response to this has been excellent. In Christianity, there has been a worldwide revival of earlier Christian approaches to meditation.

Mind Body Spirit retreats Mind Body Spirit retreats are very popular and go under a number of rather exciting titles such as *Soul Journeying, Awakening the Inner Self, Speaking with Your Angel, What Your Dreams Tell You* and *Awareness of the Inner Woman*. They are usually structured around rest, relaxation and inner discovery. The list of what is offered is extensive.

Music and dance retreats Music and dance are ancient aspects of religious worship and the praise of the sacred. The Psalms call Christians to bring forth their songs, trumpets, lutes, harps and timbrels, and to dance. Don't worry if you can't sing very well or if you don't play a musical instrument or if you have never danced. Such retreats are a joyous encounter.

Myers-Briggs retreats Isabel Myers-Briggs spent 40 years investigating personality types, building upon the research into personality done by Carl Jung. By discovering which personality type you are, you select the form of spirituality that best suits you.

Open door retreats Open door retreats provide help to make a retreat in your own home while having the direction and support of a like-minded local group.

Preached retreats Preached retreats are traditionally conducted religious Christian retreats which may be limited to a group from a parish or other organisation or may be open for anyone to join in. The retreat conductor may be a clerical, religious or lay person. Sharing together is a feature of these retreats.

Private retreats Private retreats are those in which you go alone as an individual. It is usually a silent time in which you find solitude in order to reflect, rest and meditate. You are separate from others so that you can maintain this framework of silence.

Renewal retreats Renewal retreats are Christian and aim to achieve a new awareness of the presence of Christ, a deeper experience of the Holy Spirit and a clearer understanding for the committed Christian of his or her mission in the Church.

Salesian spirituality retreats Francis de Sales (1567–1622) believed that a person did not have to enter a monastery to develop a deep spirituality. He suggested five steps for spiritual growth, which progress from a desire for holiness through the practice of virtue to methods for spiritual renewal. His methods are very gentle and have always enjoyed wide appeal among people living ordinary lives.

Silent retreats Silent retreats are an adventure into stillness. Silence is one of the most powerful of all spiritual aids.

Spa retreats Spa retreats are those held at places where facilities featured help relaxation and de-stressing and help to build up physical and emotional well-being. Such centres can be purpose-designed or part of a hotel or holiday complex as well as a facility within a retreat place, such as a yoga centre.

Shrine and temple retreats Shrine and temple retreats are increasingly popular in Asia with ordinary business travellers, who want to stay somewhere different from the usual hotel – a place where they can learn new values or simply practise meditation in suitable surroundings. Asian temples and shrines do take short-stay guests and word about them is spreading beyond the young backpacking generation.

Silver retreats go under a number of names and are quite new to the retreat scene. These are now offered at some leading-edge luxury hotels, especially those in international global business cities such as Hong Kong. You are offered a chance to devote some of your personal time during your stay to a local charitable project, usually one linked with local poverty or environment issues. This may look like a cop-out for a global money-grubber who wants to ease his or her conscience, but that is not the case. Those who must travel a lot for business are often bored with the homogeneous environment of international hotels and find the gym or spa facilities rather repetitive and meaningless. Getting out for a few hours of organised activity that is totally different makes for both a change and challenge. When it is charitable, it relates to compassion and holds meaning. Thus this new type of retreat can serve a serious spiritual purpose in the lives of materially successful people by returning them to an awareness of other people's needs and a better balance of self – aspects so often lost in a busy career and so often needed.

Teresian spirituality retreats These are based on the steps described by Saint Teresa of Avila (1515–82) in *The Interior Castle*. She wrote the text in order to lead individuals from the beginnings of spiritual growth to the heights of mysticism.

Theme and activity retreats Theme and activity retreats are a very popular type of retreat. You enter an activity, such as painting, singing, gardening, embroidery or dance, through which you bring together your feelings, senses and intuition into a greater awareness of self, of others and of God.

Weekend retreats Weekend retreats are the most popular form of retreat and usually have a theme or are about a spiritual path or practice. There will be times for lectures, practice, stillness, discussions, walks, reflection, reading and just resting. It is all simple, easy and peaceful.

Wisdom retreats Wisdom retreats are usually for women in which the spirituality of ageing is considered.

Yoga retreats Yoga retreats employ body and breathing exercises to achieve greater physical balance and mental stillness as an aid to meditation and contemplation. Yoga is a spiritual practice involving the whole person.

USING THE GUIDE

CONTACT DETAILS

Telephone and fax numbers, email and website addresses are given, but these can change. The ones we have given are those correct at time of publication as far as we could determine.

TYPE OF SPIRITUALITY

The first given is the spirituality or religion of the place, followed by what other traditions they may follow.

KEY TO THE SYMBOLS

 Highly Recommended by the Guide.

 All meals vegetarian or will serve vegetarian food.

 Practises ecological and environmental policies.

KEY TO WHAT IS OFFERED

Retreats   A place of retreat or has accommodation for personal or group stays.

Workshops and Courses   In addition to retreats, they have related programmes.

Church/Temple   They have a church, chapel, temple, meditation hall, prayer room or space set aside for quiet and contemplation.

Yoga   Yoga retreats, courses, classes, teaching or practice.

Meditation   Meditation retreats, courses, teaching, practice, community or group practice.

Spiritual Help   Able to give spiritual guidance, personal direction or talks.

Bed and Breakfast   Offer B&B only or in addition to full board.

Vegetarian Food   Vegetarian meals only or will provide vegetarian food.

Organic Food   Serves organic food as much as possible, home grown or locally bought.

Venue for Hire   Meeting and conferences rooms and space for hire to groups.

Self-Catering Space   Accommodation or space for self-catering.

Alternative Therapies   Offers or can arrange therapies and treatments.

Holistic Holidays   Offers well-being therapies, treatments and facilities for Mind Body Spirit.

Community Living   There is a resident religious or lay group at the place.

Work Retreats   Work available for learning about the resident group life or to pay for your stay.

Vocations   Offers membership in the resident lay or religious group.

Hermitages   Offers accommodation separate from the main facility away from other people.

Camping   Offers camping in grounds or allows mobile homes or caravans.

Children   Those under 16 years allowed to stay with their families.

Pets   Personal pets are allowed.

GREEN RETREATS

British retreat places are generally trying to be ecologically conscious these days and we applaud such efforts. We discovered many places did some things like changing the type of lighting or recycling. Many had written up good plans intending to be more green in the future. Some had put into effect a few of their ideas. Far too many seemed to be doing nothing. However, we wanted to find out just how many were actually managing to fulfil best green-practice requirements. So we sent them all a questionnaire asking them how green they thought they were and to list what they did. Those on the list below are the places we felt qualified as green. They have a variety of core spiritual traditions. Some of them are doing exciting advanced ecological management and projects. Regardless of religion or spirituality, they were all eco-spiritual in outlook and practice.

Name	Place
Ammerdown	England
Ard Nohoo Eco Retreat	Ireland
Ashwin Balanced Living Centre and Personal Retreat	Scotland
Baraka-Gardens Mountain and Desert Garden Retreats	Egypt
Braziers Park	England
Burren Yoga and Meditation Centre	Ireland
Caudet Radha Yoga Centre	France
Centre de la Luna	France
Cornish Tipi Holidays	England
Cum y Cyrt	Wales
Ffald-y-Brenin Christian Retreat Centre	Wales
Gatekeeper Trust	England
Hilfield Friary	England
Holy Cross Whitland	Wales
Krishnamurti Centre	England
Ladywell Centre	England
Le Tertre	France
Middle Piccadilly Spa Retreat	England
Oak Barn Workshop Centre	England
Othona Community, Bradwell-on-Sea, Essex	England
Othona Community, Bridport, Dorset	England
Viveka Yoga Retreats and Holidays	France

ENGLAND

LONDON

• •

Alternatives
St James Church
197 Piccadilly
London W1J 9LL
England

Tel: 0207 2876711
Fax: 0207 7347449
Email: admin@alternatives.org.uk
Website: www.alternatives.org.uk

Workshops and Courses • Church/Temple

Christian – Inter-denominational – Open spirituality

The intention of Alternatives is to provide a space in the heart of central London where people can explore new visions for living in a spirit of openness and community. It is a non-profit-making organisation that has run talks and workshops with great success since 1982. All events are offered in a spirit of service and are open to all. The programmes are wide ranging and cover diverse approaches to living and to spirituality. Talks are at the church and usually start at 19:00. The cost is around £10 (concession rate, £5). Workshops may be held at different venues around London.

Ananda Marga Centre
3a Cazenove Road
London N16 6PA
England

Tel: 0208 8064250
Email: london@anandamarga.org.uk
Website: www.anandamarga.org.uk

Retreats • Workshops and Courses • Yoga • Meditation

Yoga – Meditation

The Ananda Marga movement was founded by the Indian philosopher, teacher and poet P. R. Sarkar. Yoga and meditation are taught and practised as methods for self-development and self-realisation, while social service is emphasised as an outward expression of developing the human potential. Quiet, informal and friendly, there are classes in yoga postures and regular meetings for meditation. Creative writing and painting workshops are sometimes offered. Regular evenings of inspirational song, music and poetry draw the group and local community together. Weekly non-residential meditation classes are currently held at Euston, Stoke Newington and Holborn. A calendar of events and venues is on their website. There is also a centre in Chorlton (see Manchester section).

Benedictine Centre for Spirituality	Tel: 0208 4492499
Bramley Road	Email: retreats@bcsuk.wanadoo.co.uk
London N14 4HE	Website: www.benedictinecentreretreats.org.uk
England	

Retreats • Workshops and Courses • Church/Temple • Spiritual Help

Christian – Roman Catholic

The centre is at the Benedictine Parish Church of Christ the King and is adjacent to the monastery there – you may join the monks at prayer for the Divine Office and at Mass each day. On offer at the centre is a full programme of retreats and events with courses on a variety of spirituality subjects. There is a healing ministry for the sick, available to anyone, offering prayer and the laying on of hands.

OPEN: All year. Everyone welcome.
ROOMS: Please enquire about what is currently available.
FACILITIES: Chapel, prayer room, conference rooms, garden, nearby park, library, guest lounge.
SPIRITUAL HELP: Personal talks.
GUESTS ADMITTED TO: Church, chapel, prayer room.
MEALS: For day events, usually you bring a packed lunch. Otherwise for eating there, please enquire as to latest meal arrangements.
SPECIAL ACTIVITIES: Planned programme. Send for brochure or see online.
SITUATION: On the edge of a north London suburb with walks nearby and opposite a large country park in the green belt. Usually quiet but can be rather busy, especially in summer.
MAXIMUM STAY: By arrangement.
BOOKINGS: Letter, email.
CHARGES: Tea, coffee and lunch about £15 per person. Otherwise enquire for residential rates.
ACCESS: Underground: Piccadilly Line to Oakwood. Buses: 307 and 299. Car: M25 exit 24, A111.

Brahma Kumaris World Spiritual University　　Tel: 0208 7273350
Global Co-operation House　　Fax: 0208 7273351
65 Pound Lane　　Email: london@bkwsu.org
London NW10 2HH　　Website: www.bkwsu.org/uk
England

Retreats • Workshops and Courses • Meditation • Spiritual Help • Vegetarian Food

Open spirituality – Non-religious

Founded in 1937 in Karachi, the Brahma Kumaris World Spiritual University is an international organisation working at all levels of society for positive change. The University carries out a wide range of educational programmes for the development of human and spiritual values through its 3,000 branches in 62 countries. It is a non-governmental organisation affiliated to the United Nations Department of Public Information, and recipient of seven UN Peace Messenger Awards. The Brahma Kumaris World Spiritual University acknowledges the intrinsic goodness of all people and teaches a practical method of meditation that helps individuals understand their inner strengths and values. Courses, workshops, seminars and conferences covering a wide range of topics are on offer, including self-development, stress-free living, self-management, creating inner freedom, soul care, women's development and their core focus on meditation. The University operates the **Global Retreat Centre** at Nuneham Courtney near Oxford (see Oxfordshire entry).

*'Aim at heaven and you will get earth thrown in. Aim at earth
and you get neither'*
– C.S. Lewis

Buddhapadipa Temple
14 Calonne Road
Wimbledon
London SW19 5HJ
England

Tel: 0208 9461357
Fax: 0208 9445788
Email: dhammacaro@yahoo.co.uk/
dhammacaro@buddhapadipa.org
Website: www.buddhapadipa.org
Further info: The Lay Buddhist Association
Tel: 0208 9467410 / 0208 8702072
Appointments for further discussion: Venerable Phramaha Sangthong
Dhammacaro at dhammacaro@yahoo.co.uk

Retreats • Workshops and Courses • Church/Temple • Meditation
Spiritual Help • Vegetarian Food

Buddhist (Theravada tradition)

Wat Buddhapadipa was the first Buddhist temple in the United Kingdom. Its objective is to create a centre for the dissemination of theoretical and practical Buddhist teachings in Europe. The grounds cover a monastic area of approximately four acres, which includes a small grove, flower garden and an orchard. The temple, Uposatha Hall, is situated on an ornamental lake and consists of the house where the monks live and a cottage. On offer here are various forms of study and meditation courses. A summer retreat is usually held in September. Chants, which are usually in Pali, can be followed by the use of an English–Pali book, which is collected before entering the Uposatha Hall. Sometimes a monk may not be fluent in English so be patient when seeking information by telephone. There are Dharma talks and discussions in English on the programme.

OPEN: Most of the year. Receives men and women.
ROOMS: The temple itself has no facilities for guests except during the thrice-annual retreats but arrangements can be made elsewhere.
FACILITIES: Shrine room, study room, meditation garden. Sometimes part of the main garden.
SPIRITUAL HELP: 1-day retreats, personal talks, meditation, directed study.
GUESTS ADMITTED TO: Temple and most areas except community private ones.
MEALS: Everyone eats together. Vegetarian and Thai/wholefood.
SPECIAL ACTIVITIES: Telephone, email. Alternatively, write to or call the Lay Buddhist Association.
SITUATION: Urban.
MAXIMUM STAY: For duration of meditation period, class or course only.
BOOKINGS: Letter, fax, email, online booking request form.
ACCESS: Rail: Wimbledon station. Underground: District line to Putney Bridge, then Bus No. 93.

Canonesses of the Holy Sepulchre   Tel: 0207 4765490
Custom House   Website: www.canonesses.co.uk
71 Cundy Road
London E16 3DJ
England

Christian – Roman Catholic – Open to all

The sisters live in the Catholic Parish of the Royal Docks, near both St Anne's Church and the Garden Café, a meeting place for people needing support and encouragement. Their ministry is mainly with vulnerable people – asylum seekers and migrants, those with disabilities and with mental health problems, locally, in the London Borough of Newham and beyond. Once in a while, a retreat needs to be one in which you reach out to others and it seems to us that, if you live in London, why not take such a retreat with this community and help them with some of their work?

Cenacle Sisters   Email: cenaclesisters.walworth@virgin.net
142a Rodney Road   Website: freespace.virgin.net/cenacle.netley
Walworth
London SE17 1RA
England

Retreats • Workshops and Courses • Spiritual Help • Vegetarian Food
Alternative Therapies • Community Living • Vocations

Christian – Roman Catholic

The Cenacle at Walworth is a centre from which the Cenacle Sisters provide a range of programmes and therapies. Among these is an Ignatian Spirituality Course. Students are also taught for competence in the art of spiritual direction and in giving the spiritual exercises of St Ignatius. The centre does spiritual accompaniment for individuals and trains spiritual directors in the art of supervision.

Christian Meditation Centre	Tel: 0207 8339615
St Mark's	Fax: 0207 7136346
Myddelton Square	Email: uk@wccm.org
London EC1R 1XX	Website: www.christian-meditation.org.uk
England	

Workshops and Courses

Christian – Inter-denominational

This is a centre for the practice and teaching of meditation in the Christian tradition, following the method of John Main. It is under the auspices of the World Community for Christian Meditation. Other themes here are world peace and inter-faith dialogue.

Christian Meditation Retreat Centre	Tel: 0208 4491319
Monastery of Christ the King	Email: retreatcentre@wccm.org
6B Priory Close	Website: www.wccmretreatcentre.org.uk
London N14 4AS	
England	

Retreats • Workshops and Courses • Church/Temple • Yoga
Meditation • Spiritual Help • Self-Catering Space • Vegetarian food

Christian – Roman Catholic – Christian meditation

This is the retreat centre of the World Community for Christian Meditation, offering: day retreats for those beginning meditation, and those deepening their practice with personal guidance available; silent weekend retreats; themed retreats, which offer a contemplative approach to a wide variety of topics including young people's needs, addiction and bereavement.

OPEN: All year. Everyone welcome.
ROOMS: 2 singles, 6 doubles – all en suite. Also 1 double on ground floor.
FACILITIES: Church, chapel, library, meditation room.
SPIRITUAL HELP: Meditation, Divine Office, Mass. Spiritual direction is possible by prior arrangement.
GUESTS ADMITTED TO: All guest and public areas.
MEALS: Self-catering kitchen. Breakfast items usually provided.
SPECIAL ACTIVITIES: Planned retreats, specialising in meditation but other subjects on offer in programme. See online.
SITUATION: Urban, by a park, reasonably quiet.

MAXIMUM STAY: By arrangement.
BOOKINGS: Letter, telephone, email – online booking is easiest and best method.
CHARGES: Please enquire.
ACCESS: The Christian Meditation Retreat Centre is easily reached on the Piccadilly Line (alight at Oakwood).

Community of the Word of God
90–92 Kenworthy Road
London E9 5RA
England

Tel: 0208 9868511
Email: cwg90@btconnect.com

Retreats • Workshops and Courses • Church/Temple • Spiritual Help
Vegetarian Food • Self-Catering Space • Community Living

Christian – Inter-denominational

The Community of the Word of God was founded in east London in 1972. The pattern of the community's life is rather like that of a Christian family whose members seek to share the love of Christ and to encourage each other in their witness and work. Some follow secular occupations while others are home-based. The present community is made up of a small group of women who form a small evangelical lay community living in two terraced houses with a third, Emmaus House, for the guests. Although in the inner city, Emmaus House offers a place for people who are looking to get away from their daily routine. Retreats, which are usually traditional preached ones, are organised during the year and the larger ones held at different retreat venues.

OPEN: February to December. Closed January. Everyone welcome.
ROOMS: 1 or 2 singles usually available, 1 double.
FACILITIES: Chapel, garden, small library, guest lounge.
SPIRITUAL HELP: Personal talks, spiritual direction.
GUESTS ADMITTED TO: Everywhere except community living quarters.
MEALS: You may eat with the community or alone in the guest house, but self-catering facilities are limited. Traditional food. Vegetarian, special diets for medical reason.
SPECIAL ACTIVITIES: Retreats are organised during the year at various retreat places; for individual retreats they welcome you to their guest house.
SITUATION: In a city.
MAXIMUM STAY: 1 week. Longer stays negotiable.
BOOKINGS: Letter, telephone, email.
CHARGES: Donation towards costs if possible.
ACCESS: Train, bus and car all possible, but parking can be a problem.

Eagle's Wing Centre for Contemporary Shamanism and College of Shamanic Medicine BM Box 7475 London WCIN 3XX England

Tel: 01435 810233 / 01435 810308
Email: eagleswing@shamanism.co.uk
Website: www.shamanism.co.uk

Retreats • Workshops and Courses • Spiritual Help

Shamanism

All of us originate from shamanistic cultures because humans have always sought understanding and knowledge of the wider universe using a variety of experiential ways and tools. These practices are still in use in a surprisingly large number of places in the world and many shamans of indigenous cultures are now teaching Westerners. The shamanic journey, the trance dance, the vision quest and the purifying ceremony of the sweat lodge are ancient but often still relevant ways to contact the timeless reality that is invisible at first to our senses. Eagle's Wing has been established since 1985 and is a widely respected central resource for information and courses on shamanism. Leo Rutherford, who runs the centre, has been a leading and serious practitioner of this spiritual way for many years and is well known and respected for his work. Chanting, drumming, dancing, instruction in the use of the medicine wheel, ceremony and celebration are all part of the centre's teaching. There are a number of interesting day courses and workshops, which explore rich and ancient traditions of spirituality. **Highly Recommended.**

OPEN: According to programme. Receives men and women.
ROOMS: Non-residential at the centre, but accommodation on courses and workshops held elsewhere.
SPECIAL ACTIVITIES: Online for programme details.
BOOKINGS: Letter, telephone, email.
CHARGES: Rates per event, workshop or course.
ACCESS: See individual event venue for travel details.

Ealing Abbey
Charlbury Grove
London W5 2DY
England

Tel: 0208 8622100
Fax: 0208 8622206
Email: ealingmonk@aol.com
Website: www.ealingabbey.org.uk

Retreats • Workshops and Courses • Church/Temple • Spiritual Help
Community Living • Vocations • Children

Christian – Roman Catholic

The monks serve a large parish so this is a busy place, well and truly integrated into the world at large. Yet guests are welcome to share in the liturgy and community prayer, which help sustain all the various activities of the Abbey. There is a fairly large programme of events plus groups that meet regularly. These include a toddler group, *Lectio Divina* group, meditation group and Gregorian chant workshop.

Edgware Abbey
Community of St Mary at the Cross
Priory Field Drive
Edgware
London HA8 9PZ
England

Tel: 0208 9587868
Email:
info@edgwareabbey.org.uk /
nuns.osb.edgware@btclick.com
Website: www.edgwareabbey.org.uk

Retreats • Church/Temple • Spiritual Help • Vegetarian Food • Venue for Hire
Community Living • Vocations • Children

Christian – Anglican

The Anglican Benedictine Community of St Mary at the Cross Convent has an atmosphere of peace that enfolds the visitor. The provision of care has long been the mission of this Community and they welcome guests who want a retreat in tranquillity for a few days not far from the heart of London. Small comfortable guest house and day conference facilities.

The Edward Carpenter Community
BM ECC
London WCIN 3XX
England

Tel: 0870 3215121
Email: contact_ecc@
edwardcarpentercommunity.org.uk
Website: www.edwardcarpentercommunity.org.uk

Retreats • Workshops and Courses • Spiritual Help • Vegetarian Food

Open spirituality – Gay men's spirituality

The Edward Carpenter Community for Gay Men is an organisation committed to personal growth, support, trust and friendship for gay men. It offers an excellent programme of various types of residential retreats throughout the year at comfortable and established venues as well as some local meetings, conferences and events. It has been going for many years now and is named after Edward Carpenter, writer, social activist and radical thinker who lived in the early part of the last century. He was one of the first men to work openly on behalf of gay men's equality in British law and society. There is a recent biography of Carpenter which has received wide and enthusiastic media reviews: *Edward Carpenter, 1844–1929: Prophet of Human Fellowship* by Chushichi Tsuzuki. The Edward Carpenter Community have a brochure explaining the organisation as well as giving details about the organisation online – please read their statement of principles, intentions, vision and values. **Highly Recommended.**

The Grail Centre
125 Waxwell Lane
Pinner
London HA5 3ER
England

Tel: 0208 8660505 / 0208 8662195
Fax: 0208 8661408
Email: bookings@grailsociety.org.uk /
poustinias@grailsociety.org.uk
Website: www.grailsociety.org.uk

Retreats • Workshops and Courses • Church/Temple • Meditation • Spiritual Help
Vegetarian Food • Venue for Hire • Self-Catering Space • Community Living
Vocations • Hermitages

Christian – Roman Catholic – Ecumenical

Just under half an hour from Baker Street underground station, the Grail Centre stands in some 10 acres of grounds. It offers small cedar-wood chalets set in the woods where you can experience the peace of a poustinia – or hermitage. The Russian word *poustinia* can be translated as 'a place apart'. At the Grail Centre, you can live as a hermit in silence, reflection and prayer as a hermit.

The Guild of Health Ltd	Tel: 0207 5631389
St Marylebone Parish Church	Email:
17 Marylebone Road	guildofhealth@stmarylebone.org
London NW1 5TL	Website: www.gohealth.org.uk
England	

Retreats • Workshops and Courses • Church/Temple • Spiritual Help

Christian – Ecumenical

Quiet Days, seminars, retreats and events are held on aspects of healing by this ecumenical and non-denominational Christian organisation. Their work supports the **St Marylebone Healing and Counselling Centre** (see entry in this section) and they hold regular healing services.

Guy Chester Centre	Tel: 0208 8838204
Chester House	Fax: 0208 8830843
Pages Lane	Email: admin@chestercentre.org.uk
Muswell Hill	Website: www.chestercentre.org.uk
London N10 1PR	
England	

Retreats • Workshops and Courses • Church/Temple • Meditation • Spiritual Help
Bed and Breakfast • Vegetarian Food • Venue for Hire

Christian – Methodist

Muswell Hill is a popular area of north London where this centre is situated on a 10-acre site with gardens. In addition to running a large residential place for young people, they offer an extensive and interesting programme of events and courses as well as quiet retreats. Examples of current subjects on their programme are *Journey to Easter*, *Divorce Recovery Workshop*, *Advent Retreat*, *Skills Training for Meditation and Facilitation in Church* and *Meeting God – Prayer in Everyday*

Life. They also have a programme called *Toolbox for Life and Church*, which is designed to develop skills that are life-enhancing, practical, liberating and enabling.

Kagyu Samye Dzong London　　　Tel: 0207 7088969
33 Manor Place　　Email: manorplace@samye.org
London SE17 3BD　　Website: www.samye.org/london
England

Retreats • Workshops and Courses • Church/Temple • Yoga • Meditation • Spiritual Help
Alternative Therapies • Community Living • Work Retreats • Vocations • Children

Buddhist (Karma Kagyu tradition) – Tibetan

Kagyu Samye Dzong London is a branch of Kagyu Samye Ling Monastery in Scotland and the Rokpa Trust, which has branches worldwide. The Karma Kagyu tradition is one of the main schools of Tibetan Buddhism. It is renowned for its emphasis on meditation as embodied by such great masters as Marpa, Milarepa and Gampopa, whose example inspired people throughout Tibet. Kagyu Samye Dzong London Tibetan Buddhist Centre provides peace and tranquillity for all at its two centres in central London. They run a programme of courses and workshops focusing on meditation, Buddhism and holistic therapies. They also provide venues for community activities and alternative practitioners. A qualified Tibetan doctor holds regular clinics where patients can receive treatment with traditional Tibetan medicine. Evening meditation is open to the public most evenings. The centre is closed on Mondays and Fridays and is open between 14:00 and 21:00 other days. No meals or accommodation are provided. Everyone is welcome.

---

*'A man is rich in proportion to the number of things
he can afford to let alone'*
– Henry David Thoreau

Kairos Centre
Mount Angelus Road
Roehampton
London SW15 4JA
England

Tel: 0208 7884188
Fax: 0208 7884198
Email: director.kairos@psmgs.org (general) /
deputydir.kairos@psmgs.org (guest bookings)
Website: www.thekairoscentre.co.uk

Retreats • Workshops and Courses • Church/Temple • Spiritual Help
Bed and Breakfast • Vegetarian Food • Venue for Hire

Christian – Roman Catholic – Inter-denominational

Kairos is a Greek word meaning 'favourable time or graced moment'. Retreats, conference and business-meeting facilities and various courses and meetings are all on offer here at this well-placed centre located near beautiful Richmond Park and only a few miles from central London itself. You can come for their programme, a private retreat and stay over, or just come for a Quiet Day, bringing a packed lunch and they provide you with tea or coffee.

OPEN: Almost all year. Receives everyone.
ROOMS: 15 en-suite, 5 standards.
FACILITIES: Disabled and full wheelchair access, conferences, garden, prayer room, reading room, conservatory, guest lounge, TV.
SPIRITUAL HELP: Spiritual accompaniment on request.
GUESTS ADMITTED TO: Chapel, oratory.
MEALS: Everyone eats together. Traditional and simple food. Vegetarian and special diets. They can do a special range of menus from conferences and buffets to reception and wedding parties.
SPECIAL ACTIVITIES: Planned programme. Send for information.
SITUATION: Calm and peaceful centre, adjoining Richmond Park where you can enjoy walking.
MAXIMUM STAY: 1 month
BOOKINGS: Letter, telephone (08:30–16:00), fax, email.
CHARGES: Different rates apply. Currently: Quiet Day/day event, suggested offering £10/15; en-suite single B&B, £39.50 per night; en-suite sharing or standard B&B, £29.50 per night; 2-course lunch or evening meal, £10.50 per person; 3-course lunch or evening meal, £12.50 per person. Various rates for the meeting and conference rooms and facilities.
ACCESS: Rail: Barnes or Putney stations. Underground: Putney Bridge or Hammersmith Bridge. Buses: 72 (from Hammersmith or Barnes), 170, 430 (from Putney stations). Car via M4 or A3.

Leo Baeck College and the	Tel: 0208 3495600

**Leo Baeck College and the
Sternberg Centre for Judaism
80 East End Road
London N3 2SY
England**

Tel: 0208 3495600
Fax: 0208 3495619
Email: info@lbc.ac.uk
Website: www.lbc.ac.uk

Workshops and Courses

Judaism

This centre for Jewish education is dedicated to promoting the intellectual, spiritual and professional development of Progressive Judaism in Britain and Europe and stimulating Jewish religious thought and values. There are no Jewish retreat centres as such but the Sternberg Centre has in the past, however, organised youth group retreats and family retreats to provide Jewish educational, social and spiritual enrichment. There are events – not organised by this Centre – held at various retreat centres in Britain, which have courses of interest to those of the Jewish faith, such as Jewish Christian Text Studies and Inter-faith Days and on occasion other courses centred on opening Jewish–Christian dialogue. However, the centre does have a full and active programme of courses with talks by leading rabbinical teachers and speakers. For example, a recent autumn semester programme included the following themes arising from the *Books of Numbers and Deuteronomy*: *Levitical Cities And Unpursuable Refuges, Had The Job Outgrown Moses? The Decalogue, 'Heed This O Israel', Obedience Rewarded* and *What Does The Lord Require?*

**Lesbian and Gay Christian
Movement (LGCM)
Oxford House
Derbyshire Street
London E2 6HG
England**

Tel/Fax: 0207 7391249
Email: lgcm@lgcm.org.uk
Website: www.lgcm.org.uk

Christian – Inter-denominational – Ecumenical

The Lesbian and Gay Christian Movement holds annual retreats for lesbian, gay and bisexual women and men. The main one is often held in Scotland at the Macleod Centre (see the Scotland section). Such retreats are led by internationally known men and women in the field of theology with concerns in lesbian, gay and bisexual Christianity and spirituality such as James Allison, Susy Brouard, Urs Mattmann and others. There is a slow but progressive development of more retreats for lesbians, gays and bisexuals as well as for transsexuals in Britain, and more retreat houses are including such in their programmes. *The Good Retreat Guide* **welcomes this development and hopes more religious houses and retreat centres will become more inclusive of lesbian, gay, bisexual, and transsexual men and women.**

London Airport Chapels
Mini Retreats: Gatwick – Heathrow – Luton – Stansted

Church/Temple

Inter-faith – Open to all

A retreat does not have to be for a day or a weekend, it can be just a few minutes of peace and stillness – a chance to slip away for some calm, perhaps a reflection or a prayer. Next time, before you go through the gates to start your journey, why not make a mini retreat in the airport chapel. No crowds. No noise. No hectic world for a minute or two – just a bit of peace before another slice of modern busy life.

London Gatwick Airport	Tel: 01293 503857 (Anglican Chaplain) /
Gatwick, West Sussex	01293 505775 (Free Church Chaplains) /
RH6 0JH	01293 503851 (Roman Catholic Chaplains)
England	Website: www.gatwickairportchapel.org.uk

There is an inter-faith chapel at both the South Terminal (in the Village, before security) and the North Terminal (on the arrivals concourse). Both are open for private prayer. Check online for the times of the daily services. Notices of any special arrangements are displayed outside each chapel.

OPEN: Weekdays except Thursdays. Saturday and Sunday services at 12:00.

London Heathrow Airport   Tel : 0208 7454261
Hounslow, Middlesex TW6 1BP   Email: chapel-heathrow@baa.com
England   Website: www.heathrowairport.com

St George's Chapel is located below ground level, between Terminals 1, 2 and 3, close to the central bus station and opposite the entrance to the short-stay car park at Terminal 2. It is open from early morning till late at night. A prayer room for all faiths is at street level, above the main chapel. There are also prayer rooms at Terminals 2–5.

OPEN: Daily, 07:30 to 20:00.

London Luton Airport   Tel: 01582 395516
Luton, Bedfordshire LU2 9LU   Fax : 01582 395062
England   Email: chaplaincy.admin@ltn.aero
                                     Website: www.london-luton.co.uk

The Airport Chapel is located across the road from the main terminal. Follow the signs from the Onward Travel Centre, or from the main concourse in the terminal. Everyone is welcome to visit and spend some quiet time.

OPEN: Daily, 04:00 to 23:00.

London Stansted Airport   Tel: 0870 0000303
Stansted, Essex CM24 1SF   (airport information desk)
England   Website: www.stanstedairport.com

Stansted's Airport Chapel is located next to the UK Arrivals area, in check-in zone J.

OPEN: Daily, 05:00 to 23:00.

London Buddhist Vihara
Dharmapala Building
The Avenue
Chiswick
London W4 1UD
England

Tel: 0208 9959493
Fax: 0208 9948130
Email: london.vihara@virgin.net
Website: www.londonbuddhistvihara.org

Retreats • Workshops and Courses • Church/Temple • Meditation • Spiritual Help
Vegetarian Food • Community Living • Vocations • Children

Buddhist (Theravada tradition)

The London Buddhist Vihara was the first Buddhist monastery to be established outside Asia. Classes on Buddhism include those for beginners, advanced students and children, and for meditation. No residential facilities are available. There is a resident community of monks at the vihara. Evening classes explore a wide range of subjects: Bhavana (meditation) instruction and practice, beginner's Buddhism, Dharma study, Buddhist psychology, the Sinhala language and Pali, which is the language of the Buddhist Canon. A Buddhist discussion group meets monthly in an informal atmosphere. There are monthly retreats and a children's Sunday school. The vihara also caters for the needs of expatriate Buddhists from Asia, mainly Sri Lanka.

OPEN: All year. Receives everyone. Children welcome. The vihara is open daily to all devotees and visitors from 09:00 to 21:00. Details regarding the vihara's activities are displayed on the noticeboards in the main hall. A monk or a lay person will usually be present to give additional information and assistance to newcomers.
ROOMS: None.
FACILITIES: Conferences, shrine room, garden, library, payphone, bookstall.
SPIRITUAL HELP: Personal talks, meditation and directed study.
GUESTS ADMITTED TO: Everywhere except monks' rooms.
MEALS: Traditional food. Monks eat separately, everyone else together.
SPECIAL ACTIVITIES: See programme.
SITUATION: Quiet within the house.
MAXIMUM STAY: 1 day.
BOOKINGS: Letter, telephone, fax, email.
CHARGES: By donation.
ACCESS: Underground: District Line to Turnham Green. Buses: E3, 190, 237, 267, 272, 391.

London Buddhist Centre
51 Roman Road
Bethnal Green
London E2 0HU
England

Tel: 0845 4584716
Email: info@lbc.org.uk
Website: www.lbc.org.uk

Retreats • Workshops and Courses • Church/Temple • Yoga • Meditation • Spiritual Help
Vegetarian Food • Community Living • Work Retreats • Vocations • Hermitages

Buddhist – Friends of the Western Buddhist Order (FWBO)

The Friends of the Western Buddhist Order (FWBO) strive to put Buddhism's essential teachings into practice in the West through identifying core Buddhist principles and values and making them relevant to men and women living in today's modern world. The London Buddhist Centre is at the heart of a thriving spiritual community in the East End of London and is an essential part of the international and rapidly expanding FWBO movement. Buddhist practices and classes are offered as well as retreats for people at all levels of experience and of all ages. Evening and lunchtime meditation classes are available. There is no residential community so people visit by attending one of the organised retreats. You may, of course, call into the centre for a brief visit. A Buddhist Village has evolved around the centre. There are small shops and restaurants, which share common values and are run cooperatively. Bodywise Natural Health Centre (Tel: 0208 9816938), for example, offers a wide range of yoga classes, alternative healing treatments and therapies. On the retreat side of things, there is a wide variety of retreats and special spiritual events on the programme, which may include Gay Men's Retreats, People of Colour Retreats, Family Retreats, Parents' and Children's Retreats, a Summer Open Retreat of nine nights, a Working Retreat that combines meditation, study and work, and seminars on Ancient Wisdom, which may include the Buddha's advice on relationships and the practice of Dharma in everyday life. Regular retreats are held at various FWBO centres through Britain. If you are interested in Buddhism, this is a great place to get started. **Highly Recommended.**

OPEN: All year, Monday-Friday, 10:00 to 17:00. Receives everyone.
ROOMS: What is not available in London is available elsewhere on the various types of retreats – discuss accommodation with the centre when you decide what interests you on the programme. Singles, doubles, dormitories and camping available, depending on the retreat.

FACILITIES: Disabled access and garden at the centre in London.
SPIRITUAL HELP: Personal talks, group sharing, spiritual direction, personal retreat direction, meditation, directed study.
GUESTS ADMITTED TO: Everywhere.
MEALS: Everyone eats together when food is offered. Vegetarian only.
SPECIAL ACTIVITIES: Programme of events. See online or enquire at the centre.
SITUATION: In a city. Other places outside London are countryside peaceful locations.
MAXIMUM STAY: By arrangement.
BOOKINGS: Letter, telephone, email.
CHARGES: Donations vary according to event, teaching, or course of study and practice – see programme for these. Concession rates available. Longer retreats run at different rates, but there are also concessionary rates for these.
ACCESS: Underground: Central Line to Bethnal Green and then a walk. Buses: 8, 106, 254, 309, 388, D6.

The London Centre for Spirituality	Tel: 0207 6211391
The Church of St Edmund the King	Email:
Lombard Street	info@spiritualitycentre.org
London EC3V 9EA	Website: www.spiritualitycentre.org
England	

Retreats • Workshops and Courses • Church/Temple • Spiritual Help • Venue for Hire
Self-Catering Space

Christian – Anglican – Ecumenical – Inter-faith

The London Centre for Spirituality is a place of calm and space in the heart of the City of London, offering a wide range of courses, meditation and discussion groups and resources for all who are interested in spirituality. Their facilities are used by professionals and organisations working in related areas, including counselling. The centre runs a well-stocked bookshop as well.

OPEN: Most of the year. Everyone welcome.
ROOMS: Non-residential
FACILITIES: Church, hall, library, office, kitchen and enclosed garden. St Paul's Cathedral nearby.
SPIRITUAL HELP: Spiritual direction meetings are usually about an hour long (longer for a group) and typically take place every month or six weeks. Sometimes there is a fee, sometimes not.
GUESTS ADMITTED TO: All public areas.
MEALS: Limited self-catering.
SPECIAL ACTIVITIES: Programme of events and courses.
SITUATION: In a city. Close to St Paul's Cathedral and the Bank of England.
MAXIMUM STAY: Non-residential

BOOKINGS: Letter, telephone, email.
CHARGES: Please see programme for the various event costs.
ACCESS: Underground: Central, Northern and Waterloo Lines to Bank; Circle and District Lines to Monument. Rail: DLR to Bank. Buses: several bus routes stop near Bank, which is a key interchange point.

London Inter-faith Centre	Tel: 0207 3726864
125 Salusbury Road	Fax: 0207 6043052
London NW6 6RG	Email: info@londoninterfaith.org.uk
England	Website: www.londoninterfaith.org.uk

Workshops and Courses

Inter-faith – Open to all

London Inter-faith Centre was opened in 1998 when the notion of inter-faith was still a relatively new concept within mainstream Christian life. For the centre, the main focus remains the action–reflection meeting point of local mixed faith living. There are many inter-faith events and courses of study such as *Insight into Hinduism, Introduction to Buddhism, The World through Christian Eyes* and *Islam – Sunni and Shi'a.*

Methodist International Centre	Tel: 0207 3800001 (general) /
81–103 Euston Road	0207 6911437 (membership secretary)
London NW1 2EZ	Fax: 0207 3875300
England	Email: reservations@micentre.com /
	alana@micentre.com (membership secretary)
	Website: www.micentre.com

Workshops and Courses • Bed and Breakfast • Vegetarian Food
Venue for Hire • Children

Christian – Methodist – Open to all

Methodist International Centre is a social enterprise, which provides hotel services, meeting facilities and hostel facilities for students in their centre near Euston Station in central London. It supports international and home students studying in London, providing affordable accommodation in a multi-cultural, multi-faith environment. There are conferences and events as well as accommodation. The hotel has 28 guest bedrooms, offering double, twin or family rooms with an additional three members-only rooms with shared bathroom facilities and four postgraduate rooms. Rates start from about £117 per room per night B&B. There is a discounted Sunday rate of £75 per room per night, with breakfast for one person. There is a special membership club, which has discounted rates for both rooms and meals. Contact the membership secretary for more details. Disabled wheelchair access.

Mount Street Jesuit Centre	Tel: 0207 4951673
114 Mount Street	Email: lynne@mountstreet.info
London W1K 3AH	Website: www.msjc.org.uk
England	

Retreats • Workshops and Courses • Church/Temple • Spiritual Help • Vocations

Christian – Roman Catholic – Jesuit

The centre is next to the Church Of The Immaculate Conception, Farm Street, which is an oasis in the middle of the busy world of the Mayfair, Grosvenor Square and Bond Street areas. In this small, peaceful church you can find sanctuary, a little time to pray or just to sit and for a few moments leave behind that madly rushing life just outside the doors. So often at *The Good Retreat Guide* people tell us, 'I need to get away,' or 'I want some peace,' or 'I just need some space.' Yes, you can go away on a retreat – but what about during your working week? London and most other cities are full of sanctuaries like this small Jesuit church and every one offers peace and that silence which our inner life so often hungers after. Maybe it is not a full spiritual meal like a regular retreat, but nevertheless it is a bite of nourishing soul time. The Mount Street Jesuit Centre offers non-residential courses and activities, underpinned by the spiritual exercises of St Ignatius Loyola.

'The whole world is desolate because
no one reflects in their heart'
– Jeremiah 12:11

Neal's Yard Workshops and Courses   Tel: 0207 6177171
Neal's Yard Agency   Email: info@nealsyardagency.com
BCM Neal's Yard   Website: www.nealsyardagency.com
London WC1N 3XX
England

Retreats • Workshops and Courses • Yoga • Meditation • Alternative Therapies
Holistic Holidays

Mind Body Spirit – Open spirituality

A wonderful organisation that gathers together and helps any number of courses and workshops to take place – a few are at Neal's Yard itself like day talks and sessions, others are held elsewhere in London, around the country and abroad. There are arts and life skills, Body Mind, Tai Chi, yoga, healing, spiritual healing, meditation, holidays, getaways, holistic holidays, retreats – and more!

Oasis Days with the Leprosy   Tel: 01895 822863
Mission of London   Email: martind@timew.org.uk
Christ Church, Southwark   Website: www.leprosymission.org.uk
27 Blackfriars Road
London SE1 8NY
England

Retreats • Workshops and Courses • Church/Temple

Christian – Inter-denominational – Inter-faith

The Leprosy Mission of London offers Oasis Days – a day for quiet reflection and inner renewal. These popular days are held at Christ Church, as above, on the second Tuesday of each month and sometimes on a Saturday. They are led from a broad religious and denominational spectrum and the cost, which is currently about £15, covers the day's programme, materials, if any are needed, and your lunch.

Open Centre   Tel: 0207 251 1504
Third Floor   Email: ocinfo@opencentre.com
188–192 Old Street   Website: www.opencentre.com
London EC1 9FR
England

Retreats • Workshops and Courses • Yoga • Meditation • Venue for Hire

Mind Body Spirit – Self-development

Now running for almost 30 years, the Open Centre offers a programme
to increase your awareness of yourself and others and to help you take
a look at your relationships, your assumptions and your decisions
about life and work. The key ideas focus on therapy, movement, healing and growth. Courses on offer usually include such topics as Primal
Integration, Deep Bodywork, Feldenkrais Method and Bioenergetics.
There are some intensive courses that are residential in other retreat
venues, which offer accommodation. These are usually not in London
but in the countryside.

OPEN: All year. Receives men, women, groups. Also practitioners who want to use
their facilities.
ROOMS: None except group rooms used for courses or in summer courses and
workshops outside London.
FACILITIES: See above.
SPIRITUAL HELP: Group sharing.
GUESTS ADMITTED TO: Course areas.
MEALS: None unless on residential course.
SPECIAL ACTIVITIES: Programme of courses and events. See brochure.
SITUATION: In a city.
MAXIMUM STAY: For course or programme.
BOOKINGS: Letter, telephone, email.
CHARGES: Vary, but range is wide as the Open Centre offers intensive courses, day
classes, some regular group meetings, and other retreats and courses in residential
centres.
ACCESS: Underground: Northern Line to Old Street. Buses: 55, 135 and 243 stop at
Old Street; 43, 76, 141, 214 and 271 go to nearby City Road.

Providence Convent House of Prayer
8 Oakthorpe Road
Palmers Green
London N13 5UH
England

Tel: 0208 4478233
Fax: 0208 8822549
www.house-of-prayer.info
Prayer Phone Line: 0208 4478982
(19:00–21:00, Tuesdays and Thursdays)

Retreats • Workshops and Courses • Church/Temple • Spiritual Help
Vegetarian Food • Community Living • Vocations

Christian – Roman Catholic

The Prayer Phone Line is run by the sisters from their convent, in addition to their offerings of hospitality and retreats. The Prayer Phone Line, as explained by the sisters, works this way:

'Two people answer the phones and pray with the callers as they make their requests for prayers. The petitions are then taken into the Adoration Room, which is adjacent to the Phone Room, where two or more people pray especially for these requests in front of the Blessed Sacrament while the Phone Line is open. The petitions are put in a basket and when the line closes they are taken to the Convent Chapel and placed under the altar. Two Masses a month are celebrated for the intentions on the Prayer Phone Line and for the people involved.'

This praying together in the time of a person's needs and the follow-through with offering the prayer to God at his altar is a powerful spiritual support.

OPEN: Most of the year. Everyone welcome.
ROOMS: 8 singles.
FACILITIES: Chapel, lounge, garden.
SPIRITUAL HELP: You are welcome to join in community services and prayers. Prayer Phone Line (see above). Individually guided retreats possible.
GUESTS ADMITTED TO: All guest non-enclosure areas.
MEALS: Taken together. Traditional food – vegetarian possible.
SPECIAL ACTIVITIES: Day retreats and a programme of events and retreats.
SITUATION: Urban but quiet.
MAXIMUM STAY: By retreat or by arrangement.
BOOKINGS: Letter, telephone, fax.
CHARGES: Currently: The 5-Day Retreats £175 per person. The Weekend Retreats £60 per person. Days of Recollection £15 per person.
ACCESS: Rail: Palmers Green station. Underground and bus.

Royal Foundation of St Katherine
Retreat and Conference Centre
2 Butchers Row
London E14 8DS
England

Tel: 0845 4090135
Fax: 0207 7027603
Email: retreat@stkatharine.org.uk /
info@rfsk.org.uk
Website: www.stkatharine.org.uk / www.rfsk.org.uk

Retreats • Workshops and Courses • Church/Temple • Spiritual Help
Bed and Breakfast • Venue for Hire

Christian – Anglican

St Katharine's was founded in 1147 as a religious community and medieval hospital for poor infirm people next to the Tower of London. It is in a convenient and attractive setting for meetings, conferences, seminars, receptions, retreats and Quiet Days in the centre of London between the City and Canary Wharf. All the rooms have recently been refurbished and decorated.

OPEN: All year. Everyone welcome.
ROOMS: 29 singles. 7 twins. En suite accommodation for 43 people in total.
FACILITIES: Disabled access, conferences, garden, library, guest lounge, 7 meeting rooms.
SPIRITUAL HELP: Daily worship.
GUESTS ADMITTED TO: Chapel, gardens.
MEALS: Everyone eats together. Traditional food. Vegetarian and special diets.
SPECIAL ACTIVITIES: Programme of events and retreats.
SITUATION: Reasonably quiet in a city.
MAXIMUM STAY: By programme or by arrangement.
BOOKINGS: Letter, telephone, fax, email. Booking online is easy.
CHARGES: Current B&B nightly rates are about £45 for a single and £68 for a twin. Dinner per person per night is £15.50.
ACCESS: Rail: DLR or train to Limehouse station. Bus: 15 (from central London). Car: M25 exit 3, A13. St Katherine's is outside the congestion zone.

---

*'Most of the trouble in the world is caused
by people wanting to be important'*
– T.S. Elliot

Sacred Heart Priory **The Dominican Sisters** **38 Hyde Vale** **Greenwich** **London SE10 8QH** **England**	Tel: 0208 6927677

Retreats • Workshops and Courses • Church/Temple • Meditation • Spiritual Help
Bed and Breakfast • Self-Catering Space • Community Living • Vocations

Christian – Roman Catholic

Overnight accommodation for women only is offered by the community. Opportunities are here for Quiet Days, Christian meditation, scriptural sharing and a monthly retreat day with quiet prayer.

OPEN: Most of the year. Women only welcomed, with exceptions by prior agreement for 'closed groups'.
ROOMS: 6 singles.
FACILITIES: Chapel, garden.
SPIRITUAL HELP: Spiritual guidance by arrangement. IGR retreats.
GUESTS ADMITTED TO: Chapel. Guest areas.
MEALS: Self-catering available for B&B only. Meals by arrangement if staying overnight.
SPECIAL ACTIVITIES: Quiet Days, Christian meditation, guided prayer, some sharing. IGR retreats. Programme of talks and retreat days.
SITUATION: Urban.
MAXIMUM STAY: By arrangement.
BOOKINGS: Letter, telephone.
CHARGES: Please ask when booking.
ACCESS: Rail/Underground: Greenwich station. Bus, car.

School of Life **70 Marchmont Street** **London WC1N 1AB** **England**	Tel: 0207 8331010 Email: info@theschooloflife.com Website: www.theschooloflife.com

Workshops and Courses

Open spirituality – Philosophical

The School of Life is a new kind of enterprise, which is broadly based on social, philosophical, spiritual and well-being ideas. It is based in a small shop in central London and offers a variety of approaches for better everyday living and probably would not call itself a retreat in any way – but we think it fits very neatly into the modern concept of going on a retreat in order to have time to explore new values, ideas, concepts and people. What is on offer here ranges from courses, holidays, sermons and events to something called bibliotherapy; there are also meals, psychotherapy, and shopping in their shop. A quick look at some of the topics in their programme gives a feel for the diversity: *How to Spend Time Alone*, *Envy*, *Gardening*, *How to Handle Your Family*, *How to Be a Good Lover*, *How to Think about Death* and *Conversation Dinners* (which take place at a restaurant). It sounds like a strange mix but it all seems to fit together into courses and services not founded on any one dogma. However, these different approaches may lead you towards a positive outlook on your life – whether that is from a philosophical, literary or visual-arts base. Courses take place in the evenings or at weekends. The School of Life poses many inviting questions that are certainly not superficial and can lead to profound explorations about where your life is going. For example: Have you had one of those mornings lately in which you got up and wondered why you were doing a job that exhausted you or that you didn't really enjoy? Or found yourself spending the day running against the clock, too stressed to eat properly but not actually creatively challenged? Do you waste time brooding over unresolved arguments or feeling guilty for not being kinder to those in need? Such questions often arise in monastic and other traditional retreat places too because they are, at heart, deeply spiritual.

OPEN: 12:00–19:00, Monday to Friday. Usually closed in August.
ACCESS: Rail: King's Cross/St Pancras station. Underground: Piccadilly Line to Russell Square. Local bus routes include 168, 91, 59, 68, 7 and 188, as well as buses that stop along Euston Road.

Society of St John the Evangelist
St Edward's House
22 Great College Street
London SWIP 3QA
England

Tel: 0207 2229234
Fax: 0207 7992641
Email: guestmaster@ssje.org.uk
Website: www.ssje.org.uk

Retreats • Church/Temple • Spiritual Help • Community Living • Vegetarian

Christian – Anglican

The Society of St John the Evangelist is the oldest monastic community for men in the Anglican Church and here in one of its houses guests stay with the community and are not separate. A traditional monastic men's religious community, it is open for short-stay breaks, particularly for Christians and charity groups who want to live and share with the community's life. Located in central London, the guest rooms are comfortable and nicely decorated. They have a splendid roof garden from which you can see the Houses of Parliament.

OPEN: All year except August, Christmas and Easter. Receives men and women, families, groups.
ROOMS: 15 singles. No smoking, radios or mobile phones.
FACILITIES: Chapel, library, garden, guest lounge, payphone, meeting rooms, roof garden.
SPIRITUAL HELP: Personal talks, meditation, spiritual direction, personal retreat direction, directed study. Guests do not have to attend religious services but may if they want.
GUESTS ADMITTED TO: Church, chapel, refectory, library, garden.
MEALS: Everyone eats together. Food is simple and traditional. Vegetarians can be catered for but advance notice must be given. No special diets.
SPECIAL ACTIVITIES: Quiet Days and each month a planned retreat or talk..
SITUATION: In the middle of London near the Houses of Parliment. Near all London attractions if you have to have these on hand.
MAXIMUM STAY: 7 days.
BOOKINGS: Letter, telephone (after 09:30, before 21:00), email (best method).
CHARGES: Modest, and depend on meals taken. Please ask for the current charges when you book.
ACCESS: Underground: Jubilee, District, Circle Lines to Westminster; District, Circle Lines to St James's Park. Bus to Westminster Abbey.

St Mary's Church House
St Mary's Parish Office
Church Hill
Harrow on the Hill HA1 3HL
England

Tel: 0208 4222652
Email: stmarys.harrow@btinternet.com
Website: www.harrowhill.org

Retreats • Church/Temple • Venue for Hire • Self-Catering Space • Children

Christian – Anglican

St Mary's Church House is a renovated Victorian annex, which has been made into a small and comfortable conference centre, providing self-catering accommodation. It has a quiet atmosphere away from busy life, yet it is within easy reach of central London.

OPEN: All year except August. Receives groups.
ROOMS: 4 bedrooms, many with bunk beds. Can accommodate 10 people in the bedrooms.
FACILITIES: Small conferences, guest lounge, library, TV.
SPIRITUAL HELP: None.
GUESTS ADMITTED TO: Unrestricted access.
MEALS: Self-catering only. Equipped kitchen.
SPECIAL ACTIVITIES: None.
SITUATION: In an area of character amid the vast suburban sprawl of west London.
MAXIMUM STAY: By arrangement.
BOOKINGS: Letter, telephone.
CHARGES: Ask what is expected when you book. Usually very reasonable.
ACCESS: Rail/Underground: Harrow on the Hill station. Accessible by bus or car.

St Marylebone Healing and Counselling Centre
St Marylebone Parish Church
17 Marylebone Road
London NW1 5LT
England

Tel: 0207 9355066
Email: healing@stmarylebone.org
Website: www.stmarylebone.org.uk

Retreats • Workshops and Courses • Church/Temple • Meditation • Spiritual Help
Alternative Therapies

Christian – Ecumenical

This centre has been going for many years now and has a well-deserved reputation. There is an ecumenical team of spiritual directors, with professional counselling by Christian therapists. Days of prayer and courses are on offer too. The Healing and Counselling Centre offers a number of approaches to healing including professional counselling and psychotherapy, mental health support group, spiritual direction and healing prayer. There are also conferences about psychotherapy, spirituality and arts workshops.

'Peace does not dwell in outward things, but within the soul'
– François Fénelon

St Peter's Bourne Christian
Education and Spirituality Centre
40 Oakleigh Park South
London N20 9JN
England

Tel: 0208 4455535
Email: warden1@tiscali.co.uk
(guest bookings)
Website: www.stpetersbourne.com

Retreats • Workshops and Courses • Church/Temple • Spiritual Help
Bed and Breakfast • Vegetarian Food • Venue for Hire

Christian – Anglican – Ecumenical

St Peter's Bourne is set in its own large surrounding gardens and provides peaceful hospitality in which to relax, reflect, and escape from the busy world. They provide organised retreats and events and you can come for the day or stay over. The house can provide meeting rooms for small conferences and groups.

OPEN: Most of the year. Everyone welcome.
ROOMS: 7 singles, 2 twins, 1 double.
FACILITIES: Chapel, library, lounge, gardens, meeting rooms.
SPIRITUAL HELP: Ignatian guided retreats. Spiritual direction by arrangement.
GUESTS ADMITTED TO: All public areas and grounds.
MEALS: Everyone eats together. Traditional food. Vegetarian possible.
SPECIAL ACTIVITIES: Quiet Days, 8-day Ignatian retreats, preached retreats.
SITUATION: Set in a large park.
MAXIMUM STAY: By arrangement.
BOOKINGS: Letter, telephone, email.
CHARGES: Current rates per person: day rate is about £20; 24-hour residential rate, £34; B&B, £25. Separate rates for lunch or dinner only. Full rates are available online.
ACCESS: Rail: Oakleigh Park station. Underground: Northern Line to Totteridge and Whetstone stations. Buses: 34, 125, 234, 251,263, 326. Car: M25 exit 23, A1 then A5109 and A109.

'To fall provides the opportunity to get up'
– Anon.

St Peter's Centre for Meditation and Peace   Tel: 0207 7353585
308 Kennington Lane   Email: st.peterscentre@yahoo.co.uk
London SE11 5HY   Website: www.christian-meditation.org.uk/
England   public_html/web/
                                              retreats_london_saintpeters.php /
                   www.crossoverlambeth.com/Churches/Churches.htm

Retreats • Workshops and Courses • Church/Temple • Meditation • Spiritual Help
Venue for Hire • Self-Catering Space • Community Living

Christian – Anglican – Ecumenical

Retreats and workshops centred around meditation and peace and the exploration of contemporary Christian spirituality are held at this church centre in the middle of busy London. It is ecumenical in outlook and offers a monthly meditation evening and a monthly liturgy for peace and justice. St Peter's is non-residential, but there is a live-in Christian community of lay people. The centre offers a safe and secure environment in which to explore what it means to be a Christian today. You will be warmly welcomed here.

OPEN: All year with Sunday services of worship. Everyone welcome.
ROOMS: Non-residential.
FACILITIES: Meditation room, group room, office, small kitchen, 3 rooms for groups and small conferences.
SPIRITUAL HELP: Meditation, shared prayer, church services.
GUESTS ADMITTED TO: All public areas, church.
MEALS: Limited self-catering.
SPECIAL ACTIVITIES: Regular meditation times during the week. Retreats and workshops centred around meditation and peace.
SITUATION: In a city.
MAXIMUM STAY: For the meeting or workshop.
BOOKINGS: Letter, telephone, email.
CHARGES: Meeting rooms to rent. Ask about specific workshop or event charges if any.
ACCESS: Rail/Underground: Vauxhall station. Several bus routes serve this area.

'A riot is the language of the unheard'
– Martin Luther King, Jr

St Saviour's Priory
18 Queensbridge Road
Hackney
London E2 8NS
England

Tel: 0207 7399976 / 0207 7396775
(Guest Sister)
Email: info@stsaviourspriory.org.uk
Website: www.stsaviourspriory.org.uk

Retreats • Church/Temple • Spiritual Help • Vegetarian Food • Venue for Hire
Self-Catering Space • Community Living • Vocations

Christian – Anglican

This Anglican convent does not offer any organised programmes, but it is suitable for a traditional private retreat or a small self-organised group retreat. There are many traditional convents like St Saviour's Priory and they have recently gained in popularity, especially among women with busy careers who want a few days of peace and reflection.

OPEN: Most of the year. Receives men, women, young people, families. Groups for the day only.
ROOMS: 6 singles. 2 day-retreat rooms, each with kitchen facility.
FACILITIES: 2 chapels, garden, library, 2 meeting rooms: for 25 people, and for 12.
SPIRITUAL HELP: Personal talks and spiritual direction. There is not always someone immediately available so appointments have to be arranged for this guidance.
GUESTS ADMITTED TO: Chapels, garden, library.
MEALS: Traditional. Self-catering available. If vegetarian, you need to discuss it when booking.
SPECIAL ACTIVITIES: None.
SITUATION: In a city.
MAXIMUM STAY: 2 weeks.
BOOKINGS: Letter, telephone (Tuesday to Saturday, 09:00–17:00), email.
CHARGES: Donations according to means – please ask the Guest Sister what would be appropriate.
ACCESS: Rail: Cambridge Heath (London). Buses: 26, 48, 55. Car parking is difficult here.

'There is no wealth but life'
– John Ruskin

**Swaminarayan Hindu Mission
and Shri Swaminarayan Mandir
105–119 Brentfield Road
Neasden
London NW10 8LD
England**

Tel: 0208 9652651
Fax: 0208 9656313
Email: info@mandir.org
Website: www.mandir.org /
www.swaminarayan.org

Workshops and Courses • Church/Temple • Spiritual Help • Children

Hindu

The Swaminarayan Hindu Mission is a branch of the worldwide Bochasanwasi Akshar Purushottam Sanstha of India, which is a prominent and charitable Hindu organisation with a wide spectrum of activities, including a medical college. It strives to promote social, moral, cultural and spiritual values among all ages within society and has some 3,000 centres and 300 temples around the world. The London centre has now opened the largest traditional Hindu mandir (temple) in Europe and they welcome people from all faiths. The mandir has transformed the north London district of Neasden. It took three years to build and employed 1,500 sculptors, 2,000 tonnes of marble and 3,000 tonnes of limestone. Among those who have visited this temple with its nine shrines and marvelled at its design and craftsmanship have been the Prince of Wales, the late Diana, Princess of Wales, the Duke of Edinburgh, and former prime minister Tony Blair. Facilities include a community and social centre, cultural centre, school, sports and recreation facilities, library, health clinic and a programme of various activities for men, women, and families. There is a permanent exhibition on Hinduism and a video presentation on the construction of the mandir. This is a truly remarkable and inspiring spiritual place and worth the time you take to visit it. **Highly Recommended.**

OPEN: All year, 09:00–18:00. Everyone welcome.
DRESS CODE: Shorts, skirts and dresses above the knee are not permitted except by children under 10 years. Please see the website for further guidelines when visiting.
CHILDREN: Children under 17 years are not admitted except with an adult.
FOOD: No food is allowed on the premises.
MOBILES: Mobiles should be switched off before entering the premises.
ACCESS: Underground: Jubilee Line to Neasden; Bakerloo Line to Stonebridge Park; Metropolitan Line/Jubilee Line to Wembley Park and take Bus PR2 from opposite the station. Buses: 92, 112, 206, 232, PR2.

Tyburn Convent   Tel: 01717237262
8 Hyde Park Place   Website: www.tyburnconvent.org.uk
Bayswater Road
London W2 2LJ
England

Church/Temple • Spiritual Help • Vegetarian Food • Vocations

Christian – Roman Catholic

Just opposite Hyde Park, Tyburn Convent is right in the heart of London. Amid the busy outside world, the sisters preside over the perpetual exposition of the Blessed Sacrament – the chapel is open all day and retreat guests may go there at night. Guests are free to organise their time as they wish and are welcome to share in the worship of the community.

OPEN: All year. The guest facilities are mainly for women. Unattached men wishing to book should have a letter of recommendation from their parish priest or other suitable person. Tyburn Convent is the National Shrine of the Martyrs of England and Wales, so all are welcome to visit the crypt itself.

ROOMS: 7 guest rooms: 1 double; 5 at the back of the convent and away from the noise of the traffic.

FACILITIES: Chapel, small patio garden, library. Hyde Park gives space for walks.

SPIRITUAL HELP: The Sisters are not trained to give counsel or specialised advice, but a Sister is available if a guest wishes to talk about her concerns – religious or otherwise.

GUESTS ADMITTED TO: Chapel, shrine room. A sister is available 3 times a day or by appointment to give individuals or groups a guided tour of the Martyrs' Crypt.

MEALS: Vegetarian and other approved diets are catered for, and the meals are simple, home cooked and nourishing. Meals are taken together in the guests' dining room.

SPECIAL ACTIVITIES: The perpetual exposition of the Blessed Sacrament in the chapel, which is open to the public all day, a sung Divine Office and the Shrine of the Martyrs.

SITUATION: Hyde Park is across the road, but the Convent is in the very heart of busy London.

MAXIMUM STAY: 1–14 days.

BOOKINGS: Letter.

CHARGES: The suggested donation is £30 per day. This includes 2 main meals at 13:00 and 18:45, with breakfast after Mass or whenever wished.

ACCESS: Underground: Central Line to Marble Arch. Several central London buses. No parking and it is difficult to park anywhere nearby.

Yoga Biomedical Trust Tel: 0208 2456420 / 0208 3740803
PO Box 55276 Mobile: 07549 943442
London N22 9FX Email: enquiries@yogatherapy.org
England Website: www.yogatherapy.org

Retreats • Workshops and Courses • Yoga • Meditation • Spiritual Help • Vegetarian

Yoga

The Yoga Biomedical Trust, a registered charity, holds residential re-treats led by Dr Shrikrishna Bhushan and Dr Uma Krishnamurthy in peaceful and well-established retreat locations in England. The trust was established in 1983 to facilitate the integrated growth of yoga therapy in the UK. Nationally and internationally respected, the trust provides yoga therapy to the public and carries out yoga therapy re-search. For those interested in advanced-level practical training, the trust offers courses in certain aspects of yoga therapy for suitably grounded yoga teachers.

Dr Shrikrishna's retreats are for yoga therapists, yoga teachers and experienced yoga students who are interested in deeper aspects of yoga. Until recently, Dr Shrikrishna was Principal of the Kaivalyadhama Yoga Institute in Bombay, one of the oldest and best-known yoga insti-tutes in the world. He is a medical doctor and a PhD, having carried out research on respiratory physiology and pranayama at the esteemed All India Institute of Medicine. At the root of his work is the understanding that yoga acts on two levels: as a science of health, to pave the way to personal growth; as a facilitator, to enter a transcendental transper-sonal state.

Dr Uma Krishnamurthy's retreats are also suitable for yoga thera-pists, yoga teachers, experienced yoga students, as well as psycholo-gists and others interested in spirituality and mental health. She is a pioneering figure in yoga psychology, evolving a new paradigm of heal-ing that draws on both ancient and modern insights. In her retreats, she explores the psychological guidelines given by yogic masters, sages and mystics that can help us overcome sorrow and stabilise us in hap-piness. This includes exploration of yogic approaches to discovering and manifesting our positive emotions and spiritual aspirations. Dr Krishnamurthy is a psychiatrist by training with many years of experi-ence in the healing of emotions.

OPEN: Per retreat or course. Usually 10–25 people attend.

ROOMS: Usually separate rooms for each guest. The accommodation depends on the venue.

FACILITIES: The daily schedule includes yoga sessions, talks and discussions, walks and group meditation, as well as time of individual activities.

SPIRITUAL HELP: A certain amount of individual spiritual help is offered.

GUESTS ADMITTED TO: There is no restriction on where you go. Silence is usually maintained during meals and at various other times.

MEALS: Meals are taken together in a dining room. The food is vegetarian, and individual diets are catered for.

SPECIAL ACTIVITIES: As discussed above in introduction.

SITUATION: Held at quiet, peaceful retreat centres in England, usually with garden, conference and group rooms, and beautiful surrounding countryside available for walks.

MAXIMUM STAY: Duration of retreat.

BOOKINGS: Letter, telephone, email.

CHARGES: The current cost ranges from £70 to £90 per day (including full board and lodging).

ACCESS: Access varies according to the venue but is usually within easy reach by public transport and a short taxi ride.

'For all sad words of tongue and pen,
the saddest are these,
"It might have been"'
– John Greenleaf Whittier

SOUTH WEST

CORNWALL

• •

ALSTON

Hampton Manor	Tel: 01579 370494
Alston, Callington	Email: hamptonmanor@supanet.com
Cornwall PL17 8LX	Website: www.hamptonmanor.co.uk
England	

Retreats • Workshops and Courses • Church/Temple • Bed and Breakfast
Vegetarian Food • Children

Christian – Anglican – Inter-denominational

Set in two acres of land in the Tamar Valley, Hampton Manor is a quaint old Victorian house that is a place of rest and holiday with a small programme of retreats and workshops, some spiritual in nature and some not. *Bird Watching, Visiting Gardens, Painting and Prayer, Christian Ramblers Week* and *Photography Week* are among the range of programmes on offer here. All who are seeking a place of spiritual and physical refreshment are welcome. There is a small chapel.

OPEN: All year except Christmas. Receives men, women, young people, families. Children welcome.
ROOMS: 6 twin/double en suite bedrooms.
FACILITIES: Disabled access, garden, guest lounge, TV. Conference facilities for around 40 people in separate building.
SPIRITUAL HELP: None.
GUESTS ADMITTED TO: Chapel, garden. Unrestricted access everywhere.
MEALS: Restaurant. Current prices: light lunch £6.95; afternoon tea £2.95; 3-course dinner from £15.95.
SPECIAL ACTIVITIES: Planned programme. See online.
SITUATION: Very quiet. Countryside.
MAXIMUM STAY: No limit.
BOOKINGS: Letter, telephone, email, online.
CHARGES: B&B from £35 per person (single supplement £15). Special weekly rates. Please enquire for short-break, seasonal and group discounts.
ACCESS: Rail: Gunnislake station is approx. 5 miles away; pick-up by arrangement. Car: consult the brochure map or website for travel details with directions.

FOWEY

Aquae Sulis Retreat
Fowey Hall
Hanson Drive
Fowey
Cornwall PL23 1ET
England

Tel: 01726 833866
Email: reservations@foweyhall.co.uk
Website: www.foweyhallhotel.co.uk /
www.aquaesulis.com/

Venue for Hire • Bed and Breakfast • Alternative Therapies • Holistic Holidays
Children • Pets

Open spirituality – Spa

Come visit the model for Toad Hall – the kids will love it and the spa facilities are designed for relaxing and winding down in comfort. A well-established feature on the landscape, Fowey Hall was the inspiration behind Toad Hall in *The Wind in the Willows* and overlooks the sailing and fishing port of Fowey on the south Cornish coast. It still has its original walled gardens with commanding views far out to sea. The new facilities here include four treatment rooms with a spa reception area, refurbished swimming pool, and a hot tub with sea views. Fowey Hall and its spa are very family orientated and there is a selection of various childcare facilities and children's activities. The aim is that the parents get a chance to relax in comfort and take some time out – but the children are with them for a family holiday too. We like the idea that time for the inner person does not have to exclude your children – or pets for that matter who may also be part of the family visit to Aquae Sulis Retreat. The hotel is within easy reach of the many superb attractions in Cornwall, including the Eden Project and the Lost Gardens of Heligan.

'All wrong-doing arises because of mind. If mind is transformed
can wrong-doing remain?'
– Buddha

HELSTON

Trelowarren Christian Fellowship
Trelowarren Christian Centre
Mawgan in Meneage, Helston
Cornwall TR12 6AF
England

Tel: 01326 221366
Email: info@trelowarren.cc
Website:
www.trelowarrenchristiancentre.com

Retreat • Church/Temple • Bed and Breakfast

Christian – Inter-denominational

Trelowarren Christian Fellowship's aims are the deepening of spiritual awareness and fellowship among Christians of all denominations and the promotion of the healing ministry of the church. Much of the ministry of this house is through hospitality to those individuals who are in need of space, peace and quiet, and most of the time the house is able to offer full-board accommodation.

OPEN: All year except Christmas.
ROOMS: 28 people in single, double and family rooms. All rooms have tea- and coffee-making facilities and are adequately heated. Most have hand basins.
FACILITIES: Conferences and retreats. A chapel seating 100, a large drawing room with a library and sitting room with television and video. Central heating in the main house and a log fire in the drawing room.
SPIRITUAL HELP: Christian fellowship. Prayer ministry sessions by arrangement.
GUESTS ADMITTED TO: Walks in the woods and the use of the estate grounds are subject to the time of year and by arrangement, but there is an extensive woodland walk leading down to the Helford River.
MEALS: All food is home cooked. Packed lunches can be made to order.
SPECIAL ACTIVITIES: Retreats.
SITUATION: The house is set in lovely grounds in the Lizard peninsula, one of the most beautiful areas of Cornwall.
MAXIMUM STAY: By arrangement.
BOOKINGS: Telephone, letter, email.
CHARGES: Overnight stay with continental breakfast £25 per person; half board £40; full board £55. Call to check that the prices are up-to-date and for possible special concessions for those in full-time ministry in need of a retreat or just a break away from it all.
ACCESS: Trelowarren is 1.5 miles from the main road where buses are infrequent, so a car is advisable if guests wish to tour around during their stay. Cornwall can be reached by train, the most convenient station being Redruth. National coaches serve Helston and Redruth direct. Arrangement can be made to meet guests.

PENDOGGETT ST KEW

Cornish Tipi Holidays
Tregare
Pendoggett St Kew
Cornwall PL30 3LW
England

Tel: 01208 880781
Fax: 01208 880487
Email: info@cornishtipiholidays.co.uk
Website: www.cornishtipiholidays.co.uk

Venue for Hire • Self-Catering Space • Camping • Children

Eco-spirituality

Cornish Tipi Holidays combine an ancient and traditional lifestyle with the lovely Cornish countryside. The tipis are in an old valley, which is full of local flora and fauna. Nearby a large freshwater lake offers swimming, fishing and boating. Tipi accommodation consists of both medium and large tipis fully equipped for up to four to six people. Families and children have found holiday fun and relaxation in taking a tipis retreat this way. Over the years the different kinds of activities that have taken place there are amazing: drumming workshop weekends, corporate team building, university reunions, hen parties, yoga retreats, outward-bound adventures, meditation and healing, find your inner man, canoe boating, surprise birthday weekends, Brownie groups and church outings. Cornish Tipi Holidays have played host to a diverse range of visitors, including adventure trekkers and walking groups, inner-city children, fathers and sons, learner divers, bird spotters, artists, surfers and historians. *Evening Standard* and *Observer* journalists have praised it. For current rates and details of what, why and how, visit their website.

'Try to spread your loving mind and heart to all that they may
have peace and happiness in their lives'
– Ven. Dhammavijitha Thera

PENZANCE

Space for You   Tel: 01736 810409
Sancreed House   Email:claredyas@madasafish.com
Sancreed, Penzance   Website: www.spaceforyou.biz /
Cornwall TR20 8QS   www.sancreedhouse.com
England

Retreats • Workshops and Courses • Meditation • Spiritual Help • Bed and Breakfast
Vegetarian Food • Alternative Therapies

Open spirituality

Space for You is a healing retreat in a peaceful setting at Sancreed House
for those who could use an essential break or just time out from their
everyday lives. The place is in the middle of the peninsula of west Cornwall, just five miles from Land's End, and offers a good range of events
and healing therapies. This retreat is particularly suited to those open
to an alternative approach to healing, including counselling, massage
and various sorts of bodywork and healing therapies. Opportunities
also exist here for the enjoyment of being creative through art work,
pottery, music and writing. Space for You can take people who are facing life challenges and changes or suffering from stress or distress.
They have experience in helping people with mental health problems
– an explanatory brochure is available. Personally tailored and structured programmes can be agreed upon in a flexible way, but people
must be able to spend some time alone. For people in serious crisis or
whose state of mind is very fragile, a discussion must take place before
a booking is accepted as to whether Space for You is able to meet the
person's needs. Creative Wednesdays usually last for a couple of hours
either in the morning or afternoon. Some of the themes are relaxation
through movement, paintings and pottery, and wood sculpture. There
are also drop-in sessions. Unusually for a retreat, it is possible for you,
if needed, to be accompanied on your local bus trip to Sancreed House.

ST JUST-IN-PENWITH

Boswedden House
Cape Cornwall
St Just-in-Penwith, Nr Penzance
Cornwall TR19 7NJ
England

Tel: 01736 788733
Email: relax@boswedden.org.uk
Website: www.boswedden.org.uk

Retreats • Workshops and Courses • Bed and Breakfast • Vegetarian Food
Venue for Hire • Alternative Therapies • Holistic Holidays

Mind Body Spirit

Situated on the Land's End Peninsula, Boswedden House provides a tranquil and comfortable place in its almost two acres of grounds for Mind Body and Spirit. It is both a retreat centre and a hotel. They have a varied programme of workshops, retreats, and courses. There are Louise Hay workshops as well, on her excellent themes of healing yourself and your life. Cheerful open fires in winter.

OPEN: All year. Everyone welcome.
ROOMS: 5 double/twins (3 of which can take an extra bed), 1 single, 1 family room. Takes up to 18 guests with additional accommodation nearby.
FACILITIES: Large conference/meeting room holding up to 50 people. Sitting/meeting room for up to 12 persons. Indoor heated swimming pool. Golf, fishing, sea bathing and surfing not far away.
SPIRITUAL HELP: Relaxation therapies.
GUESTS ADMITTED TO: Gardens, grounds.
MEALS: 3 courses plus coffee/tea: dinner £18; lunch £14. Packed lunch £3.50.
SPECIAL ACTIVITIES: Relaxation therapies.
SITUATION: Lovely countryside.
MAXIMUM STAY: By arrangement.
BOOKINGS: Letter, telephone, email.
CHARGES: B&B £32 to £45 per night, depending on the season and length of stay.
ACCESS: By car and public transportation. To be more environmentally friendly, they suggest you come by train or coach to Penzance, then take the bus to St Just. Boswedden House is a healthy 15-minute walk from the bus stop.

ST AUSTELL

The Retreat   Tel/Fax: 01726 851404
Higher Menadue   Email: davidmead@dmretreat.freeserve.co.uk
Bugle, St Austell   Website: www.dmretreat.freeserve.co.uk /
Cornwall PL26 8QW   www.plymouth-diocese.org.uk
England

> Retreats • Church/Temple • Spiritual Help

Christian – Roman Catholic

This is a small extended farmhouse with room for five guests. A tiny stone outbuilding has been converted to serve as a chapel for Mass and the reservation of the Blessed Sacrament. The centre is a private undertaking by a Roman Catholic priest but it enjoys the blessing of the Bishop of Plymouth.

TRURO

Epiphany House   Tel/Fax: 01872 272249
Kenwyn   Email: epiphanyhouse@keme.co.uk
Truro, Cornwall TR1 3DR Website: www.epiphanyhousetruro.co.uk
England

> Retreats • Workshops and Courses • Church/Temple • Bed and Breakfast
> Vegetarian Food • Venue for Hire • Self-Catering Space

Christian – Ecumenical

This historic house on the edge of Truro, set in beautifully kept gardens with views to the country and across the city, is a former convent and bishop's residence. It is now a Christian centre for day and residential conferences and retreats and is often called 'a haven of peace in a troubled world'. As well as groups, individual guests are welcome, for example on individual retreats or pilgrimages around Cornwall's Celtic holy sites. The house has 12 bedrooms, a variety of meeting rooms and a chapel where the Eucharist is celebrated twice weekly. Events aimed at promoting spiritual life are organised on a regular basis through the year, including Quiet Days and services that are open to all. It is about 15 minutes' walk from the city centre and it is possible to get around using public transport during your stay.

DEVON

ASHPRINGTON

The Barn Rural Retreat Centre
Lower Sharpham Barton, Ashprington
Totnes
Devon TQ9 7DX
England

Tel: 01803 732661
Email:
barn@sharphamtrust.org
Website: www.sharphamtrust.org/barn

Retreats • Workshops and Courses • Church/Temple • Yoga • Meditation • Spiritual Help
Vegetarian Food • Community Living • Work Retreats • Hermitages

Buddhist tradition – Non-denominational

The underlying purpose of the Barn, which has been going for some 13 years, is to create a working meditation retreat environment. The atmosphere is contemplative. During your stay here, you will be expected to be involved in the daily schedule of activities.

OPEN: All year. Receives men and women.
ROOMS: 7 singles.
FACILITIES: Garden, library, hermitage for solitary retreats.
SPIRITUAL HELP: Personal talks when a teacher is available. Meditation teaching.
GUESTS ADMITTED TO: Unrestricted access to all areas.
MEALS: Everyone eats together. Meals are vegetarian. Special diets possible but vegetarian food only.
SPECIAL ACTIVITIES: Daily schedule.
SITUATION: Very quiet and in the countryside. Beautiful location on the Sharpham Estate, on a hillside overlooking the River Dart – no roads visible. Fantastic views.
MAXIMUM STAY: 1 week to 6 months.
BOOKINGS: Letter, telephone, email, online.
CHARGES: Fees at the Barn are subsidised by the Sharpham Trust. The current rates per week for Barn retreats and guided retreats start at £175.
ACCESS: By car is best. However, pick-up is possible at 14:30 from Totnes railway station; contact the Barn on the Friday before arrival.

Sharpham Centre for Contemporary
Buddhist Enquiry
Ashprington
Totnes
Devon TQ9 7UT
England

Tel: 01803 732542
Email: centre@sharphamtrust.org
Website: www.sharphamtrust.org
Centre Coordinator and Tutor:
Tel: 01803 732708 /
Email: tutor@sharphamtrust.org

Retreats • Workshops and Courses • Church/Temple • Meditation • Spiritual Help
Vegetarian Food • Community Living • Work Retreats

Buddhist tradition – Non-denominational

Sharpham Centre for Contemporary Buddhist Enquiry occupies a beautiful English Palladian house with views stretching down to the River Dart. It is here that the Sharpham Trust strives to create a new way of education, aiming to achieve a balance between the practical and the spiritual. Although the approach is Buddhist, it does not adhere to any particular school. It offers a unique non-sectarian environment that enables you to look into how Buddhist values can have a place in our modern world.

OPEN: Most of year. Receives men and women.
ROOMS: Singles.
FACILITIES: Garden, library, lounge, shrine room, meditation room.
SPIRITUAL HELP: Personal talks, meditation, group sharing, directed study, personal retreat direction.
GUESTS ADMITTED TO: Shrine room, work of community.
MEALS: Everyone eats together. Meals are vegetarian.
SPECIAL ACTIVITIES: Programme and events online.
SITUATION: A busy and active place but nice to be in.
MAXIMUM STAY: Duration of course, programme or event.
BOOKINGS: Letter, telephone. Email is best.
CHARGES: Please enquire at time of booking. There is a rate for programmes but the teaching is by donation.
ACCESS: By car is best. Otherwise take a train to Totnes railway station and then a taxi.

BUCKFASTLEIGH

Buckfast Abbey   Tel: 01364 645558
Buckfastleigh   Website: www.buckfast.org.uk
Devon TQ11 0EE
England

Retreats • Workshops and Courses • Church/Temple • Meditation • Spiritual Help
Bed and Breakfast • Vegetarian Food • Venue for Hire • Self-Catering Space
Community Living • Vocations • Children

Christian – Roman Catholic

Each year over a million people come to visit the Abbey, to walk through its grounds by the River Dart and to admire the work of these monks. The great church was finished in 1937, largely restored to its original form, and is filled with beautiful artefacts from the enamelled and be-jewelled Stations of the Cross to the glorious marble mosaic floor of the nave. The Lady Chapel has one of the most impressive stained-glass windows of Christ in Europe. This is a top tourist attraction with shops, walks, and receives many thousands of visitors.

OPEN: All year except early January. Men are able to stay in the monastic guest house. In the same way, women and men are welcome in Southgate Guest House. Some provision for wheelchair users.
ROOMS: Singles and doubles. There are 3 guest houses plus men can stay in the monastery.
FACILITIES: Disabled access is reasonable. Church, large garden, guest lounge, library, gift shop, bookshop, monastic products centre, restaurant.
SPIRITUAL HELP: No guided retreats.
GUESTS ADMITTED TO: Church, public buildings, guest houses and grounds.
MEALS: Taken in guest house or monastery. Traditional food. Vegetarian and special diets catered for.
SPECIAL ACTIVITIES: Programme of retreats, talks, events, and courses.
SITUATION: Beautiful location, but many tourists.
MAXIMUM STAY: 1 week.
BOOKINGS: Letter. Online contact form is best (no direct email address).
CHARGES: Please enquire.
ACCESS: Car, local bus routes. Rail: nearest stations, Newton Abbot and Totnes, are 20 minutes' drive away.

COMBE MARTIN

Wild Pear Centre
King Street
Combe Martin
Devon EX34 0AG
England

Tel/Fax: 0208 3417226
Email: juliana@wildpearcentre.co.uk
Website: www.wildpearcentre.co.uk

Retreats • Workshops and Courses • Yoga • Meditation • Spiritual Help • Vegetarian Food

Mind Body Spirit – Kum Nye Tibetan Yoga

The Wild Pear Centre is situated in a seaside village, which is a gateway to Exmoor National Park. While no garden or grounds exist at the centre, you can treat the whole area like a wild garden on your doorstep. The centre is the venue for the Primal Integration Programme. Primal Integration involves an exploration of deeper levels of experience with a view to becoming more alive and living more authentically. The comprehensive programme has been running continuously for over 30 years.

OPEN: All year for bookings. Receives everyone.
ROOMS: Up to 25 guests in 3 twins, 2 doubles, 1 triple, 8 and 4 guests in 2 dormitory spaces.
FACILITIES: Guest hall, meeting room.
SPIRITUAL HELP: None.
GUESTS ADMITTED TO: Unrestricted access.
MEALS: Everyone eats together. Wholefood/vegetarian food. Special diets. DIY facilities.
SPECIAL ACTIVITIES: None.
SITUATION: Countryside. Quiet.
MAXIMUM STAY: Short stays only.
BOOKINGS: See above.
CHARGES: The charges vary – currently the Primal Integration Summer Residential course of five days is £430, including room and full board.
ACCESS: By car, train, bus. Train to Barnstaple station, then bus or taxi to Combe Martin; alternatively take a coach to Ilfracombe, then a bus or taxi.

*'In prayer it is better to have a heart without words than words
without a heart'*
– John Bunyan

DUNSFORD

Society of Mary and Martha   Tel: 01647 252752
The Sheldon Centre   Fax: 01647 253900
Dunsford   Email: smm@sheldon.uk.com
Exeter EX6 7LE   Website: www.sheldon.uk.com
England

Retreats • Workshops and Courses • Church/Temple • Self-Catering Space
Holistic Holidays • Community Living • Vocations • Hermitages • Children

Christian – Ecumenical

The Society of Mary and Martha is a lay community with the help of a large number of volunteers. The centre is comfortably set in its own grounds and fields in a lovely spot and it offers day hospitality and overnight stays by arrangement. There is a regular programme and an open-air theatre where various performances and worship are held.

OPEN: Most of the year. Everyone welcome, including families and children.
ROOMS: There are 2 different kinds of stay-over places available. First, there are what are termed lodges for clergy on retreat. Then there are separate self-contained units. Each has a bed-sitting room or sleeping deck, small kitchen, bathroom and is centrally heated. One is adapted for disabled guests.
FACILITIES: Open-air theatre for concerts, worship, community plays, and other theatre performances.
SPIRITUAL HELP: Prayer and supportive hospitality.
GUESTS ADMITTED TO: All guest areas.
MEALS: Meals and refreshments are provided for programme events.
SPECIAL ACTIVITIES: Programme of day and weekly retreats and events including in its theatre. Ask for details or visit the website.
SITUATION: In a countryside setting with its own green fields.
MAXIMUM STAY: By arrangement or by day.
BOOKINGS: Letter, telephone, email.
CHARGES: Prices vary. See full programme online. Day retreat costs £16 including lunch. Donations are suggested for private retreats.
ACCESS: By car, train. Rail: Exeter station, then taxi; Newton Abbot station, then cycle to Sheldon. Please visit the website for travel companion information. Sheldon is 10 miles from Exeter.

'Look within; you are *Buddha'*
– Zen saying

HITTISLEIGH

Buddhafield Retreats
Trevince House
Hittisleigh, Exeter
Devon EX6 6LP
England

Tel: 01647 24539 / 07747 446040
Email: retreatinfo@buddhafield.com
Website: www.buddhafield.com

Retreats • Workshops and Courses • Church/Temple • Meditation • Yoga • Spiritual Help
Vegetarian Food • Self-Catering Space • Community Living • Work Retreats • Vocations
Camping

Buddhist – Friends of the Western Buddhist Order (FWBO)

Buddhafield retreats are Buddhist camping events that take place on various beautiful sites in the south west of England. They offer a way to take a break from everyday routines and have a fresh experience of yourself in situations of stillness, beauty and peace. On these retreats, meditation techniques are taught that are intended to bring about a calm and friendly state of mind. On Buddhafield retreats, everyone lives lightly on the land, reducing waste and reusing and recycling wherever possible.

OPEN: Everyone welcome, but you need some meditation practice, so you should discuss suitability of the event before booking. There are retreats for men and for women. On some, children are welcome with their family.
ROOMS: Tents. Space in a communal dome or bender is provided for retreatants who do not have their own tent. The WCs are earth toilets.
FACILITIES: Camping, hot tubs, shrine tent.
SPIRITUAL HELP: Meditation.
GUESTS ADMITTED TO: Mostly everywhere on the retreat site. Please note that drugs, alcohol and dogs are not allowed on site.
MEALS: Meals are vegan and mostly organic. Self-catering possible. On-site shop with advance ordering possible, so you do not need a car.
SPECIAL ACTIVITIES: Previous experience is advisable for certain retreats. Those marked 'Open' in their programme are suitable for beginners and those marked 'Regulars' are suitable for those with some experience – 6 months or more – of the mindfulness of breathing and Metta Bhavana meditation practices. The retreats are designed to deepen your connection with the elements through simple practical work combined with meditation and study. Topics on a typical programme may include such retreats as *Tree Planting*, *Women's Buddafield Mitra Study*, *Men's Buddafield Mitra Study*, *Summer Open Retreat* and a *Permaculture Retreat*. Buddhafield organises its own festival as well.
SITUATION: A festival on a beautiful site, secluded and peaceful, away from roads, with coppice woodland and plenty of space.

MAXIMUM STAY: Full retreat period of the particular event. Guests are asked to stay for the full period offered.
BOOKINGS: Letter, online. If you are in doubt about the best retreat to choose, please contact Buddhafield before booking.
CHARGES: Committed to providing affordable retreats for those with genuine need by charging on a donation basis; there are 2 suggested rates for each event (normal/concession), which includes a non-negotiable deposit.
ACCESS: Buddhafield Retreats are working to reduce their carbon footprint. Please consider coming by public transport, in which case they will pick you up from the nearest railway (Yeoford) or bus station. Good public transport links.

HONITON

Hartridge Buddhist Monastery   Tel: 01404 891251
Upottery   Email: hartridge.monastery@gmail.com
Honiton   Website: www.hartridgemonastery.org
Devon, EX14 9QE
England

Retreats • Workshops and Courses • Church/Temple • Meditation • Spiritual Help
Vegetarian Food • Community Living • Work Retreats • Vocations • Children

Buddhist (Theravada tradition)

Hartridge has been a Buddhist monastery for many years now. With over 20 acres of land, it is a small sanctuary set in a lovely spot in rural Devon. The monastery, an old farmhouse, has a small community of monks and novices. Although the monastery is a place for monastic training, visitors and guests are welcome to share the lifestyle of the community. **Highly Recommended.**

OPEN: All year. Both men and women are welcome as well as families.
ROOMS: Accommodation at Hartridge is fairly basic, with separate living spaces for men and women.
FACILITIES: Temple, gardens, fields.
SPIRITUAL HELP: One of the monks is usually available to speak with visitors on Wednesdays and Sundays from 17:00 to 18:30.
GUESTS ADMITTED TO: Everywhere except community private areas.
MEALS: All food is vegetarian. Everyone eats the one main meal together. There is a simple 'tea' in the late afternoon. Guests help the community in the necessary domestic work.
SPECIAL ACTIVITIES: Meditation, sometimes a Dharma talk.
SITUATION: Fairly isolated and in a lovely green setting. Quiet and calm.
MAXIMUM STAY: Guests coming for the first time are welcome for an initial stay of up to a week. Special consideration can be given to those from overseas.

BOOKINGS: Anyone wishing to stay overnight should book as far in advance as possible, preferably by email or post.
CHARGES: All teaching, accommodation and food at Hartridge Monastery are freely offered. Donations and offerings of requisites are accepted.
ACCESS: By car and by public transportation from Honiton railway station. See good instruction details on the website.

St Rita's Centre Tel: 01404 42601
Ottery Moor Land Email: gerald.wilson1@btopenworld.com
Honiton Website: www.stritascentre.org.uk
Devon EX14 8AP
England

Church/Temple • Spiritual Help • Venue for Hire • Children

Christian – Roman Catholic

The friars have done a complete refurbishment and upgrade job at this centre, which is in a beautiful setting in east Devon. The welcome news for the disabled is that there is now a lift to all floors. In addition, there is a new conference room, day-course rooms and a new chapel. All the bedrooms are en suite. They cannot accommodate individuals except for religious and clergy.

OPEN: Open most of year. Receives everyone but not on individual lay-person retreats. Day visits possible.
ROOMS: 6 singles with 1 for disabled, 7 twins, 2 family rooms, all en suite.
FACILITIES: Disabled access, chapel, garden, library, guest lounge, bookshop. Conference room for up to 80 and smaller meeting rooms.
SPIRITUAL HELP: Divine Office, daily Mass. Otherwise ask.
GUESTS ADMITTED TO: Chapel. Invitation to take part in Divine Office.
MEALS: It depends on the event or retreat group. Traditional food. Vegetarian and special diets possible.
SPECIAL ACTIVITIES: Group retreats and special events.
SITUATION: Quiet.
MAXIMUM STAY: By arrangement.
BOOKINGS: Letter, telephone, email, online.
CHARGES: By donation and by arrangement.
ACCESS: By car and by taxi or bus from Honiton.

IVYBRIDGE

Serene Brook   Tel: 01548 830758
20 Aylston Park
Modbury, Ivybridge
Devon PL21 0TX
England

Retreats

Christian

This small house of prayer offers Quiet Days for small groups. There is a quiet garden and a stream on the edge of the village.

LYNTON

Lee Abbey Fellowship   Tel: 01598 752621 /
Lynton   0800 389118 (UK only)
Devon EX35 6JJ   Fax: 01598 752619
England   Website: www.leeabbey.org.uk

Retreats • Workshops and Courses • Church/Temple • Spiritual Help • Bed and Breakfast Vegetarian Food • Venue for Hire • Self-Catering Space • Community Living • Hermitages Camping • Children

Christian – Inter-denominational – Ecumenical

Voted one of the top 10 spiritual places in England by BBC listeners, Lee Abbey is a very large country estate in the Exmoor National Park. While from Anglican sources in tradition, today it is ecumenical, inter-denominational and international, sharing Christ through relationships and exisiting to glorify God. In addition to planned retreats, there are breakaway weeks or weekends for those who may wish to benefit from the accommodation and facilities without joining in an organised activity. **Highly Recommended.**

OPEN: All year except some weeks for events. Receives everyone.
ROOMS: 20 singles and 15 doubles with some en suite plus other multiple combinations that add up to 135 possible guests.
FACILITIES: Disabled access, conferences, library, guest lounges, TV, chapel, shop, laundry, playroom for kids, tennis courts, sports hall, mini-golf, private beach, 280-acre estate for walking.
SPIRITUAL HELP: None.

GUESTS ADMITTED TO: Access to house and grounds, chapel.
MEALS: Everyone eats together. Traditional food. Vegetarian and special diets. There are several self-catering accommodations in the grounds.
SPECIAL ACTIVITIES: A programme of retreats and events including Bible study and group retreats, but individuals are welcome on their breakaway retreats at other times. Brochure available and see online.
SITUATION: The house is set in a 280-acre coastal estate in the Exmoor National Park. Quiet surroundings.
MAXIMUM STAY: 2 weeks.
BOOKINGS: Letter. Online contact form is best (no direct email address).
CHARGES: Stated with the individual retreat, event or weekend.
ACCESS: By car.

Monastery of Poor Clares
Lynton
Devon EX35 6BX
England

Tel: 01598 753373
Website: www.poorclares.co.uk

Church/Temple • Spiritual Help • Self-Catering Space • Community Living • Vocations

Christian – Roman Catholic

An ideal and simple place for a private retreat or for those who need a very peaceful and modest base. Lovely walks by the sea. Guests stay in self-catering facilities, which include small kitchens. The Monastery of Poor Clares is a traditional monastic house with all the rich spiritual inheritance and daily life of prayer that this implies. It is a place to put aside your materialistic and personal comfort expectations for a while at least and to get down to some serious time with God. **Highly Recommended.**

OPEN: Most of year except Christmas and Holy Week. Receives men, women, non-retreatants and religious on retreat. There are also other Poor Clare communities at Arundel, Arkley, Edinburgh and Woodchester.
ROOMS: 2 doubles – 2 separate guest flats with twin beds and self-catering facilities.
FACILITIES: Nearby beaches and moor for walking. TV. No smoking.
SPIRITUAL HELP: Personal talks only by arrangement. Regular hours of community prayer and daily Mass.
GUESTS ADMITTED TO: Church, choir.
MEALS: Self-catering. DIY facilities. Meals served for visiting religious sisters in the refectory.
SPECIAL ACTIVITIES: Prayer, mass.
SITUATION: A delightful area in which to retreat from the world at large. On the edge of Exmoor National Park in very beautiful countryside by the sea.

MAXIMUM STAY: 2 weeks or by arrangement.
BOOKINGS: Letter, telephone. Online contact form is best (no direct email address).
CHARGES: No fixed charge but a donation is welcome, to cover costs at least and hopefully more. With most retreat houses charging around £45–£68 per day for self-catering facilities, we feel most guests will want to dig deeper in their pockets than that and at least give £50 per day.
ACCESS: Car: via A39. Train, National Express coaches and buses to Barnstaple, which is about 18 miles away.

NEWTON ABBOT

Gaia House	Tel: 01626 333613
West Ogwell	Email: info@gaiahouse.co.uk
Newton Abbot	Website: www.gaiahouse.co.uk
Devon TQ12 6EN	
England	

Retreats • Workshops and Courses • Church/Temple • Meditation • Spiritual Help
Vegetarian Food • Alternative Therapies • Community Living • Work Retreats • Vocations
Hermitages • Camping • Children

Buddhist

Gaia House was founded in 1984 to provide a setting for the teaching and practice of ethics, meditation and wisdom learning. The centre is set in quiet countryside and offers a full programme with facilities for individual practice, including solitary retreats and Buddhist long retreats. There is an excellent joint Gaia House/Sharpham Centre programme, which offers a selection of weekends from taught-study weekends to weekends exploring the interrelationship of meditation and other disciplines. The environment at Gaia House is a silent one and there is opportunity to enjoy solitude. Work retreats are also available. **Highly Recommended.**

OPEN: All year. Receives men, women, young people. Family retreats are offered once a year. Groups and non-retreatants only on a 1-day retreat basis.
ROOMS: Space for 20–30 people but no guarantee of a single room; some doubles, dormitory, hermitage wing for long retreats.
FACILITIES: Meditation room, park, garden, library, guest lounge and payphone. Partial disabled access.
SPIRITUAL HELP: Meditation, personal talks, interviews with teacher of retreat.
GUESTS ADMITTED TO: Unrestricted access.
MEALS: Everyone eats together. All food is wholefood vegetarian and very good. Medical diets only are catered for.

SPECIAL ACTIVITIES: Mindfulness cognitive therapies. Group and personal retreats offered. See online programme.
SITUATION: Very quiet, in the countryside. Gaia is a silent house.
MAXIMUM STAY: Usually a week. Otherwise by arrangement.
BOOKINGS: Letter, telephone, email, online application form.
CHARGES: Currently vary from: a nightly rate of £31 for personal retreatants; weekend group retreat £87–£122; long weekend group retreat £115–162; 5-night group retreat £169–£239. See online for more details.
ACCESS: By car is best, but visit the website to find out about the online liftshare notice board.

SEATON

Peacehaven	Tel: 01297 21681
Harepath Holidays Ltd	Fax: 07092 083481
Harepath Hill	Email: stay@harepathholidays.com
Seaton	Website: www.peacehaven.org.uk
Devon EX12 2TA	
England	

Bed and Breakfast • Venue for Hire • Self-Catering Space • Children

Christian – Open spirituality

Set in five acres of peaceful picturesque east Devon countryside, enjoying panoramic views over the Axe Valley. Chapel, conference facilities and retreats for families and individuals.

OPEN: All year. Everyone welcome.
ROOMS: Flexible accommodation for a wide range of holiday and personal retreat needs from B&B for individuals to families with evening meals if required.
FACILITIES: Dining room, chapel, conference room, indoor heated swimming pool, gardens, lounges.
SPIRITUAL HELP: None.
GUESTS ADMITTED TO: All guest areas.
MEALS: Traditional food is provided, but self-catering is also possible.
SPECIAL ACTIVITIES: None. Does not at this time have any programme of retreats, but check online for up-to-date information.
SITUATION: Countryside by the sea.
MAXIMUM STAY: By arrangement.
BOOKINGS: Letter, telephone, fax, email. Online contact form is easiest and best method.
CHARGES: The rates vary with type of accommodation, number of guests in the room and time of year, so you need to ask when you enquire about booking.
ACCESS: By car, train, bus. Rail: Axminster station (6 miles from Seaton). Buses run from Axminster to Seaton, from where there are several routes to Peacehaven. See online for detailed travel directions.

SIDMOUTH

The Old Kennels
Boswell Farm
Sidford, near Sidmouth
Devon EX10 0PP
England

Tel: 01395 514162
Email: dillion@boswell-farm.co.uk
Website: www.oldkennels-boswell.co.uk

Retreats • Workshops and Courses • Yoga • Meditation • Self-Catering Space
Children • Pets

Non-religious

Just 16 miles from Exeter, the Old Kennels is a group of buildings that are available for a variety of retreats and workshops. The facility includes two excellent studios with a professionally sprung floor for dance, yoga and other floor-based activities. Tennis courts, spring water, trout pond and abundant wildlife all about you make this a cosy, attractive and up-to-date place.

OPEN: All year. Everyone welcome.
ROOMS: 7 self-catering cottages; each sleeps 4–6 guests. Good kitchens and each cottage has its own private garden area for sitting out.
FACILITIES: 2 studios, divided by sliding doors which can be opened to create a single very large space.
SPIRITUAL HELP: None.
GUESTS ADMITTED TO: All guest areas and walking among the farm's 45 acres of fields.
MEALS: Self-catering.
SPECIAL ACTIVITIES: Short programme including holistic weekends: see online. Tennis and walking.
SITUATION: Boswell Farm is within a designated Area of Outstanding Natural Beauty.
MAXIMUM STAY: By arrangement.
BOOKINGS: Letter, telephone, email.
CHARGES: You need to ask when booking what the current rates are.
ACCESS: By car or by train to Sidmouth and then taxi or other transport arrangements.

ST LEONARDS

The Devon School of Yoga
4 Barnfield Hill
St Leonards, Exeter
Devon EX1 1SR
England

Tel/Fax: 01392 420573
Email: info@devonyoga.com
Website: www.devonyoga.com

Retreats • Workshops and Courses • Yoga • Meditation

Yoga

The Devon School of Yoga brings together classes, workshops, retreats and training courses about all aspects of yoga. These are held in venues around Devon, making the yoga very accessible, particularly in rural areas. The school teaches a holistic approach to yoga and is a member of the Independent Yoga Network.

TOTNES

The Gatekeeper Trust
7 The Chapel
The Plains, Totnes
Devon TQ9 5DW
England

Tel: 01803 864680
Email: secretary@gatekeeper.org.uk
Website: www.gatekeeper.org.uk

Retreats • Workshops and Courses • Work Retreats • Camping • Children

Eco-spirituality

This is a very exciting development in eco-spirituality, linking our mind, body and spirit to our beloved Mother Earth in events that call forth our deepest sense of the sacred by visiting sacred places, celebrating them and increasing our awareness – and joy – of belonging to her. The Gatekeeper Trust works to increase our awareness of how to walk on Earth in a simple and sacred way. It is a pure way of mindfulness. These walks follow in the ancient footsteps of other sacred walking such as Hindu, Christian and Islamic pilgrimages, Australian Aborigine walkabouts and in Native American Great Father journeys. Courses and events and journeys are held in Britain and abroad. **Highly Recommended.**

WESTLEIGH

Mill House Retreats
Rockwell Manor Farm
Westleigh, near Tiverton
Exeter EX16 7ES
England

Tel: 01884 829000
Email: janetaylor@millhouseretreats.co.uk
Website: www.millhouseretreats.co.uk

Retreats • Workshops and Courses • Spiritual Help • Vegetarian Food • Venue for Hire
Self-Catering Space • Alternative Therapies

Open spirituality

Situated in Devon's heartland midway between Taunton and Exeter, Rocknell Manor Farm, home to Mill House Retreats, is an ancient Devon farmhouse dating back to the sixteenth century. The place has long settled itself in its seven acres and is within easy reach of some of Devon and Somerset's most beautiful countryside. You will be welcomed even if you just want some quiet space to read and reflect, often the best kind of retreat for those going through periods of change in their lives or those who may welcome an opportunity to explore faith outside the institution of the church. Various therapeutic treatments can be booked in advance, including massage. Guests are welcome to join the resident community for chapel times in the morning and evening. These typically include music, meditations and silence, readings and simple liturgies.

WHITESTONE

The Beacon Centre
Cutteridge Farm
Whitestone
Exeter EX4 2HE
England

Tel: 01392 811401
Email: yogameup@mac.com
Website: www.beacon-centre.com

Retreats • Workshops and Courses • Yoga • Meditation • Spiritual Help • Bed and Breakfast
Vegetarian Food • Venue for Hire • Work Retreats • Hermitages • Camping • Children

Yoga – Meditation

The centre is devoted to yoga and meditation, offering retreats, courses and teaching. The heart of the centre is a courtyard around which are the farmhouse, the centre and the residences. The centre has been running many years and is well established. **Highly Recommended.**

DORSET

BRIDPORT

The Othona Community
Coast Road
Burton Bradstock
Bridport
Dorset DT6 4RN
England

Tel: 01308 897130
Email: mail@othona-bb.org.uk
Website: www.othona-bb.org.uk

Retreats • Workshops and Courses • Church/Temple • Vegetarian Food • Organic Food
Community Living • Work Retreats • Vocations • Children

Christian – Ecumenical

Underlying everything at Othona is an experience of community. All visitors take some share in the daily life, from peeling potatoes to perhaps contributing a reading or music for chapel. It's an informal, unstuffy place – not much pious talk, but plenty of laughter. In an age of much personal isolation and epidemic stress, this experience of community is precious. It's what Christians have long called Fellowship of the Holy Spirit – though it's not the property of any one religion. The events programme ranges from family holiday weeks to times of retreat, with all kinds of courses and workshops in between. This is a green place. They treat grey water and sewage through reed beds, are in the process of converting the chapel roof to provide photo-voltaic electricity generation, and replacing their warden's bungalow using recycled local stone, solar-thermal water heating and rainwater harvesting. They manage wild grounds for species diversification and run a number of events each year that focus on wildlife and environment. One family event recently built a functioning raft to demonstrate electricity generation from waves on the beach – what one might call an in-your-face green experience. **Highly Recommended.**

Pilsdon Manor
Bridport
Dorset DT6 5NZ
England

Tel: 01308 868308
Email: pilsdon@btconnect.com
Website: www.pilsdon.org.uk

Retreats • Church/Temple • Meditation • Spiritual Help • Vegetarian Food
Community Living • Work Retreats • Vocations

Christian – Anglican – Ecumenical

Pilsdon is a community dedicated to the ideals of the Christian Gospel and these are put into real action. They live a life of simplicity within a daily structure of prayer, meals, work and recreation. The spirituality is Anglican but ecumenical in expression. People of any faith, or none, and of any race, culture or sexual orientation are made welcome. The chapel and church are open all the time and services are held four times a day and attendance is voluntary. Shelter, hospitality and spiritual refreshment for those in need of refuge without regard to gender, race or creed are truly what is offered. Such refuge is open to people in crisis, those working through depression, alcoholism, addiction, divorce or bereavement. The community also welcomes people who wish to find a time to reflect on their lives before making a change in direction, or just want time out to live as part of a community. Pilsdon is not a detoxification or treatment centre and does not accept people on methadone or similar prescriptions. There is a referral process if you wish to stay here with the community. Up to about 25 people live here at any one time. No special diets or self-catering are possible and you live as part of the community, participating, serving and belonging. Pilsdon is, indeed, that very special retreat – a sanctuary for the practice of Christian love. **Highly Recommended.**

'If you can, help others; if you cannot do that,
at least do not harm them'
– the Dalai Lama

CHARMOUTH

Monkton Wyld Court
Charmouth
Bridport
Dorset DT6 6DQ
England

Tel: 01297 560342
Email: info@monktonwyldcourt.org /
bookings@monktonwyldcourt.org
Website: www.monktonwyldcourt.co.uk

Retreats • Workshops and Courses • Meditation • Bed and Breakfast • Vegetarian Food
Venue for Hire • Alternative Therapies • Holistic • Holidays • Community Living
Work Retreats • Vocations • Camping • Children

Mind Body Spirit – Holistic education

Eleven acres of grounds surround this large Victorian rectory, which is situated in a secluded valley on the Devon–Dorset border. This green, healthy space helps people to find their inner awareness. Monkton is a leading centre for holistic education. The emphasis is on encouraging personal and spiritual growth, combined with a firm commitment to ecology, green issues and self-sufficiency.

OPEN: All of the year. Occasional closures. Receives men, women, young people, families, groups, non-retreatants. Children welcome.
ROOMS: 3 doubles, 8 dormitories, barn. A single by arrangement. Camping.
FACILITIES: Possibility of camping, garden, library, guest lounge, crafts shop, arts and crafts facilities, meditation room, massage and healing room, guest phone.
SPIRITUAL HELP: Through the courses and retreats on offer and meditation.
GUESTS ADMITTED TO: Everywhere except community living areas. Work of the community.
MEALS: Everyone eats together. Vegetarian organic wholefood.
SPECIAL ACTIVITIES: Planned programme of events. See online.
SITUATION: Very quiet, in the countryside.
MAXIMUM STAY: Depending on course being attended or by arrangement.
BOOKINGS: Letter, telephone, email. Online is best.
CHARGES: B&B £29; half board (lunch or supper) £35; full board £42. Children aged 0–4 £5 / aged 5–14 half price. Camping (without meals) 1 tent: 1 adult £10; 2nd adult £3.50; 1 child £1.50. For meals only: breakfast £3.50; lunch £6; supper £7 (children's meals are half price).
ACCESS: Rail: Axminster station is 3 miles away; taxis should be pre-booked. Car: via A35.

GILLINGHAM

Osho Leela
Thorngrove House
Common Mead Lane
Gillingham
Dorset SP8 4RE
England

Tel: 01747 821221 / 0845 6125511 (UK only)
Fax: 01747 826386
Email: info@osholeela.co.uk
Website: www.osholeela.co.uk

Retreats • Workshops and Courses • Yoga • Meditation • Spiritual Help • Vegetarian Food
Organic Food • Venue for Hire • Self-Catering Space • Alternative Therapies
Community Living • Work Retreats • Vocations • Camping

Mind Body Spirit – Osho (formerly Bhagwan Shree Rajneesh)

Osho Leela welcomes all spiritual seekers and visitors for groups and celebration events. The goal of the community seems to be to live joyously and to inspire others to do the same – the greatest of aims. A very lively, hospitable place with a truly active programme of events.

OPEN: Always open. Everyone is welcome.
ROOMS: 5 dorms, 6 mobile homes, 1 pine lodge, 2 double rooms and a campsite for up to 200.
FACILITIES: Group rooms (60 and 90 sq.m.), garden, 15 acres of grounds, internet and wireless access, yurt sauna, marquee (160 sq.m.), PA system.
SPIRITUAL HELP: Body-based therapy working strongly with emotions, and meditation.
GUESTS ADMITTED TO: Everywhere.
MEALS: Taken alone or together as you wish, but mostly together in the dining room. Self-catering facilities. Home cooking. All food is vegetarian. Special diets catered for.
SPECIAL ACTIVITIES: Regular programme of courses and retreats. Private retreats. Self-managed group retreats.
SITUATION: In the heart of the Dorset countyside.
MAXIMUM STAY: As long as you like.
BOOKINGS: Telephone, email, online.
CHARGES: Average is £40/per person per night. There is a Community Experience Programme (£70/week or £12/day) for anyone interested in experiencing life in the community.
ACCESS: Rail: Gillingham station; pick-up by arrangement, otherwise it's about £4 for a taxi. Car: please see website for detailed directions.

HILFIELD

The Friary of St Francis
Society of St Francis
Hilfield
Dorchester DT2 7BE
England

Tel: 01300 342313
Email: hilfieldproject@franciscans.org.uk /
hilfieldguests@franciscans.org.uk
Website: www.franciscans.org.uk /
www.hilfieldproject.co.uk

Retreats • Workshops and Courses • Church/Temple • Spiritual Help • Vegetarian Food
Self-Catering Space • Community Living • Vocations

Christian – Anglican

There are 19 acres of land to explore at the Friary of St Francis, made up of woodland and meadow, kitchen and formal gardens, as well as Brother Vincent's Secret Garden of rhododendrons and camellias. The friary is situated halfway between Dorchester and Sherborne in deepest Dorset, with wonderful views over the Blackmore Vale with great walks all around. It is very quiet, calm and green – both in the visual sense and the ecological one. The community – and guests over the years – have helped make the place very green indeed, with even a reed-bed sewage system. They reuse, recycle and repair all that they can, use all low-energy bulbs, try to keep their total carbon footprint small with the goal of using less electricity every year, have two wood-burning stoves, use water from a bore hole on their land, and are exploring other ways of making the energy they use. People are encouraged to visit here by public transport, and bicycles are available to borrow from the friary. The garden uses organic gardening methods and kitchen waste is composted for use in the garden. As if this were all not enough to inspire every retreat place, the friary is designated an Area of Outstanding Natural Beauty and manages the land to provide many different habitats – wood, meadow and pond. The meadows have been praised by Natural England for their diversity, as well as the orchids, the many different grasses and the wild flowers in early summer. The nearest shop is several miles away and there are no street lights. Visitors are welcome to take part in the life of the community; each working day begins with a diary meeting to which everyone is invited and during which the tasks of the day are assigned. Some examples of the type of retreats or courses here are *Buddhism, Christianity and the Violence of the Self, Working for a World without War, Making Peace where we Live, Work and Pray* and W*orld Earth Day Celebration*. **Highly Recommended.**

OPEN: The friary is open to stay or visit from Tuesday to Sunday afternoon. The self-catering cottages on the site are available at any time.

ROOMS: The Friary Guest House has 6 singles, 1 downstairs room and 2 twins. Self-catering accommodation in Juniper House with 5 singles, 1 en suite downstairs, 1 twin, and a kitchen and lounge. Bernard House has 4 singles, 1 en suite downstairs, 1 twin, 1 double, and a kitchen and lounge. The self-catering cottages have well-equipped kitchens for guests to provide their own meals.

FACILITIES: Visitors are welcome to join the community in worship at all of the services; they take place in the main Chapel of St Francis. Clare Chapel and St Mary of the Angels are both available for private prayer. The library is open to all guests as is the guest common room. A large recreation room can be used by day groups and others on request. An art room and workshops are well equipped and may also be available to guests.

SPIRITUAL HELP: Members of the community, both brothers, ordained and lay members of the community are available for spiritual direction, or spiritual companionship.

GUESTS ADMITTED TO: Everywhere except in the community's private areas.

MEALS: If you are staying at the guest house, meals can be taken alone; more commonly you would eat with the community in the refectory. The community bakes its own bread and tries to provide food from the friary's land. There is a vegetarian option with advance notice.

SPECIAL ACTIVITIES: There is an annual programme of weekends, Quiet Days and retreats, which draw upon both the community and Hilfield and outside speakers. People are welcome to come as private retreatants or bring a self-managed group.

SITUATION: In a good situation in the countryside with great views, a quiet place and dark night sky – lovely!

MAXIMUM STAY: Tuesday morning to Sunday afternoon.

BOOKINGS: Telephone, letter, email.

CHARGES: Accommodation is based on a donation recommendation of guest house £30 per person per night. Self-catering £17.50 per person per night with a minimum of 4 sharing. Retreats and courses vary but range from £85 to £100 per weekend.

ACCESS: Trains or buses arriving at Sherborne, Yeovil or Dorchester can be met.

'God in his mercy looks on you not for what you are, nor for what you have been, but for what you wish to be'
– The Cloud of Unknowing

HOLTON HEATH

Holton Lee	Tel: 01202 625562
East Holton	Fax: 01202 632632
Holton Heath, Poole	Email: admin@holtonlee.co.uk
Dorset BH16 6JN	Website: www.holtonlee.co.uk
England	

Retreats • Workshops and Courses • Church/Temple • Meditation • Spiritual Help
Bed and Breakfast • Vegetarian Food • Venue for Hire • Self-Catering Space
Alternative Therapies • Camping • Children

Open spirituality – Inter-denominational – Holistic

Lying between Poole and Wareham, Holton Lee is a centre for every-one, with lots of room and other arrangements for people with dis-abilities and for carers. Here you can find relaxation, respite, retreats, events, education activities and courses. The four aspects of Holton Lee are: Arts; Disability and Carers; Environment; Personal Growth and Spirituality. As expressed in 1993 by founder-member Faith Lees, Holton Lee is a centre to which people can come to discover new and innovative approaches, whether in practical ways or in ways that in-tegrate the spiritual, psychological and physical aspects of their lives – not separating out and compartmentalising by making a division between science and religion, able-bodied and disabled, creative and practical – thus demonstrating a holistic and a healing view of life. Such a transformative quality of life is based on the holistic integration of the four aspects of Holton Lee that are integral to and inform each other both in practice and theory. Personal assistance is provided for personal care, washing, showering, dressing and the administration of personal medication. Night-time personal assistance is for emergen-cy cover only. East Holton Driving Centre is based at Holton Lee and provides opportunities for disabled people to learn carriage driving. **Highly Recommended.**

OPEN: All year. Receives men, women, young people (under-16s must be accompanied by a guardian), families, small groups, non-retreatants. Children welcome.
ROOMS: 10 en suite twins, fully accessible bedrooms, each with its own TV and WiFi access. Accommodation for up to 20 guests in total; good for individuals, couples, families and groups. The beds provided are either adjustable for height or have a raising mechanism at the head or foot of the bed. Each bedroom has: French doors leading out to a sunny terrace; private en suite wet room with ceiling hoist and Clos-o-Mat toilet; a paging–alarm system to summon assistance if required; individual temperature controls; a ceiling hoist to provide easy transfer from wheelchair to bed

to wet room, where necessary. First-class personal assistance can be tailored to meet individual needs.

FACILITIES: Disabled access, WiFi, small conferences, sometimes camping, garden, guest lounge, TV. Holton Lee has 2 golf buggies and 5 Trampers (all terrain mobility scooters) available for guests to explore the 350-acre site. Guide dogs accepted.

SPIRITUAL HELP: Weekly time of reflection, incorporating words, music and silence. Personal talks.

GUESTS ADMITTED TO: Unrestricted access everywhere. Chapel.

MEALS: Everyone eats together. Self-catering also available. Traditional/vegetarian food. Special diets catered for.

SPECIAL ACTIVITIES: Pottery, printmaking, stone carving, carriage driving, birdwatching in hides (one overlooks a pond) – check for availability. See online for planned programme of events.

SITUATION: Quiet and in the countryside, with 350 acres of beautiful land with paths to go on.

MAXIMUM STAY: 1–3 weeks and by arrangement for shorter or longer stays.

BOOKINGS: Letter, telephone, fax, email, online.

CHARGES: The rates vary depending on the time of year, on single or twin occupancy of a room, and on B&B or full-board accommodation (continental breakfast, light lunch (or packed lunch) and evening meal). Single occupancy rates start from £65 per person; twin/double occupancy from £50 per person. Personal assistance is available both for minimal assistance and a higher level of assistance need, for which there is a charge of £30 per day.

ACCESS: Train, bus, car all possible. Poole is 6 miles away and Wareham is 4 miles away.

HOLWELL

Middle Piccadilly Spa Retreat and Wellness Centre
Holwell
Dorset DT9 5LW
England

Tel: 01963 23468
Email: dominic@middlepiccadilly.com
Website: www.middlepiccadilly.com

Retreats • Workshops and Courses • Bed and Breakfast • Vegetarian Food
Alternative Therapies • Holistic Holidays

Mind Body Spirit – Spa – Holistic

A seventeenth-century thatched cottage with attractively converted buildings, Middle Piccadilly Spa Retreat and Wellness Centre is set in beautiful Dorset countryside. It offers peaceful detox and de-stress retreats in a simple but comfortable back-to-basics atmosphere with no television, radio, road noise or light pollution. The therapies and kinds of stays are truly wide ranging.

OPEN: No more than 9 guests at any one time.
ROOMS: 2 doubles, 1 double en suite and 3 singles.
FACILITIES: Therapy rooms. An intimate aquaspa is in the garden, which is a room with a hot tub, sink, treatment bed and shower.
SPIRITUAL HELP: Through the benefits of relaxation and the healing therapies.
GUESTS ADMITTED TO: All guest areas and garden.
MEALS: All meals served at Middle Piccadilly are vegetarian. Meals are reasonably simple for maximum health benefit. Breakfast is continental in style and self-service.
SPECIAL ACTIVITIES: There is no set programme. Brochure available. Examples of what may be on offer include *Body Fresh*, *In the Spirit of Escape*, *Food for the Soul* and *Detox Juice Breaks*.
SITUATION: Middle Piccadilly nestles in the heart of the Dorset countryside.
MAXIMUM STAY: Usually about 5 nights but longer is possible by arrangement.
BOOKINGS: Telephone, letter, email.
CHARGES: To give an idea of cost, current rates are: 2 nights' accommodation, full board and consultation at £199 per person; 5 nights' accommodation, full board and consultation at £475 per person. When booking, ask about the latest charges and any special-rate stays. There are themed stays and these are priced individually.
ACCESS: Easily accessible by road or rail. Sherborne railway station is 4 miles away.

POOLE

Green Pastures
Christian Centre of
Pastoral Care and Healing
17 Burton Road
Branksome Park, Poole
Dorset BH13 6DT
England

Tel: 01202 764776 / 0845 2302680 (UK only)
Email: admin@green-pastures.org
Website: www.green-pastures.org

Retreats • Workshops and Courses • Church/Temple • Spiritual Help • Vegetarian Food
Venue for Hire • Alternative Therapies • Children

Christian – Inter-denominational

Professional counselling, spiritual direction and some healing therapies are on offer here, as well as single and double accommodation, some en suite. A peaceful place just to be and to find healing and renewal.

OPEN: All year. Everyone welcome. Special rates for children.
ROOMS: 9 singles, 11 twins/doubles, most en suite.
FACILITIES: Chapel, lounges, seasonal-use heated swimming pool, gardens, conferences, group bookings.
SPIRITUAL HELP: Crisis counselling, spiritual accompaniment and direction, Ignatian exercises, healing therapies.
GUESTS ADMITTED TO: Gardens, chapel, mostly everywhere.

MEALS: Home-cooked food. Vegetarian possible.
SPECIAL ACTIVITIES: Retreat and events programme. Downloadable online brochure. Spiritual help and counselling. Massage therapy.
SITUATION: About a mile from the sea.
MAXIMUM STAY: Minimum of 2 nights up to 21-night stay.
BOOKINGS: Online is best.
CHARGES: Currently: budget single £40; single £48; single en suite £60; double £87, double en suite £108. All rates are per night full board. Special rates for children.
ACCESS: By car, train or coach. (Take the train or coach to Bournemouth.) Good map online.

WIMBORNE

Gaunts House
Wimborne
Dorset BH21 4JQ
England

Tel: 01202 841522
Email: admin@gauntshouse.com
Website: www.gauntshouse.com

Retreats • Workshops and Courses • Church/Temple • Yoga • Meditation • Spiritual Help
Bed and Breakfast • Vegetarian Food • Venue for Hire • Self-Catering Space
Holistic Holidays • Community Living • Work Retreats • Vocations • Camping • Children

Open spirituality

Gaunts House is dedicated to the development of life on a spiritual basis. It offers space and help for spiritual and personal development with a supportive community, all set in beautiful parkland. The facilities are wide ranging from a sanctuary to healing rooms. The programme is always broad and interesting. **Highly Recommended.**

OPEN: All year. Receives men, women, young people, families and groups. Children welcome. No pets.
ROOMS: Can accommodate a great many people. Singles, doubles, camping, dormitories.
FACILITIES: Disabled access. Multimedia equipment: overhead projector, screens, flipcharts, DVD player, large-screen TV, stereo equipment, computer access. Library, conferences, the old hall, bar by request, meditation room, dining room (seats 60–84 people, extra dining space for 25 people). Alternative therapies, starhenge, labyrinth, fire circle in the grounds, camping facilities, summer swimming pool, country walks, herd of deer, bluebell woods, old Victorian walled garden. Plenty of parking.
SPIRITUAL HELP: Personal talks, group sharing, meditation, support and advice. Therapies available on request.
GUESTS ADMITTED TO: Unrestricted access to all areas, including sanctuary, work of the community.
MEALS: Vegetarian – guests can share the cooking. Food may be brought or purchased there. Provision for special diets if necessary.

SPECIAL ACTIVITIES: Planned programme of events. Send for biannual brochure.
SITUATION: Very quiet in the countryside.
MAXIMUM STAY: Unlimited.
BOOKINGS: Letter, telephone, email. Online best.
CHARGES: These vary, so email for rates. Free rooms are offered to pilgrims, monks, nuns and the ordained.
ACCESS: Train, bus, car all possible. Buses run from Poole and Bournemouth to Wimborne, and then take a taxi to Gaunts House, which is about 3 miles away.

SOMERSET

BATH

Downside Abbey
Stratton on the Fosse
Radstock, Bath
Somerset BA5 4RH
England

Tel: 01761 235161
Fax: 01761 235124
Email: monks@downside.co.uk
Website: www.downside.co.uk
(follow the link for 'Downside Abbey')
For Guestmaster of Monastery Guest House:
Tel: 01761 235153
Email: dommartin@downside.co.uk

Retreats • Workshops and Courses • Church/Temple • Spiritual Help • Venue for Hire
Self-Catering Space • Community Living • Vocations

Christian – Roman Catholic – Ecumenical

The home of a famous boys' public school with an abbey church of cathedral proportions. The community welcomes men in the Monastery Guest House who wish to share the monastic prayer and quiet or who may just want a peaceful private break.

OPEN: All year except Christmas, over Easter and at times during July and August. Receives men only in the Monastery Guest House.
ROOMS: 11 singles, all en suite.
FACILITIES: Abbey church, garden, library (by permission), guest lounge, TV, guest phone.
SPIRITUAL HELP: Personal talks, directed study.
GUESTS ADMITTED TO: Chapel. Guests are not to enter the school area.
MEALS: Everyone eats together. Traditional food. Vegetarians catered for.
SPECIAL ACTIVITIES: None.
SITUATION: Quiet, near the village, about 12 miles from Bath.
MAXIMUM STAY: 1 week.
BOOKINGS: Letter, telephone.

CHARGES: No fixed charge, but guests are welcome to leave a donation in accordance with their means. It costs currently about £30 a day to provide full board and lodging, bed and breakfast costs are £25.
ACCESS: Train to Bath Spa. Bus from Bath Spa to Stratton on the Fosse. Car: via A367.

Bainesbury House and	Tel: 01761 235114
St Bede Centre	Email: domalexander@downside.co.uk
England	Website: www.downside.co.uk
	(follow the link for 'Downside Abbey' and then 'Hospitality')

Bainesbury House is a few minutes' walk from Downside Abbey Church, where you may share in the daily worship of the monks. The house contains one single and one twin room, and three dormitories. Charges currently are £6 per person per night. There is a living room with a small library, and a dining room and kitchen. This retreat guest house is open to all Christian individuals and groups and is self-catering. **St Bede Centre** may be used for conferences, study days and retreats, as well as exhibitions. Everyone welcome.

B R I S T O L

AdventureYogi	Tel: 07929 168237
109 Richmond Rd	Email: info@adventureyogi.com
Montpelier	Website: www.adventureyogi.com
Bristol BS6 5EP	
England	

Retreats • Workshops and Courses • Yoga • Meditation • Spiritual Help • Vegetarian Food
Alternative Therapies • Holistic Holidays

Yoga

With their yoga retreats in Britain, France, Sardinia, Egypt and beyond, welcome to a fresh approach from AdventureYogi Holidays, who balance yoga for mind and body with exciting adventure sports like skiing and surfing, a choice of alternative healing treatments, and good food in beautiful locations. In Britain they also run well-being Weekends. Sun, sea, ski and surf – the choice is yours.

OPEN: Throughout the year in various locations. Everyone welcome.

ROOMS: Depends on where the accommodation is – but twin rooms mostly with a single supplement available. Some rooms are en suite while others may be sharing facilities.

FACILITIES: Garden, hot tub, yoga space, lounge, dining room.

SPIRITUAL HELP: Spiritual support through the yoga teacher throughout the week/ weekend. Healing treatments such as massage, acupuncture and Reiki and group support.

GUESTS ADMITTED TO: Everywhere.

MEALS: Together in a dining room. Food is home cooked, organic, locally sourced. Vegetarian and special diets catered for.

SPECIAL ACTIVITIES: Regular programme of courses and retreats. On offer at the retreats are action sports, such as skiing and snowboarding, surfing, climbing, hiking, walking and biking. Group meditation as part of the yoga class and silent walking meditation before yoga in the morning.

SITUATION: One retreat place often used is in the French Alps in a quiet village called La Rosiere near Les Arcs and is accessible by the snow train/Eurorail with the ski area close by for skiing. In the summer it is used for mountain summer holidays. AdventureYogi also go to Cornwall for surfing in a small and beautiful town called Polzeath on the north coast, tucked away with sea views.

MAXIMUM STAY: 1-week packages or weekends but people can come for longer.

BOOKINGS: Telephone, email. Online is easiest.

CHARGES: Average prices range from £225 for a weekend to £800 for 1 week of skiing and yoga.

ACCESS: By train/coach with pick-up to the retreat.

Elsie Briggs House of Prayer	Tel: 0117 9507242
38 Church Road	Email: warden@elsiebriggshouse.org.uk
Westbury-on-Trym	Website: elsiebriggshouse.org.uk/
Bristol	
Somerset BS9 3EQ	
England	

Retreats • Church/Temple • Meditation • Spiritual Help • Self-Catering Space • Children

Christian – Ecumenical

Elsie Briggs House is ecumenical and dedicated to Christian contemplative prayer. An ancient fifteenth-century cottage in the centre of a small village, it has long been a sacred space for prayer and retreat. All groups are open to anyone who might be interested.

OPEN: Open for visitors 15:00–17:00 on Tuesday afternoons. Everyone welcome. Individuals can book in for a day of retreat or in some cases may stay overnight by arrangement with the warden. This is on a self-catering basis. Groups can book in to use all or part of the House, either for Quiet Days or for time together. Children are welcome and special events for children are sometimes held.

ROOMS: Accommodation for 12–15 people during the day and has 2 small bedrooms for the use of occasional overnight retreatants.
FACILITIES: Parish church next door. Prayer room, upstairs meeting room, kitchen where meals may be prepared, garden, affiliated to the Quiet Garden Trust, extensive library containing books on prayer and spirituality, and a prayer hut for daytime use in the garden. Disabled access is not good as the house is so ancient.
SPIRITUAL HELP: Prayer and meditation. Church services next door.
GUESTS ADMITTED TO: All guest facilities and garden.
MEALS: Self-catering. There is a well-equipped small kitchen.
SPECIAL ACTIVITIES: Programme of events and retreats.
SITUATION: In a small country village.
MAXIMUM STAY: Usually for the day, but by agreement overnight is possible.
BOOKINGS: Letter, telephone, email.
CHARGES: A donation will be suggested when you book.
ACCESS: Accessible by bus from Bristol and car. See online for details.

Emmaus House Retreat and	Tel: 0117 9079950
Conference Centre	(09:00–15:30, Monday to Friday)
Clifton Hill	Email: administration@emmaushouse.org.uk
Clifton	Website: www.emmaushouse.org.uk
Bristol BS8 1BN	
England	

Retreats • Workshops and Courses • Church/Temple • Spiritual Help • Vegetarian Food
Venue for Hire • Alternative Therapies • Community Living • Vocations

Christian – Roman Catholic

Set in Clifton Village on the outskirts of Bristol, Emmaus House welcomes guests to workshops or simply to stay, have a meal and enjoy the splendid views. Facilities include award-winning gardens and a restaurant serving food of a high standard. There are plenty of places to pray, an art room, and spiritual companionship available for those that want it. The community here, founded by the Congregation of the Sisters of La Retraite, is noted for teaching the Enneagram in Helen Palmer's narrative tradition and for Myers-Briggs work. Known as an 'oasis in the city', this is a place for spiritual renewal and discovery in the midst of a busy world. **Highly Recommended.**

OPEN: All year except Christmas and Easter. Receives men, women, groups, non-retreatants.
ROOM : 21 bedrooms, max 31 beds, 9 en suites.

FACILITIES: Garden, chapel, oratory, meditation room, 4 meeting rooms for groups and conferences. Limited disabled access due to nature of building.
SPIRITUAL HELP: Spiritual direction by arrangement.
GUESTS ADMITTED TO: Everywhere except in meeting rooms already in use. Mass and Evening Prayer when possible.
MEALS: Dining room with home-cooked lunches and simpler (sometimes cold) suppers, often using produce from the garden. Vegetarians and those with special diets well catered for.
SPECIAL ACTIVITIES: Regular programme of courses and retreats, using both in-house guides and outside speakers. Private retreats by appointment. Self-managed groups welcome. Newsletter/programme issued twice a year.
SITUATION: In the heart of Clifton Village near the centre of Bristol. Beautiful gardens offering peace and tranquillity, yet a few minutes' walk to shops, cafés and the landmark Clifton Suspension Bridge on Bristol's Downs.
MAXIMUM STAY: Retreats generally 3–8 days, longer by negotiation.
BOOKINGS: Telephone, email, online.
CHARGES: Retreat rate £50 per 24 hours (inclusive of accommodation and all meals); courses generally £145 per weekend (Friday evening to Sunday lunchtime).
ACCESS: Bus from Bristol railway and coach stations stop nearby. Easily accessible by car; small car park with limited spaces.

COMPTON DURVILLE

Community of St Francis	Tel: 01460 240473
Compton Durville	Email: comptondurvilleecsf@franciscans.org.uk
South Petherton	Website: www.franciscans.org.uk/
Somerset TA13 5ES	Page34.htm#Compton
England	

Retreats • Workshops and Courses • Church/Temple • Spiritual Help • Vegetarian Food Venue for Hire • Self-Catering Space • Community Living • Work Retreats • Vocations Hermitages • Children

Christian – Anglican

The little hamlet of Compton Durville has the community's house, church and guest facilities on either side of the entrance street like pretty stone guardians. The welcome and hospitality here are cheerful and very friendly. We found it a pleasant and happy place and the community was very welcoming.

OPEN: All year for guests from Tuesday until Sunday. Everyone is welcome. Children welcome by prior arrangement.
ROOMS: 8 singles. The hermitage, a converted cricket pavilion a short distance away from the convent, provides a place for peace and prayer.

FACILITIES: Conferences, smaller meeting rooms, large garden, library, guest lounge, TV. Hermitage.
SPIRITUAL HELP: Personal talks by arrangement, chapel services, spiritual direction, personal retreat direction.
GUESTS ADMITTED TO: Unrestricted access except to community private areas. Work of community sometimes.
MEALS: Everyone eats main meals together. Traditional food. Vegetarian and special diets by prior arrangement.
SPECIAL ACTIVITIES: Quiet Days. Individually guided retreats. Programme of retreats and events online.
SITUATION: Very quiet, in a small village.
MAXIMUM STAY: Normally from Tuesday to Sunday unless on an 8-day Ignatian retreat or in self-catering accommodation.
BOOKINGS: Letter, telephone, email.
CHARGES: By suggested donation.
ACCESS: Train or by bus to local stations in Taunton and Yeovil. Car route is easy.

GLASTONBURY

Abbey House	Tel: 01458 831112
Chilkwell Street	Fax: 01458 831893
Glastonbury	Email: info@abbeyhouse.org
Somerset BA6 8DH	Website: www.abbeyhouse.org
England	

Retreats • Workshops and Courses • Church/Temple • Spiritual Help • Vegetarian Food
Venue for Hire

Christian – Anglican

This is the Bath and Wells Diocese Retreat and Conference House, which is set in the 40 acres of beautiful grounds of the old Benedictine Abbey in the town centre. A small resident staff manages the place. The great majority of the guests are sponsored by church groups, but private retreatants are welcome. The house enjoys a great measure of silence.

OPEN: All year. Receives men, women, young people, families, groups.
ROOMS: 18 singles and 9 twins.
FACILITIES: Disabled access, chapel, conferences, garden, park, library, guest lounge.
SPIRITUAL HELP: None.
GUESTS ADMITTED TO: Unrestricted access most of the time except when a group is resident.
MEALS: Traditional food – local produce where possible. Vegetarian and special diets by prior arrangement.
SPECIAL ACTIVITIES: Planned programme online.

SITUATION: In town but quiet since it is set in large grounds.
MAXIMUM STAY: By arrangement or by retreat or event.
BOOKINGS: Letter, telephone, email, online.
CHARGES: Retreats are full board and range in price from about £120 to £290.
ACCESS: Accessible by train, bus, coach and car. The nearest railway station to Glastonbury is at Castle Cary, which is about 11–12 miles away.

Arimathean Retreat	Tel/Fax: 01458 830230
59 High Street	Email: info@arimatheanretreat.com
Glastonbury	Website: www.arimatheanretreat.com
Somerset BA6 9DS	
England	

Retreats • Workshops and Courses • Yoga • Meditation • Spiritual Help • Bed and Breakfast
Vegetarian Food • Alternative Therapies • Holistic Holidays

Open spirituality – Non-denominational – Satyamvidya yoga

This neat cottage is an open spirituality retreat in one of Britain's best-known alternative spirituality and lifestyle towns. The place is filled with interesting people and many shops, book corners and cafes where spirituality is a common subject. At Arimathean Retreat you will find support and healing with a programme of courses and retreats including yoga and meditation as daily practices.

Chalice Well	Tel: 01458 831154
Chilkwell Street	Fax: 01458 835528
Glastonbury	Email: info@chalicewell.org.uk
Somerset BA6 8DD	Website: www.chalicewell.org.uk
England	

Retreats • Workshops and Courses • Venue for Hire • Self-Catering Space

Christian – Ecumenical – Inter-denominational

Here under entwining branches you enter a shrine that is a timeless and sacred place. In the gardens is a well or perhaps a spring, who knows, it is so ancient, and the waters are said by many people over many centuries to be of a healing nature. You may take a picnic to have in the meadows. At Little St Michaels – the retreat house for Companions of the Well and either individuals or groups – there are six rooms, each named after a tree. It is one of the most famous holy wells in Britain.

The Rowan Centre	Tel: 01458 831395 / 07789 911224
72 High Street	Email: sue@rowancentre.net (course information) /
Glastonbury	suejphd@gmail.com (books and other enquiries)
Somerset BA6 9DZ	Website: www.rowancentre.net
England	

Retreats • Workshops and Courses • Yoga • Meditation • Spiritual Help
Alternative Therapies

Open spirituality – Goddess spirituality – Yoga

Dr Sue Jennings runs this retreat studio. Her area of expertise is in drama therapy and healing. Please contact for more information as there are workshops and courses available in Britain and abroad.

Shekinashram	Tel: 01458 832300
Dod Lane	Email: info@shekinashram.org
Glastonbury	Email for enquiries in Spanish:
Somerset BA6 8BZ	gisela@shekinashram.org
England	Website: www.shekinashram.org

Retreats • Workshops and Courses • Church/Temple • Yoga • Meditation • Spiritual Help
Bed and Breakfast • Vegetarian Food • Organic Food • Venue for Hire
Alternative Therapies • Holistic Holidays • Community Living • Work Retreats
Hermitages • Children

Yoga – Bhakti yoga – Zen Buddhism – Open spirituality

Each day at Shekinashram begins with yoga practice, singing bhajans and meditating together, followed by a vegan breakfast. Shekinashram is a community dedicated to sacred space and situated at the base of Chalice Hill on the pilgrim route to Glastonbury Tor. The resident community lives according to a set of holistic principles, which include raw vegan food. There is a full programme of retreats, events and training here, including Zen retreats, sound-healing days, satsang evenings,

Bhakti yoga retreats, Thai massage, sacred chanting and silent meditation retreats.

OPEN: All year. Receives everyone.
ROOMS: 5 rooms in house – all can be used as singles or twins/doubles, 3 of which can sleep 3 people; plus cabin (sleeps 5) and yurts (1–2 people).
FACILITIES: Group meeting and work space and also to hire by groups. Hermitage, library, garden, healing therapies, sauna.
SPIRITUAL HELP: Yoga, meditation, Zen practice, chanting and singing.
GUESTS ADMITTED TO: Almost everywhere.
MEALS: Organic vegan raw food diet only. The main meal of the day is taken together at lunchtime.
SPECIAL ACTIVITIES: Morning yoga and meditation. Healing and relaxation therapies including Reiki.
SITUATION: Rather outside the village itself. Very clear plan online. Calm.
MAXIMUM STAY: Usually a week or more minimum, so longer by arrangement.
BOOKINGS: Letter, telephone, email. They prefer to be telephoned so that details can be discussed.
CHARGES: The group space can be hired from £30–£95 (rates for 20+ groups will be higher). B&B rates range from £19 (per person in shared cabin) to £80 for a triple room. Weekly events start from as little as £3. Check online for further details. Please call for group rates.
ACCESS: Public transport if possible but by car is easiest. See website for directions. The nearest railway station is at Castle Cary, which is about 11–12 miles away.

Tordown Healing Centre	Tel: 01458 832287
5 Ashwell Lane	Fax: 01458 831100
Glastonbury	Email: info@tordown.com
Somerset BA6 8BG	Website: www.tordown.com
England	

Bed and Breakfast • Vegetarian Food • Organic Food • Alternative Therapies
Holistic Holidays • Children

Mind Body Spirit

A quiet place for a B&B-type retreat with really good views from some of the bedrooms. A helpful place for those wishing some peace and rest. The hosts are Reiki trained and offer comfortable rooms, organic food and a variety of healing therapies.

OPEN: All year. Receives everyone, individuals and groups. Children welcome.
ROOMS: 6 rooms, all en suite. Can accommodate up to 14 people.
FACILITIES: Garden, park, library, guest lounge, TV.

SPIRITUAL HELP: Healing therapies.
GUESTS ADMITTED TO: Unrestricted access to garden and guest areas.
MEALS: Vegetarian organic food. Vegan and special diets by prior arrangement.
SPECIAL ACTIVITIES: A broad range of healing therapies available from Reiki to hydotherapy spa.
SITUATION: Quiet.
MAXIMUM STAY: By arrangement.
BOOKINGS: Letter, telephone, fax, email.
CHARGES: From £35 to £45 with various rates for different rooms.
ACCESS: By car is the easiest. The nearest railway station is at Castle Cary, which is about 11–12 miles away.

LANGPORT

St Gilda's Christian Centre
The Hill
Langport
Somerset TA10 9QF
England

Tel: 01458 250496
Email: ccngildas@cheminneuf.org.uk
Website: www.cheminneuf.org.uk

Retreats • Workshops and Courses • Church/Temple • Spiritual Help • Vegetarian Food
Venue for Hire • Community Living • Vocations • Children

Christian – Ecumenical – Anglican

The Chemin Neuf Community at St Gilda's Christian Centre is ecumenical in vocation and membership and is committed to promoting unity, forgiveness, reconciliation and healing. The big white eighteenth-century house in the middle of Langport, which has been called the Light on the Hill, may also be booked by individuals or a group for retreats or days. There is a very good library, a fine light chapel and in the five-acre garden there is a seasonal-use swimming pool. **Highly Recommended.**

OPEN: All year except over Christmas. Receives everyone. Children welcome.
ROOMS: 4 singles, 19 doubles, 2 dormitories.
FACILITIES: Disabled access, conferences, garden, park of 5 acres with summertime swimming pool, library, guest lounge, TV.
SPIRITUAL HELP: Personal talks. A spiritually supportive environment.
GUESTS ADMITTED TO: Unrestricted access.
MEALS: Everyone eats together. Traditional food. Vegetarian and special diets.
SPECIAL ACTIVITIES: Planned programme of events. See online or write for it.
SITUATION: Quiet, in a large village.
MAXIMUM STAY: 2 weeks usually or by retreat course or by arrangement.
BOOKINGS: Letter, telephone, email.

CHARGES: Rates vary according to the accommodation and event – download the course leaflets/booking forms online or ask when you book.
ACCESS: Train, bus and car all possible.

MINEHEAD

Croydon Hall	Tel: 01984 642200
Felons Oak	Fax: 01984 640052
Minehead	Email: info@croydonhall.co.uk
Somerset TA24 6QT	Website: www.croydonhall.co.uk
England	

Retreats • Workshops and Courses • Yoga • Meditation • Spiritual Help • Bed and Breakfast
Vegetarian Food • Organic Food • Venue for Hire • Alternative Therapies • Holistic Holidays

Open spirituality

What is on offer here is a nurturing and creative environment that is friendly, welcoming, relaxing and meditative. Meditation at Croydon Hall is the foundation of their daily life and work. Situated in the timeless beauty of the Exmoor National Park, and built over a century ago by an eccentric German count, the fully refurbished house has a colourful history and has seen many changes over the years. Croydon Hall is a perfect place to recharge your batteries and relax. **Highly Recommended.**

OPEN: All year. Receives everyone.
ROOMS: Accommodation for up to 70 guests.
FACILITIES: 5 function rooms, leisure wing with covered heated swimming, sauna, hot tub, AromaSpa and mini gym. A variety of treatments available.
SPIRITUAL HELP: Meditation.
GUESTS ADMITTED TO: Public areas.
MEALS: Vegetarian, organic, catering for various personal diets.
SPECIAL ACTIVITIES: Planned events with a variety of different programmes and retreats.
SITUATION: Croydon Hall is in one of the most beautiful parts of England. Near Minehead on edge of Exmoor National Park.
MAXIMUM STAY: Upon availability.
BOOKINGS: By telephone or email.
CHARGES: From £19.90 to £56.50 for accommodation. £23.50 for 24-hour meal and beverage package.
ACCESS: By car or train. A frequent bus service runs from the nearest train and bus stations in Taunton to Williton, the closest town to Croydon Hall. Call before boarding the bus in Taunton and a courtesy car will be arranged to pick you up in Williton.

QUEEN CAMEL

Self-Realization Meditation Healing Centre
Laurel Lane
Queen Camel
Yeovil
Somerset BA22 7NU
England

Tel: 01935 850266
Fax: 01935 850234
Email: info@selfrealizationcentres.org
Website: www.selfrealizationcentres.org

Retreats • Workshops and Courses • Yoga • Meditation • Spiritual Help
Bed and Breakfast • Vegetarian Food • Organic Food • Self-Catering Space
Alternative Therapies • Community Living • Work Retreats • Vocations

Alternative spirituality – Yoga – Non-denominational

The centre is a charitable trust run by a team of counsellors and healers, who live and work together as a family and who use the guidance of yoga, meditation and healing self-development in their work and courses. Meditation is a central feature of the centre. There is a harmony about this place and a pride in offering a warm welcome. Many people who come here on their first experience of a retreat away from their ordinary life have been pleased with the comfort and thoughtfulness of the resident community and the facilities. **Highly Recommended.**

OPEN: All year. Everyone welcome: men, women, young people, groups, non-retreatants.
ROOMS: 2 singles, 6 doubles, 2 shared en suites, 2 garden chalets. Self-catering retreat accommodation possible.
FACILITIES: 2 meditation rooms, 3 acres of beautiful gardens with ponds, oriental garden, spiritual library, 3 guest lounges (1 with log fire), large exercise room, heated indoor therapy pool.
SPIRITUAL HELP: In-depth pure meditation (Raja yoga including Kriya) course. Diploma courses in natural spiritual healing, progressive counselling and transformation Hatha yoga teacher training. Personal retreats offer spiritual guidance.
GUESTS ADMITTED TO: Group Meditation, gardens, meditation rooms, library, lounges and heated indoor therapy pool.
MEALS: Dining room for guests and course students. Self-catering accommodation also available. Vegetarian wholefood, home cooked, homegrown and organic where possible. Special diets catered for.
SPECIAL ACTIVITIES: An extensive planned programme of courses and retreats with private retreats available throughout the year. Groups by arrangement. See website.
SITUATION: Very calm and quiet, in picturesque rural village.
MAXIMUM STAY: By arrangement.
BOOKINGS: Letter, telephone, email, online.

CHARGES: Varies with programme course or event. Visit the website and download the course programme current rates.
ACCESS: By train and car. Queen Camel is 7–8 miles from Castle Cary and Yeovil Pen Mill stations.

RADSTOCK

Ammerdown Conference and Retreat Centre   Tel: 01761 433709
Ammerdown Park   Fax: 01761 433094
Radstock   Email: centre@ammerdown.org
Somerset BA3 5SW   Website: www.ammerdown.org
England

> Retreats • Workshops and Courses • Chapel • Disabled • Meditation • Spiritual Help
> Vegetarian Food • Organic Food • Venue for Hire • Self-Catering Space
> Bed and Breakfast • Community Living • Work Retreats • Children

Christian – Ecumenical

Hospitality is the motivating idea at this long-established retreat centre nestling in woods next to a stately home. It is surrounded by beautiful landscaped gardens and parkland, with an exquisitely beautiful chapel in its midst. The whole place is steeped in peace and tranquillity. No traffic noise – only birds singing! Yet it is only 12 miles from Bath and is easy of access, with free car parking on site. Ammerdown Centre was refurbished in 2004–5 and is very aware of its ecological green responsibilities. Run as an open Christian community dedicated to hospitality, spirituality and growth, it welcomes people of all faiths and none and strives to offer a space where people of all backgrounds can feel free to be themselves. Courses and events are run throughout the year. **Highly Recommended.**

OPEN: All year round. Everyone is welcome.
ROOMS: 40 en suite rooms: 16 singles, 16 twins, 7 doubles, 1 family room – includes 1 self-catering facility and 3 rooms specially equipped for disabled people.
FACILITIES: 4 conference rooms (including 2 with integral audio-visual equipment) plus several break-out rooms, full accessibility to wheelchair users (including lift), chapel, library, lounge with licensed bar, TV and computer room, WiFi access, bookshops and craft shop, heated indoor swimming pool in summertime, beautiful gardens, on-site catering facilities.
SPIRITUAL HELP: Spiritual direction, upon request.
GUESTS ADMITTED TO: Everywhere unless otherwise advised. All guests are welcome to join in prayer times.

MEALS: These can be taken alone or together. Food freshly cooked on the premises every day with a focus on wholesome food using local produce. Organic food as much as possible within budgetary constraints. Traditional English and a variety of other cuisines. Vegetarian options at every meal. Special diets – standard gluten- and diary-free. Others are considered on request, but severe allergy conditions cannot be catered for. Limited self-catering.
SPECIAL ACTIVITIES: Outside speakers. Private retreats. Courses are arranged by theme: *Personal Development, Spiritual Nurturing, Creative and Artistic, Inter-faith and Dialogue* and *Recreation and Rejuvenation*. Self-managed groups welcome.
SITUATION: Country estate, not far from Bath in Somerset with superb views.
MAXIMUM STAY: No set maximum.
BOOKINGS: Letter, telephone, fax, email.
CHARGES: Rates according to the course, event or retreat being held. See programme for details.
ACCESS: By train, bus or car. Bath Spa, the nearest train station, is 20 minutes away, and there is a regular bus service to Radstock, which is 2 miles from Ammerdown.

STREET

Creative Arts Retreat Movement	Email:
182 High Street	carmgb.info@btinternet.com
Street	Website: www.carmretreats.org
Somerset BA16 0NH	
England	

Retreats • Workshops and Courses

Open spirituality – Christian – Ecumenical

Creative Arts Retreat Movement retreats are designed to combine training in a creative art with opportunities to deepen your spiritual life. Each of the retreats focuses on one of eight key artistic and creative areas: calligraphy, creative writing, drama, embroidery, music, painting, photography or poetry. Times are set aside for prayer and personal reflection. Non-members as well as members are welcome. Bookings are by email and letter.

'Christianity, if false, is of no importance, and if true, of infinite importance. The only thing it cannot be is moderately important'
– C.S. Lewis

WILTSHIRE

HEDDINGTON

International Meditation Centre
Splatts House
Heddington
Calne
Wiltshire SN11 0PE
England

Tel: 01380 850238
Fax: 01380 850833
Email: imcuk@internationalmeditationcentre.com
Website: www.internationalmeditationcentre.org

Retreats • Workshops and Courses • Church/Temple • Meditation • Spiritual Help
Vegetarian Food • Community Living • Work Retreats • Vocation

Buddhist (Sayagyui U Ba Khin tradition) – Vipassana meditation

The International Meditation Centre, founded by the Sayagyi U Ba Khin Memorial Trust, provides the instruction and practice of Buddhist Vipassana meditation, guided by teachers who have practised and taught meditation for over 50 years. It holds monthly 10-day residential courses. The meditation practice is based on the Eightfold Noble Path as taught by the Buddha, which divides into three parts: morality, concentration and wisdom. The Light of the Dhamma Pagoda, which is very beautiful and inspiring especially when lit at night, is the focal point of the meditation centre. Many people have come here for the 10-day courses, with good results. **Highly Recommended.**

OPEN: All year for 10-day retreats. Receives men and women.
ROOMS: Dormitories and some doubles. Men and women are given separate sleeping quarters.
FACILITIES: Light of the Dhamma Pagoda, garden, library, disabled access.
SPIRITUAL HELP: Meditation. Students observe noble silence but may speak with their teacher and the staff at any time.
GUESTS ADMITTED TO: Access to most areas, Light of the Dhamma Pagoda, meditation hall, residential areas.
MEALS: Everyone eats together. Vegetarian food only. Special diets will be accommodated as far as possible.
SPECIAL ACTIVITIES: Daily schedule of meditation practice. Planned schedule for the courses. See online.
SITUATION: Quiet, on edge of a village and standing in its own 4 acres of grounds..
MAXIMUM STAY: Duration of teaching – usually 10 days.
BOOKINGS: Letter, telephone, fax, email.
CHARGES: There has never been any charge for the Buddha's Teachings. There is a suggested donation of £240 for a 10-day course, which is towards the cost of food and accommodation.

ACCESS: Rail, bus and car all possible. The nearest town with main public transport links is Chippenham. From there, it is a 10-mile taxi ride to the rural village of Heddington.

SALISBURY

Alabaré House of Prayer
Alabaré Christian Community
15 Tollgate Road
Salisbury SP1 2JA
England

Tel/Fax: 01722 501586
Email: info@alabare.org
Website: www.alabare.org

Retreats • Workshops and Courses • Church/Temple • Spiritual Help • Bed and Breakfast
Vegetarian Food • Venue for Hire • Vocations • Children

Christian – Ecumenical

A residential community and retreat centre, Alabaré House of Prayer is in the heart of Salisbury, offering retreats, days of reflection and hospitality to people seeking accommodation. This charitable organisation has a number of care centres, catering for different people for their different needs from women and children to homeless young men.

OPEN: Everyone welcome.
ROOMS: 10 twins, 2 doubles, lift available and ground-floor rooms.
FACILITIES: Disabled access, meeting rooms for hire, garden, library. B&B when possible.
SPIRITUAL HELP: Regular prayer together every day of the week at differing times and in differing styles.
GUESTS ADMITTED TO: Everywhere.
MEALS: Please ask what is available when you stay over. Many of the retreats in the programme are for the day, so you will find out when you book about the meal arrangements.
SPECIAL ACTIVITIES: Retreats, Quiet Days.
SITUATION: Peaceful accommodation in the centre of Salisbury
MAXIMUM STAY: Length or retreat or group meeting or by arrangement.
BOOKINGS: Letter, telephone, email. Online is easiest.
CHARGES: The charge for a day retreat is very low at about £10–15 but you need to enquire as to the current rate when you stay overnight.
ACCESS: By car, train, coach. Rail: Salisbury station, which is less than 1.5 miles from Alabaré.

Sarum College
19 The Close
Salisbury
Wiltshire SP1 2EE
England

Tel: 01722 424800
Fax: 01722 338508
Email: hospitality@sarum.ac.uk
Website: www.sarum.ac.uk

Retreats • Workshops and Courses • Church/Temple • Spiritual Help • Bed and Breakfast
Vegetarian Food • Venue for Hire • Children

Christian – Inter-denominational – Ecumenical

Sarum College is an ecumenical institution developed as an innovative resource for all the churches in England and Wales. Christian spirituality, theological studies, liturgy and worship, leadership and ministry, and the arts are its major areas of concentration. It occupies historic buildings, directly opposite the great Salisbury Cathedral.

OPEN: All year except Christmas. Receives everyone, but for families enquire first about accommodation available.
ROOMS: 30 singles, 10 doubles. No smoking.
FACILITIES: Disabled – lift to all floors. Conferences, seminar rooms, library, guest lounge, TV, bookshop, bar, common room, dining room.
SPIRITUAL HELP: Personal talks, spiritual direction, group sharing, meditation, directed study.
GUESTS ADMITTED TO: Mostly everywhere.
MEALS: Everyone eats together. Traditional food. Vegetarian and special diets catered for.
SPECIAL ACTIVITIES: Planned programme. Academic programme available. Send for brochures.
SITUATION: Rather busy, in a cathedral close but a beautiful house and presentation.
MAXIMUM STAY: Usually about a week but depends on arrangement and type of retreat or course you are on.
BOOKINGS: Letter, telephone, email, online.
CHARGES: Current B&B rates for rooms, singles and doubles, range from £45 to £95.
ACCESS: Centre of Salisbury; good access by train, bus, car.

WARMINSTER

Ivy House
St Denys Retreat Centre
2 Church Street, Warminster
Wiltshire BA12 8PG
England

Tel: 01985 214824
Fax: 01985 219688
Email: stdenys@ivyhouse.org
Website: www.ivyhouse.org

Retreats • Bed and Breakfast • Vegetarian Food • Organic Food • Venue for Hire • Children

Christian – Anglican – Ecumenical

Ivy House dates back to the eighteenth century and is situated about half a mile from the centre of Warminster, which was founded in Saxon times. There is a programme of various retreats and events and they have special Quiet Garden Trust days as well.

OPEN: All year except Christmas. Receives everyone.
ROOMS: 18 singles, 5 twins – ground-floor single room for disabled.
FACILITIES: Disabled access, meeting room, small conferences, garden, 2 guest lounges, prayer room, small conservatory, day facilities for up to 40 people.
SPIRITUAL HELP: Prayer room, Quiet Days.
GUESTS ADMITTED TO: Chapel. Unlimited access.
MEALS: Everyone eats together. Traditional home-cooked food. Vegetarian possible. Special diets can be catered with advance notification.
SPECIAL ACTIVITIES: See online for planned programme.
SITUATION: Quiet, in the town.
MAXIMUM STAY: 2 weeks unless doing the 30-day retreat.
BOOKINGS: Letter or telephone.
CHARGES: The current 2010 charges are as follows: House/Personal Quiet Day £17 (includes use of room, coffee, lunch and afternoon tea); full day with overnight stay from £49 (includes meals, tea/coffee, use of rooms and house facilities); B&B from £29; meals from £2.50 for coffee and biscuits to £11.50 for a 3-course meal. Quiet Garden Days are free to access the garden but contributions are welcome.
ACCESS: By car and public transport. Rail: Warminster station, Ivy House is 1 mile away. Coach/bus: services run from Bath, Bristol and Salisbury to Warminster bus station, which is 15 minutes' walk from Ivy House.

SOUTH AND SOUTH EAST

BERKSHIRE

•••

READING

Douai Abbey
Upper Woolhampton
Reading
Berkshire RG7 5TQ
England

Tel: 0118 9715300
Fax: 0118 9715305
Email: info@douaiabbey.org.uk
For Guestmaster: Tel: 0118 9715399 /
Email: guestmaster@douaiabbey.org.uk
Website: www.douaiabbey.org.uk

Retreats • Workshops and Courses • Church/Temple • Spiritual Help • Vegetarian Food
Self-Catering Space • Community Living • Vocations • Children

Christian – Roman Catholic

One of the most famous monasteries in Europe. Open to everyone for retreats, it is also a place for men to make a private retreat within an atmosphere of monastic community life and prayer. In addition to facilities in the monastery for men and the retreat house for everyone else, there is a Pastoral Programme, which organises the retreats, conferences and events and a modern guest house for both men and women. The facilities here are very much up-to-date with purpose-built rooms and dining areas. Absolutely super! **Highly Recommended.**

OPEN: All year except Christmas and mid-August to mid-September. Receives men, women, young people, families, groups. Men may stay in the monastery itself, otherwise men and women stay in the modern and very comfortable guest house.
ROOMS: 5 singles, 3 twins, 4 doubles, 1 family room; 4 rooms are disabled suitable, and 13 are en suite. The Douai Cottages, a row of three farm labourers' cottages, has been converted into a single building and sleeps 15. Well-considered and excellent accommodation.
FACILITIES: Chapel, choir, conferences, park, library, guest lounge.
SPIRITUAL HELP: Personal talks, Mass, Divine Office
GUESTS ADMITTED TO: Chapel, choir, gardens.
MEALS: Everyone eats together. Traditional food. Vegetarians. Self-catering facilities in the cottage accommodation.
SPECIAL ACTIVITIES: Planned retreats – see online programme.
SITUATION: Quiet and in the countryside.
MAXIMUM STAY: A few days usually. Otherwise by length of programme or retreat or arrangement with guestmaster.
BOOKINGS: Letter, telephone – but email best. Online booking form also available.

CHARGES: Priced by the retreat, course or event; typically £70–£185 for residential retreats, and £15–£30 for day/evening retreats. See online programme for details.
ACCESS: Douai Abbey is 1 mile north of the A4, between Reading and Newbury. Rail: Midgham station, which is 1.5 miles away; pick-up by arrangement. Bus: services run between Reading and Newbury bus stations. Car: via M4, Exit 1.

SLOUGH

Casting for Recovery UK
and Ireland
PO Box 3611
Slough
Berkshire SL3 3BY
England

Email: info@castingforrecovery.org.uk
Website: www.castingforrecovery.org.uk

In the United States:
PO Box 1123
3738 Main Street
Manchester, VT 05254
USA

Tel: +001 802 3629181 (USA)
Fax: +001 802 3629182 (USA)

Retreats • Workshops and Courses • Spiritual Help • Vegetarian Food

Open spirituality – Holistic

Casting for Recovery (CFR), founded in 1996 in America, is a national non-profit support and educational programme for breast-cancer survivors, working to enhance the lives of such women by offering no-cost retreats. These retreats promote and support mental and physical healing through shared experiences and the learning of new skills. They have held hundreds of retreats for many thousands of women and know what they are doing. The programme is run entirely by volunteers with sponsorship in Britain from Orvis and the Countryside Alliance. The retreats are held in Britain and Ireland at comfortable venues with beautiful peaceful surroundings. The retreat lasts two and a half days, during which participants learn the sport of fly-fishing. This pastime promotes physical, emotional and spiritual healing, with a balance between the physical benefits of the sport and the counselling that accompanies it on the retreat, which is by a medical/psycho-social qualified volunteer team of professionals. The weekend is also a real opportunity for meeting new friends, sharing with them and just having some fun. It is now widely accepted that taking up a new interest, including a sport, can help heal mind, body and spirit and thus aid in recovery from illness, so Casting for Recovery's signature line, 'To fish is to hope,' makes good sense. If you fly-fish and make your own flies, then perhaps the next time you sit down to do some you can make a few extra suitable for small stillwater fishing or stream fishing and send them along to Casting for Recovery UK and Ireland at the above address.

SPEEN

Elmore Abbey
Church Lane
Speen, Newbury
Berkshire RG14 1SA
England

Tel: 01635 33080
Fax: 01635 80729
Email: elmore.abbey@virgin.net

Retreats • Church/Temple • Spiritual Help • Vegetarian Food • Community Living • Vocations

Christian – Anglican

This is a distinguished Anglican abbey with a beautiful church with oak columns that seem like trees in a woodland. The little cloister courtyard at the entrance could not be prettier or more charming. All the refurbishment, rebuilding and designing have been done with obvious care and considerable talent. Everywhere is elegant and peaceful and so too seem the community of monks who live here. We find this monastery a gentle, prayerful oasis with an atmosphere of calm contentment. **Highly Recommended.**

OPEN: All year except over Christmas. Receives men, women, and those for day retreats.
ROOMS: 6 singles.
FACILITIES: Chapel, garden, library with permission.
SPIRITUAL HELP: Personal talks, individual guidance given if on a private retreat, but not guided retreats.
GUESTS ADMITTED TO: Chapel, some work of community.
MEALS: Everyone eats together. Traditional food. Vegetarians catered for.
SPECIAL ACTIVITIES: None.
SITUATION: Quiet, in the countryside.
MAXIMUM STAY: By arrangement.
BOOKINGS: Letter, telephone, email.
CHARGES: On application.
ACCESS: Rail: Newbury station (2.5 miles away), then bus or taxi. Car: M4 exit 13, then A34 and A4.

THATCHAM

Cold Ash Centre
The Ridge
Cold Ash, Thatcham
Berkshire RG18 9HU
England

Tel: 01635 865353
Email: fmmcac@aol.com

Retreats • Workshops and Courses • Church/Temple • Spiritual Help • Vegetarian Food
Venue for Hire • Community Living • Vocations

Christian – Roman Catholic – Ecumenical

The Franciscan Missionaries of Mary run a planned programme of retreats here, which offers a fairly broad range of topics and themes from
Quiet Days and preached retreats to the bio-spiritual focusing process.
There are pleasant warm rooms and fine views in this very large building and the welcome is friendly. A popular place, so you may need to
book well in advance.

OPEN: All year except August. Receives men, women, young people and groups.
ROOMS: 27 singles, 2 doubles.
FACILITIES: Conferences, garden, small library, coffee rooms, guest lounges, TV.
SPIRITUAL HELP: Spiritual direction, guided retreats.
GUESTS ADMITTED TO: Chapel, church, oratory.
MEALS: Taken in the guest house. Traditional and vegetarian food. Vegetarian and
special diets.
SPECIAL ACTIVITIES: Planned programme of events, preached retreats, bio-
spiritual focusing retreats and workshops. Send for programme.
SITUATION: Quiet, in the countryside.
MAXIMUM STAY: 1 month or by arrangement.
BOOKINGS: Letter, telephone, email.
CHARGES: According to retreat or course, otherwise enquire when booking.
ACCESS: Rail: Thatcham station (4 miles away). Bus: services run from Newbury. Car:
the centre is 4 miles from Newbury. Map available if requested.

'Ambition is like love, impatient both of delays and rivals'
– Buddha

HAMPSHIRE

ALTON

Alton Abbey
Abbey Road
Beech, Alton
Hampshire GU34 4AP
England

Tel: 01420 562145
Fax: 01420 561691
Email: altonabbey@supanet.com
Website: www.altonabbey.org.uk

Retreats • Workshops and Courses • Church/Temple • Spiritual Help • Vegetarian Food
Venue for Hire • Community Living • Vocations • Children

Christian – Anglican

Alton Abbey is a place where you may find stillness and, hopefully, that reflection which may lead to worship and prayer with the community. Benedictine hospitality helps provide a very wide range of retreats from quiet prayer days to those on icon writing.

OPEN: Most of the year except Christmas period. Receives everyone. Children welcome.
ROOMS: 12 singles, 6 twins. Silence from 20:30 until 09:30 next morning.
FACILITIES: Garden, guest lounge.
SPIRITUAL HELP: Personal talks, meditation, directed study, spiritual counsel, personal guided retreats.
GUESTS ADMITTED TO: Chapel, gardens.
MEALS: Everyone eats together in refectory. Simple traditional food. Vegetarian and special diets catered for.
SPECIAL ACTIVITIES: Planned programme. See online.
SITUATION: Quiet, in a village setting in the countryside.
MAXIMUM STAY: 8 days or by arrangement.
BOOKINGS: Letter, telephone, email.
CHARGES: Overnight/weekend stays are about £25–£55; day retreats £15. The Icon Writing Retreat is £220.
ACCESS: Train: Alton station (5 miles away), then bus or taxi. Car: Abbey is off A339.

'I am out with mirrors looking for myself'
– Emily Dickinson

AMPFIELD

Hebron Christian Retreat
Broadgate House
Hook Road
Ampfield, Romsey
Hampshire SO51 9BY
England

Tel: 02380 252673
Website: www.hebron-trust.org.uk

Retreats • Church/Temple • Spiritual Help • Vegetarian Food • Venue for Hire

Christian – Inter-denominational – Ecumenical

This ecumenical centre is open to both individuals and groups. They aim to provide space for church leadership teams, Alpha days or weekends, individual retreats, prayer ministry, friendship groups, housegroup away days, organised prayer days and holiday breaks. Guests do not have to be committed Christians. Hebron is inter-denominational and uses the same basis of faith as the Evangelical Alliance in the UK.

ALRESFORD

Old Alresford Place
Conference and Training Centre
Alresford
Hampshire SO24 9DH
England

Tel: 01962 737301
Fax: 01962 737358
Email: enquiries@oldalresfordplace.co.uk
Website: www.oldalresfordplace.co.uk

Retreats • Workshops and Courses • Church/Temple • Bed and Breakfast
Vegetarian Food • Venue for Hire • Children

Christian – Anglican – Inter-denominational

Old Alresford Place is a large old comfortable house set in five acres of garden in the heart of Hampshire. It is a Georgian complex set in extensive grounds – and the birthplace of the Mothers' Union. Run as a diocesan retreat, conference and training centre, Old Alresford Place is well decorated and furnished, and the library and meeting rooms are light, airy and modern.

OPEN: All year except usually the Christmas period. Receives everyone. Children welcome.
ROOMS: 16 en suite bedrooms, with desk and internet access, which are fully accessible. There is a lift access to the first and second floors.
FACILITIES: Chapel, 5-acre garden, car parking, library, guest lounge. As well as operating as a conference and training centre with first-class facilities, Old Alresford Place offers bed and breakfast, space for both organised and personal retreats, wedding receptions and family events.
SPIRITUAL HELP: Discuss what your needs are when you book.
GUESTS ADMITTED TO: Chapel. Unrestricted access.
MEALS: Meals taken in dining room. Traditional food. Vegetarian and special diets.
SPECIAL ACTIVITIES: Full and varied programme, which includes retreats, pilgrimage walks, Quiet Days, overnight 'time outs' and day retreats.
SITUATION: Quiet in the village and countryside.
MAXIMUM STAY: By arrangement.
BOOKINGS: Letter, telephone, email. Booking forms can be downloaded from the website.
CHARGES: Ask for current rates for event or B&B.
ACCESS: Rail: Alton station, then bus. Car: M3 exit 6, or A31; the centre is off B3046.

BORDON

Acorn Christian Healing Foundation	Tel: 01420 478121
Whitehill Chase	Fax: 01420 478122
Bordon	Email: info@acornchristian.org
Hampshire GU35 0AP	Website: www.acornchristian.org
England	

Retreats • Workshops and Courses • Church/Temple • Spiritual Help • Vegetarian Food
Holistic Holidays

Christian – Anglican tradition – Inter-denominational

A Christian retreat and healing centre set in a large nineteenth-century hunting lodge within six acres of gardens and woodlands. Christian Listening is offered here as a course, which is surprisingly rarely found in retreat programmes – surprisingly since it is truly an essential basic tool in all Christian action – indeed, we all need to learn to listen better to others because it leads us to understanding and from there into compassion and better understanding. In Christian terms, listening is three dimensional: listening to others, listening to ourselves and listening to God.

OPEN: For the duration of the programme. Receives men, women, young people and groups, religious.

ROOMS: Singles. Doubles, including twins.
FACILITIES: Disabled access, chapel, conferences, garden, library, large lounge, TV, bookshop, payphone.
SPIRITUAL HELP: Personal talks, spiritual direction (with chaplain if available), healing services. Chapel for prayer and contemplation.
GUESTS ADMITTED TO: Chapel. Unrestricted access.
MEALS: Everyone eats together in refectory. Traditional food. Vegetarian and special diets.
SPECIAL ACTIVITIES: See online for full planned programme.
SITUATION: In a small town, rural area.
MAXIMUM STAY: The day or for the duration of the course. Personal retreats by arrangement.
BOOKINGS: Letter, telephone, email.
CHARGES: Various rates and suggested donations. Please ask.
ACCESS: Car: off the A325 in Bordon. Rail: Farnham station, then bus.

BRAMDEAN

Krishnamurti Study Centre	Tel: 01962 771748
Brockwood Park	Fax: 01962 771755
Bramdean	Email: info@krishnamurticentre.org.uk
Hampshire SO24 0LQ	Website: www.krishnamurticentre.org.uk
England	

Retreats • Vegetarian Food • Self-Catering Space

Open spirituality – Non-religious

The Krishnamurti Centre in the peaceful countryside of southern Hampshire is a place of study for those interested in J. Krishnamurti's teachings. Krishnamurti, who was born in India and died in the USA in 1986, was a universal man whose major contribution to twentieth-century thought, many say, was in questioning the basis upon which we make our judgements and that this misinterpretation of our reality causes much unhappiness. He believed truth to be a pathless land. The centre is intended for the serious study of his teachings, and for people who would like for a few days to be in a quiet environment where they can devote their full attention to his teachings and the implications for their own lives. As there is no guidance or structured activity outside the programme for theme weekends and study retreats, guests may arrange their own study programme, use the library, go for walks and/ or enquire informally with others. Day guests are welcome to use the study facilities of the centre without charge. They can also, by prior arrangement, stay for a meal. Interested study groups, wanting to enquire together into Krishnamurti's teachings, may discuss a suitable programme with the centre. **Highly Recommended.**

OPEN: Open all year except January. Everyone welcome.
ROOMS: 19 rooms, all single en suite, simply but comfortably furnished and with views onto the beautiful grounds.
FACILITIES: The centre's collection of books and materials is available to all guests. The library contains all of Krishnamurti's books.
SPIRITUAL HELP: None.
GUESTS ADMITTED TO: Unrestricted except kitchen and office areas.
MEALS: Taken in dining room. Vegetarian food only.
SPECIAL ACTIVITIES: Theme weekends and study retreats for those who would like to enquire together in an atmosphere of openness with like-minded people.
SITUATION: Quiet in the countryside.
MAXIMUM STAY: The minimum stay is 2 nights.
BOOKINGS: Letter, telephone, fax, email, online.
CHARGES: Full-board nightly rates: 1 night from £68; 1 week from £360; 7 nights (including 1 night free) from £408. Day visit: with lunch £15; with lunch and supper £25. Theme weekends and study retreats are charged at higher rates. Reduced rates are also available.
ACCESS: By car, train, bus. Car: see online for detailed directions. Rail: Winchester or Petersfield stations. Bus: services run from Winchester bus station and Petersfield railway station.

FAREHAM

Park Place Pastoral Centre
Winchester Road
Wickham, Fareham
Hampshire PO17 5HA
England

Tel: 01329 833043
Email: pastoralcentre@aol.com
Website: www.parkplacepastoralcentre.co.uk

Retreats • Workshops and Courses • Church/Temple • Yoga • Meditation • Spiritual Help
Bed and Breakfast • Vegetarian Food • Venue for Hire • Self-Catering Space
Community Living • Vocations • Children

Christian – Roman Catholic – Franciscan spirituality – Yoga

The eighteenth-century elegance of Park Place is complemented by its peaceful environment. The centre exists to encourage the development of personal spiritual values, facilitated by a temporary withdrawal from the purely material demands of everyday life. People of all faiths and none are welcome.

OPEN: All year. Everyone welcome – groups and school groups and individuals.
ROOMS: The centre has a full capacity of 66 beds. There are several accommodation units.
FACILITIES: Garden, library, chapel, oratory, conference rooms, hall, ample space for car park, meditation walk.
SPIRITUAL HELP: Yes, whenever possible.
GUESTS ADMITTED TO: Guests may join in community spiritual practices and may go anywhere except in community private quarters.
MEALS: Taken together in the dining room – home cooked, traditional English. Indian meals on request. Vegetarians catered for. Self-catering facilities available.
SPECIAL ACTIVITIES: Regular programme of courses and retreats. Outside speakers. Private retreats and self-managed groups welcome.
SITUATION: Attractive grounds in a lovely part of Hampshire.
MAXIMUM STAY: 7 days.
BOOKINGS: Telephone, letter, email.
CHARGES: Residential: £41–£54. Non-residential: £20–£23. B&B: £30.
ACCESS: Almost equidistant from Portsmouth, Southampton and Winchester. Car: M27 exit 10/11, then A32. Rail: Fareham station. Bus: services run from Fareham bus station and Winchester bus station.

LYNDHURST

Furzey Christian Retreat House	Tel: 02380 812015
Furzey House	Email: daveandjill@ic24.net
Minstead, Lyndhurst	Website: www.furzey-gardens.org
Hampshire SO43 7GL	
England	

Church/Temple • Spiritual Help • Vegetarian Food • Children

Christian

Set in the heart of the New Forest at Minstead in Hampshire, this big thatched house rests in a delightful, informal garden, which was established in 1922 and is renowned for its beauty all year round. Its aim is to provide a small retreat place centred on the healing spirit of Christ where the atmosphere of peace will bring rest and renewal. In addition to the house, there are gardens, which open daily, a fine art gallery, coffee shop, lake and wetlands, arboretum, vegetable gardens and, for the children if you should be passing by for the day, tree houses and a play area.

OPEN: All year. Everyone welcome, especially those with full- or part-time ministry.
ROOMS: 2 bedrooms.
FACILITIES: Chapel, lounge, reading room for those on retreat, plus art gallery open

daily March–October. The gardens are open daily throughout the year until dusk, coffee shop, 'loft' and 'terrace', tree houses and children's area, lake and wetlands, arboretum, ancient forest cobb cottage and vegetable garden, plant sales and thatching experience.
SPIRITUAL HELP: A listening ear and prayer ministry for anyone who would like it.
GUESTS ADMITTED TO: All guest areas.
MEALS: By arrangement.
SPECIAL ACTIVITIES: There is no set programme, but they are prepared to supervise a programme if required. Small groups of up to 20 may enjoy the facilities for Quiet Days, Alpha days and seminars.
SITUATION: Countryside, set in its own well-established gardens.
MAXIMUM STAY: By arrangement.
BOOKINGS: Letter, telephone, email.
CHARGES: There is a small charge for use of the facilities and meals. Please enquire at time of booking.
ACCESS: By car is best (off the A31). Rail: Ashurst New Forest railway station (4 miles away). Bus: services run from Southampton city centre.

ROMSEY

Wisdom House Spirituality Centre Tel: 01794 830206
Wisdom House Fax: 01794 830614
Romsey reception@wisdomhouseromsey.org
Hampshire SO51 8EL Website: www.wisdomhouseromsey.org.uk
England

Retreats • Workshops and Courses • Church/Temple • Spiritual Help • Vegetarian Food
Venue for Hire • Self-Catering Space • Community Living • Vocations • Hermitages

Roman Catholic – Open spirituality – Wisdom spirituality

Wisdom House is set within beautiful gardens, and the house and bedrooms have been refurbished to a high standard, offering comfortable and peaceful accommodation. Hospitality and welcome are the keynotes here, aiming to ensure that guests have all they need to be free of concerns and preoccupations and are thus able to be fully present to the moment during their stay .

OPEN: All year except between Christmas and New Year. Both individuals and small groups are welcome.
ROOMS: 3-bedroom cottage. 1 double, 2 twins, 3 singles (1 en suite).The Poustinia is a small flatlet on the top floor of one of the houses. The remaining bedrooms are split between 2 houses on the campus, both of which house small resident communities of Daughters of Wisdom.
FACILITIES: Gardens – including a labyrinth garden (the centre is a member of the Quiet Garden Trust), prayer room, conference room, sitting room. creative room for activities such as painting, craft work and dance.

SPIRITUAL HELP: Spiritual direction on request, morning prayer, labyrinth.
GUESTS ADMITTED TO: Everywhere.
MEALS: Breakfast in own residence. Other meals can be taken alone or possibly with the small resident community. Self-catering option in Chez Nous cottage. Food is home cooked. Vegetarian option. Special diets catered for – advance notice requested.
SPECIAL ACTIVITIES: Occasional courses and residential retreats, some with outside speakers. Private retreatants welcome. Self-managed groups welcome.
SITUATION: Very tranquil.
MAXIMUM STAY: 8 days.
BOOKINGS: Letter, telephone, fax, email and online.
CHARGES: Suggested offering for full board is £45 per day.
ACCESS: By car or public transport. Rail: Romsey station. Bus: Wisdom House is walking distance from Romsey bus station. Visit the website for very clear, detailed direction.

SOUTHAMPTON

The Cenacle	Tel: 02380 453718
48 Victoria Road	Email: cenaclenetley@btinternet.com
Netley Abbey, Southampton	Website: freespace.virgin.net/
Hampshire SO31 5DQ	cenacle.netley/netley.htm /
England	www.cenaclesisters.co.uk

Retreats • Church/Temple • Spiritual Help • Alternative Therapies • Community Living Vocations

Christian – Roman Catholic

Netley Cenacle, like the ones in Walworth, London, and Ireland, is run by a community of religious sisters, which was founded to do retreat work. While all are welcome, the sisters especially offer year-round Ignatian Guided Retreats (IGR) including the 30-day retreat for individuals.

OPEN: All year. Everyone welcome.
ROOMS: 6 singles, all en suite.
FACILITIES: Prayer room, garden with summer house, library-sitting room, art room.
SPIRITUAL HELP: Spiritual direction, IGR direction.
GUESTS ADMITTED TO: Chapel. Unrestricted access.
MEALS: Everyone eats together. Traditional food. Vegetarian and special diets.
SPECIAL ACTIVITIES: Ignatian Guided Retreats, including 30-day ones, and private retreats. Ongoing spiritual direction is possible and also counselling. In the past, some complementary therapies, such as Reiki and aromatherapy massage, have been available, so please enquire what is on offer at the time of your booking.

SITUATION: Quiet in a village. Easy walk to Southampton Water.
MAXIMUM STAY: 30 days or by arrangement.
BOOKINGS: Letter, telephone, email.
CHARGES: Enquire as to day and full rates or donations when you book.
ACCESS: Train and car possible. Rail: Netley or Southampton stations. Bus: services run from Southampton. Please call for directions.

SOUTHSEA

House of Bethany	Tel: 02392 833498
7 Nelson Road	Email: ssb@sistersofbethany.org.uk
Southsea	Website: www.sistersofbethany.org.uk
Hampshire PO5 2AR	
England	

Retreats • Church/Temple • Spiritual Help • Vegetarian Food • Community Living • Vocations

Christian – Anglican

The main active work of the sisters is to offer hospitality to those who want to retreat for a time of quiet. A number of sisters have received training in spiritual direction and different aspects of retreat work, which includes leading Quiet Days and preaching.

OPEN: Most of the year. Private retreatants and non-residential groups are welcome.
ROOMS: 4 singles, 1 twin.
FACILITIES: Chapel, garden. Up to 24 people can be received as a non-residential group.
SPIRITUAL HELP: Spiritual direction. Quiet Days. Unity services and some other special Christian seasonal events.
GUESTS ADMITTED TO: All guest areas.
MEALS: For the Quiet Days, you bring your own packed lunch but drinks are available and usually soup. Please enquire about meals if you are making a private retreat.
SPECIAL ACTIVITIES: There are Quiet Days each month led by various clergy and religious.
SITUATION: In town.
MAXIMUM STAY: By arrangement
BOOKINGS: By letter to Revd Mother at above address. Online contact form also available.
CHARGES: The current cost of a Quiet Day is £6.
ACCESS: Full map details on their website. Rail: Fratton and Portsmouth stations. Bus: services run from Portsmouth and near Fratton railway station.

STROUD

The High House   Tel: 0170 262520
Stroud
Petersfield
Hampshire GU32 3PN
England

Retreats • Workshops and Courses • Venue for Hire • Self-Catering Space

Christian

A big spacious house with its own indoor swimming pool, oratory, library, garden, water garden and labyrinth. There is also a small two-bedroom flat available. A maximum of 25 people can come here at the same time, and Quiet Days, workshops, theme retreats such as painting, and Ignatian spirituality are all possible.

KENT

ADDINGTON

The Seekers Trust Healing Centre   Tel: 01732 843589
The Close   Website: www.theseekerstrust.org.uk
Addington Park, West Malling
Kent ME19 5BL
England

Retreats • Workshops and Courses • Church/Temple • Meditation • Spiritual Help
Self-Catering Space • Holistic Holidays • Community Living

Inter-denominational – Christian tradition

The Seekers Trust operates a centre of prayer for healing, spiritual guidance and protection with prayer chapels, a healing sanctuary and prayer help for anyone, regardless of their beliefs, for which there is no charge. As in the ancient tradition among places of sanctuary, they have both short-term retreat accommodation and small independent flats for those who may want to arrange a longer-term stay and become a part of the life and prayers at the centre.

OPEN: All year. Receives everyone.
ROOMS: 4 singles, 3 doubles. These are in the form of guest flats. No smoking.
FACILITIES: Disabled access if self-sufficient or accompanied. Conference rooms, garden, park, library.
SPIRITUAL HELP: Personal talks, meditation. Prayer and healing ministry. Open healing days usually each week. Otherwise, healing by request.
GUESTS ADMITTED TO: Unrestricted access except residents' quarters. Quiet in the cloisters is requested.
MEALS: Guests prepare their own food.
SPECIAL ACTIVITIES: Prayer and healing. Groups for yoga, meditation and other activities are often planned.
SITUATION: Quiet.
MAXIMUM STAY: By arrangement.
BOOKINGS: Letter, telephone.
CHARGES: The Seekers Trust depends on donations, so please enquire what the current donation rate for your stay will be when you are discussing your booking.
ACCESS: Rail: London Victoria station to Borough Green station, taxi to Addington. Car: M20 exit 3 (local map available on website).

AYLESFORD

The Friars	Tel: 01622 717272
Aylesford Priory	Fax: 01622 715575
Aylesford	Email: enquiry@thefriars.org.uk (general enquiries) /
Kent ME20 7BX	retreats@thefriars.org.uk (retreats)
England	Website: www.thefriars.org.uk

Retreats • Workshops and Courses • Church/Temple • Spiritual Help • Bed and Breakfast
Vegetarian Food • Organic Food • Venue for Hire • Community Living • Vocations • Children

Christian – Roman Catholic – Inter-denominational

The Carmelite Friars say that hope is a source of joy and that joy is a source of strength. At Aylesford they offer an open door to everyone seeking such hope and the joy of spiritual renewal. The restored shrine of Our Lady of the Assumption and St Simon Stock is a special feature. Pilgrimages, retreats, a guest house, a conference centre, excellent bookshop, craft workshops and a tearoom and shop all serve to make Aylesford Priory a full and interesting retreat experience. **Highly Recommended.**

OPEN: All year with Christmas religious services. Receives everyone. Children welcome.
ROOMS: 24 singles, 30 twins, 6 family rooms – but the medieval Priory houses an 80-bedroomed guest house set within acres of beautiful grounds and can sleep up to 100 if necessary.

FACILITIES: Chapel, shrine, conferences, guest lounge, garden, library, TV, bookshop, tea room – and some beautiful restored ancient buildings to admire.
SPIRITUAL HELP: Personal talks, spiritual direction, personal retreat direction.
GUESTS ADMITTED TO: Chapel, gardens, public areas, facilities.
MEALS: Guests eat together in the Pilgrim's Hall and are asked to help clear up after the meal. Traditional food. Vegetarian and special diets possible.
SPECIAL ACTIVITIES: Planned programme of events, exhibitions and pilgrimages. See online.
SITUATION: Can be busy but situation is excellent and quiet in a village.
MAXIMUM STAY: 1 day to 2 weeks.
BOOKINGS: Letter, telephone, fax, email.
CHARGES: Rates vary according to your stay and include special rates for senior citizens and children. Example of current shared/single room rates: full board (accommodation, supper, breakfast, lunch and afternoon tea) £44.75/45.75; B&B with English breakfast £25/£26.
ACCESS: By car, coach, train. Rail: Aylesford, Maidstone East or West Malling stations. Car: M20 exit 6 or M2 exit 3, follow signs to Eccles and The Friars.

CANTERBURY

Centrespace   Tel: 01227 462038
3 Alcroft Grange   Email: podger@centrespace.freeserve.co.uk
Canterbury CT2 9NN   Website: www.centrespace.freeserve.co.uk
England

Retreats • Workshops and Courses • Meditation • Spiritual Help • Bed and Breakfast
Vegetarian Food • Organic Food • Self-Catering Space • Alternative Therapies
Community Living • Work Retreats • Hermitages • Children

Christian – Anglican – Inter-faith – Mind Body Spirit

Silent and shared retreats to quietly rest, relax, reflect, pray and meditate and generally find some inner re-creation of spiritual awareness. Awareness training, sacred-circle dancing and group meditation practice are available. There is a quiet room, woodland and that special place of retirement – a hermit hut.

OPEN: All year. Everyone welcome – including those who come from different faith backgrounds and those who profess no particular faith.
ROOMS: 4 singles, 2 twins, 1 double with en suite for self-catering. Hermit hut. Wheelchair access bedroom – and facilities also for child's cot.
FACILITIES: Small groups, garden, library, guest lounge, quiet room, hermit hut, woodland nearby.
SPIRITUAL HELP: Daily peace prayer in Taize tradition, prayer, personal talks, group sharing, spiritual direction, personal retreat direction, meditation.
GUESTS ADMITTED TO: Almost everywhere.

MEALS: Everyone usually eats together. Wholefood, organic. Vegetarian and special diets. Self-catering possible.
SPECIAL ACTIVITIES: Planned retreats and events and daily services – see online.
SITUATION: Very quiet in the countryside.
MAXIMUM STAY: By arrangement.
BOOKINGS: Letter, telephone – mornings best, email.
CHARGES: Different rates and arrangements, so you need to ask at time of booking.
ACCESS: All visits by prior arrangement. Train/Coach: Canterbury stations. Bus: to University of Kent, then 1-mile walk. Car: plan and map online, or call for further directions.

EDENBRIDGE

Sisters of St Andrew
Eden Hall
Stick Hill, Edenbridge
Kent TN8 5NN
England

Tel: 01342 850388
Fax: 01342 851383
Email: thecentre@sisters-of-st-andrew.com
Website: www.sisters-of-st-andrew.com

Retreats • Workshops and Courses • Church/Temple • Spiritual Help • Vegetarian Food
Venue for Hire • Self-Catering Space • Community Living • Vocations • Children

Christian – Roman Catholic – Ecumenical

Quiet Days and facilities are available for groups. Individuals come here for a silent or an individually guided Ignatian retreat. which is also much in silence.

OPEN: All year. Receives men, women, young people, families. Groups for the day.
ROOMS: 25 singles, 2 twins.
FACILITIES: Chapel, conferences, garden, National Trust walk, guest lounge, TV, library.
SPIRITUAL HELP: Personal talks, spiritual direction, and personal Ignatian retreat direction. Visitors are welcome to join the community in prayer.
GUESTS ADMITTED TO: Chapel, oratory, reflection oasis, work in garden.
MEALS: Everyone eats together. Self-catering possible or meals can be taken in room. Traditional food. Vegetarian and special diets.
SPECIAL ACTIVITIES: Mainly Quiet Day retreats and Ignatian guided retreats.
SITUATION: Quiet in countryside.
MAXIMUM STAY: Up to 8 days.
BOOKINGS: Letter, telephone, fax, email. Downloadable booking forms available online.
CHARGES: Current suggested donations: residential weekend £160–£180; 24-hour self-catering £30–£40; 24-hour full board £40-£50; individually guided IGR £40–£65.
ACCESS: Car: M25 exit 6 – see online for full directions from there. Train: Edenbridge Town and Edenbridge stations, then taxi (best to book the day before arrival).

HYTHE

Cautley House
Christian Centre for
Healing and Wholeness
95 Seabrook Road
Seabrook, Hythe
Kent CT21 5QY
England

Tel: 01303 230762
Email: admin@cautleyhouse.org.uk
Website: www.cautleyhouse.org.uk

Retreats • Workshops and Courses • Church/Temple • Spiritual Help • Bed and Breakfast
Vegetarian Food

Christian – Anglican – Healing and Prayer Ministry

Cautley House is a Christian centre near the beach and famous Royal Military Canal with most of its rooms having sea views. Cautley House, whose patron is the Archbishop of Canterbury, is a place where guests can come to find wholeness in body, mind and spirit. **Highly Recommended.**

OPEN: All year. Everyone welcome.
ROOMS: 14 rooms, all en suite – a mixture of single, twin and family rooms.
FACILITIES: Chapel, lounge, gardens, creative art space for guests and visitors.
SPIRITUAL HELP: Daily services in chapel. Listening and prayer ministries. Special services for healing and wholeness with the laying on of hands are held each week.
GUESTS ADMITTED TO: Almost everywhere.
MEALS: Good food. Vegetarians catered for.
SPECIAL ACTIVITIES: A programme of varied events from *Animal Appreciation Day* to *Ways into Contemplative Prayer using The Cloud of Unknowing and Works of St John of the Cross, Exploring the Beatitudes*, and retreats on *The Psalms in Music and Art*.
SITUATION: Cautley House is situated between Seabrook and Hythe.
MAXIMUM STAY: 2 weeks.
BOOKINGS: To the administrator by letter, telephone, email.
CHARGES: These range from donations to costs per retreat based on length of stay. Example costs range from £12.50 to £160 per person.
ACCESS: : Car: Hythe is just off the A259. Train: Folkestone West/Central stations. Bus: services run from Folkestone.

MINSTER-IN-THANET

Minster Abbey Tel: 01843 821254
Church Street (for booking, write to the
Minster-in-Thanet, near Ramsgate Guest Sister instead of calling)
Kent CT12 4HF Website: www.minsterabbeynuns.org
England

Retreats • Church/Temple • Spiritual Help • Vegetarian Food • Venue for Hire
Community Living • Work Retreats • Vocations • Children

Christian – Roman Catholic

A graceful place of mainly stone with visible remains of the ancient monastery of St Mildred, founded in AD 670. A very comfortable and peaceful guest house.

OPEN: Usually January to October. During the summer months, families are welcome, as well as young women who would like a working holiday. No unaccompanied men.
ROOMS: 7 single, 2 twin, 1 double, 1 triple room, 1 double en suite with full disabilities access.
FACILITIES: Chapel, small library, conference rooms, gardens, shop.
SPIRITUAL HELP: Sharing in a prayerful environment and Benedictine way of life.
GUESTS ADMITTED TO: Guest facilities, group rooms and gardens.
MEALS: Self-service breakfast in the dining room of the guest house. Home-cooked meals are provided, with much of the produce grown in their own gardens. Vegetarian meals by prior arrangement.
SPECIAL ACTIVITIES: The public is welcome to view the ancient monastic buildings and beautiful gardens, and guided tours are given as part of the hospitality work of the sisters.
SITUATION: Peaceful.
MAXIMUM STAY: By arrangement.
BOOKINGS: Letter.
CHARGES: Ask when booking.
ACCESS: Car: Minster is off the A299 and 5.5 miles from Ramsgate. Rail: Minster station; the monastery is 3 minutes' walk away.

'God doesn't require us to succeed; he only requires that you try'
– Mother Teresa

NONINGTON

Beech Grove Community	Tel: 01304 842980
Sandwich Road	Website: www.churchcommunities.org.uk
Nonington, Dover	
Kent CT15 4HH	
England	

Church/Temple • Spiritual Help • Community Living • Work Retreats • Vocations • Children

Christian – Christian Community Life

This is one of two British Bruderhof communities that are part of a long-established Christian international community movement of single people, families and older people living together in a lifestyle based on the teachings of Jesus to love one another, to make peace, not to judge your enemies and not to worry about tomorrow. The other is **Darvell Community** in Robertsbridge (see East Sussex section). While the communities do not run retreats or any programme, they keep an open door of hospitality to anyone who desires to visit.

RAMSGATE

St Augustine's Monastery	Tel: 01843 593045
St Augustine's Road	Website: www.ramsgatebenedictines.com
Ramsgate	
Kent CT11 9PA	
England	

Retreats • Church/Temple • Spiritual Help • Community Living • Work Retreats • Vocations

Christian – Roman Catholic

Because the guest rooms are inside the monks' enclosure, they are only able to take male guests to share in the life of quiet and prayer here. You will be expected at Mass and to join the community in the Divine Offices – Evening Office of Vespers at least. Religious vocation discernment and advice are available. There is silence in the cloisters and you will be expected to follow the monks' way of community life at meal times and in other daily activities. Leave mobile phones and MP3 players at home – after all, you are getting away from it all. **Highly Recommended.**

TUNBRIDGE WELLS

Burrswood
Groombridge
Tunbridge Wells
Kent TN3 9PY
England

Tel: 01892 863637 / 01892 865988
(enquiries and reservations)
Email: admissions@burrswood.org.uk
Website: www.burrswood.org.uk

Retreats • Church/Temple • Spiritual Help • Bed and Breakfast • Vegetarian Food
Venue for Hire • Alternative Therapies • Holistic Holidays

Christian – Inter-denominational with the Anglican Church

Burrswood is a large Christian centre for healthcare and ministry, which includes a medical centre, hospital, guest accommodation and a resident community. St Michael's Guest House has recently been refurbished, offering newly decorated rooms with early Victorian features restored as much as was possible. A pool and tennis court are also available as well as the services of a physiotherapist and the use of the hydrotherapy pool (additional small charges apply). It is a good place to come for tranquillity, respite, rest and for healthy activity. Burrswood is a unique partnership between medicine and Christianity – a place of care and healing. **Highly Recommended.**

OPEN: All year. Receives everyone.
ROOMS: 7 new bedrooms for guests.
FACILITIES: Church, prayer chapel, conferences, gardens, park, library, guest lounge, hydrotherapy pool, bookshop, food and product shop, gift shop. Swimming lessons for all ages.
SPIRITUAL HELP: A very supportive place. Spiritual direction, personal retreat direction, personal talks with chaplain, healing service with laying on of hands, Eucharist, evening prayers.
GUESTS ADMITTED TO: Unrestricted access except for hospital areas.
MEALS: Taken in dining room with breakfast in room. Traditional food. Vegetarian and special diets.
SPECIAL ACTIVITIES: Various events held throughout the year. See online.
SITUATION: 220-acre estate.
MAXIMUM STAY: By arrangement.
BOOKINGS: Contact the admissions team by telephone, email or online contact form.
CHARGES: Current rates per room per night: full-board single £76, twin £122; half-board single £56, twin £102; B&B single £46, twin £82. Good discounts for stays of 2 nights or more.
ACCESS: Rail: Tunbridge Wells station, then bus or taxi. Car: access from A264.

WEST MALLING

The Pilsdon at Malling Community   Tel/Fax: 01732 870279
27 Water Lane   Email: pilsdon.malling@tiscali.co.uk
West Malling   Website: www.pilsdonatmalling.org.uk
Kent ME19 6HH
England

Retreats • Church/Temple • Spiritual Help • Vegetarian Food • Community Living
Work Retreats • Children

Christian

The Pilsdon at Malling Community has been going now for over five years and takes its ideals and ethos from the Pilsdon Community in Dorset. They seek to provide a safe and welcoming environment where people can rebuild their lives after experiencing a sudden or progressive crisis, whether that is through depression, alcoholism, addiction, divorce or bereavement. They offer friendship, hospitality and the kindness of traditional Christian charity. When you visit them, some of the community will be members who live there with their families, and there might be some longer-term guests. However, everyone – even a retreat guest – participates fully in the life of the community.

WEST WICKHAM

The Emmaus Centre   Tel: 0208 7772000
Daughters of Mary and Joseph   Fax: 0208 7762022
Layhams Road   Email: enquiries@emmauscentre.org.uk
West Wickham   Website: www.emmauscentre.org.uk
Kent BR4 9HH
England

Retreats • Workshops and Courses • Church/Temple • Spiritual Help • Bed and Breakfast
Vegetarian Food • Venue for Hire • Self-Catering Space • Community Living • Vocations

Christian – Roman Catholic – Ecumenical

The community offer hospitality in peaceful surroundings with good accommodation and a planned programme of events. There are two chapels – one grand and one more modest for quiet private prayer.

Good walks can be taken in the nearby woods. There is a small flat for silent private retreats or retreat leaders. There are a number of art-related retreats on offer as well as religious-themed or subject-focused events and retreats.

OPEN: All year except Christmas period. Receives everyone.
ROOMS: 40 rooms available: 8 singles, 32 twins. There is 1 flat and 1 en suite.
FACILITIES: Provision for disabled. Conference hall for up to 70 people, a room for up to 35, lounge, several smaller discussion rooms, 2 chapels, garden, 2 libraries, guest lounge, bookshop, internet connection, simultaneous translation equipment available.
SPIRITUAL HELP: Spiritual direction, individually guided retreats, preached retreats, spirituality workshops, personal counselling – all available by arrangement.
GUESTS ADMITTED TO: Chapel and all retreat-house facilities.
MEALS: Everyone eats together. Traditional/vegetarian food. Special diets. Self-catering in the flat.
SPECIAL ACTIVITIES: Planned programme of events, retreats and activities.
SITUATION: Quiet, on the edge of the countryside: nice views, leafy quiet garden, good walks. Also good access to public transport.
MAXIMUM STAY: By arrangement or depending on event.
BOOKINGS: Letter, telephone, fax, email. Downloadable booking form online.
CHARGES: By suggested offering given in each retreat programme. If staying on a private individual retreat, then please ask them for a donation guideline.
ACCESS: By train, car, bus. Car: off A2022. Rail: Hayes station. Local bus routes. Good map available on website.

SURREY

EAST MOLESEY

House of Prayer	Tel/Fax: 0208 9412313
35 Seymour Road	Email: info@christian-retreat.org
East Molesey	Website: www.christian-retreat.org
Surrey KT8 0PB	
England	

Retreats • Workshops and Courses • Church/Temple • Meditation • Spiritual Help
Vegetarian Food • Venue for Hire • Work Retreats • Community Living • Vocations

Christian – Roman Catholic – Ecumenical

More and more people appreciate the space and freedom available here and, located only 17 miles from London, it is remarkably convenient to get to. A spacious and comfortable house for rest and relaxation with a community who offer a daily rhythm of prayer with their work of offering retreats, spiritual help and hospitality. The community especially welcomes those who may need a retreat during an important transitional stage in their lives. **Highly Recommended.**

GODALMING

Ladywell Retreat and Spirituality Centre   Tel: 01483 419269
Ashstead Lane   Email: retreat@lady-well.org.uk
Godalming   Website: www.fmdminternational.co.uk
Surrey GU7 1ST
England

> Retreats • Workshops and Courses • Church/Temple • Spiritual Help • Vegetarian Food
> Venue for Hire • Self-Catering Space • Alternative Therapies • Community Living • Vocations

Christian – Roman Catholic

The centre borders urban Godalming and the rural Green Belt and seeks to provide a sacred place where all who come can explore their own deep desires, values and beliefs. A programme of individually guided or preached retreats, and days of prayer, based on the Roman Catholic tradition, is organised throughout the year. This is a very green-conscious retreat. In 2005 they received an award commending them for their Commitment to the Environment by the Surrey Sustainable Business Awards. **Highly Recommended.**

OPEN: The Ladywell Retreat and Spirituality Centre is open all year. Everyone welcome.
ROOMS: 24 singles, 2 doubles and 1 twin. All rooms are centrally heated.
FACILITIES: Conference Hall, an extensive library, 2 quiet rooms, 3 chapels, 3 rooms for individual direction.
SPIRITUAL HELP: Spiritual direction is available for those wishing to come for private days of prayer, but this request needs to be mentioned when booking.
GUESTS ADMITTED TO: Gardens are extensive and tranquil and freely available to all who come.
MEALS: Meals are provided for individual guests and for groups in a section of a large refectory. All food, usually traditionally English, is home cooked with a vegetarian option.
SPECIAL ACTIVITIES: Retreat programme. Also on request aromatherapy massage, reflexology and Indian head massage.
SITUATION: Rural Green Belt.
MAXIMUM STAY: By arrangement.
BOOKINGS: Letter, telephone, email. Online contact form also available.

CHARGES: There are no rates as such, but recommended offerings are given in the programme (£52–£370).
ACCESS: Car: 10 minutes off the A3. Rail: Godalming station (1 mile away).

LINGFIELD

Claridge House	Tel: 01342 832150 / 0845 3457281 (UK only)
Dormans Road	Fax: 01342 836730
Lingfield	Email: welcome@claridgehousequaker.org.uk
Surrey RH7 6QH	Website: www.claridgehousequaker.org.uk
England	

Retreats • Workshops and Courses • Yoga • Meditation • Spiritual Help • Bed and Breakfast
Vegetarian Food • Organic Food • Venue for Hire • Alternative Therapies • Holistic Holidays

Quaker – Ecumenical

A Quaker centre of healing, rest and renewal, run by the Society of Friends Fellowship of Healing and open to everyone. The centre is an old Victorian house in a small village, standing in its own two acres of lovely gardens. There are facilities for group conferences, retreats and private visits and a programme of courses on offer, many focused on healing. A warm and peaceful Quaker atmosphere with delicious vegetarian food only and open all year. **Highly Recommended.**

OPEN: All year except usually first week of January. Welcomes everyone.
ROOMS: 13 bedrooms with a mixture of single, twin and double beds.
FACILITIES: Disabled access, quiet room, conferences, garden, library, guest lounge.
SPIRITUAL HELP: Personal talks possible, group sharing, healing spiritualities and programmes.
GUESTS ADMITTED TO: Quiet Room. Unrestricted access.
MEALS: Everyone eats together. Exclusively vegetarian, with vegan and some medical diets catered for.
SPECIAL ACTIVITIES: Planned programme.
SITUATION: Quiet in a village in the countryside.
MAXIMUM STAY: By arrangement.
BOOKINGS: Letter, telephone, email, online contact form.
CHARGES: All residential course prices are inclusive of full board: Monday to Friday mid-week breaks from £170 up to £225. For 1-day retreats: £25 including lunch.
ACCESS: Rail: Lingfield station, pick-up by arrangement with notice (email: find@claridgehouse.quaker.eu.org), preferably 15:09. Coach: East Grinstead, pick-up by arrangement with notice (email as before). Car: easily accessible from the M25, M23, A22 and A264.

RICHMOND

Community of the Sisters of the Church	Tel: 0208 9408711
St Michael's Convent	Fax: 0208 9485525
56 Ham Common, Richmond	Email:
Surrey TW10 7JH	hospitality@sistersofthechurch.org.uk
England	Website: www.sistersofthechurch.org.uk

> Retreats • Workshops and Courses • Church/Temple • Spiritual Help • Vegetarian Food
> Self-Catering Space • Community Living • Vocations • Hermitages

Christian – Anglican

St Michael's has a strong commitment to hospitality, and to the provision of spiritual accompaniment/direction, counselling and psychotherapy, pastoral work and priestly ministry. The convent incorporates a spacious Georgian house, which has been extended to provide a beautiful modern chapel, well-appointed meeting rooms and comfortable guest accommodation. Ten minutes' walk from both Richmond Park and the River Thames. **Highly Recommended.**

OPEN: All year, apart from the first part of January, after Easter, and part of August. Closed on Mondays. Everyone welcome.

ROOMS: 8 single, 1 twin, self-catering flat with 2 twins.

FACILITIES: Library, chapel, refectory, centrally heated bedrooms with desks, kitchenettes for making breakfast and refreshments, bathrooms on each guest corridor, labyrinth and hermitages in the garden, green surroundings. Lift to first floor. For details on disabled access, please apply.

SPIRITUAL HELP: Spiritual accompaniment is usually available. Chapel services. Eucharist daily, except on Saturdays.

GUESTS ADMITTED TO: Guests are welcome to join in chapel services.

MEALS: Dinner and supper are taken with the sisters in the refectory, usually in silence. Vegetarian and special diets with notice.

SPECIAL ACTIVITIES: An annual programme of retreats and events is available on request and at website.

SITUATION: South-west London; quiet, green, suburban area.

MAXIMUM STAY: 6 days, or by arrangement.

BOOKINGS: Telephone, letter, email.

CHARGES: Donations are suggested. Guests: £35 per 24 hours' full board; £15 for the day with a meal; £10 for the day without a meal. Group rates for daily room hire: large meeting room (up to 25) £80; medium meeting room (up to 15) £50; small meeting room (up to 8) £25 (up to 8). See online for full cost of events.

ACCESS: Car: 5 miles from M4 exit 1; plenty of parking space. Rail: Richmond station. Bus: from Richmond railway station towards Kingston, alight at Ham Gate Avenue, then it's a few minutes' walk to St Michael's Convent.

SHERE

Harry Edwards Healing Sanctuary
Burrows Lea, Hook Lane
Shere, near Guildford
Surrey GU5 9QG
England

Tel: 01483 202054
Fax: 01483 205613
Email: info@burrowslea.org.uk
Website: www.sanctuary-burrowslea.org.uk

Retreats • Workshops and Courses • Spiritual Help • Vegetarian Food
Alternative Therapies • Holistic Holidays

Spiritual Healing

The Healing Sanctuary was founded in 1946 by the celebrated spiritual healer Harry Edwards. It is based at Burrows Lea, a magnificent Victorian country house set in 30 acres of stunning Surrey countryside, providing a sense of beauty and calm. Just a visit to these gardens and adjoining woods can refresh and nurture the mind, body and soul. People visit the sanctuary for spiritual healing, to sit quietly for prayer, for meditation or to unwind.

OPEN: Various dates in April, May, June, July, September and November.
ROOMS: 6, all en suite.
FACILITIES: Lift access, 30 acres of stunning grounds, meditation garden.
SPIRITUAL HELP: Healing appointments available as well as guided meditations.
GUESTS ADMITTED TO: Everywhere.
MEALS: All meals provided for throughout retreat. Vegetarian and other dietary requirements catered for.
SPECIAL ACTIVITIES: The Harry Edwards Healing Sanctuary offers a relaxing, totally luxurious and unique environment in which to de-stress and regenerate. They will not ask you to follow any fixed itinerary but instead offer a programme of events, a delicious menu and a bar. There is a good programme of retreats including a very popular 3-day retreat.
SITUATION: Rural setting in Surrey Hills near village.
MAXIMUM STAY: 2 nights, 3 days.
BOOKINGS: Letter, telephone, email.
CHARGES: Current retreat rates: £330 per person fully inclusive; single occupancy £360. Workshops: £50 (special offer of 3 for £125). 1-day retreats: 25–£35.
ACCESS: Train: Guildford station (9 miles away) or Dorking station (8 miles away). Car: detailed directions are available on the website.

CAMBERLEY

Tekels Park Guest House
Tekels Park
Camberley
Surrey GU15 2LF
England

Tel: 01276 23159
Fax: 01276 27014
Email: ghouse.tekels@btclick.com
Website: www.tekelspark.co.uk

Retreats • Workshops and Courses • Yoga • Meditation • Spiritual Help • Bed and Breakfast
Vegetarian Food • Organic Food • Venue for Hire • Alternative Therapies
Holistic Holidays • Children/

Theosophical – *Mind Body Spirit*

Tekels Park is owned by the Theosophical Society in England and is a wooded estate set in over 50 acres of secluded woods and fields, which form a wildlife sanctuary within 35 miles of London. There is a programme of events and talks during the year given by various spiritually inspired organisations, and guests are welcome to join in. The guest house has earned a reputation for serving excellent vegetarian and vegan food. **Highly Recommended.**

OPEN: All year. Welcomes everyone.
ROOMS: 23 bedrooms and 1 double apartment, all with wash-hand basins, and a large en suite apartment that can accommodate 3 people.
FACILITIES: Disabled access, conferences and group rooms, garden, park, library, guest lounge, TV.
SPIRITUAL HELP: Personal talks, group sharing, and directed study within the context of the various events in the Alternative Events Programme. See online.
GUESTS ADMITTED TO: Unrestricted access.
MEALS: Excellent vegetarian, vegan and whole-food cooking. No meat or fish is served. No alcohol. Guests eat together in Garden Room restaurant. Special diets catered for.
SPECIAL ACTIVITIES: Tekels Park is the venue for a number of events and talks including yoga classes, healing therapy, general spirituality, science and philosophy, and many other subjects of wide interest to many people today.
SITUATION: Quiet relaxing in the countryside.
MAXIMUM STAY: By arrangement.
BOOKINGS: Letter, telephone, fax, email, online contact form.
CHARGES: Current rates: single £44; single economy £39; twin/double £68; twin/double with single occupancy £48.
ACCESS: Car: easily accessible from A30 and M3. Rail: Camberley station (1.2 miles away), then walk or taxi.

WOKING

St Columba's House	Tel: 01483 766498
Maybury Hill	Fax: 01483 776208
Woking	Email: retreats@stcolumbashouse.org.uk
Surrey GU22 8AB	Website: www.stcolumbashouse.org.uk
England	

Retreats • Workshops and Courses • Church/Temple • Meditation • Spiritual Help
Bed and Breakfast • Vegetarian Food • Venue for Hire

Christian – Anglican – Ecumenical

St Columba's welcomes men and women of all faiths or none and provides a common ground for ecumenical discussion and prayer. It has undergone a complete refurbishment and has now been made an even more comfortable and up-to-date retreat house. Pleasant surroundings with home-style meals. There is a garden prayer walk and a collection of contemporary paintings. **Highly Recommended.**

OPEN: All year except Christmas and New Year's. Welcomes everyone.
ROOMS: 22 singles (2 with disabled facilities), 5 twins. All en suite. Lift to upper floor in main house.
FACILITIES: Disabled access, conferences, chapel, garden, library, reading room, internet access, telephone, Freeview.
SPIRITUAL HELP: Personal talks, groups sharing, spiritual direction, personal retreat direction, meditation, spiritual healing. Ignatian and Carmelite retreats can be arranged for private retreats.
GUESTS ADMITTED TO: Everywhere.
MEALS: Everyone eats together. Traditional food. Vegetarian and special diets.
SPECIAL ACTIVITIES: Planned programme of events. See online for details. Specialist facilities for business and corporate Quiet Days.
SITUATION: Very quiet, in a town.
MAXIMUM STAY: By arrangement.
BOOKINGS: Letter, telephone, fax, email. Online booking enquiry form is easiest method.
CHARGES: B&B per person: single from £56; twin single occupancy from £67; twin double occupancy from £120 (per room); weekend full board from £139pp. Full-board, group, day and conference retreat rates are all available.
ACCESS: Rail: Woking (1 mile away), then taxi or walk. Car: via Maybury Hill off the B382 – try to avoid entering Woking town itself.

EAST SUSSEX

•••

CROWHURST

Crowhurst Christian Healing Centre Tel: 01424 830033 (bookings) /
The Old Rectory   01424 830204 (general)
Crowhurst, near Battle   Fax: 01424 830053
East Sussex TN33 9AD   Email: crowhurstrectory@btconnect.com
England   Website: www.crowhursthealing.co.uk

> Retreats • Workshops and Courses • Church/Temple • Spiritual Help • Vegetarian Food
> Venue for Hire • Holistic Holidays

Christian – Healing ministry – Ecumenical – the Divine Healing Mission

Crowhurst Christian Healing Centre was founded for the purpose of developing and offering retreats and courses relating to the healing ministry of Jesus. It is a place to find emotional, spiritual and physical renewal in the experience of God's love. There is a programme of events and retreats including day, mid-week and longer breaks on a full-board basis, healing and bereavement retreats, Quiet Days, clergy retreats, prayer and painting retreats, and ones in healing in the psalms. The Chaplaincy Team presently consists of four full-time and part-time members; most are ordained members of the Anglican, United Reformed or Methodist Church, or the Salvation Army. **Highly Recommended.**

OPEN: Most of the year. Welcomes everyone.
ROOMS: 20 rooms, 6 of which are twins.
FACILITIES: Disabled access. 2 chapels. Lounge overlooking the garden with a prayer walk and stations to aid meditation and reflection, dining room, library, art room open every day, ground-floor cloakroom facilities.
SPIRITUAL HELP: Christ-centred worship, Holy Communion and twice-weekly healing services. Guided tuition is available.
GUESTS ADMITTED TO: Everywhere.
MEALS: All accommodation is full board. Meals are freshly prepared on site and include a varied choice. Special dietary requirements can be accommodated by prior arrangement.
SPECIAL ACTIVITIES: Healing services – no need to give advance notice if you are coming to a Healing Service on Tuesday evening or Thursday morning; everyone is welcome and there is no charge. Personal talks by arrangement.
SITUATION: On edge of the village, distant views of the sea and set in beautiful countryside among trees and fields.
MAXIMUM STAY: By arrangement at time of booking.

BOOKINGS: Letter, telephone, fax, email.
CHARGES: Lunch after the Thursday morning service £5; Quiet Days including lunch, coffee and tea £15; residential accommodation and all meals per night £50 (non-en suite) to £60 (en suite). See online programme for cost of individual events.
ACCESS: Rail: Crowhurst station (Old Rectory's 'garden' entrance is only 100 metres from the southbound platform exit). Car: easily accessible from the A21; clear directions are on the website.

PENHURST

Penhurst Retreat Centre	Tel: 01424 892088
The Manor House	Email: info@penhurst.org.uk
Penhurst, near Battle	Website: www.penhurst.org.uk
East Sussex TN33 9QP	
England	

Retreats • Workshops and Courses • Church/Temple • Spiritual Help
Vegetarian Food • Children

Christian – Ecumenical

Next to the parish church, Penhurst is a seventeenth-century manor house with a full annual programme of retreats and events. It is a sanctuary of peace, yet only 90 minutes from London and an hour from Gatwick Airport and the M25.

OPEN: Most of the year. Everyone welcome.
ROOMS: 5 twin, 1 double. Day groups are also welcome up to a maximum of 25.
FACILITIES: Church, chapel, garden, dining room, lounge.
SPIRITUAL HELP: Spiritual accompaniment for those seeking specific or regular guidance and support can be arranged.
GUESTS ADMITTED TO: Everywhere.
MEALS: Full board is offered. Home-cooked food. Vegetarian and special diets possible. Note that there is no self-catering provision for individual guests.
SPECIAL ACTIVITIES: Full programme of events and retreats ranging in subject, including the Art of Christian Discernment, Aspects of the Cross, using colour as a pathway to worship God, Myers-Briggs, various craft-related topics, music and dance.
SITUATION: Situated in an Area of Outstanding Natural Beauty some 10 miles from the coast in the Sussex High Weald.
MAXIMUM STAY: By event or by arrangement.
BOOKINGS: Letter, telephone, email. Online contact form is easiest method.
CHARGES: Full-board rates, per person per night: shared occupancy £42–£45; single occupancy £50–£55. Quiet Days: £20–£25. Individual retreat rates are available online.
ACCESS: Rail: Battle station (5.5 miles away), but best to ask for details when booking. Car: detailed directions are on the website.

ROBERTSBRIDGE

Darvell Community   Tel: 01580 883300
Brightling Road   Fax: 01580 883317
Robertsbridge   Website: www.churchcommunities.org.uk
East Sussex TN32 5DR
England

Church/Temple • Spiritual Help • Community Living • Work Retreats • Vocations • Children

Christian – Christian Community Life

This is a Bruderhof community, along with **Beech Grove Community** in Nonington (see Kent section). It is part of a long-established Christian international community movement whose lifestyle is based on the teachings of Jesus to love one another, to make peace, not to judge your enemies and not to worry about tomorrow. While the communities do not run retreats or any programme, they keep an open door of hospitality to anyone who desires to visit.

RUSHLAKE GREEN

The Studio and The Coach House   Tel/Fax: 01435 830203
Beech Hill Farm   Email: julia@desch.go-plus.net
Cowbeech Road, Rushlake Green   Website:
East Sussex TN21 9QB   www.sussexcountryretreat.co.uk
England

Retreats • Venue for Hire • Self-Catering Space

Open spirituality

Beech Hill Farm offers space for artistic work, some peacefulness and time to think, reflect and re-gear your creativity. It is not a centre with a programme and has no spiritual aim other than to offer that increasingly rare thing – an environment of Mind Body Spirit refreshment among the natural beauty of nature. The owner is an accomplished poet and artist and runs the organic sheep farm in which the facilities are situated.

SEAFORD

Florence House
Southdown Road
Seaford
East Sussex BN25 4JS
England

Tel: 01323 873700
Fax: 01323 873705
Email: info@florencehouse.co.uk
Website: www.florencehouse.co.uk

Retreats • Workshops and Courses • Yoga • Meditation • Vegetarian Food
Organic Food • Holistic Holidays

Open spirituality – Yoga – Meditation

With its elegant interior, Florence House is a well-established and much-appreciated venue for bespoke life-enhancing workshops and retreats. A variety of retreats is on offer, which include yoga, meditation and nutrition. These all aim to enhance a balance of life and restore a sense of calm. While maintaining the intimacy of a family home, Florence House offers comfortable accommodation including a self-contained cottage with three double bedrooms away from the main house. It is well known for creative and nutritional cuisine.

WALDRON

Monastery of the Visitation
Foxhunt Manor
Waldron, near Heathfield
East Sussex TN21 0RX
England

Tel: 01435 812619

Retreats • Church/Temple • Spiritual Help • Vegetarian Food • Community Living • Vocations

Christian – Roman Catholic

The sisters offer an environment of stillness, prayer and spiritual renewal to those women who wish to share their lives for a time. Guests are asked to stay within the enclosure throughout their stay. This is a place for silence, contemplation, and the regaining of inner peace.

WEST SUSSEX

ARUNDEL

Convent of Poor Clares
Crossbush
Arundel
West Sussex BN18 9PJ
England

Tel: 01903 882536 / 01903 883125
Email: poorclarescrossbusharundel@hotmail.co.uk
Website: www.poorclaresarundel.org

Church/Temple • Self-Catering Space • Community Living • Vocations • Hermitages

Christian – Roman Catholic

Here is a traditional convent with all the gentleness and space to pray that one could want. The surrounding countryside is beautiful, with the South Downs at hand and the sea only four miles away. The community has a small guest house where people are welcome to stay for a private retreat or just to rest and be quiet. There are two small patios and also a little woodland where guests can sit during warm weather. The dove of peace is one of the signs of this contemplative community. **Highly Recommended.**

OPEN: All year except 1 November to 8 December. Receives men, women, families in the caravans on site, groups up to 8.
ROOMS: Small guest house: 4 singles, 2 double. 2 large caravans.
FACILITIES: Guest lounge, TV.
SPIRITUAL HELP: Should anyone wish to talk with one of the sisters, they can ask the Guestmistress and this can be arranged provided there is a sister available at the time.
GUESTS ADMITTED TO: Chapel, church.
MEALS: Self-service breakfast; dinner served 12:30; self-service supper. Self-catering in the caravans.
SPECIAL ACTIVITIES: None.
SITUATION: House is quiet but on a busy road. Lovely countryside with good walks nearby. Few miles from the coast.
MAXIMUM STAY: By arrangement.
BOOKINGS: Letter, telephone, email.
CHARGES: On a donation basis. As the retreat house is a main source of their income, a donation of £25–£45 per day is suggested.
ACCESS: Rail: Arundel staion, then 10-minute walk to the convent. Car: just off the A27, a mile east of Arundel.

CRAWLEY

Monastery of the Holy Trinity
Crawley Down
Crawley
West Sussex RH10 4LH
England

Tel: 01342 712074
Email: brother.andrew@cswg.org.uk

Retreats • Church/Temple • Spiritual Help • Vegetarian Food • Community Living • Vocations

Christian – Anglican – Contemplative community

This is an enclosed contemplative order for men and remains one of our favourite retreat places. Guests are asked to respect the timetable and silence of the monks' daily life. Within the Christian vision of life, the community here offers traditional liturgy and prayer from a perspective common to both the Christian East and West. This is not a suitable retreat place for those who are under psychological stress or feel that they could not handle silence and lack of conversation. It is a place to share in the liturgical and contemplative life of a monastic community. **Highly Recommended.**

OPEN: All year except usually 1 week in spring and 1 week in December. Receives men and women. Groups only for the day.
ROOMS: 6 singles. Silence is observed.
FACILITIES: Chapel, garden, library.
SPIRITUAL HELP: Personal talks, spiritual direction, participation in the Divine Office and group prayers, which usually include the Jesus Prayer.
GUESTS ADMITTED TO: Chapel, grounds of monastery but not monastic enclosure, work of the community, refectory.
MEALS: Everyone eats together. Nice simple cooking, largely vegetarian.
SPECIAL ACTIVITIES: None.
SITUATION: Very quiet, in the midst of 60 acres of woodland.
MAXIMUM STAY: Usually 1 week.
BOOKINGS: Letter or telephone (09:45-11:45 and 14:00-17:00), email.
CHARGES: By donation and this is usually such a modest amount, currently about £25 per night inclusive of meals.
ACCESS: Car: easily accessible from M23 exit 10. Rail: East Grinstead or Three Bridges stations, then bus.

Worth Abbey	Tel: 01342 710318
Turners Hill	Fax: 01324 710311
Crawley	Email: themonastery@worthabbey.net /
West Sussex RH10 4SB	guestmaster@worthabbey.net
England	Website: www.worthabbey.net

Retreats • Workshops and Courses • Church/Temple • Spiritual Help • Vegetarian Food
Venue for Hire • Self-Catering Space • Community Living • Work Retreats • Vocations
Camping • Children

Christian – Roman Catholic – Ecumenical

A recent television programme filmed here about living a monastic life was seen by some 3 million viewers. All guests are welcome, but men only are received in the Monastic Guest House. There is other modern, comfortable accommodation for women and families. All guests staying for a few days may share in the monastic timetable in the church.

OPEN: All year except Christmas and New Year. Everyone welcome. Special programmes for young people and those men and women discerning a possible call to a religious life. Children welcome.

ROOMS: St Bruno's House: 1 single, 13 twins, 2 family rooms for 4 (groups up to 36 people). Compass House: 10 singles (1 en suite), 3 twin (1 en suite). Monastery Guest House for men only: 3 single rooms, 2 twin. There is no overnight accommodation in the abbey church complex. Refurbished Bermondsey Huts can be used as a base for summer camping and larger family gatherings and other self-catering groups.

FACILITIES: Disabled access. Day-centre meeting room for up to 35 people, camping, garden, guest lounge, library, bookshop. The large and modern abbey church can seat up to 1,400 people.

SPIRITUAL HELP: Communal prayer, monastic liturgy, group sharing, spiritual direction and personal retreat direction in IGR retreats.

GUESTS ADMITTED TO: Chapel, church, choir, gardens.

MEALS: Individual men staying in the Monastery Guest House eat with the monks in the monastic refectory. Women may stay in Compass House on a self-catering basis. Traditional food. Vegetarian and special diets.

SPECIAL ACTIVITIES: Planned Open Cloister Programme (see online). Guests are welcome to attend Divine Office as well as Mass.

SITUATION: In the countryside, with beautiful grounds.

MAXIMUM STAY: Usually 3 days.

BOOKINGS: Letter, telephone, fax, email.

CHARGES: Rates upon request.

ACCESS: Rail: Three Bridges station, then bus. Car: M23 exit 10 to East Grinstead.

HORSHAM

St Cuthman's
Coolham, Horsham
West Sussex RH13 8QL
England

Tel: 01403 74220
Fax: 01403 741026
Email: stcuthmans@dabnet.org
Website: www.stcuthmans.com

> Retreats • Church/Temple • Spiritual Help • Vegetarian Food • Venue for Hire
> Self-Catering Space • Hermitages

Christian – Roman Catholic

A tranquil environment in a beautiful rural setting with comfortable en suite rooms, central heating and log fires in the winter. The house, owned and subsidised by the Diocese of Arundel and Brighton, operates as a quiet retreat house. It is in a site of special nature conservation with a large lake, and birds abound. Open to guests of all denominations and faiths.

OPEN: All year except during Christmas and Easter weeks. Welcomes everyone.
ROOMS: 8 singles, 8 doubles/twin, all en suite – includes 1 bedroom and bathroom for disabled access. Lift. 2 self-catering hermitages in grounds.
FACILITIES: Disabled access, chapel, garden, library, guest lounges, art room, local walks, 'Garden Rooms' for group meetings and gatherings.
SPIRITUAL HELP: A simple time of prayer takes place morning and evening and Mass is celebrated regularly as well. An experienced spiritual director or retreat guide, or a listening ear, can usually be arranged for individuals, with sufficient advance notice.
GUESTS ADMITTED TO: Unrestricted.
MEALS: Traditional food. Vegetarian and special diets. Self-catering hermitages in grounds.
SPECIAL ACTIVITIES: Monthly reflection days, days of prayer, special events and some led retreats in a modest but good programme. Occasionally there are musical concerts.
SITUATION: A quiet place in countryside with large grounds, walks and lots of birds and plants.
MAXIMUM STAY: By arrangement.
BOOKINGS: Letter, telephone (09:00–21:00), fax, email, online contact form.
CHARGES: Current rate: £73 per person per night, full board, for those making a personal retreat – minimum stay 2 nights. Quiet Day rate is £25. Please ask for rates on self-catering hermitages and for groups of 16–24 people.
ACCESS: Car: on the A272, south of Horsham. Rail: Billingshurst station (4.5 miles away) or Horsham station (9 miles away).

ISLE OF WIGHT

• •

RYDE

The Garth Retreat	Tel/Fax: 01983 562602
St Cecilia's Abbey	Email: sca@stceciliasabbey.org.uk /
Ryde	info@stceciliasabbey.org.uk
Isle of Wight PO33 1LH	Website: www.stceciliasabbey.org.uk
England	

Retreats • Church/Temple • Spiritual Help • Self-Catering Space • Vocations

Christian – Roman Catholic

Divine Office is sung in Gregorian chant by this Benedictine community of nuns. The Garth, adjacent to the monastery, offers self-catering
guest accommodation to those wishing to spend some days in an atmosphere of prayer and recollection.

OPEN: Most of the year except Christmas week. Receives women, families, small
groups and young people.
ROOMS: 3 twins, 1 single annex.
FACILITIES: Chapel. Small garden, library, guest lounge
SPIRITUAL HELP: Personal talks possible.
GUESTS ADMITTED TO: External chapel of the abbey church.
MEALS: Self-catering only.
SPECIAL ACTIVITIES: None.
SITUATION: Quiet, on the outskirts of a seaside town.
MAXIMUM STAY: 1 week.
BOOKINGS: Letter with stamped addressed envelope if possible, telephone or fax
(10:30–18:30), email.
CHARGES: No fixed charge – donations accepted.
ACCESS: Ferry: from Portsmouth, Southampton or Lymington. From Portsmouth
Harbour to Ryde Pier Head, it is a short train ride to Ryde Esplanade, then take a taxi or
bus, or walk (20–30 minutes) to the abbey. Excellent details given online at website.

'There is no remedy for love but to love more'
– Henry David Thoreau

Quarr Abbey	Tel: 01983 882420 / 01983 884850 (Guestmaster)
Ryde	Email: guestmaster@quarrabbey.co.uk
Isle of Wight PO33 4ES	Website: www.quarrabbey.co.uk
England	

Retreats • Church/Temple • Spiritual Help • Vegetarian Food • Community Living • Vocations

Christian – Roman Catholic

Here you may share for a few days in the life and rhythm of a contemplative Benedictine men's monastic community, following their daily life of prayer and work. The purpose of your retreat should be for prayer and to draw nearer to God.

> *'All major religious traditions carry basically the same message;*
> *that is, love, compassion and forgiveness – the important thing is*
> *they should be part of our daily lives'*
> *– the Dalai Lama*

EAST AND EAST ANGLIA

BEDFORDSHIRE

TURVEY

Monastery of Christ Our Saviour
Jacks Lane
Turvey
Bedfordshire MK43 8DH
England

Tel: 01234 881211
Email: turveymonks@yahoo.co.uk
Website: www.turveyabbey.org.uk

Retreats • Workshops and Courses • Church/Temple • Spiritual Help • Vegetarian Food
Venue for Hire • Self-Catering Space • Community Living • Work Retreats
Vocations • Children

Christian – Roman Catholic

The monks' guest house has been converted from a stone barn. The rooms are spacious and comfortable with lots of books to read and an easy chair in every room, and there is a guest kitchen where self-catering is possible. It is a place where personal silence is very much respected and so, if you are on a private retreat, you will be left in peace to get on with it. As it is a very small community of monks and lay men and women, help in the garden is usually welcomed. The life here is deliberately kept simple. Guests are expected to respect the silence of others. There is a large park of trees and birds; just behind the monastery property are fields and plenty of places to walk. Within the monastery grounds is the Turvey Centre for Group Therapy, which was founded by the community some years ago. Nothing is grand here, everything is real – a peaceful place. **Highly Recommended.**

OPEN: All year except Christmas and Easter seasons. Everyone welcome.
ROOMS: Singles and usually a double in the main guest house. In the garden, there are some newly built guest/meeting rooms in a separate building.
FACILITIES: Conferences, garden, library, guest lounge, kitchen, payphone, nearby fields in which to walk.
SPIRITUAL HELP: Daily Mass, Divine Office in the chapel, personal talks possible.
GUESTS ADMITTED TO: Chapel, gardens, some outside work of community.
MEALS: Taken in the guest house, often with a self-catering lunch, with breakfast and evening meal being provided. Full catering for groups if required. Provision for vegetarians if requested.
SPECIAL ACTIVITIES: None.

SITUATION: The village has a lot of traffic, but the guest house and gardens are quiet.
MAXIMUM STAY: By agreement.
BOOKINGS: Letter, telephone (leave message on answer phone), email.
CHARGES: Suggested donations depending on what the meal arrangements are going to be.
ACCESS: Rail: Bedford or Northampton stations, then bus (not frequent) or taxi. Car: via M1, exit 14 to Olney, then on to Turvey via A428.

Priory of Our Lady of Peace	Tel: 01234 881432
Turvey Abbey	Website: www.turveyabbey.org.uk
Turvey	
Bedfordshire MK43 8DE	
England	

Retreats • Workshops and Courses • Church/Temple • Spiritual Help • Vegetarian Food
Self-Catering Space • Community Living • Work Retreats • Vocations

Christian – Roman Catholic

Although Turvey Abbey is next to a busy road, the sisters have created an oasis of peace and prayer in this picturesque stone village by the River Ouse. The nuns are a lively community, who warmly welcome their guests and put them immediately at ease. The chapel is modern, full of light and simply decorated by work of the community, who are famous for the quality of the design and execution of their projects. The meals are served either in the small guest dining room or in a beautiful stone carriage house attached to the chapel. The programme of icon painting and prayer workshops are excellent. **Highly Recommended.**

OPEN: Most of the year, Everyone welcome.
ROOMS: 5 singles, 1 single en suite, 2 twins, 1 twin en suite.
FACILITIES: Chapel, small conferences, garden, park, nearby woodlands and fields, library, guest lounge, day retreats possible.
SPIRITUAL HELP: Guests are welcome to join in the Divine Office and are provided with books, which are easy to follow even if you never have attended such a service before. Daily Mass.
GUESTS ADMITTED TO: Chapel, Divine Office, library, occasionally work of the community.
MEALS: Meals are taken in a guest house or separate dining room. Traditional food. Vegetarian provision and special diets – not too complicated.
SPECIAL ACTIVITIES: Planned programme of events. See brochure or online.
SITUATION: In the village near countryside with fields to the rear and side.

MAXIMUM STAY: By arrangement.
BOOKINGS: Preferably by letter.
CHARGES: Ask for charges information.
ACCESS: Rail: Bedford or Northampton stations, then bus (not frequent) or taxi. Car: via M1, exit 14 to Olney, then on to Turvey via A428.

CAMBRIDGESHIRE

CAMBRIDGE

The Institute for Orthodox Christian Studies
Wesley House
Jesus Lane, Cambridge
Cambridgeshire CB5 8BJ
England

Tel: 01223 741037
Fax: 01223 741370
Email: info@iocs.cam.ac.uk
Website: www.iocs.cam.ac.uk

Retreats • Workshops and Courses • Church/Temple • Spiritual Help • Vocations

Christian – Orthodox

Although the Institute for Orthodox Christian Studies (IOCS) is non-residential, it is able to provide a list of local B&B guest houses if you wish to visit or attend any of their various events. A programme is run with lectures, courses and weekends on Orthodox Christianity and there is choir practice as well. The institute's approach to learning is to engage the whole human person. It seeks to integrate the learning cycle into the liturgical cycle. The services in English and moments of prayer during the courses form an essential part of the programme. For all enquiries regarding the excellent distance-learning programmes of the Institute, please contact Dr Constantinos Athanasopoulos by email: ca356@cam.ac.uk. **Highly Recommended.**

'He is able who thinks he is able'
– Buddha

ELY

Bishop Woodford House	Tel: 01353 663039
Retreat and Conference Centre	Fax: 01353 665305
Barton Road, Ely	Email: bwh@ely.anglican.org
Cambridgeshire CB7 4DX	Website: www.bwh.org.uk
England	

> Retreats • Workshops and Courses • Church/Temple • Vegetarian Food
> Venue for Hire • Children

Christian – Anglican

A modern place with lawns, it is easy to find in the grounds of an old theological college. The chapel is large and traditional. Both individual and group day retreats are welcome, and accommodation can be booked. There is a bookshop and a bar, and the staff here are welcoming and helpful. The house is five minutes' walk from Ely Cathedral, the river and the town.

OPEN: All year. Everyone, adults and children, welcome.
ROOMS: 4 twin en suite, 10 single en suite, 13 singles. Day groups up to 60 people.
FACILITIES: Chapel, guest lounge, library, bookshop, dining room, meeting rooms, rehearsal room, Woodford room and bar.
SPIRITUAL HELP: None.
GUESTS ADMITTED TO: Unrestricted access.
MEALS: Everyone eats together. Traditional food. Vegetarian and special diets possible.
SPECIAL ACTIVITIES: Planned open events. See online.
SITUATION: In a town and next to a school – quiet in the school holidays and at night.
MAXIMUM STAY: By arrangement.
BOOKINGS: Letter, telephone, fax, email. Availability can be easily checked online, and booking forms can be downloaded.
CHARGES: Please enquire at time of booking. Tariffs vary for residential stays (bed only, B&B, half board, full board available), day groups and room hire.
ACCESS: Rail: Ely station, then 10-minute walk or taxi. Coach: Cambridge, then bus. Car: via A10. Good directions are given on the website.

HORSEHEATH

Mill Green House
Mill Green
Horseheath
Cambridgeshire CB21 4QZ
England

Tel: 01799 584937
Email: suewalker619@btinternet.com /
graemewalker619@btinternet.com
Website: www.millgreenhouse.co.uk

Retreats • Church/Temple • Spiritual Help • Bed and Breakfast • Vegetarian Food
Venue for Hire

Christian – Inter-denominational

Mill Green House is an old sixteenth-century family house, which is available for all who wish to have time and quiet in which to pray, read and wait upon God. Individual counselling, day retreats and opportunities for individuals to be alone and for groups to do their own programme are on offer.

OPEN: All year except August. Everyone welcomed.
ROOMS: 2 doubles.
FACILITIES: Conferences, garden, chapel/library, guest lounge.
SPIRITUAL HELP: Personal talks, spiritual direction, personal retreat direction.
GUESTS ADMITTED TO: Everywhere.
MEALS: Everyone eats together. Traditional simple food. Vegetarians catered for.
SPECIAL ACTIVITIES: Please enquire when booking if there are any events or special days planned.
SITUATION: Quiet in the countryside.
MAXIMUM STAY: By arrangement.
BOOKINGS: Letter, telephone (09:00–17:00), but email is easiest.
CHARGES: There is a range of rates from B&B and just lunch or supper to full board and a rate for day hire by groups as well as donations for spiritual direction/retreat. Ask for current charges and suggested donations when you are booking.
ACCESS: Rail: Cambridge station (15 miles away) or Audley End station (13.5 miles away). Car: easily accessible from M11/A11.

'Be kind whenever possible. It is always possible'
– the Dalai Lama

HUNTINGDON

Houghton Chapel Centre   Tel: 01480 469376
Chapel Lane   Email: wardens@houghtonchapelcentre.org.uk
Houghton, Huntingdon   Website: www.houghtonchapelcentre.org.uk
Cambridgeshire PE28 2AY
England

Retreats • Church/Temple • Venue for Hire • Self-Catering Space • Children

Christian – United Reform Church

Houghton Chapel Centre is a residential centre near St Ives, which is run by the United Reform Church and welcomes everyone. There is accommodation for 30 people in six small dormitories, a modern kitchen and meeting room with full range of audio-visual equipment. Groups will normally be self-catering, but catering can be arranged.

LITTLE GIDDING

Ferrar House   Tel: 01832 293383
Little Gidding   Email: info@ferrahouse.co.uk
Huntingdon   Website: www.ferrarhouse.co.uk
Cambridgeshire PE28 5RJ
England

Retreats • Church/Temple • Spiritual Help • Bed and Breakfast • Vegetarian Food
Venue for Hire • Self-Catering Space • Children

Christian – Anglican

Little Gidding is famous for the visit in the mid-1930s of the poet T. S. Eliot, who later wrote the poem 'Little Gidding' as the final part of his masterpiece *Four Quartets*. It is now a small retreat centre, which offers retreat hospitality, quiet space for personal retreats, facilities for groups and overnight accommodation.

OPEN: Most of year. Everyone welcome.
ROOMS: 4 rooms, of which 2 are family rooms, so there is accommodation for up to 12 people.
FACILITIES: Church, sitting rooms, self-catering kitchens near rooms, meeting room, dining room, small shop, gardens (member of the Quiet Garden Trust).
SPIRITUAL HELP: None.
GUESTS ADMITTED TO: Everywhere.

MEALS: B&B, full board and self-catering. Vegetarian and special diets catered for with prior arrangement.
SPECIAL ACTIVITIES: Church. Personal and small group retreats.
SITUATION: Peaceful countryside.
MAXIMUM STAY: By arrangement.
BOOKINGS: Email, online contact forms.
CHARGES: Current rates per person: B&B from £30; full board from £45; self-catering £30. Except for self-catering, rates are slightly higher for single occupancy.
ACCESS: By car is best – excellent instructions and a map are on the website.

ESSEX

BRADWELL-ON-SEA

Othona Community	Tel: 01621 776564
East Hall Farm	Fax: 01621 776207
East End Road, Bradwell-on-Sea	Email: bradwell@othona.org
Southminster, Essex CMO 7PN	Website: www.bos.othona.org
England	

Retreats • Workshops and Courses • Church/Temple • Vegetarian Food • Venue for Hire
Self-Catering Space • Community Living • Work Retreats • Hermitages
Camping • Children

Christian – Ecumenical – Open spirituality

This place is in the far reaches of the Essex estuary, which stretches right out into the North Sea. You drive and drive and the lanes get narrower; you find a farm and then – surprise! Here in the middle of nowhere is the Othona Community. A purpose-built place, centrally heated, provides lots of space for visitors. There are dormitories and rooms, which are comfortable. School groups and families can visit here too. Hidden around the grounds are tiny hermitages, without toilets or electricity, for those that may want a real desert spirituality experience. A Site of Special Scientific Interest (SSSI) is here because of the abundant birds and it is a well-known spot for birdwatching enthusiasts. It is a rather haunting scene of birds, people, silence, peace and wilderness. This is one of two Othona Communities; the other is in Bridport, Dorset (see the South West section). The setting being so close to a SSSI, a nature reserve and the sea makes this a very special retreat place for those who are keen on nature and wildlife. The community has use of the seventh-century chapel of St Ceed, which dates from AD 645. We had very good vegetarian food when we visited. **Highly Recommended.**

OPEN: All year. Everyone welcome including families, young people and children.
ROOMS: Lots of rooms – singles, doubles, dormitories; tents available, barn, hermitages.
FACILITIES: Chapel, conference rooms, camping, garden, park, guest lounge.
SPIRITUAL HELP: Depends on programme course. The community works closely with the local churches.
GUESTS ADMITTED TO: Everywhere except community private areas.
MEALS: Everyone eats together. Simple, wholefood. Vegetarian and special diets. Self-catering facilities available.
SPECIAL ACTIVITIES: See online for planned programme.
SITUATION: Quiet and remote with its own beach, fields, orchards, woodlands and ancient chapel.
MAXIMUM STAY: By arrangement.
BOOKINGS: Letter, telephone, fax, email, online enquiry and booking forms.
CHARGES: Currently: B&B about £19; adult £28.25 per day; student £20.15 per day. Rates for children, groups, schools, drop-in meals, working retreats and the unwaged all available.
ACCESS: Rail: Southminster Station (10 miles away), then bus to the King's Head pub in Bradwell; pick-up by arrangement from the pub. Car: see the website for detailed directions.

St Peter's Chapel on the Wall
The Rectory
East End Road, Bradwell-on-Sea
Southminster, Essex CMO 7PX
England

Tel: 01621 776203
Website: www.bradwellchapel.org

Church/Temple

Christian – Anglican – Ecumenical – Inter-denominational

Open all the time and to everyone, this is one of the loveliest and most ancient chapels in Britain. It sits on a windswept and grassy rise on the edge of the sea. Empty of furnishings and built of weathered stone, it speaks of prayer and of aloneness with God. Today the religious tradition is continued at the chapel by a Eucharist celebration each Wednesday morning, followed most weeks by breakfast at the **Othona Community**, which offers retreat and guest accommodation (see previous entry).

BRENTWOOD

Abbotswick   Tel: 01277 373959
Diocesan House of Prayer   Email: bookings@abbotswick.org
Navestock Side, Brentwood   Website: www.abbotswick.org
Essex CM14 5SH
England

Retreats • Workshops and Courses • Church/Temple • Spiritual Help • Bed and Breakfast
Vegetarian Food • Venue for Hire • Vocations • Hermitages • Children

Christian – Roman Catholic

Set in 14 acres of beautiful grounds, the House of Prayer provides hospitality for making a quiet retreat. There are a caravan and a small hermitage in the grounds for people wishing to experience more solitude.

*'Love every leaf, every ray of light. Love the animals, love the
plants, love each separate thing.
If thou love each separate thing thou wilt perceive The Mystery
of God in all'
– Fyodor Dostoyevsky*

COLCHESTER AND CHELMSFORD

Canonesses of the Holy Sepulchre Tel: 01206 867296
74 Howe Close Website: www.canonesses.co.uk/colchester.html
Colchester
Essex CO4 3XD
England

Canonesses of the Holy Sepulchre Tel: 01245 604108
43 Anderson Avenue Website:
Chelmsford www.canonesses.co.uk/chelmsford.html
Essex CM1 2DA
England

Canonesses of the Holy Sepulchre Tel: 01245 604128
22 Anderson Avenue Website:
Chelmsford www.canonesses.co.uk/chelmsford.html
Essex CM1 2BZ
England

Retreats • Church/Temple • Spiritual Help • Community Living • Vocations

Christian – Roman Catholic

This religious community, until very recently, ran the school at New Hall in Essex and offered a very good retreat programme with accommodation in a beautiful renovated barn on the school campus. Their hospitality was excellent. Now that they have moved on, they are currently offering spiritual accompaniment and offer, as always, open and warm hospitality to everyone.

'Even the rich are hungry for love, for being cared for, for being wanted, for having someone to call their own'
– Mother Teresa

MALDON

The Patriarchal Stavropegic	Tel: 01621 816471
Monastery of St John the Baptist	
The Old Rectory	
Tolleshunt Knights, Maldon	
Essex CM9 8EZ	
England	

Church/Temple • Spiritual Help • Community Living • Vocations

Christian – Orthodox

The Patriarchal Stavropegic Monastery of St John the Baptist is a monastic community for both men and women, directly under the Ecumenical Patriarchate. It is the oldest Orthodox religious community in the UK. Currently, the majority of the community are nuns with a smaller number of monks. If you wish to visit, please write to them in the first instance.

PLESHEY

The Retreat House	Tel: 01245 237251
Chelmsford Diocesan	Fax: 01245 237594
The Street	Email: info@retreathousepleshey.com
Pleshey, Chelmsford	Website: www.retreathousepleshey.com
Essex CM3 1HA	
England	

Retreats • Workshops and Courses • Church/Temple • Meditation • Spiritual Help
Vegetarian Food • Venue for Hire • Self-Catering Space • Children

Christian – Anglican – Inter-denominational

This retreat house has been a place of prayer for 100 years and in the village of Pleshey for over 600 years. The House of Retreat has been called the New Jerusalem. It is just off the M25.

OPEN: Most of the year. Everyone welcome.
ROOMS: 22 single bedrooms, 1 of which is on the ground floor and equipped for disabled. Gatehouse adjoining the house with 4 bedrooms, which is also possible for self-catering.
FACILITIES: Disabled access, chapel, garden, library, day conferences, guest lounge, separate meeting room for up to 30 people. There are several other rooms at Pleshey that can be used for meetings.

SPIRITUAL HELP: Personal talks, personal retreat direction, directed study, spiritual direction.
GUESTS ADMITTED TO: Everywhere including chapel.
MEALS: Everyone eats together. Traditional simple food. Vegetarian. Special diets – on limited basis. Self-catering facilities possible.
SPECIAL ACTIVITIES: Myers-Briggs retreats, open retreats, Quiet Days, course for spiritual directors – check details online.
SITUATION: Quiet, in historic Essex village in countryside village.
MAXIMUM STAY: By programme event or 7 days.
BOOKINGS: Letter, telephone, email. Booking forms can be downloaded from their website.
CHARGES: Current rates range from £20 to £300 for planned retreats and events. Please enquire as to private stays, full board, self-catering and group rates.
ACCESS: Rail: Chelmsford station, then bus. Car: via M11 or M25/A11.

STANSTED

The Arthur Findlay College	Tel: 01279 813636
Stansted Hall	Fax: 01279 8160225
Stansted	Email: info@arthurfindlaycollege.org
Essex CM24 8UD	Website: www.arthurfindlaycollege.org
England	

Retreats • Workshops and Courses • Meditation • Spiritual Help • Bed and Breakfast
Vegetarian Food • Venue for Hire • Alternative Therapies • Holistic Holidays

Spiritualism – Spiritualists' National Union

The Arthur Findlay College for the Advancement of Psychic and Spiritual Science has been going since 1964 and is the world's foremost such college. The seven principles of Spiritualism are: the Fatherhood of God, the Brotherhood of Man, the Communion of Spirits and the Ministry of Angels, the Continuous Existence of the Human Soul, Personal Responsibility, Compensation and Retribution hereafter for all good and evil deeds done on Earth, and the Eternal Progress open to every human soul. The college runs an extensive series of courses and programmes; read about them on their website or send for their brochure to fully understand the range available and the various costs involved. Some examples might be as follows: *Crystal Enlightenment, Dance of the Spirits, Psychic Art Weekend, Spiritualist Healing Mediumship, Your Inner Spirit* and *Investigating the Paranormal.* The topics covered in various areas include mediumship, trance mediumship, meditation, colour and hypnosis. **Highly Recommended.**

OPEN: All year, according to programme.
ROOMS: 14 singles. 2 double plus other rooms available.
FACILITIES: Conferences, garden, library, guest lounge, TV.
SPIRITUAL HELP: Personal talks, group sharing, spiritual direction, personal retreat direction, meditation, directed study. Spiritual healing, private spiritual sittings/ readings.
GUESTS ADMITTED TO: Unrestricted access.
MEALS: Everyone eats together. Traditional/vegetarian food. Special diets.
SPECIAL ACTIVITIES: Planned programme – brochures available and see website.
SITUATION: Set in 15 acres of parkland and woods.
MAXIMUM STAY: By course or arrangement.
BOOKINGS: Letter, telephone, email, online booking form.
CHARGES: Day visit, residential, therapies and spiritualist sitting at various rates. No charge normally for healing.
ACCESS: Rail: Bishop's Stortford, Stansted Mountfitchet or Stansted Airport stations, then taxi. Car: via M11 exit 8a.

HERTFORDSHIRE

BARNET

Fellowship of Contemplative Prayer	Tel: 0208 4496495
117 Leicester Road	Email: crolder@tiscali.co.uk
Barnet	Website: www.contemplative-prayer.org.uk
Hertfordshire EN5 5EA	
England	

Retreats • Workshops and Courses

Christian – Inter-denominational

The Fellowship of Contemplative Prayer is a an association of individuals and groups who follow the way of prayer taught by the founder Robert Coulson, which is called the Prayer of Stillness. Central administration is kept minimal and, while groups and retreats are largely self-run, there is a planned programme of events and retreat. These are held at various venues around the country, many at retreat houses or places listed by us. This is updated and detailed on their website. They have publications available and welcome new members.

HEMEL HEMPSTEAD

Amaravati Buddhist Monastery Tel: 01442 842455
St Margarets Lane Fax: 01442 843721
Great Gaddesden Email: guestmonk@ amaravati.org (for men) /
Hemel Hempstead guestnun@amaravati.org (for women)
Hertfordshire HP1 3BZ Website: www.amaravati.org
England

Retreats • Workshops and Courses • Church/Temple • Yoga • Meditation • Spiritual Help
Vegetarian Food • Community Living • Work Retreats • Vocations

Buddhist (Theravada tradition)

This is a community of Buddhist monks and nuns of the Theravada tradition, but people of any or of no formal religious affiliation are welcomed. In fact, from time to time, you may well meet nuns and monks from other faiths visiting here and, certainly, people who are new to Buddhism. Retreats are held in separate facilities away from the often busy life of the Armarvati religious community itself. Guests are asked to attend morning and evening meditation and to help in the kitchens in the morning or to join in the morning work period with others. Accommodation is fairly basic and no shoes are worn indoors. The shrine room is very grand and beautiful with a large enclosed courtyard through which you enter the temple with a beautiful reclining Buddha. At the time of our visit there was another smaller room behind the temple room. There is a full calendar of events, talks and long and short retreats, so have a look at the programme online. It is possible by arrangement and at their discretion for you to stay with the monastic community for a time, but you must participate fully in their daily routine of meditation, meals and work. **Highly Recommended.**

OPEN: April to December for planned retreats. Closed January to end of March. Receives men, women, teenagers for a special annual retreat and young people over 15 years of age, families and groups for organised retreats.
ROOMS: 4 rooms for men. 8 rooms for women. Dormitory for men only. Up to 40 guests can be accommodated. Men and women are separated in accommodation and certain other areas.
FACILITIES: Temple, garden, park, library.
SPIRITUAL HELP: Personal talks on the retreats, otherwise evening talks. Guided meditation. Walking meditations possible in nearby woodlands.
GUESTS ADMITTED TO: Shrine room, work of the community, all daily work routines.

MEALS: Everyone eats together. Vegetarian food based on Thai, Sri Lankan and British dishes and served buffet style. No special diets, but variety of food at most meals gives a wide choice among vegetarian dishes.

SPECIAL ACTIVITIES: Festivals, retreats, workshops, courses, long retreats. Morning and evening chanting and meditation. A quiet contemplative atmosphere is maintained.

SITUATION: Quiet.

MAXIMUM STAY: First stay 1 week. After that 1 month at discretion of the Guest Monk.

BOOKINGS: Letter or email to the Guest Monk or the Guest Nun, depending on your gender.

CHARGES: Donations are welcomed at end of your stay to help towards running costs.

ACCESS: Coach/Rail: Hemel Hempstead, then taxi, or bus to Great Gaddesden or Nettleden followed by 15-minute walk. By car is the easiest option, but please drive very slowly and carefully, as the lanes to the centre are narrow; detailed directions are given on the website.

Monastic Community	Tel/Email/Website as above
Amaravati Buddhist Monastery	
Great Gaddesden, Hemel Hempstead	
Hertfordshire HP1 3BZ	
England	

In the monasteries, men stay with the monks, women with the nuns. Write to either the Guest Monk or the Guest Nun, depending on your gender. If received as a monastic guest, you will be expected to follow fully the regular daily monastic schedule of the monks or nuns, including all meditation and work.

Retreat Centre	Tel: 01442 843239
Amaravati Buddhist Monastery	Fax: 01442 843 721
Great Gaddesden	Email: retreats@amaravati.org
Hemel Hempstead	Website: www.amaravati.org
Hertfordshire HP1 3BZ	Related websites:
England	Amaravati Newsletter: www.forestsangha.org
	Amaravati Dhamma Talks: www.dhammatalks.org.uk
	Amaravati Lay Events: www.buddhacommunity.org
	Amaravati Family Events: www.amaravati.org

Group retreats are mostly held in silence, with a routine that emphasises formal meditation practice and instruction. Guests have access to the monastery meditation rooms. Retreats may be for a weekend or up to 10 days. Retreatants are expected to respect the retreat schedule. Open April to December. Everyone is welcome.

ST ALBANS

SPEC Centre and The Loft
All Saints Pastoral Centre, Shenley Lane
London Colney, St Albans
Hertfordshire AL2 1AG
England

Tel: 01727 828888
Fax: 01727 822927
Email: spec@rcdow.org.uk
Website: www.spec-centre.org.uk

Retreats • Workshops and Courses • Church/Temple • Spiritual Help • Vegetarian Food Venue for Hire • Children

Christian – Roman Catholic

With so many retreats for adults and so few that cater for young adults and children, we are pleased to see the continuation of the hospitality and work at SPEC and the Loft. SPEC is a residential centre that works with young people aged 14–20 years, with a team of trained staff and volunteers who deliver a planned programme. The focus at the Loft is on children and offers opportunities for spiritual and personal growth to young people aged 7–14. Booking online.

WATFORD

Bhaktivedanta Manor
Hilfield Lane
Aldenham, Watford
Hertfordshire WD25 8EZ
England

Tel: 01923 851000
Fax: 01923 852896
Email: info@krishnatemple.com
Website: www.krishnatemple.com/home

Retreats • Workshops and Courses • Church/Temple • Yoga • Meditation • Spiritual Help Vegetarian Food • Organic Food • Community Living • Children

International Society for Krishna Consciousness – Brahma-Madhva Gaudiya sampradaya lineage – Hinduism

In a lovely spot in the countryside, Bhaktivedanta Manor was donated to the Hare Krishna movement in the early 1970s by the former Beatle

George Harrison. Weekend retreats are on offer, which teach practices of mantra meditation and Bhakti yoga in ways that are attuned to the modern world. Topics on their excellent and beautifully illustrated website are fully explained. These include the spiritual heritage of the movement, vegetarianism, reincarnation, mantra meditation, yoga, karma, spiritual-practice principles.

OPEN: Most of the year and according to programme. Everyone is welcome.
ROOMS: Please enquire what is available at the time of your booking enquiry. Venues by arrangement.
FACILITIES: Temple, shrine, gardens, in-house Hindu weddings.
SPIRITUAL HELP: Mantra meditation, yoga, devotional practices.
GUESTS ADMITTED TO: Temple. All public areas.
MEALS: All vegetarian food.
SPECIAL ACTIVITIES: Daily devotions, festivals, open days, Ratha-Yatra (annual street festival).
SITUATION: In countryside.
MAXIMUM STAY: Usually the day or by arrangement.
BOOKINGS: Letter, telephone. Online booking enquiry is the best method.
CHARGES: Please ask what the arrangements are when you discuss visiting.
ACCESS: Rail: Watford Junction (5 miles away), Radlett (3 miles away). Underground: Jubilee Line to Stanmore (6 miles away); Northern Line to Edgware (7 miles away); Metropolitan Line to Watford (5.5 miles away). Bus: from Watford High Street. By car is the easiest; very good map and directions on the website, but do read the correct postcode on their website for sat-nav devices.

LINCOLNSHIRE

BOURNE

Edenham Regional House
Church Lane
Edenham, Bourne
Lincolnshire PE10 0LS
England

Tel/Fax: 01778 591358
Email: athawes@tsicali.co.uk
Website: www.erh.org.uk

Retreats • Workshops and Courses • Church/Temple • Spiritual Help • Bed and Breakfast
Vegetarian Food • Venue for Hire • Self-Catering Space • Children

Christian – Anglican – Ecumenical

This is a Queen Anne vicarage set in a lovely garden, which welcomes both individuals and small groups. Edenham Regional House offers a programme for Quiet Days and study courses and individual Ignatian retreats (IGR). There are a church, chapel, gardens and group meeting space. The guided retreats take place in an atmosphere of quiet and provide the maximum opportunity for prayer, rest and reflection. There are a lot of steps in part of the facility, making it unsuitable for the less mobile.

OPEN: Most of the year. Everyone welcome.
ROOMS: 4 rooms and 1 bedsit/kitchen/dining area on the second floor of the house. There is twin-bedded en suite accommodation adapted for wheelchair users.
FACILITIES: Disabled access, church, chapel, drawing room, library, garden, summer house.
SPIRITUAL HELP: Spiritual direction, guided retreats, church and chapel services, shared prayer.
GUESTS ADMITTED TO: Everywhere.
MEALS: There is a kitchenette that enable guests to self-cater, but meals can be provided.
SPECIAL ACTIVITIES: Individual Ignatian retreats.
SITUATION: Quiet, nearby great park and walks.
MAXIMUM STAY: By arrangement.
BOOKINGS: Letter, telephone, email.
CHARGES: Please enquire at time of discussing your individual or group needs.
ACCESS: By car is easiest, on the A151.

HORNCASTLE

Dev Aura   Email: sallym@asiact.org / enquiries@asiact.org
Little London   Website: www.asiact.org / www.aura-soma.net
Tetford, Horncastle
Lincolnshire LN9 6QL
England

Retreats • Workshops and Courses • Yoga • Meditation • Spiritual Help • Vegetarian Food
Organic • Venue for Hire • Alternative Therapies

Alternative spirituality – Mind Body Spirit

Dev Aura, the home of ASIACT, means 'House of Light' because the power of light and colour and colour education are what Dev Aura is about. The place is an old restored rectory standing in two acres with a garden where there is a meditation sanctuary. At Deva Aura, courses are held where you can learn about colour and discover what an important part colour plays in your life. Colour and light are increasingly being recognised as valuable forms of treatment for a growing number of conditions and the concept is international now.

OPEN: All year. Everyone welcome.
ROOMS: 11 bedrooms comprising 2 singles, 5 twins and 4 triples. Each room has its own hand basin, but bathrooms and shower rooms are shared.
FACILITIES: Teaching room, meditation room, meeting and consultation room, garden, library, and dining room.
SPIRITUAL HELP: Colour therapy.
GUESTS ADMITTED TO: All guest areas and garden.
MEALS: All vegetarian food using local organic produce where possible.
SPECIAL ACTIVITIES: Education, consultations, therapy.
SITUATION: Lincolnshire Wolds.
MAXIMUM STAY: For duration of course.
BOOKINGS: Email.
CHARGES: The rates are according to the course or consultation and can run from as little as £15 for a day visit to over £600; higher rates are inclusive and usually for 3- to 5-day stays.
ACCESS: Rail: Horncastle station, then bus. Car: access from A16 or A158.

LINCOLN

The Edward King Centre   Tel: 01522 504075
The Old Palace   Website: www.bishopedwardking.org
Minster Yard, Lincoln
Lincolnshire LN2 1PU
England

Retreats • Church/Temple • Venue for Hire

Christian – Anglican

Once the residence of the Bishops of Lincoln, this beautiful and historic house offers a place where Christians can come to address the issues of their calling, as individuals and as a Church. Other individuals and groups can be resources in pursuing their work and other interests, and here Church and world can meet, share and seek to collaborate on issue of significance.

'Better than a thousand hollow words,
is one word that brings peace'
– Buddha

NORFOLK

Buddhafield East Retreats

Tel: 07715 151149
Email: buddhafieldeast@hotmail.com

Retreats • Yoga • Meditation • Spiritual Help • Vegetarian Food • Self-Catering Space
Holistic Holidays • Community Living • Camping • Children

Buddhist – Friends of the Western Buddhist Order (FWBO)

Buddhafield East is a community of people who come together to put on Buddhist retreat camps and similar events in beautiful East Anglian countryside areas. They offer a way to take a break from everyday routines and to have a fresh experience of yourself in situations of stillness, beauty and peace. On these retreats, meditation techniques are taught, which are intended to bring about a calm and friendly state of mind. Also, everyone lives lightly on the land, reducing waste and reusing and recycling wherever possible.

NORWICH

All Hallows House
Community of the Sacred Passion
Rouen Road, Norwich
Norfolk NR1 1QT
England

Tel: 01603 624738
Website: www.all-hallows.org

Retreats • Church/Temple • Spiritual Help • Vegetarian Food • Vocations

Christian – Anglican

Though it is on a busy street, All Hallows has a peaceful atmosphere inside. St Julian's Church is next door and contains a chapel that is built on the site of the cell of the fourteenth-century mystic Julian of Norwich. Her *Revelations of Divine Love* is a classic Christian mystical work and can be obtained through all good bookshops. Reading her book, then coming here for a retreat built around some of her writings may well prove a worthwhile spiritual journey. All Hallows house is run by tbe sisters of the **Community of All Hallows**, which is based in Ditch-ingham. near Bungay. (See their separate entry in the Suffolk section.)

SURLINGHAM

Padmaloka Buddhist Retreat Centre for Men   Tel: 01508 538112
Lesingham House   (Monday–Friday 09:30-13:00, 14:30-17:00)
Surlingham, Norwich   Email: info@padmaloka.org.uk
Norfolk NR14 7AL   Website: www.padmaloka.org.uk
England

Retreats • Workshops and Courses • Church/Temple • Yoga • Meditation • Spiritual Help
Vegetarian Food • Community Living • Work Retreats • Vocations

Buddhist – Friends of the Western Buddhist Order (FWBO)

Here, no time is wasted in getting you into stillness and simplicity, and the study of what is the fastest-growing spiritual tradition in the West. In addition to meditation and other related classes, you can discover how to make spiritual practice work in your career through talks by men who have achieved it. They may be managing directors of suc-cessful companies or even medical school lecturers, but all have devel-oped what Buddhists term 'right livelihood'. Disabled can come too and there are a garden and a small delightful courtyard. A happy, peaceful and justly famous place for men. **Highly Recommended.**

OPEN: All year. Welcomes men.
ROOMS: Comfortable enough.
FACILITIES: Disabled access, garden, park, library, guest lounge, bookshop.
SPIRITUAL HELP: Personal talks, spiritual direction, group sharing, meditation, directed study, yoga, Buddhist devotional practice.
GUESTS ADMITTED TO: Shrine room. Work of community. Unrestricted access except to ordination team and support team areas.
MEALS: Everyone eats together. Vegan food.
SPECIAL ACTIVITIES: Planned programme of retreats throughout the year – see details online.
SITUATION: Old country house surrounded by farmland, quiet, in a village and countryside.
MAXIMUM STAY: By retreat event or by arrangement.
BOOKINGS: Letter, telephone, email, online booking.
CHARGES: Currently, retreats run from £65 and go up to £425. Request the brochure or view it online for costs per course.
ACCESS: Rail/Coach: Norwich, then taxi or bus to Surlingham village. Car: Padmaloka is off the A146 Norwich to Lowestoft road.

SUTTON

St Fursey's Orthodox Christian Study Centre   Tel: 01692 580552
St Fursey's House
111 Neville Road, Sutton
Norfolk NR12 9RR
England

Retreats • Workshops and Courses • Church/Temple • Spiritual Help • Vegetarian Food
Work Retreats

Christian – Orthodox Christian in the Patriarchate of Antioch

St Fursey's House is a small Orthodox Christian home and study centre, in a modern house, set in the Norfolk Broads. It exists to help nurture the Orthodox Christian faith in an English context through regular Quiet Days and talks on Orthodox spirituality, weekly ecumenical Bible studies and evenings of discussion. There are facilities for overnight stays and individual retreats. **Highly Recommended.**

WALSINGHAM

Shrine of Our Lady of Walsingham   Tel: 01328 820239
Hospitality Department   Fax: 01328 824206
The Milner Wing   email: accom@olw-shrine.org.uk
Common Place, Walsingham   Website:
Norfolk NR22 6BP   www.walsinghamanglican.org.uk /
England   www.walsingham.org.uk
(for both Anglican and Roman Catholic links)

Retreats • Workshops and Courses • Church/Temple • Bed and Breakfast
Vegetarian Food • Children

Christian – Anglican – Roman Catholic – Ecumenical

Walsingham Shrine is an ancient place of Christian pilgrimage and this is a famous, busy pilgrimage centre. This means that you will not normally find facilities for silence or for spiritual guidance. To go on a pilgrimage to a holy place is a long-established religious practice of most major world faiths. It can, and ought to, be regarded as a kind of retreat, especially as the pilgrim hopes for a deepening of personal spirituality.

The centre is a pleasant place to stay, from which you can visit either the Anglican shrine or the Roman Catholic one situated a mile away. Both continue to attract many thousands of people every year.

Sue Ryder Retreat House   Tel: 01328 820622
47–51 High Street
Walsingham
Norfolk NR22 6BZ
England

> Retreats • Church/Temple • Vegetarian • Hermitages • Children

Christian – Inter-denominational

Facilities are offered here for groups and individuals to make private retreats. There are no retreat programmes or spiritual direction available. Groups usually have their own facilitator. The staff concentrates on providing for the practical needs of visitors. Children are welcome.

SUFFOLK

BECCLES

Ringsfield Hall Trust Eco-Study Centre   Tel: 01502 713020
Ringsfield Hall   Fax: 01502 710615
Ringsfield, Beccles   Email: info@ringsfield-hall.co.uk
Suffolk NR34 8JR   Website: www.ringsfield-hall.co.uk
England

> Retreats • Workshops and Courses • Church/Temple • Bed and Breakfast
> Vegetarian Food • Venue for Hire • Self-Catering Space • Holistic Holidays
> Community Living • Hermitages • Children

Christian – Educational Christian Foundation – Eco-spirituality

This is a large brick house set in 14 acres of grounds, offering an amazing variety of amenities that include woodlands, meadows, ponds, and gardens and an up-to-date hermitage. In addition, there is a playing field with football pitch, adventure play equipment, camp fire circle and barbecue, a small chapel and a renovated hermitage set in a new woodland. In summary, Ringsfield Hall offers full board or self catering, day facilities, Quiet Days and group retreats, residential programmes, school and church-based workshops, and workshops for teachers and leaders – all with the aim of fostering the spirit and education of children and young people to support their physical, social and emotional development.

OPEN: Open all year for self-catering, otherwise for programme. Welcomes everyone, especially children and youth groups.
ROOMS: 2 singles, 6 twins, 1 triple, 4 dormitories (for 4–12 people), hermitage, cottage with 9 beds.
FACILITIES: Chapel, conferences, garden, park, library, guest lounge, games facilities, tennis court, nature trails, playing fields, solitary retreat hermitage.
SPIRITUAL HELP: Group sharing, personal retreat direction.
GUESTS ADMITTED TO: Unrestricted access.
MEALS: Everyone eats together. Traditional food. Vegetarian and special diets. Self-catering facilities.
SPECIAL ACTIVITIES: Planned programme relating to faith and environment, as well as Quiet Day retreats.
SITUATION: Quiet in the countryside in 14 acres of grounds.
MAXIMUM STAY: 1 week usually.
BOOKINGS: Letter, telephone, fax, email.
CHARGES: Full-board rates depend on number of nights stayed and size of the group. Self-catering group rates are per person per night. There is a youth weekend tariff as well. Hermitage is by daily donation to the Ringsfield Hall Trust. Please call for details.
ACCESS: Rail: Beccles station (3 miles away). Car: best option, A12 or M11.

'When a man surrenders all desires that come to the heart and by the grace of God finds the joy of God, then his soul has indeed found peace'
– The Bhagavad Gita

BUNGAY

Community of All Hallows
Belsey Bridge Road
Ditchingham, Bungay
Suffolk NR35 2DT
England

Tel: 01986 892840 / 01986 892749
(community/retreat information)
Email: allhallowsconvent@btinternet.com
Website: www.all-hallows.org

> Retreats • Workshops and Courses • Church/Temple • Meditation • Spiritual Help
> Bed and Breakfast • Vegetarian Food • Venue for Hire • Self-Catering Space
> Community Living • Work Retreats • Vocations • Children • Pets

Christian – Anglican

The Anglican Community of All Hallows run three small retreat houses at Ditchingham and **All Hallows House** in Norwich (see Norfolk section), which may be booked by individuals or small groups for a maximum stay of two weeks. At Ditchingham are **All Hallows House**, **St Mary's Lodge** and **Holy Cross House**, which is the guest wing of the convent for those seeking to share in the worship of the community. There is also a complex with all modern facilities, **St Gabriel's Conference Centre**. There is a happy and positive atmosphere in this community, and group retreatants often return on an individual basis. Open retreats of various kinds are held, often bearing such titles as *Beginners*, *Light out of Darkness*, *Julian and Healing*, *Pottery and Prayer*, *Celtic Retreat* and *Praying with George Herbert*, while Advent and summer courses are available for residential groups. As to **All Hallows House** itself – well, it can hardly be faulted for hospitality with its comfort, nice food and pleasant sitting room. The choice of accommodation with this community is excellent and the church and domestic arrangements are among the best. **Highly Recommended.**

Contact details for the individual sites:

All Hallows House, Ditchingham Tel: 01986 892840

Holy Cross House Tel: 01986 894092

St Mary's Lodge Tel: 01986 892731

St Gabriel's Conference Centre Tel: 01986 892133 /
Email: saint.gabriels@btinternet.com

All Hallows House, Norwich Tel: 01603 624738

Quiet Waters Christian Retreat House
Flixton Road
Bungay
Suffolk NR35 1PD
England

Tel: 01986 893201
Email: mail@quietwaters.org.uk
Website: www.quietwaters.org.uk

Retreats • Spiritual Help • Bed and Breakfast • Vegetarian Food • Venue for Hire

Christian – Inter-denominational

Quiet Waters aims to provide hospitality and an opportunity for Christians to seek God in a peaceful and safe environment.

OPEN: Most of the year. Everyone welcome.
ROOMS: 3 singles, 6 twins, 1 double. 2 ground-floor rooms are available with access for the less able, along with a specially equipped downstairs bathroom. Wheelchair ramps to the house. Please discuss any access needs that you may have.
FACILITIES: Small chapel, 2 sitting rooms, dining room, summer house, group bookings up to 19 and for the day only 20 persons.
SPIRITUAL HELP: Rest, refreshment, quiet, and the space and time for prayer and reflection.
GUESTS ADMITTED TO: Guest areas and gardens.
MEALS: Flexible catering arrangements up to full board. Vegetarian and special diets possible.
SPECIAL ACTIVITIES: Check the website for latest events.
SITUATION: Quiet countryside. Bungay is about a mile away.
MAXIMUM STAY: By arrangement.
BOOKINGS: Letter, telephone, email.
CHARGES: B&B £36.50; half board £47; full board £52; weekend to include board and room from £109.50. Separate pricing available just for lunch, dinner or day retreat.
ACCESS: Bus/Coach: to Bungay. Rail: Halesworth or Beccles stations. Car: accessible from M11 and A12. See website for travel directions and pick-up costs.

'It is better to be silent and real than to talk and be unreal'
– Saint Ignatius of Antioch

CLARE

Clare Priory	Tel: 01787 277326 (Monday–Friday 09:30–15:00)
Ashen Road	Fax: 01787 278688
Clare, Sudbury	Email: clare.priory@virgin.net
Suffolk CO10 8NX	Website: www.clarepriory.org.uk
England	

Retreats • Workshops and Courses • Church/Temple • Spiritual Help • Vegetarian Food
Venue for Hire • Community Living • Work Retreats • Vocations • Children

Christian – Roman Catholic

In Clare, near the old railway station, you can cross a bridge and follow a path grown wild with weeds to a door set in a stone wall. When you open it, you step into the peace of Clare Priory, the first home of the Augustinian monks in England. Spread before you in this once-secret garden lies a spring coverlet of white violets. Set in eight acres of secluded gardens beside a river, Clare Priory remains in the same solitude and quiet that it has enjoyed for all these long centuries. Now it is a place to share the daily routine of the Augustinian friars and the lay community. Private or guided retreats for individuals and groups are available as well as a programme of events, including reflective days with creation and scripture, praying and walking, art work or 'just being' with the Lord, silent directed retreats, holistic approach to prayer, and spirituality retreats. Each year a popular craft fair is held at the Priory. Spiritual guidance is available by arrangement. The Shrine is dedicated to Our Lady, Mother of Good Counsel, and is housed in one of the oldest parts of the priory. Ancient yet comfortable, filled with its long history of prayer and with an open heart to all, Clare Priory is rightfully a jewel among the retreat houses of England. **Highly Recommended.**

OPEN: Most of the year. Everyone welcome – for a retreat or just for a visit during the day to enjoy the peace and quiet.
ROOMS: The Stable House offers 7 single rooms and 1 double room (all with en suite and disabled facilities), 2 small meeting rooms and a small prayer room. In the Priory, there are 2 rooms with 3 beds, a family room with 1 double and 2 singles, and 1 twin room.
FACILITIES: Disabled access, oratory, library, gardens, shrine, small cloister.
SPIRITUAL HELP: Spiritual guidance, daily life of the community, individual Ignatian retreats.
GUESTS ADMITTED TO: All guest areas, library, gardens.
MEALS: Taken together in dining room. Vegetarian possible.
SPECIAL ACTIVITIES: Retreat programmes, private and guided retreats for either individuals or groups, Quiet Days.

SITUATION: Set in 8 acres of land beside the river. Lovely gardens.
MAXIMUM STAY: By arrangement.
BOOKINGS: Letter, telephone (see times above), email.
CHARGES: The current suggested offerings are £45 per person per overnight stay, £10 day visit, £12 day visit with soup and roll lunch, or £15 day visit with full lunch, weekdays only. The community emphasise that these are suggestions only and that no one is to feel excluded because of limited economic circumstances. See the online events page for cost per retreat.
ACCESS: Rail: Sudbury station (10 miles away). By car is best, via A1092. Excellent detailed travel directions on website.

MICKFIELD

St Andrew's Christian Centre   Tel: 01449 711640
Mickfield   Email: markfaith@tiscali.co.uk
Suffolk IP14 5LR
England

> Retreats • Church/Temple • Spiritual Help • Bed and Breakfast • Venue for Hire
> Community Living • Hermitages • Children

Christian – Anglican

St Andrew's is a Grade 1 listed medieval parish church that has been restored once again to a place of worship and hospitality, this time as a Christian centre. It offers individual and group retreat days, accommodation and daily prayer services, as well as space and time for contemplation and rest. The surrounding grounds are being developed under the influence of medieval church garden design and intent, and now the centre offers a paradise garden with a hermitage for contemplative solitude.

OPEN: Most of the year. Everyone welcome.
ROOMS: 1 double in church tower, others located nearby in parish; 5 double rooms in all. Groups up to 30 for day visits and 10 overnight guests possible. Hermitage for contemplation.
FACILITIES: Church chancel for daily prayer services. Paradise garden, hermitage, meeting areas, gallery.
SPIRITUAL HELP: Daily prayer service, spiritual guidance, personal talks, group sharing.
GUESTS ADMITTED TO: Everywhere.
MEALS: B&B, simple lunch. Evening meals taken locally – 2 pubs a short distance away that provide meals.
SPECIAL ACTIVITIES: Morning and evening prayers, development of an informal community and a traditional choral emphasis in the services, Quiet Days and contemplation space.

SITUATION: Village.
MAXIMUM STAY: By arrangement.
BOOKINGS: Letter, telephone, email.
CHARGES: Please ask for current situation.
ACCESS: Car: 12 miles north of Ipswich, via A140. Rail: Ipswich station, with weekday bus service linked to train times.

NEWMARKET

Old Stable House Centre　　　　　　　　Tel/Fax: 01638 667190
3 Sussex Lodge　　　Email: bookings@oldstablehouseretreats.org.uk
Fordham Road, Newmarket　　　　　　　　　　　　Website:
Suffolk CB8 7AF　　　www.oldstablehouseretreats.org.uk
England

Retreats • Workshops and Courses • Church/Temple • Spiritual Help • Bed and Breakfast
Vegetarian Food • Organic Food • Venue for Hire • Self-Catering Space • Children

Christian – Roman Catholic

Very close to Newmarket Heath, this retreat house offers a warm, comfortable environment with as much freedom as possible for individuals and groups to work on their personal and spiritual development. The atmosphere is informal and home-like.

OPEN: Most of the year. Welcomes everyone. Children welcome but over 14 years of age.
ROOMS: 2 singles, 6 twins. Also Bethal flat, which is on the first floor and is self-contained with large sitting room, 2 singles and 1 twin.
FACILITIES: Prayer room, conferences, library, garden, park.
SPIRITUAL HELP: Guided retreats by arrangement.
GUESTS ADMITTED TO: Unrestricted access.
MEALS: All self-catering.
SPECIAL ACTIVITIES: Groups and individual retreat stays.
SITUATION: Quiet, with a small woodland area and paddock, and 5 minutes' walk from the local town and supermarkets. National Racing Stud nearby. 12 miles from Cambridge.
MAXIMUM STAY: 1 week.
BOOKINGS: Letter, telephone (09:00–18:00), fax, email.
CHARGES: Suggested donations from about £11 non-residential to £22 residential for the night. Other various rates depend on type of stay and size of group.
ACCESS: Rail: Newmarket station (15 minutes' walk away); services are infrequent. Coach: coach stop is on the High Street (10 minutes' walk away). Car: via the A14. Good travel directions are on the website.

OTLEY

Otley Hall
Hall Lane
Otley
Suffolk IP6 9PA
England

Tel: 01473 890264
Fax: 01473 890803
Email: enquires@otleyhall.co.uk
Website: www.otleyhall.co.uk

Retreats

Christian – Inter-denominational – Inter-faith

A wonderful, romantic medieval hall and still a family home, Otley Hall is set in 10 acres of gardens in lovely countryside. It offers guided Quiet Days, which include silence and enjoyment of the peacefulness of the place. There are lots of seats in the garden and swans and ducks to watch. During your day there, a ploughman's lunch is served and you get to have both a time of stillness and a time to talk and socialise. Altogether a very civilized way to have a quiet and reflective day and perhaps a moment in which to say, 'Aren't we lucky!'

OPEN: From March to December. Everyone welcome.
ROOMS: No overnight accommodation but can receive up to 40 people.
FACILITIES: Gardens, conferences, private dinners, quiet and open days, wedding receptions.
SPIRITUAL HELP: None.
GUESTS ADMITTED TO: Guest areas.
MEALS: Lunch on the Quiet Day retreats.
SPECIAL ACTIVITIES: Quiet Days.
SITUATION: Countryside.
MAXIMUM STAY: The day as programmed.
BOOKINGS: Letter, telephone, email. Booking online is easy.
CHARGES: Depends on the event or booking.
ACCESS: Otley is 8 miles north of Ipswich off the B1079. By car is best, otherwise take the train to Ipswich and then a taxi.

'We can never know God until we first know clearly our own soul'
– Julian of Norwich

WALSHAM LE WILLOWS

Vajrasana   Tel: 0845 4584716 (solitary retreats)
Potash Farm   Email: solitaries@lbc.org.uk (solitary retreats)
Walsham le Willows   Website: www.lbc.org.uk
Suffolk IP31 3AR
England

Retreats • Workshops and Courses • Church/Temple • Meditation • Spiritual Help
Vegetarian Food • Community Living • Work Retreats • Vocations • Hermitages

Buddhist – Friends of the Western Buddhist Order (FWBO)

Vajrasana is run by the **London Buddhist Centre**, specifically for re-treats (see London section). There are some retreats for beginners as well as for experienced practitioners. Classes are taken by full-time practising Buddhists who are members of the Friends of the Western Buddhist Order. There are also courses about Buddhism where you can learn who the Buddha was, what he taught and what relevance his teaching has for us in the West today. Retreats are booked through the website for the London Buddhist Centre, but call or email for solitary retreats (see details above).

*'Silence of the heart practised with wisdom will see a lofty depth
and the ear of the silent mind will hear untold wonders'
– Hesychius of Jerusalem*

CENTRAL

BIRMINGHAM AND WEST MIDLANDS

BIRMINGHAM

Woodbrooke Quaker Study Centre   Tel: 0121 4725171
1046 Bristol Road   Fax: 0121 4725173
Birmingham B29 6LJ   Email: enquiries@woodbrooke.org.uk
England   Website: www.woodbrooke.org.uk

Retreats • Workshops and Courses • Church/Temple • Yoga • Meditation
Bed and Breakfast • Vegetarian Food • Venue for Hire • Alternative Therapies • Children

Quaker

Woodbrooke welcomes all of any faith or none and runs a programme of courses, retreats and events, in addition to offering retreat facilities with twice-daily meetings for worship. The centre is set in 10 acres of organically managed grounds – an oasis in the city. Woodbrooke is Europe's only Quaker study centre and offers a unique campus for learning, ecumenical and international relationships, short courses, various retreats from those concerned with non-violence to using creativity and the arts. **Highly Recommended.**

OPEN: All year. Receives everyone.
ROOMS: 69 rooms, 55 of which are en suite. Disabled adapted rooms.
FACILITIES: Disabled access, quiet room, conferences, gardens, park, library, guest lounge, TV, art room, silent room, bookshop.
SPIRITUAL HELP: Directed study, Quaker worship.
GUESTS ADMITTED TO: Public rooms, meeting room, silent room.
MEALS: Everyone eats together. Vegetarian and special diets.
SPECIAL ACTIVITIES: See online for planned programme of events, courses and retreats
SITUATION: Quiet in city.
MAXIMUM STAY: By arrangement.
BOOKINGS: Letter, telephone, email, online enquiry form. Downloadable list of retreats.
CHARGES: B&B starts at £38.25. Half-/full-board rates are also offered. Visit the website or enquire at the time of booking for further details.
ACCESS: Rail: Birmingham New Street, then bus. Car: A38, 6 miles from M42.

MOSELEY

Birmingham Buddhist Centre Tel: 0121 4495279
11 Park Road Email: info@birminghambuddhistcentre.org.uk
Moseley, Birmingham Website:
West Midlands B13 8AB www.birminghambuddhistcentre.org.uk
England

Retreats • Workshops and Courses • Church/Temple • Yoga • Meditation • Spiritual Help
Vegetarian Food

Buddhist – Friends of the Western Buddhist Order (FWBO)

All Buddhism and meditation classes at the centre are led by ordained
members of the Friends of the Western Buddhist Order, who have
many years' experience of teaching and practising Buddhism and
meditation. Introductory and regular practitioner classes, retreats and
yoga are offered here.

WOLVERHAMPTON

Parkdale Yoga Centre Tel: 01902 424048
10 Parkdale West Email: yabyum@connectfree.co.uk
Wolverhampton Website: www.heartyoga.co.uk
West Midlands WV1 4TE
England

Retreats • Workshops and Courses • Yoga • Meditation • Spiritual Help • Vegetarian Food
Organic Food • Alternative Therapies

Yoga – Open spirituality

Located in the southern part of Wolverhampton, the Parkdale Yoga
Centre is in a Victorian house and has been going now for some years.
It focuses on yoga practice and teaching, organic growing and holistic
living. There are many yoga classes held here, so you need to check
the programme and call or email to discuss your level and requirements. Beginners' yoga and intermediate and advanced classes available. There are both summer and weekend yoga retreats on offer, plus
a special weekend yoga retreat for beginners. Some complementary
therapies are offered.

OPEN: Most of the year. Everyone welcome.
ROOMS: Usually the classes, courses and retreats are for the day only, but there are weekend and longer courses and workshops for which limited guest accommodation may be available.
FACILITIES: Yoga room, garden, vegetable and fruit gardens, lounge.
SPIRITUAL HELP: Yoga, group sharing, personal talks.
GUESTS ADMITTED TO: Everywhere.
MEALS: Lots of home-grown and cooked organic food. Vegetarian.
SPECIAL ACTIVITIES: Yoga, alternative and complementary therapies, painting, writing, music making, sewing, gardening and other creative activities.
SITUATION: In town.
MAXIMUM STAY: For duration of the course, class or retreat, or by arrangement.
BOOKINGS: Letter, telephone, email (easiest method).
CHARGES: There are charges for many of the courses and workshops but overnight stays are often given as part of the centre hospitality.
ACCESS: Rail: Wolverhampton station (2 miles away). Bus: local routes available. Car: Parkdale Yoga Centre is just off the A41.

BUCKINGHAMSHIRE

AMERSHAM

The Quiet Garden Trust
Kerridge House
42 Woodside Close, Amersham
Buckinghamshire HP6 5EF
England

Tel: 01494 434873
Email: quiet.garden@ukonline.co.uk
Website: www.quietgarden.co.uk

Christian – Ecumenical – Inter-faith

The Quiet Garden Trust movement began in 1992 and was the vision of Revd Philip D. Roderick. The trust encourages provision of local venues where there is an opportunity to set aside time to rest and prayer. A quiet garden comes into being when someone opens their home and garden for occasional days of stillness and reflection. It may also be in a retreat centre or local church. Another development has been to offer quiet spaces in cities to give space and opportunities for prayer, hospitality and healing.

CHALFONT ST PETER

Mount Carmel Prayer House   Tel: 0208 9972858
Holy Cross Convent   Email: holycross@hcengland.co.uk
Chalfont St Peter   (contact: Sister Imelda Fleming)
Buckinghamshire SL9 9DW
England

Retreats • Church/Temple • Venue for Hire • Self-Catering Space

Christian – Ecumenical

Self-catering accommodation with six singles. There are a chapel, lounge and conference room. All rooms are on ground level.

LEE COMMON

Lee Common Methodist Chapel   Tel: 01494 874386
Oxford Street   (office number)
Lee Common   Email: pwandersen@aol.com
Buckinghamshire HP16 9JP   (contact: Revd Preben Andersen)
England   Bookings secretary: 01494 837479 (Marian Tomkins)
                                 or 01494 837594 (Jan Moseley)

Church/Temple • Spiritual Help • Venue for Hire • Self-Catering Space • Children

Christian – Ecumenical

Lovely Lee Common, with its green centre and surrounding hills, fields and woods, is one of the most charming villages in Buckinghamshire. The houses are old, warm and friendly or sturdy and dignified. Quiet with many walks. A once-upon-a-time place.

'The reason for love is love'
– Stafford Whiteaker

MILTON KEYNES

The Well at Willen Tel: 01908 242190
Newport Road Fax: 01908 242187
Willen Village, Milton Keynes Email: bookings@thewellatwillen.org.uk
Buckinghamshire MK15 9AA Website: www.thewellatwillen.org.uk
England

Retreats • Workshops and Courses • Church/Temple • Bed and Breakfast
Vegetarian Food • Venue for Hire • Hermitages

Christian

A lay community offers hospitality in a house set in three acres of garden and grounds, which is close to a park and an old church. People of all faiths or none are welcome to come here for a programmed retreat or an individual one by arrangement.

OPEN: All year. Welcomes everyone.
ROOMS: 1 single, 1 twin, 1 double. 2 retreat lodges.
FACILITIES: Meeting room, library, gardens, labyrinth walk. Please read about what is available on their website as they have various hospitality facility arrangements.
SPIRITUAL HELP: Individual retreats. Spiritual direction by arrangement.
GUESTS ADMITTED TO: All public rooms.
MEALS: Traditional food. Vegetarian possible. Check website for details.
SPECIAL ACTIVITIES: Respite and healing Quiet Days, Spiritual Explorers Programme, individual retreats, group retreats and a planned programme of events and retreat.
SITUATION: A village in a city – but leafy and green and plenty of walks.
MAXIMUM STAY: For duration of event or retreat and by arrangement.
BOOKINGS: Letter, telephone (08:30-12:30), email, online booking request form..
CHARGES: Visit the website for the latest charges. Call the above number for special event details.
ACCESS: Rail: Milton Keynes Central station (4.5 miles away), then bus or taxi. Car: via M1 exit 14.

'Tread softly! All earth is holy ground'
– Christina Rossetti

DERBYSHIRE

....

CLAY CROSS

The Portiuncula
Franciscan House of
Prayer and Solitude
St Clare's Convent, Stretton Road
Clay Cross, Derbyshire S45 9AQ
England

Tel: 01246 251870 / 01246 862621
Email: info@stclaresconvent.fsnet.co.uk
Website: www.stclaresconvent.fsnet.co.uk

> Retreats • Church/Temple • Spiritual Help • Vegetarian Food • Self-Catering Space
> Community Living • Vocations • Hermitages

Christian – Roman Catholic – Franciscan

We have waited at the guide for many years to be able to list an English retreat place created for solitary retreats and providing the necessary hermitages. At last there is one, and the hermitages here are new, modern and exactly right as far as we are concerned. The sisters at the convent have created five hermitages under one roof and, in the company of Saint Francis, each guest hermit is invited and challenged to explore the spirituality of a particular hermitage by journeying into the depths of his or her own heart and into the Heart of God. Each hermitage, in the tradition of both the Calmodese and the Carthusian cells, looks out on to its own view and there is no visual sense of a hermitage next door. This is an exciting development in view of the increasing numbers of men and women who are drawn to explore the eremitic life. **Highly Recommended.**

> *'There are two ways to go about getting enough –*
> *one is to continue to accumulate more and more.*
> *The other is to desire less'*
> *– G.K. Chesterton*

HOPE

Breathing Space Tel: 01433 620350
Manor House
Pindale Road, Hope
Derbyshire S33 6RN
England

Retreats • Workshops and Courses • Spiritual Help • Venue for Hire

Christian

Breathing Space offers a studio with kitchen as a self-contained and self-catering place near a river in the beautiful Peak District. The studio is available for individuals and groups up to ten people. There is a programme of planned workshops in creativity and spirituality.

HORSLEY WOODHOUSE

Sozein (A Churches' Ministry of Healing Trust) Tel: 01332 780598
The Old Vicarage Email: enquiries@sozein.org.uk /
Church Lane, Horsley Woodhouse neil.broadbent@sozein.org.uk
Derbyshire DE7 6BB Website: www.sozein.org.uk
England

Retreats • Workshops and Courses • Church/Temple • Spiritual Help • Alternative Therapies

Christian – Ecumenical – Anglican

The word *Sozein* is a New Testament verb signifying the setting free, making safe and healing of the individual or the community. It refers to God's work on behalf of us all. This defines the purpose and the work carried out at the Old Vicarage by the Revd Neil Broadbent and his wife. Healing services, group prayer, the offering of a quiet healing environment, homeopathy and the laying on of hands are some of the activities here.

OPEN: Open by arrangement – but closed for Christmas, Holy Week. Everyone welcome.
ROOMS: Only day retreats recently but please enquire what is currently on offer.
FACILITIES: Chapel, garden, new reference library.
SPIRITUAL HELP: Personal talks, spiritual direction, personal retreat direction, prayer, Anglican Sacraments, healing ministry.
GUESTS ADMITTED TO: Prayer room, library, kitchen access. This is a family house.

MEALS: Taken together, but please ask what is available if going just for the day.
SPECIAL ACTIVITIES: Healing and prayer, exploration of spiritual ideas and questions, the writings of spiritual mystics and other spiritually inspired people, homeopathy, and other planned events.
SITUATION: Quiet in the countryside with hills in background.
MAXIMUM STAY: For the day usually, but ask before arrival.
BOOKINGS: Letter, telephone, email.
CHARGES: By donation per day, depending on individual spiritual talks and direction. Please enquire when booking.
ACCESS: Rail: Derby station (11 miles away). Bus: there is a local service from Derby. Car: via M1 exits 16 or 28, or A38 then A609.

OAKWOOD

Community of the Holy Name	Tel: 01332 671716 (convent) /
Convent of the Holy Name	01332 670483 (guest house)
Morley Road, Oakwood	Fax: 01332 669712
Derbyshire DE21 4QZ	Email: bursarsoffice@tiscali.co.uk
England	Website: www.chnderby.org

Retreats • Church/Temple • Spiritual Help • Venue for Hire • Community Living • Vocations

Christian – Anglican – Ecumenical

The sisters offer a modern guest cottage with rooms for about eight people. There is a chapel daily service, which you are welcome to join. It is a peaceful place in which to retreat either as an individual or as a small group to stay or just for the day.

> *'Try to spread your loving mind and heart to all that they may have peace and happiness in their lives.'*
> *– Ven. Dhammavijitha Thera*

UNSTONE

Unstone Grange
Crow Lane
Unstone, Dronfield
Derbyshire S18 4AL
England

Tel/Fax: 01246 412344
Email: admin@unstonegrange.co.uk
Website: www.unstonegrange.co.uk

Retreats • Workshops and Courses • Church/Temple • Meditation • Spiritual Help
Bed and Breakfast • Vegetarian Food • Organic Food • Venue for Hire • Self-Catering Space
Alternative Therapies • Holistic Holidays • Work retreats • Community Living
Work Retreats • Camping • Children

Open spirituality – Mind Body Spirit

With over two acres of organic gardens and orchards set amid lovely Derbyshire countryside, Unstone Grange welcomes individuals, groups and community and youth groups of all kinds. All may use the centre to express their creative spirit through dance, drama, craftwork, writing, painting, music, meditation, bodywork, healing and a wide range of other activities. There is a planned programme of events and courses as well, including courses on cooking good healthy food and learning about growing your own. The guiding principle of the Unstone Grange Trust is 'Unity in diversity'.

OPEN: All year. Everyone welcome.
ROOMS: Up to 35 beds available plus camping and a barn.
FACILITIES: Conferences and groups, barn, garden and vegetable/fruit growing.
SPIRITUAL HELP: Meditation, healing therapies.
GUESTS ADMITTED TO: Everywhere.
MEALS: Catered or self-catering. Vegetarian provided.
SPECIAL ACTIVITIES: The Organic Gardening for Health Project.
SITUATION: Countryside.
MAXIMUM STAY: By arrangement.
BOOKINGS: Letter, telephone, email. Downloadable booking forms are on the website.
CHARGES: Example of current costs (for 24-hour stay per person): self-catering £20; full board £50. Download the booking information leaflet from the website for full details. There is a discount rate for groups who are all vegetarians.
ACCESS: Rail: Dronfield (1.5 miles away) or Chesterfield (4 miles away) stations. Bus: local routes from Sheffield, Chesterfield or Dronfield. Car: via M1 exits 29 or 30; via A61 from Sheffield.

WHALEY BRIDGE

Whaley Hall   Tel: 01663 732495
Community of the King of Love   Email: whaley@whaleyhallckl.org.uk
Reservoir Road, Whaley Bridge   Website: www.whaleyhallckl.org.uk
Derbyshire SK23 7BL
England

Retreats • Workshops and Courses • Church/Temple • Spiritual Help • Vegetarian Food
Venue for Hire • Community Living • Vocations • Children

Christian – Ecumenical

Whaley Hall is an 1853 gritstone house built for a mill-owner and has now been run for many years as a retreat centre. The community is ecumenical and composed of both men and women. This is a warm and welcoming house run along peaceful and unhurried lines where you are made to feel at home. The lounge is full of comfortable chairs and the dining room is a cheerful and lively place during meals. There is a new oratory and daily services. Close by are good walks. **Highly Recommended.**

GLOUCESTERSHIRE

MAY HILL
May Hill Methodist Church   Tel: 01452 855477
May Hill   Email: dkah1963@hotmail.co.uk
Gloucester
Gloucestershire GL17 0NL
England

Retreats • Workshops and Courses • Church/Temple • Spiritual Help • Venue for Hire
Self-Catering Space • Children

Christian – Methodist

Non-residential for Quiet Days, retreats and conferences. Facilities include a comfortable chapel, kitchen and several meeting rooms. It is in a small village near beautiful countryside. The above contact details are for Revd Denise Hargreaves.

NYMPSFIELD

Marist Centre
Front Street
Nympsfield, Stonehouse
Gloucestershire GL10 3TY
England

Tel: 01453 860228
Fax: 01453 861331
Email: maristconvent@btconnect.com

Retreats • Workshops and Courses • Church/Temple • Meditation • Spiritual Help
Bed and Breakfast • Vegetarian Food • Venue for Hire • Self-Catering Space
Community Living • Vocations

Christian – Roman Catholic – Ecumenical

All people of every spiritual persuasion or none are welcome in this delightful convent tucked away in the beautiful Cotswolds. Situated midway between Bristol and Cheltenham and Gloucester, Nympsfield is a village of great antiquity containing many charming stone houses. There is a kind and warm welcome here from the community, who are flexible and accommodating. Gentleness is the key word here.

OPEN: All year. Receives everyone.
ROOMS: 19 singles/doubles.
FACILITIES: Conferences, garden, park, library, guest lounge, TV.
SPIRITUAL HELP: Spiritual direction. Groups usually bring their own spiritual director.
GUESTS ADMITTED TO: Chapel and all areas not private to the community.
MEALS: Taken in guest house together. DIY kitchens. Meals can be provided if needed. Vegetarian and special diets.
SPECIAL ACTIVITIES: Some planned events.
SITUATION: Quiet in a village.
MAXIMUM STAY: 1 week.
BOOKINGS: Letter, telephone, email.
CHARGES: Please contact them for self-catering, full-board and day retreat rates.
ACCESS: Rail/bus: nearest stations are in Stroud, which is 4 miles away. Call for directions from there. Car: accessible from M5 exit 13 and A46 .

'Fame is nothing but an empty name'
– Charles Churchill

STROUD

Hawkwood College	Tel: 01453 759034 / 01453 764045 (guestline)
Painswick Old Road	Fax: 01453 764607
Stroud	Email: info@hawkwoodcollege.co.uk
Gloucestershire GL6 7QW	Website: www.hawkwoodcollege.co.uk
England	

> Retreats • Workshops and Courses • Meditation • Spiritual Help • Bed and Breakfast
> Vegetarian Food • Venue for Hire • Self-Catering Space • Alternative Therapies
> Holistic Holidays • Work Retreats • Camping • Children

Anthroposophical – Rudolf Steiner tradition

Situated at the head of a small Cotswold Valley, Hawkwood provides a beautiful setting in over 40 acres of land for retreat, groups, adult education courses and conferences. The variety of subjects and groups and conference meetings here is widely spiritual and includes music, Celtic studies, alternative lifestyle exploration, arts and crafts, bodywork, meditation, prayer, eco-spirituality and educational training. The college works with ecological and sustainable land management practices, using organic and biodynamic methods. **Highly Recommended.**

OPEN: All year. Everyone welcome.
ROOMS: Can accommodate more than 50 guests on site with 14 single, 14 double (2 on ground floor and wheelchair accessible) and 3 triple rooms. Additional camping or campervan spaces are also available.
FACILITIES: Conferences, garden, library, guest lounge. A range of course facilities is available, including meeting rooms, lecture hall and studios. Outside courses accommodated where possible.
SPIRITUAL HELP: Spiritual direction, meditation, courses in many healing and complementary therapies.
GUESTS ADMITTED TO: Public areas.
MEALS: Everyone eats together. Delicious traditional and wholefood. Organic where possible. Vegetarian and special diets catered for.
SPECIAL ACTIVITIES: Planned events. Lots to do – from homeopathy healing and arts to wetlands ecological courses. See online programme or send for their brochure.
SITUATION: 42-acre estate with Cotswold valley views.
MAXIMUM STAY: Open.
BOOKINGS: Letter, telephone, email. Online booking available and easy to use.
CHARGES: Prices can vary, so ask when you book for specific details for course or individual stay.
ACCESS: Rail: Stroud station (just over 1 mile away), then taxi. The college is 25 minutes' walk from the railway station. Car: accessible from M5 exit 13 and A46.

HEREFORDSHIRE

••

HAREWOOD END

Dhamma Dipa
Vipassana Meditation Centre
Harewood End, Hereford
Herefordshire HR2 8JS
England

Tel: 01989 730234
Fax: 01989 730450
Email: info@dipa.dhamma.org
Website: www.dipa.dhamma.org

Retreats • Workshops and Courses • Meditation • Spiritual Help • Vegetarian Food
Community Living • Children

Vipassana meditation – Sayagyi U Ba Khin tradition

Vipassana means 'to see things as they really are', and *Dhamma Dipa* means 'Island of Dhamma'. It is a way of self-purification by self-observation and is one of India's most ancient meditation techniques. It is grounded in reality of self and there are no visualisation, verbalisation or mantras involved but careful observation of the body and self. Today in India over 600 Roman Catholic nuns, for example, use the Vipassana techniques and there is an increasing demand for it around the world in both Eastern and Western cultures. The Vipassana Trust offers courses in the tradition of Sayagyi U Ba Khin as taught by S. N. Goenka. You need to give all your effort on these courses, observing the rules of the house and taking your study seriously. If you are a married couple, it is best to come at different times because the retreats are intensive and demand full personal attention from each partner. There are local practising Vipassana groups in London, Bedfordshire, Bristol, Liverpool, Suffolk, Sussex, Devon and Wales. This is a serious spiritual centre with established programmes, basic accommodation and a peaceful setting for those looking for increased self-awareness and development and who want to stop talking about it and get down to doing it. Over 10,000 people from all walks of life have taken Vipassana retreats here. **Highly Recommended.**

OPEN: All year. Receives men, women. Also children and young people for specifically designed courses.
ROOMS: A few singles are available; 15 doubles; 3 dormitories. **Men and women are segregated and restricted to their own areas.** The rooms for men are basic but beds and central heating are good. The toilet/shower block is modern and clean. Women's quarters are slightly more comfortable (we are not sure why).

FACILITIES: All the facilities are divided into those for men and those for women. There is a garden. A meditation hall holds 120 guests.

SPIRITUAL HELP: Meditation. Teachers are available to guide students and answer questions about technique. There are some group discussions and also usually daily lectures or 'talks'.

GUESTS ADMITTED TO: Almost everywhere, but **male and female guests have designated and separate areas.**

MEALS: Men and women eat separately. The food is vegetarian and simple. There are morning and midday meals and that is it, with only fruit consumed until the next morning – most people find this no problem. It keeps you alert and attentive. Special diet arrangements only for specific medical reasons; your medical condition and your medication should not interfere with the meditation, and you will be asked a series of appropriate questions to determine if meditation is suitable for you at this time. You are not allowed to bring your own food.

SPECIAL ACTIVITIES: Very specific courses are on offer. Send for information, which fully explains what is on offer and how the courses are run.

SITUATION: Quiet in the countryside.

MAXIMUM STAY: None but there is a minimum stay of 10 days unless it is specifically a 3-day course.

BOOKINGS: Letter, telephone, fax, email, online application form.

CHARGES: Voluntary donations only, according to what people wish to give. In effect the previous student donates to your retreat.

ACCESS: Details are online and will be sent with booking information. Rail: Hereford station. Bus: from Gloucester and Hereford; pick-up available from local bus stop (2 miles away). Car: accessible from M4, M5 and M50. The centre is located up a long lane.

HEREFORD

Belmont Abbey
Hereford
Herefordshire HR2 9RZ
England

Tel: 07799 811646 (retreat bookings) /
01432 374747 (Hedley Lodge)
Email: retreats@belmontabbey.org.uk /
hedley@belmontabbey.org.uk
Website: www.belmontabbey.org.uk /
www.hedleylodge.com

Retreats • Workshops and Courses • Church/Temple • Spiritual Help • Vegetarian Food
Venue for Hire • Community Living • Vocations • Children

Christian – Roman Catholic

The community at Belmont Abbey offers very modern and comfortable guest and conference facilities in Hedley Lodge, as well as a full programme of organised and private retreats for individuals and group retreats. The facilities are a mixture of monastic and modern living environments.

KINGS CAPLE

Poulstone Health Education Centre   Tel: 01432 840251
Poulstone Court   Email: mel@poulstone.com
Kings Caple   Website: www.poulstone.com
Herefordshire HR1 4UA
England

Retreats • Workshops and Courses • Yoga • Meditation • Spiritual Help • Vegetarian Food
Venue for Hire • Alternative Therapies • Holistic Holidays

Mind Body Spirit – Open spirituality

All food is vegetarian here and the centre is regularly used for courses in meditation, healing, counselling and yoga. The programme is online and very well designed, explaining the course or retreat in detail and giving links and contacts for further information, so you get a full chance to understand what is on offer and usually to discuss it with the facilitator via email.

OPEN: Most of the year. Everyone welcome. Some retreats and courses are open, others closed just for the group running them.
ROOMS: Plenty of rooms – 10 bedrooms.
FACILITIES: Gardens, small shop, guest lounge, meeting rooms, workshop space.
SPIRITUAL HELP: Personal talks. Group discussions.
GUESTS ADMITTED TO: All guest areas.
MEALS: Vegetarian, taken in dining room. Special diets possible.
SPECIAL ACTIVITIES: A confirmed programme of events and courses from Buddhism to Holotropic Breathwork and Shamanic healing. See online.
SITUATION: Countryside.
MAXIMUM STAY: By arrangement or by event and course.
BOOKINGS: Letter, telephone, email, online enquiry form. See the online programme for individual course booking.
CHARGES: Please enquire when making your booking.
ACCESS: Rail: Hereford station, then taxi. Car: accessible from M4 and M5 – see the website for details.

'Men speak of perfection but they do precious little about it'
– Abba Alonius, Desert Father

LEICESTERSHIRE

COALVILLE

Mount St Bernard Abbey	Tel: 01530 839162 (guestmaster)
Coalville	Fax: 01530 814608
Leicestershire LE67 5UL	Email: msbgh@btconnect.com
England	(guestmaster)
	Website: www.mountsaintbernard.org

Retreats • Church/Temple • Vegetarian Food • Community Living • Vocations

Christian – Roman Catholic – Cistercian

In the fine and very large granite church, Latin Mass is sung once a month and the vernacular Mass celebrated daily. Rooms are clean, comfortable and have good beds. The abbey has a large working pottery, as well as carpentry and printing shops. Meals are traditional. Located in the middle of the famous Quorn Hunt country, the abbey offers good walking over hill, pasture and moor. This monastery is a very popular place and you may find it hard to get accommodation except by booking well in advance.

EAST NORTON

Launde Abbey	Tel: 01572 717254
East Norton	Fax: 01572 717454
Leicester	laundeabbey@leicester.anglican.org
Leicestershire LE7 9XB	Website: www.launde.org.uk
England	

Retreats • Workshops and Courses • Church/Temple • Spiritual Help • Vegetarian Food
Venue for Hire • Self-Catering Space • Work Retreats • Hermitages • Children

Christian – Anglican – Ecumenical

This is a huge redbrick house built by Thomas Cromwell in 1540 on the site of an early Augustinian priory. It retains today the old-fashioned comfort and charm of a distinguished private country mansion with a cheerful drawing-room fire, a panelled dining room and games room.

A beautiful chapel, still intact from the fifteenth century, is the jewel of Launde Abbey. Refurbishment work to the buildings has been going on since 2009. Everyone is welcome here.

UPPER WREAKE (FRISBY-ON-THE-WREAKE AND HOBY)

Frisby Centre   Tel: 01664 840479
29 Main Street   Email: denjenbarsby@yahoo.co.uk
Frisby-on-the-Wreake, Melton Mowbray
Leicestershire LE14 2NJ
England

Hoby Centre   Tel: 01664 434543
3 Chapel Lane   Email: methodist@hobyparish.freeserve.co.uk
Hoby, Melton Mowbray
Leicestershire LE14 3DW
England

Retreats • Workshops and Courses • Church/Temple • Venue for Hire
Self-Catering Space • Children

Christian – Methodist – Inter-denominational

Refurbished in the last few years, these **Chapels of the Upper Wreake** offer suitable group meeting space and Sunday worship, which alternates between the two Methodist churches so one is almost always available for a quiet group or individual weekend retreat. Kitchen facilities are at both places for any necessary self-catering. Good walking all around and meals available in local public houses. This refurbishment and increased use of local small churches and chapels, which is gradually taking place across Britain, adds tremendously to the continued use of such facilities, to the restoration of many somewhat neglected places, and to the building of a sense of community.

OPEN: All year. Everyone welcome.
ROOMS: Non-residential meeting room. Hoby takes up to 15 people and Frisby up to 30.
FACILITIES: Church, worship area, meeting room, kitchen facilities, disabled access.
SPIRITUAL HELP: Worship, prayer, group sharing.
GUESTS ADMITTED TO: Everywhere.
MEALS: Self-catering.
SPECIAL ACTIVITIES: Quiet Days, Sunday worship, self-managed group and individual retreats.

SITUATION: Quiet villages in the countryside near Melton Mowbray.
MAXIMUM STAY: By arrangement.
BOOKINGS: Letter, telephone, email.
CHARGES: Please enquire.
ACCESS: By car is best, via A46 or A607.

REMPSTONE

Community of the Holy Cross
Holy Cross Convent, Ashby Road Hall
Rempstone, Loughborough
Leicestershire LE12 6RG
England

Tel: 01509 880336
Fax: 01509 881812
Email:
chc.rempstone@webleicester.co.uk
Website: www.holycrosschc.org.uk

Retreats • Church/Temple • Self-Catering Space • Community Living
Vocations • Hermitages

Christian – Anglican – Benedictine

The sisters offer self-catering or eating together in their refectory during your stay with them. There are two singles and one twin on offer in a guest cottage and a hermitage is also available. Day groups up to 20 people are also received. The community has recently purchased a rural farming property and has started work on developing a new convent and retreat there. You can keep up with this progress on their website, but meanwhile they will warmly welcome you to Holy Cross. Bookings by letter, telephone, fax or email.

'If tomorrow was the legendary Day of Judgement, what evidence
of your love would you place before the angels?'
– Stafford Whiteaker

STATHERN

Stathern Retreat Centre
Chapel Path
Chapel Lane, Stathern
Leicestershire LE14 4HA
England

Tel: 01949 860455 (09:00–21:00)
Email: gumsmitstat@aol.com

Retreats • Workshops and Courses • Church/Temple • Venue for Hire
Self-Catering Space • Children

Christian – Methodist – Ecumenical

This is a non-residential centre with wheelchair access set in a small village. It is used as a day-retreat centre, offering a chapel, kitchen and gardens. If you are writing, please contact Mr Graham Smith, 36 Penn Lane, Stathern, Melton Mowbray, Leicestershire LE14 4JA.

NORTHAMPTONSHIRE

KELMARSH

Nagarjuna Buddhist Centre
The Old Rectory
Kelmarsh
Northamptonshire NN6 9LZ
England

Tel: 01604 686778
Fax: 01604 686767
Website: www.meditation-nagarjuna.org

Retreats • Workshops and Courses • Church/Temple • Meditation • Spiritual Help
Vegetarian Food • Venue for Hire • Community Living • Work Retreats • Vocations
Children

Buddhist (New Kadampa tradition)

Nagarjuna Buddhist Centre is set in the beautiful countryside of Northamptonshire where it serves as a special place of peace and refuge for everyone.

OPEN: All year. Everyone welcome.
ROOMS: A range of single, twin and dormitory accommodation, all en suite facilties. For dormitory rooms, please bring a sleeping bag and towel.

FACILITIES: 3 meditation rooms, World Peace Tea Room, resident teacher, study programmes, chanted meditations, group and school visits, retreat venue, working holidays and a shop.
SPIRITUAL HELP: Meditation, group sharing.
GUESTS ADMITTED TO: Everywhere.
MEALS: Accommodation includes breakfast and evening meal, all vegetarian.
SPECIAL ACTIVITIES: Full programme of events, retreats and courses. Send for information or see online.
SITUATION: Countryside.
MAXIMUM STAY: By course or by arrangement.
BOOKINGS: Letter, telephone, fax, email, online enquiry form.
CHARGES: Please ask about current arrangements.
ACCESS: Car: A14 exit 2, then A508 between Market Harborough and Northampton. Look out for the signpost in Kelmarsh village for 'Buddhist Centre/Haselbech'; they are 100m up this small road.

RUSHTON

Homefield Grange Retreat   Tel: 01536 712219
Manor Road   Email: enquiries@homefieldgrangeretreat.co.uk
Rushton   Website: www.homefieldgrangeretreat.co.uk
Northamptonshire NN14 1RH
England

Yoga • Meditation • Vegetarian Food • Organic Food • Alternative Therapies
Holistic Holidays

Spa – Open spirituality

Homefield Grange Health Retreat is comfortable, rather cosy and set in 23 acres of countryside. Therapies, nutritional and educational talks and demonstrations are all available. Homefield Grange aims to give clients quiet time, rest, weight-loss help if needed, detox programmes and advice on how to look after their health.

OPEN: Most of the year. Welcomes everyone but only takes a limited number of guests at any one time.
ROOMS: High standard and comfortable bedrooms
FACILITIES: Aqua gym, beauty treatment rooms, exercise classes, gym, gardens, group bookings, sauna, juice bar, massage treatment rooms, meditation room, pilates studio, spa packages, swimming pool, workshops, yoga studio.
SPIRITUAL HELP: Rest, relaxation, caring environment.
GUESTS ADMITTED TO: All public areas.
MEALS: Fresh fruit salads, juices, broths, raw food and other health-giving dishes.
SPECIAL ACTIVITIES: Planned programmes for a stay here. See online or call/ email to discuss with them.

SITUATION: Countryside.
MAXIMUM STAY: As the programme selected or arranged.
BOOKINGS: Letter, telephone, email.
CHARGES: The rates are modest compared to many hotel spas and centres. For example, currently a weekend detox runs from £303 to £445.
ACCESS: Rail: Kettering station, then 10-minute taxi ride. Car: easily accessible from M6 exit 1, M1 exit 19, then A14 and A6003, or M1 exit 15, then A43.

NOTTINGHAMSHIRE

BRAMCOTE

St John's College Nottingham
Chilwell Lane
Bramcote
Nottingham NG9 3DS
England

Tel: 0115 9251114
Fax: 0115 9436438
Email: enquiries@stjohns-nottm.ac.uk
Website: www.stjohns-nottm.ac.uk

Retreats • Workshops and Courses • Church/Temple • Bed and Breakfast
Venue for Hire • Self-Catering Space • Children

Christian – Anglican – Ecumenical

Set in large open grounds and close to Nottingham and Derbyshire, St John's College is a training place for theological students, but it also offers distance learning, away-day retreats, retreat weekends and personal retreat stays, conference and meeting rooms, and full or part board. There is a good programme of study courses and events including a summer school.

'Riches are not from abundance but from a contented mind'
– Hadith, Sayings of the Prophet Mohammed,
peace be upon him

SOUTHWELL

Sacrista Prebend Retreat House   Tel: 01636 816833
4 Westgate   Email: mail@sacrista-prebend.co.uk
Southwell   Website: www.sacristaprebend.wordpress.com
Nottinghamshire NG25 0JH
England

Retreats • Workshops and Courses • Church/Temple • Spiritual Help • Bed and Breakfast
Venue for Hire • Self-Catering Space

Christian – Anglican

Sacrista Prebend is a Georgian house in the heart of Southwell, offering facilities for retreats, conferences, Quiet Days and courses. It is set
in large peaceful gardens and is a member of the Quiet Garden Movement. The house is open to individuals, parish and church groups, pilgrims and searchers who wish to stay overnight as B&B guests, and for
conferences and meetings.

OXFORDSHIRE

ABINGDON

St Ethelwold's House   Tel: 01235 555486
30 East St Helens Street   Email: ethelwoldhouse@btinternet.com
Abingdon   Website: www.ethelwoldhouse.org.uk
Oxfordshire OX14 5EB
England

Retreats • Workshops and Courses • Church/Temple • Yoga • Meditation • Spiritual Help
Bed and Breakfast • Venue for Hire • Self-Catering Space • Children

Inter-faith

A retreat place on an interesting old Oxfordshire street in the centre
of Abingdon. The Fellowship of St Ethelwold was founded in 1971 by
Dorothea Pickering, a visionary Christian who dedicated her life to
furthering understanding between people of different faith traditions.
While drawing on its Christian roots, it is open to the wisdom and practices of other traditions. Individuals and small groups are welcome to

organise their own Quiet Days and retreats, and the centre has its own events programme as well. The current one illustrates the breadth of their events and courses: *Opening Doors: A series of conversations on Meditation, Patchwork Appliqué, More than Pretty Pictures: Expressing our relationship with God through creative art and writing, Meditations for Living Well with Pain and Illness, Tai Chi and Qi Gong* and *Foundation Training in Nonviolent Communication*, as well as Islamic classes for children, and yoga workshops. Their meeting room can accommodate up to 25 people.

ASTON TIRROLD

Centre for Reflection   Tel: 01235 850423
Aston Tirrold United Reformed   Email:
Church, Spring Lane   coordinator@reflect.freeuk.com
Aston Tirrold, Didcot   Website: www.reflect.freeuk.com
Oxfordshire OX11 9EJ
England

Retreats • Workshops and Courses • Church/Temple • Meditation • Spiritual Help
Venue for Hire • Self-Catering Space • Children

Christian – United Reform Church

Built in 1728, the church is a fine example of eighteenth-century free-church architecture, with a beautiful interior decorated in its original style. The centre is a more modern, recently renovated building offering space for Quiet Days, group retreats, drop-in days, church away days and other events. It has a good kitchen and meeting facilities. Outside is a nice garden with a water feature and there are meditative footpaths and walks. Although no accommodation is offered, B&B can be arranged. Regular workship services and a weekly meditation group are also on offer here.

'Practise random acts of kindness and senseless acts of beauty'
– Xtine Hankinson

BEGBROKE

**Community of St John Baptist
and the Companions of Jesus
the Good Shepherd
Priory of St John Baptist
2 Spring Hill Road
Begbroke, Kidlington
Oxfordshire OX5 1RX
England**

Tel: 01865 855320 /
01865 855327 (Guest Sister)
Fax: 01865 855336
Email: information@csjb.org.uk /
sisterjane@csjb.org.uk
Website: www.csjb.org.uk

Retreats • Church/Temple • Spiritual Help • Vegetarian Food • Venue for Hire
Community Living • Work Retreats • Vocations

Christian – Anglican

The Anglican Communities of St John Baptist and the Companions of
Jesus the Good Shepherd live together in this lovely priory which has
been a religious house for more than 100 years. This is a good place for
rest, reflection and prayer.

OPEN: All year. Everyone welcome.
ROOMS: 9 single (2 of which are disabled suitable), 1 double.
FACILITIES: Chapel, lounge, large garden.
SPIRITUAL HELP: Personal talks and some retreat guidance possible by prior
arrangement. Eucharist and Daily Offices of Prayer.
GUESTS ADMITTED TO: All guest areas.
MEALS: Everyone eats together. Traditional food – vegetarian possible.
SPECIAL ACTIVITIES: Quiet Days. Day groups welcome.
SITUATION: Countryside.
MAXIMUM STAY: By arrangement.
BOOKINGS: Letter, telephone or email Guest Sister.
CHARGES: Please enquire when discussing your booking.
ACCESS: Rail: Hanborough station (4 miles away), then taxi. Car: via A44.

'Happiness is a matter of changing troubles'
– Colette

BOARS HILL

| Carmelite Priory | Tel: 01865 730183 |
| Boars Hill | Fax: 01865 326478 |

Oxfordshire OX1 5HB   Website: www.carmelite.org.uk/Oxford.html
England

Retreats • Workshops and Courses • Church/Temple • Spiritual Help • Vegetarian Food
Venue for Hire • Community Living • Vocations

Christian – Roman Catholic – Carmelite

Boars Hill is an ideal location for this recently refurbished centre, which is run by the Teresian Discalced Carmel Friars. The centre stands in its own 17 acres of woodland. It aims to provide courses on prayer and spirituality, special attention being given to the teaching on prayer of the great Carmelite writers such as St Teresa of Avila, St John of the Cross and St Teresa of Lisieux. There is an annual vocation weekend open to all young men interested in the religious life and the Carmelites in particular. The programme of planned group and individual retreats and events is usually an intelligent and inviting one.

CHARNEY BASSETT

Charney Manor   Tel: 01235 868206
Quaker Conference Centre   Email: charneymanor@quaker.org.uk
and Retreat House   Website: www.charneymanor.demon.co.uk
Charney Bassett, near Wantage
Oxfordshire OX12 0EJ
England

Retreats • Workshops and Courses • Spiritual Help • Vegetarian Food
Venue for Hire • Children

Quaker

Charney Manor is a Grade 1 listed house and one of the oldest inhabited buildings in the Vale of the White Horse. It is well maintained, very clean and has a country-home feeling with an old-fashioned sitting room. The rooms are neat and modern with meals professionally prepared. There are Quakers living here, so a warm welcome awaits all guests. Quakers say, 'Each person is unique, precious, a child of God.' Short courses and retreats on offer may include exploration of radical faithfulness and Quaker marriage, spiritual music, calligraphy and meditation. Many of those who have stayed here say they came away feeling uplifted at sharing troubles and with renewed hopes for the future. Charney Manor has accommodation for disabled as well as a disabled-access conference room.

OPEN: All year. Receives men, women, young people, families and groups. Children welcome.
ROOMS: Accommodates up to 36 people. Self-catering cottage, the Gilletts, in the grounds.
FACILITIES: Disabled access, conferences, garden to walk in with places to sit, library, guest lounge, TV, craft and workshops. Small Anglican church almost in the garden – Sunday services.
SPIRITUAL HELP: None
GUESTS ADMITTED TO: Unrestricted access everywhere.
MEALS: Everyone eats together. Traditional food. Vegetarian and special diets.
SPECIAL ACTIVITIES: Planned programme of retreats and events.
SITUATION: Very quiet, village in countryside.
MAXIMUM STAY: By arrangement.
BOOKINGS: Letter, telephone, email.
CHARGES: See online room and conference rate information for details of the various charges and combinations of prices.
ACCESS: Rail: Didcot Parkway staion, then taxi. Car: the route is easy, via A420.

NUNEHAM COURTNEY

Global Retreat Centre
Nuneham Park
Nuneham Courtney
Oxfordshire OX44 9PG
England

Tel: 01865 343551
Fax:01865 343576
Email: info@globalretreatcentre.com
Website: www.globalretreatcentre.com

Retreats • Workshops and Courses • Church/Temple • Meditation • Spiritual Help
Vegetarian Food • Children

Open spirituality

The **Brahma Kumaris World Spiritual University** (see London entry) runs this international centre in a magnificent Palladian villa built by the Earl of Harcourt in 1796. George II called it 'the most enjoyable place I know' and Queen Victoria wrote after one of her many visits: 'This is a most lovely place, with pleasure grounds in the style of

Claremont.' About 15 minutes' drive from Oxford, the house is situated by the River Thames in 55 acres of land and gardens. As well as regular retreats lasting from one day to one week, there is a variety of seminars, workshops and courses offering a range of opportunities to learn meditation, develop personal skills, and explore the common values essential to world harmony. **Highly Recommended.**

OPEN: All year. Everyone welcome. The building is open to the public during certain weekends of the year.
ROOMS: Lots of rooms and en suite.
FACILITIES: Conferences, garden, park, guest lounge.
SPIRITUAL HELP: Group sharing, meditation, personal talks, spiritual direction.
GUESTS ADMITTED TO: Unrestricted access.
MEALS: Everyone eats together. Vegetarian food and special diets. **No alcohol or smoking is allowed.**
SPECIAL ACTIVITIES: Planned programme. Guests are expected to attend the scheduled programme. Ask for information or go online to see current programme and events.
SITUATION: Very quiet in its own parkland surrounded by countryside.
MAXIMUM STAY: By event or by arrangement.
BOOKINGS: Letter, email. Online residential retreat and course registration forms.
CHARGES: No charges are made but voluntary donations are welcome.
ACCESS: Train: Oxford station (7 miles away), then taxi. Car: accessible from M4; on A4074 south of Oxford. Good details on the website.

OXFORD

The Community of the Sisters	Tel: 01865 721301
of the Love of God	Fax: 01865 250798
Convent of the Incarnation	Email: guests@slg.org.uk
Fairacres, Parker Street	Website: www.slgpress.co.uk (publications)
Oxford OX4 1TB	
England	

Retreats • Church/Temple • Spiritual Help • Self-Catering Space • Community Living
Vocations

Christian – Anglican

Tucked into one of the busy residential parts of east Oxford, the Convent of the Incarnation offers a haven of peace where silence and solitude are hallmarks of the contemplative life. Founded in 1906, the Community of the Sisters of the Love of God was the first contemplative community for women in the Church of England. The simple, dedicated life of witness and prayer spanning nearly 100 years contributes to a stability and depth of peace that make this a very special place. There is very comfortable accommodation for a limited number of guests, who stay either in the guest house or in self-contained bungalows. The emphasis is on solitude and self-directed retreats, so anyone coming on retreat for the first time would probably be offered a room in the guest house. There is a beautiful chapel within the grounds where silent participation in the Eucharist and Divine Office is encouraged. Also, there is a small guest garden and shared use of some of the community's grounds. As well as welcoming guests, they have a small publishing department, SLG Press.

OPEN: Most of the year.
ROOMS: 4 rooms. 2 self-contained bungalows.
FACILITIES: Chapel, guest gardens, self-catering.
SPIRITUAL HELP: Chapel services. Guests can ask to see a sister, but you should mention this when booking.
GUESTS ADMITTED TO: Visitors' chapel, refectory for the main meal at midday, and the guests' garden.
MEALS: The midday meal is eaten with the sisters; guests get their own breakfasts and suppers. The guest house and each bungalow have their own small kitchens with a small range of food provided. Drinks can be made at any time.
SITUATION: In urban south-east Oxford, but in a usually quiet area, and close to the Thames Path.
MAXIMUM STAY: By arrangement.
BOOKINGS: Letter, email. If it is your first visit, they prefer requests for bookings to be accompanied by a reference.
CHARGES: No set charges, but donations accepted
ACCESS: Rail: Oxford station. Coaches from London are frequent and stop within 20 minutes' walk of the convent. Car: from Oxford Ring Road take the A4158 towards the city centre.

PARMOOR

St Katharine's
Parmoor, Frieth
Henley-on-Thames
Oxfordshire RG9 6NN
England

Tel/Fax: 01494 881037
Email: office@srpf.org.uk
Website: www.srpf.org.uk

Retreats • Church/Temple • Bed and Breakfast • Vegetarian Food • Venue for Hire

Christian – Ecumenical – Non-denominational

This is a retreat house run by the Community of Sue Ryder Prayer Fellowship. It is set in lovely and generous grounds. The facilities include day groups, conferences and private residential retreats for individuals and groups. Everyone is welcome.

OPEN: All year. Everyone welcome.
ROOMS: St Katharine's offers 15 mixed twins and doubles (4 can take 1–2 extra beds), 2 singles. St Joseph's Annex offers 6 singles, 3 twins.
FACILITIES: Chapel, sitting room, small sitting room, dining room, library, inner library, gardens.
SPIRITUAL HELP: Prayer groups. Space for rest and renewal.
GUESTS ADMITTED TO: All public areas and grounds.
MEALS: Professionally prepared in house kitchen. Fresh eggs from the chickens. Vegetarian and special diets catered for.
SPECIAL ACTIVITIES: None.
SITUATION: Lovely grounds.
MAXIMUM STAY: By group booking or by arrangement.
BOOKINGS: Letter, telephone, fax, email.
CHARGES: Individual B&B room rates: single £55, twin/double £70 (these are more likely to be available mid-week when there is not a group retreat). Full-board residential rates: weekday £50 per person; weekend £110 per person. Self-catering is about £30 per person per day. Quiet Days £15–£30.
ACCESS: Rail: High Wycombe station (7 miles away) or Henley-on-Thames station (6.5 miles away), then taxi. Car: via M40 exits 4 or 5; M4 exit 8/9. See the website for travel directions.

SHIPTON-UNDER-WYCHWOOD

Ruth White Yoga Centre
Lane House Farm, Milton Road
Shipton-under-Wychwood
Oxfordshire OX7 6BD
England

Tel: 01993 831032
Fax: 01993 831400
Email: info@ruthwhiteyoga.com
Website: www.ruthwhiteyoga.com

Retreats • Workshops and Courses • Church/Temple • Yoga • Vegetarian Food

Yoga – Mind Body Spirit

The Ruth White Yoga Centre, now in Oxfordshire, has been running for over 25 years. Taught and inspired by India's yoga master B. K. S. Iyengar, Ruth White is recognised as one of Britain's leading yoga teachers. Retreats are usually on the weekends but there are also four-day breaks and a summer holiday. Workshops are held throughout Britain and all are in peaceful country residences with pleasant surroundings suitable for yoga spirituality and practice. Ruth White is an exceptionally able teacher and well known in Europe, and has several yoga centres operating. **Highly Recommended.**

OPEN: Receives everyone.
ROOMS: At place of venue in programme. Otherwise Church Farm House has 30 bed spaces.
FACILITIES: See online programme.
SPIRITUAL HELP: Meditation, yoga breathing and postures, Karuna yoga.
GUESTS ADMITTED TO: Access to whatever are the guest areas.
MEALS: Full board for groups. Guests eat together. Wholefood, vegetarian.
SPECIAL ACTIVITIES: Planned programme of events. Send for brochure or see online. Guest groups received.
SITUATION: Quiet in good venues.
MAXIMUM STAY: By course and event.
BOOKINGS: Letter, telephone, fax, email; online contact form is best.
CHARGES: Specific for each event and venue.
ACCESS: Provides directions for the individual venue or see online programme for addresses of the various venues.

STANTON ST JOHN

Stanton House
Stanton St John
Oxford
Oxfordshire OX33 1HQ
England

Tel: 01865 358807
Email: office@stantonhouse.org.uk
Website: www.stantonhouse.org.uk

Retreats • Workshops and Courses • Church/Temple • Vegetarian Food • Organic Food

Christian

Stanton House is a Christian retreat centre offering very comfortable accommodation in an informal family atmosphere – where home cooking is definitely a speciality! The emphasis is on peace and quiet and guests, whether individuals or groups, are encouraged to relax and rest as much as they need to. There is no formal structure to the day, but guests are welcome to use the prayer room in the house or the prayer cabin in the grounds. The village church is a short and secluded walk through the grounds and over a stream that cascades down a series of gentle waterfalls. All guests are encouraged to take the time and space offered to find and experience God for themselves.

SUTTON COURTENAY

The Abbey
Sutton Courtenay
Abingdon
Oxordshire OX14 4AF
England

Tel: 01235 847401
Fax: 01235 847608
Email: admin@theabbey.uk.com
Website: www.theabbey.uk.com

Retreats • Workshops and Courses • Meditation • Vegetarian Food • Venue for Hire
Self-Catering Space • Community Living • Work Retreats • Vocations • Camping • Children

Inter-faith – Christian traditions

The Abbey, with its charming inner courtyard, flowers and surrounding meadow-like areas, has been going for a number of years and the current community is small but dynamic. The programme of events is designed to encourage personal, social and ecological transformation and nourishment of our inner lives. There are many excellent and interesting courses on offer at the Abbey, which can include Qi Gong, Tibetan healing exercises, Iyengar yoga and prayer retreats. **Highly Recommended.**

OPEN: All year by arrangement but sometimes closed for community needs. Everyone welcome.
ROOMS: Some rooms in the Abbey itself. The guest house in the grounds accommodates up to 14 sharing in self-catering accommodation.
FACILITIES: Conferences and group space, camping, 4-acre garden, library with Gandhi archive, guest lounge. 4 public rooms available for hire within the thirteenth- to sixteenth-century main Abbey building.
SPIRITUAL HELP: Meditation.
GUESTS ADMITTED TO: Unrestricted access except community members' rooms. Work of the community.
MEALS: All meals are vegetarian and meals can be provided for seated groups of up to 35. Up to 80 can be catered for on a non-residential, buffet basis. Self-catering possible in guesthouse.
SPECIAL ACTIVITIES: Planned programme. Send for brochure or see online. Spiritual healing, Reiki and spiritual direction available on request, by donation.
SITUATION: Surrounded by 4 acres of wooded grounds, the Abbey is of archaeological importance because of the underlying Roman and Saxon remains. Location is quiet, in a village.
MAXIMUM STAY: Usually 1 week.
BOOKINGS: Letter, telephone, fax, email.
CHARGES: Please ask when enquiring about booking.
ACCESS: Train: Didcot Parkway station (3 miles away), then taxi. Bus: regular service from Oxford. Car: via A34.

WALLINGFORD

Braziers Park
Ipsden
Wallingford
Oxfordshire OX10 6AN
England

Tel/Fax: 01491 680221
Email: admin@braziers.org.uk
Website: www.braziers.org.uk

Retreats • Workshops and Courses • Yoga • Meditation • Vegetarian Food • Organic Food
Venue for Hire • Community Living • Work Retreats • Vocations • Camping • Children

Eco-spirituality – Evolutionist

Braziers Park is a non-religious residential adult college deep in the south Oxfordshire countryside and is not a retreat house as such. However, it is receptive to other organisations running retreats here. Individual guests making their own retreat time and spaces are welcomed. Their programme of events and courses takes you into areas of concern and learning that are spiritual, especially where personal creativity and the environment are concerned as well as in the deeper elements of yoga and Tai Chi and North American Native spiritual rituals. For example, the programme may include: permaculture events and courses, yoga, North American Sweat Lodge, Apple Day, Work Week, Alexander Techniques, Creativity Sunday, Tai Chi retreat, and courses on non-violent communication and psychodrama. Braziers Park is a big place, with a large main house, rambling buildings, gardens, grounds, big stretches of vegetables growing, compost bins, and everywhere is that bit of lovely mess, which spells a real concern for trying to help the environment and live a more simple lifestyle that stays connected with planet Earth and with others. We like it. **Highly Recommended.**

OPEN: All year except Christmas period. Everyone welcome.
ROOMS: 10 singles. 4 doubles. Camping. Sometimes a caravan.
FACILITIES: Conferences, camping, garden, park, library, guest lounge.
SPIRITUAL HELP: Personal talks.
GUESTS ADMITTED TO: Unrestricted access.
MEALS: Everyone eats together. Traditional plus vegetarian food. Special diets possible with notice. It is possible to be self-catering if you are camping – but really the ethos here is to share meals and to be together.
SPECIAL ACTIVITIES: Lots to do here from garden composting to Tai Chi – see the programme for a variety of events and courses.
SITUATION: Countryside.
MAXIMUM STAY: By event duration or by arrangement.
BOOKINGS: Letter, telephone, email.

CHARGES: The cost per person depends on the course and the level of catering and accommodation you want. A current guide price for a group is from £57.50 shared accommodation per 24-hour period, including room hire, overnight accommodation, all meals, tea and coffee.

ACCESS: Rail: Reading or Oxford stations. Bus: a service runs between Reading and Oxford. Car: accessible from M4 exit 8/9, then A4130 and A4074. See the website for very good travel directions.

WANTAGE

Community of St Mary the Virgin	Tel: 01235 763141 /
St Mary's Convent	01235 760170 (Guest Wing)
Challow Road, Wantage	Email: guestwing@csmv.co.uk
Oxfordshire OX12 9DJ	
England	

Retreats • Church/Temple • Spiritual Help • Vegetarian Food • Community Living • Vocations

Christian – Anglican

Within walking distance of the town centre, St Mary's is a large, rather institutional but open-spirited convent that dates from 1848. There are two chapels, the larger of which is used for the Divine Office and Eucharist. Guests are free to use the time and space as they wish, and are asked to observe silence in accordance with the life of the community. Creative expression is encouraged in an art room.

'Every human being is the author of his own health or disease'
– Buddha

SHROPSHIRE

BETTISFIELD

Taraloka Buddhist Retreat Centre for Women Tel: 01948 710646 /
Bettisfield, Whitchurch   0845 3304063
Shropshire SY12 2LD   Email: admin@taraloka.org.uk
England   Website: www.taraloka.org.uk

Retreats • Workshops and Courses • Church/Temple • Yoga • Meditation • Spiritual Help
Vegetarian Food • Community Living • Work Retreats • Vocations

Buddhist – Friends of the Western Buddhist order (FWBO)

Situated peacefully on the plains of the Welsh borderlands, this Buddhist women's community, Taraloka, acts as a focal point for women throughout the world from various walks of life. It provides inspiration and affords a glimpse of new spiritual and personal vistas for all who come. **Taraloka is one of the few retreat centres specifically run by women for women and it has developed a kind and gentle space in which all women may find relaxation and be well supported in their spiritual journey.** The retreats are for complete beginners to committed practising Buddhists. Guests come on one of the retreats or events in the published programme. Those with no experience of meditation and Buddhism can come for an introductory course weekend. Other features are yoga weekends, spiritual life and motherhood, and retreats. The facilities are modern, light and airy. They have been converted from farm buildings, and women did almost all of the work. There are a garden, views, a pond and flowers – in the early spring white magnolias are in bloom. The place is high on a hill rise and you can go for a walk in safety. Everywhere shines out with cleanliness and there is an art room for those who want to paint and make. Taraloka has made a solitary suite for a private retreat with a bedroom, small kitchen and conservatory, which could make you want to stay forever as it is so delightful. On your stay you meet a selection of other women you might not ordinarily encounter and this too can be a very spiritual experience. There is a strong emphasis here on ethical practice, aiming for more kindness, generosity, contentment, truthful speech and clarity of mind. Taraloka is a place of peace, self-discovery and transformation. One of our most favourite places and where we would happily send our sisters, mother, aunts and any woman we know for a retreat whether they were Buddhist or not. **Highly Recommended.**

OPEN: Specific programme of retreats for women – no other guests received.
ROOMS: Singles, dormitories.
FACILITIES: Shrine room, guest lounge, camping, garden.
SPIRITUAL HELP: Personal talks, group sharing, meditation, directed study, personal retreat direction, spiritual direction.
GUESTS ADMITTED TO: Shrine room.
MEALS: Taken in guesthouse. Vegetarian and vegan food. Special diets.
SPECIAL ACTIVITIES: Planned events only available. Send for brochure.
SITUATION: Very quiet, in the countryside with beautiful country walks – near the Shropshire Union Canal. Nearby is a peat moss of special scientific interest.
MAXIMUM STAY: For the duration of the retreat.
BOOKINGS: Letter, telephone, email. Downloadable booking form on the website.
CHARGES: Very modest – please enquire. Weekend and concession rates possible.
ACCESS: Rail: Whitchurch (Shorpshire) station (6–7 miles away), then taxi. Car: via A49 or A495. Map and details are on the website and will be provided with booking confirmation.

CLEE ST MARGARET

Oak Barn Workshop Centre
Nordybank Nurseries
Clee St Margaret, Craven Arms
Shropshire SY7 9DT
England

Tel: 01584 823609
Email: info@oak-barn.co.uk
Website: www.oak-barn.co.uk

> Retreats • Workshops and Courses • Vegetarian Food • Organic Food • Venue for Hire
> Self-Catering Space • Holistic Holidays • Camping • Children

Eco-spirituality – Music

For over 10 years Oak Barn has been a place of retreat for healing, singing, making music and taking care of Mother Earth. It welcomes all who share in this ethos of environmental and ecological desire for oneness with nature. The centre is situated in some of the most lovely countryside in all of England – hills, walks, distant views, sheep peacefully grazing, pastures, ancient trees and abundant verges of green herbs and wildflowers. Not to be missed.

OPEN: All year. Everyone welcome
ROOMS: Accommodation in different buildings and yurts and camping. Single occupancy or shared.
FACILITIES: All groups are self-led and individuals make their own retreat structure. If you want to help in any of the garden work, you probably can.
SPIRITUAL HELP: None.
GUESTS ADMITTED TO: Whole site, including land, garden and hill walks.

MEALS: Self-catering, but they can provide lunch and evening meals if required. All food served is vegetarian and vegan, home cooked and organic if possible. Wheat-free options.
SPECIAL ACTIVITIES: Programme of singing and healing events each year. Details online.
SITUATION: Rural, peaceful, situated in the Brown Clee Hills of beautiful Shropshire.
MAXIMUM STAY: 1 week or by arrangement.
BOOKINGS: Letter, telephone, email, online booking form.
CHARGES: Currently, £15–£20 per person per night for groups of two people or more. Longer-stays rate is negotiable or for groups above 10 people. Hire of centre for courses or workshops is £50 per day.
ACCESS: Rail: Ludlow station; pick-up available (no local public transport). Car: via A49.

ELLESMERE

The Grange
Grange Road
Ellesmere
Shropshire SY12 9DE
England

Tel: 01691 623495
Fax: 01691 623227
Email: rosie@thegrange.uk.com
Website: www.thegrange.uk.com

Retreats • Workshops and Courses • Meditation • Spiritual Help • Bed and Breakfast
Vegetarian Food • Venue for Hire • Alternative Therapies

Inter-faith

A lovely short drive hedged with cherry trees and magnolias and in spring masses of daffodils brings you to this mellow, comfortable and welcoming old country family house. Rooted in Christianity but open to all faiths, the Grange continually updates itself with bright and light new decorations and more landscaping of the gardens. The retreat and relaxation approach here takes the idea of offering a country house retreat with the slogan: 'Here is the house, let's use it for peace and quiet!' It offers traditional bed and breakfast accommodation for a peaceful stay as well as a programme of courses. The garden has a labyrinth based on the one in Chartres Cathedral; this garden plus woodland and pasture give a guest over 10 acres in which to wander. For older women there are weekends and courses to reflect, reassess and search for new personal potential within the security of a small group. Indeed, one of the main concerns here has long been to explore and celebrate the second half of life for women. These sessions have grown in strength over the years. Peace, harmony and kindness are to be found here. **Highly Recommended.**

OPEN: March to November inclusive. Everyone welcome.
ROOMS: 5 singles, 4 twins, 4 doubles, 1 triple. Most rooms have en suite and tea/coffee facilities.
FACILITIES: Accompanied disabled access. Conferences, meditation, garden, fields and woodland, small library, guest lounge, TV.
SPIRITUAL HELP: None – but group talks on courses.
GUESTS ADMITTED TO: Access everywhere except private family rooms.
MEALS: Everyone eats together. Lots of vegetarian food, innovative cooking with interesting menus, making the most of the organic produce from the garden. Special diets possible.
SPECIAL ACTIVITIES: The aim of the courses is to promote inner understanding and spirituality. The aim of the house is also to offer non-retreatants a place for stillness and enjoyment. Send for information or see programme online.
SITUATION: Quiet, about 10 minutes' walk from a small town.
MAXIMUM STAY: About 5 days usually.
BOOKINGS: Letter, telephone, email.
CHARGES: Different charges for B&B and for the various events and courses. Please see online for the latter and enquire about the current charge for B&B per night.
ACCESS: Train: Shrewsbury station (17 miles away), then taxi; Gobowen station (8 miles) – pick-up possible if arranged in advance. Buses: infrequent services. Car: via A528 from Ellesmere.

LYDBURY NORTH

Silent Presence   Tel: 01588 680663
The Granary   Tel: 01743 884963
Lydbury North   Email: focusinshropshire
Shropshire SY7 8AS   @brickett-thegranary.fsnet.co.uk
England

Retreats • Workshops and Courses • Meditation • Vegetarian Food • Alternative Therapies

Open spirituality

The aim of Silent Presence is to create an experience of 'being in the present moment' during the retreat. On these retreats you are first introduced to the basics of breathwork and focusing, and how they can be helpful when you are in silence. A Silent Presence retreat offers suggestions, but does not tell you what you must do nor insist on a certain form of meditation. It is about sensing in your body for what is appropriate for you in the present moment. A large part of the retreat is in silence with alternating periods of sitting and walking meditation.

MARCHAMLEY

Hawkstone Hall	Tel: 01630 685242
Redemptorist International Pastoral Centre	Tel: 01630 685616 /
Marchamley, Shrewsbury	01630 685620 (guests)
Shropshire SY4 5LG	Fax: 01630 685565
England	Email: hawkhall@aol.com
	Website: www.hawkstone-hall.com

Retreats • Workshops and Courses • Church/Temple • Spiritual Help • Vegetarian Food
Venue for Hire • Community Living • Vocations

Christian – Roman Catholic – Redemptorist

Hawkstone Hall and its lavish gardens are splendid and listed of Grade 1 importance. It is a large place with a grand approach, extensive parks and grounds. Run by the Redemptorists as an international renewal centre for both the lay and religious, guests come from all over the world to this beautiful place. There are both short and long three-month courses, plus a retreat programme running through most of the year. The programme continues to explore new ideas and subjects relative to its mission and welcomes both individuals and groups.

'It is not so much the organism or the species that evolves,
but the entire system, species and environment.
The two are inseparable...'
– Alfred Lotka, 1925

STAFFORDSHIRE

CANNOCK WOOD

Reflections
Little Hayes, Beaudesert Park
Cannock Wood, Rugeley
Staffordshire WS15 4JJ
England

Tel/Fax: 01543 674474
Email:
polhill@reflectiongardens.org.uk
Website: www.reflectiongardens.org.uk

Retreats • Workshops and Courses • Spiritual Help • Venue for Hire
Self-Catering Space • Hermitages

Christian – Eco-spirituality

Reflections is a hermitage retreat set in a series of gardens, which have
been created to illustrate the connections between care for the environment and the Christian spiritual journey. Five different gardens
comprise Reflections and follow this Christian spiritual journey using the ideas of St Ignatius. Each garden also expresses an ecological
concern, so the spiritual and the ecological inform and enlighten each
other – and thus the visitor. The gardens are called: the Loving Creator,
the Loved and Forgiven Sinner, Discipleship, the Passion, and Resurrection. These themes are echoed in a set of original triptychs, each designed and executed with imagination and skill. Visitors are welcome
at Reflections's open days and at other times by arrangement. Some
programmes are available with themes that challenge you by linking
environmental issues with Christian spirituality. Additional accommodation is available at Beaudesert Park nearby. Here, there is a campsite,
which is held in trust for the benefit of young people, and also chalets
for self-catering. Guests can contribute some time during their stay to
help with work at the site. There are a chapel, an open-air worship
space and a covered barbecue area. **Highly Recommended.**

OPEN: Most of the year. Everyone welcome.
ROOMS: Self-catering hermitage. Additional accommodation possible at nearby
Beaudesert Park Campsite.
FACILITIES: The hermitage and gardens. Additional accommodation and meeting
space at Beaudesert Park.
SPIRITUAL HELP: Spiritual guidance and direction. Personal talks possible.
GUESTS ADMITTED TO: Gardens.
MEALS: Self-catering.

SPECIAL ACTIVITIES: Ignatian retreats, spiritual direction. See online for retreat and event programme.
SITUATION: Countryside.
MAXIMUM STAY: By arrangement.
BOOKINGS: Letter, telephone, email – send for their booking form.
CHARGES: No charge is made for use of the Hermitage. Visitors are invited to make a donation to the Rivendell Trust, a registered charity that funds their work.
ACCESS: By car: Cannock Wood village can be accessed from the A460, A5190 and A51. Reflections is about half a mile due east of Castle Ring, a nearby ancient monument, and less than a mile north of the village of Gentleshaw.

HORTON

Croft Meadows Farm   Tel: 01782 513039
Horton
Leek
Staffordshire ST13 8QE
England

> Retreats • Church/Temple • Bed and Breakfast • Vegetarian Food • Venue for Hire
> Self-Catering Space • Children

Non-denominational

A spacious self-contained cottage with three single bedrooms, one twin and one double on the ground floor with disabled access. The cottage is set in countryside on a farm. There are a chapel and garden and it offers a quiet retreat place for up to 16 people, either for the day or residential self-catering.

'If a care is too small to be turned into a prayer, it is too small to be made into a burden'
– Corrie ten Boom

ROCESTER

Hartley Woods Retreat   Tel: 01889 590755
Hartley Woods, Hollington Road   Email: rogdelf@aol.com
Rocester, Uttoxeter   Website: www.hartleywoods.co.uk
Staffordshire ST14 5HY
England

Retreats • Church/Temple • Bed and Breakfast • Vegetarian Food • Venue for Hire • Children

Non-denominational

A family-run retreat house in the countryside for both individuals and small groups up to 12. Home-cooked meals, comfortable lodging and close to many historic attractions and various activities – for example it is only three miles from Alton Towers. The grounds are varied with over 60 species of trees and an abundance of wildlife, and the owners have a long-established herd of red deer.

STONE

Shallowford House   Tel: 01785 760233
Lichfield Diocesan Retreat and   Fax: 01785 760390
Conference Centre   Email: info@shallowfordhouse.org
Shallowford, Stone   Website: www.shallowfordhouse.org
Staffordshire ST15 0NZ
England

Retreats • Workshops and Courses • Spiritual Help • Vegetarian Food • Venue for Hire

Christian – Anglican

This is a big old house, which is the centre of the Lichfield Diocese. The aim of Shallowford is to offer Christian hospitality to all who visit. There is a planned programme throughout the year, which ranges from Quiet Days and topics like *Stress and the Spiritual Life* to individually guided retreats. You will find details on their website, well detailed under the heading 'Diary'. Shallowford, set in four acres of countryside, is a place of warm welcome, nice food and pleasant surroundings.

OPEN: All year. Receives men, women, young people, families, groups.
ROOMS: 27 bedrooms: 12 twins, 15 singles – 7 of the bedrooms are en suite. There is a ground-floor en suite room with full disabled facilities. Groups up to 40 people.
FACILITIES: Disabled access, conferences, garden, bookstall, guest lounge, TV.
SPIRITUAL HELP: Individually guided retreats.
GUESTS ADMITTED TO: Unrestricted.
MEALS: Everyone eats together. Vegetarian, special diets possible.
SPECIAL ACTIVITIES: Planned programme of events. Send for brochure or visit the website.
SITUATION: Quiet and in the countryside.
MAXIMUM STAY: By arrangement.
BOOKINGS: Letter, telephone, fax, email, online contact form.
CHARGES: For full-board and day visits, including meals, please enquire when booking. The various events and retreats are individually priced in the programme.
ACCESS: Train: Stafford station (5 miles away), then taxi. Car: 3 miles from M6 exit 14. See the website for detailed directions to Shallowford House.

WARWICKSHIRE

MANCETTER

Purley Chase Centre
Purley Chase Land
Mancetter, Atherstone
Warwickshire CV9 2RQ
England

Tel: 01827 712370
Email: enquiries@purleychasecentre.org.uk
Website: www.purleychasecentre.org.uk

Retreats • Workshops and Courses • Church/Temple • Meditation • Spiritual Help
Bed and Breakfast • Vegetarian Food • Organic Food • Venue for Hire
Self-Catering Space • Children

Christian – Swedenborg spirituality

This centre's spirituality welcomes people of all backgrounds and beliefs and is rooted in a Swedenborgian approach to Christianity. They welcome open dialogue between people of all religions and those with none at all. Their events programme aims to meet a wide range of personal and spiritual needs, and caters for both adults and young people.

OPEN: Most of the year. Everyone welcome.
ROOMS: A total of 60 beds in all: 8 single en suite, 8 twin en suite (2 for disabled), 2 bedsits, 8 standard rooms, each sleeping 3–8 people.
FACILITIES: Disabled access, chapel, activity room, conservatory, games room, dining

room, adventure-play area, bar, TV, several good conference and meeting rooms.
SPIRITUAL HELP: Personal talks by arrangement.
GUESTS ADMITTED TO: All public areas and outside grounds and gardens.
MEALS: Full dining service. Vegetarian and special diets possible.
SPECIAL ACTIVITIES: Events and retreat programme. Send for information or visit the website.
SITUATION: Countryside.
MAXIMUM STAY: By arrangement.
BOOKINGS: Letter, telephone, email.
CHARGES: Full-board rates per person are £38/£48 for dormitories/en suite; corresponding B&B rates are £25/36. Special rates for children and young people, and meals only. For details, see the website.
ACCESS: Rail: Nuneaton station (7 miles away) or Atherstone station (2 miles away). Car: Purley is near Atherstone, 1.5 miles south of the A5.

OFFCHURCH

Offa House
Village Street
Offchurch, near Leamington Spa
Warwickshire CV33 9AS
England

Tel: 01926 423309
Email: offahouse@btconnect.com
Website:
www.offahouseretreat.co.uk

Retreats • Workshops and Courses • Church/Temple • Spiritual Help • Bed and Breakfast
Vegetarian Food • Venue for Hire • Self-Catering Space • Children

Christian – Anglican

The Coventry Diocesan Retreat House and Conference Centre are situated in an old Georgian vicarage, which has a large garden. The house has been organised in such a way that all visitors can feel that this is their own special place, and the staff try to be as non-intrusive as possible.

OPEN: All year. Everyone, including children, welcome.
ROOMS: 18 singles, 3 twins, 4 double (15 of which are en suite); accommodates 25–32 guests. Self-contained cottage, sleeps 5.
FACILITIES: Disabled access, church, conferences, chapel, garden, library, guest lounge, TV. Some facility improvement plans have been started; please visit the website for news about further facilities.
SPIRITUAL HELP: Personal talks, personal retreat direction, spiritual direction.
GUESTS ADMITTED TO: Everywhere.
MEALS: Everyone eats together. Traditional. Vegetarian and special diets catered for.
SPECIAL ACTIVITIES: Planned programme of events. Send for brochure and see online for downloadable brochure.
SITUATION: Quiet, in the village and countryside.

MAXIMUM STAY: By arrangement.
BOOKINGS: Letter, telephone, email. Downaloadable booking forms.
CHARGES: Current standard rates per person: 24-hr £60; weekend £120; day conference £33. Lower rates for charities and church organisations available. Please enquire for B&B, half-day and evening meeting rates.
ACCESS: Rail: Leamington Spa station (3 miles away), then taxi. Car: about 1 mile from Radford Semele, which is on the A435. View the website for clear travel directions.

PRINCETHORPE

**Princethorpe Retreat and Conference Centre
Coventry Road
Princethorpe, Rugby
Warwickshire CV23 9QF
England**

Tel: 01926 633357 / 07901 858687
Email: info@princethorperetreatcentre.org
Website: www.princethorperetreatcentre.org

Retreats • Workshops and Courses • Church/Temple • Spiritual Help • Venue for Hire
Self-Catering Space

Christian – Inter-denominational – Ecumenical

A calm atmosphere in a comfortable old house with views across the fields and wildflowers in the summer. Owned by the Roman Catholic Missionaries of the Sacred Heart, Princethorpe Retreat has its own planned programme and is also open to groups and individuals for retreats.

OPEN: Most of the year. Everyone welcome.
ROOMS: 7 bedrooms (accommodates 10 people in total).
FACILITIES: Chapel, 2 conference rooms, dining room, self-catering kitchen. The house is available for conferences, meetings and groups.
SPIRITUAL HELP: Spiritual accompaniment.
GUESTS ADMITTED TO: Everywhere.
MEALS: To keep costs low, most planned programmes are self-catering. Outside caterers can be used to assist with the running of your event. Please discuss your requirements with Princethorpe Retreat.
SPECIAL ACTIVITIES: A programme, including spiritual accompaniment training.
SITUATION: Countryside – on the edge of the grounds of Princethorpe College.
MAXIMUM STAY: By arrangement.
BOOKINGS: Letter, telephone or email to request a booking form.
CHARGES: Currently, programmed day retreats cost about £12.50 per person. Other rates on request.
ACCESS: Rail: Coventry station (7–8 miles away). Bus: services run from Coventry. Car: via A423. Good driving directions are on their website.

SNITTERFIELD

Red Hill Christian Centre   Tel/Fax: 01789 731427
Snitterfield   Email: enquiries@red-hill.org
Stratford upon Avon   Website: www.redhillchristiancentre.co.uk
Warwickshire CV37 0PQ
England

> Retreats • Workshops and Courses • Spiritual Help • Bed and Breakfast • Vegetarian Food
> Venue for Hire • Self-Catering Space • Camping • Children

Christian – Evangelical

This centre is set in some 50 acres of land and offers excellent retreat facilities, including a beautiful renovated barn for meetings and conferences. The whole place has had careful attention to its renovation and building renewal. Meals can be provided for booked retreats, including day retreats, but otherwise you get a continental breakfast and then you fix your own lunch and dinner. Programme of events and retreats available.

WORCESTERSHIRE

CHADWICH

Community for Reconciliation   Tel: 01562 710231
Barnes Close   Fax: 01562 710278
Chadwich, Bromsgrove   Email: cfrenquiry@aol.com
Worcestershire B61 0RA   Website: www.cfrbarnesclose.co.uk
England

> Retreats • Workshops and Courses • Church/Temple • Spiritual Help • Bed and Breakfast
> Vegetarian Food • Venue for Hire • Work Retreats • Vocations • Children

Christian – Ecumenical

Enjoying close links with the United Reform Church through founder members, prayer and financial support, the community here has developed ecumenically in its team, membership and patterns of work.

Barnes Close is a group of buildings situated on the southern slopes of Waseley Hill with five acres of grounds. It is near a country park and just 12 miles from Birmingham. There are fine views of the Malvern Hills and beyond towards the Cotswolds. Accommodation is comfortable in a homey way and some rooms are en suite. There is a common room with real fire, a chapel, library, coffee bar, seminar rooms, two conservatories, craft stall and bookshop. The programme has a number of retreats based around prayer, reflection, peace and rest. If you want a private silent retreat, then you should discuss this first when you contact the community. The community has a network of friends who help with the work of reconciliation and justice and there are charitable projects going in Romania, Africa and other countries.

CROPTHORNE

Holland House (Retreat, Conference and Laity Centre)
Main Street
Cropthorne, Pershore
Worcestershire WR10 3NB
England

Tel: 01386 860330
Fax: 01386 861208
Email: enquiries@hollandhouse.org
Website: www.hollandhouse.org

Retreats • Workshops and Courses • Church/Temple • Spiritual Help • Bed and Breakfast
Vegetarian Food • Venue for Hire • Children

Inter-denominational

Holland House was set up to help people who are trying to relate their prayer life more closely to the world around them. It is a big seventeenth-century place, with lots of thatch and gardens laid out by Sir Edwin Lutyens. A good place for your retreat with a wide-ranging and interesting programme, coupled with comfortable accommodation.

OPEN: All year except Christmas and the week after Easter. Everyone, including children, welcome.
ROOMS: 18 singles, 7 twins. Shared bathroom/shower facilities.
FACILITIES: Chapel, garden, library, TV.
SPIRITUAL HELP: Holy Communion. Group sharing on certain courses. Personal talks.
GUESTS ADMITTED TO: Unrestricted access.
MEALS: Everyone eats together. Traditional food. Vegetarian and special diets.
SPECIAL ACTIVITIES: Planned programme of events. Send for the brochure or download it from the website.

SITUATION: Quiet, in the village and countryside.
MAXIMUM STAY: 1 month.
BOOKINGS: Letter, telephone during office hours, email, online contact form.
Download booking form.
CHARGES: Rates depend on your stay and whether it is an event or programmed
retreat. A comprehensive list of the tariffs can be downloaded from the website, or
enquire when booking.
ACCESS: Train: Evesham station (3.5 miles away). Buses: services run from Evesham.
Car: via M5 exit 7, then A44.

GLASSHAMPTON

Society of St Francis	Tel: 01299 896345
St Mary at The Cross	Fax: 01299 896083
Glasshampton, Shrawley	Email: glasshamptonssf@franciscans.org.uk
Worcestershire WR6 6TQ	Website: www.franciscans.org.uk/
England	Page34.htm#Glasshampton

Retreats • Workshops and Courses • Church/Temple • Spiritual Help • Vegetarian Food
Community Living • Work Retreats • Vocations

Christian – Anglican – Franciscan

Up a road beyond cultivated fields or other houses, Glasshampton sits
waiting for you. If you take the bus to Glasshampton, you will have a
good long walk to get to St Mary at The Cross and this may well be a
perfect meditation time before commencing your retreat. The monastery is well established and was built from the stable blocks of a once
very grand house that burned down years ago. It is a simple place with
a certain elegance about it – homey and silent, yet charming and welcoming. Services in chapel are open to guests. The guest rooms are
modern and pleasant and there is a library, which has books by Brother
Ramon, a now deceased member of this community and famous for his
writings on spirituality. We especially commend to you his books *Franciscan Spirituality* and *The Prayer Mountain*. This Franciscan house has
a lifestyle based on ideals of simplicity, hospitality and prayer. It has
that quiet air of happiness that so many today long for in their lives.
This is a serious place for a private retreat. **Highly Recommended.**

OPEN: Around the year except on Mondays to Tuesday afternoons during the week
and at Christmas and Easter seasons. Welcomes everyone.
ROOMS: 3 singles. 2 twins.
FACILITIES: Garden, library, guest area.

SPIRITUAL HELP: Brothers may be available, if arranged in advance, to spend time with individuals or groups, for spiritual direction, talks and Quiet Days. We suggest that you give a donation for these ministries.

GUESTS ADMITTED TO: Chapel, library.

MEALS: Everyone eats together. Very plain traditional food. Vegetarians. Special diets only within reason, so discuss before you go.

SPECIAL ACTIVITIES: None.

SITUATION: Very quiet and peaceful, in the countryside.

MAXIMUM STAY: 6 days.

BOOKINGS: Letter, telephone, fax, email.

CHARGES: Suggested current donations: 24-hours residential full board £25; day groups and individual visitors £7.50 for the day if you bring your lunch, otherwise £10 if you join the community for lunch. Groups are asked to add an appropriate donation if a brother gives a talk or helps to run your retreat day, or spends personal ministry time with you as an individual.

ACCESS: Rail: Kidderminster station (8 miles away). Bus: services run from Kidderminster and Worcester. Car: via A443, A451.

HARVINGTON

Harvington Hall	Tel: 01562 777846
Harvington Hall Lane	Fax: 01562 777190
Harvington, Kidderminster	Email: harvingtonhall@btconnect.com
Worcestershire DY10 4LR	Website: www.harvingtonhall.com
England	

Church/Temple • Vegetarian Food • Organic Food • Children

Christian – Roman Catholic

A moated Tudor manor house, owned and restored by the Archdiocese of Birmingham, it features among other things three chapels, gardens, a visitor's centre, a bookshop and a restaurant. Everyone is welcome for a visit, to see the house and gardens, and for Quiet Days and parish-group away days. Non-residential.

'A right delayed is a right denied'
– Martin Luther King, Jr

NORTH

CHESHIRE

••

BOLLINGTON

Savio House	Tel: 01625 573256
Ingersley Road	Fax: 01625 560221
Bollington	Email: retreatoffice@saviohouse.org.uk /
Cheshire SK10 5RW	saviooffice@saviohouse.org.uk
England	Website: www.saviohouse.org.uk

Retreats • Workshops and Courses • Church/Temple • Spiritual Help • Vegetarian Food
Self-Catering Space • Community Living • Vocations • Children

Christian – Roman Catholic – Ecumenical

Savio House is a retreat centre especially for young people. All young people, Christian or not, are welcome here. It is run by a Catholic religious congregation called the Salesians of Don Bosco. St John Bosco was a nineteenth-century Italian priest who dedicated his life to working for the benefit of young people. The Savio House Community celebrates God's presence in all people – particularly the young. Their aim in their work and life is to journey alongside others towards a deeper awareness of God's love. During the last 25 years there have been many changes here to meet the modern expectations of the young and to be able to offer them the right retreat facilities. The barns have been turned into accommodation for residential groups of up to 40 young people in self-catering facilities. The farm cottage was converted to be used by small self-catering residential groups and, at the moment, it is home to the Youth Ministry Office of the Salesians and houses many of the lay retreat team here.

'God is beauty'
– Saint Francis of Assisi

CHESTER

Chester Retreat House   Tel: 01244 321801
11 Abbey Square   Email: chester.retreat@tiscali.co.uk
Chester
Cheshire CH1 2HU
England

Retreats • Workshops and Courses • Church/Temple • Bed and Breakfast
Vegetarian Food • Venue for Hire

Christian – Inter-denominational

Chester Retreat House consists of two elegant Georgian houses, now joined, which are situated in a quiet corner near Chester Cathedral. Facilities include a sitting room, library and a large well-maintained garden. Both dining room and meeting rooms, plus disabled lavatory, are on the ground floor and there are en suite rooms. While groups use this centre, individuals are welcome and very often last-minute bookings for a room are possible – so it is worth a try if you suddenly decide that a few days away for some interior meditation and time alone are what you need. Parking is difficult because of the central location of the house, but public transport is available.

FRODSHAM

Foxhill   Tel: 01928 733777
Tarvin Road   Fax: 01928 551041
Frodsham   Email: foxhillwarden@aol.com
Cheshire WA6 6XB   Website: www.foxhillconferences.co.uk
England

Retreats • Church/Temple • Vegetarian Food • Venue for Hire • Children

Christian – Anglican

Foxhill is set in a wonderful garden of 70 acres with many trees and woodlands. It has modern conference facilities, a dining room, its own chapel, and 18 en suite bedrooms, with two fully equipped for a disabled person and a carer. There are facilities for up to 108 people for day meetings. One of the most notable aspects of this spiritual retreat house is the arboretum, noted for its fine variety of trees and its views across Cheshire.

STOCKPORT

Shalom Spirituality Centre Tel: 0161 2927270
1 Adswood Lane West
Stockport
Cheshire SK3 8HT
England

Christian – Roman Catholic

Here, a small community of sisters have undertaken a new adventure in caring and community in what was once a novitiate house. This developing centre for spirituality work aims to provide day group retreats and various ways of experiencing the benefits of stillness, silence, solitude and the Good News of Christian spirituality. This is done through scripture, dialogue, silence, symbol, music, hand massage and reflexology. So far it all seems to be working, and visitors come for a day retreat or event. This place shows what can be achieved in providing a small and simple oasis of Christian peace in the middle of a densely populated and busy urban setting.

WARRINGTON

Tumble Trust Tel: 01925 635662 / 07817 798896
7 Grammar School Road Email: tumble-trust@yahoo.co.uk
Warrington Website: www.tumbletrust.co.uk
Cheshire WA4 1JN
England

Retreats • Workshops and Courses • Yoga • Meditation • Vegetarian Food • Children

Inter-faith

Tumble Trust, now over 10 years old, runs organised relaxation spirituality courses at some of the most hospitable retreat centres in the UK. Tumble's aim is to relax, enlighten, encourage and sustain you –

laughter is part of the deal here. Taking its main inspiration from the Christian contemplative tradition, Tumble put an emphasis on community and shared spiritual journeys. Some of the titles of their courses are very inviting: *Enneagram, Way of Transformation, Relaxation and the Art of Foolishness* and *For God's Sake, Relax!* Remember, please, just in case you forgot, that being relaxed and enjoying life can be combined with contemplative prayer – indeed, relaxing and being filled with joy are a great way to greet God. The psalms tell us that God does not want sacrifice but thanksgiving – so what better way to say thanks for life than through your happiness? For all-inclusive prices for weekend current events and for their summer week, visit the website. Excellent value. **Highly Recommended.**

WISTASTON

Oblate Retreat and Spirituality Centre   Tel: 01270 568653
Wistaston Hall, 89 Broughton Lane   Fax: 01270 650776
Wistaston, Crewe   Email: director@oblateretreatcentre.org.uk
Cheshire CW2 8JS   Website: www.oblateretreatcentre.org.uk
England

Retreats • Workshops and Courses • Church/Temple • Spiritual Help • Bed and Breakfast
Vegetarian Food • Venue for Hire • Community Living • Work Retreats
Vocations • Children

Christian – Roman Catholic

This is a 200-year-old cheerful-looking country house, set in five acres of garden and peaceful countryside. The centre is staffed by Oblate Fathers and some 40 guests can be accommodated. The aim is to enable those who come here to wind down from the stresses and strains of modern living and to enter into a deeper experience of prayer and reflection in the presence of Christ. Much effort goes into making guests feel comfortable with professional catering for meals and log fires in the winter months. The retreats and courses on offer are wide ranging. Private retreats with spiritual accompaniment can be arranged.

CUMBRIA

AMBLESIDE

Rydal Hall	Tel: 01539 432050
Rydal	Fax: 01539 434887
Ambleside	Email: mail@rydalhall.org
Cumbria LA22 9LX	Website: www.rydalhall.org
England	

Retreats • Workshops and Courses • Church/Temple • Spiritual Help • Vegetarian Food
Venue for Hire • Self-Catering Space • Work Retreats • Camping • Children

Christian – Anglican – Ecumenical

There is a relaxed atmosphere in this big Georgian house, which is set in the heart of the Lake District and within a 30-acre estate with waterfalls and formal gardens. It is mainly used by groups, but individuals are welcome and there is no pressure to join in any activities that may be taking place. There are led retreats and activity events. A lovely place.

GRASMERE

Glenthorne Country Guest House	Tel: 01539 435389
Easedale Road	Website: www.glenthorne.org
Grasmere	
Cumbria LA22 9QH	
England	

Retreats • Workshops and Courses • Bed and Breakfast • Vegetarian Food • Venue for Hire
Self-Catering Space • Children

Quaker

Glenthorne is a fairly large country house that is both a holiday centre and a Quaker retreat house for those wishing an atmosphere of peace and friendship. It is a few minutes' walk from the village centre and there are open views to the fells. Located on the Coast to Coast path, walking groups regularly use Glenthorne as a base. Individuals and families are both welcome. The website has an online enquiry form.

STROTH

Monastery of St Francis　　　　Tel: 01524 762292 (10:00–16:30)
Chapel Gap, Storth Road　　　　Email: brothersean5@aol.com
Storth, Milnthorpe　　Website: www.monasteryofsaintfrancis.com
Cumbria LA7 7JL
England

Retreats • Church/Temple • Meditation • Spiritual Help • Vegetarian Food
Community Living • Vocations

Christian – Inter-faith – Tau Inter-faith Community of St Francis

This small monastery has been called the Assisi of the South Lakes. As members of the Tau Inter-faith Community of St Francis, the monks, friends and oblates live to a simple rule by honouring the Divine within everything and everyone that moves, lives and breathes. The friendly monastic guest house endorses a Charter of Compassion by welcoming brothers and sisters from the Abrahamic Faith Community – that is the children of Abraham, who in religious terms are considered the Jews, Christians and Muslims – and all other faith communities who seek stillness, peace and respite in relaxed surroundings.

ULVERSTON

Manjushri Kadampa Meditation Centre　　　Tel: 01229 584029
Conishead Priory　　　　　　　　　　　　　Fax: 01229 580080
Ulverston　　　　　　　　　　　　Email: info@manjushri.org
Cumbria LA12 9QQ　　　　Website: www.nkt-kmc-manjushri.org
England

Retreats • Workshops and Courses • Church/Temple • Meditation • Spiritual Help
Vegetarian Food • Community Living • Work Retreats • Vocations • Children

Buddhist (Kadampa tradition)

Manjushri Kadampa Meditation Centre is located at Conishead Priory near Ulverston, south of the Lake District and just a short woodland stroll from the western shore of Morecambe Bay. Conishead Priory is a listed Romantic-gothic mansion, and in the former kitchen garden of the estate the Buddhist Centre has constructed a stunning 'Kadampa

World Peace' Temple. The temple is richly decorated both inside and out. Inside, a display case takes up most of the western wall and contains many fine representations of the Buddha, including an eight-foot bronze statue cast in Britain. The temple normally seats up to 750 people, and is extended to seat over 2,000 participants during two annual Buddhist Festivals. It is a place of great tranquillity. The centre has a resident community of about 100 people, both lay and ordained Buddhists. Throughout the year, residents and local non-residents follow three structured programmes of Buddhist study and retreat at different levels, and there is a year-round programme of residential weekend courses and retreats for visitors. The resident teacher of Manjushri Centre is Gen-la Kelsang Khyenrab, an English monk of great experience. The study and retreat programmes at the centre were designed by the Spiritual Director of the centre, Venerable Geshe Kelsang Gyatso, a fully accomplished meditation master and internationally renowned Buddhist teacher and author. Geshe Kelsang has been based at at the centre since 1977, and has worked tirelessly to promote Kadampa Buddhism, founding a worldwide association of Buddhist centres called the 'New Kadampa Tradition – International Kadampa Buddhist Union'. One member of our guide team had this to say of his experience there: 'I found the summer festival to be a really rewarding experience. During the festival the centre had a welcoming, friendly and family atmosphere with a mix of people of all ages from around the world. There were even a crèche and a clown to keep children and some adults entertained. I was extremely impressed with the teachings that I received; Geshe Kelsang Gyatso delivered them with great humour and humility.' **Highly Recommended.**

Rookhow Centre	Tel: 01229 860231
Rusland	Email: straughton@btinternet.com
Ulverston	Website: www.swarthmoorquakers.co.uk/rookhow
Cumbria LA12 8LA	
England	

Retreats • Self-Catering Space

Quaker – Open spirituality

In 14 acres of woodland, Rookhow provides accommodation in a set of former stables for individual and groups for guided group retreats and self-directed retreats. It is very popular with local hikers and backpackers.

Swarthmoor Hall	Tel: 01229 583204
Ulverston	Email: info@swarthmoorhall.co.uk /
Cumbria LA12 0JQ	swarthmrhall@gn.apc.org
England	Website: www.swarthmoorhall.co.uk

Retreats • Workshops and Courses • Bed and Breakfast • Venue for Hire
Self-Catering Space • Children

Quaker – Open spirituality

Swarthmoor Hall was the original centre in the 1600s for the spread of Quakerism and today this historic property offers group and individual retreats, places for meetings and conferences, and a quiet place for rest and reflection hospitality. Courses held there include craft such as stone walling. It is in a rural setting set among farmlands and fields.

OPEN: All year. Everyone welcome.
ROOMS: 3 units, which sleep 4–6 people. In total there are 6 twins; 2 single and a sofa bed. (1 twin is en suite.)
FACILITIES: Self-contained and self-catering units (1 of which is wheelchair friendly), gardens and grounds, meeting rooms. Day workshop space for 10–35 people.
SPIRITUAL HELP: None.
GUESTS ADMITTED TO: Everywhere.
MEALS: Self-catering or B&B.
SPECIAL ACTIVITIES: Retreats, pilgrimages and holidays. Programme of events includes topics from spirituality to craft.
SITUATION: Countryside with gardens, fields, farmland.
MAXIMUM STAY: By arrangement.
BOOKINGS: Letter, telephone, email.
CHARGES: Please enquire when booking. Rates per week for the units start at £280.
ACCESS: Rail: Ulverston station (half a mile away, but it can be wet and muddy in winter). Car: via M6 exit 36 and A590.

'It is only with the heart that one can see rightly; what is
essential is invisible to the eye'
– Antoine de Saint-Exupery

COUNTY DURHAM

••

CONSETT

Minsteracres Retreat Centre
Near Consett
County Durham DH8 9RT
England

Tel: 01434 673248
Fax: 01434 673540
Email: info@minsteracres.org
Website: www.minsteracres.org

Retreats • Workshops and Courses • Church/Temple • Spiritual Help • Vegetarian Food
Venue for Hire • Self-Catering Space • Work Retreats • Hermitages • Camping • Children

Christian – Roman Catholic – Ecumenical

Giant Wellingtonia sequoia trees line the drive to this former mansion, set in 60 acres of grounds and once the home of the Silvertop family. It is a large place with distant views. It's all very informal and relaxed here, with an emphasis on providing a service to the local parish and dioceses, which means it can be a busy place. There are guided weekend retreats in such topics as *Celtic Spirituality* and *Exploring Liturgy*, but individuals are welcome any time and, if you really want to be alone, a charming Poustinia is available – with its own tiny chapel.

OPEN: February to mid-December, closed January and latter part of July. Receives everyone.
ROOMS: Main house contains group rooms for 10–90 people; dining room; 11 singles, 6 twins and 3 doubles; chapel; a poustinia; and a library. The retreat house, an old stable block, has a lecture room for 55 people; lounge and TV room; small meeting room; kitchen; bar; bookshop; 8 singles and 24 twins; 2 ground-floor en suite singles with disabled facilities (1 has an adjoining carer's room). The youth centre consists of 2 dormitories, lounge/dining room and kitchen.
FACILITIES: Conferences, camping, garden, park and as given above for the main house, retreat house and youth centre.
SPIRITUAL HELP: Personal retreat direction, spiritual direction, meditation, group sharing, personal talks.
GUESTS ADMITTED TO: Church, chapel, oratory, work of community.
MEALS: Everyone eats together. Traditional food. Vegetarian and special diets. Self-catering also – see above.
SPECIAL ACTIVITIES: Planned retreats and events. See online or send for brochure.
SITUATION: A little busy but in the countryside in 60 acres of grounds with lots of walks and super views. There are plenty of quiet corners to be found here both in the house and outside.
MAXIMUM STAY: 1 week.
BOOKINGS: Letter, telephone, email. Downloadable booking form.
CHARGES: Please enquire when booking.
ACCESS: Rail: Stocksfield station (6 miles away), then taxi. Car: via A68.

DURHAM

St Antony's Priory   Tel/Fax: 0191 3843747
Ecumenical Spirituality Centre   Email: durhamstant@aol.com
74 Claypath   Website: www.stantonyspriory.co.uk
Durham DH1 1QT
England

Retreats • Workshops and Courses • Church/Temple • Spiritual Help • Bed and Breakfast
Vegetarian Food • Venue for Hire • Self-Catering Space

Christian – Ecumenical – Anglican

Formerly the vicarage of St Nicholas Parish Church in the city market-place, this 150-year-old house has been developed into an ecumenical spirituality centre. It provides hospitality and weekday worship as well as an annual programme of Quiet Days and workshops led by individuals drawn from differing denominations and none. Also available are prayer guidance, Quiet Days and workshops, space for small groups, individually guided retreats (by request), counselling and spiritual guidance.

LANCASHIRE

CARNFORTH

Capernwray Bible School and   Tel: 01524 733908
Capernwray Holidays   Fax: 01524 736681
Capernwray Hall   Email: info@capernwray.org.uk (general) /
Carnforth   registrar@capernwray.org.uk (Bible school) /
Lancashire LA6 1AG   holidays@capernwray.org.uk (holidays)
England   Website: www.capernwray.org.uk

Retreats • Workshops and Courses • Church/Temple • Spiritual Help
Vegetarian Foods • Children

Christian – Missionary – Bible school studies

'Where God changes lives' is the slogan of Capernwray. Here the Capernwray Missionary Fellowship of Torchbearers runs a well-planned

Christian holiday place and scripture-based courses, including those with internationally famous speakers on the Word of God. The Bible school has an excellent reputation for its study programme. The programme is a good one, full of interesting courses and conferences that will help to move you ahead in your Christian commitment and bring you inspiration and group sharing of your faith. Young people in particular seem to enjoy this venue and the accommodation is shared, which for this age group is a positive aspect. There are some single rooms available.

Monastery of Our Lady of Hyning	Tel: 01524 732684
Warton	Fax: 01524 720287
Carnforth	Email: hyningbookings@yahoo.co.uk
Lancashire LA5 9SE	Website: www.bernardine.org/hyninge.html
England	

Retreats • Workshops and Courses • Church/Temple • Spiritual Help • Vegetarian Food
Venue for Hire • Community Living • Vocations

Christian – Roman Catholic

Particularly suitable for private retreats and day retreats, the monastery is set in private grounds. In some rooms, cheerful fires greet you in winter, while there is a peaceful and welcoming atmosphere everywhere. A barn has been converted into a church where guests may join the sisters in their daily schedule of prayer.

OPEN: All year except for mid-July to late August. Receives everyone.
ROOMS: 7 single, 1 double, 12 twins.
FACILITIES: Conference room, garden, library, guest telephone.
SPIRITUAL HELP: Resident chaplain. Personal talks, one-to-one guidance by arrangement.
GUESTS ADMITTED TO: Chapel, choir.
MEALS: Large dining room and small dining room, serving mainly traditional food. Vegetarian and special diets catered for.
SPECIAL ACTIVITIES: Groups and individuals welcomed for day retreats, one-to-one retreats by arrangement, programme of events.
SITUATION: Quiet and in the countryside.
MAXIMUM STAY: By arrangement.
BOOKINGS: Letter, telephone, email.
CHARGES: Ask for the tariff.
ACCESS: Rail: Carnforth station (3 miles away). Bus: local routes from Carnforth to Warton. Car: via M6 exit 35, then A6.

Old School   Tel: 01524 732336
Yealand Conyers
Carnforth
Lancashire LA5 9SH
England

Venue for Hire • Self-Catering Space

Quaker

The Old School is adjacent to the Meeting House and offers simple accommodation for self-catering at very reasonable prices. There are no beds but dormitory arrangements so you bring your own sleeping bags. Groups up to 30 can be accommodated. There are lots of local attractions like the RSPB bird reserve at Leighton Moss.

PRESTON

Tabor Carmelite Retreat House   Tel: 01772 717122
169 Sharoe Green Lane   Fax: 01772 787674
Fulwood, Preston   Email: tabor@carmelite.net
Lachashire PR2 8HE   Website: www.tabor-preston.org/
England

Retreats • Church/Temple • Spiritual Help • Self-Catering Space • Alternative Therapies
Holistic Holidays • Community Living • Vocations

Christian – Roman Catholic

Here a small community offers self-catering accommodation, spiritual guidance, alternative therapies, a chapel with Eucharistic celebration, a good conference room, and a retreat and events programme. Tabor Retreat House retains many of the features of the original nineteenth-century farmhouse from which it was recently converted. There is always a warm welcome from the community here.

WHALLEY

Whalley Abbey
The Sands
Whalley, Clitheroe
Lancashire BB7 9SS
England

Tel: 01254 828400
Fax: 01254 825519
Email: office@whalleyabbey.org
Website: www.whalleyabbey.co.uk

Retreats • Workshops and Courses • Vegetarian Food • Venue for Hire
Self-Catering Space • Children

Christian – Anglican

The *Good Retreat Guide* team found Whalley Abbey to be a very comfortable and gracefully furnished house within the historic ruins of an ancient Cistercian abbey. Whalley Abbey was once the ecclesiastical power centre for northern England, but like so many others was destroyed during the Reformation. An elegant manor house was built in the sixteenth century and it is this building that is used today for retreats and conferences. The accommodation has recently been refurbished with a selection of rooms – many of which have wonderful views over the ruins and gardens. Meals, which are delicious, are served in a Jacobean-style dining room with all the refinements of a first-class restaurant. Whalley Abbey offers a warm and gentle Christian hospitality that is conducive to deep rest and relaxation. You will be very well looked after! **Highly Recommended.**

OPEN: All year except Christmas/New Year. Receives everyone. Children welcome.
ROOMS: 10 twins, 6 singles, 1 double. All en suite with TV, telephone, tea-making facilities and computer point. Accommodation received 4-star rating from Visit Britain.
FACILITIES: Disabled access, conferences, garden, guest lounge, TV, gift shop, coffee shop.
SPIRITUAL HELP: Spiritual direction.
GUESTS ADMITTED TO: Unrestricted access.
MEALS: Everyone eats together. Traditional food. Vegetarian and special diets.
SPECIAL ACTIVITIES: Planned programme. Send for brochure or go online.
SITUATION: Quiet and peaceful environment, with beautiful tranquil gardens where there is the ruin of a fourteenth-century Cistercian abbey.
MAXIMUM STAY: Usually 5-7 days.
BOOKINGS: Letter, telephone, fax, email.
CHARGES: Ask for latest rates.
ACCESS: Train: Whalley station (10 minutes' walk away). Bus: local routes serve Whalley. Car via A59 to Whalley.

MANCHESTER

●●

CHORLTON

Ananda Marga Centre   Tel: 0161 2829224
42 Keppel Road   Email: london@anandamarga.org.uk
Chorlton   Website: www.anandamarga.org.uk
Manchester M21 0BW
England

Retreats • Workshops and Courses • Yoga • Meditation

Yoga – Meditation

The Ananda Marga movement was founded by the Indian philosopher, teacher and poet P. R. Sarkar. Yoga and meditation are taught and practised as methods for self-development and self-realisation, while social service is emphasised as an outward expression of developing the human potential. This centre is in a Victorian terraced house in south Manchester, but there are other courses and classes across the UK, including London. Their website details what is available and where. Quiet, informal and friendly, there are classes in yoga postures and regular meetings for meditation. Creative writing and painting workshops are sometimes offered. Regular evenings of inspirational song, music and poetry draw the group and local community together. The classes, being usually weekly, are non-residential, but there is a programme of retreats at countryside venues.

'It is not that someone else is preventing you from living happily; you yourself do not know what you want. Rather than admit this, you pretend that someone is keeping you from exercising your liberty. Who is this? It is you yourself'
– Thomas Merton

MANCHESTER

Manchester Buddhist Centre Tel: 0161 8349232
16–20 Turner St Email: info@manchesterbuddhistcentre.org.uk
Northern Quarter Website: www.manchesterbuddhistcentre.org.uk
Manchester M4 1DZ
England

Bodywise Tel: 0161 8332528
2nd Floor Email: health@bodywisenaturalhealth.co.uk
Manchester Buddhist Centre Website:
www.bodywisenaturalhealth.co.uk

Retreats • Workshops and Courses • Yoga • Meditation

Buddhist – Friends of the Western Buddhist Order (FWBO)

An old Victorian warehouse right in the heart of Manchester's city centre, sensitively restored, this is now a Buddhist centre offering classes in meditation and Buddhism. Exposed brick and natural wood contribute to an atmosphere of calm, while the integrity of architecture, building materials and voluntary human effort are an inspiration. There are two shrine halls: a larger one for groups and a smaller one for private meditation or prayer. Introductory classes are offered in meditation and Buddhism. Upstairs the natural health centre **Bodywise** (see above) offers a spacious yoga studio, a wide range of yoga classes, Qi Gong classes and treatment rooms for massage, reflexology, pain management, acupuncture and Shiatsu. There are a bookshop and reference library and the award-winning vegan Earth Café is a haven of healthy eating and drinking. The Buddhist Centre is non-residential, but weekend retreats are organised in venues in surrounding areas.

*'The ocean is the same ocean as it has been of old;
the events of today are its waves and its rivers'
– Sayyid Haydar Amuli*

Manchester Chan Group
Western Chan Fellowship
Friends Meeting House
6 Mount Street
Manchester M2 5NS
England

Email: manchester@
westernchanfellowship.org
Website: www.westernchanfellowship.org

Retreats • Workshops and Courses • Meditation • Spiritual Help

Chinese Zen Meditation

Chan is the Chinese ancestor of Zen Buddhism. The Western Chan Fellowship is an association of lay Chan practitioners in England and Wales, but they also have connections in Europe, principally in Norway, Poland, Germany, Croatia and Switzerland. Their retreats and other activities are open equally to both Buddhists and non-Buddhists. They lead intensive meditation retreats at their main retreat centre in Wales, **Maenllwyd Retreat Centre**, and also at other meditation centres in England and Scotland. On offer are facilities for solitary, Zen, Buddhist, meditation and silent retreats. Some of the Zen meditation retreats follow closely the traditional methods of Chan teaching and practice, while others include adaptations from other Buddhist schools to match the needs of Westerners. There are Chan meditation groups meeting at various locations across the UK. The Manchester group holds day classes and group practice rather than residential retreats. The Western Chan Fellowship's intensive meditation retreats are residential and held at Maenllwyd Retreat Centre; these are detailed on their website as detailed above (follow the link for 'Events').

*'The two places where people don't smile are in churches and
health food shops'
– James of Winford Manor*

MERSEYSIDE

• •

FRESHFIELD

St Joseph's Prayer Centre   Tel: 01704 874343
Holy Spirit Prayer Community
Blundell Avenue, Freshfield
Liverpool L37 1PH
England

Retreats • Church/Temple • Spiritual Help • Venue for Hire

Christian – Roman Catholic

Only half a mile from the sea and set near National Trust land, the centre offers Ignatian retreats, Quiet Days, Alpha groups and retreats for reflection and prayer or just for relaxation. There 15 single rooms and three twin rooms. For information on retreat programme and booking, you need to apply in writing.

LIVERPOOL

Sandymount House of Prayer   Tel: 0151 9244850
16 Burbo Bank Road
Blundellsands
Liverpool L23 6TH
England

Retreats • Church/Temple

Christian – Ecumenical

Just by the seashore and available for both staying guests and for non-residential visits, Sandymount has a programme of retreats. The house can accommodate up to 15 guests.

The Cenacle
Tithbarn Grove
7 Lance Lane
Liverpool L15 6TW
England

Tel: 0151 7222271
Email: cenacleliverpool@btconnect.com

Retreats • Workshops and Courses • Church/Temple • Spiritual Help
Community Living • Vocations

Christian – Roman Catholic

The Sisters of the Cenacle offer individually directed retreats and a programme of various retreats and events. If you wish to come for a quiet time or a day of prayer and reflection, contact the sisters' retreat team.

OPEN: All year, except July, August. Everyone welcome, for the day only.
ROOMS: Non-residential.
FACILITIES: Garden, library.
SPIRITUAL HELP: Spiritual direction, personal retreat direction, meditation, prayer ministry.
GUESTS ADMITTED TO: Everywhere.
MEALS: Everyone eats together. Traditional food.
SPECIAL ACTIVITIES: Day retreats and some workshops. Leaflet available.
SITUATION: In city but quiet.
MAXIMUM STAY: As arranged.
BOOKINGS: Letter, telephone.
CHARGES: Very modest charge for the day.
ACCESS: Rail: Liverpool Lime St station. Bus: regular services from Liverpool. Car: via M62, then A5058.

PRESCOT

Loyola Hall Spirituality Centre
Warrington Road
Rainhill, Prescot
Merseyside L35 6NZ
England

Tel: 0151 4264137
Fax: 0151 4310115
Email: mail@loyolahall.co.uk
Website: www.loyolahall.co.uk

Retreats • Workshops and Courses • Church/Temple • Spiritual Help • Vegetarian Food

Christian – Roman Catholic – Ecumenical

This is a Jesuit retreat centre and that usually means some hard work on prayer, personal introspection and spiritual growth if you want to undertake an individually guided retreat. In addition to this form of retreat, there are preached ones, days of prayer and reflection, guided prayer weeks, theme retreats on icons and the Enneagram, women's retreats and special courses for those who work with young adults. The centre itself is set in a park and consists of a combination of older buildings and functional new ones. The facilities are modern and excellent. The centre has a special programme aimed at the 18–30 age group. The colour brochures available are exceptionally well designed and informative and there are details of the programme online.

OPEN: All year except Christmas week. Everyone welcome.
ROOMS: 40 single en suite room.
FACILITIES: Disabled facilities – lift and loop system provided. Conferences, garden, park, library, guest lounge, art room, exercise room, jacuzzi. Prayer rooms available.
SPIRITUAL HELP: Personal talks, group sharing on some retreats, meditation, directed study. Individually guided retreats in the tradition of St Ignatius Loyola. Courses on spiritual direction, prayer guidance.
GUESTS ADMITTED TO: Unrestricted access.
MEALS: Eaten in the guest dining rooms. Traditional food. Vegetarian and special diets.
SPECIAL ACTIVITIES: Planned programme of events, including conferences, courses on spiritual direction, lecture programme, parish retreats. Send for brochures or see online.
SITUATION: Quiet, in a village.
MAXIMUM STAY: Up to 30 days depending on programme course undertaken plus a stay of 3 months if you are doing that retreat.
BOOKINGS: Letter, telephone, fax, email, online enquiry form.
CHARGES: The rates here vary enormously because of the various lengths of each retreat from day or weekend to 3 months. You need to consult the price of each event in the programme.
ACCESS: Rail: Rainhill station. Bus: several local routes. Car: via M62 exit 7 to Prescot.

'It is because Man is able to say No that his Yes is so full of resonance'
– Paul Evdokimo

NORTHUMBERLAND

CARRSHIELD

Throssel Hole Buddhist Abbey   Tel: 01434 345204
Carrshield, Hexham   Fax: 01434 345216
Northumberland NE47 8AL   Email: gd@throssel.org.uk
England   Website: www.throssel.org.uk

Retreats • Workshops and Courses • Church/Temple • Meditation • Spiritual Help
Vegetarian Food • Community Living • Work Retreats • Vocations

Buddhist (Soto Zen tradition)

Throssel Hole is a monastery and retreat centre in the Order of Buddhist Contemplatives in the Soto Zen tradition. They have been here in northern England for some 40 years. The Serene Reflection Meditation tradition (Soto Zen) emphasises the practice of meditation, living by the Buddhist precepts, expressing compassion in daily life and training to realise one's spiritual potential. There is a clear and strict structure to daily life here in which guests are expected to take part. This ensures the continuity of monastic life for the community but also offers an invaluable opportunity to let worldly distractions fall away and to experience the benefits of mindfulness for oneself. Whether eating, working or resting, attention is given to integrating the openness, awareness and compassion of meditation into every aspect of daily life. Smaller monastic and community centres are found throughout the UK and also across many places in Europe. Visit the website *www.obcon. org* to find out more about the other groups and temples of the Order of Buddhist Contemplatives. **Highly Recommended.**

'The purpose of our lives is to be happy'
– the Dalai Lama

HARNHAM

Aruna Ratanagiri Buddhist Monastery   Tel: 01661 881612
and Kusula House   Email: www.ratanagiri.org.uk
2 Harnham Hall Cottage
Harnham, Belsay
Northumberland NE20 0HF
England

> Retreats • Workshops and Courses • Church/Temple • Meditation • Spiritual Help
> Vegetarian Food • Community Living • Work Retreats • Vocations

Buddhist (Theravada tradition)

Aruna Ratanagiri Buddhist Monastery is a Theravadin Buddhist monastery, and an adjacent lay retreat facility known as Kusala House is open to all. The frequency of retreats varies each year and for current information you need to visit the website. If you want to stay here, write to the guestmaster and include some information about yourself – for example, age, gender, background, and your interest and experience in Buddhism and meditation. Access is by car, coach or bus; there are full bus and coach details on the monastery's website (above). Visit the website *aruno.org* for information about the Dhamma teachings given at Aruna Ratanagiri. **Highly Recommended.**

HOLY ISLAND OF LINDISFARNE

Marygate House   Tel/Fax: 01289 389246
Holy Island of Lindisfarne   Email: ian@marygateho.freeserve.co.uk
Berwick-upon-Tweed   Website: www.marygatehouse.org.uk
Northumberland TD15 2SD
England

> Retreats • Church/Temple • Spiritual Help • Vegetarian Food • Work Retreats • Pets

Christian – Inter-denominational

Marygate House is situated on an island that is famous in Christian history and that remains even today a place of pilgrimage and tourism. The centre is very quiet in winter but busy and popular in the summer.

Two houses form the centre. One is Marygate House, which is the home of the small community who run the centre. This house accommodates up to 22 people for religious, educational or cultural purposes. The other house, Cambridge House, is for private retreats, study time or for a few days of peace and quiet. Please note that there is no medical care on Holy Island and that life on the island is dominated by the coming and going of the tides. It is safe only to cross the causeway for a period of about six hours, twice in every 24 hours. **Highly Recommended.**

OPEN: 4 January to 15 December. Receives everyone except children as it is a place for adult quiet retreats.

ROOMS: Marygate House: 7 rooms (1–4 beds in each). Cambridge House: 4 singles, 1 double, 1 twin. There is an annex to Cambridge House for those who require wheelchair access or who have difficulty with stairs. Bring your own towels. Warm windproof clothes are suggested.

FACILITIES: Disabled access, conferences, garden, library, guest lounge, guest telephone. **Pets are welcome** but not to come into the kitchen, dining room or library. **No medical care on the island.**

SPIRITUAL HELP: Personal talks, group sharing, spiritual direction, personal retreat direction, directed study. Quiet place set aside for prayer and there are regular prayer times. Local Roman Catholic and Anglican churches.

GUESTS ADMITTED TO: Unrestricted access.

MEALS: Everyone eats together. Traditional, wholefood, simple food. Vegetarian and special diets.

SPECIAL ACTIVITIES: None.

SITUATION: An island accessed by car when tide is low.

MAXIMUM STAY: 2 weeks.

BOOKINGS: Letter, telephone, email.

CHARGES: Donations only – suggested amount, so ask when booking. As always with donations for a retreat stay, we suggest you be as generous as you can. Currently it costs them about £30 a day for a guest – so take it from there.

ACCESS: Rail: Berwick-upon-Tweed station (14 miles away). Bus: infrequent service from Berwick-upon-Tweed. Car: via A1, 7 miles south of Berwick-upon-Tweed.

'Do not dwell in the past, do not dream of the future, concentrate the mind on the present moment'
– Buddha

The Open Gate Retreat House
Community of Aidan and Hilda
Holy Island of Lindisfarne
Berwick-upon-Tweed
Northumberland TD15 2SD
England

Tel: 01289 389222
Email:
opengate@aidanandhilda.demon.co.uk
Website: www.aidanandhilda.org

Retreats • Church/Temple • Spiritual Help • Vegetarian Food • Self-Catering Space

Christian – Celtic spirituality – Inter-denominational

The Open Gate is an old farmhouse on the island of Lindisfarne, a place of ancient spiritual history. The Guardian of the Community of Aidan and Hilda, Ray Simpson, is a leading figure in the Celtic tradition and facilitates workshops here as well as in other centres. The community's main aim in offering retreats is to allow people to reconnect with God, especially through scripture, creation and Celtic Christian spirituality. Retreat themes such as *Walking in the Steps of the Saints*, *Prayer Walking with St Cuthbert*, *St Hilda's Weekend* exemplify the way in which prayer, the saints, pilgrimage and nature are woven together by this community. Simple home cooking is offered to those staying on retreat. **Highly Recommended.**

St Cuthbert's Centre
Fiddlers Green
Holy Island of Lindisfarne
Berwick-upon-Tweed
Northumberland TD15 2RZ
England

Tel: 01289 389254
Email: centre@holyisland-stcuthbert.org
Website: www.holyisland-stcuthbert.org

Retreats • Church/Temple • Self-Catering Space • Hermitages

Christian – United Reform Church

This is a fresh and bright and modern Christian centre for church and group hire. Everyone is welcome here for a day visit, and private and guided retreats can be arranged. There are prayer walks and public worship. The programme is short but nice with subjects like *Christian Skills for Peaceful Living*. As to staying here, there is room for one person – rather in keeping with the life of St Cuthbert who was at heart, and in much of his life, a hermit by religious calling. The room available is called the Bothy and people stay here for a variety of reasons, but essentially so that they can be alone with themselves and with God. In exchange for free accommodation, a Bothy resident guest stewards the centre for five hours a day, providing an opportunity for Christian service to the many visitors who call in to browse, to pick up leaflets and to look at the various displays. This steward scheme runs from Easter to the end of October only. Alternatively, those who wish to do so can make a private retreat without stewarding the centre. A fee of about £20 for the first night and £17.50 per night thereafter is payable for the self-catering accommodation.

RIDING MILL

Shepherds Dene Retreat House   Tel: 01434 682212
Riding Mill   Fax: 01434 682311
Northumberland NE44 6AF   Email: enquiry@shepherdsdene.co.uk
England   Website: www.shepherdsdene.co.uk

Retreats • Workshops and Courses • Church/Temple • Spiritual Help • Bed and Breakfast
Vegetarian Food • Venue for Hire • Self-Catering Space • Children • Pets

Christian – Anglican – Inter-denominational

An old Victorian house tucked away behind this pretty Northumbrian village, Shepherds Dene nestles in extensive grounds with its own medieval labyrinth in the style of Chartres Cathedral. It offers a variety of Quiet Days and creative spirituality retreats, as well as space for non-guided personal retreats. Warm and homely with its own chapel, this is a centre that caters mostly for groups. However, individuals are welcome as they always try to extend hospitality or even refuge to people to recharge their batteries. The retreat house can usually accommodate an individual guest alongside other guests, but you need to check out availability with them.

WHITFIELD

Burnlaw Healing And Retreat Centre
Whitfield
Hexham
Northumberland NE47 8HF
England

Tel: 01434 345359
Email: gvs38@hotmail.com
Website: www.burnlaw.org.uk

Retreats • Workshops and Courses • Church/Temple • Spiritual Help • Vegetarian Food
Venue for Hire • Self-Catering Space • Work Retreats • Camping • Children

Baha'I

Burnlaw is a small north Pennines upland farm in an area of outstanding natural beauty. Here a community of Baha'I live and work together, specialising in sustainable lifestyle and holistic living. The centre was established to provide a space where people could realise 'the sacredness of all existence'. Hill walking, painting, dancing, singing, horticulture, conservation work are all part of the life here – and whether you are visiting for a short break, or taking part in a working holiday, there is plenty to nourish and sustain. Festivals, weddings and business groups can all be arranged here.

OPEN: Most of year. Everyone welcome.
ROOMS: Community house rooms, bunk houses for 16 people, camping.
FACILITIES: Temple, Quaker burial garden, circular meditation garden, labyrinth, lounge, meeting rooms.
SPIRITUAL HELP: Group talks.
GUESTS ADMITTED TO: Everywhere.
MEALS: Everyone eats together.
SPECIAL ACTIVITIES: Event and retreat programme.
SITUATION: Countryside.
MAXIMUM STAY: By arrangement.
BOOKINGS: Letter, telephone, email.
CHARGES: Currently: Community house rooms £12 per night without breakfast; bunk houses £10-£13; meeting rooms and group rates by request; camping adults £5 per night, children £3 per night.
ACCESS: By car is best, via A69.

'In the death of the self, lies the life of the heart'
– Iman Ja'Far Al-Sadiq

YORKSHIRE (NORTH)

AMPLEFORTH

Ampleforth Abbey and The Grange
Ampleforth
York
North Yorkshire YO6 4EN
England

Tel: 01439 766889 /
01439 766486
Fax: 01439 766755
Email: pastoral@ampleforth.org.uk
Website: www.ampleforth-hpo.org.uk

Retreats • Workshops and Courses • Church/Temple • Vegetarian Food
Community Living • Work Retreats • Vocations

Christian – Roman Catholic

All the facilities at this large and busy monastery are excellent. There are sometimes single rooms in the monastery for men, but to stay in the monastery you need to write to the guestmaster there. The course and retreat programme is extensive and Roman Catholic in spirit. A very well-known and popular place to go on retreat.

BROMPTON-BY-SAWDON

Wydale Hall and Emmaus Centre
Brompton-by-Sawdon
Scarborough
North Yorkshire YO13 9DG
England

Tel: 01723 859270
Fax: 01723 859702
Email: admin@wydale.org
Website: www.wydale.org

Retreats • Workshops and Courses • Church/Temple • Spiritual Help • Vegetarian Food
Venue for Hire • Self-Catering Space • Children

Christian – Anglican – Inter-denominational

An old house set in 14 acres with formal gardens with good views to the Yorkshire Wolds. Quiet Christian hospitality is on offer here with the purpose of trying to create a place where people can unwind, rest and perhaps draw nearer to God. The retreats and one-day workshops cover a wide range from assertiveness skills and stress management to a creative arts retreat movement, and a painting and prayer retreat.

OPEN: 9 January to 28 December. Receives men, women, young people, families, groups, non-retreatants. Children welcome.
ROOMS: 6 singles, 12 twins, 8 doubles, 5 family rooms – 32 en suite rooms in all.
FACILITIES: Disabled access, chapel, conferences, garden, library, guest lounge, bookstall, TV, payphone. Guide dogs only. Self-catering in the Emmaus Centre.
SPIRITUAL HELP: Personal talks possible.
GUESTS ADMITTED TO: Unrestricted access, except staff areas.
MEALS: Everyone eats together. Traditional food. Vegetarian and special diets.
SPECIAL ACTIVITIES: Programme of events. Send for brochure or visit their new website.
SITUATION: Quiet and in the countryside.
MAXIMUM STAY: By arrangement.
BOOKINGS: Letter, telephone, fax, email.
CHARGES: Ask for details as there are a number of rate charges.
ACCESS: Rail: Scarborough station (9 miles away). Buses: services from Scarborough stop 1 mile from Wydale. Car: Wydale Hall is 1 mile north of A170.

SCARBOROUGH

Fountains Court Holistic Health Hotel   Tel/Fax: 01723 381118
120/122 Columbus Ravine   Email: info@fountainscourt.com
Scarborough   Website: www.fountainscourt.com
North Yorkshire YO12 7QZ
England

Retreats • Workshops and Courses • Bed and Breakfast • Vegetarian Food
Alternative Therapies • Holistic Holidays

Mind Body Spirit – Non-denominational

A small neat hotel that specialises in holistic healing holidays and re-treats. While it is in an urban area with houses surrounding it, there are parks nearby for walking, and the hotel is quiet and peaceful inside. There are some 35 different therapies on offer here, as well as planned events and retreats. A Zen garden with a terrace and a jacuzzi is an unusual feature. The bedrooms are fresh and well decorated. Online booking is available.

'To say that I am made in the image of God is to say that love is
the reason for my existence, for God is love'
– Thomas Merton

SKIPTON

Parcevall Hall	Tel: 01756 720213
Skyreholme Lane	Fax: 01756 720656
Appletreewick, Skipton	Email: parcevall@bradford.anglican.org
North Yorkshire BD23 6DG	Website:
England	www.parcevall.bradford.anglican.org

Retreats • Workshops and Courses • Church/Temple • Spiritual Help • Vegetarian Food
Venue for Hire • Work Retreats • Hermitages

Christian – Anglican – Ecumenical

This is an Elizabethan manor house with grand views in a super setting and whose interior is filled with oak and atmosphere. Legends and history abound; the nine acres of garden are said to have been admired by the late Queen Mary. It is a traditional place for either a private retreat or participation in the programme of events, which includes many parish-group retreats but also retreats with such titles as *The Spirituality of Julian of Norwich*, *Painting and Prayer* and *Spring Walkers' Weekend Retreat*.

OPEN: All year except Christmas period. Everyone welcome.
ROOMS: 7 singles, 8 twins, 1 double, 1 triple.
FACILITIES: Poustinia, chapel, conferences, garden, library, guest lounge, TV.
SPIRITUAL HELP: Personal talks, spiritual direction, personal retreat direction.
GUESTS ADMITTED TO: Everywhere, including chapel services.
MEALS: Everyone eats together. Professionally cooked traditional food with provision for vegetarian and special diets by prior arrangement.
SPECIAL ACTIVITIES: Programme of events. Send for brochure or visit the website for the programme.
SITUATION: Very quiet, in the countryside.
MAXIMUM STAY: 1 week.
BOOKINGS: Letter, telephone, fax, email, online contact form.
CHARGES: Currently, the retreats in the programme run from £12 for day visitors to £300 for some of the longer retreats. Check the programme first for current retreats. Please enquire for 24-hour full-board rates for a personal retreat.
ACCESS: Rail: Skipton station, then taxi. Car: via A65, 9 miles north of Skipton.

SWAINBY

The Sanctuary   Tel: 01642 700782
White Gables, 66 High Street   Email: hintja@aol.com
Swainby, Northallerton
North Yorkshire DL6 3DG
England

Retreats

Christian

A non-residential and peaceful place with a lovely garden and nice views. It is available for personal retreats and small groups. There is a diverse programme of themed retreats on Saturdays, which include painting and prayer, *Lectio Divina* and journalling. Member of the Quiet Garden Trust.

TADCASTER

The Peace Centre   Tel: 01937 833752
Inholmes, Leeds Road   Fax: 01937 530440
Tadcaster   Email: theguardian@thepeacecentre.co.uk
North Yorkshire LS24 9LP   Website: www.thepeacecentre.co.uk
England

Retreats • Workshops and Courses • Meditation • Spiritual Help • Vegetarian Food
Self-Catering Space

Christian – Anglican

The Peace Centre is part of a large private house set in gardens. They are developing a continuing and extending healing and caring service as well as the offering of retreats to groups and individuals. When they discover a real community need, they try to help – for example, in their development of a luncheon club for the elderly. We look forward to hearing more in the future of the good work of the Peace Centre.

OPEN: Most of year. Everyone welcome, including groups.
ROOMS: 2 singles, 4 twins – all en suite. In addition, 4 singles, 1 double (not en suite).
FACILITIES: Dining and sitting rooms, meditation room, gardens and large grounds, swimming pool in summer, walking meditation garden.
SPIRITUAL HELP: Personal talks on spiritual and holistic health issues. The Guardian of the Peace Centre is a chartered psychologist.

GUESTS ADMITTED TO: Everywhere.
MEALS: Self-catering. Good large kitchen
SPECIAL ACTIVITIES: Groups and individuals for Quiet Days and private retreats.
SITUATION: Near town, in countryside.
MAXIMUM STAY: By arrangement.
BOOKINGS: Letter, telephone, email.
CHARGES: Please enquire when booking.
ACCESS: Rail: Ulleskelf (5 miles away) and Wetherby station (9 miles away). Bus: local services stop a mile away in Tadcaster. Car: via A64. Ask for details when booking.

THIRSK

Holy Rood House Centre for   Tel: 01845 522580
Health and Pastoral Care   Email: enquiries@holyroodhouse.org.uk
10 Sowerby Road   Website: www.holyroodhouse.org.uk
Thirsk
North Yorkshire YO7 1HX
England

Retreats • Workshops and Courses • Meditation • Spiritual Help • Vegetarian Food
Venue for Hire • Children • Pets

Christian – Ecumenical – Residential Therapeutic Centre

This special place welcomes people of all ages and backgrounds, who come on retreat here for many different reasons. Holy Rood House follows a gentle Christian ethos and offers counselling, psychotherapy and a holistic approach to well-being. Reflection, exploration and discovery, working towards justice, peace and ecological awareness are some of the core aims here. They have an excellent reputation for home cooking and all diets can be accommodated. There is a policy that no one should ever feel unable to stay because of cost. This is also the home of the Centre for the Study of Theology and Health, which offers Easter retreats, art exhibitions and a summer school, as well as women's spirituality, research and theological courses. Thorpe House, adjacent to Holy Rood, provides excellent conference facilities for day or residential groups. **Highly Recommended.**

OPEN: All year, occasional exceptions. Welcomes everyone – all ages and backgrounds. Children and pets welcome.
ROOMS: 6 singles, 2 doubles, 6 twins.
FACILITIES: Disabled access – ground-floor room and chair lift to first floor. Chapel and garden chapel, creative gardens with smallholding, libraries, guest lounges, TV.
SPIRITUAL HELP: Ministry of healing, personal retreat, spiritual direction, daily

prayer life, meditation, creative liturgies. Art therapy, professional counselling and psychotherapy, drama therapy, body therapies, relaxation and stress management, theology courses and women's spirituality courses.

MEALS: Everyone eats together. Good wholesome cooking. Vegetarian and special diets.

SPECIAL ACTIVITIES: Planned programme of events and courses. Send for brochure or see online. Occasional self-catering holidays and annual events.

SITUATION: Quiet village location; close to Thirsk market town centre, public swimming pool, cinema and river walks.

MAXIMUM STAY: 3 weeks.

BOOKINGS: Letter, telephone (Monday to Friday), email. Printable booking form on the website.

CHARGES: Please enquire when booking. Suggested donation basis for having professional therapy. Courses offered with suggested donation depends on the nature of the retreat or event.

ACCESS: Good train and coach connections, with pick-up by arrangement. Rail: Thirsk station (1.5 miles away). Bus: local routes serve Thirsk. Car: via A61 to B1448, or A19 and A168.

WHITBY

Sneaton Castle Centre	Tel: 01943 600051
Whitby	Fax: 01947 603490
North Yorkshire YO21 3QN	Email: sneaton@globalnet.co.uk
England	Website: www.sneatoncastle.co.uk

Retreats • Workshops and Courses • Church/Temple • Spiritual Help • Bed and Breakfast
Vegetarian Food • Venue for Hire • Community Living • Vocations • Children

Christian – Anglican

A huge and imposing place with room for 100 guests, Sneaton Castle Centre is nevertheless peaceful and a picturesque location providing Christian venues for conferences, B&B, music workshops and personal retreats. It is situated in beautiful and extensive grounds adjacent to St Hilda's Priory, which is the Mother House of the Order of the Holy Paraclete, an Anglican religious community. Although Sneaton Castle Centre specialises in group accommodation, it also provides space for families or individuals who just want to come for a break. In summary, the situation, garden and grounds and facilities here are first-rate.

OPEN: All year but Christmas weeks. Receives everyone.

ROOMS: They have rooms to accommodate 100 people – many are en suite and there are two rooms especially adapted for disabled.

FACILITIES: Disabled access, church, chapel, conferences, garden, guest lounges, TV. There is a loop system in one of the chapels and some of the conference rooms.

SPIRITUAL HELP: Personal talks if needed.
GUESTS ADMITTED TO: Public rooms, church and chapel.
MEALS: Everyone eats together. Vegetarian and special diets.
SPECIAL ACTIVITIES: A short event programme over the year.
SITUATION: Walking distance of the picturesque seaside town of Whitby and the entrance way to the wonderful moors.
BOOKINGS: Letter, telephone, email.
CHARGES: There is an excellent and detailed rates schedule on their website, explaining the different charges from residential rates to those for school groups.
ACCESS: Train: Scarborough station (20 miles away). Bus/coach: regular services to and from Whitby. Car: via A19, then A171 or A19 and A64 . Clear directions are on the website.

St Hilda's Priory	Tel: 01947 602079
Sneaton Castle	Fax: 01947 820854
Whitby	Email: ohppriorywhitby@btinternet.com
North Yorkshire YO21 3QN	
England	

Retreats • Church/Temple • Vegetarian • Community Living • Work Retreats • Vocations

Christian – Anglican

The priory itself is not a retreat house as such but the home of the sisters of the international Order of the Holy Paraclete. Central to the Order's life in all its houses are the Divine Office and Eucharist, and a strong emphasis on corporate activity. Guests come for a quiet retreat on an individual basis and there is no structured programme other than the daily pattern of worship.

OPEN: Open all year except 3 weeks in August. Everyone welcome.
ROOMS: 6 singles, 2 doubles.
FACILITIES: Disabled access, garden, library, guest lounge.
SPIRITUAL HELP: Personal talks may be available.
GUESTS ADMITTED TO: Chapel, refectory.
MEALS: Main meals taken together. Vegetarian and special diets.
SPECIAL ACTIVITIES: None.
SITUATION: In the countryside, edge of town and near national park.
MAXIMUM STAY: 1 week.
BOOKINGS: Letter, telephone, email.
CHARGES: Suggested donations.
ACCESS: See previous details for Sneaton Castle.

St Oswald's Pastoral Centre
Woodlands Drive
Sleights, Whitby
North Yorkshire YO21 1RY
England

Tel: 01947 810496
Email: ohpstos@globalnet.co.uk
Website: www.stoswaldspastoralcentre.co.uk

> Retreats • Church/Temple • Spiritual Help • Vegetarian Food • Self-Catering Space
> Community Living • Vocations

Christian – Anglican

St Oswald's Pastoral Centre is a small complex of buildings set in the wonderful surroundings of the North Yorkshire Moors. The centre is run by the Anglican Order of the Holy Paraclete and several sisters live at the centre. The purpose of the centre is to offer private and conducted retreats, as well as quiet times for rest or study. The sisters extend a warm welcome to small groups or individuals. It is a happy place to stay.

OPEN: All year except Christmas and August; normally closed Sunday afternoon to late Monday afternoon. Everyone welcome.
ROOMS: 10 singles, 3 twins; also 3 self-contained, self-catering 1-bed apartments are available and suitable for extended stays.
FACILITIES: Chapel, garden, library, guest lounge.
SPIRITUAL HELP: Personal talks, meditation, group sharing, directed study.
GUESTS ADMITTED TO: Chapel. Unrestricted access except to community quarters.
MEALS: Everyone eats together. Traditional simple food. Vegetarian and special diets catered within reason.
SPECIAL ACTIVITIES: Planned programme of events. Send for the brochure or see online.
SITUATION: Very quiet, in the countryside near to the moors.
MAXIMUM STAY: 1 week.
BOOKINGS: Letter, telephone (mornings best), email.
CHARGES: By donation. Current suggestions for private retreats: weekend £70, weekday (two nights) £55 and thereafter £40 per 24 hours; Cuthbert Lodge £42 per 24 hours, per person. For conducted retreats an additional donation is suggested: open retreat about £5 a day; individual guided retreat about £9 a day.
ACCESS: Rail: Sleights station (less than a mile away); York or Scarborough station and then coach/bus to Whitby. Bus: services run from Whitby. Car: via A169. Visit the website for more detailed travel directions.

YORK

St Bede's Pastoral Centre   Tel: 01904 464900
17 Blossom Street   Email: info@stbedes.org.uk
York   Website: www.stbedes.org.uk
North Yorkshire YO24 1AQ
England

The Bar Convent   Tel: 01904 643238
17 Blossom Street   Fax: 01904 631792
York   Email: info@bar-convent.org.uk
North Yorkshire YO24 1AQ   Website: www.bar-convent.org.uk
England

> Retreats • Workshops and Courses • Church/Temple • Meditation • Spiritual Help
> Bed and Breakfast • Vegetarian Food • Children

Christian – Roman Catholic

St Bede's was founded in 1987 as a joint venture by the Middlesborough
Diocese and the Ampleforth monks. It is a base for ecumenical work
right in the heart of York and next door to the historic Bar Convent. St
Bede's is a lovely place with a museum, café, shop and gallery around
a central courtyard. There is a pretty, small garden at the rear that is
very pleasant. There are events, exhibitions and talks throughout the
year, including Julian meetings, Bible study, and prayer and reflection
courses. It is a friendly and welcoming place in the heart of a great and
hospitable city. Bar Convent has B&B accommodation and a popular
café for other meals. There are a chapel and a garden – it is a happy,
busy place with a welcoming atmosphere.

OPEN: All year except Christmas. Receives everyone. Children welcome.
ROOMS: Available at the Bar Convent are 18 guest bedrooms situated on 3 floors for
a maximum of 30 guests: 9 singles, 3 twins (1 en suite), 2 doubles (1 en suite) and 1
family room (1 en suite).
FACILITIES: Chapel, disabled access, conferences, garden, library, 2 guest lounges,
TV, payphone, museum, shop, exhibition hall, café.
SPIRITUAL HELP: Spiritual direction possible.
GUESTS ADMITTED TO: Chapel and areas open to the public..
MEALS: B&B at Bar Convent if you are staying over. Otherwise, food at the Bar
Convent café, which is open to everyone.
SPECIAL ACTIVITIES: Programme of events and courses at St Bede's. Send for
brochure and see online.
SITUATION: Busy and in the city, but once inside quite peaceful.

MAXIMUM STAY: Day only at St Bede's; B&B at Bar Convent.
BOOKINGS: Letter, telephone, email (easiest and best method of contact for both places).
CHARGES: Ask for current charges for B&B at Bar Convent. St Bede's events and retreats programme has prices per event.
ACCESS: Rail: York station, which is 5 minutes' walk away. Bus/coach: several routes serve York. Car: easily accessible on the south-west side of York. Detailed directions are on the website.

YORKSHIRE (SOUTH)

DONCASTER

Hexthorpe Manor   Tel: 01302 310133
Centre for Health and Pastoral Care   Email:
Old Hexthorpe, Doncaster   hexthorpe.manor@yahoo.co.uk
South Yorkshire DN4 0HY   Website:
England   www.holyroodhouse.freeuk.com/hexthp.html

Open spirituality – Ecumenical – Inter-denominational

'Are you 18–30 years old? Been through a rough time? Could do with being part of a community following recovery from trauma or illness?' Hexthorpe Manor believes they may be the right place for you, providing a new and supportive way of living. Guests are invited to live at the Manor to build their skills and confidence, to prepare for independent living. Hexthorpe Manor is an extension of the work of **Holy Rood House**, a therapeutic centre in Thirsk (see previous North Yorkshire section). With a gentle Christian ethos and open and inclusive policy, Hexthorpe Manor offers short residential semi-self-catering retreats, day groups and long-term residential community space for young adults following recovery from trauma or illness. A professional counselling service is available. Situated a few minutes' taxi ride from Doncaster station, visitors are taken through an inner-city area to this lovely house overlooking parkland and close to the River Don. This place provides a warm welcome from a community of hospitality, and also offers inclusive church, theological reflection, creative arts and spiritual direction. Visitors needing residential therapeutic support will be referred to Holy Rood House, just an hour away. If you think this place could be right for you, then take a retreat with them – it could change your life.

SHEFFIELD

The Listen Centre
Glen Mount, Rivelin Glen
Sheffield
South Yorkshire S6 5SE
England

Tel: 0114 2517679 / 07515 399981
Email: thelistencentre@aol.com /
adrianscott@mac.com /
wilmascott@mac.com
Website: www.thelistencentre.com

Retreats • Workshops and Courses • Spiritual Help • Vegetarian Food • Venue for Hire
Self-Catering Space • Hermitages

Christian

The Listen Centre is secluded and peaceful yet only 20 minutes or so from the centre of the city. This is also a family home, so the atmosphere is warm but with some boundaries (visits are by arrangement only). There is a well-stocked spirituality and theology library open to guests. Food is simple and home cooked. Retreat space for individuals is to enable them to make a silent and/or guided retreat. Facilities comprise an en suite single room and private chapel, with a small seminar room for small group Quiet Days and workshops. A hermitage is available for those who wish to make a more rugged retreat. In addition to this, the Listen Centre has a four-bedroomed cottage in the Peak District village of Castleton (30 minutes' drive from the Listen Centre), available for small group retreats and gatherings.

Whirlow Grange Conference Centre
Eccleshall Road South
Sheffield
South Yorkshire S11 9PZ
England

Tel: 0114 2363173
Fax: 0114 2620717
Email: info@whirlowgrange.co.uk
Website: www.whirlowgrange.co.uk

Retreats • Workshops and Courses • Church/Temple • Spiritual Help • Vegetarian Food
Venue for Hire • Children

Christian – Anglican

The centre occupies a grey-stone house on a rise on the outskirts of Sheffield, near Peak District beauty spots. The place is a little institutional, but it has very comfortable rooms and modern facilities. There are various retreats on offer with a wide range of themes, for example healing seminars, Christmas, Myers-Briggs work, sacred-dance group weekends and Franciscan directed retreats. The centre's programme has a strong focus on modern as well as traditional core spirituality issues.

OPEN: All year. Receives men, women, young people, families, groups, non-retreatants. Children welcome.
ROOMS: 21 singles, 7 twin, 2 doubles. One of the singles is for the disabled. All rooms en suite.
FACILITIES: Disabled access, chapel, conferences for day groups up to 120 people, garden, bookstall, library, guest lounge, TV.
SPIRITUAL HELP: Group sharing. Personal talks and directed study are possible by prior arrangement.
GUESTS ADMITTED TO: Chapel. Unrestricted access.
MEALS: Taken in guest house. Professionally prepared traditional food. Special menus for events and functions possible by arrangement. Vegetarian and special diets catered for.
SPECIAL ACTIVITIES: Planned programme of events. Send for brochure or see online.
SITUATION: Quiet and on the outskirts of the city. Peak District National Park within easy reach.
MAXIMUM STAY: Open.
BOOKINGS: Letter, telephone, fax, email, online booking form.
CHARGES: On application.
ACCESS: Rail: Sheffield station. Bus: regular services from Sheffield Interchange. Car: easily accessible via M1 exit 29 and A617, M1 exit 33 and A630, and via A625.

YORKSHIRE (EAST)

KINGSTON-UPON-HULL

The Endsleigh Centre
481 Beverley Road
Kingston-upon-Hull
East Yorkshire HU6 7LJ
England

Tel: 01482 342779
Fax: 01482 448859
Email: endsleigh@endsleigh.karoo.co.uk
Website: www.endsleighcentre.org.uk

Retreats • Workshops and Courses • Church/Temple • Spiritual Help • Bed and Breakfast
Vegetarian Food • Venue for Hire • Children

Christian – Roman Catholic – Ecumenical

This a large imposing building with two chapels and a warm welcome for both individual retreats and groups. There is a full programme of courses and seminars and they also offer Ignatian guided retreats.

OPEN: Most of the year. Everyone welcome.
ROOMS: 27 comfortable singles, 3 en suite doubles, 3 en suite twins. 1 suite of a sitting room with TV and separate en suite bedroom.
FACILITIES: Disabled access – a lift is available between all floors. Large chapel (seats 400), smaller chapel (seats 30), prayer room, main hall (200 guests), bridge room, function room (50–70 guests), garden lounge, gardens, 2 smaller meeting rooms (12–20 guests), dining room. Lots of facilities and space for groups and conferences.
SPIRITUAL HELP: Chapel, guided retreats.
GUESTS ADMITTED TO: Chapels, all guest and public areas.
MEALS: Full board and B&B available. Traditional food. Vegetarian and special diets catered with prior notice. Special menus possible for special occasions such as weddings and family celebrations.
SPECIAL ACTIVITIES: Summer and Advent retreat.
SITUATION: Idyllic situation within 10 minutes' drive from the city.
MAXIMUM STAY: By arrangement.
BOOKINGS: Telephone, fax, email.
CHARGES: B&B at very reasonable prices from £30 per person. Call or visit the website for retreat charges, as well as Ignatian retreats, individual stays and group conferences or courses.
ACCESS: Easily accessible from Hull. Rail/coach: Hull Paragon Interchange (2 miles away). Bus: several services from Hull. Car: 10 minutes from Hull, on A1079.

POCKLINGTON

Madhyamaka Kadampa Buddhist Centre
Kilnwick Percy Hall
Pocklington
East Yorkshire YO42 1UF
England

Tel: 01759 304832
Fax: 01759 305962
Email: info@madhyamaka.org
Website: www.madhyamaka.org

Retreats • Workshops and Courses • Church/Temple • Meditation • Spiritual Help
Bed and Breakfast • Vegetarian Food • Community Living • Work Retreats
Vocations • Children

Buddhist (Kadampa tradition)

The centre is located in a very large and beautiful Georgian country mansion built in 1784. Its aim is to preserve and promote the teachings and traditions of Buddhism. There is a large Kadampa Buddhist community here, ranging in age from 20 to 70 years, who regard this as their home. Some are ordained and all of them work and study together. Many are outstanding Buddhist teachers. There are group discussions, weekend and day courses throughout the year, plus a summer school. Some of the retreat courses have great titles such as *The Hitchhiker's Guide to the Mind*. But, make no mistake, Madhyamaka Kadampa

Buddhist Centre is a serious spirituality place. Courses are on offer for beginners and those who are able to do more in-depth teachings. If you would like to sample life in the community, they offer working retreats for a week's stay. They also have a new B&B place called the Wolds Retreat. **Highly Recommended.**

OPEN: All year. Everyone welcome, including children.
ROOMS: Doubles, dormitories, camping.
FACILITIES: Shrine room, camping, garden, library, guest lounge, payphone.
SPIRITUAL HELP: Meditation, directed study, spiritual direction.
GUESTS ADMITTED TO: Unrestricted access, shrine room, work of community.
MEALS: Everyone eats together. Vegetarian.
SPECIAL ACTIVITIES: There is a special programme, including working holidays. Send for brochure or see online.
SITUATION: Quiet, in the countryside.
MAXIMUM STAY: Open.
BOOKINGS: Letter, telephone, fax, email, online booking available.
CHARGES: There are various suggested donations for classes, but they are modest. Visit the website for the costs of the various courses and retreats.
ACCESS: Rail: York station (10 miles away). Bus: infrequent services run from York. Car: Madhyamaka Centre is on the B1246, about 1.5 miles outside Pocklington, which is off the A1079. Ask for directions when you book; a map is online on their website.

YORKSHIRE (WEST)

HALIFAX

Stod Fold Barn
Ogden
Halifax
West Yorkshire HX2 8XL
England

Tel: 01422 244854
Email: stodfold@yahoo.co.uk
Website: www.stodfold.co.uk

Retreats • Vegetarian Food • Venue for Hire • Self-Catering Space • Children

Christian – Open spirituality

A lovely old place right on the edge of the moors, which has hosted writers' circles, meditation groups, family holidays, Christian prayer groups, theatre troupes, girl guides and many others. There is space for creative activities and workshop courses. It is a good venue for small groups wanting to run their own retreat or for a Quiet Day together.

This is a place for those who find living in simplicity to their taste and helpful to their spirituality. A separate space for reading, meditation or prayer has been created in the nearby pigeon loft.

OPEN: All year but busy in summer. Everyone welcome.
ROOMS: 3 bedrooms, sleeping 9 people. 1 single and 1 double futons available without bedding.
FACILITIES: Main barn with kitchen. Limited parking, so travel sharing suggested.
SPIRITUAL HELP: None.
GUESTS ADMITTED TO: All grounds and fields and guest areas around barn.
MEALS: Self-catering.
SPECIAL ACTIVITIES: None; groups organise themselves.
SITUATION: Countryside.
MAXIMUM STAY: By arrangement.
BOOKINGS: Letter, telephone, email (best method).
CHARGES: Current rates for 9 people: first night/23 hrs with own sleeping bags £78, subsequent nights £62; per week £400. Extras: bedding per person £4; towel per person £1. Use of room and facilities only £40 (10:00–17:00).
ACCESS: Stod Fold is only 4 miles from Halifax, 7 miles from Bradford. Rail: Halifax station. Bus: services from Halifax stop a mile away in Illingworth. Car: via A629.

HEPWORTH

Foster Place Retreat House   Tel: 01484 688680
Hepworth
Holmfirth
West Yorkshire HD9 7TN
England

Retreats

Christian

Foster Place Retreat House is a large 400-year-old farmhouse and converted barn nested among trees. It has a library specialising in the history of spirituality, whether from a psychological perspective or a religious one. Foster Place offers a programme of one-day events and a series of ongoing reading and study groups, all with the aim of radical questioning and learning. They hold a Learning to Listen programme and do specialised meetings on the work and philosophy of René Girard. A quiet Eucharist is held from time to time.

ILKLEY

Briery Retreat Centre
38 Victoria Avenue
Ilkley
West Yorkshire LS29 9BW
England

Tel: 01943 607287
Fax: 01943 604449
Email: srscp@aol.com
Website: www.briery.org.uk

Retreats • Workshops and Courses • Church/Temple • Spiritual Help • Vegetarian Food
Venue for Hire • Self-Catering Space • Community Living • Vocations

Christian – Roman Catholic

The Briery Retreat Team are Sisters of the Cross and Passion and their programme is firmly spiritually based in such traditions as the Rosary, preached retreats and transformation retreats.

OPEN: All year except Easter Week and over Christmas and New Year. Receives men, women, young people over 18 years and groups.
ROOMS: 23 singles, 4 twins including some en suite, 1 flat. Self-catering cottage.
FACILITIES: Limited disabled facilities. Conferences, garden, guest lounge, TV, payphone.
SPIRITUAL HELP: Personal talks, meditation, spiritual direction, group sharing, Ignation guided retreat (IGR), personal retreat direction.
GUESTS ADMITTED TO: Unrestricted access.
MEALS: Everyone eats together. Traditional food.
SPECIAL ACTIVITIES: Planned programme of events. Send for the brochure or visit the website for description of retreats on offer.
SITUATION: 10 minutes' walk from Ilkley town but in countryside and surrounded by Ilkley Moor.
MAXIMUM STAY: 10 days.
BOOKINGS: Letter, telephone, fax, email.
CHARGES: While subject to your personal circumstances, the suggested offerings are: full board per day £50; 6-day preached retreat and IGRs £330; themed weekend £105; Day of Reflection £20. Day groups can have coffee, lunch and tea for £12.
ACCESS: Rail: Ilkley station (1 mile away). Bus: regular services from Keighley, Skipton, Leeds and Bradford. Then it's a 15-minute walk or a taxi ride to Briery. Car: via A65.

'Hospitality has to be total. It is first and foremost of a practical kind. The ideal to strive for, however, is hospitality of the heart'
– Catherine de Hueck Doherty

LEEDS

Hinsley Hall
62 Headingley Lane
Leeds
West Yorkshire LS6 2BX
England

Tel: 0113 2618000
Fax: 0113 2242406
Email: info@hinsley-hall.co.uk
Website: www.hinsley-hall.co.uk

Retreats • Church/Temple • Vegetarian Food • Organic Food • Venue for Hire

Christian – Roman Catholic

A very imposing place with any number of very comfortable, bright, modern, high-standard rooms and facilities. There are a lovely chapel, a library and a bookshop. The chapel has continuous circle seating, arranged round the altar for praying and celebrating together, which we liked. The Yorkshire Dales are within easy reach. If you want a silent, more solitary place, then Hinsley Hall is probably not for you – but the facilities are excellent and the chapel and grounds are there for prayer and meditative walking.

MIRFIELD

House of the Resurrection
Stocksbank Road
Mirfield
West Yorkshire WF14 0BN
England

Tel: 01924 494318
Fax: 01924 490489
Email: guestmaster@mirfield.org.uk /
ogartside@mirfield.org.uk
(Guest Brother)
Website: www.mirfieldcommunity.org.uk

Retreats • Church/Temple • Spiritual Help • Bed and Breakfast • Vegetarian Food
Community Living • Work Retreats • Vocations

Christian – Anglican

Here is a famous community, which finds its roots in the monastic tradition of the Christian Church – a tradition concerned with the quest for God in prayer and worship in the common life and in work and service. The church, the chapel and the buildings are splendid. There is a good programme of courses, retreats and events for clergy, individuals, and group.

OPEN: All year except July. Everyone welcome, including groups.
ROOMS: 20 singles, 2 doubles.
FACILITIES: Chapel, park, library, guest lounge.
SPIRITUAL HELP: Personal talks, spiritual direction, personal retreat direction, directed study. All chapel services are open to the public.
GUESTS ADMITTED TO: Unrestricted access.
MEALS: Everyone eats together either with the community or in the new refectory. Traditional food. Vegetarian.
SPECIAL ACTIVITIES: Planned programme and details of retreats at other houses, including Hemingford Grey in Huntingdonshire. Visit the website for more details.
SITUATION: Quiet in countryside.
MAXIMUM STAY: 2 weeks.
BOOKINGS: Letter, telephone, fax, email, online enquiry form (best method).
CHARGES: Suggested donations: weekend retreat £115; Bank Holiday retreat £140; Monday–Friday (4 nights, usually for priests) £140. If you cannot afford this level of donation, then please discuss it with the Guest Brother.
ACCESS: Rail: Wakefield Westgate station. Coach: Sheffield to Dewsbury. Bus: local services run through Mirfield. Car: M1 exit 40 or M62 exit 25; then A644.

'India will teach the West the tolerance and gentleness of the mature mind, the quiet content of the unacquisitive soul, the calm of the understanding spirit and a unifying, pacifying love for all living things'
– Will Durrant

WALES

CLWYD

CORWEN

Vajraloka Buddhist Meditation Centre	Tel: 01490 460406
Tyn-y-Ddol, Treddol	Email: info@vajraloka.com
Corwen	Website: www.vajraloka.org
Denbighshire LL21 0EN	
Wales	

Retreats • Workshops and Courses • Church/Temple • Meditation • Spiritual Help
Vegetarian Food • Community Living • Vocations • Hermitages

Buddhist – Friends of the Western Buddhist Order (FWBO)

Vajraloka is a well-established and efficiently run Buddhist intense meditation centre whose purpose is to provide facilities for the practice of such meditation. There are retreats suitable for those who have been practising meditation for at least three months, retreats for experienced meditators, and special retreats for those with a beginner's level of experience. The centre is set in the beautiful countryside of north Wales and it is a very peaceful place. There are facilities for solitary retreats. **Highly Recommended.**

'A nation that continues year after year to spend more money on military defence than on programs of social uplift is approaching spiritual doom'
– Martin Luther King, Jr

HAWARDEN

St Deiniol's Library
Church Lane
Hawarden
Flintshire CH5 3DF
Wales

Tel: 01244 532350
Fax: 01244 520643
Email: enquiries@st-deiniols.org
Website: www.st-deiniols.com

> Workshops and Courses • Church/Temple • Bed and Breakfast • Vegetarian Food
> Venue for Hire • Work Retreats

Christian – Ecumenical – Open spirituality

One of Britain's finest residential libraries, with 250,000 texts, St Deiniol's is unique. This outstanding library attracts scholars and others from around the world, and it also offers bed and board in beautiful surroundings, and various interesting talks and courses. This is a particular place, but if it seems right for you, then it could be the ideal retreat. **Highly Recommended.**

PANTASAPH

Franciscan Friary
Monastery Road
Pantasaph, Holywell
Flintshire CH8 8PE
Wales

Tel: 01352 711053
Email: pantasaph@gmail.com
Website: www.pantasaph.org.uk

> Retreats • Workshops and Courses • Church/Temple • Spiritual Help
> Self-Catering Space • Community Living • Work Retreats • Vocations • Children

Christian – Roman Catholic – Franciscan

Preached retreats are held here, as well a programme of various retreats. The Pantasaph Seekers' Programme at the Seekers' Centre runs a series of events for people who are interested in Catholic spirituality but who are not necessarily members of the Church. There is plenty of space for relaxation and wandering around the friary grounds, where there is a rosary walk. Other spiritual facilities include confession, accompanied prayer, and, most importantly, Mass.

OPEN: Most of the year, usually closed in January for the month. Receives men, women, families, groups.

ROOMS: More than enough rooms: 24 singles, 2 twins and a 6-bedroom holiday house.

FACILITIES: Garden, library, guest lounge, chapel, St Pio's Shrine, St David's Church.

SPIRITUAL HELP: Personal talks, preached retreats, RC confession, Mass.

GUESTS ADMITTED TO: Chapel, choir, church.

MEALS: Everyone eats together in Pantasaph Retreat Centre. DIY facilities. Traditional food.

SPECIAL ACTIVITIES: Planned programme of retreats and events.

SITUATION: Quiet.

MAXIMUM STAY: By arrangement.

BOOKINGS: Letter, telephone, email.

CHARGES: Suggested donations per person per night: public retreat £40; private retreat £35. Visit the website for other suggested donations or charges depending on the programme.

ACCESS: Rail/coach: services stop at Flint, which is 7.5 miles away; pick-up possible if arranged in advance. Car: via A56.

TREMEIRCHION

St Beuno's Ignatian Spiritual Centre	Tel: 01745 583444
St Asaph	Fax: 01745 584151
Tremeirchion	Email: info@beunos.com
Denbighshire LL17 0AS	Website: www.beunos.com
Wales	

Retreats • Workshops and Courses • Church/Temple • Spiritual Help
Vegetarian Food • Vocations

Christian – Roman Catholic

This is a leading Jesuit centre of spirituality for the teaching and study of the spiritual exercises of St Ignatius Loyola for Christians from all over the world. These famous exercises are a series of scripture-based, Christ-centred meditations and contemplation, designed to help each retreatant to discover his or her hidden self. There are courses designed to last six or eight days, others which are given in eight-day periods over three months, and the full course of spiritual exercises involving a continuous period of some 30 days. The Ignatian exercises are among the most famous and rigorous of all spiritual retreats. You should first read about this form of retreat and perhaps discuss it with your spiritual adviser or priest before deciding to go. This is a place for a serious religious retreat in seeking God. **Highly Recommended.**

OPEN: All year except January. Everyone welcome.
ROOMS: 48 singles, 1 twin – 3 rooms only are en suite.
FACILITIES: Limited disabled access, garden, library.
SPIRITUAL HELP: Meditation, one-to-one retreats, 3-month courses in apostolic spirituality for Christians, 30-day retreats, 2-month training courses.
GUESTS ADMITTED TO: Unrestricted access.
MEALS: Everyone eats together. Traditional food. Vegetarian and special diets catered for.
SPECIAL ACTIVITIES: Send for brochure that explains.
SITUATION: Very quiet in the countryside.
MAXIMUM STAY: The 3-month course.
BOOKINGS: Letter, telephone, fax, email. Downloadable booking from.
CHARGES: Invited offerings of about £410 for a 7-day retreat but check the website as the offerings depend on the length and kind of retreat.
ACCESS: Rail: Rhyl station (7 miles away). Bus: services run from Rhyl. Car: via A56.

DYFED

• •

FISHGUARD

Fflad-y-Brenin Retreat Centre	Tel: 01348 881182
Pontfaen	Email: info@ffald-y-brenin.co.uk
Fishguard	Website: www.ffald-y-brenin.org
Pembrokeshire SA65 9UA	
Wales	

Retreats • Workshops and Courses • Church/Temple • Spiritual Help • Vegetarian Food
Organic Food • Community Living • Vocations • Camping • Children

Christian

At its heart, Ffald-y-Brenin is a committed Christian House of Prayer. Everything that happens is soaked in prayer. Guests are welcome to join with the resident community and welcome Jesus into their lives during the three set prayer times each day. A warm welcome is given to everyone: 'individuals, families, groups of friends, church leaders, house groups, church groups of various sorts; art groups, study groups, youth groups; those searching to discover the reality of God revealed in Jesus.' This retreat centre is truly green. They have won, among other awards: the Prince of Wales award for the sensitive development of an uplands farm into a Christian Retreat Centre; the Templeton Project Trust prize; the Pembrokeshire Coast National Park annual project award for the planting and development of a wood. At the Centre they sow wild flowers and produce organic meat, eggs and vegetables. **Highly Recommended.**

OPEN: Most of the year and everyone is welcome, but please note that at this particular Christian Retreat Centre, they do not accommodate any alternative religious worship or practices.

ROOMS: Simple, comfortable, very recently refurbished accommodation for groups, families and individuals: 34 beds plus some camping space. Kitchens are well equipped. Duvets, pillows and blankets are provided. An old stone cottage across the valley is also available, built in a similar style to the main centre. It has 2 bedrooms and a galleried bedroom.

FACILITIES: Common room, beehive chapel, library area, prayer room, meeting rooms, vestry a few minutes away (seats 120), barbeque facilities, gardens (plus prayer garden being developed), walks, grounds. Note that pets are not allowed and smoking outside the buildings only.

SPIRITUAL HELP: Prayer, chapel.

GUESTS ADMITTED TO: Almost everywhere.

MEALS: Organic mostly and local or home produced. Vegetarian served. Please ask when booking.

SPECIAL ACTIVITIES: Retreats, events, talks, discussions, individual retreat stays, day visitors. See their website for the latest information.

SITUATION: Wonderful in a deep valley, with views and splendour.

MAXIMUM STAY: By arrangement and by day.

BOOKINGS: Letter, telephone, email.

CHARGES: Donations are wecome. For other charges, please ask when you discuss your booking.

ACCESS: Car: via A40 or A487. Detailed travel directions are on their website.

LAMPETER

Cwrt y Cylchau
Llanfair Clydogau
Lampeter
Ceredigion SA48 8LJ
Wales

Tel: 01570 493526
Email: info@courtofcircles.org.uk
Website: www.courtofcircles.org.uk

Meditation • Spiritual Help • Self-Catering Space • Alternative Therapies
Holistic Holidays • Work Retreats • Camping

Holistic

Cwrt y Cylchau is a stone Welsh 'long-house' with five acres of beautiful, peaceful land situated in the hills – six miles from Lampeter and one and a half miles from the village of Llanfair Clydogau – and it offers self-managed retreats in an ecologically managed green environment in the Welsh countryside. Lampeter is a small market town with a university, lots of cafés and two good organic food suppliers. Llanfair Clydogau itself is an attractive village on the River Teifi and has a very well-stocked village shop with a good selection of wholefoods. The ethos of Cwrt y Cylchau is to encourage simple sustainable living and manage the land in a wildlife-friendly manner. Cwrt has its own natural well water and is a green site, hosting volunteers to work on the land and learn about permaculture and sustainable living, growing and coppicing wood for future energy supply and managing the land for biodiversity.

OPEN: Cwrt y Cylchau is open to individuals and small groups all year round.
ROOMS: There are a single and a double bedroom in the house and guests share living room, bathroom and kitchen facilities with residents. In the summer months there is the possibility to camp and use the house facilities. Other facilities from April to September include a 20ft yurt and a large stone camping barn, which is basically equipped with comfortable chairs, futon, mattresses and Baby Belling cooker.
FACILITIES: Camping, forest orchard, gardens, woodlands, river.
SPIRITUAL HELP: Meditation, deep ecology, alternative therapies.
GUESTS ADMITTED TO: Full access to the gardens and land with its meadows, forest orchard garden, vegetable growing areas, ponds, woodland and river. There are sometimes sheep grazing the land and dogs are not permitted.
MEALS: All guests are expected to self-manage their own retreat and be self-catering.
SPECIAL ACTIVITIES: Qualified and experienced hypno-psychotherapy, massage, and group facilitation, guidance in meditation, and treatments on site in massage and stress management. The host is an active member of the thriving Lampeter Permaculture Group, is involved in Transition Town and has trained and facilitated deep ecology practices, which follow the work of Buddhist scholar and social activist Joanna Macy, now known as 'The Work that Reconnects'.
SITUATION: Lovely countryside, green hills, peaceful.
MAXIMUM STAY: The length of stay is negotiable but must be booked in advance.
BOOKINGS: Contact Gina Heathersprite by email or telephone (see above details).
CHARGES: The cost of staying in the house is £10 per person per night, £15 per couple sharing. Camping charges can be arranged and depend on use of facilities.
ACCESS: Rail: Carmarthen station (28 miles away) or Aberystwyth station (25 miles away). Bus: services run to Lampeter with connections to Llanfair Clydogau. Guests without cars will need to be prepared to walk from the village, which is 1.5 miles away. The host does not run a car and encourages walkers and cyclists.

LLANDEILO

Kites' Nest
Bryndolau
Cwmifor, Llandeilo
Carmarthenshire SA19 7AT
Wales

Tel: 01558 824514
Email: davidsteel@mypostoffice.co.uk
Website: www.kitesnestcottage.co.uk

Retreats • Workshops and Courses • Bed and Breakfast • Vegetarian Food
Venue for Hire • Self-Catering Space • Holistic Holidays • Children

Open spirituality – Christian

What is on offer here is a quiet, comfortable cottage and a double room
in the main house for bed and breakfast. A limited number in a group
can come here and lunch can be arranged. Focus Days for retreat and
reflection are held here twice a year and are led by local clergy. The
programme is mainly prayer and meditation. Llandeilo is a small village in the Brecon Beacons, which has easy access to local footpaths for
walking in this lovely countryside.

LLANDYSUL

Ceridwen Centre
Penybanc Farm
Velindre, Llandysul
Ceredigion SA44 5XE
Wales

Tel/Fax: 01559 370211
Email: info@ceridwencentre.co.uk
Website: www.ceridwencentre.co.uk

Retreats • Workshops and Courses • Yoga • Meditation • Bed and Breakfast
Vegetarian Food • Organic Food • Venue for Hire • Self-Catering Space
Alternative Therapies • Holistic Holidays • Camping • Children

Open spirituality

Ceridwen Centre is a purpose-built residential centre for small groups
at a farm in south-west Wales. It is a working organic farm and the
site overlooks a beautiful valley of trees. Very clean, comfortable and
nicely furnished rooms and dormitories. Camping is possible. Health
and healing and arts and crafts are some of the event subjects here.
Everyone is welcome, including children and families. Various alterna-

tive healing treatments as well as beauty treatments can be arranged. A very pleasant place.

LLANPUMSAINT

The Community of the Many Names Of God   Tel: 01559 384421
Skanda Vale Monastery   Fax: 01559 384999
Llanpumsaint   Website: www.skandavale.org
Carmarthenshire SA33 6JT
Wales

Retreats • Workshops and Courses • Church/Temple • Yoga • Meditation • Spiritual Help
Vegetarian Food • Community Living • Work Retreats • Vocations • Children

Spiritual teachings of Lord Krishna as in the Bhagavad-Gita

This is a very special place. Tucked away on a wooded hillside a few miles north of Carmarthen, Skanda Vale is something out of the ordinary. Indian temples, devotional chanting, a deer park, an elephant ... step into this world and it's difficult not to be charmed, uplifted and deeply moved by the genuine love and inspiration that started the community nearly 30 years ago and which has seen it grow into a place of pilgrimage for thousands every year. The spiritual head of the community is a Sri Lankan known as Guruji, whose determination to set up and run a community where God comes first has meant a radical refusal to be bothered by the pressures of money. There are no charges here and the centre is financed solely through donation. The community of swamis, monks and nuns live by strict rules. **Women visitors are requested to come in pairs, unless they are already known by the community. The traditional custom of segregation in the temple is followed, and it is important to have eaten a vegetarian diet for three days before entering the temple. There is a certain caution towards single women, but everyone is welcome here – provided they respect the rules of this traditional monastic community.**

Prayers, or poojas, are joyful occasions and take place regularly throughout the day in one of the three temples. The most stunning of which is the Sri Ranganatha Temple, which was built without a roof and without walls: an outdoor water temple. In the middle of a small lake, a divine figure lies prostrate on a stone bed. Around the lake, other figures – including Krishna, Shiva, Buddha – remind us of the many forms of God. A short, but steep, walk up the hill through woodland

and some of the wonders of God's creation await – Skanda Vale has its own deer park, bird sanctuary and elephant. Valli was an orphaned elephant given as a gift in the 1980s and is now a much-loved member of the community. At the Maha Shakti Temple is where the community gathers for prayer three times a day.

The community is actively involved in hospice work: respite care in people's homes has been operating for several years and they have just opened a day-care centre, with plans for a residential hospice in the near future. Skanda Vale receives thousands of pilgrims and visitors every year and this can be a very busy place. Guests and retreatants are expected to work four hours a day in exchange for their board and accommodation. So don't come here if you want to get away from it all! But do come for any other reason – after all, a retreat is about stepping out of your ordinary life for a while and the Community of the Many Names Of God is surely just the place to do it. We confess that we could not resist a retreat with an elephant, particularly one named Valli. She is a marvel of Creation – as are all the other animals kept here, every one treated with the respect and honour that they deserve. Having said this, Skanda Vale is a place of honest and real pilgrimage, so you should be a serious spiritual seeker in coming here.

The Community of the Many Names of God was founded on the worship of God in his Universality in accordance with the spiritual teachings of Lord Krishna as in the *Bhagavad-Gita*. It was established as a monastic centre in Wales in 1973, although the temple had been founded 20 years previously in London. The present 115-acre site was originally three adjacent farms and a small block of woodland, which were separately purchased and amalgamated by the community as the grounds of Skanda Vale Monastery. Its first temple dedicated to Lord Subramanium was registered as a place of public worship in 1975. The community became a registered charity in 1980 and is administered by a board of trustees whose chairman is Guru Sri Subramanium, the community's founder and spiritual director. In addition to this monastery, they run a local day hospice and have a retreat facility in Switzerland (see below). **Highly Recommended.**

Skanda Vale Hospice

Skanda Vale Hospice Day Care Centre, founded by the Skanda Vale Community, is situated between Carmarthen and Cardigan on the A484, in the village of Saron. The central location puts them at the heart of the peaceful rural communities of Carmarthenshire and Ceredigion. The hospice is open five days a week, usually from 09:30 until 16:00. They currently offer a full respite care service and can arrange for clinical care to be provided by visiting nurses or GPs. Their policy is to be as patient-centred as possible in all matters, so opening hours can be flexible to suit the requirements of visitors and their families.

Skanda Vale in Switzerland

In 1994 the Swiss Association of Skanda Vale was formed by supporters, mostly from Switzerland and Germany, and a mountain chalet was purchased near Fideris in Canton Graubünden about 30km from Davos at a height of almost 2000m. The chalet was to be a permanent venue for the seminars and devotions with the long-term aspiration of establishing a temple. Thereafter the seminars were formalised to coincide with the intervals between the festivals in Skanda Vale, normally in June, July, September and October. The themes of the seminars revolve around learning to develop a partnership with God in one's everyday life, dealing with all aspects of living – this ranges from physical health, emotional attachments, relationships, parenting, professional responsibilities, suffering and death to the practice of mantras, concentration, breathing, devotion, the diverse manifestations of the divine, karma, liberation and our relationship with the planet. The structure of the teaching is in the form of informal discourses and question-and-answer sessions.

ST DAVID'S

St Non's Retreat Centre	Tel: 01437 720224 / 01437 720161
St David's	Email: stnonsretreat@aol.com
Pembrokeshire SA62 6BN	Website: www.stnonsretreat.org.uk
Wales	

Retreats • Workshops and Courses • Church/Temple • Yoga • Meditation • Spiritual Help
Vegetarian Food • Venue for Hire • Alternative Therapies • Community Living
Work Retreats • Vocations • Children

Christian – Roman Catholic – Ecumenical

St Non's is a lovely bay on the Pembrokeshire coast and has a graceful little chapel, an oratory and a library, as well as comfortable accommodation. It is managed by a Community of the Sisters of Mercy. There is a programme and the place is quiet and warmly welcoming.

OPEN: Most of year. Everyone welcome, including groups.
ROOMS: 10 single rooms or 10 twin-bedded rooms plus 1 single. Groups of up to 21 can be accommodated.
FACILITIES: Oratory, library, meeting rooms and places for reflection and prayer. Garden.
SPIRITUAL HELP: Please ask.
GUESTS ADMITTED TO: Everywhere except private community areas.
MEALS: Vegetarian and special diets possible, so please discuss when writing to book.
SPECIAL ACTIVITIES: The kind of retreats on offer here vary ranging from the traditional to Tai Chi. Some current programme topics give the flavour: mid-life retreat, 6-day preached retreat, yoga, meditation, painting and reflection, bereaved parents' retreat, pilgrim adventure retreat, Tai Chi, Sacred Dance. Brochure available.
SITUATION: Set in St Non's Bay.
MAXIMUM STAY: By retreat programme or by arrangement when booking.
BOOKINGS: Letter, with downloadable booking form on the website.
CHARGES: Suggested donations, but there is a policy of facilitating people who might find these offerings too high for their circumstances: parish-group weekend £75; full board £42 per person; day groups £7 per person; day groups with a cooked meal £14 per person; yoga weekend £80 per person.
ACCESS: Boat: St Non's bay is 30 minutes' drive from Fishguard Harbour. Rail: Haverfordwest station (16.5 miles away). Car: via M4, A48, A40 and A487. Travel directions are available on the website.

WHITLAND

Holy Cross Abbey
Velfrey Road
Whitland
Carmarthenshire SA34 0QX
Wales

Tel: 01994 240725
Email: coeddcrist@googlemail.com
Website: www.hcawhitland.co.uk

Church/Temple • Spiritual Help • Vegetarian Food • Community Living • Vocations

Christian – Roman Catholic

This Cistercian community of nuns is situated in a beautiful part of west Wales with views to the Preseli hills. As Cistercians, their particular spirituality is Benedictine and they live a quiet and straightforward traditional monastic lifestyle. The community earns its living making altar breads, used at the celebration of the Eucharist. Each member of the community has some involvement in this industry and the altar breads are dispatched all over the country and abroad. There is a small monastic guest house and a quiet garden for guests. The community has five acres and more, which they have planted up for biofuel and for helping wildlife. While everyone is welcome, only women are received as staying guests. Once on a retreat course, a member of the *Good Retreat Guide* team met a member of this community. She was talented, full of laughter and brightness and joy and very at ease with the world – yet had only been out visiting it just a few times in more than half a life as a nun. So, if as a woman, you should be looking for a private retreat of real – and that means deep – monastic quality or considering the idea of a vocation to the religious life, then perhaps Whitland Abbey should be on your must-visit list.

OPEN: Most of year. Closed over the Christmas period, Holy Week and Easter week. Receives women only as guests.
ROOMS: 3 independent en suite rooms and can accommodate up to 4 guests. **Not** suitable for disabled guests.
FACILITIES: Chapel, daily Mass, Divine Office. Walks in the 5 acres of woodland, and you can help with some gardening if you want.
SPIRITUAL HELP: Personal talks by request sometimes possible.
GUESTS ADMITTED TO: Chapel, gardens, woodlands.
MEALS: All food is provided with option of a cooked vegetarian midday meal.
SPECIAL ACTIVITIES: None.
SITUATION: Quiet in the countryside.
MAXIMUM STAY: 1 week.
BOOKINGS: Letter or email. Try not to telephone unless truly necessary.
CHARGES: Charges currently are £20–£25 per day. If this is beyond your means, then discuss it with the guestmistress.
ACCESS: Rail: Whitland station (1 mile away). Car: via A40.

'Let all guests that come be received like Christ'
– Monastic Rule of Saint Benedict

SOUTH GLAMORGAN

LLANDOW

Ty Teilo Day Retreat House
The Rectory
Llandow, Cowbridge
Vale of Glamorgan CF71 7NT
Wales

Tel/Fax: 01656 890205
Email: peter@theleonards.org.uk
Website: www.churchinwales.org.uk/
Llandaff (follow the link from 'Faith')

Church/Temple • Venue for Hire • Self-Catering Space

Christian – Anglican

Ty Teilo Retreat House is in the grounds of the Llandow rectory at Llandow, situated in the countryside of the Vale of Glamorgan. A conversion from the rectory stable, Ty Teilo offers a meeting place for groups of up to 25 people. There is no accommodation. The chapel is open and available for Eucharist celebrations. There are simple catering facilities and it is disabled friendly. Contact the warden for booking arrangements.

'Glance at the sun. See the moon and stars.
Gaze at the beauty of earth's greenings. Now, think'
– Hildegard of Bingen

GWENT

CWMBRAN

Tŷ Croeso Centre
Llantarnam Abbey
Cwmbran
Torfaen NP44 3YJ
Wales

Tel: 01633 867317
Fax: 01633 872435
Email: tycroeso@talktalk.net
Email: www.tycroesocentre.co.uk

> Retreats • Workshops and Courses • Church/Temple • Meditation • Spiritual Help
> Bed and Breakfast • Vegetarian Food • Venue for Hire • Self-Catering Space
> Community Living • Vocations • Hermitages

Christian – Roman Catholic – Ecumenical – Monastic

The Tŷ Croeso Centre is the retreatant part of the large and rather charming old Llantarnam Abbey, which is situated in large grounds and surrounded by woodlands, hills and rivers. The abbey is built on the site of an older monastery and has been a Sisters of St Joseph Community for more than half a century now. The surrounding area is excellent for walking, rambling and cycling. There is a hermitage cottage as well as rooms. In the large gardens there is a labyrinth. Events and retreats programme with details are on the website.

MONMOUTH

Society of the Sacred Cross
Tymawr Convent
Lydart, Monmouth
Monmouthshire NP5 4RN
Wales

Tel: 01600 860244 / 01600 860808
Email: tymawrconvent@btinternet.com
Website: www.churchinwales.org.uk/~tymawr/

> Retreats • Church/Temple • Spiritual Help • Vegetarian Food • Community Living
> Work Retreats • Vocations

Christian – Anglican Monastic

You will feel well looked after in this house, which has views across a lush valley of green fields in the Wye Valley. If you want the experience of living alongside a spiritual community, the convent occasionally offers this for one or two months for young women and young men. The resident community is a contemplative one – hence there is much silence here. Lots of vegetables and fruit are grown by the sisters at this popular place, so the food is fresh if plain.

OPEN: Almost all year – enquire about closed weeks. Receives men, women, young people.
ROOMS: 9 singles, 3 doubles.
FACILITIES: Chapel, garden, library, guest telephone.
SPIRITUAL HELP: Personal talks by arrangement.
GUESTS ADMITTED TO: Chapel, choir, work of the community.
MEALS: Traditional food taken guest dining room. Vegetarian. Self-catering facilities.
SPECIAL ACTIVITIES: None.
SITUATION: Very quiet, in the countryside; 65 acres of land in Wye Valley.
MAXIMUM STAY: By arrangement.
BOOKINGS: By letter, email or if necessary telephone (18:45–19:45).
CHARGES: About £25 per person per night full board; £20 self-catering per day. However, ask about the current rate when you are booking.
ACCESS: Tymawr Convent is 4 miles south of Monmouth. Rail: Chepstow station (13 miles away). Bus: services from Monmouth and Chepstow stop 0.5–1 mile from the convent. Car: via A40 (best method).

GWYNEDD

ANGLESEY

Sue Rowlands Centre for Psychic and Spiritual Studies
Tre-Ysgawen Hall
Capel Coch, Llangefni
Isle of Anglesey LL77 7UR
Wales

Tel: 01248 750750
Fax: 01248 750035

Retreats • Workshops and Courses • Meditation • Spiritual Help • Bed and Breakfast
Vegetarian Food • Venue for Hire • Alternative Therapies • Holistic Holidays

Mind Body Spirit – Psychic spiritualism

This is a country-house hotel in the heartland of Anglesey with all the facilities you would expect of such a place, from the 1882 drawing room and library to an American-type bar, four-poster beds and jacuzzi baths. However, even though they do offer luxury surroundings, the

Sue Rowlands Centre for Psychic and Spiritual Studies at Tre-Ysgawen Hall runs a serious programme of events designed to deepen spiritual awareness and the gaining of self-revelation. The range of courses is wide, from meditation practices to healing, mediumship and awareness courses and training.

OPEN: All year except Christmas. Receives all guests.
ROOMS: 19 bedrooms plus.
FACILITIES: Disabled access, conferences, garden, park, guest lounge, TV in rooms.
SPIRITUAL HELP: Personal talks, spiritual direction, meditation.
GUESTS ADMITTED TO: Unrestricted access except for staff areas.
MEALS: Restaurant .
SPECIAL ACTIVITIES: A planned programme. Contact the centre for details.
SITUATION: Very quiet and tranquil in countryside.
MAXIMUM STAY: Usually for a course or by arrangement in B&B.
BOOKINGS: Letter, telephone, fax.
CHARGES: £295 tariff per course, everything included, plus £35 course fee. The single supplement is about £60. Various discounts for booking early, so do ask. There are day visiting rates as well with prices for any food provided.
ACCESS: Rail: Llanfairpwll station (11 miles away). Car: via A55 – ask for brochure, which details routes.

BANGOR

Dru Yoga Retreats
Snowdonia Mountain Lodge
Nant Ffrancon, Bangor
Gwynedd LL57 3LX
Wales

Tel: 01248 602900
Fax: 01248 602004
Email: hello@druworldwide.com
Website: www.druworldwide.com/
www.druyoga.com

Retreats • Workshops and Courses • Yoga • Meditation • Spiritual Help
Vegetarian Food • Alternative Therapies • Holistic Holidays • Community Living
Work Retreats • Vocations

Yoga – Dru Yoga – Mind Body Spirit

Situated in the beautiful Welsh mountains of Snowdonia National Park, this is the head office and main retreat centre for Dru Yoga. The team at the centre are from a wide range of backgrounds who have come together to provide spiritual awareness, self-empowerment and self-development courses. Specialities include Dru Yoga, Dru Sound Develop and Dru Dance courses, and meditation retreats. They also run retreats around the UK and Ireland – visit the website for more details.Tools for transformation sums this enterprise up best.

OPEN: For retreat and course programme. Receives men, women and groups.
ROOMS: Single, double, twin and family rooms. All en suite, and with internet access.
No smoking. No alcohol.
FACILITIES: At Snowdonia Mountian Lodge, there are 2 spacious halls, a holistic
shop, multimedia facilities (DVD and data projection) and relaxing therapies (enquire
about availability).
SPIRITUAL HELP: Inner self-development, self-help tools, yoga, meditation.
GUESTS ADMITTED TO: Unrestricted access.
MEALS: Everyone eats together. All meals are vegetarian.
SPECIAL ACTIVITIES: Programme of events and retreats throughout the year and
around the country.
SITUATION: Welsh mountains of Snowdonia National Park.
MAXIMUM STAY: Duration of retreat or course experience.
BOOKINGS: Letter, telephone, email, online booking available.
CHARGES: In the region of £260–£480. Visit the website or ask for current rates as
these depend on the course or retreat offered. Lower rates are available if you book
early enough.
ACCESS: Rail: Bangor station (8 miles away), then taxi. Car: on the A5.

DOLGELLAU

Carmelite Monastery   Tel: 01341 422546
Cader Road   Website: www.carmelite.org.uk/Dolgellau.html
Dolgellau
Gwynedd LL40 1SH
Wales

Church/Temple • Spiritual Help • Self-Catering Facilities • Vocations

Christian – Roman Catholic – Monastic

The Carmelite monastery of Dolgellau is the only Carmel in Wales. It is
situated on a road ascending the Cader Idris mountain range in truly
beautiful surroundings. This monastery of stone buildings with modern additions is a traditional Carmelite Community, meaning that the
community of nuns live an enclosed life – they do not go out and about.
The lifestyle is influenced by the sisters' vows of poverty, chastity and
obedience and they live a life of solitude and silence in allegiance to
Jesus Christ, tracing their origins back to the hermits living on Mount
Carmel in the Holy Land in the twelfth century. If you feel drawn towards a Christian contemplative life, then here perhaps is a place to
commence that hard yet joyous journey. **Highly Recommended.**

OPEN: All year. Receives women, men, young people, religious, non-retreatants.

ROOMS: Guest house.
FACILITIES: Garden, TV, books to read.
SPIRITUAL HELP: Personal talks may be arranged if needed.
GUESTS ADMITTED TO: Chapel.
MEALS: Self-catering facilities for all.
SPECIAL ACTIVITIES: None.
SITUATION: Quiet and in the countryside with opportunities for walks in the mountains.
MAXIMUM STAY: 1 week.
BOOKINGS: Letter.
CHARGES: Donation by agreement. Ask for guidelines.
ACCESS: Rail: Blaenau Ffestiniog station (22 miles away) or Bangor station (49 miles away). It is possible to reach Dolgellau by bus from these two locations. Car: via A470.

LLANDUDNO

Loreto Centre	Tel: 01492 878031 (centre/group bookings)
Abbey Road	Tel: 01492 878542 (Clifton/retreats/self catering)
Llandudno	Email: loretocentre@yahoo.co.uk
Gwynedd LL30 2EL	Website: www.loretollno.org.uk
Wales	

Retreats • Workshops and Courses • Church/Temple • Spiritual Help
Self-Catering Space • Community Living • Work Retreats • Vocations • Children

Christian – Roman Catholic – Monastic

The Loreto Centre is run by the Loreto Sisters and is located near the west shore of Llandudno at the foot of the Great Orme. It is only a 10-minute walk from town, parish church and the east shore. This is a huge place and there are a number of types of accommodation.

'Be real, embrace simplicity, put others first, desire little'
– Tao Te Ching

POWYS

BRECON BEACONS

Buckland Hall
Bwich
Brecon Beacons
Powys LD3 7JJ
Wales

Tel: 01874 730330
Fax: 01874 730740
Email: info@bucklandhall.co.uk
Website: www.bucklandhall.co.uk

Retreats • Workshops and Courses • Bed and Breakfast • Vegetarian Food
Venue for Hire • Alternative Therapies • Holistic Holidays

Open spirituality

Buckland Hall is a large well-established place, which caters for a variety of retreat, events and personal celebrations such as weddings. Everything is tailored to your group's requirements. They have developed a residential retreat package and service, and you can review this online before calling to discuss your specific needs. Improvements and development of facilities are ongoing here to improve what is on offer. A very complete facility for a group retreat – but you can also stay as an individual.

OPEN: All year. Everyone welcome.
ROOMS: Accommodation in very comfortable bedrooms with en suite bathrooms.
FACILITIES: Activity rooms, conference rooms, meeting rooms, lounges, snooker room, gardens. All the equipment you might need is at hand. And more – the facilities are really very complete – and they are making a new spa and more new bedrooms. The choice of what is on offer expands every year. Look on their website and be impressed.
SPIRITUAL HELP: None.
GUESTS ADMITTED TO: All guest areas and gardens.
MEALS: All meals are wholly vegetarian with as much local and organic produce as practical. Lunches and dinners are served to the table 'home style', which enhances the convivial atmosphere.
SPECIAL ACTIVITIES: Retreats, training and courses, team building and outdoor activities, health, well-being and holistic events, family and community get-togethers.
SITUATION: Countryside.
MAXIMUM STAY: By arrangement of your booking.
BOOKINGS: Letter, telephone, fax, email, online enquiry form.
CHARGES: You must discuss this as it depends on what you want, how many people, and so on – all the usual details for individual or group bookings.
ACCESS: Rail: Abergavenny station (15 miles away), then taxi. Car: on the A40. Detailed directions are on the website, including printable road directions.

Coleg Trefeca
Trefeca
Aberhonddu
Powys LD3 0PP
Wales

Tel: 01874 711423
Fax: 01874 712212
Email: colegtrefeca@ebcpcw.org.uk
Website: www.trefeca.org.uk

Retreats • Workshops and Courses • Church/Temple • Spiritual Help • Bed and Breakfast
Vegetarian Food • Venue for Hire • Vocations • Children • Pets

Christian – Presbyterian Church of Wales

Coleg Trefeca is a lay training centre owned by the Presbyterian Church of Wales. Courses and conferences are regularly held and every effort is made by the staff to create a relaxing atmosphere. The centre consists of a group of eighteenth-century buildings and a modern block, standing in five acres of grounds set in the Brecon Beacons National Park. It was once the home of Howell Harris (1714–73), one of the leaders of the evangelical revival in Wales. The programme brochure and retreats are in both Welsh and English and are available on their website. The following programme topics give an idea of the retreats offered: women's retreat, in-service training for ministers, older folks' fellowship, and youth weekend. There are healing retreats and sometimes a children's weekend as well. A good place for a stimulating retreat firmly based on Christian precepts and for mixing with other like-minded people.

OPEN: All year. Receives men, women, young people, families, groups and non-retreatants. Children welcome. Pets sometimes by arrangement.
ROOMS: 19 twin-bedded doubles.
FACILITIES: Some facilities for disabled but do enquire. Conferences, garden, library, guest lounge, TV and payphone.
SPIRITUAL HELP: Personal talks if requested. Group sharing on the healing retreats. Directed study as part of courses. An ordained minister may be available.
GUESTS ADMITTED TO: Unrestricted access.
MEALS: Everyone eats together. Traditional home cooking with provision for vegetarian and special diets by prior arrangement only.
SPECIAL ACTIVITIES: Planned programme. Groups, churches and secular organisations may follow their own programme.
SITUATION: Very quiet, in an area of outstanding natural beauty; 10 miles from Brecon and an ideal centre for those who wish to walk, climb, pony-trek, or simply admire the views.
MAXIMUM STAY: By retreat or by arrangement.
BOOKINGS: Telephone, letter, email. You must complete a booking form, which is downloadable from the website.

CHARGES: Full-board rates for groups for 2 nights range from £45 to £109 per person. B&B is £25 per night. There are reductions for children, youth, people with disabilities and people in hardship. Day conferences are £19 per person.
ACCESS: Rail: Abergavenny station (18 miles away), then taxi. Car: Coleg Trefeca is in Trefeca village on the B4560 between Talgarth and Llangors.

Llangasty Retreat House	Tel: 01874 658250
Llangasty	Email: enquiries@llangasty.com
Brecon	Website: www.llangasty.com
Powys LD3 7PX	
Wales	

> Retreats • Workshops and Courses • Church/Temple • Meditation • Spiritual Help
> Bed and Breakfast • Vegetarian Food • Self-Catering Space • Children

Christian – Church in Wales (Anglican)

This isolated and large stone house, hidden away from roads and the busy world, is comfortable, cheerful and overlooks a marvellous lake. There are magnificent views to the Black Mountains and superb walking. It has long been a place for Christian worship and prayer but all are welcome.

OPEN: All year. Receives men, women, young people, families, groups. Children welcome.
ROOMS: 11 singles, 6 twins – includes 2 disabled friendly. Cottage with a single and 2 twin bedrooms.
FACILITIES: Chapel, conferences, garden, library, dining room, guest lounge, prayer area.
SPIRITUAL HELP: Eucharistic prayer, chapel.
GUESTS ADMITTED TO: Unrestricted access except for the kitchen and other working areas.
MEALS: Everyone eats together. Traditional food. Vegetarian and special diets by arrangement.
SPECIAL ACTIVITIES: Planned events including drop-in days. Programme online.
SITUATION: Very quiet, in the countryside.
MAXIMUM STAY: By arrangement.
BOOKINGS: Telephone, email, online contact form.
CHARGES: Current rates: weekday full board £50, B&B £27 and weekends £28–£54. See website for the latest rates.
ACCESS: Rail: Abergavenny station (15.5 miles away), then taxi. Car: via A40 and B4560.

Llannerchwen
Llandefaelog Fach
Brecon
Powys LD3 9PP
Wales

Tel: 01874 622902
Email: retreats@llannerchwen.org.uk
Website: www.llannerchwen.org.uk

Retreats • Workshops and Courses • Church/Temple • Yoga • Meditation • Spiritual Help
Self-Catering Space • Community Living • Vocations • Hermitages

Christian – Roman Catholic

Llannerchwen has been a spiritual sanctuary for a number of years and is now run by the Society of the Sacred Heart, a Roman Catholic congregation of women who are committed to a life of contemplation and active service. They do have a very quiet and peaceful place to stay either for a private retreat or on an Ignatian retreat in which they specialise. The accommodation is very suitable for this latter type of retreat as most are small hermitages with all you need for simple self-catering and comfort. The sisters are helped by an ecumenical team of both religious and lay men and women. The aim here is hospitality for all, creating and keeping an atmosphere of solitude, managing their resources in a harmonious and ecologically sound way, and to be there for guests but in an unobtusive way. We suggest this is not only a good place to undertake an Ignatian retreat but also a place where those wanting a more solitary hermitage retreat may find it most suitable.

OPEN: Closed in January. Everyone welcome.
ROOMS: 6 self-contained spaces, each with its own entrance, which are composed of 3 separate hermitages, 2 in a bungalow, and 1 on the upper floor of a cottage. Each space has a bed, shower, toilet, fridge and cooking facilities. Most have a microwave.
FACILITIES: Chapel, hermitages, garden, communal prayer, creative arts cabin.
SPIRITUAL HELP: Individually guided retreat with daily spiritual accompaniment. Chapel always open for private prayer and used once a day for communal prayer. Transport into Brecon for church services on Sundays and Holy Days of Obligation.
GUESTS ADMITTED TO: Everywhere except community private and work areas.
MEALS: Main midday meal in your room when you are on an individually guided retreat. Special diets must cater for themselves. Otherwise self-catering.
SPECIAL ACTIVITIES: Ignatian retreats.
SITUATION: Countryside near Brecon.
MAXIMUM STAY: 1 day to several months.
BOOKINGS: Letter, telephone.Online is easiest as there is a booking form.
CHARGES: By donation. Current suggestions: self catering £23 per night; cooked midday meal when on Ignatian retreat £7 per day; non-residential day of prayer £11–£17; spiritual direction session £15–£25. Individually guided retreats: 8 days self-catering £330; 8 days with cooked lunch £385; 30 days with cooked lunch £1,370.
ACCESS: Rail: Abergavenny station (24 miles away), then taxi. Bus/coach: Brecon Interchange – pick-up by arrangement. Car: via A40 or A470, then B4520. Further details are on their website.

KERRY

Monstery of St Barnabas the Encourager   Tel: 01686 630575
Lower Brynmawr   Website: www.saintbarnabas.co.uk
Kerry, Newtown
Powys SY16 4NQ
Wales

Church/Temple • Spiritual Help • Self-Catering Space • Hermitages

Christian – Anglican – Ecumenical

St Barnabas Monastery is in a beautiful part of Powys with green hills and quiet lanes abounding. Here a resident former Anglican clergyman who is married lives out an Anchorite monastic-type life with the aim of prayer and hospitality. The chapel holds up to 10 people and there are four set prayer times each day. The accommodation is self-catering, simple and sufficient for a private retreat. For those who want greater solitude and silence, there is a hermitage hut. You will get a warm welcome at this small retreat with a big heart.

OPEN: All year. Everyone welcome to stay or just for a restful and prayerful pause.
ROOMS: 1 room sleeping 3 people; it is en suite with a kitchenette sitting area. Hermitage hut.
FACILITIES: Hermitage, chapel, garden, and places to prayer, walk and rest.
SPIRITUAL HELP: Personal talks if required.
GUESTS ADMITTED TO: Mostly everywhere.
MEALS: Self-catering.
SPECIAL ACTIVITIES: Private retreats.
SITUATION: Countryside, set in the woods.
MAXIMUM STAY: By arrangement.
BOOKINGS: Letter, telephone.
CHARGES: You must ask.
ACCESS: Car: via A483 or A489.

'Our hearts were made for you, O God, and will not rest
until they rest in you'
– Saint Augustine

LLANDRINDOD

Spirit Horse Foundation	Tel: 07882 522878 (Erica)
PO Box 66	Email: info@spirithorse.co.uk (general enquiries only)
Llandrindod	Website: www.spirithorse.co.uk
Powys LD1 9AH	
Wales	

Retreats • Workshops and Courses • Vegetarian Food • Self-Catering Space
Community Living • Work Retreats • Camping • Children

Mind Body Spirit – Warriors, Heroes and Visionaries

Nearly all events by the Spirit Horse Foundation are held in the summertime under canvas in a magnificent green and hidden Welsh valley. These range from personal tents you bring with you to Turkomangers, yurts and tipis. There is a large Celtic roundhouse. Many of the structures have fallen into some disrepair, but do not worry about it – everyone helps during the retreat to do a bit of work on them and they are being restored. This work helps create a sense of community, which is a vital ingredient in these retreats. The structured courses on offer cover Shamanic practice and ceremony, meditation, children's retreats, work retreats and aspects of both Buddhism and Celtic mythology. It is an archaic, ceremonial environment, close to nature with a variety of different courses enabling a rediscovery of self through spiritual practices, healing and mythology. Influential sources used are Tibetan Buddhism, Celtic spirituality and North American Indian traditions. Sweat lodge, stone medicine healing, storytelling, Arabic dancing, song and voice work, Buddhist visionary instruction and much more can be involved in the Spirit Horse programme. Although many of the retreatants are younger, some with children, we feel that older people could benefit greatly by this kind of retreat that dislodges them from a lot of creature comforts and conveniences they enjoy at home. This kind of displacement with attendant initial discomfort often ends by lifting the spirits and bringing inner reawakening of self. Such a process has always been part and parcel of traditional Christian pilgrimages, so why not give it a go with a hidden valley retreat with Spirit Horse? If you want to start in a safer zone, they do have some winter retreats in a mountain centre, which is warm.

OPEN: Summer only. Everyone welcome.
ROOMS: Special tents.

FACILITIES: Conferences possible, camping.
SPIRITUAL HELP: Personal talks, group sharing, meditation, directed study.
GUESTS ADMITTED TO: Unrestricted access.
MEALS: Traditional food. Vegetarians catered for.
SPECIAL ACTIVITIES: See brochure or online for programme. There are some retreats abroad as well and a year's study course on offer.
SITUATION: Peaceful to the point of paradise.
MAXIMUM STAY: 5-10 days.
BOOKINGS: Letter, telephone.
CHARGES: Rates range from £25 to £350 for 1-, 3-, 5- and 10-day events and courses. Meals are usually included.
ACCESS: Depends on the event. By car, sometimes via a train; transport sharing possible.

LLANDRINDOD WELLS

Dyffryn Farm	Tel: 01597 811017
Llanwrthwl	Fax: 01597 810609
Llandrindod Wells	Email: stay@dyffrynfarm.co.uk
Powys LD1 6NU	Website: www.dyffrynfarm.co.uk
Wales	

Retreats • Meditation • Spiritual Help • Bed and Breakfast • Self-Catering Space
Vocations • Children • Pets

Christian – Anglican – Inter-denominational

Situated in mid-Wales in a beautiful part of the Wye Valley, this seventeenth-century house and farm of 20 acres has pastures, springs, old stone walls and in winter welcoming warm fires. There are two comfortable self-catering cottages in idyllic situation with superb views of the Wye Valley. Both cottages are green with wood stoves and solar heating, supplementing central heating. Ideal place for kite flying, bird-watching, walking, cycling, fishing or just relaxing. Spiritual direction, retreat weekends, guided walks, maps for walking, and space to pray and reflect can be found here. The hosts have both been trained as clergy appraisers and Gaynor Tyler is a Church in Wales priest while her husband Richard is a mediator and retired solicitor. By using the self-catering accommodation together with the rooms in the house, they are able to offer groups accommodation up to 10 people. **Highly Recommended.**

OPEN: All year. Receives everyone.

ROOMS: Accommodation consists of 1 double/twin room (with en suite), another double and a single room. Well-equipped 3-bedroomed self-catering cottage attached to the barn.
FACILITIES: Garden, guest lounge, TV.
SPIRITUAL HELP: Personal talks if needed. Personal/ministry appraisal.
GUESTS ADMITTED TO: Mostly unrestricted access.
MEALS: Self-catering. B&B in main house.
SPECIAL ACTIVITIES: All of nature – birdwatching, walking, cycling, fishing.
SITUATION: Countryside and beautiful.
MAXIMUM STAY: 2 weeks. Otherwise extended by arrangement.
BOOKINGS: Letter, telephone, email, online contact form.
CHARGES: Prices currently £195–£395 depending on number of guests and season. This includes heating with a reasonable supply of wood in the stable, lighting and bedlinen and towels. B&B prices from £25 to £30 per person per night.
ACCESS: By train: Llandrindod Wells (9 miles away). By car: via A470.

LLANFAIR CAEREINION

Tan y Foel Farm Holidays Tel: 07855 060241
Tan y Foel Farm Email: tanyfoelfarmholidays@yahoo.co.uk
Llanfair Caereinon Website: www.tan-y-foel-farm-holidays.co.uk
Powys SY21 0HY
Wales

Retreats • Workshops and Courses • Meditation • Spiritual Help • Vegetarian Food
Organic Food • Self-Catering Space • Alternative Therapies • Holistic Holidays • Children

Eco-spirituality – Multi-faith – Alternative spirituality

Here is a special place in the magic of Wales – a farm that has set itself up to receive guests in a few caravans placed in lovely situations in the midst of Welsh valleys and muntains. Well, you might think there are lots of farms that have gone this way, offering some countryside stays for the restless and dispirited workers from the grand cities and the dormitory suburbs. That is true – but at Tan y Foel you get the whole farm retreat package done in the correct and inviting way for inner renewal and rest. There are alternative healing treatments, from Indian head massage to Reiki, courses and workshops, life stories about the farm animals, wells and springs reputed to have healing properties, the possibility of fresh organic veggie boxes, and loads of beautiful views and hidden places to sit and read or just relax – and you can bring the kids. We believe this to be a wonderful place for inner healing and for becoming more conscious of the present in your life. As to being green, Tan y Foel sources everything on site – quite an accomplishment these days. It is worth noting just what this means to them: all fencing and paths are made using trees that were taken down for safety reasons; the materials used to build the car park were sourced on the farm, so involve no road miles; fully organic, they grow and sell own produce, which includes goat's milk, eggs, fruit, salad, vegetables and wool; a 10-bin composting system is in operation; all animal wastes are used in the gardens; they produce all feeds for the animals. Everything is recycled: a rainwater harvesting system is used for all water for growing and for the animals; all waste water, including toilets, is dealt with via a reed-bed system; a large proportion of the house is lit using solar power; all heating is produced using renewable resources that are produced on site; every light is low energy; every toilet has a hippo water-saving device; recycling bins are available for every single item; product purchases are sourced locally; car use is kept to a minimum. All products used in the treatments suite are organic and recycleable. If all this were not ecologically dazzling enough, the farm has turned over half of its land to a wildlife programme, which includes a wetland area, a lake, a pond and a wildlife field. **They offer a discount on their prices to members of the Centre for Alternative Technology, Friends of the Earth, Greenpeace and those subscribing to permaculture.**

LLANGUNLLO

The Samatha Centre
Greenstreete
Llangunllo
Powys LD7 1SP
Wales

Tel: 01348 811583
Email: info@samatha.org
Website: www.samatha.org

Retreats • Workshops and Courses • Church/Temple • Meditation • Spiritual Help
Vegetarian Food • Organic Food • Community Living

Buddhist (Theravada tradition)

The Samatha Centre is run by the Samatha Trust, a Buddhist group that practises a traditional Thai form of meditation based on attending to the breath, in the broader context of Theravada Buddhism. It is practised and taught by British people leading ordinary lives and so is organically adapted to the West and open to a range of spiritual influences. But not all who practise or even teach it consider themselves Buddhist, and there is no expectation that those who learn the meditation will become so. They run several introductory courses a year for people who wish to learn this particular meditation technique. Meditation on the breath is very versatile, suited to all types of people and adaptable to different needs. The particular form they teach includes different ways of attending to the breath, and different lengths of breath, which gives it a physical, yogic dimension. As well as presenting the various aspects of the technique, and of meditation in general, the courses provide space for individual practice, walks, group discussions and one-to-one discussions with the teachers. There are follow-up weekends for people who wish to develop the meditation further, or they can join a local group if there is one in their area. Everyone is welcome here to learn this gentle and effective way of meditation. There are regular classes for the more experienced and some for beginners.

OPEN: During organised weekends and weeks. Receives men and women.
ROOMS: Accommodation is in rooms in the farmhouse or nearby cabins, with rooms shared with at most one other person, and numbers are limited to about 15 participants.
FACILITIES: Disabled access, garden, park, library.
SPIRITUAL HELP: Individual instruction on Samatha meditation, directed study. There is always an experienced teacher to whom a person can talk on their practice. This is an important aspect of the courses here.
GUESTS ADMITTED TO: Unrestricted access everywhere. Shrine room, work of community.
MEALS: Food is home cooked, and meals are eaten together. Vegetarians and people with special diets can be catered for. Participants need to give some help with a few tasks like washing up.
SPECIAL ACTIVITIES: Meditation practice. See programme and details online.
SITUATION: The centre has 88 acres of land just outside a small village. The land includes hill top and valley bottom, woods, streams and fields. A wetland with a small lake has been created and the land is steadily being developed, with trees being planted and paths made.
MAXIMUM STAY: Length of retreat, usually a weekend or week.
BOOKINGS: To book, email Rachael Hall (rmh1001@cam.ac.uk) or call her on 01223 249732. They are unable to offer retreat facilities outside specific courses.
CHARGES: The cost is £50 for the weekend, including food and accommodation – no charge for the teaching.
ACCESS: Rail: Llangynllo station is 20 minutes' walk from the centre; pick-up possible if lifts from further away can't be arranged. No local buses. Car: via A44 and A483.

MACHYNLLETH

Eco Retreats
Plas Einion
Furnace, Machynlleth
Powys SY20 8PG
Wales

Tel: 01654 781375
Mobile: 07702 598909 / 07962 186563
Email: chananb@ecoretreats.co.uk
Website: ecoretreats.co.uk

Retreats • Meditation • Spiritual Help • Self-Catering Space • Alternative Therapies
Holistic Holidays • Community Living • Camping • Children

Eco-spirituality

Wales is an increasingly popular destination and with such wonderful landscapes, forests, hills, mountains and rivers it is not surprising. Eco Retreats is a chance to appreciate the natural beauty of Wales, while camping in traditional and authentic style in tipis or in a yurt. Instead of just reading about ecological living, you can get right down to it here. The 21-foot diameter tipis are surprisingly spacious. Each one is furnished with a double bed with a proper mattress, organic bedlinen, cushions and a coffee table, sheepskin rugs and a central wood-burning type of stove. Wood and kindling are supplied along with candles and lanterns. There is a two-ring gas stove for cooking, complete with all utensils, crockery and cutlery. Each tipi has its own washing and toilet unit, with a spring-water shower and basin situated just a few yards outside. There is also a yurt, which is furnished in the same way as the tipis. Eco Retreats often recommend the yurt to families or larger groups. Amplified music or portable stereo systems and pets are not allowed on site – but children and teenagers and friends as extra guests are all warmly welcomed. You even get a Fairtrade product hospitality pack. The whole style here speaks of a new approach to our living with Mother Earth. Try it and have some fun with simplicity.

OPEN: April until November. Everyone welcome, individuals, families and children.
ROOMS: Tipis and a yurt.
FACILITIES: Reiki, healing therapies. Nature. Please note that mobile reception is limited.
SPIRITUAL HELP: Reiki, spiritual healing, guided meditation, simple living.
GUESTS ADMITTED TO: Mostly everywhere.
MEALS: Self-catering.
SPECIAL ACTIVITIES: Natural healing treatments and guided meditation sessions. Reiki and spiritual healing.
SITUATION: Countryside and in nature. Very pleasant.

MAXIMUM STAY: Standard stay is for 2 nights, both weekends and in mid-week, but longer stays are possible by arrangement.
BOOKINGS: Letter, telephone, email. Note that the above is the office address, not the address where Eco Retreats take place.
CHARGES: Prices are for 2 guests staying 2 nights, including a Reiki session each, meditation, tickets for the Centre for Alternative Technology at Pantperthog and an organic welcome hamper: tipis £305–£339; Yurt: £315–£359; extra nights £65–£75. For other overnight guests: children under 4 are free; children aged 5–15 £7.50; adults £15.
ACCESS: The address given above is the address of the office, not the retreat site. Rail: Machynlleth station (11 miles away), then taxi. Bus: nearest village served by buses is Ceinws; pick-up available. Car: head for Machynlleth via A487/A489; they will give you a map to follow from there.

WELSHPOOL

Abhed Ashram
Camlad House
Forden, Welshpool
Powys SY21 8NZ
Wales

Tel/Fax: 01938 580499
Email: contact@abhedashram.org
Website: www.abhedashram.org/camlad.html

Retreats • Workshops and Courses • Church/Temple • Yoga • Meditation • Spiritual Help
Vegetarian Food • Venue for Hire • Self-Catering Space • Community Living • Children

Yoga – Vedanta traditions

A Grade II listed building of historical importance, Camlad House is situated in peaceful surroundings with lovely views over the Severn Valley. It has 29 acres of land and consists of three floors with accommodation, plus two apartments to let. This ashram and meditation centre accommodates people who have committed their lives to the study and practice of a spiritual life in the methods of yoga and Vedanta traditions, which are two systems of Indian philosophy. The ashram has been established in Wales since 1983 under the auspices of the Universal Confluence of Yoga–Vedanta Luminary Trust. It welcomes people interested in this spiritual way. The centre has regular day and weekend programmes.

OPEN: All year. Receives men and women.
ROOMS: Singles, twin and family rooms available, as well as 2 guest apartments.
FACILITIES: There are increasing facilities here as refurbishment and enlargement are continuous.
SPIRITUAL HELP: Guidence in practice of these 2 spiritual traditions of yoga and Vedanta.

GUESTS ADMITTED TO: All public and guest areas and outside grounds.
MEALS: Vegetarian. Self-catering guests are asked to follow the vegetarian-only diet here.
SPECIAL ACTIVITIES: Contact the ashram for their latest programmes and course schedule.
SITUATION: 29 acres in quiet countryside.
MAXIMUM STAY: 1 week in first instance.
BOOKINGS: Letter, telephone, fax, email.
CHARGES: Low rates and many programmes are free or by donation. Please enquire for current charges.
ACCESS: Car: One hour from M6/M56 and less from the M54; via A483 and A490. Rail/coach: Welshpool (6 miles away), then taxi or pick-up by arrangement.

'All things appear and disappear because of the concurrence
of causes and conditions. Nothing ever exists entirely alone;
everything is in relation to everything else'
– Buddha

SCOTLAND

ARGYLL AND BUTE

DALMALLY

Craig Lodge
Family House of Prayer
Dalmally
Argyll PA33 1AR
Scotland

Tel: 01838 200216
Email: mail@craiglodge.org
Website: www.craiglodge.org

Retreats • Workshops and Courses • Church/Temple • Spiritual Help • Vegetarian Food
Community Living • Work Retreats • Children

Christian – Roman Catholic

Craig Lodge Family House of Prayer is a Catholic retreat centre in a traditional country house and sits on the banks of the River Orchy with mountains all around. It is a place of outstanding beauty. The community is a mixture of young people who have given up a year of their lives to live here and grow closer to God through prayer and hospitality. They welcome everyone from all backgrounds and traditions for retreats, refreshment, healing and renewal. The accommodation and food are homely and comfortable, in keeping with a family atmosphere. People of all generations ramble in and out; sometimes children and teenagers are as much involved in the domestic chores and the devotions as everyone else. There is a chapel where the Eucharist is reserved and exposed for adoration throughout the day. Divine Office is prayed morning and evening and the rosary three times a day. The aid organisation Scottish International Relief (SIR) is a fruit of this community and gives the opportunity to reach out to some of the world's poorest people. Mary's Meals is SIR's campaign to set up school feeding projects in places where poverty and hunger prevent children from gaining an education. SIR was conceived during the Bosnian conflict in 1992 when the organisation's founders delivered aid to Medjugorje in Bosnia, The first project began in Malawi in 2002 and today over 350,000 children receive a daily meal. To find out more about the work of SIR and how you can get involved, please visit www.marysmeals.org.

DUNBEG BY OBAN

Ashwhin Balanced Living Centre
and Personal Retreat
Dunstaffnage Mains Farm
Dunbeg by Oban
Argyll PA37 1PZ
Scotland

Tel: 01631 567192
Email: derby@ashwhin.com
Website: www.ashwhin.com

Retreats • Self-Catering Space • Alternative Therapies • Holistic Holidays

Mind Body Spirit – Healing spirituality

Ashwhin is run by Derby Stewart-Amsden. Though it was originally an holistic health centre, the centre is now open for personal retreats to meet the needs of people who want to take some time away from their hectic lives to regain their perspective, rest and relax, and to reconnect with themselves. Ashwhin is composed of old farm buildings, built in the early 1700s, and is unusual in hosting only one or two people at a time. This provides a highly personal service. Reiki attunements, shamanic work or continued coaching and counselling, along with a number of healing therapies, are on offer – plus spectacular scenery, fresh seafood, and lots of wildlife to watch.

ISLE OF ERRAID

Isle of Erraid Centre
Isle of Erraid
Fionnphort, Isle of Mull
Argyll PA66 6BN
Scotland

Tel: 01681 700384
Email: erraid@live.co.uk
Website: www.erraid.com

Retreats • Meditation • Spiritual Help • Bed and Breakfast • Vegetarian Food
Organic Food • Holistic Holidays • Community Living • Work Retreats • Children

Open spirituality – Non-sectarian spiritual community

A tiny island, close to the ancient Isle of Iona, Erraid offers a mini-paradise of golden beaches, moorland and rocky shoreline. Here you can unwind for a week or two, living with the small resident community and participating in meditation, work, play and celebration. This is an island for the whole family – children will love the freedom and adventure of the natural world in an environment that is safe and contained. The Isle of Erraid belongs to the Findhorn Foundation community, but is an independent project. If you're looking for simplicity and a chance to live close to the elements, Erraid is very much a place to bear in mind. Programme details are available on the website.

OPEN: Almost all year. Men, women, young people, families, groups and non-retreatants.
ROOMS: 10 singles, 2 doubles.
FACILITIES: Garden, lounge, TV.
SPIRITUAL HELP: Meditation. Communal working together.
GUESTS ADMITTED TO: Unrestricted access. Sanctuaries.
MEALS: Taken together. Organic food: they have had their own growing gardens for many years now. Vegetarian possible.
SPECIAL ACTIVITIES: Mass, often daily.
SITUATION: Isolated, beautiful.
MAXIMUM STAY: By arrangement, but if you want to stay on, discuss it with them.
BOOKINGS: Telephone, email. Confirm by letter.
CHARGES: Full-board weekly rates range from £150 to £300; the level of contribution is chosen by the guest after discussion of what the money will be used for.
ACCESS: Boat: ferry from Oban to Craignure, Mull, then connecting bus service to Fionnphort, Mull. The Erraid minibus can be arranged to meet you there. Ask for directions when booking.

ISLE OF IONA

Cnoc a' Chalmainn ('Hill of The Dove')   Tel/Fax: 01681 700369
Catholic House of Prayer   Email: mail@catholic-iona.com
Isle of Iona   Website: www.catholic-iona.com
Argyll PA76 6SP
Scotland

Church/Temple • Spiritual Help • Community Living

Christian – Roman Catholic

Founded in 1997 as a place of quiet retreat on Iona for pilgrims of all faiths, Cnoc a' Chalmainn is a small house up a rough track on a hillside overlooking the Sound of Iona. There is an oratory where the Blessed Sacrament is reserved, and which is open to all for quiet prayer and meditation. By maintaining a Eucharist Centre and reserved accommodation for visiting priests, Cnoc a' Chalmainn ensures that there is daily Mass or Communion on Iona throughout the year, and collaborates with the Iona Community to offer these services at St Michael's Chapel in Iona Abbey on Sundays from Easter to October. This is a very peaceful house in a beautiful location.

Iona Abbey
Iona Community
Isle of Iona
Argyll PA76 6SN
Scotland

Tel: 01681 700404
Fax: 01681 700460
Email: ionacomm@iona.org.uk

Retreats • Workshops and Courses • Church/Temple • Meditation • Spiritual Help
Vegetarian Food • Venue for Hire • Self-Catering Space • Community Living
Work Retreats • Children

Christian – Ecumenical

On the remote island of Iona stands the ancient monastic building of Iona Abbey, restored by the late Revd George Macleod and now home to the world-renowned Iona Community. The Iona Community is an ecumenical movement of ordained and lay Christians and welcomes more than 150,000 people to this ancient holy island every year. People come from all over the world, from all walks of life, to share in the daily work and worship of the community. The essence of their approach is the integration of spirituality and social concern. With a strong emphasis on social justice, there have been controversial times in the community's history, but it continues to show courage and conviction. It was on this tiny, peaceful island in AD 563 that St Columba from Ireland began his mission to bring Christianity to Scotland. A Benedictine abbey was built here in the Middle Ages and, until the Reformation, this offered hospitality to pilgrims. The present Iona Community began with the rebuilding of the cloistral buildings of the abbey – 'the place of the common life' – in the mid-twentieth-century, then continued its mission of work for political and social change and the renewal of the church. The abbey itself is splendid: very little of the original Benedictine monastery remains, but the rebuilding of the abbey in traditional style means that the cloisters, the refectory and the church itself are reminiscent of the lives of the monks that once lived here. The library is very special – rather like the cabin of a ship and full of interesting tomes. St Columba's Shrine too is a place for a moment of quiet prayer and reflection. While some of its members are dispersed throughout Britain to pursue their vocation in their daily lives, the ecumenical Iona Community runs two residential centres on Iona and an adventure camp on the Island of Mull, welcoming guests from March to October for programmes focusing on themes of concern to the Community and a wide range of intrest. These usually run for six days, offering an opportunity to experience a common life of worship, work, discussion and relaxation, with a weekly pilgrimage around the whole island every Tuesday. Celtic spirituality is a strong influence on the style of worship, which expresses the ecumenical and inclusive nature of Iona Community. Private retreats are possible in November, with the chance to join in daily worship in the abbey, share chores and take turns in leading services. This is not a particularly quiet place. It is filled with many visitors and is an active facility, which involves everyone in participating in all aspects of the community life including daily chores. The idea is that people come to join the community for a minimum of three nights, which allows guests to get to know one another, eating together, doing chores and talking part in discussions. The Iona Community also runs the **Camas Adventure Centre** (see Isle of Mull entry) and the **MacLeod Centre** (see below). In general, Iona is a place for finding a sense of belonging to God through community and shared activity. **Highly Recommended.**

MacLeod Centre
Iona Community
Isle of Iona
Argyll PA76 6SN
Scotland

Tel: 01681 700404
Fax: 01681 700460
Email: mac.bookings@iona.org.uk
Website: www.iona.org.uk

Retreats • Workshops and Courses • Church/Temple • Spiritual Help • Vegetarian Food
Venue for Hire • Community Living • Work Retreats • Children

Christian – Ecumenical

Run by the Iona Community, the MacLeod Centre welcomes youth clubs, school classes, church and community groups – all of whom live in dormitory accommodation and take part in the daily tasks of running the centre as well as in their own group work. Among the facilities are a multi-purpose community room, a craft room, sitting areas, a library and a quiet room. This is a lively, spirited place and fun and happiness are very much a part of the expression of a spiritual life. Fully accessible for disabled.

ISLE OF MULL

Camas Centre   Tel: 01681 700367
Ardfenaig, Bunessan   Email: camas@iona.org.uk
Isle of Mull   Website: www.iona.org.uk
Argyll PA67 6DX
Scotland

Retreats • Workshops and Courses • Church/Temple • Yoga • Meditation • Spiritual Help
Vegetarian Food • Self Catering • Community Living • Work Retreats • Children

Christian – Ecumenical – Open spirituality

Here is an opportunity to experience the simple life, with its challenges and rewards. It has been said that the peace and beauty of Camas create an atmosphere where the mind can wander and the body revive; it is a special place. The programme includes lots to do, which is fun too – even a children's weekend. The centre is run by the Iona Community and is an ideal setting for team building. Visit the website or contact the centre for the current programme. The Camas Centre's commitment to inclusive spirituality makes for a welcoming place on the south-western tip of Mull.

---

*'The human body, at peace with itself, is more precious than the
rarest gem. Cherish your body, it is yours this one time only'*
– Tsongkapa

DUMFRIES AND GALLOWAY

KIRKBEAN

Thomas Bagnall Centre
St Mary's, New Abbey
Kirkbean
Dumfries DG2 8DW
Scotland

Tel: 01387 880201
Email: bagnallcentre@sky.com /
info@thomasbagnallcentre.org
Website: www.thomasbagnallcentre.org

Church/Temple • Venue for Hire • Self-Catering Space • Children

Christian – Roman Catholic – Ecumenical

The Thomas Bagnall Centre, in the Diocese of Galloway, is a Christian retreat centre for small groups to pray, rest and renew. There is a special welcome for priests, with or without a group, or with family and friends, and to celebrate Mass here. The building, which dates from 1824, lies within the precincts of the ancient wall of the nearby thirteenth-century Cistercian monastery of St Mary, commonly known as Sweetheart Abbey. As part of the Parish of St Andrew's in the town of Dumfries, Sunday Mass is celebrated in St Mary's. The centre is available for spiritual and pastoral uses for exclusive use for small groups within the Christian community. Groups and individuals are welcome to come for a quiet stay or for their own organised retreat with a leader of their choice. It is available, on a self-catering basis, daily or for longer periods such as weekends, or weekly.

OPEN: All year. Everyone welcome.
ROOMS: Accommodation for a group of up to 10, sharing 3 large bedrooms and having exclusive use of the centre. New Abbey has two inns, which offer extra accommodation.
FACILITIES: Group meeting rooms, church.
SPIRITUAL HELP: None direct.
GUESTS ADMITTED TO: Every part of the facility when using it.
MEALS: Self-catering.
SPECIAL ACTIVITIES: Groups organise their own programme.
SITUATION: Picturesque village.
MAXIMUM STAY: By booking.
BOOKINGS: Letter, email. Visit the website for indication of availability.
CHARGES: The Thomas Bagnall Centre is a non-profit organisation and is available for a single overall donation rather than a per-person basis. The suggested offerings are: day £20; weekend £50; weekly £100 or whatever can be afforded.
ACCESS: Rail: Dumfries station (13 miles away). Bus: limited services from Dumfries to Kirkbean. Car: via A710. Ask for directions when booking.

ESKDALEMUIR

Kagyu Samye Ling Monastery	Tel: 01387 373232
and Tibetan Centre	Fax: 01387 373223
Eskdalemuir, Langholm	Email: scotland@samyeling.org
Dumfries DG13 0QL	Website: www.samyeling.org
Scotland	

Retreats • Workshops and Courses • Church/Temple • Yoga • Meditation • Spiritual Help
Vegetarian Food • Self-Catering Space • Alternative Therapies • Community Living
Work Retreats • Vocations • Hermitages

Buddhist (Tibetan Karma Kagyu tradition)

This Tibetan monastery set in the rolling hills of southern Scotland is one of the leading Buddhist centres in the Western world. Founded in 1967, Kagyu Samye Ling was the first major Tibetan Buddhist centre in Europe and it is still regarded as the 'mother' centre of the many Kagyu centres that have been established since. The temple is magnificent and is the heart of the community's life of daily prayer and practice. Samye Ling is home to an increasing number of resident lay and ordained sangha practitioners. The centre also continues to attract thousands of visitors who come to tour the beautiful temple and grounds or to attend one of the many courses on offer. Under the direction of Abbot Lama Yeshe Losal Rinpoche, Samye Ling has also initiated a system of long-term retreats in which the ancient meditation practices of the Karma Kagyu tradition are taught and practised. Guests are welcome to attend any of the meditation and prayer sessions. The programme on offer here is extensive and includes yoga, Tai Chi, garden courses and Buddhist home study. For those who are looking for a rest, Samye Ling offers a wide range of options. From working in the organic garden to helping out in the kitchens, from taking part in weekend courses to relaxing in the Tibetan tea rooms, there is plenty to do – or not do! There are lovely walks, within the grounds and further away and whether it's a meditative stroll around the stupa or a hearty stride into the hills, the benefits of a little exercise and fresh air are all part of life here. There is no expectation or pressure and guests are free to choose their own programme of activity within the framework of the Five Golden Rules. These rules safeguard the well-being of everyone and are: to protect life and refrain from killing; to respect other's property and refrain from stealing; to speak the truth and refrain from lying; to encourage health and refrain from all intoxicants; to respect others and refrain from sexual misconduct.

Less than a quarter-mile from the main centre is Purelands, a smaller independent centre where longer retreats are held and where you may hire the space for your own work. Here the atmosphere is calm and peaceful, conducive to more inward-focusing work. It can get pretty busy at the main centre, especially in the summer. As well as the ongoing programme of building development and the continuing programme of courses, teachings, empowerments and visits from Lamas and Rinpoches, there is a flourishing programme of humanitarian activity. The original founder, Dr Akong Tulku Rinpoche, has set up initiatives to help the poor and homeless in the UK, Tibet and other countries. He also founded Tara Rokpa Therapy, a system of psychotherapy that works with the principles of Buddhism to heal patterns of emotional and mental suffering. The development of places of long retreat and of the Holy Island project have made Samye Ling an enterprise in the deepest traditions of spiritual life. It welcomes people from all faiths in the understanding that Buddhism is a way of life rather than a religion. Nevertheless, there is a strong tradition of Tibetan Buddhism underpinning the work at this centre and a commitment to preserve the culture and heritage of Tibet. No one is expected to adopt Buddhism, but the opportunities to learn more about this profound philosophy and spiritual tradition are there for anyone who is open and interested. **Highly Recommended.**

OPEN: All year. Receives everyone but not families for overnight stays.
ROOMS: A large variety of rooms and dormitories and other accommodation is available. You need to bring adequate bedding and equipment if you are camping, as these are not provided. Rennaldburn self-catering farmhouse, 2 miles south of the monastery, is suitable for family accommodation.
FACILITIES: Disabled access, camping, garden, temple, walks. The facilities are numerous and in more than just one place, so you need to visit their website and spend some time exploring what is on offer here – which is a very great deal.
SPIRITUAL HELP: Meditation, personal retreat direction, weekend courses and short retreats, long retreats.
GUESTS ADMITTED TO: Unrestricted access.
MEALS: Everyone eats together. Simple vegetarian food only.
SPECIAL ACTIVITIES: A huge planned programme of events, courses and study. Visit the website or send for a brochure.
SITUATION: Rather isolated and quiet, but busy in summer. There can be lots of people visiting here at any time of the year but summer especially.
MAXIMUM STAY: No limit.
BOOKINGS: Telephone in normal office working hours, email, online contact form and online booking available.
CHARGES: Rates start from £15 per person and vary considerably according to type of accommodation, from dormitory and single/twin rooms to camping. See the website for full details.
ACCESS: Rail: Lockerbie station (16 miles away). Bus: services run from Lockerbie. Car. Via M6, then A7 or A744.

ASSOCIATED KAGYU SAMYE DZONGS AND ROKPA CENTRES IN UK AND IRELAND

Holy Island, c/o Holy Island Office   Tel: 01387 373232
Kagyu Samye Ling Monastery Tibetan Centre   Fax: 01387 373223
Eskdalemuir, Langholm   Email: office@holyisland.org
Dumfries DG13 0QL
Scotland

Kagyu Samye Dzong Glasgow   Tel: 0141 3329950
7 Ashley Street   Email: admin@ksdglasgow.org
Woodlands
Glasgow G3 6DR
Scotland

Kagyu Samye Dzong Edinburgh   Email: info@edinburgh.samye.org
28 Great King Street   Website: http://www.edinburgh.samye.org
Edinburgh EH3 6QH
Scotland

Kagyu Samye Dzong Cardiff   Tel: 02920 860054
2a–4a Cardiff Road   Email: info@meditateinwales.net
Caerphilly CF83 1JN   Website: http://www.meditateinwales.net
Wales

Samye Dzong Dundee   Tel: 01382 872020
51 Reform Street   Fax: 01382 872010
Dundee DD1 1SL
Scotland   Email: info@dundee.rokpa.org

Kagyu Samye Dzong London (Manor Place)   Tel: 0207 7088969
33 Manor Place   Email: manorplace@samye.org
London SE17 3BD   Website: www.london.samye.org
England

Kagyu Samye Dzong Northamptonshire   Tel: 07812 567496
4 Whitehill Road   Email: kettsamyedzong@aol.com
Desborough   Website: www.samyedzongnorthants.org
Northamptonshire NN14 2JZ
England

Kagyu Samye Dzong Chichester   Tel: 01243 671309
Southern Comfort, West Bracklesham Drive   Fax: 01243 672872
Bracklesham Bay, Chichester   Email: chichester@samye.org
West Sussex PO20 8PF
England

Kagyu Samye Dzong Cork
High Meadows, 6 Upper Panorama Terrace
Sunday's Well, Cork
County Cork
Ireland

Kagyu Samye Dzong Dublin   Tel: +353 (0)1453 7427
Kilmainham Well House   Fax: +353 (0)1453 7427
56 Inchicore Road   Email: info@buddhism.ie
Kilmainham, Dublin 8
Ireland

EDINBURGH AND EAST LOTHIAN

EDINBURGH

House of Prayer   Tel: 01314 471772
Society of the Sacred Heart of Jesus   Fax: 01314 469122
8 Nile Grove   Email: nilegrove@rscj.freeserve.co.uk
Edinburgh EH10 4RF
Scotland

Retreats • Workshops and Courses • Church/Temple • Meditation • Spiritual Help
Vegetarian Food • Community Living • Vocations

Roman Catholic – Inter-denominational – Monastic

Located in a suburban area, the House of Prayer embraces all denominations and tries to promote a non-sensational Christian spiritualism. Meditation is encouraged and there are two chapels. The community and the retreat team are members of the Society of the Sacred Heart of Jesus, an international congregation for women. Rooms are clean and bright, and surrounding the house is a fine garden. There are plenty

of courses to choose from in the programme along the following lines:
30-day retreats, women in scripture and tradition, Taize prayer days,
work with icons. Individually guided retreats in the tradition of the
Ignatian Exercises are available.

HADDINGTON

Sancta Maria Abbey	Tel: 01620 830223 /
Nunraw	01620 830228 (guest house)
Haddington	Fax: 01620 830304
East Lothian EH41 4LW	Email: guesthouse@nunraw.com
Scotland	Website: www.nunraw.org.uk

Retreats • Workshops and Courses • Church/Temple • Meditation • Spiritual Help
Bed and Breakfast • Vegetarian Food • Self-Catering Space • Community Living
Work Retreats • Vocations • Children

Christian – Roman Catholic – Monastic

With sometimes 60 people in their guest house and around 6,000 visitors a year, this monastery, home to a community of Cistercian monks, must be one of the most popular in Britain today. Nunraw offers a wide choice of informal retreats. Individuals or families can visit for a day, overnight or longer if they wish, with full-board accommodation. The guest house is run in keeping with the contemplative nature of a monastic life. The surrounding countryside is very beautiful and the abbey runs a large agricultural establishment. This is a place of silence and deep spirituality where you may truly put aside the burdens of everyday living and open yourself to the benefits of silence and solitude. The purpose in coming here is to seek God. **Highly Recommended.**

OPEN: All year except February. Receives men, women, young people, families, groups and non-retreatants. Children welcome.
ROOMS: Singles, doubles, dormitory rooms in the guest house. 4 family rooms.
FACILITIES: Park, library, guest lounge.
SPIRITUAL HELP: Personal talks, spiritual direction.
GUESTS ADMITTED TO: Chapel, church, gardens, grounds. Sometimes helping with work.
MEALS: Simple food in keeping with the monastic way, taken in the guest house. Self-catering possible.
SPECIAL ACTIVITIES: Divine Office and Mass.
SITUATION: Very quiet in the countryside, with woodlands, lakes, moorland, farmland.

MAXIMUM STAY: 1 week usual or by arrangement with guestmaster.
BOOKINGS: Letter, telephone, email.
CHARGES: Donation only. Ask for a guideline when you book.
ACCESS: Rail: Edinburgh station (26 miles away). Bus: a service runs from Edinburgh to Haddington (7.5 miles from the abbey), then take a taxi from there. Car: via A1.

FIFE

FALKLAND

Tabor Retreat Centre
Key House, High Street
Falkland
Fife KY15 7BU
Scotland

Tel: 01337 857705
Email: lynda@keyhouse.org /
ann@keyhouse.org
Website: www.keyhouse.org

> Retreats • Church/Temple • Meditation • Spiritual Help • Bed and Breakfast
> Vegetarian Food • Venue for Hire • Self-Catering Space • Holistic Holidays
> Community Living • Vocations

Christian – Ecumenical

Tabor, a very pretty eighteenth-century house, is on the High Street, next door to Falkland Palace and situated in a garden with views of the Lemon Hills. It is an ecumenical house, welcoming men and women of all traditions or none. The name of the centre comes from Mount Tabor, where Jesus chose to be apart for a time, the place of change. As the resident community is small, an informal atmosphere prevails and there is a mixture of silence and family-style life. Retreats include individual ones and regular weekend retreats. A popular place, so you need to book well in advance. **Highly Recommended.**

OPEN: All year Tuesday to Sunday. Receives men, women, young people and groups.
ROOMS: 4 doubles but can be booked as singles.
FACILITIES: Chapel, oratory, garden, guest lounge.
SPIRITUAL HELP: Personal talks, spiritual direction, meditation, personal retreat direction.
GUESTS ADMITTED TO: Unrestricted access.
MEALS: Everyone eats together – in the kitchen usually. Wholefood, simple, mainly vegetarian. Special diets.
SPECIAL ACTIVITIES: Planned programme.
SITUATION: Quiet in a conservation village.

MAXIMUM STAY: 5 nights.
BOOKINGS: Letter, telephone, email. Printable booking form.
CHARGES: By donation; current suggestions per person are: full board £35; bed and
dinner £30; B&B £20; non-programme day retreats (includes tea, coffee and lunch)
£15; professional groups £20; programmed and guided day retreats £20; groups of 8 or
more £17; programmed weekend event £75.
ACCESS: Rail: Markinch station (5 miles away), then bus. Bus: local routes serve
Falkland. Car: via A91 and A92, on the A912. Detailed directions are on the website.

GLASGOW

GLASGOW

Ignatian Spirituality Centre   Tel: 0141 3540077
35 Scott Street   Email: admin@iscglasgow.co.uk
Glasgow G3 6PE   Website: www.iscglasgow.co.uk
Scotland

Retreats • Workshops and Courses

Christian – Roman Catholic – Ecumenical

Training courses, retreats and events based on the spiritual exercises
of St Ignatius of Loyola for all who seek God in their lives are precisely
what these retreats are about. There are day and evening events as
well as longer courses. While this is a non-residential centre, retreats
are held in various other venues where you can stay, such as in Iona
and even abroad in Spain. However, everyone is welcome here who
seeks an oasis in the city for quiet space, private prayer and reflection
during weekdays.

'Be generous in prosperity, and thankful in adversity'
– Baha' Allah

HIGHLAND

CANNICH

Sancti Angeli Benedictine Skete
Marydale
Cannich, near Beauly
Inverness IV4 7TT
Scotland

Tel: 01456 415218
Email: sancti.angeli@ukonline.co.uk
Website: www.sanctiangeli.org

Retreats • Workshops and Courses • Church/Temple • Spiritual Help • Vegetarian Food
Self-Catering Space • Community Living • Work Retreats • Vocations • Hermitages

Christian – Roman Catholic

In the Highlands, this Skete is a large hermitage dedicated to silence and prayer. Activities here are formation for prayer integrated into daily life, and icon writing. All visitors live alongside a monastic life with the community. Only women are permitted to stay inside the monastery and men are received to stay in a nearby self-catering place, but men may attend the midday meals and all regular prayer times. There are weekend monastic study breaks for students and young professional women, as well as longer stays to work as helpers. A summer school and an online icon-writing course are offered as well. The website is one of the best monastic websites and it explains all about Skete tradition and history in Christianity. All visitors do some monastic studies and have one-to-one meetings regarding vocational discernment and the place of prayer in their lives. **Highly Recommended.**

'It is sad not to be loved, but it is much sadder
not to be able to love'
– Miguel de Unamuno

KILMUIR

The Coach House
Coach House Kilmuir Trust
Kilmuir, North Kessock
Inverness IV1 3ZG
Scotland

Tel: 01463 731386
Email:
coachhouse@kilmuir.fsbusiness.co.uk
Website: www.coachhousekilmuir.org

Retreats • Workshops and Courses • Spiritual Help • Bed and Breakfast • Vegetarian Food

Christian – Open spirituality

The Coach House is a lay retreat place where you can relax, reflect, study and recover some inner direction to face the strains of your ordinary life. We found it an extremely restful place, with spectacular views over the Moray Firth and marvellous woodland and beach walks – the wild flowers and bird life are renowned. The work here is to provide the space and guidance for spiritual growth and insight to happen with individual retreats and workshops, many Ignatian-based including 30-day Ignatian retreats. A caring and nurturing environment.

OPEN: March to December. Receives everyone.
ROOMS: 4 singles in house plus 1 single in cottage. 2 doubles.
FACILITIES: Garden, library, guest lounge.
SPIRITUAL HELP: Personal talks, group sharing, spiritual direction, personal retreat direction, meditation, directed study, Ignatian exercises.
GUESTS ADMITTED TO: Unrestricted access.
MEALS: Everyone eats together. Traditional/vegetarian food. Special diets catered for.
SPECIAL ACTIVITIES: Planned programme online.
SITUATION: Very quiet, overlooking the Firth with woods, beach and hill walking at hand.
MAXIMUM STAY: Open.
BOOKINGS: Letter, email, online contact form.
CHARGES: By donation. Current suggestions: B&B £30 per night; full board £40 per night; 6-day retreat £280 (7 nights); 8-day retreat £360 (9 nights).
ACCESS: Rail: Inverness station (6 miles away). Bus: coaches run to Inverness. Air: Inverness airport (13 miles away). Pick-up possible from Inverness airport and bus and railway stations, with donation towards petrol costs. Car: via A82, A9 or A96.

SCORAIG

Shanti Griha Retreat
Scoraig
Dundonnell
Wester Ross IV23 2RE
Scotland

Tel: 01854 633260
Email: shantigriha@hotmail.com
Website: www.shantigriha.com

Retreats • Workshops and Courses • Yoga • Meditation • Spiritual Help
Bed and Breakfast • Vegetarian Food • Organic Food • Alternative Therapies
Holistic Holidays • Community Living • Hermitages

Yoga – Astanga Yoga – Zen Buddhism

Shanti Griha was established in 1999 and its name means 'house of peace'. It is very remote – when you finally leave your transportation, you walk about an hour to get there. It is in a wild, wonderful and back-to-real-life place. Fresh air, pure water, tranquillity, walks and wildlife abound. And just look at the retreats and courses on offer: Yoga, Thai massage, meditation, Tai Chi and Qi Gong, lots of singing, windpower and how to make and create it, vegetarian cooking, hypnosis and regression work, individual retreats and Gaelic language immersion courses. All of these are led by expert teachers and practititoners. Scoraig is an almost forgotten peninsula in the Highlands and one of the last wildernesses of Europe. Shanti Griha is set in its own two acres, just a few yards from the sea and at the foot of a great mountain. Electricity here is provided by small windmills. There are only about 30 houses stretched out along the area. Among these you will find a violin maker, boat builder, pony breeder, weaver and a potter. No pub, no corner shop, no noise, no crowds, nothing but you and Mother Earth and a few like-minded people learning to live more deeply, singing, meditating, doing yoga – and eating plain real food. Start walking up the path to Shanti Griha now. **Highly Recommended.**

OPEN: Courses at Shanti Griha take place between April and October and are limited to 8 participants. Everyone welcome.
ROOMS: 5 bedrooms – singles, double, twin, triple, 2 bathrooms. A cabin in the woods sleeps one to two. Note that shoes are not allowed indoors so you'll need to wear slippers, socks or sandals.
FACILITIES: Meditation room/yoga studio, an open kitchen and dining room, and a cosy living room with an open fire and library.
SPIRITUAL HELP: Yoga, group sharing, healing therapies.
GUESTS ADMITTED TO: Everywhere.

MEALS: Vegetarian food. Organic. Home-baked bread and cakes. Vegan is possible and special diets for medical or ethical reasons are by arrangement.
SPECIAL ACTIVITIES: Special programme. Visit the website for current and full details.
SITUATION: Truly remote and filled with wonderful scenery.
MAXIMUM STAY: Usually a week or so, but also by arrangement.
BOOKINGS: Online booking form is the easiest and best method, but the booking form can also be downloaded if you wish to send a letter.
CHARGES: Currently courses can go up to £750 per week (full board), but the average for a programme retreat is about £500. For personal retreats, the minimum stay is 4 nights and the full-board rate is £50 per night, with meditation guidance if required.
ACCESS: Car: via A9, A835 and A832 to Badrallach, then it is a 3-mile walk. This is a remote place as you will see from these instructions: 'Take the footpath that leads off from the parking area [at Badrallach] and is marked by the sign saying "unsuitable for vehicles".' The travel directions are very well detailed on their website.

ISLE OF SKYE

Skye Yoga Holidays   Tel: 01470 592367
West House   Email: info@skye-yoga-holidays.co.uk
Stein, Waternish   Website: www.skye-yoga-holidays.co.uk
Isle of Skye IV55 8GA
Scotland

Retreats • Workshops and Courses • Yoga • Meditation • Spiritual Help
Self-Catering Space • Alternative Therapies • Holistic Holidays • Children

Yoga

Skye Yoga Holidays is based in an old traditional Isle of Skye stone-house with a front garden that runs down to the Lochbay shore. There is a purpose-built yoga studio. The host here trained at the Yoga for Health Foundation as a yoga teacher and a remedial yoga teacher. This means she can teach those who are less able and also children, so do not hesitate to discuss your requirements with her.

'Ultimately faith is the only key to the universe'
– Thomas Merton

TONGUE

Fir Chlis House of Prayer and Healing Tel: 01847 611788
Old Kyle Road, Rhian Email: firchlishouseofprayer@hotmail.co.uk
Tongue, by Lairg Website: www.angelforce.co.uk/firchlis
Sutherland IV27 4XL
Scotland

Retreats • Spiritual Help

Christian – Anglican – Ecumenical

This Ecumenical retreat is a place devoted to prayer and healing. Fir Chlis has stunning views over Ben Loyal, which is often referred to as the Queen of Scottish Mountains. Marvellous coastlines, abundant wildlife and a quiet remote location give enchantment to this retreat. Life at Fir Chlis revolves around regular prayer times – morning, noon and evening, with Communion celebrated once a month. The Reserved Sacrament is kept in the house for contemplation. In a nutshell, this retreat is about seeking the presence of God – no alternative therapies, no mixed bag of spiritual traditions – just peace, silence and the time and space for you, as St Benedict said, to listen.

OPEN: Most of the year. Everyone welcome.
ROOMS: 1 single. 2 en suite twins.
FACILITIES: Garden.
SPIRITUAL HELP: Regular times of prayer, Communion, Reserved Sacrament.
GUESTS ADMITTED TO: Everywhere.
MEALS: The 3 meals a day are simple and sufficient. A packed lunch can be done if you plan to go walking.
SPECIAL ACTIVITIES: Prayer, rest.
SITUATION: Remote and wonderful. Coast and mountains.
MAXIMUM STAY: Visits may be from as little as a day.
BOOKINGS: Letter, telephone, email.
CHARGES: Donations for short, medium or longer-term stays are invited.
ACCESS: Rail: Lairg station (38.5 miles away). Bus: limited services from Lairg, Durness and Thurso. Car: via A9 and A836.

STRUY

Centre of Light	Tel: 01463 761254
Tighnabruaich	Email: lindachristie@ecosse.net
Struy	Website: www.centreoflight.co.uk
Inverness IV4 7JU	
Scotland	

> Retreats • Workshops and Courses • Meditation • Spiritual Help • Bed and Breakfast
> Vegetarian Food • Self-Catering Space • Alternative Therapies
> Holistic Holidays • Hermitage

Alternative spirituality – Mind Body Spirit

This is a centre for healing and retreats set in the Highlands, which we have recommended for many years now. The core direction is on meditation and Resonance Kinesiology, which is opening the heart to the higher self, building better connections between yourself and the Creator Being, and understanding human and planetary progression and your place in the scheme of things. Resonance Kinesiology is an opening to a new way of working with kinesiology that looks in depth at all levels and areas of your life. Reality has many facets, some seen, some unseen, and these may all be approached and understood using this method. Over time it can unlock creative potential and provide insights into life. Linda Christie, the retreat owner, has written a book about Resonance Kinesiology, which can be ordered from her website. The centre, set in five acres, is situated in a beautiful glen, there are mountains all around, rivers, trees and even a waterfall. Facilities are light, airy and clean. **Highly Recommended.**

OPEN: All year. Receives everyone.
ROOMS: You will have a cottage of your own to stay in during your retreat. It is light and spacious, the perfect place to relax, write, meditate and explore the highland countryside. The cottage has a large double room, a living area and a shower room. There is a small kitchen area for drinks and snacks while the main kitchen is housed across the garden where you can cook and watch TV should you feel the need to keep in touch with the world.
FACILITIES: Garden, park, library.
SPIRITUAL HELP: Personal talks, meditation, Resonance Kinesiology.
GUESTS ADMITTED TO: Unrestricted.
MEALS: All food will be provided for you on a self-catering basis. Accommodation-only retreats are totally self-catering.
SPECIAL ACTIVITIES: Planned retreats, courses and traning. Visit the website for details.
SITUATION: A supportive landscape for a retreat.

MAXIMUM STAY: By arrangement, usually 3–7 days.
BOOKINGS: Letter, telephone, email.
CHARGES: Currently the rates are as follows: sessions with Linda £40 per hour; to create your own retreat £400 per week or £55 per day (minimum stay 3 days); 5-day meditation retreat £475 (including food and accommodation).
ACCESS: Rail: Inverness station. Air: Inverness airport. Pick-up can be arranged from Inverness for £40 return. Car: on A831; if you plan to drive, directions can be emailed to you.

MORAY

ELGIN

Pluscarden Abbey	Tel: 01343 890257
Elgin	Fax: 01343 890258
Moray IV30 8UA	Email: monks@pluscardenabbey.org
Scotland	Website: www.pluscardenabbey.org

Retreats • Church/Temple • Spiritual Help • Vegetarian Food • Self-Catering Space
Community Living • Vocations

Christian – Roman Catholic – Monastic

The complete Benedictine Divine Office is sung in Latin to Gregorian chant at Pluscarden, wonderfully well too. You can buy a CD to take home if you want. The monks here do market gardening, book binding and work with bees. Year by year their reputation increases in their gifts of hospitality. If you are a man and want a retreat that is truly monastic in a far place with great depth in the prayer life, then go to Pluscarden. Women guests are normally accommodated in a separate guest house, St Scholastic's, where it is self-catering. Guests are admitted to the side chapels of Pluscarden Abbey, and to the ornamental garden in front of St Benedict's. Facilities include a quite well-stocked shop. Retreats are less structured here than in many other retreat places. What is offered is the regular monastic day with the eight services of prayer and the daily Mass. This is one of the very best frameworks for seeking God, as millions of men and women have discovered over the centuries. People who come here normally return. **Highly Recommended.**

OPEN: All year, 04:30–20:30. Receives everyone over 16 years of age; those under 16 should be accompanied by an adult.

ROOMS: There are two guest houses: one with 14 rooms for men where meals are taken with the monks; the other has 12 rooms and is self-catering and this is where women guests stay. Each guest house has its own warden or guestmaster. See their website for details of the accommodation.

FACILITIES: Disabled facilities are good in both guest facilities. Church, chapel, garden, library, guest lounge.

SPIRITUAL HELP: Personal talks, spiritual counselling.

GUESTS ADMITTED TO: Chapel, church, guest areas.

MEALS: Men eat together lunch and supper. Otherwise taken in guest house. Traditional food. Vegetarians and simple special diets. Self-catering facilities for women guests.

SPECIAL ACTIVITIES: Some events but no particular organised programme (see above).

SITUATION: Very far north and very quiet.

MAXIMUM STAY: 2 weeks.

BOOKINGS: Letter, email, online enquiry form. Bookings are not taken by telephone.

CHARGES: Donations. Ask for what is suggested.

ACCESS: Rail/bus: to Elgin (6–7 miles away), then taxi. Car: via A96 and B9010.

FINDHORN

Findhorn Foundation	Tel: 01309 691653
The Park, Findhorn	Email: bookings@findhorn.org
Forres	Website: www.findhorn.org
Moray IV36 3TZ	
Scotland	

Retreats • Workshops and Courses • Meditation • Spiritual Help • Bed and Breakfast
Vegetarian Food • Self-Catering Space • Alternative Therapies • Holistic Holidays
Community Living • Work Retreats • Vocations • Camping • Children

Open spirituality – Mind Body Spirit

This is a famous and popular place and can get very crowded in the summertime. The Findhorn Foundation community was founded in 1962 by three people, who believed in the principles that the source of life or God is accessible to each person and that nature, including earth, is intelligence and part of a much greater plan. Nature spirits, or devas, are said to have allowed them to raise vegetables and exotic flowers from a barren soil of sand and gravel. Today Findhorn is a highly organised and very large operation, and one of the largest private communities in Britain, maybe even in the world. Enthusiasm, harmony and love are the precepts by which they all try to work and there is a strong emphasis on meditation. They believe that humanity is in an evolutionary expansion of consciousness and Findhorn seeks to develop new ways of creating a better world in which we may live. Tens of thousands of visitors are welcomed here every year and the Findhorn reputation is known internationally. Courses of all descriptions, length and type run throughout the year. Subject specialities include alternative lifestyles and technology, meditation, food and gardening, health and healing, arts and crafts, inner process, prayer and self-expression – to name but a few. Such is the popularity of this place that accommodation usually needs to be booked many months in advance. It is definitely not a place for a private retreat as understood in the Christian or Buddhist traditions. The Community offers a live-work-meditate lifestyle for those who wish to share it. There are also secondary island retreat centres of the Foundation. Visit their website and be amazed at what is on offer.

OPEN: All year. Receives men, women and families. Children welcome if supervised.
ROOMS: Many rooms and other accommodation too numerous to list. These vary in quality and type, so ask what is on offer when you book, but there are singles and doubles.
FACILITIES: Disabled access possible, conferences, garden, park, library, payphone, large indoor space, several smaller working spaces. The facilities range from houses, chalets, caravans and campsites plus all manner of shared things like a visitors' centre and retail shopping. You name it, they probably have it.
SPIRITUAL HELP: Personal talks, meditation, workshop participation.
GUESTS ADMITTED TO: Most places, including the sanctuaries when on a programme. Day visitors can spend hours here.
MEALS: Meals include vegetarian provision and special diets.
SPECIAL ACTIVITIES: Planned programme of events.
SITUATION: Quiet in places but busy and those seeking silence may be out of luck here.
MAXIMUM STAY: According to programme and by arrangement.
BOOKINGS: Letter, telephone, email, online contact form.
CHARGES: These vary, but there is a fixed-prices system. Visit the website for full event details.
ACCESS: Rail: Forres station (5.5 miles away). Bus: services run between Forres and Findhorn. Car: Findhorn is 5 miles from Forres on the A96. Air: Inverness airport (24 miles away) and Aberdeen airport (74 miles away). See the website for detailed instructions.

'Prayer and love are really learned in the hour when prayer becomes impossible and your heart turns to stone'
– Thomas Merton

Shambala Retreat Centre for
Healing and Compassion
Findhorn
Forres
Moray IV36 0YY
Scotland

Tel: 01309 690690
Email: info@shambala-retreat.org
Website: www.shambala-retreat.org

Retreats • Workshops and Courses • Church/Temple • Meditation • Spiritual Help
Bed and Breakfast • Vegetarian Food • Organic Food • Venue for Hire • Self-Catering Space
Community Living • Work Retreats • Vocations • Camping • Children

Buddhist

Here is a new and exciting retreat, only a few minutes' walk from Findhorn Park. Shambala Retreat Centre for Healing is devoted to universal compassion with the aim of promoting harmony, tolerance and understanding among all who seek the spiritual in all religious and spiritual traditions. It offers a sanctuary to the many students and practitioners of all Buddhist traditions, as well as regular study and practice groups. There is space for both individual and group retreats. *Shambala* is a Sanskrit word for 'pure land' or 'paradise' and this retreat centre in its beautiful and freshly renovated house encourages you to keep focused on that spiritual vision. It is situated in six acres of gardens and grounds on the edge of the famous Findhorn Bay. Much work is still to be done here and they welcome those who might wish to come on a working retreat. If this interests you, please discuss it with them.

OPEN: All year. Everyone welcome.
ROOMS: Accommodation for 24 guests with private or en suite facilities. All rooms are equipped with orthopedic mattresses and natural bedding. Many rooms offer glorious views over Findhorn Bay.
FACILITIES: Ideal space for individual reflection and contemplation. Meditation hall, seminar room, Buddhist library, Finnish sauna, south-facing terrace with views of the bay, massages and holistic treatments.
SPIRITUAL HELP: Daily meditations, retreat coaching, alternative treatments.
GUESTS ADMITTED TO: Everywhere.
MEALS: Taken together. Organic vegetarian food and use of fresh local organic produce. Catering only for dairy/egg-free and wheat/gluten-free special diets.
SPECIAL ACTIVITIES: Meditations, courses and retreats. See the website for the full programme.
SITUATION: 5 minutes' walk from Findhorn Park.
MAXIMUM STAY: By arrangement.
BOOKINGS: Letter, telephone, email. Online payment possible (using PayPal).

CHARGES: Currently B&B rates start from £35 for single room and £25 per person in double/twin room. The complete list of prices is on the website.
ACCESS: Rail: Forres station (5.5 miles away). Bus: services run between Forres and Findhorn. Car: Findhorn is 5 miles from Forres on the A96. Air: Inverness airport (24 miles away) and Aberdeen airport (74 miles away).

FORRES

Newbold House Community	Tel: 01309 672659
111 St Leonards Road	Fax: 01309 672512
Forres IV36 2RE	Email: office@newboldhouse.org
Scotland	Website: www.newboldhouse.org

> Retreats • Workshops and Courses • Church/temple • Yoga • Meditation
> Spiritual Help • Bed and Breakfast • Vegetarian Food • Alternative Therapies
> Holistic Holidays • Community Living • Work Retreats

Open spirituality

This is one of the Findhorn Foundation community's centres, dedicated to retreats and workshops in healing and transformation. It is a large Victorian mansion in a pretty setting, with a resident core team who share the same vision. All spiritual traditions and religions are welcomed to come here and explore their inner awareness and life either by themselves or through the various retreats and workshops on offer.

OPEN: Most of year. Everyone welcome.
ROOMS: Accommodation for up to 24 people in mainly shared rooms.
FACILITIES: Sanctuary, gardens, various workrooms.
SPIRITUAL HELP: Retreats and workshops, group sharing.
GUESTS ADMITTED TO: Everywhere.
MEALS: Traditional vegetarian, lots from their own garden. Special diets for medical reasons.
SPECIAL ACTIVITIES: Retreats and workshops. Daily meditation. Subject to availability: educational programme and exploring spiritual themes through discussion. For an additional fee, you can follow other activities such as the transformation, life-coaching and healing courses.
SITUATION: Old house with gardens and woodlands. Specimen trees.
MAXIMUM STAY: By retreat, workshop and longer by arrangement.
BOOKINGS: Letter, telephone, email. Downloadable booking form. Online contact form available, and online booking will be coming soon.
CHARGES: Check the website for prices per event, workshop, course or stay.
ACCESS: Rail: Forres station (1.5 miles away). Bus: a service runs from Aberdeen and Inverness; local service runs to Newbold House. Car: via A96. Air: Inverness airport (20.5 miles away) and Aberdeen airport (73 miles away).

LETTERFOURIE

Letterfourie   Tel: 01542 832298
Drybridge, Buckie
Banffshire AB56 2JP
Scotland

Retreats • Workshops and Courses • Church/Temple • Bed and Breakfast
Vegetarian Food • Venue for Hire • Self-Catering Space

Christian – Inter-denominational

Letterfourie welcomes all people of all denominations or of none for self-organised retreats, conferences, workshops, church weekend, quiet restful breaks, and renewal and just for space and study. The 300-acre site has plenty to see, with ample opportunities to walk, observe and find beauty and nature in abundance. Letterfourie Chapel is very handsome and seats 60 people. The place has quietness, harmony and a friendly hospitality. Letterfourie House itself was built in 1773, designed by Robert Adam, and after additions in 1806 has remained virtually unchanged except, of course, for modern updating of necessary facilities. In addition to going on a private retreat here, there is the Woolworks Studio at Letterfourie, which means you might combine a workshop with wool with a retreat – in fact the combination of manual work and prayer is a traditional way to reflect and find spiritual space within.

OPEN: All year. Open to all.
ROOMS: 6 singles, 4 doubles, family room with double and 2 singles.
FACILITIES: Chapel, conferences, garden, park, lounge, bookstall, TV, guest telephone, large and extensive grounds.
SPIRITUAL HELP: Personal talks, group sharing, spiritual direction, personal retreat direction, directed study.
GUESTS ADMITTED TO: Chapel and 300 acres of ground plus guest areas.
MEALS: Traditional, wholefood meals available. Self-catering facilities available.
SPECIAL ACTIVITIES: Spinning, natural dyeing, felting, and lots of walking if you like.
SITUATION: Set in 300 acres of countryside on an organic farm.
MAXIMUM STAY: None at present.
BOOKINGS: Letter, telephone.
CHARGES: Please contact Letterfourie for details.
ACCESS: Rail: Keith station (14 miles away) or Elgin station (18 miles away), then bus to Buckie. Bus: local routes serve to Buckie, which 3 miles from Letterfourie. Car: 2 miles south of A98/A942 junction.

NORTH AYRSHIRE

ISLE OF ARRAN

Holy Isle Project	Tel/Fax: 01770 601100
Centre for World Peace and Health	Email:
Lamlash Bay, Holy Isle	reception@holyisland.org
Isle of Arran	Website: www.holyisland.org
North Ayrshire KA27 8GB	
Scotland	

> Retreats • Workshops and Courses • Church/Temple • Yoga • Meditation
> Spiritual Help • Vegetarian Food • Self-Catering Space • Alternative Therapies
> Holistic Holidays • Community Living • Work Retreats • Vocations

Inter-faith – Open spirituality – Buddhist (Tibetan Karma Kagyu tradition)

This is a very special place: an environmental and spiritual sanctuary that was once the home of the sixth-century Celtic hermit St Molaise and is now under the guardianship of the Tibetan Buddhists of **Kagyu Samye Ling Monastery** (see Dumfries and Galloway section). Holy Isle has been designated a Sacred Site in the UK and is home to a rich natural heritage of flora and fauna, seabirds, wild ponies, goats and Soay sheep. The coastal waters, warmed by the Gulf Stream, attract seals, dolphins and the occasional basking shark (and jellyfish too are common), so swimming is not advisable in many areas. St Molaise's Cave still exists and marks the beginning of an informal pilgrimage walk linking the two ends of the island. A healing spring and rock paintings depicting Tibetan Buddhist deities and saints bring the traditions of Christianity and Buddhism together in easy, harmonious relationship. The Buddhists acquired Holy Isle in 1992 and have made every effort to protect the natural environment and to re-establish a living tradition of spiritual practice. At the south end of the island, lighthouse cottages have been refurbished as cloistered long retreats for Buddhists; visitors to the island are asked to respect the privacy of this secluded area. At the north end of the island, the old farmhouse and additional buildings form an attractive courtyard complex for the new Centre for World Peace and Health. Everything has been done to the highest standards. The centre offers retreat and conference facilities for inter-faith, complementary health and environmental groups. Individuals are welcome for private retreat, but priority is given to groups during the summer months. Accommodation is spacious, modern, comfortable and light; the vegetarian meals are delicious. Some of the produce is grown on the island and there is a delightful peace garden where rock paintings, a labyrinth peace walk, meditation corners, herbs and shrubs combine to soothe the senses and calm the mind. Guests and visitors are asked to respect the Five Golden Rules, which are there to protect the well-being of all sentient beings and the island's pure environment. These are: to protect life and refrain from killing; to respect other's property and refrain from stealing; to speak truthfully and refrain from lying; to encourage health and refrain from all intoxicants; to respect others and refrain from sexual misconduct. Whether you come alone or as part of a group, for a day visit, a course or a private retreat, Holy Isle will not disappoint – just be prepared to wait to come on or off the island. Weather conditions are renowned for disrupting ferry crossings! The Abbot of Kagyu Samye Ling Monastery and director of this project, has said about this place: 'May every wonderful and wholesome thing arise here and may its goodness and happiness spread throughout the entire world.' **Highly Recommended.**

OPEN: All year except winter when ferry crossing is too difficult. Receives men, women and groups. **No smoking, drugs, alcohol or pets are allowed on the island.**
ROOMS: Singles, doubles, dormitories.
FACILITIES: Conference, library.
SPIRITUAL HELP: Meditation and personal retreat direction in some cases on a specific retreat.
GUESTS ADMITTED TO: Unrestricted access in the spaces designated as open to the public.
MEALS: Vegetarian food only.
SPECIAL ACTIVITIES: At the north of the island there is the Centre for World Peace and Health, where an ongoing retreat and course programme takes place. Guests are also welcome to stay at the centre for personal retreats or holiday breaks. A closed Buddhist retreat takes place at the south of the island. As well as staying at the centre, you are encouraged to visit Holy Isle for the day. The island is divided into several areas, some of which are reserved for birds and animals, others for their native-tree-planting project. Visitors are requested to never bring any animals on to the island and to stay on the designated pathways. Full programme of retreats and events on the website.
SITUATION: A beautiful sacred Scottish island.
MAXIMUM STAY: Open.
BOOKINGS: Letter, telephone, email. Printable booking form.
CHARGES: Between March and October, a course programme takes place at the Centre for World Peace and Health. Courses vary in price according to who is teaching. Rates include meals. Visit the website for current course fees.
ACCESS: Boat: at Ardrossan Harbour take the ferry to Brodick on the Isle of Arran, then the bus to Lamlash Pier where you board the ferry to Holy Isle. Visit the website for a travel timetable to Holy Isle, which shows links from Glasgow Central, Glasgow Airport and Prestwick Airport. Call for travel directions when you have booked. Day visitors can contact the Holy Isle ferry directly (email tomin10@tiscali.co.uk or telephone 01770 600998).

ISLE OF CUMBRAE

Island Retreats
College of the Holy Spirit and
Cathedral of the Isles
Millport, Isle of Cumbrae
North Ayrshire KA28 0HE
Scotland

Tel: 01475 530353
Fax: 01475 530204
Email: cumbrae@island-retreats.org /
tccumbrae@argyll.anglican.org
Website: www.island-retreats.org

Retreats • Workshops and Courses • Church/Temple • Spiritual Help • Bed and Breakfast
Vegetarian Food • Venue for Hire • Self-Catering Space • Children

Christian – Anglican – Scottish Episcopalian

Visitors have said that the college is a combination of a very upmarket guest house and a Christian retreat house. Easily accessible by public transport with only a 10-minute ferry crossing from Largs, the college built in 1851 is attached to one of Britain's smallest cathedrals, the Cathedral of the Isles. Both stand in eight acres of gardens, fields and woods, and they present an appearance of tranquillity and peace. The Cathedral of the Isles is home to the local congregation of St Andrew's Millport and is a centre for Christian worship on the island. The warden there may be available to provide spiritual direction and to lead both individual and group retreats on request. Guests have the use of the library and two common rooms. The cathedral is open every day for services or simply quiet times and reflection. The small but very beautiful island of Cumbrae enjoys wonderful views of the surrounding mountains and islands and is known for its marvelous bird life and wild flowers. The retreats here and at **Bishop's House** on the Isle of Iona (details given below) are managed by Island Retreats, a company within the Diocese of Argyll and the Isles. Both the College of the Holy Spirit and Bishop's House are very special places in very special settings. Everyone is welcome to come and stay, regardless of faith or belief and whether you want a retreat, a quiet restorative time or an active holiday, you will be welcomed. The College of the Holy Spirit is also available for conferences, functions and weddings, so at certain times it can be busy.

Bishop's House
Isle of Iona
Argyll PA76 6SJ
Scotland

Tel: 01681 700111
Fax: 01681 700101
Email: iona@island-retreats.org

KILWINNING

Smithstone House of Prayer
Dalry Road
Kilwinning
North Ayrshire KA13 6PL
Scotland

Tel: 01294 552515
Fax: 01294 559081
Email: office@smithstonehouse.org.uk
Website: www.smithstonehouse.org.uk

Retreats • Workshops and Courses • Church/Temple • Spiritual Help
Community Living • Vocations

Christian – Roman Catholic – Ecumenical

Smithstone is a house and lodge that developed through the eighteenth and nineteenth centuries and is now a peaceful and beautifully situated retreat house of prayer run by the Sacred Heart Fathers. The aim here is to promote the spirituality of the heart. There is a short programme of events (visit the website for details). Accommodation is for up to 40 people for a day event; for overnight stays, there are 4 singles and 5 twin-bedded rooms. The facilities are just a little old-fashioned for a retreat these days, but for all that it is a comfortable place, which is welcoming.

---

*'The spirit is present in every human being. It may be
totally concealed but it is always there and without it we
cannot be fully human'*
– Bede Griffiths

ORKNEY

●●●

ORKNEY

Woodwick House	Tel: 01856 751330
Evie	Fax: 01856 751383
Orkney KW17 2PQ	Email: mail@woodwickhouse.co.uk
Scotland	Website: www.orknet.co.uk/woodwick

> Retreats • Bed and Breakfast • Vegetarian Food • Organic Food • Venue for Hire
> Community Living • Children

Open spirituality – Non-denominational

Woodwick House is a guest house in a particularly lovely situation, which makes it a good place for a private retreat in what is not a religious or a particularly spiritual domestic environment. Woodwick House is a peaceful place set in 12 acres of bluebell woodland with its own burn and bay in the beautiful islands of Orkney. This is a bit unusual because Orkney is mostly bare of trees, so Woodwick feels like a self-contained and enclosed space. There are open fires and nicely prepared meals, using as much local produce as possible. Bird and seal watching, painting, walking or just sitting in front of the fire and reading a book from the house library are all possible here. It is a good venue for small group retreats as well. There are a number of concerts each year, mainly folk, jazz, and other similar types of music. Poetry readings, plays and art expositions are also activities at Woodwick House.

OPEN: All year. Receives everyone.
ROOMS: Singles, twin, and doubles, some en suite at various rates.
FACILITIES: Disabled access, conferences, performance room, garden, library, guest lounge, TV.
SPIRITUAL HELP: None.
GUESTS ADMITTED TO: Everywhere except private household areas.
MEALS: Traditional food, organic where possible. Vegetarian and special diets.
SPECIAL ACTIVITIES: Special music, literary and art events and exhibitions.
SITUATION: Unique situation of river, woodland, and near secluded bay.
MAXIMUM STAY: No limit.
BOOKINGS: Letter, telephone, email.
CHARGES: B&B rates per person per night range from £34 to £70.
ACCESS: Rail: Thurso station, then bus to Scrabster or Aberdeen. Coach: connection service from Inverness/Wick to Gills Bay; routes also go to Scrabster or John O'Groats in Caithness. Boat: routes run from Aberdeen, Scrabster, Gills Bay and John O'Groats (the latter is a summer-only, passenger-only service). Air: Orkney can be reached by air from Glasgow, Aberdeen, Edinburgh, Inverness and Sumburgh (all served by Flybe, operated by Loganair). It is best to ask for travel directions when booking.

PERTH AND KINROSS

CALLANDER

Lendrick Lodge
Brig O'Turk
Callander
Perth FK17 8HR
Scotland

Tel: 01877 376263
Email: enquiries@lendricklodge.com
Website: www.lendricklodge.com

Retreats • Workshops and Courses • Yoga • Meditation • Spiritual Help
Bed and Breakfast • Vegetarian Food • Venue for Hire • Alternative Therapies
Holistic Holidays • Community Living • Work Retreats

Alternative spirituality – Mind Body Spirit

Whatever your beliefs, you are welcome here – there is no specific religious tradition but respect for all and a strong commitment to love and acceptance. Lendrick Lodge is home to the world-renowned Sundoor International Firewalking School. Whether you are inspired to 'walk the path' of the shaman, undertake healing therapies, or simply to relax in the magnificent surroundings of the lodge, you will have comfortable accommodation and good vegetarian food. The grounds, set amid the mountains and lochs of the Trossachs, are peaceful: trees and a meandering stream offer places to be alone and to reflect, while other areas have been set aside for the Sweat Lodge and Firewalking ceremonies. Retreat and course leaders are professional teachers, masters and mystics. The following retreat topics give an idea of what is on offer here: *Yoga Weekend*, *Reiki Practitioner Course* , *Soul Retrieval Practitioner Course* and *Focusing on the Power of Soul Firewalk*. There is a volunteer programme. A new and very modern building has been created recently, which is the River Retreat – lots of natural wood, just by the river, and up-to-date, with space and peacefulness. **Highly Recommended.**

OPEN: All year. Everyone welcome.
ROOMS: Standard bedrooms sleep 3–4 people. In addition, single and twin rooms available for a supplement, River Retreat accommodation is en suite twin and twin/triple bedroom.
FACILITIES: The River Retreat offers a rebirthing pool, a holistic clinic, workshop space, and excellent accommodation.
SPIRITUAL HELP: Personal direction, yoga, alternative spiritualities, healing therapies.
GUESTS ADMITTED TO: Everywhere.

MEALS: Vegetarian. Everyone eats together. However, for a £5 per-day per-person charge the following diets are offered with at least 7 days' notice: vegan, dairy-free, wheat-free and mushroom-free.
SPECIAL ACTIVITIES: Acupuncture, craniosacral treatment, massage treatment, Reiki treatment, and harmonising pool treatment. 1-day courses on topics like *Reiki Healing*, *Yoga and Shamanism Sweat Lodge* and *Firewalking*.
SITUATION: Rural, by a river.
MAXIMUM STAY: Retreat, course or by arrangement.
BOOKINGS: Letter, telephone, email. Online booking form is best.
CHARGES: Treatments run about £35 per session. Full-board rates are about £45 per person, but check when booking.
ACCESS: Rail: Dunblane station (18.5 miles away). Car: off A821. Air: Edinburgh International (51 miles away), Glasgow International (40 miles away). In tourist season, allow 2 hours' driving from either airport.

DUNBLANE

Scottish Churches House	Tel: 01786 823588
1 Kirk Street	Fax: 01786 825844
Dunblane	Email: reservations@scottishchurcheshouse.org
Perth FK15 0AJ	Website: www.scottishchurcheshouse.org
Scotland	

Retreats • Workshops and Courses • Church/Temple • Spiritual Help • Vegetarian Food
Venue for Hire • Self-Catering Space • Vocations • Children

Christian – Inter-denominational – Ecumenical

This is a conference centre, belonging to all the mainstream churches in Scotland, but daily retreats are organised for individuals. The centre consists of a row of converted and renovated eighteenth-century cottages and a church along two sides of Cathedral Square. The atmosphere is quiet and not at all overpowering for such a large place. There is accommodation for 41 people, a conference hall, dining room, plus six more meeting rooms with lots of lounges and other facility space. Weddings and other special celebrations are possible in the medieval chapel in the garden. There are a programme and a good website with all details. Retreats are led by the Epiphany Group, a group working ecumenically in Ignatian spirituality; see www.epiphanygroup.org.uk for more details.

OPEN: All year except Christmas and New Year. Receives everyone.
ROOMS: 9 singles: 3 en suite, 1 disabled. 14 twin: 8 en suite. 1 family room. Day group facilities for up to 70 people.
FACILITIES: Disabled access, chapel, conferences, garden, guest lounge.

SPIRITUAL HELP: Personal talks, spiritual direction, meditation, directed study during planned retreats, all as requested.
GUESTS ADMITTED TO: Unrestricted access.
MEALS: Everyone eats together. Wholefood and vegetarian. Special diets catered for.
SPECIAL ACTIVITIES: Planned programme of conferences, retreats, events and seminars are available on the website.
SITUATION: Quiet in a cathedral close.
MAXIMUM STAY: Open.
BOOKINGS: Letter, telephone, fax, email.
CHARGES: Vary according to the retreat and kind of stay, so enquire when booking or visit the website.
ACCESS: Rail: Dunblane station; the centre is less than 10 minutes' walk away. Bus: regular bus services to Dunblane. Car: easily accessible from the M9 and A9.

KILGRASTON

Garden Cottage
Orchard and Apple House
Kilgraston, Bridge of Earn
Perth PH2 9HN
Scotland

Tel: 01738 813618
Email: adminorchard@btconnect.com
Website:
www.gardencottagespirituality.org.uk

Retreats • Church/Temple • Yoga • Meditation • Spiritual Help • Self-Catering Space
Alternative Therapies • Holistic Holidays • Community Living • Vocations • Hermitages

Christian – Roman Catholic – Ecumenical

A small community of the Society of the Sacred Heart offers space for rest and spiritual refreshment in two small stone cottages run together. They offer the option of guided retreats, either in the Ignatian mode or inspired by the interconnectedness of Eastern and Western spiritualities. The Orchard Centre is in a walled garden where a number of courses are on offer, including holistic spirituality, Enneagram, De Mello exercises, creation spirituality, yoga, Reiki, Shiatsu and massage as meditation. The community is ecumenical in outlook and aims to promote a holistic way of life and seeks to respond to the particular needs of individual guests. There is a little chapel where one can join in the morning and evening silent meditation periods. The accommodation is plain, offering one single in the main cottage and a hermitage; both are self-catering. For walks, there is a formal garden in front, a large walled paddock with old fruit trees at the back, rolling hills and woods over the road.

LOCHEARNHEAD

Dhanakosa
Buddhist Retreat Centre
Balquhidder, Lochearnhead
Perth FK19 8PQ
Scotland

Tel: 01877 384213
Email: info@dhanakosa.com
Website: www.dhanakosa.com

Retreats • Workshops and Courses • Church/Temple • Yoga • Meditation • Spiritual Help
Vegetarian Food • Alternative Therapies • Community Living • Work Retreats
Vocations • Hermitages

Buddhist – Friends of the Western Buddhist Order (FWBO)

Situated on the shores of Loch Voil in a beautiful glen, Dhanakosa is in a haven of natural beauty and tranquillity. Dhanakosa is run by the Friends of the Western Buddhist Order as a retreat centre for Buddhists and non-Buddhists alike. Throughout the year, weekend and week-long courses provide opportunities to learn meditation and introductory Buddhism. There is a special emphasis on integrating mind and body through a wide range of retreats, which include Yoga, hillwalking, Tai Chi, and arts and alternative health themes – all of which complement a programme of introductory meditation teaching that is open to anyone. The programme also usually has gay men's retreats, solitary retreats and working retreats. The atmosphere is very relaxed, warm and friendly. There is always time for retreatants to simply 'be' – and whether that means a stride up the hills, a swim in the loch, a quiet read or a snooze, it's all okay. Accommodation is comfortable; small dormitories with en suite facilities provide an experience of community. Dhanakosa itself is home to a small residential community and it is this strong sense of spiritual community that permeates the experience of being on retreat here, making it a very enriching stay indeed.

OPEN: Everyone welcome. In order not to disturb ongoing retreats, Dhanakosa is not open to drop-in visitors.
ROOMS: Dhanakosa was once a hotel, so it is centrally heated and generally comfortable. Rooms are shared between 1–3 people. Most rooms are en suite. Sleeping arrangements are always on a single-gender basis. There are usually between 15 and 32 people on a retreat, including the team. Single-room accommodation is not normally available, but if you are disabled or have special medical needs, then please discuss this with them at the time of booking.
FACILITIES: Meditation room, gardens, walks.
SPIRITUAL HELP: Meditation and Buddhist study. Personal meditation talks sometimes can be arranged.

GUESTS ADMITTED TO: Everywhere.
MEALS: All food is vegetarian. You will be asked to help with chopping vegetables and washing up.
SPECIAL ACTIVITIES: Introductory, regular and solitary retreats.
SITUATION: Natural beauty on the shores of a lake.
MAXIMUM STAY: By the retreat or programme. There are other longer-term stays, so you can discuss this with them.
BOOKINGS: Telephone during office hours, email.
CHARGES: Suggested current donations are £140 for a weekend and £330 for a week. There are lower suggested rates for those on low wages or who are unwaged. Contact Dhanakosa for further details or visit the website.
ACCESS: Rail/coach: Stirling station, then take a bus to Kingshouse and a taxi from there. Car: via A84. Comprehensive details are available on the website.

PERTH

Redemptorist Institute of Spirituality Tel: 01738 624075
St Mary's Monastery Fax: 01738 442071
Hatton Road, Kinnoull Email: copiosa@kinnoullmonastery.org
Perth PH2 7BP Website: www.kinnoullmonastery.org/index.html
Scotland

Retreats • Workshops and Courses • Church/Temple • Spiritual Help • Vegetarian Food
Community Living • Vocations

Christian – Roman Catholic – Monastic

This a large, rather institutional retreat centre, which overlooks Perth and enjoys peaceful seclusion. There is plenty of accommodation and a wide range of retreat and renewal courses available, which are firmly Christian based. Example of courses titles are: *The Bible in Liturgy*, *Mercy and Forgiveness* and *Spirituality for the Third Age*. Renewal retreats also for religious and priests. Individuals are welcomed throughout the year.

OPEN: All year except Christmas season. Receives everyone.
ROOMS: A lot of rooms here: some 20 singles, 16 twin.
FACILITIES: Disabled access, conferences, garden, library, guest lounge, TV.
SPIRITUAL HELP: Personal talks, group sharing, meditation, directed study, spiritual direction, personal retreat direction.
GUESTS ADMITTED TO: Unrestricted access.
MEALS: Everyone eats together. Traditional food. Vegetarian and special diets.
SPECIAL ACTIVITIES: Planned programme. Visit the website for details.
SITUATION: Quiet, on edge of town.
MAXIMUM STAY: Open.

BOOKINGS: Letter, telephone, email. Downloadable booking forms with course descriptions.
CHARGES: Enquire about charges when you book. The individual charges are given in the downloadable course details and booking forms.
ACCESS: Rail: Perth station (1.5 miles away). Bus: coaches run to Perth; local bus routes from Perth. Car: via M90, A90, A9 or A85.

TIBBERMORE

The Bield at Blackruthven	Tel/Fax: 01738 583238
Blackruthven House	Email: info@bieldatblackruthven.org.uk
Tibbermore	Website: www.bieldatblackruthven.org.uk
Perth PH1 1PY	
Scotland	

Retreats • Workshops and Courses • Church/Temple • Meditation • Spiritual Help
Bed and Breakfast • Vegetarian Food • Organic Food • Venue for Hire • Self-Catering Space
Alternative Therapies • Holistic Holidays • Community Living • Work Retreats • Children

Christian – Anglican – Eucumenical

The Bield is a huge estate, which holds a spectacular Georgian house, a walled garden with organic vegetables, an orchard with fruit trees and flowers, an indoor swimming pool and an art room – you name it and the Bield either provides it or is trying to offer it. A centre of Christian spirituality but open to all, this retreat offers healing and spiritual renewal both in the traditional and in the widest senses. The team here is numerous, from those who work in the garden and smallholding to an Episcopalian priest, a qualified counsellor, an art therapist and a horticulturalist/ecologist specialist. They are available as desired to listen, counsel, guide and support you on your personal journey. Daily prayers in the chapel and a Sunday Eucharist give structure to your day here and help to keep you anchored in the spirit. The 370-acre farm employs organic practices, including how the pigs, cows, and chickens are raised. The accommodation and conference rooms are in a converted steading – comfortable and well appointed, and providing a mostly vegetarian diet, using organic produce from the garden whenever available. Guests may enjoy all these resources for rest and relaxation or for prayer, reflection or healing. Southton Smallholding is their therapeutic farm project, offering supported part-time employment to adults with learning difficulties. Revd Robin Anker-Petersen, Director of Healing for St Andrew's Episcopal Diocese and tutor with the Acorn Christian Foundation in Scotland, offers spiritual direction, listening, prayer and group facilitation. Believing that Christ desires to heal in mind, spirit and body, prayer is available with the laying on of hands and anointing with oil for those who may wish it. All in all, the Bield is a continuing successful effort to provide the very best in a Christ-centred retreat open to all. **Highly Recommended.**

SCOTTISH BORDERS

HAWICK

Beshara School of Esoteric Education	Tel: 01450 88215
Chisholme House	Fax: 01450 880204
Roberton, near Hawick	Email: secretary@beshara.org
Roxburgh TD9 7PH	Website: www.beshara.org
Scotland	

Retreats • Workshops and Courses • Meditation • Spiritual Help • Vegetarian Food
Community Living • Work Retreats • Camping • Children

Open spirituality – Non-denominational – Educational charity

The Chisholme Institute has been the home of the Beshara School for more than 30 years. The Beshara School focuses on esoteric education. The subject matter is the human reality: who we are, and what our potential and purpose here in the world are, striving towards an understanding of the unity of existence. This study of spiritual awareness is quite demanding as it encompasses many mystical traditions, especially Sufism and in particular the works of Muhyddin Ibn Arabi. Residential courses of differing lengths, from a weekend to six months, are available. The study consists of periods of meditation, work, study and devotional practices; visitors are always welcome and invited to participate in this daily rhythm. In some ways it seems a spiritual mix of esoteric teaching, warm hospitality and love for the environment, which in this day and age strikes a chord in most people. The cooking, flower arrangements in the house, bedrooms, kitchen gardens and re-forestation programme all show love, care and impeccable taste. The house itself is Georgian, the accommodation simple but comfortable enough, and the food well prepared. They aim to produce about 70 per cent of their own food on some 200 acres of land, so you are eating

more or less organic the whole time. The staff and students are helpful, relaxed and very welcoming. The school follows no one particular
religious tradition or spiritual way. As to the word *Beshara* – it means
'good news'. It is reputed to be the word the Angel Gabriel used when
he announced the coming of Christ to Mary. **Highly Recommended.**

OPEN: All year but limited visiting during the 6-month winter residential course.
Receives everyone except groups.
ROOMS: Accommodation is shared, in double, triple or dormitory-style rooms. A
limited number of single rooms are available on request. There are no bedrooms with
en suite facilities.
FACILITIES: Disabled access: ground-floor rooms with wheelchair access, and one
bathroom with toilet and shower suitable for disabled users. Please discuss your
requirements. Garden, library.
SPIRITUAL HELP: The study course itself, personal talks, meditation, directed
personal study.
GUESTS ADMITTED TO: Main building and work of the resident community.
MEALS: Everyone eats together in the main house's dining room. Food may include
meat. Vegetarians are catered for, but any other dietary requirements will need to be
discussed with the secretary when booking. Special diets for medical conditions only.
SPECIAL ACTIVITIES: Planned events. Full course details are on the website.
SITUATION: Set in 200 acres of moorland and pasture; a very quiet place.
MAXIMUM STAY: By programme course and by arrangement.
BOOKINGS: Letter, telephone, fax, email.
CHARGES: By donation. Suggested daily rate: adult £30; teenager £12; child £7. All
education and tuition is free.
ACCESS: Rail: Edinburgh station (57 miles away) or Carlisle station (46 miles
away). Bus: from Edinburgh or Carlisle to Hawick, then take a taxi from there; pick-up
possible. Car: via A7. Air: Edinburgh, Newcastle or Glasgow airports; best to take a train
to Edinburgh, but pick-up is available on request.

STOBO

Stobo Castle Health Spa	Tel: 01721 725300
Stobo	Fax: 01721 760294
Peebles EH45 8NY	Email: reservations@stobocastle.co.uk
Scotland	Website: www.stobocastle.co.uk

Retreats • Workshops and Courses • Vegetarian Food • Organic Food
Alternative Therapies • Holistic Holidays

Holistic – Spa

Situated in the wonderful countryside of the Scottish Borders, Stobo
Castle offers a complete range of health and spa facilities and treatments, as well as specially designed programmes for a healing and re-

laxing retreat here. You can take as much exercise or not as you prefer, and dine expansively or follow a stricter regime. The spa facilities are quite complete, ranging from indoor pool to fully equipped gym. The bedrooms are first-class, and the surrounding gardens and grounds offer gentle strolling. There is an additional selection of treatments for men. You can come for the day or a longer stay – alone, with a partner or a group of friends.

OPEN: All year. Everyone over 14 years is welcome.
ROOMS: 50 en suite bedrooms.
FACILITIES: Full health spa – gym, pool, holistic treatments, fitness and well-being department, special men's range of treatments and therapies, hair salons, luxury comfort – in fact, the works!
SPIRITUAL HELP: None.
GUESTS ADMITTED TO: Everywhere.
MEALS: Everyone eats together in dining room. Excellent food. All diets catered for.
SPECIAL ACTIVITIES: Spa treatments and fitness classes.
SITUATION: Very calm in countryside.
MAXIMUM STAY: No maximum stay.
BOOKINGS: Letter, fax, telephone, email, online contact form.
CHARGES: They have an excellent brochure giving details of what is on offer with each rate for your stay. Details are also on their website.
ACCESS: Rail: Edinburgh station (30 miles away), then bus via Peebles. Coach: regular services to Peebles, then taxi. Bus: routes stop in Stobo, which is about a mile from the castle. Car: via A27 or A701.

'This is my simple religion. There is no need for temples; no need for complicated philosophy. Our own brain, our own heart is our temple; the philosophy is kindness'
– the Dalai Lama

CHANNEL ISLANDS

GUERNSEY

Les Cotils
Christian Retreat and Conference Centre
Les Cotils L'Hyureuse
St Peter Port
Guernsey GY1 1UU
Channel Islands

Tel: 01481 727793
Fax: 01481 701062
Email: reception@lescotils.com
Website: www.lescotils.com

Retreats • Workshops and Courses • Bed and Breakfast • Vegetarian Food
Venue for Hire • Children

Christian – Ecumenical

Les Cotils is a grand white place on a hill with glorious views to the port and sea. Set in 12 acres with wonderful views of the port, the sea and onwards to France, which is only 30 miles away, it offers first-class comfort, pretty furnished rooms and a coffee shop and tea room. This is retreating in style – if you can't relax here, then where else? For those on retreat, peace and quiet are possible even if other non-retreatant guests are staying – there is an active management policy to try and maintain this balance. There is a programme of ecumenical retreats and workshops, which range from men's retreats, drop-in days for carers, and musical events, to retreats on *Abundant Life in Jesus* and marriage-study courses.

OPEN: All year. Everyone welcome, including families with children.
ROOMS: 26 rooms, all en suite – singles, twin, doubles and family. Some with sea views.
FACILITIES: Disabled access, conferences, garden, park, good library, 3 guest lounges, TV.
SPIRITUAL HELP: Group sharing and spiritual direction on retreats. Morning and evening prayers led by members of different Christian traditions.
GUESTS ADMITTED TO: All public rooms.
MEALS: Everyone eats together. Traditional and vegetarian food. Special diets. Sample menus can be seen on their website, which we wish more retreat places would give.
SPECIAL ACTIVITIES: Special programme of events – see online for details.
SITUATION: Situated above the beautiful port in a large garden and park with great views.
MAXIMUM STAY: Open.
BOOKINGS: Letter, telephone. fax, email, online enquiry form.

CHARGES: Singles from about £24 to £47, doubles £48 to £80 – all are B&B and depend on time of year and type of accommodation. Special rates for children. Discounts for groups and low season. Full-board, half-board and dinner rates are all available; the various prices are on the website.
ACCESS: By air or sea. Les Cotils is 3.5 miles from Guernsey airport, and just over 1 mile from the St Peter Port harbour ferry terminal. The website gives links to the various transportation services. Discount car hire available on the island.

Lihou Charitable Trust
La Cachette, Rue Des Mares
St Pierre Du Bois
Guernsey GY7 9PZ
Channel Islands

Tel: 01481 266294 / 07781 120421
Email: warden@lihouisland.com
Website: www.lihouisland.com

Retreats • Workshops and Courses • Venue for Hire • Self-Catering Space • Children

Open spirituality

In 1995 the States of Guernsey bought Lihou Island and the house there to guarantee that the people of Guernsey and visitors alike could have access to this beautiful and inspiring island. In 2006 the Lihou Charitable Trust took over the lease to continue the work, ensuring that the house remained open to all. The house is orientated towards youth and school groups, but also accommodates adult gatherings for any purpose from workshops to parties. The house is now available to be booked by groups for single-night, weekend or multiple-night stays. All prices are kept as low as possible – currently, for example, a youth group might pay £9.50 per person and a family group £22 per person, or a business group £30 per person. These are for 24-hour sole use of the house and all have minimum numbers for the group rates. Online booking will be available soon; in the meantime contact the warden (Richard Curtis), using the above details.

'Know that the lower soul, the Devil, and the Angel, the higher soul, are not external to you. You are they'
– Najam al Din Kubra

IRELAND AND NORTHERN IRELAND

ANTRIM

ARMOY

Knocklayd Retreat Centre
Corrymeela Community
28 Stroan Road, Armoy
County Antrim BT53 8RY
Northern Ireland

Tel: 028 20751521
Email: knocklayd@corrymeela.org.uk
Website: www.corrymeela.org/

Retreats • Workshops and Courses • Vegetarian Food • Organic Food
Self-Catering Space • Children

Christian – Ecumenical

Knocklayd comprises a house and annex set in pretty gardens, and the place itself is high up a mountain. For accommodation there is a mix of single and double rooms, plus kitchens for self-catering stays, but home-cooked meals are also available. There is a ground-floor room with a shower and toilet, so wheelchair-disabled guests may be possible. This retreat centre is about eight miles from the Corrymeela community centre in Ballycastle. Knocklayd offers a programme of weekend retreats and quiet days, which range from gardening weekends to retreats on the spirituality of Thomas Merton.

OPEN: Most of year. Everyone welcome.
ROOMS: Up to 16 guests in single and double rooms.
FACILITIES: Conferences, lounge, dining room, gardens.
SPIRITUAL HELP: Group sharing on retreats.
GUESTS ADMITTED TO: Everywhere.
MEALS: Everyone eats together. Traditional, vegetarian and other dishes. Self-catering also possible.
SPECIAL ACTIVITIES: Programme of events and courses. Visit the website for progamme details.
SITUATION: On the slopes of Knocklayd Mountain.
MAXIMUM STAY: For the event or retreat or by arrangement.
BOOKINGS: Letter, telephone, email.
CHARGES: Please ask.
ACCESS: Rail: Ballymoney (13 miles away). Car: accessible via the A2 and A26.

LARNE

Drumalis Retreat Centre
47 Glenarm Road
Larne
County Antrim BT40 IDT
Northern Ireland

Tel: 028 28272196 / 028 28276455
Fax: 028 28277999
Email: drumalis@btconnect.com
Website: www.drumalis.co.uk

Retreats • Workshops and Courses • Church/Temple • Spiritual Help • Vegetarian Food
Venue for Hire • Self-Catering Space • Children

Christian – Roman Catholic – Inter-denominational

The Drumalis vision statement says it all: 'Drumalis is a place of welcome, an oasis on the journey of life. A living community where all may experience the power of God's love and compassion; discover and value their gifts; seek to be healers in a divided world; grow in their relationship with God and all Creation. We draw our life and strength from sharing and prayer.' The house itself is a rambling late Victorian mansion with a view across Larne Harbour, which has been called awe-inspiring. It was recently renovated and a splendid new modern building has been added, which has 40 new twin/double en suite bedrooms with conference rooms and a chapel area. The programme here can include, for example, directed retreats, a healing touch workshop, Celtic spirituality, Enneagram weekends, and prayer and painting retreats.

OPEN: All year except Christmas and Easter. Receives men, women, young people, families, groups, non-retreatants.
ROOMS: Single, doubles, plus a new 40-bedroom accommodation, all en suite. Parkview Cottage in the grounds of Drumalis comprises 3 bedrooms (2 twin and 1 single), a bathroom with electric shower, a lounge, a sitting room and a fitted kitchen with adjoining dining area. There is private parking outside as well as an enclosed patio area.
FACILITIES: Chapels, conferences, garden, library, guest lounge.
SPIRITUAL HELP: Personal talks, group sharing, meditation, personal retreat direction, spiritual direction.
GUESTS ADMITTED TO: Almost unrestricted access.
MEALS: Everyone eats together. Traditional food. Vegetarian and special diets.
SPECIAL ACTIVITIES: Retreats for lay people, parishes, religious. renewal courses, folk and prayer groups, inter-church work, Christian fellowship groups, Celtic spirituality, Cursillo weekends. Send for brochures and see online information.
SITUATION: Quiet with spacious grounds overlooking the sea.
MAXIMUM STAY: By arrangement.
BOOKINGS: Letter, telephone, fax, email.
CHARGES: The costs vary according to the retreat on offer.

ACCESS: Boat: ferry services from Cairnryan, Troon and Fleetwood. Car: from Belfast, take M2 and leave at exit A8; from the harbour, follow signs for the Coast Road. Drumalis is on the right before Bankhands Lane just before leaving the town.

PORTGLENONE

Our Lady of Bethleham Abbey	Tel: 028 25821211
11 Ballymena Road	Fax: 028 25822795
Portglenone, Ballymena	Email: kelley@unite.net
County Antrim BT44 8BL	Website: www.bethlehem-abbey.org.uk
Northern Ireland	

Retreats • Church/Temple • Spiritual Help • Vegetarian Food • Community Living • Vocations

Christian – Roman Catholic

Our Lady of Bethlehem Abbey is a Cistercian monastery. The monks live a secluded, contemplative life in which prayer holds a central focus. The monastery has a guest house for those wishing to make short retreats, a repository, a gift shop and a coffee shop. Although the abbey is in the countryside, it can be very busy with day visitors.

OPEN: Weekdays and sometimes weekends. Welcomes everyone.
ROOMS: 2 singles, 8 doubles.
FACILITIES: Conferences, park, lounge. Bookshop with books, crafts, religious objects.
SPIRITUAL HELP: Mass, Divine Office, Sacrament of Reconciliation.
GUESTS ADMITTED TO: Church, public areas.
MEALS: Taken in guest house. Traditional food. Vegetarian and special diets catered for.
SPECIAL ACTIVITIES: None.
SITUATION: At edge of village in countryside.
MAXIMUM STAY: 5 days.
BOOKINGS: Letter, telephone, email.
CHARGES: None fixed, so by suggested donation or by other arrangement.
ACCESS: Rail: Ballymoney station (15 miles away). Car: Portglenone is just off the A42 and A54. Please enquire for bus directions.

CAVAN

•••

BAWNBOY

Jampa Ling Tibetan Buddhist Centre
Owendoon House
Bawnboy
County Cavan
Ireland

Tel: +353 (0)49 9523448
Fax: +353 (0)49 9523067
Email: info@jampaling.org
Website: www.jampaling.org

Retreats • Workshops and Courses • Church/Temple • Meditation • Spiritual Help
Vegetarian Food • Venue for Hire • Self-Catering Space • Community Living
Vocations • Hermitages

Buddhist (Tibetan tradition)

Jampa Ling was established in 1990 under the guidance and spiritual direction of Panchen Ötrul Rinpoche and the patron is His Holiness The Dalai Lama. The centre, a large Victorian house called Owendoon, is in 13 acres of meadow, woodland and gardens, and it borders a lake. It is run by a small group of Panchen Ötrul Rinpoche's students, who are supported by many others around the world. It is open to visitors, both Buddhist and those of other traditions. The name *Jampa Ling* means 'place of infinite loving kindness'. There is an annual programme of events, courses and study. These have included the following: *White Tara Retreat* – a weekend retreat for those already initiated in the practice of Tara; *Saga Dawa* – a family day to celebrate the Buddha's birth, enlightenment and parinirvana which occurs on the full moon; *Summer Solstice* – Tibetan Buddhist prayers to purify the environment. Usually always on the agenda are *Introduction to Buddhism* and *Meditation*. Jampa Ling recently converted Tara House, a nineteenth-century coach house, which is ideal for workshops and courses of all kinds, as well as being fully equipped for self-catering family holidays.

The aims of Jampa Ling are: to preserve the Tibetan Buddhist tradition and culture through teaching meditation and Dharma practice; to assist in the re-establishment of monasteries in Tibet; to work for the re-establishment of Buddhism in Mongolia and relieve the difficulties of the Mongolian people; to promote inter-faith dialogue at a deep spiritual level in the context of the work for peace in this island; to support Tibetan refugees and their monasteries in India; to work for peaceful coexistence between all living beings; to encourage conservation of Earth's natural resources and to develop an awareness of the interdependence of existence. When you visit their website, please do take time to explore the information about the present situation of the Mongolian people who have already suffered very much from the change in global climate on top of their long struggle for social and political stability and progress. **Highly Recommended.**

OPEN: All year. Welcomes all people.
ROOMS: Singles, doubles and dormitories are available. Tara House provides accommodation for groups of up to 20 people. A mobile home at the end of the walled garden for longer solitary retreats is also available. Plans have been made to develop further retreat facilities in other farm buildings.
FACILITIES: Shrine room, temple, guest areas.
SPIRITUAL HELP: Directed meditation and retreats. Personal and group talks by arrangement.
GUESTS ADMITTED TO: Everywhere.
MEALS: Everyone eats together. All vegetarian food.
SPECIAL ACTIVITIES: Meditation, study of Dharma, talks, planned programme – see online or send for information.
SITUATION: Quiet. In the countryside.
MAXIMUM STAY: For the course or by arrangement and type of retreat.
BOOKINGS: Letter, telephone, fax, email, online contact form.
CHARGES: Current cost for teaching weekends: residential 215€, non-residential 160€. Full-board accommodation rates per person: dormitory 36€; double room 36€, or 45€ for a single occupancy. The mobile home, which is a hermitage for solitary retreats, is about 20€ per night with electricity charged separately. See programme for individual rates for retreat courses and events.
ACCESS: Car: via N3/N87, or via A32/N87. Good directions are on their website.

'Happiness cannot be found through great effort and willpower,
but is already there, in relaxation and letting go'
– Ven. Lama Gendun Rinpoche

CLARE

••

SIXMILEBRIDGE

Sunyata Retreat Centre
Snata
Sixmilebridge
County Clare
Ireland

Tel: + 353 (0)61 367073
Email: info@sunyatacentre.com
Website: www.sunyatacentre.com

Retreats • Workshops and Courses • Yoga • Meditation • Spiritual Help • Bed and Breakfast
Vegetarian Food • Venue for Hire • Self-Catering Space

Buddhist – Open spirituality

Sunyata is a beautiful 10-acre property set in the rolling hills of west Ireland – a spacious haven outside the bustle of modern life with time for relaxation, contemplation and self-development. There is a varied programme of retreats and workshops on offer and the unique workshop venue is also available for hire. The retreats provide an opportunity to explore and develop serenity, health and well-being, wisdom and compassion, through meditation, mindfulness and affiliated practices in a supportive environment. The teachers provide guidance through various means including meditation instruction, talks, chanting, yoga or Qi Gong, individual or group discussions, as the different workshops indicate. The meditation retreats are usually held in an atmosphere of meditative silence, guided by the teacher to allow a deepening of the practice. All retreats and workshops are suitable for beginners or more experienced practitioners, unless otherwise stated. Self-catering accommodation for personal retreats is also available outside the retreat programme. **Highly Recommended.**

OPEN: All year round to all. Everyone welcome.
ROOMS: Shared accommodation, 2–4 per room. The centre can accommodate up to 15 guests.
FACILITIES: Meditation room, dining room, office, self-catering room. The whole centre can be reserved for group bookings.
SPIRITUAL HELP: All teachers provide expert advice and guidance in meditation or relevant discipline.
MEALS: Wholesome, simple vegetarian food.
SITUATION: The centre is set on a hillside on 10 acres and has a lovely creek and waterfall. Many walks nearby join up to the marked East Clare Way.

BOOKINGS: Application forms can be requested via email or telephone. Call for a full brochure of events or check the website for details. Online contact form is on the website.

CHARGES: Vary slightly: most weekend retreats cost around 160€, covering accommodation, all meals and facility costs. A donation for the teacher is made separately unless the programme indicates ' Teacher fee included'.

ACCESS: Rail: Limerick station, then bus. Bus: services run from Limerick and Shannon airport to Sixmilebridge, which is 6.5 miles from the centre. From there, take a taxi. Car: via N18. The centre is 30 minutes' drive from Limerick, Shannon or Ennis, on a hillside half a mile off the Sixmilebridge–Broadford road. Good directions are given on the website.

CORK

BALLYVOLANE

Cenacle Sisters
16 Mervue Lawn
Ballyvolane
County Cork
Ireland

Tel: +353 (0)21 508059
Email: cenacle@iol.ie

Retreats • Workshops and Courses • Church/Temple • Spiritual Help
Community Living • Vocations

Christian – Roman Catholic

This and their sister community in Killiney, County Dublin (see Dublin section), work for transformation by awakening and deepening people's faith and by promoting a society that has a spirituality of justice at its core. The Cenacle Sisters aim to accomplish this through the offering of development workshops, directed retreats, spiritual direction on a one-to-one basis, counselling, individual and group retreats, and directed and guided prayer.

'Live simply that others might simply live'
– Elizabeth Seaton

COBH

St Benedict's Priory
The Mount
Cobh
County Cork
Ireland

Tel: +353 (0)21 4811354
Website: www.tyburnconvent.org.uk/
monasteries/ireland/ireland.html

Retreats • Church/Temple • Spiritual Help • Vegetarian Food • Venue for Hire
Community Living • Vocations

Christian – Roman Catholic

This Benedictine community aims to provide a place of silence and solitude where guests may be able to recollect and dwell within themselves at peace. Rooms are comfortable enough and they have lovely harbour views – some bedrooms have balconies even. This is a peaceful and restful place. You can come for the day to visit their Bible Garden.

OPEN: All year. Receives men, women, young people and small groups up to 8.
ROOMS: 6 singles, 2 doubles.
FACILITIES: Garden, Bible garden in 1.5 acres with pool and stream, library, guest lounge. No rooms on ground floor.
SPIRITUAL HELP: Personal talks, directed study by prior arrangement, Daily Mass and Exposition of Blessed Sacrament, share in the liturgy of the Community.
GUESTS ADMITTED TO: Chapel. Helping in garden possible.
MEALS: Everyone eats together. Self-catering facilities for breakfast. Traditional food, some grown in own garden. Provision for vegetarian and special diets possible.
SPECIAL ACTIVITIES: None.
SITUATION: Very quiet, in a picturesque town on an island in Cork Harbour, so the sea is at hand. All rooms have view of harbour with some having balconies.
MAXIMUM STAY: 2 weeks.
BOOKINGS: By letter or telephone (10:30–12:30).
CHARGES: Suggested donation per day – ask when you book.
ACCESS: Cork is 13 miles from Cobh. Rail: from Cork to Cobh. Air: Cork airport. Boat: ferry from France or England to Cork. Car: via N25.

'Yesterday is a cancelled cheque, tomorrow is a promissory note,
today is cash in hand; spend it wisely'
– Anonymous

ENNISMORE

St Dominic's Retreat Centre
Ennismore
Montenotte
County Cork
Ireland

Tel: +353 (0)21 4502520
Fax: +353 (0)21 4502712
Email: ennismore@eircom.net /
marziareeb@yahoo.com
Website: www.ennismore.ie

Retreats • Workshops and Courses • Church/Temple • Meditation • Spiritual Help
Bed and Breakfast • Vegetarian Food • Venue for Hire • Self-Catering Space
Work Retreats • Vocations

Christian – Roman Catholic – Inter-denominational

Although located in an urban area of Cork, St Dominic's offers an oasis of green lawns and quiet views with much peace and quiet. The excellent food is prepared in an old-fashioned kitchen – the homemade soup and bread are delicious. The gardens surrounding this ambling large house have plenty of benches and there is a charming old walled garden with box-hedge paths. All in all, a perfect place for a stroll and a good think. The facilities here are numerous and include an 1824 stable block converted into the Meditation House with two buildings of bunks for retreats, which is modern and comfortable. Next to that a separate hermitage is available to sleep up to six people, with a specially designed meditation room, a lounge and large conference area. Altogether a nice group of stone buildings around a pretty courtyard down the drive away from the main house. For the disabled, there is a modern lift and other special arrangements. A number of courses are on offer here from the resident Dominican community, ranging from courses on healing to retreats centred on scriptural passages. **Highly Recommended.**

OPEN: All year. Receives men, women, young people, families, groups and non-retreatants.
ROOMS: 40 rooms. The hermitage accommodates 6 people. There is another separate accommodation for 20 people.
FACILITIES: Disabled access, simple chapel with lots of light, meditation room, conferences, garden, library, hermitage.
SPIRITUAL HELP: Mass, personal talks, group sharing, meditation, community prayers, personal retreat direction.
GUESTS ADMITTED TO: Unrestricted access. Chapel.
MEALS: Taken in the guest house. Traditional/wholefood. Vegetarian and special diets. Self-catering available.
SPECIAL ACTIVITIES: Planned programme of events; *Bio-spirituality Focusing, Christian Meditation, Enneagram, Myers-Briggs* and *Celtic Spiritual Heritage* are examples of what is on offer. Send for brochure or visit the website.

SITUATION: Quiet in the countryside, but near the town so can be rather busy.
MAXIMUM STAY: 1–2 weeks.
BOOKINGS: Letter, telephone, email.
CHARGES: Please enquire for any costs for courses and events. For private residential retrats, B&B is currently 25€ (plus 12€ for lunch, 7€ for supper).
ACCESS: Rail/air: to Cork. Bus: a service runs from the city centre. Car: Ennismore is off the N8, about a mile from Cork city centre.

GARRANES

Dzogchen Beara (Rigpa Ireland)   Tel: +353 (0)27 73032 (general) /
Garranes   +353 (0)27 73147 (accommodation)
Allihies   Fax: +353 (0)27 73177
West Cork   Email: info@dzogchenbeara.org
Ireland   Website: www.dzogchenbeara.org / www.rigpa.ie

Retreats • Workshops and Courses • Church/Temple • Meditation • Spiritual Help
Vegetarian Food • Self-Catering Space • Community Living • Work Retreats
Vocations • Children

Buddhist (Tibetan tradition)

This meditation and retreat centre for Buddhist study and practice on the Beara Peninsula is 400 feet up on the cliffs above Bantry Bay, with a vast panorama of the Atlantic Ocean. The Dzogchen Beara is run under the spiritual direction of Sogyal Rinpoche, and is affiliated to the Rigpa Fellowship; it serves as Rigpa's main retreat centre. Sogyal Rinpoche was born in Tibet and raised as a son by one of the most revered spiritual teachers of this century, Jamyang Khyentse Chökyi Lodrö. Rinpoche studied at university in Delhi and Cambridge and has been teaching in the West since 1974. He is the author in English of *The Tibetan Book of Living and Dying* and founder and spiritual director of Rigpa, an international network of centres and groups that follow the teachings of the Buddha under his guidance. Sogyal Rinpoche and other Tibetan masters lead retreats at Dzogchen Beara several times a year. *Rigpa* is a Tibetan word which means 'the innermost nature of the mind'. **Rigpa International** is a Buddhist organisation with centres in nine countries around the world, dedicated to practising the techniques of the Buddha under the guidance of Sogyal Rinpoche, and to making these teachings available to benefit as many people as possible. **Rigpa Ireland** centres offer a variety of courses based on the book *The Tibetan Book of Living and Dying* – visit the website to find out more. The centre also offers a range of retreats and courses on various aspects of Buddhism, such as meditation, compassion and spiritual care for the dying, most of which are open to beginners. Visitors are also welcome at other times and to attend daily meditation classes or simply relax in the beautiful and peaceful environment of the place. **Highly Recommended.**

OPEN: All year. Everyone welcome, including children.
ROOMS: Guest house, dormitories, self-catering cottages.
FACILITIES: Temple, conferences, retreats, meditation hall, garden, book and gift shop.
SPIRITUAL HELP: Meditation, directed study for students following the Rigpa Study and Practice Programme.
GUESTS ADMITTED TO: Shrine room, grounds.
MEALS: During most retreats, vegetarian lunch and supper are provided. Breakfast is self-catering.
SPECIAL ACTIVITIES: Programme of planned events on the website. Daily meditation classes to which beginners are welcome. Good walking with sporting facilities in vicinity.
SITUATION: Very quiet in countryside with dramatic and beautiful views.
MAXIMUM STAY: By arrangement.
BOOKINGS: Letter, telephone, fax, email. Downloadable booking forms.
CHARGES: Ask for current charge rates.
ACCESS: Dzogchen Beara is 100 miles west of Cork city. Rail/air/coach: Cork, then national bus service to Castletownbere (52 miles). From there, take a taxi to Dzogchen Beara. Car: via N71. See the website for travel directions.

LEAP

Missionaries of the Sacred Heart	Tel: +353 (0)28 33118 /
Myross Wood House	+353 (0)28 34078
Leap, Skibbereen	Fax: +353 (0)28 33793
County Cork	Email: mscmyross@eircom.net
Ireland	

Retreats • Workshops and Courses • Church/Temple • Spiritual Help • Vegetarian Food

Christian – Roman Catholic

Missionaries of the Sacred Heart run this house set in lovely west Cork among woodlands, streams and near the sea. There is a programme of individual and group retreats throughout the year. Private retreats are welcomed. There are mostly single rooms, which can accommodate up to 38 guests. You need to contact the centre, as the programme on the diocesan website is not very detailed. Ask for further information on the specific event, the charge and what meals are available.

DONEGAL

BURNFOOT

St Anthony's Retreat Centre
Dundrean
Burnfoot
County Donegal
Ireland

Tel: +353 (0)74 9368370
Email: sarce@eircom.net

Retreats • Church/Temple • Spiritual Help • Vegetarian Food • Hermitages

Christian – Roman Catholic

This is a place of seclusion and peace amidst the sheep and rolling hills that straddle the border between County Derry and County Donegal. Consisting of five hermitages discreetly placed beyond an old farmhouse, St Anthony's offers space, privacy, places to pray and long walks in the beautiful countryside. A pilgrim garden has been created in the immediate surroundings of the farmhouse, reflecting scriptural themes and the Celtic Christian tradition. The hermitages are simple and small but comfortable.

CREESLOUGH

Ards Friary Retreat and
Conference Centre
Creeslough
Letterkenny
County Donegal
Ireland

Tel/Fax: +353 (0)74 9138909
Email: info@ardsfriary.ie
Website: www.ardsfriary.ie

Retreats • Church/Temple • Bed and Breakfast • Vegetarian Food • Venue for Hire
Hermitages • Children

Christian – Roman Catholic

With 200 acres of grounds and many beaches, Ards Friary hosts some spectacular views. Its peace and serenity are not to be missed; take the opportunity to wonder and explore. Ards Country Park is next door and walks from the friary extend into it, allowing you to venture even further. The programme includes a variety of retreat subjects; individual retreats are also possible for those looking just for a quiet time.

OPEN: February to December. Everyone welcome.
ROOMS: Many singles and doubles. Hermitage.
FACILITIES: Conferences, garden, park, guest lounge, TV.
SPIRITUAL HELP: Personal talks possible.
GUESTS ADMITTED TO: Church, chapel.
MEALS: Everyone eats together. Simple, wholesome food, vegetarian if requested. A new daily service is available, which is a full lunch at about 15€, and a children's menu at 8€. Please book in advance for lunch on +353 (0)74 9138909.
SPECIAL ACTIVITIES: Planned programme available.
SITUATION: Very quiet in the countryside near seaside with forest walks.
MAXIMUM STAY: By arrangement.
BOOKINGS: Letter, telephone, email, online contact form.
CHARGES: Full board is available – please enquire for current year's rates. The costs of retreats vary greatly depending on topic and length.
ACCESS: Bus: bus/coach services run to Cresslough, including McGinley Bus from Dublin; pick-up is possible. Car: to Letterkenny via N13/N14, then N56 to Creeslough.

PETTIGO

St Patrick's Purgatory   Tel/Fax: +353 (0)71 9861518
Lough Derg   Email: info@loughderg.org
Pettigo   Website: www.loughderg.org
County Donegal
Ireland

Retreats • Church/Temple • Spiritual Help • Self-Catering Space

Christian – Roman Catholic – Open to all

St Patrick's Purgatory has been a place of prayer and pilgrimage for at least 1,000 years. This island sanctuary located on Lough Derg challenges human frailty but may bring a deep and richly rewarding experience of spirituality, enabling participants to find peace of mind and giving them new strengths for continuing their life's journey. A historic centre of Celtic spirituality, St Patrick's Purgatory remains a unique place of prayer and penance. The traditional pilgrimage is a three-day undertaking of fasting and incorporates a 24-hour vigil, which means you do not go to bed for that period; it is meant to be penitential. The fast means just that too – a simple meal of dry toast and black tea each day. You must be in normal health, at least 15 years old and be able to walk (including barefoot) and to kneel unaided. You fast from midnight prior to leaving the next day by boat to the island. This type of pilgrimage, deeply Christian and Catholic in nature and also highly ritualistic, is not to be undertaken without great seriousness of purpose in the seeking of God. There is a less arduous one-day retreat, which does not require fasting or walking barefoot. As in all great places of spiritual pilgrimage, demand is great and prior booking is essential. A multipurpose facility provides amenities for school retreats, youth groups, and one-day retreats and facilities for meditation and prayer during the traditional Three-Day Pilgrimage retreat season.

OPEN: April to October. Closed in winter. Receives men, women and those over 15 years of age.
ROOMS: 11 en suites, 9 doubles, 10 singles and hostel. No mobile phones.
FACILITIES: Disabled access, church, chapel, oratory, conferences, library, guest lounge, TV.
SPIRITUAL HELP: Personal talks, group sharing, spiritual direction, personal retreat direction, meditation, Way of the Cross, Eucharist.
GUESTS ADMITTED TO: Unrestricted access.
MEALS: Everyone eats together. See comments above on the Three-Day Pilgrimage as to fasting.
SPECIAL ACTIVITIES: Brochure available in English plus several other languages explaining what is offered and details of pilgrimage retreats. Visit the website for more details.
SITUATION: Isolated, very quiet on an island.
MAXIMUM STAY: 1 week.
BOOKINGS: You need to book a long time in advance here. Letter, telephone. fax, email – using the online booking/enquiry forms is best.
CHARGES: Currently 55€ for the Three-Day Pilgrimage. Other rates on application or given in details of the event or retreat.
ACCESS: Car: via A35 or A47 to Pettigo; the sanctuary is 7 miles north from there.

ROSSNOWLAGH

Franciscan Friary Tel: +353 (0)71 9851342 / +353 (0)71 9852035
Rossnowlagh Fax: 353 (0)71 9852206
County Donegal Website: www.franciscans.ie
Ireland

Church/Temple • Vegetarian food

Christian – Roman Catholic – Franciscan

This is a centre of peace and reconciliation. The buildings are modern with all necessary facilities and close to the sea. The extensive grounds have been laid out to include several grottoes, peace gardens and an outdoor Way of the Cross. The view over the bay is quite dramatic. This centre is much used by religious orders, especially in summer. **La Verna**, the modern retreat house, situated over the road from the friary, is extremely comfortable.

OPEN: All year except for Christmas to first week of January. Receives everyone.
ROOMS: 19 rooms.
FACILITIES: Garden, park, bookshop, library, guest lounge, TV.
SPIRITUAL HELP: Daily Mass, personal talks, Sacrament of Reconciliation.
GUESTS ADMITTED TO: Chapel, choir, shrine room, repository. Everywhere except community living quarters.
MEALS: Retreat house has a kitchen and dining room. Vegetarian and special diets possible.
SPECIAL ACTIVITIES: Send for planned programme.
SITUATION: Very quiet in the countryside with nearby swimming and surfing. Summer can be busy.
MAXIMUM STAY: A week to 10 days.
BOOKINGS: Letter, or telephone then in writing to confirm.
CHARGES: Rates for 24-hour stays and for 6-day retreats available. Contact the friary for current charges.
ACCESS: No public transport. Car: Coast road R231 between Donegal Town and Ballyshannon, via N15. Rossnowlagh is about 5 miles from Ballyshannon.

DOWN

NEWRY

Dromantine Retreat and Conference Centre   Tel: 028 30821964
Society of African Missions   Fax: 028 30821963
Newry   Email: admin@dromantineconference.com
County Down BT34 1RH   Website: www.dromantineconference.com
Northern Ireland

Retreats • Workshops and Courses • Church/Temple • Spiritual Help • Vegetarian Food
Venue for Hire • Children

Christian – Roman Catholic

Only 70 miles from Dublin or 30 miles from Belfast, Dromantine is a very large centre situated in beautiful countryside with good walks at hand. While groups with their own programme usually come here, it is open for private retreat. There is a regular programme of retreats and events; more details are on their website.

OPEN: All year except Christmas. Everyone welcome.
ROOMS: 42 singles, 30 doubles, 1 self-contained apartment with 3 singles. All bedrooms are en suite and have telephones, broadband service, with many having views of the grounds. around the house. 4 rooms are designed for disabled access.
FACILITIES: Disabled access, conferences, chapel, lounge, library, coffee shop.
SPIRITUAL HELP: Only by arrangement.
GUESTS ADMITTED TO: Chapel, all public areas.
MEALS: Meals taken in guest house. There are 2 dining rooms, one of which seats 180 people. The food is professionally prepared at the centre. Vegetarian and special diets catered for.
SPECIAL ACTIVITIES: Visit the website for their programme of courses and retreats.
SITUATION: Quiet in countryside about 6 miles from nearest town.
MAXIMUM STAY: By arrangement.
BOOKINGS: Letter, telephone, fax, email, online enquiry form.
CHARGES: Depend on size of group, length of stay and what facilities and catering are arranged. Ask for rates for a private retreat.
ACCESS: Car: via M1/A1; can be reached from either Dublin or Belfast. A local road map is available on the website.

ROSTREVOR

Christian Renewal Centre
44 Shore Road
Rostrevor, Newry
County Down BT34 3ET
Northern Ireland

Tel: 028 41738492
Fax: 028 41738996
Email: crc-rostrevor@lineone.net
Website: www.crc-rostrevor.org

Retreats • Workshops and Courses • Church/Temple • Spiritual Help • Bed and Breakfast
Vegetarian Food • Venue for Hire • Community Living • Work Retreats
Vocations • Children

Christian – Inter-denominational

This community was founded in 1974 by a group of Christians who were drawn together to seek to demonstrate and proclaim the uniting and healing love of Christ. The first churches were Roman Catholic and Protestant, but since then membership has been drawn from the new Community and Fellowship Churches. Reconciliation, particularly for all of Ireland, revival and renewal are central to the work and prayer here. The place is large, part old but modernised, and there are other newer buildings too. Renewal weekends and three-day break retreats are a speciality. Although doing so is optional, guests are invited to join in prayers, which are daily in morning and evening. While this community has always had a charismatic flavour, it now mostly focuses on intercessory prayer for Ireland.

OPEN: All year except Christmas period. Receives men, women, children, young people and groups.
ROOMS: Rooms are mainly twin and single, with 1 family room. They also have a ground-floor single room with easy access for a wheelchair.
FACILITIES: Disabled access, conferences, garden, library, guest lounge, TV, guest phone.
SPIRITUAL HELP: Personal talks, group sharing, prayer ministry with guests as requested.
GUESTS ADMITTED TO: Gardens, prayer room, quiet room, TV, lounge.
MEALS: Everyone eats together. Traditional food. Vegetarian and special diets.
SPECIAL ACTIVITIES: Special programme. Send for brochure or see the website.
SITUATION: Very quiet in a village at the foot of the Mourne Mountains, with a glorious sweeping view of Carlingford Lough.
MAXIMUM STAY: 1 week.
BOOKINGS: Letter, telephone, fax. Email and online booking form are easiest.
CHARGES: Suggested donations: B&B £18 and full board £30 per day. They have special rates for children, families, students and the unwaged. See online for latest rates.
ACCESS: Rail: Newry station, then bus. Bus: from Belfast or Dublin airport to Newry Courthouse, then bus to Rostrevor. Car: follow signs from Newry for Warrenpoint on the A2.

DUBLIN

DUBLIN

Catholic Youth Council
20/23 Arran Quay
Dublin 7
Ireland

Tel: +353 (01) 872 5055
Fax: +353 (01) 872 5010
Email: info@cyc.ie
Website: www.cyc.ie

Retreats • Workshops and Courses • Church/Temple • Spiritual Help
Self-Catering Space • Community Living • Work Retreats • Children

Christian – Roman Catholic

The mission of this leading youth organisation is to promote a youth work response that is caring, compassionate and Christian and that enables young people to participate more fully in the life of society and church. The CYC offers a number of holiday centres for youth groups, some with disabled facilities. Groups primarily use the centres for

holidays and training as well as for retreat purposes. The holiday centres **Teach Chaoimhin** and **Teach Lorcain** (in the valley of Glendasan
near Glendalough) are designed particularly for prayer and religious
retreats. Groups make their own programmes, but there are usually no
resident staff. **Coolure House**, about 60 miles away in County West-
meath, is a staffed centre located near Lough Derraghvara and it has a
wide range of services for retreats plus extensive indoor and outdoor
facilities. A new youth facility, **The White House**, was opened recently
in Ballogan by Dundrum-Rathdown Youth Service. Most CYC centres
are in beautiful rural and coastal areas and there are planned summer
project activities.

OPEN: All year. Receives young people.
ROOMS: Dormitories. Teach Chaoimhin accommodates 31 guests and Teach Lorcain
sleeps 15.
FACILITIES: See above.
SPIRITUAL HELP: Self-directed.
GUESTS ADMITTED TO: Unrestricted on site usually.
MEALS: Self-catering.
SPECIAL ACTIVITIES: None.
SITUATION: See above.
MAXIMUM STAY: None.
BOOKINGS: Letter, fax. Downloadable booking form.
CHARGES: These vary depending on centre and how long the stay will be; send for
rate sheet.
ACCESS: Ask for directions for particular centre when booking.

Dominican Retreat and Pastoral Centre   Tel: +353 (0)1 4048189 /
St Mary's Priory   +353 (0)1 4048123
Tallaght   Fax: +353 (0)1 4596080
Dublin 24   Email: retreats@dominicanstallaght.org
Ireland   Website: goodnews.ie/tallaghthome.htm /
                www.dominicans.ie/friars/communities/tallaght.html

Retreats • Workshops and Courses • Church/Temple • Spiritual Help • Bed and Breakfast
Vegetarian Food • Venue for Hire • Community Living • Vocation • Children

Christian – Roman Catholic

Square in the middle of Ireland's fourth most populated area and surrounded by urban sprawl, the centre is in the peaceful grounds of St
Mary's Priory and it's a surprisingly first-rate place for anyone going

on retreat. The guest house is very comfortable with its own big reading room, tea and coffee bar, bookshop and all the other facilities one could want, from hairdryers to a TV room. But the real delight is the gardens with ancient walkways and many fine old trees. The community is fairly large and, unusual today in the religious life, is composed of all ages. They are hospitable and friendly in their welcome of both groups and individuals. As this is a major priory of the Dominican Friars, it is a place of prayer and contemplation.

Dublin Buddhist Centre
Friends of the Western
Buddhist Order – Ireland
5 James Joyce Street
Dublin 1
Ireland

Tel: +353 (0)1 8178933
Email: info@dublinbuddhistcentre.org
Website: www.dublinbuddhistcentre.org

Buddhist – Friends of the Western Buddhist Order (FWBO)

The Dublin Buddhist Centre will provide information on the activities of the Friends of the Western Buddhist Order and the various events, classes, courses of study and retreats available in Ireland.

Jesuit Centre of Spirituality
Manresa House
426 Clontarf Road
Dollymount, Dublin 3
Ireland

Tel: +353 (0)1 8331352
Fax: +353 (0)1 8331002
Email: manresa@jesuit.ie.
Website: www.manresa.ie

Retreats • Workshops and Courses • Church/Temple • Spiritual Help • Vegetarian Food
Venue for Hire • Children

Christian – Roman Catholic – Ecumenical

Situated on the north side of Dublin on the coast road, Manresa is set well back in its own extensive grounds, next to the 400 acres of St Anne's Park, with its glorious rose garden, as well as overlooking Dublin Bay and the wild bird sanctuary of Bull Island. The Jesuit Centre of Spirituality is open to everyone who wants to take time out to nourish the spirit and find peace in God. Based on the wisdom of St Ignatius Loyola, especially as found in his spiritual exercises, the centre offers many kinds of retreats from full 30-day retreats to a few hours in the afternoon for peace and reflection. One-to-one accompaniment, training in spiritual direction and De Mello Evenings are on offer, as well as courses and seminars addressing areas of topical concern, including leadership, addiction, the family and the arts. An oasis in a busy metropolis where space, peace and a silent atmosphere help you touch base with yourself and with God.

The Sanctuary	Tel: +353 (0)1 6705419
Stanhope Street	Fax: +353 (0)1 6728086
Dublin 7	Email: enquiries@sanctuary.ie
Ireland	Website: www.sanctuary.ie

Retreats • Workshops and Courses • Yoga • Meditation • Spiritual Help • Venue for Hire
Alternative Therapies

Mind Body Spirit – Open spirituality

The Sanctuary is a holistic spiritual centre in the heart of the city of Dublin. It was designed to provide space and time to busy and stressed-out people, where they can develop balance and harmony between their public and private selves in terms of their work and lifestyle. A beautiful contemplative space, including a peaceful garden, has been created both inside and outside the house, where the team offer programmes, courses, workshops and individual treatments to nourish, illuminate and build inner strength and wisdom. While none of this is residential, the Sanctuary is offering the equivalent of what is often looked for in retreat settings: the chance to step back, take stock and find peace within one's everyday life. Everyone is welcome here. Open Monday to Fridays with some weekend events and courses. Contact the Sanctuary for brochures or visit their website. This is not a residential centre.

'Belief consists of accepting the affirmations of the soul; unbelief in denying them'
– Ralph Waldo Emerson

KILLINEY

Cenacle Sisters Tel/Fax: +353 (0)1 2840175
3 Churchview Drive Email: cenacledublin@eircom.net
Killiney
County Dublin
Ireland

Retreats • Workshops and Courses • Church/Temple • Spiritual Help
Community Living • Vocations

Christian – Roman Catholic

This community and their sister one in Cork (see Cork section) work for transformation through awakening and deepening people's faith and through promoting a society that has a spirituality of justice at its core. They aim to accomplish this by offering development workshops, directed retreats, spiritual direction on a one-to-one basis, counselling, individual and group retreats, and directed and guided prayer.

GALWAY

ATHENRY

Esker Monastery and Tel: +353 (0)91 844007 (monastery) /
Retreat House +353 (0)91 844549 (retreat house)
Athenry Fax +353 (0)91 845698
County Galway Email: cssresker@eircom.net (monastery) /
Ireland eskerret@indigo.ie (retreat house)
Website: www.eskercommunity.net

Retreats • Workshops and Courses • Church/Temple • Meditation • Spiritual Help
Bed and Breakfast • Vegetarian Food • Venue for Hire • Self-Catering Space
Community Living • Work Retreats • Vocations • Children

Christian – Roman Catholic

As you leave Athenry, you drive into a flat and unattractive valley dotted with houses and the stone walls so common in this part of Galway. Soon Esker Monastery looms in the distance – the only sizeable structure in sight. As you enter Esker's drive, the trees are all around and you are in a world of rich greenery and grassy pastures. Close up, the monastery is friendly if somewhat institutional at first sight. Rooms are comfortably furnished. Many members of the community are retired after many years of work, but one or more may join you in the lounge or for a meal. It is a friendly, old-fashioned place with activities, retreats and courses in its programme. Here, wisdom and a vision of the future have prevailed and a completely separate Youth Village has been created and set aside for younger groups only. There are garden walks and creative workshops, which include painting courses, wood-carving and creative writing. Food is plentiful and traditional. There are Stations of the Cross in the garden along a bluebell walk through trees where violets and primroses glow in the shade. The Stations are in an elegant Italian style. Esker is a prayerful place.

OPEN: All year. Receives men, women, children, young people, families, groups and non-retreatants.
ROOMS: 45 rooms – can accommodate up to 71 people.
FACILITIES: Church, oratory, guest lounge, TV, conferences, gardens, woodland park, lots of walks in grounds and in surrounding countryside.
SPIRITUAL HELP: Personal talks, group sharing, spiritual direction, personal retreat direction.
GUESTS ADMITTED TO: Church, chapel, choir, oratory.
MEALS: Full board, half board or B&B. Everyone eats together. Food by professional chefs with provision for vegetarian and special diets. Self-catering available too.
SPECIAL ACTIVITIES: There is an extensive planned programme. You can download the brochure from the website.
SITUATION: Very quiet in countryside.
MAXIMUM STAY: Open.
BOOKINGS: Letter, telephone, email.
CHARGES: Please enquire for current B&B and full-board charges. Youth Village and group rates by arrangement.
ACCESS: Rail/bus: to Galway, which is about 15 miles from Athenry; pick-up possible by arrangement. Car: easily accessible from the A6. A map is available in the brochure.

'To gain that which is worth having, it may be necessary to lose everything else'
– Bernadette Devlin

KINVARA

Burren Yoga and Meditation Centre
Lig do Scith, Cappaghmore
Kinvara
County Galway
Ireland

Tel: +353 (0)91 637680
email: dave@burrenyoga.com
Website: www.burrenyoga.com

Retreats • Workshops and Courses • Yoga • Meditation • Spiritual Help
Vegetarian Food • Organic Food

Open spirituality – Yoga

The Burren Yoga and Meditation Centre is a purpose-designed yoga centre with the prime motivation of introducing genuine yoga and meditation to beginners, and deepening the practice of those already practising. The centre was set up by Dave Brocklebank, who has been meditating for over 30 years and practising yoga for over 20 years and is a fully trained Satyananda yoga teacher. The centre uses only the most highly trained yoga teachers from all over the world. Dave personally picks these teachers as being the best and also very good with people, as the course participants live and eat and go on the out-door trips each day with the teacher, as well as taking the yoga and meditation classes with them. They teach about eight different types of yoga, which range from very gentle meditative yoga to strong dynamic forms. The number of people on each course is limited to 15. A very important aspect of all the courses are the organised outdoor trips into the beautiful unspoiled Burren hills and by the sea. Dave believes this time spent in nature is food for the soul and complements the time spent practising yoga and meditation in the centre. The centre is very comfortable with under-floor heating throughout, and with floor-to-ceiling windows, which offer spectacular views of the Burren hills. The centre is green and there is a new yoga centre, which uses solar-heated hot water, a wood-pellet stove for heating, and passive solar design to capture warmth from the sun. It will recycle all grey water for use in toilets, and utilize green materials for building where possible. The atmosphere is informal, friendly and relaxed and the whole feeling is one of peace and tranquillity. As if this were not enough one has the fabled joy of the sociable Irish people. **Highly Recommended.**

OPEN: All year . Everyone welcome.

ROOMS: 15 people maximum. 2 rooms for 4; 1 room for 6; 3 single rooms; 2 double rooms. The accommodation is sharing in some rooms for 4 or 6, but some are singles and doubles.

FACILITIES: Yoga room, lounge, reading area.

SPIRITUAL HELP: Yoga and meditation.

GUESTS ADMITTED TO: Everywhere.

MEALS: Meals are eaten together in the main kitchen. Tea or coffee in the kitchen at any time. Food is mainly organic and local produce, all vegetarian. The chef ran a restaurant in Galway city for over 12 years, so the food is restaurant standard. Special diets from vegan to wheat- or dairy-free and catering for allergies.

SPECIAL ACTIVITIES: Residential courses consist of a full daily programme of yoga classes, meals, outdoor activities and organised trips into the surrounding countryside, meditation and relaxation classes and rest/free time. The classes are all given by highly trained and very loving yoga teachers. The outings are organised and led by Dave Brocklebank, the founder. All the courses are organised and run by the centre and they do not hire the centre out to external groups. All guests stay as part of one of their retreats. Send for the brochure or visit the website.

SITUATION: Located in the middle of nowhere at the foot of the Burren hills on the west coast of Ireland. The Burren hills are a spectacular area about 30 miles long and 15 miles wide, consisting of spectacular shaped hills that plunge down into the Atlantic Ocean. The area is protected and has very few houses, and very few inhabitants. The retreat is surrounded by nature on all sides and the nearest village is 5 miles away. It is very tranquil, calm and quiet.

MAXIMUM STAY: Retreats of 1 week long. It is possible to sign up for 2 or 3 consecutive courses.

BOOKINGS: Email or phone to check availability, then book online.

CHARGES: Currently 690€ for a full-board week-long course, and 300€ for a weekend course.

ACCESS: Accessible by air, train, and bus; very good, detailed information is on their website. Nearest airport at Galway is 30 miles away, but Shannon or Dublin airports are also possible; reduced-fare taxi arrangement available. Local buses come to nearest village, Kinvara, which is 5 miles away. Car: Kinvara is just off the N67.

MOUNTBELLEW

Holy Rosary Convent	Tel/Fax: +353 (0)90 9679311
Mountbellew	Email: info@christian-retreat.org
County Galway	Website: www.christian-retreat.org
Ireland	

Retreats • Workshops and Courses • Church/Temple • Meditation • Spiritual Help
Community Living • Vocations

Christian – Roman Catholic

The community here provides Christian meditation, prayer groups, spiritual direction, supervision for spiritual directors and counselling.

They offer 24-hour stays, which include full board. Spiritual direction is on offer by prior arrangement. Everyone is welcome. There is a programme of events; enquire for costs and availability when booking, which may be done by letter, telephone or email.

NEWCASTLE

Sisters of La Retraite
The Hermitage
2 Distillery Road, Newcastle
County Galway
Ireland

Tel: +353 (0)91 524548
Website: www.laretraite.ws/en/0.htm

Retreats • Church/Temple • Spiritual Help • Self-Catering Space • Vocations • Hermitages

Christian – Roman Catholic

This is a small community and usually only one person is received on retreat at a time. There are space and time for silence in a self-catering hermitage, which is a small two-bedroom house with its own kitchen/sitting room. A small oratory links this with the main house. You may join the community for prayer if you wish.

OPEN: All year. Receives women only.
ROOMS: Self-contained hermitage.
FACILITIES: Chapel.
SPIRITUAL HELP: Personal talks. Retreat and spiritual direction may be possible by prior arrangement.
GUESTS ADMITTED TO: Chapel, oratory.
MEALS: Self-catering.
SPECIAL ACTIVITIES: None.
SITUATION: Town.
MAXIMUM STAY: 8 days.
BOOKINGS: Letter is best.
CHARGES: Donation suggested – if you can be generous, please be so.
ACCESS: Rail: Galway station, the community is about a mile away in Galway city. Bus: ask for direction when booking. Car: Galway can be reached via major routes in Ireland.

'Often we simply do not know what it is we love'
– Stafford Whiteaker

KERRY

Ardfert Retreat Centre	Tel: +353 (0)66 7134276
Ardfert	Fax: +353 (0)66 7134867
Tralee	email: ardfertretreat@eircom.net
County Kerry	Website: www.ardfertretreatcentre.ie
Ireland	

Retreats • Workshops and Courses • Church/Temple • Spiritual Help • Vegetarian Venue for Hire

Christian – Roman Catholic

While the centre is basically used for group bookings, individuals wishing to join any Saturday or Sunday parish-group retreat are welcome to do so by prior arrangement with the secretary of the centre. There is also a planned programme of events and talks. A brochure is available and a schedule of events is on the website.

OPEN: September to July inclusive. Everyone welcome.

ROOMS: 29 singles.

FACILITIES: This is a diocesan retreat centre in use by parish groups and schools. Chapel, garden, conference and group rooms.

SPIRITUAL HELP: Personal talks, spiritual direction, group sharing.

GUESTS ADMITTED TO: Almost unrestricted access except for certain areas of the house.

MEALS: Meals taken together in dining room. Limited self-catering. Home-cooked wholefood. Traditional Irish dishes. Vegetarian options. Special diets possible.

SPECIAL ACTIVITIES: These range from residential weekends of prayer and Enneagram or Myers-Briggs workshops to days of prayer. Send for brochure or see online.

SITUATION: Very quiet, in the countryside.

MAXIMUM STAY: Usually residential weekend, but there are also 6-day retreats and day and evening retreats.

BOOKINGS: Letter, telephone, fax, email.

CHARGES: Current offering rates: 30€ per person for a day-only parish retreat; 160€ for a residential weekend retreat; 360€ for a 6-day retreat. Day and evening retreat rates available also.

ACCESS: Rail/bus: to Tralee, then taxi to centre, which is 5 miles north. Car: via N21, N69, N70 and N86.

KILLARNEY

Franciscan Prayer Centre	Tel: +353 (0)64 31334
Killarney	Fax: +353 (0)64 37510
County Kerry	Email: friary@eircom.net
Ireland	Website: homepage.eircom.net/~franciscanprayercentre

Retreats • Workshops and Courses • Church/Temple • Spiritual Help • Vegetarian Food
Venue for Hire • Community Living • Vocations

Christian – Roman Catholic

Killarney is one of the most beautiful places in the world and no one can resist the beauty of its lakes, forests and mountains. The Franciscan Prayer Centre in the heart of this wondrous place of nature seems ideally placed for the search for God. It is also in the heart of the town of Killarney, but the centre is set up from the road, above the noise. Meals, while taken with other guests, can be taken with the resident community. The rooms are clean and comfortable and the beds are very good. The church has much wall and ceiling decoration combined with a stunning old-fashioned altar with various ornamentation and mosaics circa 1917. A special feature is the sound of running water, which does move one to think of the living waters of faith. This may help some with their contemplation – for others it will be a distraction. Overall, an atmosphere of friendly caring. It is only a few minutes to some of the glorious lakes of Killarney – not to be missed for true inspiration of the wonder of creation. You can take a cart and pony just near the centre and be driven to see it all.

OPEN: Most of the year except Christmas/New Year/Easter seasons. Receives men, women, young people and groups.
ROOMS: 6 en suite singles.
FACILITIES: Church, garden, park, library, small bookshop, guest lounge, TV.
SPIRITUAL HELP: Spiritual direction, group prayer, Friday evening Divine Office together with community in church, personal talks and meditation.
GUESTS ADMITTED TO: Chapel, choir, oratory.
MEALS: Guests eat together usually. Traditional food. Vegetarians catered for.
SPECIAL ACTIVITIES: Planned directed retreats; send for information. Private retreats with spiritual direction if wanted.
SITUATION: Quiet in a small town.
MAXIMUM STAY: By arrangement. Range of 8–30 days.
BOOKINGS: Letter.
CHARGES: Daily rates: directed retreat 55€; private retreat 50€; day events including snacks 25€. Special consideration will be given to the unwaged.
ACCESS: Killarney is easily accessible by air, rail and bus/coach. Car: via N22, N71 and N72.

KILDARE

•••

BALLYMORE EUSTACE

Avelin	Tel: +353 (0)45 864524
Bishopland	Fax: +353 (0)45 864823
Ballymore Eustace	Email: begg@iol.ie
County Kildare	Website: www.avelin.hitsplc.com
Ireland	

Retreats • Workshops and Courses • Church/Temple • Spiritual Help
Bed and Breakfast • Vegetarian Food

Christian – Ecumenical

At Avelin there is an experiential approach to Celtic spirituality through visiting ancient, prehistoric and early Christian sites. Each day ends with prayer in the Celtic tradition. There is a maximum of six people for these courses, which are called *Celtic Journeys and Pilgrim Walks*. They have had wide media publicity and people come from around the world to participate in these special Celtic-tradition-based retreats.

LEITRIM

•••

DROMAHAIR

Ard Nahoo Eco Retreat	Tel: +353 (0)71 9134939
Ard Nahoo, Mullagh	Fax: +353 (0)71 9164733
Dromahair	Email: info@ardnahoo.com
County Leitrim	Website: www.ardnahoo.com
Ireland	

Retreats • Workshops and Courses • Yoga • Meditation • Bed and Breakfast • Vegetarian
Food • Organic Food • Self-Catering Space • Alternative Therapies • Holistic Holidays

Eco-spirituality – Yoga

How green can you get these days? Some would answer by going to Ard Nahoo Eco Retreat, where one of the most important aspects is their

Eco Policy. Their hard work to be green resulted in being granted the EU Flower, the only sign of environmental quality recognised throughout Europe. This status means that they are meticulous about energy consumption, recycling and natural produce. In 2007 they undertook a massive renovation, extending their health farm to include a new yoga studio and indoor/outdoor wet area and the addition of two new Eco Cabins. The building was done using green principles – sustainable cedar from County Donegal, hemp insulation, limited concrete, no petrochemicals and natural paints throughout. All their Eco Cabins are heated using pellet stoves and have an underground recycling facility. Compost bins are collected regularly for their organic vegetable patch. With six acres of land untouched by chemicals and maintained in keeping with their natural state, Ard Nahoo offers a beautiful and spacious environment. The retreat weekends are well known now. Recently, they were voted one of the Top Ten Retreats Worldwide by the British newspaper the *Guardian*. The most popular weekends are the *Yoga, Walking and Relaxation Retreat*, and the *3-Day Detox Retreat*. Choose from a short no-nonsense list of treatments. Alongside the treatment room there's a steam room and an Epsom float room. There are numerous beautiful walks that begin on the doorstep and take in the mountainous scenery. **Highly Recommended.**

OPEN: All year round. Everyone is welcome.
ROOMS: 3 self-catering Eco Cabins, sleeping 17 in total. Fully equipped kitchens, bathrooms, private decking areas and surrounded by flower and vegetable patches.
FACILITIES: A custom-built yoga studio, outdoor area with detox sauna and hot tub, health farm offering variety of massages and craniosacral therapy, a Celtic Nature Trail and Wise Woman Mandala.
SPIRITUAL HELP: Yoga. No other specific spiritual assistance.
GUESTS ADMITTED TO: Individual Eco Cabins are private, but otherwise the grounds are open.
MEALS: As part of a retreat, meals are taken together. These are organic, home-made and local where possible. On private holidays, Eco Cabins are self-catering, though they have a caterer who can provide meals direct. There is also an organic vegetable box and Irish artisan cheese board available. All Eco Cabins come with an organic welcome pack.
SPECIAL ACTIVITIES: All activities are included in organised retreats. These include yoga, walking, meditation and sessions in the sauna/hot tub. Guests can join in weekly yoga classes or book in for private sessions, or for a massage.
SITUATION: About a mile outside a small village in the west coast of Ireland, surrounded by beautiful rugged scenery .
MAXIMUM STAY: No maximum stay. Retreats are typically 2–3 nights long.
BOOKINGS: Letter, telephone, fax, email, online booking form.
CHARGES: Between 280€ and 395€ per person for the retreats. Prices for the Eco Cabins start from 190€ (for 2–3 nights, arriving on a Wednesday, for 2–4 people).
ACCESS: Rail/bus: to Sligo, which is 10 miles away. Air: an hour's drive from Knock airport, 3 hours from Dublin airport. Car: accessible from the N4 and N16.

LIMERICK

CASTLECONNELL

Irish Harp Centre
The Old Schoolhouse
Castleconnell
County Limerick
Ireland

Tel: +353 (0)61 372777
Fax: +353 (0)61 372712
Email: info@irishharpcentre.com
Website: www.irishharpcentre.com

> Retreats • Workshops and Courses

Christian – Sanctuary for Music

The centre is a mid-nineteenth-century listed school house, with neighbouring cottages, and is magnificently situated on the shores of the River Shannon by the ancient castle and historic village of Castleconnell. In the tradition of the ancient monastic places of learning in Ireland, the Irish Harp Centre and Music School is a place of culture and learning, of natural and architectural beauty, of sanctuary and a centre for the pursuance of excellence in the traditional arts. It is located only 20 minutes from Shannon airport, six miles from Limerick city, and two miles from the University and the Irish World Music Centre. The facilities include exhibition and small conference rooms, teaching rooms, conservatory, dining room, reference library, rehearsal space for orchestra and performers, and accommodation in adjacent village and hotel. The music school runs daily throughout the year and includes music for children.

MURROE

Glenstal Abbey
Murroe
County Limerick
Ireland

Tel: +353 (0)61 386103
Fax: +353 (0)61 386328
Email: guestmaster@glenstal.org
Website: www.glenstal.org

> Retreats • Workshops and Courses • Church/Temple • Meditation • Spiritual Help
> Vegetarian Food • Self-Catering Space • Community Living • Work Retreats • Vocations

Christian – Roman Catholic

A long, elegant drive leads up to this great abbey of stone, but the large castle-like building only houses the school run by the monks here.

Their monastery and the guest area are much more modest – in fact they are fashioned from the old stable block. Rest assured, however, the monks are not deprived, for their place quietly surrounds a pretty cloister away from students and visitors. The church standing to one side by itself is a stunner inside. The decorations of ceiling and altar are in vibrant colours of geometric designs with an oriental theme. Somehow this modernity combined with plain walls and simple furnishings works well. The gardens are large and have long walks through woods and by water with azaleas blooming in the late spring. There is a walled and terraced early seventeenth-century garden, which may be locked, but ask if you can go inside. The monks are very hospitable and the guest house has extremely comfortable accommodations. The guestmaster is usually in the guest house to welcome guests and converse with them. Evening meals, which are taken in the monastic refectory with the monks, are quite solemn, graced with readings from something informative or enriching to the mind. Glenstal – founded in 1927 on ground owned by a medieval abbey – has a tradition of involvement in arts, crafts and liturgical renewal. **Highly Recommended.**

OPEN: All year except Christmas and the Community's own annual retreat. Receives men and women. Guests are expected to attend daily liturgy services in the church.
ROOMS: 12 rooms, all en suite.
FACILITIES: Disabled access, with one wheelchair-accessible bathroom. Men and women accommodated in the same guest house. Small guest-house library, church, large grounds with long and varied walks through the surrounding woods.
SPIRITUAL HELP: Personal talks, spiritual counsel if requested, personal retreat direction.
GUESTS ADMITTED TO: Church, most of the grounds.
MEALS: Breakfast is self-catering in the guest house, lunch is served to guests in a small dining room, and dinner is in the monastery refectory with the monks. Traditional food. Vegetarians.
SPECIAL ACTIVITIES: Programme of courses. Online meditation.
SITUATION: Very quiet and in the countryside.
MAXIMUM STAY: 3–7 days.
BOOKINGS: Letter, telephone, email.
CHARGES: By donation.
ACCESS: Rail: to Limerick, then taxi. Car: 12 miles from Limerick, off the N7.

'He who would travel happily must travel light'
– Antoine de Saint-Exupery

MAYO

••

CLAREMORRIS

Ballintubber Abbey	Tel: +353 (0)94 9030934
Ballintubber, Claremorris	Fax: +353 (0)94 9030018
County Mayo	Email: btubabbey1@eircom.net
Ireland	Website: www.ballintubberabbey.ie

Retreats • Workshops and Courses • Church/Temple

Christian – Roman Catholic – Ecumenical

Ballintubber is the thirteenth-century abbey that refused to die – the surrounding community stubbornly continued to worship here long after the roof had been demolished in the Penal Times. The restoration of this simple but majestic old abbey was begun in the nineteenth century and completed by the end of the twentieth. The retreat and pilgrimage experience at Ballintubber includes the chance for a day of quiet on nearby Church Island (sacred from pre-Christian times), an optional 22-mile walk to the summit of Croagh Patrick, a day of prayer in the atmospheric grounds around the abbey, and immersion in the Neolithic and Celtic roots of Irish Christianity at a nearby cultural heritage museum. As well as theme retreats for confirmation groups, older students and adults, Ballintubber is used for private retreats in surroundings that deepen the sense of connectedness to the distant past.

OPEN: All year, but theme retreats are not offered in June.
ROOMS: Guests and retreatants are all accommodated in local B&Bs, with mostly good facilities, though not all en suite or with disabled access. It is possible to find accommodation for up to 30 adults, though only 15 at a time can travel on the little ferry to Church Island.
FACILITIES: Abbey, conference room, shop, video presentation, the Way of the Cross, the Way of Mary, the Way of Patrick, Celtic Furrow, Church Island (adults only).
SPIRITUAL HELP: Spiritual accompaniment, personal talks, Sacrament of Reconciliation, daily Eucharist.
MEALS: In local restaurant or cafeteria.
SPECIAL ACTIVITIES: The Ballintubber Experience (including Church Island, Croagh Patrick, Ballintubber Abbey and the Celtic Furrow), or one or more of these elements. Passion Play in Holy Week. Themed retreats for young people and adults.
SITUATION: A quiet village, 8 miles to the south of Castlebar, with views across to the Connemara mountains and Croagh Patrick.
MAXIMUM STAY: 5 days, or by arrangement for private retreatants.
BOOKINGS: Letter, phone or email.
CHARGES: Please enquire as to current charges for programmes.
ACCESS: Rail/bus: to Castlebar; pick-up can be arranged. Car: along the N84 from Castlebar or Galway.

SLIGO

•••

SKREEN

Holy Hill Hermitage
Skreen
County Sligo
Ireland

Tel: +353 (0)71 9166021
Fax: +353 (0)71 9166954
Email: holyhill@eircom.net
Website: www.spirituallifeinstitute.org

Retreats • Church/Temple • Spiritual Help • Self-Catering Space • Vocations • Hermitages

Roman Catholic – Ecumenical – Eremitical

One of the foundations of the Spiritual Life Institute, here a group of men and women live as hermits in the Carmelite tradition, with a passion for God and his creation. As there are only six hermitages for retreatants, they tend to be booked well in advance, but it is worth checking if there are cancellations. For those who feel the need of complete silence and solitude, Holy Hill radiates peace amid great natural beauty and some inspired gardens created or restored by the monks. The hermitage cabins are complete in themselves, very comfortable and simply furnished and equipped. From Holy Hill there is a magnificent view across the hills to Donegal Bay – the beach is only four miles away – and to Ben Bulben, and there are wonderful hikes into the Ox Mountains. The old manor house and outbuildings have been lovingly and creatively restored.

'Why not listen a little? Why not slow down some, hush up a bit,
sit still a moment, turn on your dreams and listen to the wind, to
the woods, to the water? Bend over and look down into the dark
pool of your own depths and do not be afraid.'
– Matthew Kelty

TIPPERARY

•••

KILSHEELAN

Glencomeragh House
Kilsheelan
Clonmel
County Tipperary
Ireland

Tel: +353 (0)52 6133181
Fax: +353 (0)52 6133636
Email: info@glencomeragh.ie
Website: www.glencomeragh.ie

Retreats • Workshops and Courses • Church/Temple • Spiritual Help • Vegetarian Food
Venue for Hire • Vocations • Hermitages

Christian – Roman Catholic

Glencomeragh sits at the foot of the Comeragh Mountains looking out over the valley of the River Suir. This splendid nineteenth-century house has very attractive rooms, tastefully decorated like a small, elegant country hotel with pretty wallpaper and curtains. The bathrooms are sparkling clean and generously equipped. The community went for professional advice on the decorating and it is a great success. With such outstanding attention to comfort and detail (even down to writing stationery in the desks) plus central heating, large dining room, library, church, hall, spacious gardens, ornamental ponds and streams, the Rosminian House of Prayer at Glencomeragh is one of the best retreat houses in Europe. For exercise, there is a variety of forest walks, countryside rambles and mountain hills, all easily available. In addition to the main house, there is Glen Lodge, a separate modern and well-furnished self-catering house which is ideal for private retreats, groups and workshops. The community makes everyone feel at home. There is a daily Mass with a Taize Mass on the last Saturday of each month and both a Medjugorje evening as well as a Maranatha Rosary group each week. This neat-as-a-pin place is just right for a spirituality and retreat programme that combines deep religious traditions and retreats with new thinking. For example, the Eucharist may be celebrated outdoors by a waterfall in the hills and there are Creation Retreats using animals such as horses, and riding. As to the food, it is honest and plain with home-made pies and other good dishes. Frankly, we just couldn't get enough of their delicious Irish soda bread. As the song says, it may well be a long, long way to Tipperary, but if you're headed to this Rosminian House of Prayer, the journey is worth it. **Highly Recommended.**

OPEN: All year but self-catering at Christmas and New Year. Receives men, women, groups and religious.
ROOMS: 16 singles, 4 doubles, 4 hermitages.
FACILITIES: 8 rooms on ground level. Conferences, garden with ponds, library, TV, direct-dialling phone.
SPIRITUAL HELP: Personal talks, private meditation, spiritual direction available, daily Mass with a Taize Mass monthly, Sacrament of Reconciliation.
GUESTS ADMITTED TO: Chapel. Residential guests have freedom of the house.
MEALS: Everyone eats together. Wholefood and traditional. Vegetarian and special diets catered for.
SPECIAL ACTIVITIES: Special programme, including a 12-Step Spirituality programme, De Mello weekend courses and preached and directed retreats. Creation Retreats. Brochure available on request.
SITUATION: Very quiet in the countryside.
MAXIMUM STAY: By arrangement.
BOOKINGS: Letter, telephone, email.
CHARGES: Current daily/nightly rates: full board from 80€; self-catering from 60€ single and 80€ double.
ACCESS: Bus: Bus Éireann runs to Kilsheelan village; pick available from there. Car: easily accessible from the N24 and N76.

ROSCREA

Mount St Joseph Abbey	Tel: +353 (0)0505 25600
Roscrea	Fax: +353 (0)0505 25610
County Tipperary	Email: info@msjroscrea.ie
Ireland	Website: www.msjroscrea.ie

Retreats • Church/Temple • Spiritual Help • Bed and Breakfast • Vegetarian Food
Community Living • Vocations

Christian – Roman Catholic

This Cistercian monastery's guest house is a large one with wide, cool hallways and much silence. Night prayers with the community in the huge, grey-stone, vaulted monastic church is a deeply enriching experience as their liturgy is inspiring. The abbey is set in quiet countryside and is conducive to prayer and relaxation. In this monastic splendour – combined with a simplicity of lifestyle – the atmosphere remains friendly and warm from a community busy seeking God and living out full lives in Christ.

OPEN: All year except from 10 December to 10 January. Everyone welcome.
ROOMS: 20 singles, 30 doubles.
FACILITIES: Church. Prayer room in guest house with Blessed Sacrament reserved. Garden, lovely park and grounds, guest lounge. Nice walks in extensive grounds are a retreat advantage.

SPIRITUAL HELP: Mass daily, Divine Office, Sacrament of Confession available.
GUESTS ADMITTED TO: Church, chapel, oratory.
MEALS: Everyone eats together in the guest house. Traditional wholesome good food. Vegetarians catered for.
SPECIAL ACTIVITIES: No planned programme.
SITUATION: In quiet countryside.
MAXIMUM STAY: 7 days.
BOOKINGS: Letter, telephone, fax, email.
CHARGES: B&B and full board possible; please ask for rates when you are booking.
ACCESS: The guest house is 2.5 miles from Roscrea. Rail: Roscrea station, then taxi. Bus: good services to Roscrea. Car: via N62 or N7.

TYRONE

COOKSTOWN

Tullycoll Trust Foundation	Tel: 028 86758785
Tullycoll House	Fax: 028 86758815
10 Tullycoll Road, Cookstown	Email: tullycoll@hotmail.com
County Tyrone BT80 9QY	
Northern Ireland	

Retreats • Workshops and Courses • Meditation • Spiritual Help • Vegetarian Food
Alternative Therapies • Holistic Holidays • Community Living • Vocations • Children

Mind Body Spirit – Spiritual development – Course in Miracles

Tullycoll is a developing spiritual community set in the heart of mid-Ulster with newly constructed bunkhouse accommodation for up to 24 people. The community is guided by the teachings of *A Course in Miracles* and is an open fellowship of people united by commitment to spiritual growth and a desire to support themselves and others in a loving environment, thereby creating a safer, more loving Earth on which we may all live. The following retreat courses can be typical of what is on offer: *Group Rebirthing Workshops, Sweat Lodge Ceremony, Men's Talking Circle and Workshops* and *Spiritual Mastery Training.* You need to email them for detailed information on what is available on their programme and the costs.

WATERFORD

•••

CAPPOQUIN

Mount Melleray Abbey   Tel: +353 (0)58 54404
Cappoquin   Email: guestmaster@mountmellerayabbey.org
County Waterford   Website: www.mountmellerayabbey.org
Ireland

Retreats • Church/Temple • Self-Catering Space • Community Living • Vocations

Christian – Roman Catholic – Cistercian

Mount Melleray Abbey is a community of Cistercian monks. Their monastery is situated on the slopes of the Knockmealdown Mountains and they have a retreat house available for quiet private retreats. This is a good monastic environment for a silent retreat of prayer and reflection.

OPEN: Most of the year. Men and women welcome.
ROOMS: Accommodation is in the guest house.
FACILITIES: Church, chapel, the repository/bookshop, the heritage centre, The Cloisters restaurant and the tea rooms.
SPIRITUAL HELP: It may be possible to arrange to speak personally with a monk by special arrangement.
GUESTS ADMITTED TO: All guest areas, plus public garden area and chapel.
MEALS: Taken in guest house.
SPECIAL ACTIVITIES: None.
SITUATION: Countryside.
MAXIMUM STAY: 1 week or by arrangement.
BOOKINGS: Letter, email.
CHARGES: While no set fee is asked, guests staying here should donate a reasonable amount to help offset the costs of running the retreat house.
ACCESS: Car : via N72.

'It matters not how a man lives, but how he dies'
– Samuel Johnson

WATERFORD

Grace Dieu Manor Retreat	Tel: +353 (0)51 374417
and Conference Centre	Fax: +353 (0)51 874536
Tramore Road	Email: gracedieu@ireland.com
Waterford	Website: homepage.eircom.net/~gracedieu
County Waterford	
Ireland	

Retreats • Workshops and Courses • Church/Temple • Meditation • Spiritual Help
Vegetarian Food • Venue for Hire

Christian – Roman Catholic

A large and very busy place, which offers a wide variety of retreats from Scripture Study weekends to Earth Ecological retreats and extends the opportunity in all their retreats for a person to develop more profound insights. The old house, which is the retreat centre, was build about 1810 but has an equally large modern extension. The grounds are not extensive but offer mature trees, private sitting areas and a pleasant walk among trees and nearby pastures of almost a mile. All ages and all kinds of retreat programmes are catered for here with a chapel, simple in design and into which light pours from all sides. The resident community is friendly and has a wide range of interests. There are good facilities for the disabled – not long ago 16 disabled people with their own helpers were accommodated on a retreat.

OPEN: Open all year. Receives men, women, young people and groups.
ROOMS: 33 en suite single, twin-bedded and double rooms. Several rooms located on ground floor and intended for disabled guests.
FACILITIES: Chapel, conferences, guest lounge.
SPIRITUAL HELP: Spiritual direction, personal guided retreats, guided meditation group.
GUESTS ADMITTED TO: Chapel, work of community.
MEALS: Guest dining room. Traditional food. Vegetarian and special diets.
SPECIAL ACTIVITIES: Programme of retreats. Send for brochure and download the programme on the website.
SITUATION: Quiet.
MAXIMUM STAY: 7 days.
BOOKINGS: Letter, telephone, email, easy online booking form.
CHARGES: Currently, a week's retreat runs at about 510€ and a weekend about 170€. Rates for short stays available.
ACCESS: Rail: Waterford station. Bus: coach services are available. Air: Waterford airport is 4.5 miles from the city; Dublin airport is a 2.5-hour drive away; Cork Airport is 90 minutes away. Car: via N9, N24 and N25. Ask for directions when booking.

WICKLOW

• •

DONARD

Chrysalis Holistic Centre
Donard
County Wicklow
Ireland

Tel/Fax: +353 (0)45 404713
Email: peace@chrysalis.ie
Website: www.chrysalis.ie

> Retreats • Workshops and Courses • Meditation • Spiritual Help • Bed and Breakfast
> Vegetarian Food • Venue for Hire • Self-Catering Space • Alternative Therapies
> Holistic Holidays • Hermitages

Mind Body Spirit – Holistic

This holistic centre, founded in 1989 for renewal and growth, is a former rectory dating from 1711, now restored. It specialises in residential courses in personal growth and spirituality. The house is charming and welcoming. While the main concern here is with Mind Body Spirit spirituality approaches, there are often Christian traditions within the workshop programme such as De Mello exercises. This quiet sanctuary, which has now been running for some years, offers space for diverse spiritual traditions with one of the most extensive programmes of residential and one-day courses on offer anywhere in Ireland. These include topics such as *Search for Inner Freedom*, *Journey of Transition and Transformation*, *De Mello Retreats*, *Touch and Relaxation*, *Facing Co-dependency* and *Journal Writing*, as well as *Healing and Transformation*, *Inner Yoga* and *Imagery* workshops. Vegetarian food and two hermitages in a Zen garden add to the considerable attractions of this place. **Highly Recommended.**

OPEN: All year except Christmas. Receives men, women and groups.
ROOMS: 3 singles, 5 twin/doubles, 2 dormitories, 2 hermitages. Mobiles should be switched off when staying here.
FACILITIES: Conferences, lovely garden, park, library.
SPIRITUAL HELP: Personal talks, group sharing, meditation, directed study. Two hermitages for silence and private reflection.
GUESTS ADMITTED TO: Guest areas and grounds.
MEALS: Everyone eats together. Vegetarian food only. Vegan possible. Self-catering possible in hermitages.
SPECIAL ACTIVITIES: Planned programme. Conferences. Workshops. Brochure available and programme information is also on the website.
SITUATION: Very quiet in the countryside.
MAXIMUM STAY: By programme or event or by arrangement.

BOOKINGS: Letter, telephone (office hours), fax, email. Online booking is easy.
CHARGES: All charges are listed in the extensive programme brochure. Can be about 350€–400€ for a weekend course, all inclusive. Fully self-catering, the hermitages are available for a minimum 2-day stay at 60€ per day for one person and 85€ per day for 2 people.
ACCESS: Bus: service runs from Dublin. Car: via N81 – within an hour of Dublin. Very clear travel directions are on the website.

GLENDALOUGH

Glendalough Hermitage
St Kevin's Parish Church
Glendalough
County Wicklow
Ireland

Tel/Fax: +353 (0)40 445777
Email: glendalough2000@eircom.net
Website: www.glendalough.dublindiocese.ie

Retreats • Church/Temple • Spiritual Help • Self-Catering Space • Hermitages

Christian – Roman Catholic

Glendalough, an ancient monastic site surrounded by the majestic splendour of the Wicklow Mountains, draws large numbers of visitors today – just as it has done for some 1,500 years. It is still possible in this lovely spot to make a peaceful hermitage retreat a little off the beaten track . You go up a quiet road overlooking the valley to St Kevin's Parish Church. There are five tastefully designed retreat hermitages here – each complete with bathroom, kitchenette and an open fire (there are also storage heaters) – and a bench outside on which to sit and gaze across the valley. Retreatants cater entirely for themselves, provisions to be brought or obtained locally. The monastic site is well worth lingering in, but go early in the morning or evening if you prefer to do it in a contemplative atmosphere. There are countless beautiful walks by lakes, streams, woods and hills. Marvellous! **Highly Recommended.**

'There are a thousand doors to let out life'
– Phillip Massinger

FRANCE

There are many organised retreats available in France for groups and individuals. The majority of these programmes still have a Christian orientation, particularly Roman Catholic, and most are offered in French. There are many traditional retreat programmes with established faith-awakening themes – such as *Introduction to Bible Reading* and *Silence in the Carmelite Tradition* – but increasingly more French Catholic retreat houses are offering contemporary approaches to spirituality that suit modern ideas of living. Buddhist and yoga retreats and courses are now very popular, and France has sped ahead with Mind Body Spirit, eco-spirituality and holistic healing retreats and programmes. In addition, herbal treatments, Ayurvedic medicine, permaculture, nature walking and treatments such as Reiki and massage of various types are widely available. However, group pilgrimages to various sacred sites or routes remain popular, usually organised by parish churches or by walking clubs and youth groups.

Language You need an adequate understanding of French for most retreats, but it is possible to manage without fluency in the language. It is worth asking whether a retreat centre offers retreats in English, as this is happening much more frequently now.

Disabled It is worth contacting the organisation **Office Chrétien des Personnes Handicapées**. (Tel: +33 (0)1 53 69 44 30. Website: www.och.assoc.fr) The French are working hard to bring access to the disabled everywhere, but in general the level of access is perhaps not yet as high as in Britain.

Paris If you are staying in or near Paris for a while, there are plenty of evening talks and day retreats. The French daily national newspaper *La Croix* usually has a short-listing of spiritual and religious talks taking place.

Buddhism Buddhism is the most rapidly expanding religion by conversion in France today, with over 5 million people claiming interest in this spiritual path. For those keen to discover and learn more about Buddhist teachings and retreats, the choice of places to go in France is wide. Note that French Buddhist centres expect you to be with them for spiritual intentions and, while you often need or should have some previous experience of meditation, it is not always mandatory or even necessary. There are plenty of beginners' courses on offer now.

Christianity Most Christian religious communities and the lay people associated with them offer modern guest-house facilities, which are often striking in design and concept, and as comfortable as a good hotel. The old monasteries are huge buildings, originally built to house large communities and, consequently, such places can strike one as very institutional. However, most of these rambling places have comfortable refurbished guest rooms, some with en suite bedrooms – but the French expectation of en suite provision is well behind that of the British.

Mind Body Spirit and Alternative Spirituality Mind Body Spirit and alternative spirituality facilities and programmes have increased in France by leaps and bounds, with a continuing expansion of courses, workshops, training and retreats. French readers, please see l'Association Psychotherapie Vigilance below.

Yoga in France Yoga is now taught all over France and is as popular as it is in Britain.

Retreat Meals Do not expect the meals in monastic France to reflect necessarily the fame of that nation's reputation for cooking. Although the cuisine can be great, some dishes may not so appetizing. Vegetarians on retreat in France sometimes get lucky – but where the French differ from the British is in their understanding of the latter's fashion for personal diets.

Retreat Costs As to costs for your retreat in France, the rates are about the same as for Britain, sometimes marginally lower.

INFORMATION POUR LES LECTEURS FRANÇAIS

Nous vivons maintenant dans une communauté planetaire et cela s'applique tout autant aux retraites qu'elles soient en France, Angleterre, Italie ou ailleurs. La France foisonne de retraites de toutes sorte, depuis la solitude des chartreux a la Chartreuse de Sélignac juqu'au boudhisme à Thìch Nhat Hanh's Le Village des Pruniers et de l'ecospiritualité au Blé en Herbe aux Retraites et Vacances Viveka Yoga a Festes-et-Saint-André. Dans la plus grande partie de l'Europe la langue n'est plus la barrière qu'elle était a une epoque. Si vous êtes Français, il y a de nombreux endroits en dehors de la France pour aller en retraite où vous vous sentirez bienvenus et a l'aise. Evidemment, si vous ne parlez pas bien l'anglais ni d'autres langues, choisissez une retraie qui ne vous impose pas d'aller a de nombreuses conférences. Il y en a beaucoup qui vous sont ouvertes de l'Irlande a l'Inde s'etalant des chrétiennes traditionnelles aux boudhistes a celles de l'esprit et du corps en ce qui concerne le fait de traiter les soins en station thermale ou « Spa » et les vacances conçues autour de thera-pies de bien-être comme des retraites spirituelles. Il est peut-être sage de rappeler ce que Bouddha avait à dire sur l'importance de nos corps: Garder le corps en bonne santè est un devoir sinon nous ne porrons pas garder un esprit fort et clair. Il est certain que sans cet etat d'espirit nous ne pouvons pas entrer dans notre voyage spirituel, sans se soucier de savoir si nous avons dejà la foi ou cherchons encore des rèponses spi-rituelles. Qu'importe oú vous déciderez d'aller en retraite dans le belle France ou á l'etranger que ces mots de St Francis de Salles vous guident: Dieu est partout et dans tout, il n'y a pas de lieu dans ce monde où on ne le trouve.

L'Association Psychotherapie Vigilance Si vous avez des inquietudes au suject des stages ou therapies que quiconque vous-offre vous pouvez vous adresser á l'association pour en apprendre plus: www.PsyVig.com. Ce site de Psychothérapie Vigilance a été conçu pour recueillir et donner la parole. Pour soutenir et accompagner les structures, les associations et les particuliers luttant au quotidien contre les thérapeutes recourant à des techniques et des méthodes dites de manipulation mentale ou de sujétion psychologique. Pour rendre hommage aussi à tous les opérateurs et professionnels de la santé mentale qui, dans une démarche scientifique authentiquement respectueuse du droit et de la dignité des demandeurs d'aide psychologique ou de développement personnel exercent leur métier avec humilité, dévouement et compétence. Pour s'incliner aussi devant les malades et leurs souffrances, pour leur dire notre compassion, pour accueillir les doléances de leur entourage et les aider à trouver la solution la plus adaptée à leur situation. Le site de Psychothérapie Vigilance est indépendant et n'a aucune vocation commerciale. Il est entièrement financé par des fonds privés et toutes les contributions apportées le sont à titre gracieux.

RETREAT CENTRES AND PLACES

The retreat places in this section are listed by the departments of France, which each have a number. For example, the number for the Pyrénées-Haute is 65 and for Paris it is 75.

AIN (01)

BOURG-EN-BRESSE

Auris   Tel: +33 (0)4 74 22 48 86
6 Rue Viala
01000 Bourg-en-Bresse
France

Yoga – Alternative spirituality (Yoga – Spiritualité Alternative)

Yoga, de-stressing, meditation, chanting, voice workshops and personal therapies are all on offer here. Send for a brochure for more information.

LE PLANTAY

L'Abbaye Notre-Dame des Dombes   Tel: +33 (0)4 74 98 14 40
Le Plantay   Fax: +33 (0)4 74 98 16 70
01330 Villars-les-Dombes   Email: nddombes@chemin-neuf.org
France   Website: chemin-neuf.org/dombes/index.html

Roman Catholic – Trappist (Catholique – Trappist)

The community of Trappist monks here receive men, women and groups who desire a retreat of silence and prayer. Accommodation for 40; disabled facility for one. Camping, woods, domitory and barn.

Les moines font divers produits, y compris les fruits séchés et petits fours, et ont une petite boutique.

SIMANDRE

Maison St Bruno   Tel/Fax: +33 (0)4 74 51 79 20
Chartreuse De Sélignac   Email: chartreusedeselignac@selignac.org
01250 Simandre   Website: www.selignac.org
France

Roman Catholic – Carthusian (Catholique – Carthusian)

This is a lay religious house that follows Carthusian spirituality. All who come here follow the small resident lay community in prayer, solitude and silence in their cell, supplemented by work in the gardens or the kitchen. **Silence is maintained**. This is not an ideal place if you have not previously lived in silence. Required minimum stay of eight days.

*En 2001, l'Ordre des Chartreux a confié la maison de Sélignac à quelques laïcs, appelé à y poursuivre, après le départ des moines, une présence de prière et d'accueil dans l'esprit de Saint Bruno. Une retraite une durée minimum de huit jours est requise. L'exigence du **respect absolu du silence** étant équivalent dans tout le monastère.*

ALLIER (03)

CHANTELLE

L'Abbaye Bénédictine Saint-Vincent   Tel: +33 (0)4 70 56 62 55
Rue Anne de Beauzier   Fax: +33 (0)4 70 56 15 30
03140 Chantelle   Email: contact@benedictines-chantelle.com
France   Website: www.benedictines-chantelle.com

Roman Catholic (Catholique)

This Benedictine community receives men, women and accompanied disabled. The abbey has 27 rooms, five conference rooms, a library, a chapel and a choir. Personal talks and meditation are offered.

27 chambres. Des entretiens personnels, la méditation.

DOMPIERRE-SUR-BESBRE

L'Abbaye Notre Dame de Sept-Fons   Tel: +33 (0)4 70 48 14 90
03290 Dompierre-sur-Besbre   Fax: +33 (0)4 70 48 14 87
France   Email: septfons@septfons.com
                                  Website: www.abbayedeseptfons.com

Roman Catholic (Catholique)

Men for religious retreats only are received here. Personal talks are possible.

Les hommes et religieux de retraites seulement.

ALPES-DE-HAUTE-PROVENCE (04)

FAUCON DE BARCELONNETTE

Couvent Saint-Jean de Matha   Tel: +33 (0)4 92 81 09 17
04400 Faucon-de-Barcelonnette   Fax: +33 (0)4 92 81 49 26
France   Email: couvent.matha@wanadoo.fr

Roman Catholic (Catholique)

This community of religious men welcomes individuals or groups for stays of not more than 21 days. The rates are about 50€ full board per day.

Cette communauté religieuse hommes acceptent des gens seuls ou en groupes pour des séjours de pas plus de 21 jours.

'Le mesure de l'amour c'est d'aimer sans mesure.'
– Saint Augustine

HAUTES-ALPES (05)

••

LARAGNE

Terre Nouvelle   Tel: +33 (0)4 92 65 24 25
Boite Postal 52
05300 Laragne
France

Alternative spirituality (Spiritualité alternative)

A place like the **Findhorn Foundation** community in Morayshire, Scotland. There are many workshops in the summer.

Nombreux ateliers à l'été.

SAINT ETIENNE DE LAUS

Hotellerie Notre-Dame du Laus   Tel: +33 (0)4 92 50 30 73
05130 Saint-Etienne-de-Laus   Fax: +33 (0)4 92 50 90 77
France   Email: accueil@notre-dame-du-laus.com
                              Website: www.notre-dame-du-laus.com

Roman Catholic (Catholique)

A very large establishment that accommodates 400-plus, it is based at the pilgrimage destination of Sanctuaire Notre-Dame du Laus. The sanctuary is very popular and bookings need to be made at least four months in advance. With a view of the mountains, this retreat house offers disabled facilities, library, lounges, personal talks, conferences, chapel, choir, Mass and courses. Full-board rates vary but are in the range of 40€ to 60€.

Avec vue sur les montagnes, maison de retraite offre installations pour personnes handicapées, bibliothèque, salons, entretiens personnalisés, conférences, chapelle, choeur et Mess.

LA TRINITÉ

Sanctuaire de Notre-Dame de Laghet   Tel: +33 (0)4 92 41 50 50
06340 La Trinité   Fax: +33 (0)4 93 41 50 59
France   Email: sanctuairelaghet@orange.fr
Website: www.sanctuaire-laghet.cef.fr

Roman Catholic (Catholique)

The sisters of the Sacred Heart receive pilgrims and men and women for retreats. They offer 60 rooms, guest lounges, library, personal talks, conferences. The full-board rates are about 55€ per day.

Retraites et les pèlerins.

ARDÈCHE (07)

ROCHESSAUVE

Aleph   Tel: +33 (0)4 75 65 10 99
07210 Rochessauve   Fax: +33 (0)4 75 65 08 02
France

Alternative spirituality (Spiritualité alternative)

It is claimed that this centre is like no other. It is certainly true that it is in a magical place in the Ardèche – a marvellous situation of gorges, mountains, prehistoric sites and sacred places. The aim of Aleph is to help you to make contact with nature and, in turn, with your own nature.

On prétend que ce centre est comme aucun autre. C'est certainement vrai que c'est dans un endroit magique en Ardèche. Voici une merveilleuse situation de gorges, de montagnes, de sites préhistoriques, et de lieux sacrés. Ce qui se passe à Aleph vise à vous aider à prendre contact avec la nature et, à son tour, avec votre propre nature. D'information envoi sur leur philosophie et les cours.

ROSIÈRES

Le Mas Bleu
07260 Rosières
France

Tel: +33 (0)4 75 39 93 75
Email: info@lemasbleu.com
Website: www.lemasbleu.com

Alternative spirituality – Spa (Spiritualité alternative – Spa)

This old eighteenth-century farmhouse has gardens and views of vineyards, fruit trees and forested hills. It's an informal place with Provençal decoration, offering apartments and a range of alternative therapies from a team of experienced therapists. There is an outdoor pool, indoor jacuzzi with whirlpool, hammam and treatments ranging from reflexology, massage, yoga and Shiatsu to aqua-relaxation Jahara. This last is used internationally in aquatic rehabilitation as well as being available at many spa facilities.

Parmi les traitements disponibles ici est l'eau: thérapie pour la détente.

SAINT-ÉTIENNE-DE-LUGDARÈS

L'Abbaye Notre-Dame des Neiges
07590 Saint-Laurent-les-Bains
France

Tel: +33 (0)4 66 46 59 00
Fax: +33 (0)4 66 46 59 08
Email: info@notredamedesneiges.com
Website: notredamedesneiges.com

Roman Catholic (Catholique)

Open from Easter to All Saints Day, the abbey receives all. Groups are possible. Expect much silence and an austere life.

Haute montagne – beaucoup de silence et vie austère.

'To rejoice at another person's joy is like being in heaven'
– Meister Eckhart

AUDE (11)

FESTES-ET-SAINT-ANDRÉ

Viveka Yoga Retreats and Holidays Tel: +33 (0)4 68 20 07 72
Hameau de Marses Email: viveka@franceyogaretreats.com
11300 Festes-et-Saint-André Website: www.franceyogaretreats.com
France

Yoga – Meditation (Yoga - Méditation)

Situated in the still wild romantic landscape of the Aude between the Mediterranean coast and the Pyrenées, Viveka offers yoga retreats for adults and families with children. Near to Spain and about an hour's drive from Carcassonne, it is in the former land of the Cathars. There are one-week yoga retreats, two daily yoga classes and 10-day family yoga holidays with child-care activities during the summer holidays. Organic vegetarian food, massages, walking and other activities, such as eco-building projects, walking to the nearby lake, felt-making, singing, and bread-making, help complete the picture of this welcoming place. It is run by several families and offers you a choice of three languages and a chance to meet like-minded people. **Highly Recommended.**

*Un choix de trois langues et une chance de rencontrer quelqu'un ayant les animés des mêmes sentiments. **Fortement – Recommandé.***

RENNES-LE-CHÂTEAU

Lavaldieu Tel/Fax: +33 (0)4 68 74 23 21
11190 Rennes-le-Château Email: info@lavaldieu.com
France Website: www.lavaldieu.com

Mind Body Spirit – Yoga (L'Esprit, L'Âme et Le Corps – Yoga)

Self-directed retreats and working holidays here are set in a landscape that is inspiring. Yoga, breath work, Earth mysteries, food and gardening, healing, shamanism practice and yoga are all subjects that can take place here. Camping and vegetarian meals are offered, and it is open to all ages, including children, with about 20 bed spaces.

Retraites de vacances-travail, qui peuvent aussi être une forme de retraite pour échapper à ce que vous faites ordinairement d'habititude – tou ici dans un paysage qui inspire. Le Yoga, souffle travail de la respiration, mystères de la terre, l'alimentation et l'horticulture, de la guérison de la pratique du chamanisme, et d'yoga sont tous les sujets que peuvent intéresser lieu ici dans cette belle partie du monde. Camping, repas végétariens, interdiction de fumer, ouvert à tous les âges, y compris les enfants avec environ 20 places lit.

AVEYRON (12)

MUR-DE-BARREZ

Monastère Sainte-Claire Tel: +33 (0)5 65 66 00 46
2 Rue de la Berque Fax: +33 (0)5 65 66 00 90
12600 Mur-de-Barrez Email: steclaire.mur@wanadoo.fr
France Website: www.steclairemur.org

Roman Catholic (Catholique)

This community of Poor Clares welcomes women and families with children. Much peace and solitude can be found here. Facilities include a chapel, a library, TV, meeting rooms, with personal talks and spiritual direction possible. Rates are about 48€ full board per day or self-catering.

Beaucoup le calme et la solitude.

'Do not seek to follow in the footsteps of the Masters;
seek what they sought'
– Zen saying

BOUCHES-DU-RHÔNE (13)

● ●

AIX-EN-PROVENCE

Carmel de Notre Dame de l'Assomption   Tel: +33 (0)4 42 21 40 58
4 Monteé Saint-Joseph
Route du Tholonet
13090 Aix-en-Provence
France

Roman Catholic (Catholique)

Women and young women – two or three at a time – are received here
by the Carmelite nuns.

Les femmes et jeunes femmes seulement.

GRANS

Le Domaine de Petite   Tel: +33 (0)4 90 55 93 60
Association Culture et Promotion   Fax: +33 (0)4 90 55 87 74
Route de Saint-Chamas D16   Website: www.domainedepetite.com
13450 Grans
France

Roman Catholic (Catholique)

Receives everyone for spiritual retreats, seminars and courses. This is
an isolated house with a very large woodland park. It has 20 single
rooms, 19 doubles, four dormitories, eight meeting rooms, TV, a Pilgrim's Way, a chapel and a library. Rates are about 42€ full board and
30€ demi-pension.

C'est une maison isolée avec un très grand parc avec des arbes anciens.

TARASCON-SUR-RHÔNE

Hôtel Saint-Michel   Tel: +33 (0)4 90 90 52 70
L'Abbaye Saint-Michel de Frigolet   Fax: +33 (0)4 90 95 75 22
13150 Tarascon-sur-Rhône   Website: www.frigolet.com
France

Roman Catholic (Catholique)

A magical place of herbs set in the summer beauty of Provence, the abbey is open to all, including pilgrims. The hotel has 36 rooms, and there is a restaurant that is also open for day visitors. There are meeting rooms, TV, a chapel and choir, and personal talks are possible. Your presence at least at one daily office is requested as a sign of the spiritual activity you have undertaken.

Un lieu magique de fines herbes beauté de l'été la en Provence. Ouvert à tous, y compris les pèlerins. 36 Chambres, un restaurant qui est aussi ouvert aux visiteurs dans la journée. Il y a des salles de réunion, une chapelle, le chœur des moines, et des entretiens personnels possibles.

CALVADOS (14)

JUAYE-MONDAYE

L'Abbaye Saint-Martin de Mondaye   Tel: +33 (0)2 31 92 58 11
14250 Juaye-Mondaye   Fax: +33 (0)2 31 92 08 05
France   Website: www.mondaye.com

Roman Catholic (Catholique)

Open all year, the abbey is set in a magnificent green setting that is typical of Normandy. All guests are welcome and are housed in different buildings dedicated to the hotel or camping areas. Disabled guests are possible. Special Open Door Retreats are offered in summer, and participation in Divine Office is warmly welcomed. There is accommodation for about 60 people, three lounges and two workshops, a library and chapel; personal talks are possible.

Ouvert toute l'année. Dans un magnifique décor vert typique de la Normandie – pommes et les vaches garanti- et dans la vraie campagne – le

premièr café-bar est au moins deux kilomètres. Dans cet calme, la com-
munauté vous accueille pour une période de retraite, de repos, de mise
au point. Tous les invités sont les bienvenus. Très populaire – louez plu-
sieurs mois à l'advance.

LISIEUX

Saint Thérèse de l'Enfant Jésus (1873–97)

Lisieux is another international Christian place of pilgrimage that is
located in France. Saint Thérèse de l'Enfant Jésus, or 'the Little Flower'
as she is affectionately called, was the daughter of a watchmaker. At the
early age of 15, she obtained permission to enter the Carmelite convent
at Lisieux. She wrote about 20 prayers and an autobiography, *L'Histoire
d'une Âme* (*The Story of a Soul*), which has been translated into 50 languages and remains the best spirituality seller after the Bible. She is
one of the most famous and beloved saints in the world. Her popularity
lies in her appeal to ordinary people.

Saint Thérèse a dépassé la pensée religieuse de son temps et elle a mon-
tré, avec une perspicacité inspirér une nouvelle route vers Dieu sur la
base du message central de l'évangile: l'amour.

Communauté la Providence   Tel: +33 (0)2 31 32 92 19
14 Chemin de Rocques
14100 Lisieux
France

Roman Catholic (Catholique)

This is a very large place where a lot of groups and school groups come
on retreat – but individual retreats are possible.

Les retraites individuelles sont possibles.

L'Ermitage Sainte-Thérèse   Tel: +33 (0)2 31 48 55 10
23 Rue du Caramel   Fax: +33 (0)2 31 48 55 27
14100 Lisieux   Email: hermitage-ste-therese@therese-de-lisieux.com
France   Website: www.therese-de-lisieux.catholique.fr

Roman Catholic (Catholique)

This is a centre for pilgrims, and it is open most of the year. There is a calendar of retreats and both individuals and groups are received.

Un centre pour les pèlerins ouvert toute l'année.

CHARENTE (16)

MONTMOREAU-SAINT-CYBARD

L'Abbaye Sainte-Marie de Maumont   Tel: +33 (0)5 45 60 34 38
16190 Juignac   Fax: +33 (0)5 45 60 29 02
France   Email: maumont.accueil@wanadoo.fr
               Website: www.maumont.com

Roman Catholic (Catholique)

This abbey is open to individuals or groups for stays of up to eight days. There are 23 rooms, and you need to book 15 days in advance. It has a chapel and choir. Personal talks are possible by arrangement.

Pour venir en visite, faire une retraite, réviser ses examens au calme l'hôtellerie du monastère est ouverte à tous, toute l'année et l'on peut y faire des séjours. Pour ceux qui n'habitent pas loin, la chapelle est ouverte aux heures des offices et l'on peut venir y chanter avec les soeurs. Des week-ends spirituels sont organisés à l'hôtellerie.

'Be in general virtuous, and you will be happy'
– Benjamin Franklin

CHER (18)

SAINT-DOULCHARD

Monastère de l'Annonciade	Tel: +33 (0)2 48 65 57 65
115 Route de Vouzeron	Website: catholique-bourges.cef.fr/
18230 Saint-Doulchard	communaute/religieuses/annonciade
France	

Roman Catholic (Catholique)

Individuals and groups for retreats are received here by Ordre de l'Annonciade (or the Order of the Virgin Mary), with about 20 rooms available. The maximum stay is eight days. There is a daily Mass and the chapel services are in French.

Reçoit personnes seules et les groupes de retraites, durée du séjour maximum huit jours, 20 chambres disponibles. Messes á la offices Chapelle services en français. Messe tous les jours.

CORRÈZE (19)

AUBAZINE

Monastère de la Théophanie	Tel: +33 (0)5 55 25 75 67
Le Ladeix	Website: www.sjlpmelkites.fr
19190 Aubazine	
France	

Byzantine Catholic (Catholique Byzantin)

The monastery is an old farmhouse, high up in the Massif Central. This small community of nuns of the Melkite Greek Catholic Church receives men, women, young people and very small groups; one of the nuns speaks English. Courses on Byzantine spirituality and on the art and theology of icons are sometimes offered. Vegetarian food is available on request. For retreatants, there are 11 single rooms and three double rooms, with central heating in winter. There is also a guest lounge, library and chapel. Personal talks are possible. This is a busy place; during Easter and summer, you need to book at least a month in advance. When visiting the above website, click on 'Spritual Life' and then 'Spiritual Retreat' to find out more about the monastery.

Le monastère est une vieille ferme en hauteur dans le Massif Central. Des cours la sur spiritualité byzantin et sur l'art et de la théologie d'icônes sont parfois offerts. 11 chambres simples, trois doubles, chauffage central en hiver, salon, bibliothèque, chapelle. Un monastère tres occupé – pour Pâques et pour l'été vous devez réserver au moins un mois à l'avance. Lorsque vous visitez le site ci-dessus, cliquez sur 'Spiritual Life' et puis 'Retraite Spirituelle' pour en savoir plus sur le monastère.

CORSE-DU-SUD (20)

VICO

Couvent Saint-François	Tel: +33 (0)4 95 26 83 83
20160 Vico	Fax: +33 (0)4 95 26 64 09
France	

Roman Catholic (Catholique)

The community receives everyone for a few days or a weekend. The convent is high up on the mountain with views. There are about 40 beds, at the daily rate of 38€ full board.

La Communauté reçoit tout le monde pour un retraite individuel ou en retraite groupe. Vous pouvez venir pour quelques jours ou un week-end de réflexion et de prière. Le couvent est en hauteur sur la montagne avec vue.

'Where there is no love, put love and you will find love'
– St John of the Cross

CÔTE-D'OR (21)

•••

FLAVIGNY-SUR-OZERAIN

L'Abbaye Saint-Joseph de Clairval   Tel: +33 (0)3 80 96 22 31
21150 Flavigny-sur-Ozerain   Fax: +33 (0)3 80 96 25 29
France   Website: www.clairval.com

Roman Catholic (Catholique)

Stays at the abbey are reserved for organised and individual retreats. The organised retreats last for five days and follow the spiritual exercises of St Ignatius. Please note that the retreats are for men only (aged 17 upwards); some are conducted in English. The abbey can be contacted by email via the website.

Lorsqu'on séjourne à l'Abbaye, deux options sont possibles. Tout au long de l'année sont organisées des retraites prêchées par les pères du Monastère. Elles se déroulent en cinq jours en s'inspirant des exercices de Saint Ignace de Loyola. Accueil individuel à l'hôtellerie, avec participation à la liturgie quotidienne avec accompagnement spirituel possible. Cet accueil se déroule exclusivement en dehors du temps des retraites prêchées.

CÔTES-D'ARMOR (22)

•••

SAINT-JACUT-DE-LA-MER

L'Abbaye Saint-Jacut de la Mer   Tel: +33 (0)2 96 27 71 19
Boite Postal 1   Fax: +33 (0)2 96 27 79 45
22750 Saint Jacut-de-la-Mer   Email: abbaye.st.jacut@wanadoo.fr
France   Website: www.abbaye-st-jacut.com

Roman Catholic (Catholique)

Managed by the association La Providence, this retreat house is open from September to the end of June for both individuals and groups who wish to make a retreat. They run a programme of courses, retreats and events. The atmosphere here is peaceful. In terms of facilities, the abbey offers disabled facilities, 95 bedrooms, meeting rooms, guest lounges, tennis court, a library, TV, a chapel and choir.

Avec son cadre de verdure, son parc et ses jardins,et des randonnées,et un espace de paix l'Abbaye offre un espace pour le silence pour une paix sereine. Ici ést une communauté religieuse avec la vie spirituelle dans la prière et la réflexion. 95 chambres tout confort,4 salles à manger de 12, 20, 50 et 120 couverts et des locaux adaptés aux personnes handicapées. Chapelle, crypte et l'oratoire, 2 salles de conférence, 7 salles de groupes de 10 à 25 places, salon de lecture, bibliothèque, court de tennis, parc et aire de jeux pour enfants.

ST HELEN

La Ville Davy   Tel: +33 (0)2 96 83 33 53
22100 St Helen   Email: villedavy@orange.fr
France   Website: www.lavilledavy.org

Buddhist – Soto Zen tradition (Bouddhiste – Tradition de Zen de Soto)

La Ville Davy is a converted farm in Brittany, north-west France. It dates from some 400 years ago and today provides comfortable retreat accommodation. It is is very convenient if you are coming from England. The place is set within three acres of secluded and peaceful gardens on the fringe the Forest of Coetquen, with a variety of trail walks and wildlife. La Ville Davy is run by experienced lay Buddhist practitioners who follow the Serene Reflection Meditation tradition (Soto Zen). The centre offers space for regular Buddhist retreats and there is a schedule of mindfulness courses for both beginners and regular practitioners. In addition are residential and appointment-based therapeutic assistance by registered UK and Jersey States Health Service psychotherapists. People can also simply come for a quiet personal rest, renewal and reflection. **Highly Recommended.**

*La Ville Davy est une ferme en Bretagne dans le nord ouest de la France. Elle a quelques 400 ans et aujourd'hui fournit un logement en vue d' une retraite confortable. **Fortement – Recommendé.***

CREUSE (23)

LA CELLETTE

Le Blé en Herbe   Tel/Fax: +33 (0)5 55 80 62 83
Le Puissetier   Email: maria.sperring@wanadoo.fr
23350 La Cellette   Website: bleenherbes.free.fr
France

Eco-spirituality (Éco-spiritualité)

Open from February to December, everyone is welcome here. Set in the rolling foothills of the Massif Central, this well-established place has been run for many years by Maria Sperring. It has a lovely organic garden of 7.5 acres with wild-flower fields and is surrounded by unspoiled countryside. The lifestyle here is one of simplicity and closeness to nature. There are different options for courses or events and retreats, which change from time to time, but the main focus is on permaculture. The food is vegetarian and organic. B&B and camping are possible. When contacting by email, please note that short messages only are possible. **Highly Recommended.**

*Le Blé en Herbe est un site permaculturel de 7.5 acres. Il est composé d'un moon garden et d'un sun garden, agrémentés de champs, d'un bois et d'une rivière. C'est un lieu harmonieux et agréable, où il fait bon vivre, travailler ou se détendre. Différents stages sont organisés: permaculture, danse, etc. et vous pouvez faire du travail bénévole dans le jardin. La cuisine végétarienne est très bonne. En entrant en contact par l'email, les messages courts seulement sont possibles. **Fortement – Recommendé.***

'Tout comprendre, c'est tout pardonner.'
– Voltaire

DORDOGNE (24)

CUBJAC

Moulin de Chaves
Le Maine
24640 Cubjac
France

Tel: +33 (0)5 53 05 97 46
Email: mail@moulindechaves.org
Website: www.moulindechaves.org

Buddhist – Yoga – Vipassana meditation (Bouddhiste – Yoga – Méditation de Vipassana)

Located in the green rolling hills of the Dordogne, Le Moulin is a meditation centre that practises Vipassana in the Thai Buddhist Forest tradition. In addition to meditation, they offer yoga, Tai Chi and other courses geared to contemporary approaches to living, including mindfulness-based stress-reduction classes. All food is vegetarian.

Séjourner au Moulin, c'est l'occasion d'explorer votre Cœur et votre esprit à travers le méditation silencieuse, des introspections guidées individuellement et en groupe. Ici, ils font la pratique bouddhiste Vipassana méditation – cette méditation est de la tradition « Thaï bouddhiste dans la forêt » – voir les choses telles qu'elles sont. Ils offrent le yoga, Tai Chi, et d'autres cours adaptés aux méthodes spirituelles contemporaines. Toute la nourriture est végétarienne. Les brochures sont disponibles en anglais et français.

MONESTIER

Centre Sainte-Croix
24240 Monestier
France

Tel: +33 (0)5 53 63 37 70
Fax: +33 (0)5 53 61 31 05
Email: centresaintecroix24@wanadoo.fr
Website: www.centresaintecroix.net

Romanian Orthodox (Orthodoxe Roumaine)

A study and prayer centre which offers various retreats, courses, workshops and summer sessions of study.

*Le **Centre est** ouvert à tous ceux qui sont en quête de Dieu. Ils vous propose: Une étude approfondie de l'anthropologie chrétienne, une approche* *de la thérapie chrétienne dans l'héritage des Pères du Désert, un accompagnement spirituel, une introduction de la vie de prière dans l'esprit de la Philocalie, des ateliers d'art liturgique, et des temps de reflexions.*

SAINT-LÉON-SUR-VÉZÈRE

Dhagpo Kagyu Ling	Tel: +33 (0)5 53 50 70 75
Landrevie	Fax: +33 (0)5 53 50 80 54
24290 Saint-Léon-sur-Vézère	Email: accueil@dhagpo-kagyu.org
France	Website: www.dhagpo-kagyu-ling.org

Buddhist – Tibetan Karma Kagyu tradition (Bouddhiste – Tradition Tibétaine de Kagyu de Karma)

This is one of three international centres, the others being in Sikkim and America. Practice is in Tibetan, but information is available in English. Accommodation ranges from dormitories to singles and doubles. All meals are vegetarian.

Dhagpo vous propose tout au long de l'année pendant les vacances scolaires et les week-ends des enseignement et des méditations, des retraites guidées, des rencontres avec de grands maîtres, des stages d'étude de la philosophie bouddhiste, des séminaires de réflexion sur l'accompagnement des personnes en deuil ou en fin de vie, sur l'éducation, ainsi que des stages adolescents ou jeunes adultes. Repas végétariens.

Songtsen, Chanteloube	Tel: +33 (0)5 53 50 75 24
La Bicanderie	Fax: +33 (0)5 53 51 02 44
24290 Saint-Léon-sur-Vézère	Email: chanteloube@songtsen.org
France	Website: www.songtsen.org

Buddhist – Vajrayana Tibetan tradition (Bouddhiste – Tibétain de Vajrayana)

Situated in a green valley, not far from Brive in the direction of Bordeaux. Spiritual practices are in Tibetan, but information is available in English and French. Three-year guided retreats are possible here, as well as various programmes of study, which are at a modest cost. Accommodation is single and double rooms.

La Bicanderie est dans une valle verte, dans la direction de Bordeaux. Les pratiques spirituelles sont en tibétain mais les renseignements sont disponibles en français.

DOUBS (25)

BESANCON

La Roche D'Or   Tel: +33 (0)3 81 51 42 44
25042 Besancon
France

Roman Catholic (Catholique)

Retreats of six days, groups (often children or adolescents), weekends of evangelism and individual retreats are all possible. Some people staying here may be on pilgrimages to the Holy Land and Greece. La Roche D'Or welcomes some 5,000 people a year – Christians of all ages, all backgrounds and all continents, as well as non-believers who are spiritually searching.

Les retraites de six jours, accueillant souvent des groupes d'enfants ou d'adolescents, les week-ends d'évangélisation, ainsi que les retraites itinérantes en Terre Sainte et Grèce. Elles rassemblent environ 5,000 personnes par an, des chrétiens de tous âges, toutes origines et de tous continents, ainsi que des non croyants en recherche de foi.

LES FONTENELLES

Les Soeurs de la Retraite Chretienne   Tel: +33 (0)3 81 43 71 79
17 Rue de Couvent   Fax: +33 (0)3 81 43 79 96
25210 Les Fontenelles   Email: rm.prongue@scolafc.org /
France   collegestjoseph.fontenelles@wanadoo.fr

Christian – Roman Catholic (Chretien – Catholique)

Founded in 1789 by the Sisters of Christian Retreat, this centre is situated on the high plateau of the Haut-Doubs Horloger at an altitude of 900 metres, just a few kilometres from the Swiss border between Morteau and Maîche. They welcome everyone for a spiritual retreat, especially for sessions of *Lectio Divina*, prayer and contemplation. It is a place of peacefulness. Access is by train at Morteau, which is about 20 km away, or by car.

Bienvenue a tout le monde pour une retraite spirituelle.

DRÔME (26)

GRIGNAN

Dominicaines des Tourelles   Tel: +33 (0)4 75 46 50 37
Prieuré de l'Emmanuel   Fax: +33 (0)4 75 46 53 49
26230 Grignan   Email: dom_tou@club-internet.fr
France   Website: dom.tourelles.free.fr

Roman Catholic (Catholique)

This priory receives everyone looking for peace and reflection. The retreats and courses are on biblical subjects; a brochure is available. For guests, there are nine rooms and two dormitories (17 beds in all), a guest lounge, a meeting room for up to 25 persons. Camping is possible. Meals are served here. Surrounding the priory are woods and lavender fields.

Reçoit tous ceux qui cherchent paix et réflexion. Retrsaites et stages sur sujets biblique. Brochure disponible. 9 chambres, 2 dortoirs – la possibilité de camping. Repas servis. Bois et champs de lavande autour !

'I know but one freedom, and that is the freedom of the mind'
– Antoine de Saint-Exupery

EURE (27)

LE BEC-HELLOUIN

L'Abbaye Notre-Dame du Bec   Tel: +33 (0)2 32 44 86 09
27800 Le Bec-Hellouin   Fax: +33 (0)2 32 44 96 69
France   Website: www.abbayedubec.com

Roman Catholic (Catholique)

This is a grand monastery of the Benedictine Olivetan order in France. Set in green pastures and near to the Channel ports, Notre-Dame du Bec is open to all. Men stay with the monks individually or in groups and take meals in the refectory. There are about 30 rooms available in two areas: one is inside the monastery for guests who wish to join the community in their silence and prayer, while the other accommodation is outside and reserved for groups and young people on retreat and for study and various courses. The Divine Office is sung in Gregorian chant and in French. Women guests stay in the nearby convent **Monastère Sainte-Francoise Romaine** (Tel: +33 (0)2 32 44 81 18 / Fax: +33 (0)2 32 45 90 53). **Highly Recommended.**

C'est un grand Monastère Bénédictin de l'ordre Olivetan afin en France. Située dans de verts pâturages et près de ports de la Manche, le Bec est ouvert à tous. Les hommes séjournent avec les moines individuellement ou en groupes et prennnent les repas dans le réfectoire. ***Fortement – Recommendé.***

FINISTÈRE (29)

PLOUNÉVENTER

Monastère de Kerbenéat   Tel: +33 (0)2 98 20 47 43
29400 Plounéventer   Fax: +33 (0)2 98 20 43 03
France

Roman Catholic (Catholique)

Everyone is welcome here. A tree-lined lane leads to the church reflecting a setting for this monastery, which is near woods with fields on most sides. There are 10 singles, two family rooms, a meeting room, two guest lounges, a library, chapel and choir; personal talks are possible. The charges vary greatly so it is best to enquire; write well in advance to book.

Reçoit tout le monde. Un endroit tranquille avec la possibilité de visiter un ermitage voisin.

GARD (30)

CONGÉNIES

Le Centre Quaker de Congénies
11 Avenue des Quakers
30111 Congénies
France

Tel: +33 (0)4 66 71 46 41
Email: centre.quaker.congenies@gmail.com
Website: www.maison-quaker-congenies.org

Quaker (Les Société Religieuse des Amis)

Open to all, this is the oldest Quaker Meeting House in France and unique in that it is the only one ever purpose-built. It is now restored as a centre for retreats and cultural, leisure, educational and other related activities. There are a number of meeting rooms of varying size, bedrooms and a self-contained area. Camping is sometimes permitted in the grounds. The programme and brochure are available in English and French or you can visit the website. If you telephone, it is likely that the person who answers will speak English as well as French. **Highly Recommended.**

*La Maison Quaker de Congénies, avec son ancien cimetière ombragé, n'est pas seulement un lieu de recueillement Quaker, c'est aussi un Centre Culturel, où sont oragnisés des rencontres-partages, des tables rondes, des week-ends d'études, des retraites, des ateliers, et des sejours de vacances. Le Centre accueille également des personnes et des familles ainsi que d'autres groupes organisant eux-mêmes leurs activités. **Forte-ment – Recommendé.***

HAUTE-GARONNE (31)

BLAGNAC

Monastère Notre-Dame des Sept   Tel: +33 (0)5 34 60 53 90
Douleurs et de Sainte-Catherine de Sienne
60 Avenue Général-Compans
31700 Blagnac
France

Roman Catholic (Catholique)

This community of Dominican nuns welcomes everyone. Guest accommodation is separate from the monastery. On offer are guest lounges, a library, chapel and choir. Individual or groups retreats with leaders are welcome to stay or visit for reflection and prayer. This is a beautiful setting in a quiet place by the river.

Belle situation dans un endroit tranquille prés de la rivière.

TOULOUSE

L'Ecole de Yoga et de Méditation   Tel: +33 (0)5 61 25 17 69
46 Rue de Metz   Email: ecole@yogaetmeditation.fr
31000 Toulouse   Website: www.yogaetmeditation.fr
France

Yoga – Satyananda yoga (Yoga – Yoga de Satyananda)

This school focuses on traditional yoga and meditation techniques inspired by the Tantric tradition, which is a type of yoga often referred to as Satyananda yoga. The spiritual master of this school is the Danish yogi Swami Janakananda. For the time being what is on offer is one long retreat at the end of July (14 days), one short retreat around Easter (six days) and a weekend course at the beginning of November at the **Centre de la Luna** in the south of France (see below). The school in Toulouse is a branch of the **Scandinavian School of Yoga and Meditation**, the largest yoga institution in Scandinavia, which also organises similar retreats at other times of the year in Denmark, Sweden, Norway, Finland and Germany. The retreats are in principle open to everybody and in practice are attended by beginners as well as advanced students. **Highly Recommended.**

*Le maître spirituel de cette école est le yogi danois Swami Janakananda. Les cours ont lieu à l'adresse ci-dessous. L'école de Toulouse est issue de l'Ecole Scandinave de Yoga et de Méditation, qui est la plus importante institution de yoga en Scandinavie, avec des écoles au Danemark, en Suède en Norvège et en Finlande ainsi qu'en Allemagne. **Fortement – Recommendé.***

Centre de la Luna
Layrol
09200 Saurat
France

GERS (32)

MARSOLAN

Caudet Radha Yoga Centre	Tel: +33 (0)5 62 68 87 95
Caudet	Email: info@radhacaudet.com
32700 Marsolan	Website: www.radhacaudet.com
France	

Karma yoga (Yoga de karma)

The centre is a renovated old stone French farmhouse, redone in a comfortable simple style, using traditional materials where appropriate. The centre grow their own vegetables organically, and these supply most of their needs during the summer months at least. Organic, locally grown produce is bought when possible. All retreat and course teachers have trained at Yasodhara Ashram, Canada. There are two acres of grounds within gently rolling arable countryside, where wheat and sunflowers are the main crops. The view from the upper terrace is stunning.

Belle campagne où le blé et le tournesol sont les principales cultures.

BOULAR

L'Abbaye Cistercienne   Tel: +33 (0)5 62 65 49 39
Sainte-Marie de Boulaur   Fax: +33 (0)5 62 65 49 37
32450 Boulaur   Email: hotellerie@boulaur.org
France   Website: www.boulaur.org

Roman Catholic (Catholique)

Open May to September, this Cistercian abbey receives women, young
people, groups and families only, with groups only in winter. Men are
only allowed to stay if they are in a family group. The minimum stay is
two nights. The abbey has 53 guest beds.

*Les Cisterciennes Sainte-Marie de de Boulaur reçoivent toute l'année des
groupes organisés de laïques, de prêtres et séminaristes pour retraites et
sessions, week-end, et rencontres de prières. Du mois d'avril à la fin du
mois de septembre, les soeurs accueillent les particuliers: dames seules,
familles, pour des séjours en pension complète – minimum deux nuits.
Pas d'hommes laïques invités sauf ceux de la famille.*

GIRONDE (33)

BORDEAUX

Centre Louis-Beaulieu   Tel: +33 (0)5 57 57 32 32
145 Rue de Saint-Genès   Fax: +33 (0)5 57 57 32 33
33082 Bordeaux Cedex   Email: clb.beaulieu@wanadoo.fr
France   Website: www.catholique-bordeaux.cef.fr

Roman Catholic (Catholique)

This retreat centre, which welcomes individuals and groups, is on the
Lourdes–Compostelle route so it is also a centre for pilgrims. Situated
in Bordeaux, it has 30 rooms, six with four beds each, a guest lounge,
meeting rooms, library, park and sports facilities. Full-board rates are
offered.

*Le Centre Louis Beaulieu est un lieu d'accueil et d'hébergement pour les
groupes, pour les personnes accompagnant les malades hospitalisés à
l'Institut Bergonié. Le Centre Louis Beaulieu accueille le Séminaire Saint*

*Joseph, l'Institut Pey-Berland – Service diocésain de la formation – la bib-
liothèque diocésaine ainsi que de nombreux autres Services diocésains et
Mouvements d'Eglise.*

RIONS

Monastère du Broussey	Tel: +33 (0)5 56 62 60 90
5 Le Broussey Sud	Fax: +33 (0)5 56 62 60 79
33410 Rions	Email: accueil.broussey@carmel.asso.fr
France	Website: www.carmel.asso.fr

Christian – Roman Catholic – Discalced Carmelites (Chrétien – Catholique –Carmélites)

This is a traditional Carmelite monastery where a life of prayer and
contemplation takes place. If you come here, you come to share in this
way of spiritual life, to find rest and renewal. Here you will find calm
and silence. Languages spoken, if needed, are French, English, Italian,
Spanish and Portuguese. Other places of Carmelite brothers in France
are given below.

*C'est un monastére y traditionel Carmélit où on offre une vie de prière et
de contemplation.*

PROVINCE DE PARIS

Couvent des Carmes, 4 Cité du Sacré-Cœur, 75018 Paris.
Tel: +33 (0)1 42 88 01 18. Fax: +33 (0)1 45 20 94 15.

**Couvent des Carmes, 1 Rue du Père Jacques, 77215 Avon
Cedex.**
Tel: +33 (0)1 60 72 28 03 (Community). Tel: +33 (0)1 60 72 28 45
(Spiritual Centre). Fax: +33 (0)1 64 23 48 39.

Couvent des Carmes, 99 Rue des Stations, 59800 Lille.
Tel: +33 (0)3 20 57 39 49. Fax: +33 (0)3 20 13 76 87.

Couvent des Carmes, 42 Rue du Docteur Lesigne, 14100 Lisieux.
Tel: +33 (0)2 31 31 44 77. Fax: +33 (0)2 31 31 66 14.

PROVINCE D'AVIGNON-AQUITAINE

Couvent des Carmes, 10 bis Rue Moquin Tandon, 34000 Montpellier.
Tel: +33 (0)4 99 23 24 90. Fax: +33 (0)4 99 23 24 99.

Monastère du Broussey, 33410 Rions.
Tel: +33 (0)5 56 62 60 90. Fax: +33 (0)5 56 62 60 79.

Couvent des Carmes, 33 Avenue Jean Rieux, 31500 Toulouse.
Tel: +33 (0)5 62 47 33 70. Fax: +33 (0)5 62 47 33 71.

Couvent des Carmes Saint Désert Notre-Dame de Pitié, Route des Cavalières, 83520 Roquebrune-sur-Argens.
Tel: +33 (0)4 94 44 18 18.

HÉRAULT (34)

LE BOUSQUET-D'ORB

Monastère Orthodoxe Saint-Nicolas   Tel: +33 (0)4 67 23 41 10
La Dalmerie   Fax: +33 (0)4 67 23 44 83
34260 Le Bousquet-d'Orb   Email: st.nicolas@dalmerie.com
France   Website: www.dalmerie.com

Orthodox – Eastern Rite (Chrétiens Orthodoxes Rite Oriental)

The monastery is open from Easter to October for spiritual retreats only, with a maximum stay of seven days. According to the custom of the Orthodox monastic tradition, only men are received. Only those of the Orthodox Church receive Holy Sacraments.

Situé à 85 km à l'ouest de Montpellier et à 60 km au nord-est de Béziers, le monastère orthodoxe Saint-Nicolas est installé depuis 1965 au hameau de la Dalmerie. Ici, les sept moines étant tous français d'origine, les offices y sont intégralement chantés et célébrés en français, selon le rite de l'Eglise orthodoxe, avec les particularités du typicon de Constantinople. Selon l'usage de la tradition monastique orthodoxe, le monastère ne reçoit que des hommes.

ROQUEREDONDE

L'Arche de Lanza del Vasto　　Tel: +33 (0)4 67 44 09 89
La Borie Noble　　Fax: +33 (0)4 67 57 20 20
34650 Roqueredonde　　Email: cremersylvia@hotmail.com
France　　Website: www.arche-nonviolence.eu

Ecumenical – Christian (Oecuménique – Chrétien)

The main house of the charitable organisation la Communauté de l'Arche is high up in the mountains and not easy to find or get to. The community here live a simple and austere life based on Gandhian principles. Open all year round, it receives men, women, young people, families and groups. You can also share in their community life in a work retreat for a week. If you do not know about the work of l'Arche, which has houses in Britain and elsewhere, you may find it rewarding to find out, especially if you are young and want to help people less fortunate than yourself within a community life context, even if only for a short time. **Highly Recommended.**

*La Communauté de l'Arche vivre une vie simple fondée sur les principes de Gandhi. Vous pouvez partager dans leur vie communautaire dans un stage pour une semaine. **Fortement – Recommendé.***

Lerab Ling　　Tel: +33 (0)4 67 88 46 00
L'Engayresque　　Fax: +33 (0)4 67 88 46 01
34650 Roqueredonde　　Email: lerab.ling@rigpa.org
France　　Website: www.lerabling.org

Buddhist – Tibetan Nyingma School (Bouddhiste – École Tibétaine de Nyingma)

The Lerab Ling retreat centre was founded in 1991 by Sogyal Rinpoche, world-renowned Tibetan Buddhist teacher and author of the *Tibetan Book of Living and Dying*. Sogyal Rinpoche is also the founder and spiritual director of Rigpa, an international network of 130 Buddhist centres and groups in 41 countries around the world. Located to the north west of Montpellier in France, Lerab Ling has established itself as one of the leading centres of Tibetan Buddhist culture and learning in Europe. His Holiness the Dalai Lama has on two occasions visited here. **Highly Recommended.**

La Lerab Ling centre de retraite a été fondée en 1991 par Sogyal Rinpoche, et l'auteur célèbre du Livre Tibétain de la Vie et de la Mort. ***Fortement – Recommendé.***

ILLE-ET-VILAINE (35)

SAINT-GEORGES-DE-REINTEMBAULT

La Grande Connais Christian Centre   Tel: +33 (0)2 99 97 00 16
35420 Saint-Georges-de-Reintembault   Email:
France   info@christianbreaks.com
Website: www.christianbreaks.com

Christian (Chrétien)

Large and small groups, couples and individuals are welcomed here. The centre is an old stone farmhouse in the countryside and within easy reach of Channel ports. There is good walking in nearby hills, field, and beaches. Full-board and self-catering stays are possible in this centre, which has six bedrooms.

Le Centre est une vieux ferme en pierre a la campagne et non loin des ports de la Manche.

LANDES (40)

MUGRON

L'Abbaye Notre-Dame de Maylis   Tel: +33 (0)5 58 97 68 12
315/455 Avenue de la Chalosse   Fax: +33 (0)5 58 97 72 58
40250 Mugron   Email: accueil@maylis.org
France   Website: www.abbaye-de-maylis.com

Roman Catholic (Catholique)

This abbey houses Benedictine monks of the Olivetan Order as at **L'Abbaye Notre-Dame du Bec** (see above). The monastery is situated in lovely country in the midst of this vast department of France, which has millions of trees. The community has retreats usually for groups, but individuals who want a personal retreat for spiritual reasons are welcome. There are many ancient churches in the area. Nearby at the hilltop town of St Sever, there is an annual summer exhibition with demonstrations by outstanding artisans, including bookbinding, woodturning and weaving.

Dans le logis des hôtes, les retraitants profitent de chambres individu-elles ou de dortoirs. Quelques salles sont á la disposition des groupes, adultes, jeunes ou enfants, qui veulent organiser des périodes spirituels.

SAINT-VINCENT-DE-PAUL

Hôtellerie Saint Joseph	Tel: +33 (0)5 58 55 97 97
Le Berceau	Fax: +33 (0)5 58 55 97 96
600 Impasse de l'Oeuvre	Email: oeuvre.berceau@wanadoo.fr
40990 Saint-Vincent-de-Paul	Website:
France	www.leberceaudesaintvincent.com

Roman Catholic (Catholique)

Here in the birthplace of St Vincent de Paul, the founder of an order that continues today to serve the poor throughout the world. There is a retreat guest house, which welcomes individuals and groups for retreats and courses. There are a number of tourist sites in the area. Disabled guest stays are possible. The retreat house offers accommodation for 56 in single and double rooms, as well as meeting rooms, a guest lounge, library, TV and chapel. Personal talks are possible, and pilgrims are welcome.

Le Berceau est la mémoire de Saint Vincent, on y trouve des reliques, des objets qui lui ont appartenu, on y retrace sa vie et on y explique son ray-onnement et ses pensées. Plus de 50.000 personnes de tous pays viennent chaque année visiter le Berceau. C'est la raison pour laquelle le Berceau est en constante évolution et entre dans la réalisation de grands projets pour les années à venir. L'Hôtellerie du Berceau accueille les retraites, sessions et pélérinages. Elle dispose de 56 chambres avec WC et douches dont 32 peuvent être doubles.

LOIRET (45)

●●●

NEUVILLE-AUX-BOIS

Château du Yoga Sivananda   Tel: +33 (0)2 38 91 88 82
26 Impasse du Bignon   Email: orleans@sivananda.net
45170 Neuville-aux-Bois   Website: www.sivananda.org/orleans
France

Yoga – Méditation – Mind Body Spirit (Yoga – Méditation – L'Esprit, L'Âme et Le Corps)

The Château du Yoga Sivananda belongs to the International Sivananda Yoga Vedanta Centre, whose aim is to spread ancient teachings of yoga to all. This place, formally an ashram, is located about 100 kilometres south of Paris and very close to the city of Orléans. It is a large property in a calm and peaceful setting near one of France's largest forests. Activities take place throughout the year.

La pratique du Yoga intégral au coeur de la nature conduit à une relaxation profonde et à un ressourcement intérieur. La méditation élève l'esprit tandis que les exercices de respiration revitalisent le corps entier. Ici, la nourriture est végétarienne. Le conférences sur la philosophie Vedanta apporte une vision positive de la vie. Les débutants sont les bienvenus. Les cours et les conférences sont donnés en anglais et en français avec une traduction simultanée dans ces deux langues.

LOT (46)

●●●

ROCAMADOUR

Centre d'Accueil Notre-Dame   Tel: +33 (0)5 65 33 23 23
Le Château   Fax: +33 (0)5 65 33 23 24
46500 Rocamadour   Website: www.notre-dame-de-rocamadour.com
France

Roman Catholic – Ecumenical (Catholique – Oecuménique)

This centre is run by the Diocesan of Cahors and is open all year for individuals or groups on retreat. Rocamadour has a church from the

Middle Ages, in which there is a sanctuary. Christian pilgrims consider this sanctuary to be a holy place and it is, indeed, a mysterious and spiritual place set in a rugged and equally mysterious countryside. Inside is an ancient wooden statue of Mary holding the child Jesus; it is simple yet deeply dramatic and possibly a great work of art. In the retreat centre, there are 46 rooms, guest and meeting rooms, a library, TV, chapel and choir. There are disabled facilities, but the sanctuary has steps and the place itself is steep and not very easy to access. Personal talks are possible. Please enquire for the latest rates. If you stay here, try to visit the sanctuary. There are lots of tourists about in the summer, but the atmosphere inside is haunting, mysterious and peaceful.

Ici, à l'intérieur ce sanctuaire depuis le XIIème siècle, la Vierge Noire, visage recueilli, sourire ébauché et mains tendues, présente son fils aux pèlerins venus de toute l'Europe des chemins de Compostelle et maintenant des bouts du monde.

LOT-ET-GARONNE (47)

LOUBÈS-BERNAC

Le Village des Pruniers
Hameau du Bas
Meyrac
47120 Loubès-Bernac
France

Tel: +33 (0)5 53 94 75 40
Email: lh-office@plumvillage.org /
lowerhamlet@wanadoo.fr
Website: www.plumvillage.org

Buddhist – Vietnamese School of Mahayana – Unified Buddhist Church (Bouddhiste – École Vietnamienne de Mahayana – Eglise Bouddhique Unifiée)

Plum Village is world famous because it is the home of Thich Nhat Hanh – monk, poet, scholar, author, legendary teacher of meditation and nominee for the Nobel Peace Prize. Plum Village consists of several rural retreat hamlets over three departments of France: Dordogne, Gironde and Lot-et-Garonne. **Hameau du Bas** is set among grape vines and the celebrated plum trees of the Agen area of Lot-et-Garonne, and the community receives men, women and married couples. **Hameau du Haut** is a monastery, receiving men only. **Hameau Nouveau** is a nuns' convent, receiving women. Hundreds of people a year attend these places for meditation. Plum Village is a big, busy and serious site, with at least three major retreats organised each year. All meals are vegetarian. Send for information, which is available in English, because Buddhist places often have different requirements regarding meditation technique experience and other aspects of Buddhism before you come on a retreat. You will need to book three months in advance. **Highly Recommended.**

Le Village des Pruniers est un monde célèbre tout simplement parce qu'il est le foyer de Thich Nhat Hanh – moine, poète, auteur, légendaire professeur de méditation, et candidat au le Prix Nobel. Est-qu'ici une retraite est bonne? Super! Géant! **Fortement – Recommendé.**

Hameau du Haut	Tel: +33 (0)5 53 58 48 58
Le Pey	Email: uh-office@plumvillage.org
24240 Thénac	
France	

Hameau Nouveau	Tel: +33 (0)5 56 61 66 88
13 Martineau	Email: nh-office@plumvillage.org /
33580 Dieulivol	newhamlet@wanadoo.fr
France	

MORBIHAN (56)

BRÉHAN

L'Abbaye Notre-Dame de Timadeuc	Tel: +33 (0)2 97 51 50 29
Boite Postal 17	Fax: +33 (0)2 97 51 59 20
56580 Bréhan	Email: timadeuc.abbaye@wanadoo.fr
France	Website: www.abbaye-timadeuc.fr

Roman Catholic (Catholique)

This Cistercian community receives men and women for stays of up to eight days, with 41 rooms available. Near the monastery are two further guest centres for young people. The atmosphere is peaceful and you join the community in much silence. Enquire for full-board charges. There are two guest lounges, disabled facilities, a library, chapel and choir. Personal talks are possible.

Les hommes et les femmes peuvent rester avec cette communauté Cister-cienne pendant jusqu'à huit jours. Il y a 41 salles, deux salons, installa-tions pour personnes handicapées, bibliothèque, chapelle et chœur.

SAINT-GILDAS-DE-RHUYS

L'Abbaye de Rhuys	Tel: +33 (0)2 97 45 23 10
Place Mgr Ropert	Fax: +33 (0)2 97 45 10 32
56730 Saint-Gildas-de-Rhuys	Email: abbaye.de.rhuys@wanadoo.fr
France	Website: www.abbaye-de-rhuys.fr

Christian – Roman Catholic (Chrétien – Catholique)

We like Saint-Gildas-de-Rhuys and confess that some of the team take holidays there, so we are not quite impartial. Having said that, Brittany is really a glorious land, filled with ports, seashores, sunshine and storm, ancient archeological monuments, good food and welcoming people. It is best explored by car, but if you are a walker or biker you can get along just fine that way; little roads and main ones are most often flat or gently sloping. The Abbaye de Rhuys is a cultural and spiritual centre, with full board for some 80 rooms. Conference and meeting rooms are available for groups and you can walk the 200 metres from the garden down to the sea. They welcome everyone and have a retreat programme on offer. In July and August, traditional holiday times for the French, the centre is very busy, but there is always space for quiet reflection and prayer.

Dans cette ancienne abbaye bénédictine les soeurs de la Charité de Saint Louis offrent des retraites et week-ends organisés par la maison, celle-ci peut accueillir des groupes pour les sessions, journées de réflexion, séminaires, et colloques. Elle accueille aussi des personnes seules en quête de lieux de silence et de repos. L'abbaye n'est qu' á de 200 mètres de la mer. Nous aimons Saint Gildas de Rhuys et avouons que certains membres de notre équipe y passent des vacances, donc nous ne sommes pas tout à fait impartiaux. Cela étant dit, la Bretagne est vraiment une région splendide, mer et plages en soleiliées, de nombreux ports, beau temps ou tempête, monuments archéologiques, bonne nourriture, et accueil chaleureux.

NORD (59)

MOUSTIER-EN-FAGNE

Monastère Notre-Dame des Pres   Tel: +33 (0)3 27 61 81 28
59132 Moustier-en-Fagne
France

Christian – Roman Catholic (Chrétien – Catholique)

This is a Benedictine Olivetan community so you will be assured of
a warm welcome in a very homely and peaceful atmosphere. Usually
closed in September and October, the monastery receives men, wom-
en, young people and groups. There are five rooms and a separate self-
catering annex for groups with their own leader. Stays of up to five days
are possible. There is a Byzantine chapel, with Byzantine liturgy once
a week, and icon painting is a speciality of the community. It is easily
possible to walk to Belgium from here.

*Un monastére benedictin. Séjours justqu'a 15 jours. Il y a une chapelle
byzantine et l'icone est une spécialtité de la communauté. Aucun programme de cours ni stages sauf pour l'icône.*

ORNE (61)

MONTGAUDRY

Le Tertre   Tel: +33 (0)2 33 25 59 98
61360 Montgaudry   Fax: +33 (0)2 33 25 56 96
France   Email: letertre61@french-country-retreat.com
                    Website: www.french-country-retreat.com

Open spirituality – Yoga (Spiritualité laïque – Yoga)

Le Tertre is an oasis of peace situated in the heart of the Perche, an area
of France noted for the quality and diversity of its landscapes, with forests, copses and meadows, and it sits astride the ancient pilgrimage route
to Mont-Saint-Michel. With no visible neighbours, it is left to the birds to

wake you in the morning. Le Tertre is environmentally friendly with two air-to-water heat pumps installed in 2007 to provide the central heating and the ground floor is heated by an under-floor low-temperature system. Anne Morgan, who runs this pleasant place, maintains a small kitchen garden where vegetables are grown organically, and she makes her jams from her fruit trees and hedgerows. She offers three approaches for a retreat: hire of a self-catering unit for retreats with a group facilitator; catered retreats for groups who have their own leader; and private retreats for individuals with no more than two persons at any one time. A private retreat with meals can include Hatha yoga, walks, meditation, Reiki and spa.

Anne Morgan, la propriétaire, maintient un petit jardin où les légumes sont cultivés avec des engrais organiques et elle fait ses confitures avec les arbres fruitiers et les baies de son jardin.

PUY-DE-DÔME (63)

SAINT-AMANT-TALLENDE

L'Abbaye Notre-Dame de Randol   Tel: +33 (0)4 73 39 31 00
63450 Saint-Amant-Tallende   Fax: +33 (0)4 73 39 05 28
France   Email: postmaster@randol.org
                              Website: www.randol.org

Roman Catholic (Catholique)

Benedictine monks receive men only here. A new monastery opened in 1971 of very modern architectural design, dramatically set on the very edge of a steep gorge in an isolated position. The views are staggering! A similar-looking place to the modern Prinknash Abbey in England, but Abbaye Notre-Dame de Randol is much grander and more imposing. 5 days maximum stay. Retreatants must respect the silence and attend services if at all possible. Library, chapel, personal talks possible. No preached retreats but spiritual direction is sometimes possible.

Dans la solitude des monts d'Auvergne, mais facile d'accès, l'Abbaye bénédictine de Randol conjugue, en effet, architecture moderne avec liturgie en latin et chant grégorien, tenant le regard en éveil et le cœur en paix. Retraitants doivent respecter le silence et assister aux services dans l'église si possible.

PYRÉNÉES-ATLANTIQUES (64)

URT

L'Abbaye Notre-Dame de Belloc Tel: +33 (0)5 59 29 65 55
64240 Urt Fax: +33 (0)5 59 29 44 08
France Email: belloc.abbaye@wanadoo.fr
Website: www.belloc-urt.org

Roman Catholic (Catholique)

This community of Benedictine monks receives men, married couples and small groups of men for retreats from one day to a week in an isolated monastery in one of the loveliest parts of France – a situation of mountains and valleys lush with wildflowers and trees. Sheep abound, as do tiny villages where life seems to continue much as it has for centuries in spite of everything. It is possible here to imagine that indeed all is well with the world. This has not always been so – during the Second World War, the abbot and his prior were sent to Buchrenwald and Dachau concentration camps because of the help they and the monastery community gave to refugees and resistance fighters. After the war, the abbey community was awarded the honour of the Cross of War. Today the abbey continues to offer hospitality to all in accordance with the Rule of Saint Benedict that all guests should be received as if Christ himself. There are 18 singles, 10 doubles, four dormitories, guest lounges, library, chapel and choir, with personal talks possible. Conferences are also possible. A programme of activities is sometimes available; ask for the brochure. The monks are attentive to the needs of busy modern people who are looking for a time and situation in which to find peace and silence to seek the spiritual. For a number of years, the Anglican community of Pau has come here for an annual retreat. There is a community of Benedictine sisters nearby at the **Monastère Sainte-Scholastique**, 64240 Urt (Tel: +33 (0)5 59 70 20 28) who also offer hospitality. **Highly Recommended.**

*Moines bénédictins. Reçoit les hommes, les couples mariés, les petits groupes d'hommes pour le jour des retraites et jusqu'à 1 semaine. Le monastère est isolé dans une des plus belles régions de France – une situation de la montagne et vallées riche en fleurs sauvages et arbres. Il est possible ici d'imaginer que tout va bien dans le monde. **Fortement – Recommendé.***

HAUTES-PYRÉNÉES (65)

●●

BANIOS

Yourtes Mongoles	Tel: +33 (0)5 62 95 36 08
Dévathcot	Email: herve.carenzi@laposte.net
65200 Banios	Website: www.yourtes-chambres.com
France	

Open spirituality (Spiritualité laïque)

If staying in the middle of real nature makes you relax and brings you renewal, and you have always wanted to experience of staying in a traditional Mongolian yurt, then Banios is the place to try. This tiny village is perched high up in the Pyrénées with mountains all around, the beautiful spa town of Bagneres de Bigorre only a short drive away, and truly wild forests at your fingertips. If you take a walk here from April until late autumn, you will be surrounded on all sides by wild flowers. A member of the *Good Retreat Guide* team once counted over 200 different flowers in just 10 minutes, while walking along the winding road in Banios. Yourtes Mongoles has been running for a number of years and know what they are doing. The yurts are set below the main house in green pastures on a hill with far views. They are traditional and comfortable, and the welcome is warm. The current rates for a yurt for two people is 60€–300€, breakfast included. A yurt for four to six people is 82€–500€. You can stay from one to seven nights; as you can see the rates vary greatly depending on length of stay so it is best to check the website for details. Firewood, if needed, is not included in the accommodation price (it is about 5€ per night). There is a dormitory yurt for up to 10 people, which is about 14€ per person per night with breakfast included. They also have three rooms available for B&B stays; the current rate is 53€ for two people with breakfast. It is possible to book a main meal with them for about 14€ each. Access is by car. **Highly Recommended.**

Des forêts sauvages a portée de main. Yourtes mongol. **Fortement – Recommandé.**

LASLADES

La Sève Tel/Fax: +33 (0)5 62 35 08 34
Madame Julia Huppert Email: j.huppert@wanadoo.fr
46 Route de Tarbes Website: www.francenature.fr/
65350 Laslades association-la-seve--laslades-1000052559
France

Mind Body Spirit (L'Esprit, L'Âme et Le Corps)

La Sève offers a programme of healing courses and experience of self, including discovering your relationship in the Zodiac signs, essential oil therapies and rediscovery of the senses of taste, sight, hearing, touching and smelling. La Sève welcomes those with disabilities.

La Sève est un lieu d'accueil et d'activités et vous propose plusieurs services. Très orientés vers la découverte et le développement de soi, les thérapies naturelles et les échanges de tous ordres, les propriétaires gérants du gîte et de l'association « Chrysalide » sont attirés par tous les publics à particularités. Les déficients mentaux que les propriétaires gérants reçoivent régulièrement, et les déficients moteurs plus ponctuellement, sont vraiment les bienvenus.

LOURDES

Lourdes is one of the three most popular places of religious pilgrimage in the world. It is visited by millions of people every year so it is always very crowded, except early in the morning at dawn. The history of this great Christian shrine is a simple one. A 14-year-old poor peasant girl Marie-Bernarde Soubirous (1844–79) received 18 apparitions of the Blessed Virgin Mary at the Massabielle Rock in Lourdes over a period of months. During this time, a spring appeared in the grotto of the rock, the waters of which are believed to be miraculous. Almost from the beginning, people visited the grotto to seek cures for their illnesses and fulfilment of their prayers. The girl later became a nun and is known today as Saint Bernadette. The Catholic Church is medically and ethically extremely rigorous in deciding if any claim of a cure is authentic. There have been a small but impressive number of cases declared to be so over the years and you may read about these in detail. The grotto itself is filled with candles and has remained relatively simple. People here are quite silent and all attention is on spiritual intentions – the atmosphere is unique and conducive to prayer in spite of the number of people gathered together. However, an enormous church has been built on the site, with religious chapels and sanctuaries plus a museum and all the various facilities related to handling millions of visitors each year. Many of the visitors are ill, infirm, in wheelchairs or on stretchers. Indeed, those suffering from illnesses and handicaps come by the coach and planeload each year. At all times, there are visitors who may not be Christians or who have doubts about the existence of God but have been attracted to Lourdes by its global fame. Along with many Christians, they may be appalled by the commercial aspects of Lourdes, such as the streets lined with shops and tables selling religious trinkets like rosaries, statues and bottles of holy water from the grotto spring, the distress of ill pilgrims and the harsh realities of how men and women may behave when driven by their religious yearnings. But all great religious shrines and places of pilgrimage through the ages, whether Christian or not, suffer this kind of commerce and Lourdes is no exception. A visitor who is not a pilgrim or believer needs to put to one side this human economic foible and think about the spiritual awareness that draws pilgrims here by the millions. All have taken time to devote a few days to prayer and God. And is it such a bad thing that some hope, no matter how little or how much, may be afforded to the sick and the incurable when they feel that all hope may be lost? So the shrine at Lourdes and its huge church are well worth a visit if for no other reason than compassion. Forget the streets lined with tourists and religious trinkets; instead concentrate on the prayerful atmosphere of the shrine with its many candles of inspiring light. Afterwards you might take a picnic lunch to Lourdes Lake nearby and drift in a pedal-boat – it is a kind of day retreat that lifts the heart. There are many hotels and guest houses in all price ranges in Lourdes and, of course, a number of religious houses, some of which take guests. The Lourdes tourist information offices will help you find accommodation. The official website **www.lourdes-infotourisme.com** gives details about the place, while at **www.lourdes-France.com** a virtual tour can be experienced.

Oublier les rues bordées de tourisme religieux de boutiques a babioles et se concentrer sur l'atmosphère de prière du sanctuaire avec ses nombreux des bougies qui d'inspire la lumière. Ensuite vous pourriez aller en pique-nique à Lourdes au lac de Lourdes à proximité et vous laisser deriver en pédalo – c'est un genre de jours de retraite qui élève l'âme

Carmel Notre-Dame de Lourdes   Tel: +33 (0)5 62 94 26 67
17 Route de Pau   Fax: +33 (0)5 62 94 50 44
65100 Lourdes
France

Roman Catholic (Catholique)

Receives men and women for day retreats and in the summer months for longer stays.

Reçoit les hommes et femmes en d'été pour de longs séjours.

Foyer Familial   Tel: +33 (0)5 62 94 07 51
2 Avenue Saint-Joseph   Fax: +33 (0)5 62 94 57 14
65100 Lourdes   Email: foyerfamilial.dominicaines@wanadoo.fr
France   Website: www.dominicaines-lourdes.com

Roman Catholic (Catholique)

Run by the Dominican sisters, the house and garden are situated in town, about 15 minutes' walk to the shrine and sanctuary area. It has 12 singles, nine doubles and five family rooms. Full board per person is about 35€ and half board about 33€. Special rates are available for group bookings.

Pension complète et chambre par personne a environ 35€ et demi-pension environ 33€. Tarifs spéciaux pour différents groupe ayant reservé.

Résidence de la Pastourelle   Tel: +33 (0)5 62 94 26 55
34 Rue de Langelle   Fax: +33 (0)5 62 42 00 95
65100 Lourdes
France

Ecumenical (Oecuménique)

This large residence is in the centre of Lourdes and is basically for the disabled with physical care services possible and all facilities. Although near the shrine, it is a peaceful place. If you are the carer of another person, then perhaps you can make arrangements here for your visit with him or her to Lourdes.

Cette grande résidence est dans le centre de Lourdes. C'est pour les hand-icapés physiques avec des services de soins possible et tous les équipe-ment et aménagements.

Maison Sainte-Thérèse   Tel: +33 (0)5 62 94 35 16
32–34 Rue du Sacré-Cœur   Fax: +33 (0)5 62 94 70 13
65100 Lourdes   Email: emmalourdes@wanadoo.fr
France

Roman Catholic (Catholique)

The Community of Emmanuel receives guests for up to seven days who may participate in the life of the community. It is about 15 minutes' walk from the shrine. Accommodation is for up to 60 guests, with full-board rates at about 20€ per night. Languages spoken include English.

La communauté d'Emmanuel reçoit invités jusqu'à sept jours, ils peuvent participer à la vie de la Communauté.

Monastère des Dominicaines   Tel: +33 (0)5 62 46 33 30
Avenue Jean Prat   Fax: +33 (0)5 62 94 89 76
65100 Lourdes   Email: hotmoplourdes@free.fr
France   Website: moplourdes.com

Roman Catholic (Catholique)

The sisters here offer monastic hospitality to all, whether as individu-als or in groups, as well as private retreats. The maximum stay is 15 days and there are 22 rooms; full board is about 28€ per day. Languag-es spoken include English.

Hospitalité monastique pour tous.

SAINT-PÉ-DE-BIGORRE

Monastère du Désert de L'Immaculée   Tel: +33 (0)5 62 41 88 49
65270 Saint-Pé-de-Bigorre
France

Roman Catholic (Catholique)

Nuns of the Community of Bethlehem, Assumption of the Virgin and of Saint Bruno – a religious community in the Carthusian tradition – have made and built a small monastery high above the town. You drive up through trees and hills until you turn into the drive where all is peaceful and silent. This is an enclosed order in the hermit tradition so you are unlikely to meet more than the Guest Sister if you are staying here. **This monastery is not run as a retreat house**, but it offers a simple hermitage at the gate for a single person and this is usually going to be a priest, nun or monk. However, it is well worth the detour for its charm and setting, and for taking an hour out to pray and be silent during your travels in south-west France. The chapel is absolutely beautiful and built of limed timber. You are able to join in the Offices or when Mass is held by entering a door and sitting above the sisters, who come in below to form their choir. Mass is sometimes conducted in Spanish, otherwise in French or Latin. You are usually welcome to help with the trees and hedges outside and around the monastery, and the nuns make delicious jams and jellies, which are on sale in a small open-door room next to the visitor's door to the chapel.

Mérite le détour pour son charme et pour y passer une heure à prier. La chapelle est absolument superbe avec toutes les boiseries chaulées.

TOURNEY

L'Abbaye Notre-Dame de Tournay   Tel: +33 (0)5 62 35 70 21
18 Avenue Toulouse   Fax : +33 (0)5 62 35 25 72
65190 Tournay   Website: www.abbaye-tournay.com
France

Roman Catholic (Catholique)

This community of Benedictine monks receives men and women. Services are held in French. For accommodation, there are 30 singles for men plus dormitories, and 12 rooms for women. Men take meals in the refectory, while women guests eat separately. The abbey is in a quiet location, close to a river. This is a lovely area of south-west France and is regularly visited by local people. From Tournay you can drive into the Baronnies, one of the most beautiful regions in all of the Pyrénées.

Saint Benoît dit: Toutes les personnes qui arrivent au monastère seront reçues comme le Christ, car lui-même dira un jour: J'ai demandé l'hospitalité, et vous m'avez reçu.

BAS-RHIN (67)

KUTTOLSHEIM

Sakya Tsechen Ling
Institut Européen de Bouddhisme
Tibétain
5 Rond-Point du Vignoble
67520 Kuttolsheim
France

Tel: +33 (0)3 88 60 74 52
Fax: +33 (0)3 88 87 79 06
Email: sakya.tsechen.ling@orange.fr
Website: www.sakya.eu

Buddhist – Vajrayana Tibetan (Bouddhiste – Vajrayana Tibétain)

The goals of the Sakya Tsechen Ling Institute are the study and practical application of the traditional teachings of Mahayana Buddhism. The main activities here are monthly sessions of teaching, retreats, study of Tibetan language and root texts, study and training of rituals, training courses and conferences. It is about 20 minutes' drive from Strasbourg. Daily meditation and devotional practice takes place here. Languages used include French, English, German and Tibetan.

L'Institut Européen de Bouddhisme Tibétain á Sakya Tsechen Ling est pour l'étude et la pratique des enseignements traditionnels du Bouddhisme Mahayana ainsi que leur préservation. Les activités sont des sessions mensuelles d'enseignement, des retraites, l'étude du tibétain et de textes a la source, l'étude et l'apprentissage de rituels, des stages et des conférences. Environ 20 minutes de route de Strasbourg.

STRASBOURG

Temple Zen Kosanryumonji	Tel: +33 (0)3 88 75 06 50
Centre Zen de Strasbourg	Email: secretariat@zenstrasbourg.org
21 Rue des Magasins	Website: www.zenstrasbourg.org
6700 Strasbourg	
France	

Buddhist – Soto Zen tradition (Bouddhiste – Tradition de Zen de Soto)

This centre was created in 1970 by a number of groups in France and southern Germany. Three weekends a year are organised, including a beginner's session; send for the programme. There is regular practice of Zazen here, in English, German and French.

Tous les moines et nonnes du dojo de Strasbourg vous accueilleront avec beaucoup de simplicité si vous souhaitez vous informer ou faire l'expérience de zazen, la méditation assise.

HAUT-RHIN (68)

LANDSER

Monastère Saint Alphonse	Tel: +33 (0)3 89 81 30 10
68440 Landser	Fax: +33 (0)3 89 26 87 56
France	

Roman Catholic (Catholique)

The nuns here receive everyone for retreats. Located in the heart of the village, high up in the mountains, the monastery has a large park, six bedrooms, a guest lounge, TV, meeting room, chapel and choir. Personal talks are possible. Full-board rates are about 25€; write a month in advance.

Les moniales recevoir tout le monde pour les retraites. Huit jours maximum.

OELENBERG

L'Abbaye de Notre-Dame d'Oelenberg   Tel: +33 (0)3 89 81 91 23
Oelenberg   Fax: +33 (0)3 89 81 86 07
68950 Reiningue   Email: hotellerie@abbaye-oelenberg.com
France   Website: www.abbaye-oelenberg.com

Roman Catholic (Catholique)

This brethern community follows the Rule of Saint Benedict. They receive male retreatants, with 12 single and 12 double rooms available. English, French, German and Spanish are all spoken here. Full-board rates are about 25€; stays are for a maximum of eight days.

Haut lieu de spiritualité, unique monastère masculin en Alsace.

RHÔNE (69)

L'ARBRESLE

Centre Thomas More   Tel: +33 (0)4 74 26 79 70
Couvent de la Tourette   Fax: +33 (0)4 74 26 79 99
Route de la Tourette   Email: accueil.couventdelatourette@orange.fr
69210 Éveux   Website: www.couventlatourette.com
France

Roman Catholic (Catholique)

Designed by Le Corbusier, the centre in the Dominican convent of La Tourette is for weekend retreats of reflection on religion and society. If writing to them, note that their postal address is: **Couvent de la Tourette, Boite Postal 105, 69591 L'Arbresle, France.**

Weekend conferences de réflexion sur la religion et la société.

SAÔNE-ET-LOIRE (71)

BRUAILLES

Terre du Ciel
Domaine de Chardenoux
71500 Bruailles
France

Tel: +33 (0)3 85 60 40 33
Fax: +33 (0)85 60 40 31
Email: infos@terre-du-ciel.fr
Website: www.terre-du-ciel.fr

Eco-spirituality – Mind Body Spirit (Éco-spiritualité – L'Esprit, L'Âme et Le Corps)

After 14 years of existence, development and diversification – and now affecting almost 3,000 people a year – Terre du Ciel is established at le Domaine de Chardenoux, where they offer exciting and thought-provoking weekend courses and conference retreats. **Highly Recommended.**

*Terre du Ciel s'installer dans le Domaine de Chardenoux avec la mission d'en faire un lieu témoin et transmetteur des valeurs de spiritualité, écologie, solidarité. Le Domaine de Chardenoux est l'espace pédagogique au service des valeurs de spiritualité, écologie, et solidarité. Le programme d'activités qu'ils vous y proposent comprend stages, séminaires et retraites. – de permettre une petite exploitation d'agriculture biologique (maraîchage, fruits, œufs). **Fortement – Recommandé.***

TAIZÉ

Communauté de Taizé
71250 Taizé
France

Tel: +33 (0)3 85 50 30 02
Fax: +33 (0)3 85 50 30 16
Email: meetings@taize.fr
Website: www.taize.fr

Ecumenical (Oecuménique)

In founding the Taizé Community, Brother Rogers opened ways to heal the divisions between Christians and, through reconciliation of Christians, to overcome certain conflicts in humanity. In his own words, he felt that 'the Church can be a leaven of community and peace in the entire family'. Today the community includes over 80 brothers, both Protestant and Catholic, from over 20 countries. This is one of the most popular retreat places in the Western world – in some years there have been more than

6,000 visitors in a single week. Taizé receives men, women and especially young people for whom it is a very popular place. There are 30 rooms plus dormitories, camping and caravans. While all activities take place in Taizé itself, most adult accommodation is in villages nearby. Disabled guests and families with children are welcome. Personal talks, meditation and group discussions are all available here. There are special meetings for different age groups – for example, special activities for younger people and other events for the over-60s. Everyone eats together and the food is very simple, but there are no provisions for vegetarians or special diets. It is so crowded in summer that older people are advised to come before or after that period. In spite of all these crowds and popularity, Taizé remains a place where you may find inner peace and joy.

Before deciding to go there, it is a good idea to send for information, which lists the various meetings and gives important details that you need to know before visiting. You must write at least two months before your intended stay and wait for a reply before making any firm arrangements. When writing with regards to meetings, add the heading 'Accueil' to the postal address (as above). It is also useful to make first contact via the registration form on their website, which is available in many languages. **Highly Recommended.**

Taizé demeure un lieu où vous pouvez trouver la paix intérieure et la joie. Fortement – Recommandé.

SARTHE (72)

SOLESMES

L'Abbaye Saint-Pierre de Solesmes	Tel: +33 (0)2 43 95 03 08
Père Hôtelier, I Place Dom Guéranger	Fax: +33 (0)2 43 95 03 28
72300 Solesmes	Email: hospes@solesmes.com
France	Website: www.solesmes.com

Roman Catholic (Catholique)

Founded in 1010 and occupied until 1790, the abbey was again opened in 1833 and later refurbished and rebuilt. The guest house is in the enclosure and receives men only for retreats of a few days to a maximum of one week. The work of the monks here is divided between prayer, manual work and intellectual endeavor and study. It is a silent place. There is an outstanding collection of Gregorian music.

Reçoit des hommes seulement.

HAUTE-SAVOIE (74)

•••

SAINT-GERVAIS-LES-BAINS

Assomption Fleur des Neiges   Tel: +33 (0)4 50 93 41 96
287 Chemin des Granges d'Orsin   Fax : +33 (0)4 50 93 49 56
74170 Saint-Gervais-les-Bains   Email:
France   assomption.fleurdesneiges@wanadoo.fr

Roman Catholic (Catholique)

This small community of Nuns of The Assumption is beautifully situated in the mountains, with Mont Blanc only two kilometres away. All are welcome to join in the community's life of prayer and the monastic offices. For guests, there are 20 singles, five doubles, a library, guest area, TV and chapel. Personal talks, small conferences and directed retreats are all possible here. Camping is by arrangement. Full-board rates start from about 50€ per person per day.

Magnifiquement situé dans les montagnes avec Le Mont Blanc a 2 km seulement.

PARIS (75)

•••

PARIS

L'Abbaye Sainte-Marie   Tel: +33 (0)1 45 25 30 07
3 Rue de la Source   Fax: +33 (0)1 45 24 56 12
75016 Paris   Email: stemarie@club-internet.fr
France

Roman Catholic (Catholique)

The abbey has a well-known library, which is open by arrangement for study purposes. The Benedictine community of monks receives men only for spiritual retreats of silence and solitude – it is not a place for tourist stays. Personal talks are possible, and there are sometimes courses. Both men and women are accepted for a few hours of silence and reflection or for a day retreat; everyone eats together. This is a sanctuary of peace in the midst of a rushing, noisy and beautiful city.

C'est un sanctuaire de paix pour les hommes au milieu d'une ville belle et bruyant.

Centre Sivananda de Yoga	Tel: +33 (0)1 40 26 77 49
Vedanta de Paris	Fax: +33 (0)1 42 33 51 97
140 Rue du Faubourg Saint Martin	Email: paris@sivananda.net
75010 Paris	Website: www.sivananda.org/paris
France	

Yoga – Méditation – Mind Body Spirit (Yoga – Méditation – L'Esprit, L'Âme et Le Corps)

With centres and ashrams around the world, this organisation has trained almost 10,000 yoga teachers. Swami Vishnudevananda founded the centre and it is run as a non-profit organisation, whose purpose is to propagate the teachings of yoga and Vedanta as a means of achieving physical, mental and spiritual well-being and self-realisation. Retreats are held at the **Château du Yoga Sivananda** in Neuville-aux-Bois.

Avec les centres et ashrams autour du monde, cet organisme a formé près de 10,000 enseignants de yoga.

Monastère de l'Adoration-Réparatrice	Tel: +33 (0)1 43 26 75 75
39 Rue Gay-Lussac	Fax: +33 (0)1 43 25 95 54
75005 Paris	
France	

Roman Catholic (Catholique)

This monastery receives men and women for individual retreats all year, except during July and August.

Les personnes souhaitant quelques jours de retraite sous le rayonnement de l'eucharistie peuvent être accueillies.

Monastère de la Visitation   Tel: +33 (0)1 43 27 12 90
68 Avenue Denfert-Rochereau
75014 Paris
France

Roman Catholic (Catholique)

A welcome here is extended to those who wish to join the sisters in silence and solitude.

Les personnes souhaitant quelques jours de retraite sous le rayonnement de l'eucharistie peuvent être accueillies.

Mont Thabor – Myriam-Salomé   Tel: +33 (0)1 47 43 95 04
Léonore Gottwald (Secrétariat)
30 Rue Clause Lorrain
75015 Paris
France

Christian – Alternative spirituality (Chrétien – Spiritualité alternative)

This association, formed by the Marianist priest Bernard Rérolle, offers Christian and Eastern spirituality, meditation, Tai Chi, sacred rituals and body-in-spirit exercises. There is a good weekend programme, as well as prayer groups.

Conférences spirituelle et séminaires.

'A partir de notre vécu, se découvre une voie d'éveil du cœur et de l'esprit, simple et universelle. Elle constitue le fond commun de tout cheminement authentique'
– Lama Denys

SEINE-MARITIME (76)

ROGERVILLE

Fraternité du Père Arson   Tel: +33 (0)2 35 20 42 57
14 Rue du Père Arson   Fax: +33 (0)2 35 55 58 84
76700 Rogerville
France

Roman Catholic (Catholique)

A Franciscan welcome is given to all at this retreat house, which is open all year. There are 15 bedrooms, conferences rooms, a guest lounge, TV and chapel; personal talks are possible.

Il y a 15 chambres, salles de conférences, salon, télévision, et chapelle.

YVELINES (78)

VERSAILLES

St Mark's English Church   Tel: +33 (0)1 39 02 79 45
31 Rue du Pont Colbert   Email: office@stmarksversailles.org
78000 Versailles   Website: www.stmarksversailles.org
France

Anglican (L'Église de l'Angleterre)

This is a Church of England in the Diocese of Europe and under the patronage of the Intercontinental Church Society. Everyone is welcome. There is regular Sunday worship, a crèche, children's and teenage groups, and during the weekdays Bible Study, social events and a mother and toddlers group. There are also services at St Paul's Church, Chevry, and at Gif-sur-Yvette on Sunday afternoons. All services and studies are in English.

L'église St Mark de Versailles est une communauté vivante et en croissance de personnes de toutes origines, à l'ouest de Paris. Célébrations des cultes en anglais.

DEUX-SÈVRES (79)

MONTMARQUET

Mill Retreat Centre
Moulin de Breteuil
Route du Tréport D316
80430 Montmarquet
France

Tel: 0845 3108063 (UK contact)
Email: info@millretreatcentre.com
Website: www.millretreatcentre.com

Open spirituality (Spiritualité laïque)

The Mill Retreat Centre, located near Dieppe in northern France, is a centre for personal and spiritual growth. The centre is for hire to self-contained groups or guests are welcome to join in programmes that run throughout the year, including those run by **Stillness Retreats** (see below). Only four hours' drive from London, with a private mini-bus pick-up from London direct, the Mill Retreat Centre offers good value with current prices starting from about £45 per person per night. There are many accommodation and meal options for groups of up to 50 people, with 20 bedrooms. Groups from all spiritual paths and backgrounds are very welcome to enjoy the centre's special energy and spectacular grounds. There is a large 10-acre lake, which has many rare wild birds and swans and is teeming with fish, from trout to pike. The 30 acres of grounds include wild wetlands, woodland, river wildlife and lake habitats, all of which combine to provide an extraordinary rich area of plants and wildlife – a wonderful place to explore, go for walks, meditate or just relax. It tries to be a centre of excellence in maintaining high environmental standards and preservation. For example, hydro-electricity is in the process of being set up using the river and the original millworks. The historic local town of Aumale is five minutes away by car, and it has shops and services for most needs, as well as a railway station. **Highly Recommended.**

Le centre essaie d'être un centre d'excellence dans le maintien de bons environnements. ***Fortement – Recommandé.***

Stillness Retreats
Mill Retreat Centre
Moulin de Breteuil
Route du Tréport D316
80430 Montmarquet
France

Tel: 01243 785333 / 07809 655453
Email: info@stillnessretreats.com
Website: www.stillnessretreats.com

Open spirituality – Buddhist Approach (Spiritualité laïque –
Approche Bouddhiste)

Stillness Retreats at the Mill Retreat Centre are hosted by Barbara and Mike Boxhall ensuring well-supported and organised residential courses and retreats. They ran retreats in Britain at Duncton Mill for many years and earned many accolades over the years. They have now settled at this wonderful place in northern France, just across the Channel. They share the Mill Retreat Centre with the owner and are open for bookings throughout the year, except Christmas and the New Year, providing a venue for hire to groups. Mike's teaching is on 'spirituality as revealed in the body' and Barbara teaches painting and drawing from stillness. To hire the retreat centre or for any questions, contact Barbara (see above details). Currently the hire rates are £75 per person per night for groups of 14–35. The price includes use of all facilities, meals, snacks, drinks and accommodation. The Mill is an impressive house, which has been recently converted. It is comfortable, warm and well maintained. The main workshop/studio is huge, with a cathedral-like domed, wooden ceiling. This space lends itself to a wide range of activates, from yoga and meditation, conferences and team building to dance, the arts, bodywork and other therapies. Other group rooms are available for flexible usage. Meals are taken together in the dining room. Imaginative vegetarian food, using locally sourced, and where possible organic, produce are offered. Special diets for medical reasons and wheat- and dairy-free options are possible, with notice at time of booking. Indoor facilities include a wide range of multimedia and other equipment. The centre is fully equipped for yoga classes and for bodywork courses, with massage tables and chairs. Note that the postal address is: **Stillness Retreats Ltd, 5 High Street, Oving, Chichester PO20 2DD, England. Highly Recommended.**

*Ce grand lieu avec un beau parc est géré par des anglais qui ont de nombreuses années d'expérience dans le domaine d'offres de retraites. **Fortement – Recommandé.***

TARN (81)

••

DOURGNE

L'Abbaye Saint-Benoît d'en Calcat　　　Tel: +33 (0)5 63 50 32 37 /
En Calcat　　　+33 (0)5 63 50 84 10 (guest house)
81110 Dourgne　　　Fax: +33 (0)5 63 50 34 90
France　　　Email: hote@encalcat.com
　　　Website: www.encalcat.com

Roman Catholic (Catholique)

We very much like this place for a private individual retreat. Between
60 and 70 monks live a life of contemplation and prayer here and they
are also involved in many different activities and programmes. Set in
a quiet location in the countryside, the monastery receives everyone
and that includes not just the various Christians, but non-believers, the
non-baptized, divorced people and people of other faiths. The monks
do not organise retreats themselves, but groups do come on retreat
here with their own leaders. It is open to men in the monastery, all
others stay in the guest house. There are 26 singles, 39 doubles, guest
lounge, TV, chapel, choir and meeting rooms. Guest-house visitors eat
separately from the community. There is a library open to the public, and a special library of over 100,000 volumes that is open under
certain conditions. Here, the monks make a form of zither called a
psalterion (*cithare*), which is now used in monasteries and churches
throughout the world as well as for private accompaniment for singing
the psalms. They also produce a delicious honey and CDs of their Gregorian chant and have glass and pottery workshops. It is a highly popular place to visit, with visitors often exceeding 60,000 in a year. This is
a hard-working community of men who extend a warm welcome and
it is a restful, comfortable and beautiful place in which to pray, reflect
and be at peace. This is in *Belle France* too! Could you want anything
more? **Highly Recommended.**

*Le communauté d'hommes offre un accueil chaleureux et reposant, con-
fortable, un lieu magnifique et dans le quel on peut prier, réfléchir et être
en paix. Il est possible de rencontrer un moine pour un accompagnement
spirituel. Le séjour est limité à une semaine. Fortement – Recommandé.*

VAR (83)

COGOLIN

Trimurti   Tel: +33 (0)4 94 54 44 11
Chemin du Val Périers   Fax: +33 (0)4 94 54 63 31
83310 Cogolin   Email: trimurti@orange.fr
France   Website: www.trimurti-seminaires.com

Alternative spirituality (Spiritualité alternative)

Trimurti is a centre for courses and workshops, as well as resources for knowing yourself and for personal development. Situated in the south of France in the countryside behind Saint Tropez, there is much on offer here with good facilities for guests. Send for information on the current year's programme.

Trimurti accueille plus de 80 séminaires sur l'année – philosophes, psychologues, thérapeutes, écrivains, artistes venant du monde entier apportent richesse et variété dans les thèmes abordés.

VAUCLUSE (84)

AVIGNON

Centre ATMA   Tel/Fax: +33 (0)4 90 27 35 14
50 Rue des Lices   Mobile: +33 (0)6 88 16 59 24
84000 Avignon   Email: centreatma@orange.fr
France   Website: www.centreatma.fr

Yoga (Yoga)

The centre is open all year for courses and workshops in yoga and massage. They also organise a group expedition to India each year. Visit the website for more details.

Le Centre ATMA est une association qui souhaite promouvoir et faire connaître la culture indienne par l'enseignement du Yoga et du massage Ayurvédique. Une à deux fois par an elle organise des spectacles de musique ou de danse avec les artistes indiens.

MONTFAVET

Monastère Sainte-Claire   Tel: +33 (0)4 90 31 01 55
de Notre-Dame-des-Miracles   Fax: +33 (0)4 90 32 31 77
1454 Chemin de la Verdière   Email: claire.a.la.verdiere@wanadoo.fr
84140 Montfavet   Website: www.clarisses-montfavet.eu
France

Roman Catholic (Catholique)

Located five kilometres from Avignon, this monastery receives men
and women in a very peaceful atmosphere for retreats of up to eight
days. If contacting them in writing, please note that the postal address
is: La Verdière, Boite Postal 28, 84141 Montfavet Cedex, France.

*Le monastère accueille ceux qui sont en quête de silence pour se remettre
en présence de Dieu.*

YONNE (89)

VÉZELAY

Fraternités Monastiques de Jérusalem   Tel: +33 (0)3 86 33 39 53
Secrétariat Jérusalem Vézelay   Fax: +33 (0)3 86 33 36 93
Presbytere   Email: retraites@vezelay.cef.fr
89450 Vézelay   Website: www.vezelay.cef.fr
France

Roman Catholic (Catholique)

This is a World Heritage Site and one of the most spiritually famous
places in all of France. The basilica is staggeringly beautiful and sits
majestically on a high hill above all the surrounding countryside. Vézelay is a very small town and almost car-free because of its very narrow
ancient streets. It has few shops but several other religious houses of
friars, monks and nuns. One has the feeling that for centuries nothing
has changed here. There is a small pension in the town and at the bottom, where you can park, there are several places of accommodation.
The monastic community celebrates the Divine Office every day and
it is still a place devoted to God. If you hear the community is sing-

ing but they are not in the choir stalls in the church, then walk to the right through the stone arch into the next part where you will probably discover them. While we would be hard-pressed at the *Good Retreat Guide* to choose a single best retreat site in France, we have to admit our heart goes out to Vézelay. **Highly Recommended.**

La basilique a une longue histoire et est un monument national – mais elle a aussi une spiritualité vivante. Différentes possibilités vous sont proposées pour en découvrir les richesses avec les monastiques de Jérusalem.
Fortement – Recommandé.

ESSONNE (91)

SAINT-SULPICE-DE-FAVIÈRES

La Maison Saint Dominique   Tel: +33 (0)1 64 58 54 15
Dominicaines de Béthanie
11 Rue de Rochefontaine
91910 Saint-Sulpice-de-Favières
France

Roman Catholic (Catholique)

Situated just 40 kilometres from Paris in a lovely valley, La Maison Saint Dominique welcomes groups for retreats as well as individuals and families. There are 24 bedrooms, a grand garden and a conference room, along with the chapel for worship and prayer.

Situé à 40 kilomètres de Paris, dans la vallée de la Renarde, à proximité d'une très belle église du XIIIème (gothique rayonnant), la maison Saint-Dominique est destinée aux groupes de retraite, de réflexion, de travail, ainsi qu'aux adultes et familles qui recherchent un lieu de silence et de paix en vue d'une réflexion spirituelle.

EVANGELICAL CHURCHES IN FRANCE
(Évangélique Églises en France)

There are a number of evangelical fellowships throughout France. **Les Fédération Évangélique de France (FEF)** will provide information on these as well as for the Centres Évangéliques de Vacances.

Fédération Évangélique de France	Tel: +33 (0)5 46 74 79 51
Boite Postal 10070	Fax: +33 (0)5 46 93 79 86
17103 Saintes Cedex	Email: contact@lafef.com
France	Website: www.lafef.com

YOGA IN FRANCE

Yoga is taught all over France, from village community centres to leisure centres and fitness clubs to fully equipped yoga centres for retreats and courses as well as regular weekly sessions. A national organisation for further information is:

La Fédération Nationale des	Tel: +33 (0)1 42 70 03 05
Enseignants de Yoga (FNEY)	Fax: +33 (0)1 42 78 06 27
3 Rue Aubriot	Email: info@fney.asso.fr
75004 Paris	Website: www.lemondeduyoga.org/htm/fney)
France	

SELECTED YOGA PLACES IN FRANCE

All the underlined places are featured in this guide.

L'Association Provençale de Hatha Yoga, 12 Rue Jean Daret, Aix-en-Provence, France. Tel: +33 (0)5 42 64 18 54.

Auris, 6 Rue Viala, 01000 Bourg en Bresse, France. Tel: +33 (0)4 74 22 48 86.

La Buissière Yoga Retreat Centre, Duravel, 46700 Lot Valley, France. Tel: +33 (0)5 65 36 43 51. Website: www.yogafrance.com

Centre ATMA, 50 Rue des Lices, 8400 Avignon, France. Tel: +33 (0)4 90 27 35 14.

Centre de Yoga Iyengar de Lyon, 40 Rue Roger Radisson, 69005 Lyon, France. Tel: +33 (0)4 78 36 03 84

Centre Eviel, Les Granges, 24590 Saint-Crépin-Carlucet. Tel: +33 (0)5 53 28 93 27. Fax: +33 (0)5 53 28 81 17.

Centre Sivananda de Yoga Vedanta de Paris, 140 Rue du Faubourg Saint Martin, 75010 Paris, France. Tel: +33 (0)1 40 26 77 49. Fax: +33 (0)1 42 33 51 97.

Le Chartrou Belmonet, 46800 Montcuq. Tel: +33 (0)5 65 31 90 23

Château de Valclérieux, Saint-Bonnet de Valclérieux, 26350 Crépol. Tel: +33 (0)4 75 71 70 67. Website: www.chateaudesaintbonnetdeval-clerieux.com

Château du Yoga Sivananda, 26 Impasse du Bignon, 45170 Neuville-aux-Bois, France. Tel: +33 (0)2 38 91 88 82.

L'Ecole Francaise de Yoga du Sud-Est, 18 Rue Victor Leydet, 13100 Aix en Provence. Tel: +33 (0)4 42 27 92 20. Website: www.conserva-toire-du-yoga.net

L'Ecole de Yoga et de Méditation, 46 Rue de Metz, 31000 Toulouse, France. Tel: +33 (0)5 61 25 17 69. Website: www.yogaetmeditation.fr

Fédération Inter-Enseignements de Hatha-Yoga, 322 Rue Saint Honoré, 75001 Paris. Tel: +33 (0)4 42 60 32 10.

La Fédération Tantra Kundalini Yoga, 37 Rue Robillard, 33240 Saint-André-de-Cubzac, France. Tel: +33 (0)5 57 47 47 17. Website: www.ftky.org

La Fédération des Yogas Traditionnels, André Riehl, 65 Rue des Cèdres, 84120 Pertuis. Tel: +33 (0)4 90 09 65 27.

Kaivalyadhama-France, Lozeron, 26400 Gigors-et-Lozeron. Tel: +33 (0)4 75 76 42 13. Website: www.kdham.org

Lavaldieu, 11190 Rennes-le-Château, France. Tel/Fax: +33 (0)4 68 74 23 21. Website: www.lavaldieu.com

La Sève, 40 Route de Tarbes, 653560 Laslades. Tel: +33 (0)5 62 35 08 34.

La Yoga Thérapie, Christine Campagnac-Morette, 5 Place du Général Beuret, 75015 Paris.

BUDDHIST FACILITIES AND PROGRAMMES

L'Association Un Pas vers les Tibétains Tel: +33 (0)1 43 28 47 24
26 Chaussée de l'Etang Email: danielesens@gmail.com
94160 Saint Mandé Website: tibetanway.free.fr
France

Friends of the Western Buddhist Tel: +33 (0)1 44 53 07 31
Order – France Email: centrebouddhisteparis@gmail.com
Centre Bouddhiste de l'Ile de France Website:
25 Rue Condorcet www.centrebouddhisteparis.org
75009 Paris
France

Institut Karmapa Tel: +33 (0)4 93 60 90 16
35 Chemin Rural de la Ferriére Fax: +33 (0)4 93 60 48 75
06750 Valderoure Email: institut.karmapa@wanadoo.fr
France Website: www.institut-karmapa.net

Nyima Dzong Tel: +33 (0)4 94 76 90 88
Institut Européen de Fax: +33 (0)4 94 85 68 27
Bouddhisme Tibétain Email: nyima@wanadoo.fr
Château de Soleils
04120 Castellanne
France

ITALY

Italy, an eternal treasure house of beautiful monasteries and famed religious and pilgrim sites, always attracts people wanting a religious-type retreat. St Francis and Assisi, and other saints and places of pilgrimage, call to people's hearts as strongly as ever. For Catholics, Rome remains the magnificent centre point of their Church. So pilgrimage tours, monastic retreats and Christian events and courses remain a dominant feature of retreats in Italy. However, yoga, holistic holidays, spa retreats and alternative spiritualities are rapidly establishing themselves too. There are numerous and excellent guides to religious places in Italy and a great many travel agencies also specialise in arranging such visits and tours. Abbeys, hostels and hotels near religious sites, and monastic communities all offer programmes and special visits or, at the very least, accommodation. If you do not know the Slow Food Movement, then read up on it before going to Italy, because it will send you searching for delicious authentic local food there and increase your awareness of buying locally from small producers back home. By doing so, you will have joined a global eco-gastronomic movement involving tens of thousands of people to help ensure that our food and our traditional agriculture remains a way of life and that our food and its production does not continue to lead to the homogenisation of flavour and, hence, to erosion of culture. In its deepest sense, the Slow Food Movement is a spiritual idea. In this guide, we give just a few retreat ideas along with some outstanding monastic houses, which might get you thinking about making a retreat in Italy. Many of the retreat places have community members who speak some English and the closer the facility is to the French border, the more likely French is also spoken.

ASSISI

Assisi Retreat Centre
Alle Porte del Paradiso
06081 Assisi PG
Italy

Tel: +39 (0)349 4991293
Email: info@assisiretreats.org
Website: www.assisiretreats.org

Inter-faith

The teachings here include the steps of spiritual development practised by St Francis. The environment is one of silence and contemplation. Assisi Retreat Centre, a renovated historic monastery, is located in the Umbrian countryside, just five minutes by car from the centre of Assisi itself. The centre is situated on 26 acres of farmland; it has gardens, forest meditation spots and a great choice of country walks. They offer meditation retreats with meditation teaching in the mornings with your afternoons free to explore Assisi and surrounding towns and countryside.

CASPERIA

Sunflower Retreats　　　　　Tel: +39 (0)333 1893092
Via Tito Tazio, 11　　　　　Fax: +39 (0)765 639015
Casperia　　　　Email: mail@sunflowerretreats.com
02041 Rieti　　　Website: www.sunflowerretreats.com
Italy

UK contact details:
Sunflower Retreats Holidays　　　　Tel: 01273 782330
Suite 232, Regency House
91 Western Road
Brighton BN1 2LB
England

Yoga – Eco-spirituality – Mind Body Spirit

Sunflower Retreats is a small independent company that has been going for a number of years and was the first of its kind in Italy. They have renovated village houses for their guest accommodation, and employ local people and work with the community. A part of their profits goes to support local festivals and functions each year. With their retreat holidays, they aim to promote eco-tourism and protection of nature. At the moment, they are restoring a thirteenth-century building to its former glory to become accommodation for eco-retreats in the forest-covered mountains of Casperia. The yoga practice and teaching is by well-qualified teachers.

COSTIGLIOLE

Agriturismo Cascina Papaveri   Tel: +39 (0)141 962044
Str. Chiesa San Michele, 8   Mobile: +39 (0)347 0404144
14055 Costigliole   Email: info@cascinapapaveri.com
D'Asti (AT)   Website: www.cascinapapaveri.com
Italy

Alternative spirituality – Open spirituality

The retreat, which is an old Piedmont farmhouse set within its own vineyard and kitchen gardens, runs culinary experiences and Pilates activities every week from the middle of February until the end of November. The Poppy Farmhouse, as it is called in English, offers guests the possibility of taking both Pilates and Italian cooking courses. Golf, cycling and skiing can also be arranged, but guests can either participate in the various activities going on here or just chill out. The situation is no less than stunning in a region of Italy that is famous for its food and wine. The Pilates courses are often run by visiting teachers from both Britain and America.

FERRARA

Centro Alkaemia   Tel: +39 (0)2 4265216
Scuola Yoga-Reiki-Massaggio   Email: info@alkaemia.it
Via Pontegradella, 370   Website: www.alkaemia.it
Ang. via Pioppa
44100 Ferrara
Italy

Yoga – Mind Body Spirit

Ferrara is a splendid old town with tiled roofs, colourful buildings and seemingly a large number of joyful young Italian students. The bars, cafes, clubs, music, fashion and shops are everything you might want in a modern Italy – but it is all set in a venerable and beautiful place. Centro Alkaemia runs classes and courses in Integral Yoga, gymnastic posture and rehabilitation work, meditation, Reiki of the Mikao Usui tradition, Karuna Reiki, massage, Qi Gong, Bach Flower Therapy, and counselling (if you speak Italian). There is no resident accommodation, but there are plenty of local small hotels and other lodging near-by. They also have special arrangements for students and guests, with three places for B&B.

GALEAZZA DI CREVALCORE

Castello di Galeazza	Tel: +39 (0)51 985170
Via Provanone, 8585	Email: info@galeazza.com
40014 Galeazza di Crevalcore (BO)	Website: www.galeazza.com
Italy	

Open spirituality

The Castle of Galeazza is home to the cultural association Reading Retreats in Rural Italy and its founder, Clark Lawrence. The association hosts year-round concerts, art exhibitions and seasonal events, and is open as a guest house to members, who come from Italy and abroad to read, relax and meet each other in a friendly and tranquil atmosphere. The castle, 40 minutes north of Bologna, features frescoed ceilings and a library of thousands of books, and sits amidst extensive gardens and a 10-acre woodland. Guests span a wide range of ages, nationalities and walks of life, from professors and actors to local farmers and ironworkers. All who stay at the castle pitch in with cooking, gardening and other daily tasks. Although Castello di Galeazza has been going for years, it is still quite unique. It is funky, fun, unpredictable, sometimes noisy and over the top, often so quiet you could hear a pin drop, both super-efficient and madly disorganised – a real treat for tired souls, a beautiful spot to just be and a happy place to let go of your worries and to chill out. You live in a castle and read a book – if you want to – as well as sleep a lot, eat well with lots of delicious light Italian food (and share in the cooking too), listen to music, hold conversations, make new friends, go for bike rides, or just sit around doing nothing. From time to time, there are concerts, art displays and other art and cultural activities. If you are used to traditional Christian retreats, this place can still suit you, for the retreats are different but still broadly spiritual. We tested this out by sending an Anglican priest to stay who was accustomed to going on traditional places. He loved it. **Highly Recommended.**

MAGNANO

Comunita Monastica di Bose
Cascina Bosa, 6
13887 Magnano (BI)
Italy

Tel: +39 (0)51 679185
Fax +39 (0)51 679294
Email: ospiti@monasterodibose.it
(for information only)
Website: www.monasterodibose.it

Christian – Ecumenical

The monastic community of Bose, founded by Brother Enzio Bianchi in the late 1990s, is an ecumenical community with each member retaining his or her own church membership after joining Bose. Living under the Rule of Saint Benedict, the community today has over 80 members. It remains close to the ideals and spiritual values of the early Desert Fathers. Among other activities, they run a publishing house, which enjoys a worldwide reputation. The Monastery of Bose is a very popular place with some 15,000 visitors a year, so you need to plan and book early for your retreat. The brothers of Bose at Ostuni in the Apulia region of Italy also welcome guests and pilgrims who seek a place of solitude and silence, and a quiet place where they can pray, listen to the Word of God, and experience community life. There is limited accommodation for guests at their Ostuni establishment. You can get more information by sending them an email via the main Bose website. **Highly Recommended.**

MARTINA FRANCA

Santa Maria Del Sole World Yoga Retreat
Martina Franca
Puglia
Italy

Tel: +39 (0)80 4490224
Mobile: +39 (0)347 9678133
Email: info@santamariadelsole.it
Website: www.santamariadelsole.it

Yoga – Mind Body Spirit

About 300 acres surround this white village, which is dedicated to yoga and healing. It offers studios and courses, a swimming pool, lovely fields of flowers in the spring and three meals a day with red wine at dinner. It is not far from the port and airport of Brindisi, which makes Santa Maria Del Sole a great choice for a relaxing time with yoga teaching and practice.

SARDINIA

Yoga in Sardinia
Bosa Yoga Studio
Bosa, Sardinia
Italy

Tel: + 39 (0)348 2738644
Email: info@yoga-breaks-italy.co.uk
Website: www.yogabreaksitaly.co.uk

UK contact details:
Melanie Willsher
472 Earlham Road
Norwich, Norfolk NR4 7HP
England

Fax: 01603 451182
Email: melaniewillsher@onetel.com
(bookings)

Yoga

Based in Sardinia and the UK, Melanie Willsher is a qualified British Wheel of Yoga Teacher. She organises non-residential yoga holidays, retreats and workshops based in her studio apartment in the small town of Bosa on this beautiful Mediterranean island. The yoga holidays run for a week and you choose your apartment, hotel or B&B accommodation, which is then booked for you. The current cost for six days of yoga teaching and practice is 250€. Massage therapies are also available with a number of local therapists.

VENICE

Foresteria Valdese
Castello, 5170
30100 Venezia
Italy

Tel: +39 (0)41 5286797
Fax: +39 (0)41 2416238
Email: foresteriavenezia@diaconiavaldese.org
Website: www.foresteriavenezia.it

Christian

The Foresteria Valdese in Venice is a fantastic and cheap religious hostel run by the Waldesian and Methodist Church. It is a few minutes' walk from St Mark's Square and has both private rooms and shared (but non-coed) dormitories and excellent bathrooms with lots of hot water. The hostel overlooks the canals on both sides of the building, and gives you free breakfast and a storage locker. There normally isn't a lock-out hour – which counts for much when you are in the spring of life's adventure. This tourist, traveller, pilgrim and holiday retreat accommodation is best summed up by one young guest's comment: 'This hostel is awesome!'

ZOLLINO

Associazione YIS 'Yoga in Salento'
Le Campine Eco Resort
Via Stazione, 116
73010 Zollino (LE) Lecce
Italy

Tel: +39 (0)836 802108
Mobile: +39 (0)348 9117272
Email: info@yogainsalento.com
Website: www.yogainsalento.com

Yoga – Holistic Holiday

Yoga in Salento Centre is an international association, which was established by accomplished yoga instructors and practitioners dedicated to the proliferation and promotion of the yoga lifestyle. The association has devoted itself to a high degree of excellence in all aspects of the yoga experience, including gorgeous accommodations offering a wide array of speciality foods, an excellent staff and inspiring activities in a lively and fun atmosphere. Within the 20 acres of Le Campine Eco Resort, there is a park with ancient trees, a swimming pool, large organic vegetable garden, olive trees and an outdoor gazebo where meals are taken together. A car park with solar panels provides clean energy to the entire place. While yoga is for every age from childhood to the last years of life, this centre has a young following and we think it is most suitable for those 40 years and under.

ITALIAN MONASTIC RETREATS AND STAYS

The following are monastic houses, most of which take private retreat guests. Some are so ravishingly beautiful you will want to jump on the next flight to get to them. If you have difficulty in accessing them through your search engine, then go to the website for Italian monasteries, which offers links to all these places and more: **www.cattolici. org/monasteriositalia**

Abbazia Benedettina Santa Maria di Finalpia

Abbazia Benedettina San Pietro di Sorres, Borutta

Abbazia Cistercense di Casamari (Silent Order)

Abbazia del Santi Nazzario e Celso

Abbazia del Goleto

Abbazia di Borzone

Abbazia di Chiaravalle di Fiastra

Abbazia di Monte Oliveto Maggiore (This is among the greatest of Italian historic monasteries and it has had a Roman Catholic community of the Benedictine Olivetan Order since 1344. See also **Turvey Abbey**, Bedfordshire, in the England section.)

Abbazia di Novacella

Abbazia di San Bartolomeo

Abbazia di San Benedetto

Abbazia di San Benedetto Po

Abbazia di San Giovanni Evangelista, Parma

Abbazia di San Martino di'Bocci

Abbazia di San Paolo, Roma

Abbazia di San Paolo, Roma

Abbazia di Sant Egidio

Abbazia di Sant'Agata

Abbazia di Santa Giustina

Abbazia di Sassovivo, Foligno

Abbazia di Vallombrosa

Abbazia di Villanova di San Bonifacio, Verona

Abbazia Sacra di San Michele

Carmelo S. Anna di Carpineto Romano

Clonard Monastery

Comunità Monastica di Germagno

Comunita Trappiste di Valserena (Silent Order)

Famiglia Monastica Fraternità di Gesù

Fraternità Monastica della Trinità

Monache Agostiniane, Schio

Monasteri Benedettini di Subiaco (See also **Quarr Abbey**, Isle of Wight, in the England section.)

Monastero Camaldolese (Eremetical Order)

Monastero Carmelo Santa Anna (Enclosed Order)

Monastero Carmelo, Sorano

Monastero Certosa di Pavia

Monastero Cistercense Dominus Tecum di Bagnolo, Piemonte (Silent Order)

Monastero delle Clarisse S. Maria delle Grazie Farnese

Monastero di Bastia Capuchins (English and Spanish also on the website)

Monastero di Lanuvio

Monastero di Pra'd Mill

Monastero di San Biagio Mondovi

Monastero di San Domenico Abate, Sora

Monastero di Sant'Anna, Salerno

Monastero di Santa Chiara

Monastero di Vitorchiano, Rome (Trappist Silent Order)

Monastero Eremo San Silvestro in Monefano (For serious short-stay retreats, joining in monastic prayers and life with some courses and individually guided retreats.)

Monastero Monache Domenicane Santa Maria della Neve

Monastero Nostra Signora di San Giuseppe (Trappist Silent Order)

Monastero San Benedetto, Modica

'The journey to God is an inward one'
– Najam al Din Kubra

SPAIN

Spain continues to delight with its sunshine and culture, and more tourists than ever are discovering the rich spiritual heritage of this magnificent country. You can easily find a wide choice of traditional monastic hospitality, as well as yoga, holistic holiday and health centres and any number of established Buddhist places. Then there is the world famous pilgrims' route to Santiago de Compostela, which is walked by thousands of people every year, both those of faith and those with no particular religious beliefs. Everyone we have talked with who has undertaken this ancient adventure by foot, has been full of praise for the hospitality they received and for the sheer joy of the Spanish countryside. If you are interested in the sacred sites and pilgrim routes of Spain – or just want some real insights into the country – we recommend *The Spiritual Traveler: Spain* by the American writer and cultural anthropologist Beebe Bahrami. It is informative, easy to read and a notable achievement in travel books.

YOGA IN SPAIN

A fantastic choice of yoga retreats now exist in Spain, many run by qualified British teachers. Some are open all year and some are for programmes that change from year to year in terms of venue and what is offered. Most yoga centres today are vegetarian and into organic food and local produce. In addition to our selection, you might try the following websites:

www.yogaholidays.net
www.holistic-online.com
www.yoga-centres-directory.net/spain
www.spainyoga.com
www.yogafinder.com
www.yogabreaks.org.uk

BUDDHIST

As in the rest of Europe, the last few years in Spain has seen a considerable expansion in the number of Buddhist monasteries and guest houses. We have featured some in the *Good Retreat Guide*.

MONASTIC RETREATS

Spain is a treasure house of peaceful and welcoming monasteries, open to tourists and those seeking a retreat. They are not hotels, and the monks and nuns are inspired by values of simplicity, silence and seclusion. While you will be expected to respect their way of life, your personal religious beliefs, or lack of them, will not pose any problem. Charges are usually modest. You could try combining hotel accommodation with monastery visits, staying at one of the Spain's *paradores* (luxury hotels in often historic buildings). For example, if you are a lover of art and architecture, you may choose to stay at the **Parador de Santo Domingo de la Calzada** (Plaza del Santo 3, Santo Domingo de la Calzada) en route to visiting such famous monasteries as the **Monasterio de Santo Domingo de Silos**, south of Burgos, and the **Monasterio de San Millan de la Cogolla** – and these places are in or near Spain's wine-growing area of La Rioja. We also especially like the *hospedería* at the **Abadía Benedictina de la Santa Cruz del Valle de los Caídos**, which is near Madrid. Spain is a big country and a Catholic one for centuries, so the choice of monastic places to stay is considerable.

MIND BODY SPIRIT & HOLISTIC HEALING HOLIDAYS

The warm weather and the relaxed atmosphere of Spain provide restful settings for many healing and holistic holiday renewal programmes, as well as spas. These include de-stressing courses, relaxation techniques, complementary health methods and courses for the development of deeper self-awareness. Such courses and retreats are much like the ones you would find in Britain. Often set in sunny holiday sites like Granada or further down in the very popular Malaga area, the core aim of these places is to get you to relax within a holistic approach. One of the most successful retreat centres running along these lines is **Cortijo Romero** (see below).

PILGRIMS' ROUTE TO SANTIAGO DE COMPOSTELA

The pilgrims' route to Santiago de Compostela is tremendously popular these days, with thousands of people from all over the world. Pilgrims, from teenagers to those over 70, walk from the interior of France to Spain and down to Santiago de Compostela, following ancient roads and paths and enjoying themselves – this route has become a backpacker's dream. Most realise by the end of their adventure that the spiritual nature of a pilgrimage is not in the arrival but in the journey itself. The travellers usually stay in hostels, refuges or in monasteries along the way, which are often located in some of Spain's most lovely countryside. Many of the historic places and churches contain great works of art. Given the limited number of rooms in such guest places and the thousands of people doing this route, try to book well in advance. If, like most pilgrims, you fall behind in your walking schedule and just happen to discover a nearby monastery as night falls, a knock on their door will probably find you both a bed and a meal. After all, the monks on this route have been dealing with pilgrims for hundreds of years.

ORGANISED TRAVEL RETREATS AND PILGRIMAGES

For those desiring an organised retreat in Spain that ties up all the loose ends from booking travel tickets to a welcoming retreat leader, there are companies who specialise in such programmes. If you are Catholic look in the *Catholic Herald* or the *Tablet*, and if you're Anglican try the *Church Times* for advertisements, particularly for pilgrimages.

USING THIS SECTION

The retreats in the section below are listed according to the regions of Spain and then by province or town.

'True nobility is exempt from fear'
– William Shakespeare

ANDALUCIA

ALMERÍA

**Casa Blanca Yoga and Reiki Therapy
and Retreat Centre
Casa Blanca 9
04660 Arboleas
Almería
Spain**

Tel: +34 950 439 020
Mobile: +34 635 350 772
Email: lizyoga@hotmail.com
Website: www.casablancayogareiki.com

Yoga – Alternative spirituality

Casa Blanca is a traditional Spanish manor house, offering yoga and Reiki retreats, courses and teachings. There are wonderful views of orange and lemon groves with great vistas of the mountains in the distance. Accommodation is in two comfortable twin-bedded rooms with vegetarian meals on the terrace. They do special-offer weeks that include airport transfers, accommodation, all vegetarian meals, yoga twice a day, Reiki healing sessions and a visit to a local famous monastery. Currently this offer is priced at about 350€ per person, which seems good value to us. They also hold regular weekly yoga classes, which include lunch.

GRANADA

**Cortijo Romero
18400 Órgiva
Granada
España**

Tel: +34 958 784 252

**Cortijo Romero (Bookings and Information)
PO Box 813, Amersham
Buckinghamshire HP6 9ER
England**

Tel: 01494 765775
Fax: 01494 766577
Email: cr@cortijo-romero.co.uk
Website: www.cortijo-romero.co.uk

Mind Body Spirit – Alternative spirituality

Cortijo Romero has been established for many years now and enjoys a good reputation, attracting much press coverage. Such applause is hardly surprising as it is a beautiful alternative holiday centre, serving good food with excellent accommodation, and is set in magnificent Andalucian mountains with a very sunny climate. The courses here are designed for personal rest and renewal and for the enrichment and discovery of self. Examples of what is on offer range from *Movement and Stillness* and *Yoga for Form and Feeling* to courses dealing with issues of human development. Yoga, Tai Chi, dance, massage and more are available. **Highly Recommended.**

Kaliyoga Retreats (Andalucian Office)	Tel: +34 958 784 496
Apartado de Correos 171	Email: enquiry@kaliyoga.com
18400 Órgiva	Website: www.kaliyoga.com
Granada	
España	

UK contact details:	
Jonathon and Rosie Miles	Tel: 01373 814663
Kaliyoga Retreats	
1 The Rock, Mells	
Somerset BA11 3PF	
England	

Yoga – Open spirituality

Kaliyoga is a retreat centre offering yoga and detox courses in one of the most enchanting regions in Andalucia. Though not a purpose-built spa place, it maintains a home-from-home atmosphere for people who want beautiful landscapes, yoga and tranquillity. The yoga retreat adopts a workshop-style approach, developing the practice while keeping the basics in focus. Yoga classes are founded on the dynamic yoga method and set within the context of Patanjali's classical yoga. You practice yoga for two hours each morning and one and a half hours in the evening. Beginners are always welcome. The detox retreat is a seven-day cleanse to revitalise your mind and body, working with yoga movement, guided meditation, raw organic juices and consultations with their detox specialists. Holistic therapies are available in the afternoons and include Thai yoga massage, Chinese five-elements acupuncture, aromatherapy massage, deep tissue massage, McTimoney chiropractic adjustment, intuitive kinesiology and Indian head mas-

sage. Beauty treatments are available. There is also a trip to a traditional hammam in Granada (hot salt-water baths and massage), nurturing
country walks, outdoor hot tub, sauna and aqua-therapy sessions designed to stimulate circulation. In the evening, the atmosphere is usually jovial, warm and familiar, with a book and CD library for you to
use. The group can enjoy informative evening talks around the fire, or
watch movies or documentaries on the home cinema before retiring to
bed with a hot-water bottle and a cup of sleepy-time tea. The events of
each day are complemented with lots of question-and-answer sessions
so guests feel informed and supported through every aspect of their
experience. **Highly Recommended.**

Mumonkan Centre	Tel: +34 958 768 806
Calle Baja 21	Email: info@mumonkan.co.uk
18440 Cádiar	Website: www.mumonkan.co.uk
Granada	
España	

Open spirituality – Holistic Holidays

Open to all, the Mumonkan Centre in the beautiful valley of Las Alpu-
jarras offers alternative holiday retreats for singles, couples or groups.
There are workshops, seminars, courses and retreats aimed at nurturing mind, body and spirit to increase inner balance and harmony. Based
in a very comfortable and stylish country hotel with private rooms and
swimming pool, you may chose meditation, mountain walking, Qi Gong
or other practices among a selection of workshops and retreats that
include some in the crafts field.

'When one is a stranger to oneself,
then one is estranged from others too'
– Anne Wilson Schaef

MALAGA

Montaña Palmera SC   Tel: +34 952 536 506
El Cañuelo   Fax: +34 952 536 506
29710 Periana   Email: montpalmera@hotmail.com
Málaga   Website: www.montanapalmera.com
España

Yoga

Montaña Palmera is a rural mountain retreat in Alta Axarquias near Malaga where you can escape and relax for a week or so with walking or on mountain bikes, which are provided, or by horseback if you like riding. Otherwise feel free to laze around the pool, which has marvellous distant views. There is a regular programme of yoga and Tai Chi residential courses with qualified instructors, most of whom are from Britain.

Spirit of Yoga   Tel: +34 653 302 748
Bhakti Kutir   Email: maggielevien@yahoo.co.uk
El Carrion 125   Website: www.youareyoga.com
29792 Iznate
Málaga
España

Yoga (Hindu yoga tradition)

Spirit of Yoga retreats are held in several venues, all of which are quiet and with natural views. Some of their yoga retreats are in Andalucia, Spain, and others are in Rishikesh, India.

> *'If everyone demanded peace instead of another television set,*
> *then there'd be peace'*
> *– John Lennon*

ARAGON

••

TERUEL

Monasterio de Nuestra Señora de El Olivar   Tel: +34 978 752 300 /
Comunidad de Religiosos Mercedarios   +34 978 727 009
44558 Estercuel
Teruel
España

Christian – Roman Catholic

You can take the train to Alcaniz and get a bus from there to reach this monastery. The building was founded in 1627 and is situated 700 metres up a mountain. There are 23 rooms, though camping is also possible. Men, women, groups and children with their parents are all welcome. The costs are very modest.

▬▬▬▬▬▬▬▬▬▬▬▬▬▬▬▬▬▬▬▬▬▬▬▬▬▬▬▬▬▬▬▬▬▬▬

BALEARIC ISLANDS

••

IBIZA

Jardin de Luz   Tel: +34 971 334 644
School for Yoga and   Email: thegardenoflight@hotmail.com
Human Development   Website: www.thegardenoflight.net
PO Box 1126
07800 Ibiza
Islas Baleares
España

Yoga – Holistic spirituality – Holistic healing

Jardin de Luz is open from May to October, welcoming men, women and groups. A spacious place in a forest about two kilometres from the beach, it has been established for some years and is very popular with all age groups. Although they are not given to over-provision of luxury here as in some Spanish secular retreats, they have made a place of beauty with an authentic emphasis on creativity and simplicity. Accommodation is in various facilities, including Lotus House (a small, independent house with kitchen facilities, bathroom and private terrace) and Shanti House, which has spacious rooms for up to three people. In all about 32 people can be accommodated. There are conferences and a programme of interesting retreats, in addition to yoga. Everyone eats together; they serve vegetarian food only. **Highly Recommended.**

CANTABRIA

●●

CÓBRECES

Abadía Cisterciense de Viaceli
39320 Cóbreces
Cantabria
España

Tel: +34 942 725 017
Fax: +34 942 725 086
Email: ocso.viaceli@confer.es

Christian – Roman Catholic

This Cistercian community receives men only, for stays of up to one week. This is a place to stay if you are going on a serious religious retreat and not just to rest and relax. The atmosphere is strict, silent, and deeply spiritual.

CASTILE AND LEÓN

●●

BURGOS

Abadía Benedictina de
Santo Domingo de Silos
Calle Santo Domingo 2
09610 Santo Domingo de Silos
Burgos
España

Tel: +34 947 390 049 / +34 947 390 068
Fax: +34 947 390 033
Email: hospedero@abadiadesilos.es
Website: www.abadiadesilos.es

Christian – Roman Catholic

This Benedictine abbey receives men only. There are 21 rooms, which are much above the average in comfort with individual bathrooms and central heating. The minimum stay is three days and the maximum eight. The cost is very modest: currently about 38€ per day for room and full board. There is a peaceful and serious atmosphere here, with the Divine Office in Gregorian chant. The Holy Week religious services are impressive and justly famous. **Highly Recommended.**

Monasterio Cisterciense de   Tel: +34 947 290 033
San Pedro de Cardeña   Email: spc-hospederia@hotmail.com
09193 Castrillo del Val
Burgos
España

Christian – Roman Catholic

Founded in 899, this was the first Benedictine monastery in Spain. It has a long and colourful history, surviving invasions and wars. Housed in a Cistercian abbey, the community receives men only who wish to share in the spiritual life of the community. The maximum stay is eight days; there are 24 rooms within the monastery and full board is offered. Silence and an atmosphere of contemplation prevail here.

Monasterio de Santa María   Tel: +34 947 206 045
La Real de Las Huelgas   Website: www3.planalfa.es/lashuelgas
Burgos
España

Christian – Roman Catholic

The 36 nuns in this Cistercian monastery form a community of prayer, work and welcome in solitude and silence. They offer room and board hospitality to women only in an annex guesthouse.

---

*'There is an inner-most centre in us all
where truth abides in fullness'
– Robert Browning*

Monasterio de Palacios de Benaver　　　　Tel: +34 947 450 209
09132 Palacios de Benaver
Burgos
España

Christian – Roman Catholic

This convent has four guest rooms, and welcomes men and women as guests and visitors. There are Gregorian chants at the services.

Monasterio de Santa María de la Vid　　Tel: +34 947 530 510
Ctra. de Soria, s/n　　　　　　　　　　Fax: +34 947 530 429
09471 La Vid de Aranda　　　　　Email: licet@retemail.es
Burgos　　　　　　Website: www.agustinos-es.org/lavid
España

Christian – Roman Catholic – Augustinian

With many styles of architecture ranging from Roman to Baroque, this monastery founded in 1162 is in an imposing position above the village among trees. The guest inn receives up to 90 women, men and families in single, double or triple rooms with private bathrooms. There is a lift for the less able. Modest charges for rooms start at 10€ (per person per day) and full-board rates from 28€. There is also a fully equipped self-catering hostel. La Vid has a beautiful church and several chapels, a conference room, meeting rooms, a lounge, TV, satellite, Internet cafe and wireless system. You may participate in the Eucharist and other prayer times. The great library alone is worthy of visiting this site. It is one of the architectural treasures of Spain. **Highly Recommended.**

'People ask me what my religion is.
I tell them, "My religion is compassion"'
– The Dalai Lama

LEÓN

Monasterio de San Pedro de las Dueñas   Tel: +34 987 780 150
Sahagún
León
España

Christian – Roman Catholic

Benedictine nuns receive both men and women in a guest house at the monastery. Visitors may come here just to relax and rest or for a retreat for which the charges are lower than many other places.

PALENCIA

Abadía de San Isidro de Dueñas   Tel: +34 979 770 701
Venta de Banos   Website: www.abadiasanisidro.es
34208 San Isidro de Dueñas
Palencia
España

Christian – Roman Catholic

This Trappist monastery is open to men, woman and married couples seeking a retreat. The guest accommodation is very comfortable.

SALAMANCA

Monasterio de Carmel Dascatros   Tel: +34 923 437 133
Las Mostas
La Alberca
Salamanca
España

Christian – Roman Catholic

A strictly religious place where men only may go for spiritual retreat – but visits are only by prior written request and with permission. It is not open to tourists. The film director Luis Buñuel stayed here once and fell in love with the beautiful Las Batuecas valley where the monastery is situated. He called it a paradise on Earth. It is important that you remember to write first to the monastery to make arrangements to stay.

Real Colegio de Escoceses　　　　　　Tel: +34 923 254 011
Calle Henry Collet 51–65 bajo　　Email: realcolescoceses@planalfa.es
37007 Salamanca　　　　　Website: www.scots-college-salamanca.org
España

Christian – Roman Catholic

The Royal Scots College in Salamanca has been the Scottish Roman Catholic Seminary in Spain for almost 400 years. It trains priests for the Scottish Mission, whose priority continues to be the formation of priests. However, it also offers a place of pilgrimage, study and relaxation in the heart of Spain for all who wish to experience its spiritual atmosphere and excellent facilities.

CATALONIA

BARCELONA

Abadía de Montserrat　　　　　　Tel: +34 938 777 701
Montserrat　　　　　Website: www.abadiamontserrat.net
Barcelona
España

Christian – Roman Catholic

This Benedictine community receives men, women and children. The accommodation is situated in the marvellous, high mountain setting of Montserrat Natural Park, 50 kilometres north west of Barcelona. There is a lot to discover here – a wonderful view, a library of over 300,000 books and a museum rich in treasures, including paintings by El Greco. There are concerts and various cultural events during the year. There are 48 singles and four doubles available, as well as a place to eat. Charges are reasonable for accommodation and board. **Highly Recommended.**

Kagyu Samye Dzong España   Tel: +34 934 362 626
Centro de Meditacion de Budismo Tibetano Fax: +34 934 334 241
Rambla de la Muntanya 97   Email: barcelona@samye.es
08041 Barcelona   Website: www.samye.org/spain
España

Buddhist (Tibetan Karma Kagyu tradition)

Kagyu Samye Dzong España is a centre for Tibetan Buddhist medita-tion in Spain, organised by the **Kagyu Samye Ling Tibetan Centre** in Dumfries, Scotland (see entry in that section). There are four open centres in Spain where lessons are taught regularly. Outside Barcelona, there are centres at **Manresa** and **Santa Coloma de Farners**, which runs the four-year retreats. The smallest centre is in **Las Palmas de Gran Canaria** in the Canary Islands and there are two study groups in **Madrid** and **Coruña**.

Samye Dzong Manresa   Tel: +34 938 720 254
C/ Bruc 42   Email: manresa@samye.es
08240 Manresa
Barcelona
España

Kagyu Samye Ling La Fradera Castanyet Tel: +34 972 178 339
17430 Santa Coloma de Farners
Girona
España

Kagyu Samye Dzong Las Palmas   Tel: +34 699 716 863 /
Calle La Naval 183, 4°   +34 630 411 896
35008 Las Palmas de Gran Canaria   Email:
España   samyedzonglp@hotmail.com

Samye Dzong Madrid   Tel: +34 606 992 569
Calle de Pérez Ayuso 18 bis, 2°   Email: madrid@samye.es
28002 Madrid
España

TARRAGONA

Abadía de Poblet
43448 Poblet
Tarragona
España

Tel: +34 977 870 089
Email: info@poblet.cat
Website: www.poblet.cat

Christian – Roman Catholic

Founded in 1151, the main buildings in the abbey complex are grand and have for the most part retained their original character. The thirteenth-century chapter house is intact as is the thirteenth-century kitchen, which still contains the huge stone hearths on which meals were once prepared. The abbey currently houses a Cistercian community, which receives men only within the abbey itself. Such guests are expected to keep to the community's monastic timetable. Everyone eats together in the refectory.

EXTREMADURA

CÁCERES

Monasterio de San Jerónimo de Yuste
10430 Cuacos de Yuste
Cáceres
España

Tel: +34 927 172 197
Fax: +34 927 172 347
Website: www.patrimonionacional.es
(follow the link 'Monasterios y Conventos')

Christian – Roman Catholic

A monastery of the Order of St Jerome, it has a very royal history and today enjoys the distinction of being designated an European Heritage Site. Carlos I, the King of Spain, decided in 1556 to give up his throne and retire to this monastery, where he lived until he died. Today the monks here welcome men only for stays of up to a week.

'Even God cannot change the past'
– Agathon

GALICIA

••

LA CORUÑA

Monasterio Cisterciense de   Tel: +34 981 787 509 /
Santa María de Sobrado   +34 650 246 958 (hospitality)
15813 Sobrado Dos Monxes   Fax: +34 981 787 626
La Coruña   Email: sobradohospederia@gmail.com (guestmaster)
España   Website: www.planalfa.es/sobrado

Christian – Roman Catholic

The guest inn at this Cistercian monastery accommodates up to 35 men
and women in single and double rooms. It is set in a beautiful location.

MADRID

••

Abadía Benedictina de la Santa   Tel: +34 918 905 611 /
Cruz del Valle de los Caídos   +34 918 901 398
28209 Valle de Cuelgamuros   Fax: +34 918 905 544
Madrid
España

Hospedería Santa Cruz   Tel: +34 918 905511
Abadía Benedictina de la Santa
Cruz del Valle de los Caídos
28209 Valle de Cuelgamuros
Madrid
España

Christian – Roman Catholic

Located on the historically important site of Valle de los Caídos ('Valley
of the Fallen'), the monks have made their abbey – a royal monastery –
a prayerful place of welcome. Although it is strategically set apart from
the purely touristic route, it can still be quite busy at times. Valle de
los Caídos is a huge monument, conceived by General Franco, to hon-

our the fallen soldiers of the Spanish Civil War; however, it remains a point of contention. The granite Basílica de la Santa Cruz bears the tallest memorial cross in the world and it attracts many tourists. The resident Benedictine community are responsible for the continuity of divine worship and the Liturgy within the Basilica, as well as the lodging of guests. There are very good views of the countryside and you can enjoy a relaxed and peaceful rest within a privileged environment, surrounded by the beauty of nature. It is also an appropriate place for personal study and work if you wish.

Men and woman are received in two different facilities. One is in the monastery itself and this is reserved for men wishing to join in the spiritual life of the community. The other accommodation is **Hospedería Santa Cruz** outside the monastery, which has 110 rooms with bathrooms. The charges are modest. **Highly Recommended.**

Centro de Yoga Sivananda	Tel: +34 913 615 150
Calle Eraso 4	Fax: +34 913 615 194
28028 Madrid	Email: madrid@sivananda.org
España	Website: www.sivananda.org

Yoga

This centre is part of the international Sivananda Yoga Vedanta Centre, based in France and founded by Swami Vishnudevananda. The purpose of this non-profit organisation is to teach yoga and Vedanta as a means of achieving physical, mental and spiritual well-being and self-realisation.

Monasterio Benedictino	Tel: +34 918 691 425
Santa María de El Paular	Website: www.monasterioelpaular.com
28741 Rascafría	
Madrid	
España	

Christian – Roman Catholic

The altar area here has amazingly painted religious figures and scenes; it is very beautiful and shows how colourful the inside of so many churches were before the contemporary preference for leaving the original stone unadorned. Male guests are received for a minimum stay of three days and a maximum of 10. All the rooms have bathrooms. This community expects you to stay for a serious monastic retreat of prayer and reflection. For example, guests must attend morning and night Divine Offices and there are strict rules about being in cloister. Bookings are by telephone only with the monastic Guest Brother.

NAVARRA

Monasterio de La Oliva	Tel: +34 948 725 006
31310 Carcastillo	Fax: +34 948 715 055
Navarra	Email: hospederia@monasteriodelaoliva.eu
España	Website: www.monasteriodelaoliva.eu

Christian – Roman Catholic

Men and women are received here in a place that is a wonderful example of Cistercian architecture. The monastery was restored in the early twentieth century and it is now inhabited by a community of Cistercian monks, who farm and make wine. There is a peaceful cloister, and the atmosphere is calm yet still busy and hard working.

Monasterio de San Salvador de Leyre	Tel: +34 948 884 011
31410 Yesa	Fax: +34 948 884 230
Navarra	Email: info@monasteriodeleyre.com
España	Website: www.monasteriodeleyre.com

Leyre Hotel-Hospedería	Tel: +34 948 884 100
31410 Yesa	Fax: +34 948 884 137
Navarra	Email: hotel@monasteriodeleyre.com
España	Website: www.hotelhospederiadeleyre.com/

Christian – Roman Catholic

High in the mountains, the abbey looks down on the plain. It was restored by the government to the religious community in 1961. Mass and religious offices are sung in Gregorian chant. Men only are received in the monastery, but fathers may bring their children, if over seven years, by arrangement. Stays of three to 10 days are permissible. There are eight rooms within the monastery, with modest daily full-board charges at about 25€ per person. There is a 3-star guest hotel outside the monastery itself, which is charming and very comfortable and to which everyone, including families, are welcome. A double room is under 100€.

VALENCIA

ALICANTE

Guhyaloka Buddhist Retreat Centre
Finca El Morer
03579 Sella
Alicante
España

Tel: +34 647 240 791 (mobile)
Email: info@guhyaloka.com
Website: www.guhyaloka.com

Buddhist – Friends of the Western Buddhist Order (FWBO)

Guhyaloka Buddhist Retreat Centre is a magical place of peace and austere simplicity for men. It is set high in a remote and secret place in the Spanish mountains, not far from Alicante. The deep silence here offers a chance for you to deepen your meditation experience. The resident monastic community is devoted to study, meditation and work in this place, with the offering of hospitality to visitors. While the vihara was set up for long and three-month retreats, you can still enjoy here a summer retreat, group retreat, solitary retreat, winter semi-working retreat or working retreat. The working retreat gives you a chance to spend an extended period away from the ordinary busy life of towns and cities, but there is ample time for exploring the valleys and mountains around the centre. Three very comfortable self-catering solitary chalets are set in different places in the hillside or pine woods. **Highly Recommended.**

VALENCIA

Centro Budhista de Valencia
Calle de Segunto 97 bajo
46009 Valencia
España

Tel: +34 963 480 892
Website: www.budismo-valencia.com

Buddhist – Friends of the Western Buddhist Order (FWBO)

Meditation, yoga and Tai Chi are all on offer here in the form of classes and courses. There are also winter retreats, as well as retreats in meditation teaching for children 6–10 years old.

'Once we dare to free ourselves from our own culture and all its value judgements, then we can also descend, as it were, into our own minds and be freed from all the judgements passed upon us in the past – and they are many'
– Gregory van der Kleij, OSB

OTHER RETREATS IN EUROPE

BULGARIA

Ancient and beautiful Bulgaria is amazingly scattered with monasteries, just as so much of Europe once was, and they remain part of Bulgarian culture today. Few of these monasteries, even those with religious communities, offer retreats as we understand them in Britain and France, but many do welcome guests and visitors. With over 100 monasteries, Bulgaria has witnessed increasing tourist interest in the last few years. Some of the monasteries, which date back to Byzantine times, have played a key role in keeping up the Bulgarians' national social and cultural consciousness over many centuries of change, political domination, wars and peace. A great many are located in beautiful and wild remote parts of Bulgaria and they offer to the visitor wonderful icons and wall paintings and unique architectural designs. You really need to book through the current travel agencies that specialise in monastic visits to Bulgaria rather than try to organise a visit yourself – it is easier all around. Listed in this section are some of the most famous or often visited monasteries. Two excellent websites that give abundant information are **bulgarianmonasteries.com** and **bulgarianmonastery.com**

Aladzha Monastery, in north-eastern Bulgaria, is dug out high above ground in steep rock and has some very brightly coloured wall paintings, which date back to the early Middle Ages. Few frescoes remain, however. The monastery dates back to the twelfth century. There is a small museum. No accommodation or food is offered as there is no resident community here.

Bachkovo Monastery, the second largest monastery in the country, is located on the right bank of the spectacular Chepelare River. The monastery was founded in 1083 by a Byzantine military commander, and it was patronised by Tsar Ivan Alexander. This is one of the most visited monasteries. Around it is a neighborhood that has developed tourist sights, small shops, stalls and restaurants. Herbs, home-made jams of wild fruit, yogurt, cheese made of sheep or buffalo's milk, and carpets are among the sort of things found in the shops. The monastery welcomes guests, with accommodation for the night for up to 200. It is very popular so early summer-time booking is advisable.

Dragalevtsi Monastery is considered one of Bulgaria's most beautiful monasteries. Its foundation dates back to 1345 and there are lovely frescoes and wall paintings. The monastery is a functioning cloister, but it does not offer accommodation or food except for a limited choice of refreshments. There are restaurants nearby, and it is about 17 miles from Sofia.

Dryanovo Monastery is situated in the picturesque gorge of the Dryanovo River and was founded in the twelfth century. The history of this monastery is closely connected with the National Liberation Movement in Bulgaria. The Dryanovo Monastery offers accommodation in double and triple rooms, and nearby are a couple of restraurants with local cuisine.

Kalofer Monastery lies in a scenic valley on the bank of the Byala Reka River, surrounded by mountains. The entrance to the Central Balkan National Park is just a few minutes' walk behind the monastery, with an eco-trail, camp and a children's centre there. The monastery offers accommodation in apartments and four-bed rooms. Food is not offered. There is a simple coffee shop nearby.

Samokov Convent of the **Athos Hilendarski Monastery** is open to visitors every day. One of the monastery's buildings is used for accommodation of visitors, and the religious community also runs a charity kitchen for the poor, but visitors – presumably not poor or they would hardly afford to travel to foreign lands – can have a meal in one of the many restaurants in the town of Samokov.

Troyan Monastery, founded in the sixteenth century and the third largest monastery in Bulgaria, is situated in the northern part of the country in the Balkan Mountains, on the banks of the Cherni Osam River. The richly decorated interior and exterior of the church were painted in the middle of the nineteenth century. The Troyan Monastery is also famous for its incredible wood-carvings. The monastery has a big hotel part with modern rooms.

CROATIA

Long famous for its beauty, the Republic of Croatia is a country stretching from the Alps down to the Adriatic Sea and up to the banks of the Danube River. Croatia grew from the ruins of the Roman Empire and today has once again taken its place among the modern nations of Europe. Here the Mediterranean, the mountains and the remarkable Pannonian plains come together in harmonious natural beauty. With 1,185 islands, beaches, valleys, mountains and lakes, Croatia is an exciting and romantic land.

DIKLIC'I

Transition: Lifestyle Retreat in Croatia   Tel: +385 52 422077
Shirley Heyward   Mobile: +385 91 1758763
Istria   Email: shirley@retreatincroatia.co.uk
Diklic'i   Website: www.retreatincroatia.co.uk
Croatia

Open spirituality

The owners of Transition, an old refurbished stone house in the village of Istria, Shirley and Nigel Heyward, are passionate about Croatia and the retreat that they have made there. The house is some 200 years old and has been renovated to a high standard, where peacefulness and comfort are key notes. The whole aim is for you to relax and rejuvenate. There are four bedrooms, a lounge, kitchen, utility room and a large terrace outside. All this has been done in a rustic style, perserving the traditional Croatian features as much as possible, yet bringing in the latest in modern living, including English-language television for those who want it. A swimming pool is located in the garden, which has several quiet areas designed for reading or meditation. Transitions is a retreat for adults and children over 16 years of age. Therapies such as aromatherapy massage, Reiki and reflexology are carried out in a secluded private area of the garden during the warm summer months. In the cooler months, therapies are offered to guests in the privacy of their own rooms. With access to the sea, sightseeing in nearby ancient hilltop villages and an all-around view of the beautiful natural landscapes, Transitions offers a retreat with a real difference in a place that is still new and exciting.

CZECH REPUBLIC

PRAGUE

International Baptist Theological Seminary
Nad Habrovkou 3
Praha 6
CZ 25741683
Czech Republic

Tel: +420 296 392311
Email: info@ibts.eu
Website: www.ibts.eu

Christian – Baptist

The International Baptist Theological Seminary of the European Baptist Federation (IBTS), located just 40 minutes from the airport, is composed of 13 buildings on a 14-acre site, which includes housing for students, a large theological library, and dining and conference facilities. The hillside campus overlooks the beautiful green Šárka Valley, which is a national nature preserve. IBTS is a leading centre of postgraduate theological study for Baptist Christians and other evangelical believers. The students are from over 30 nations. In addition to all the courses they run, as well as receiving individuals and self-led groups, they do a special Baptist Group Visit of four days. The group sees different pro-reformation sites in Prague and ends the last morning with worship in the Šárka Community Baptist Church, which is based in the grounds of the seminary. This package is for at least 15 people at the amazing current price of £99. This includes three nights' lodging and breakfast, a guided tour of central Prague and a celebration dinner back at Jenerálka, the hotel of the seminary. A marvellous idea for a different kind of retreat, yet one linked to one's faith. Five of their research institutes run specialist conferences each year.

'Clay is moulded into a pot, but it is the
emptiness inside that makes it useful'
– Tao Te Ching

TOUŽIM

Převorství Nový Dvůr – OCSO
Dobrá Voda 20
364 01 Toužim
Czech Republic

Tel: +420 353 300500
Fax: +420 353 300521
Email: email@novydvur.cz /
bratr.hostitel@novydvur.cz (Guest Brother)
Website: www.novydvur.cz

Christian – Roman Catholic – Cistercian

The Monastery of Nový Dvur was designed by London architect John Pawson and his colleagues. The former farm consists of a residential building and three wings of outbuildings around a courtyard with a well in centre. The restoration project combines contemporary construction to maintain the necessary elements of monastic life with a style that is consistent with the Cistercian simplicity. The construction of the monastery began in May 2000, and foundations of the church were completed the next year. Some parts are still under construction as funding is difficult and slow for the community, which is poor. Staying here is limited to priests and a few male guests at any one time. Any help with the work is gratefully received. The site is beautiful and lonely on a high plateau and just an hour from Prague.

GREECE

Being the cradle of Western civilization, our source of the idea of democracy, and the dream islands of sunlight and the ancient gods, who would not want to go to Greece on retreat? The many centres and retreats that take place in Greece offer yoga, alternative spirituality, healing therapies, meditation and self-discovery courses. Indeed, Greece seems to have quickly become the place for yoga retreats.

EVIA

Zarka Centre
Zarakes
34017 Krieza
Evia, Greece

Tel: +30 222 3053991
Mobile: +30 694 6827391
Email: info@zarkacentre.com
Website: www.zarkacentre.com

Yoga – Holistic Holiday

The Zarka Centre is on the edge of a valley of once-deserted old houses, most of which are now restored and comfortable. The centre's theme is the exploration of health and creativity, and the teachers are well trained. Their skills range from British-trained Inter-faith Ministry members, who do spiritual counselling, to qualified teachers in yoga, transpersonal psychology, reflexology, aromatherapy and Reiki; there are also postgraduate experts in botany – one of whom has a doctorate in the bluebells of Greece. Set in an old olive grove on top of a hill, the centre is surrounded by landscaped gardens around a swimming pool. The main facility is a large circular hall with adjoining rooms for catering, therapy work, library, toilets and changing rooms. With excellent open space, activities such as seminars, meetings, lectures, dance, music, yoga and art classes can be held. There has been a recent ongoing development programme for the construction of accommodation units and an arts workshop.

LESBOS

Sam Rao Yoga – Greece
98 Pinehill Road
Crowthorne
Berkshire RG45 7JR
England

Tel: 01344 769050
Mobile: 07775 770526
Website: www.samraoyoga.com

Yoga – Hatha yoga

Sam Rao is an experienced Hatha yoga teacher in England, who runs regular yoga retreats there and in Greece, usually on the lovely sunny island of Lesbos, which is famous for being the home of the classical Greek poet Sappho. The retreat group is limited to 20 people. Sam Rao is an experienced teacher from the Ruth White Karuna Yoga School and teaches weekly classes in his home area. Ruth White is one of the leading yoga masters in Europe. Sam Rao's teaching is done in an atmosphere of expertise, fun and well-being. He carefully explains techniques to his students to help them visualise how they are working with the inner body. His Greek retreats are usually scheduled for the early autumn when the summer heat has ended but the days are still long and beautiful.

PAROS

Tao's Centre	Tel: +30 228 4028882
PO Box 47936	Fax: +30 228 4028882
Naoussa	Email: taos@taos-greece.com
Paros 84401	Website: www.taos-greece.com
Greece	

Yoga – Meditation – Buddhism (Zen tradition)

Tao's Centre is a retreat and meditation centre located on a beautiful Greek island, bathed in sunshine and dreams. It offers guests a number of events, retreats and ongoing courses. Daily and weekly activities include morning and evening meditation, daily Tai Chi and Qi Gong practice, yoga lessons, Zen sessions, dance lessons and activities for children. Some of the courses have inviting titles such as *Walking through Walls, Karmic Laws of Relationships, Life Management, Trilotherapy Training* and *Secrets of Qi Gong*. There is a long-stay internship work and study programme. The centre has no resident accommodation and guests stay at local hotels, but the centre does have its own treatment room for a variety of massages, a Thai-Oriental restaurant and Internet cafe bar.

PELOPONNESE

Spirit of Life Holistic Centre	Tel: +30 272 1078240
Agios Nikolaos	Email: sol@thespiritoflife.co.uk
Messinia	Website: www.thespiritoflife.co.uk
Peloponnese T24024	
Greece	

Yoga – Holistic Holiday

Spirit of Life Holistic Centre offers holistic workshops, pilgrimages and retreats with different themes, including yoga, healer retreats and their special Dream Healing Pilgrimage. It is worth quoting how they describe this pilgrimage because its aim is one of deepening spiritual awareness: 'A modern-day pilgrimage for those looking for deeper answers and searching for deeper healing. Our Dream Healing Pilgrimage brings the ancient principles of dream healing and holistic health into the modern world. During the pilgrimage we will visit both ancient and modern holy sites, immersing ourselves in their mysteries and opening up to new possibilities.' Most of those who come on the retreats here are women. This is not surprising as it is women who constitute the greater percentage of people practising yoga today. Some guests bring a non-yoga participating partner. The age range averages 30–50, but some are over 70 years old and one was just 15. Levels of yoga experience among guests ranges from beginners to those in deeper practice. On a retreat morning yoga sessions are held and during the week there are various sessions of meditation. Therapies and healing treatments are not included in the price, but may be booked separately when you arrive. Among those on offer are Shiatsu, Thai and Thai yoga massage, aromatherapy, deep tissue massage, healing and Reiki, and life coaching. The size of the groups is excellent at a maximum of 12 people.

SKYROS

Skyros Centre
Skyros
Greece

UK Postal Address:
Skyros	Tel: 01983 865566
9 Eastcliff Road	Fax: 01983 865537
Shanklin	Email: office@skyros.com
Isle of Wight PO37 6AA	Website: www.skyros.com
England	

Yoga – Holistic Holiday

The most famous of all holistic retreat places in Greece, Skyros enjoys a worldwide reputation as Europe's first ever alternative holiday centre. Still going strong and very popular, it was established by American psychologist Dr Dina Glouberman and Greek journalist Dr Yannis Andricopoulos. Skyros pioneered a holistic approach to life, inspired by classical Greek holistic understandings. Both founders have written a number of books that explain and explore their approaches. The courses and facilities at Skros and its other centres are, as you would expect, excellent. The best way to find out all about them is to go to their website, which tells the Skyros story and gives all the details you could possibly want to know, as well as online booking. If you are 20–35 years old, going on a first-time holistic retreat in Greece and want everything to be lots of fun, then Skyros is a sound bet. **Highly Recommended.**

NORWAY

GARMO

Sandom Retreat Centre
Garmo-Lom
N-2685 Garmo
Norway

Tel: +47 61 21 27 45
Email: retreat@sandom.no
Website: www.sandomstiftelsen.no

Christian – Church of Norway – Evangelical Lutheran

Sandom is the oldest retreat centre in Norway, and for some 50 years has been a pioneer for progressive movement within the Church of Norway. The guest house is a converted old hay barn and the centre is simply furnished but comfortable. It is a hospitable place with a warm welcome and long experience in running retreats. They hold three- and five-days retreats frequently throughout the year and plenty of Christian fellowship takes place. Individuals and groups are both welcome here for stillness and rest, Christian-focused meditation and reflection, and prayer. Personal talks and counselling are possible on request. In addition to its normal retreats, Sandom has a range of other activities on offer, all of which are linked to the ideas and themes of a retreat. These include meditation, mountain hiking, rafting and glacier walking.

GRIMSTAD

Bibelskolen Catering and Gjestehus
Østerhus
N-4879 Grimstad
Norway

Tel: +47 37 25 68 00
Fax: +47 37 25 68 01
Email: post@bibelskolen.no
Website: www.bibelskolen.no

Christian

The Bible School Catering and Guest House is idyllically situated by the seaside in the south of Norway and about four kilometres outside Grimstad itself. The guest house is open all year and they can accommodate up to 98 guests. In addition, there is a large caravan site. The house caters for training courses, conferences and youth camps, as well as personal retreats. Many places like this enjoy youth group visits during the summer months and facilities are geared in this direction and for family holidays.

KOPPANG

Lia Gård Tel: +47 62 46 65 00
2481 Koppang Fax: +47 62 46 65 10
Norway Email: retreat@liagard.no
Website: www.liagard.no

Christian – Ecumenical

A sensational get-away-from-the-world place, as exotic as winter snow can make it, as green as Norway's famed summers, and right on our European doorstep. Lia Gård lies high up in the mountains with Lake Storsjøen below. The nearest neighbour lives four kilometres away. The views are simply astonishing and the potential of the power of nature is all around you – if you feel yourself 'in charge' of things, this situation will remind you of how fragile and impotent we humans are when faced with the dynamic presence of Mother Earth. Lia Gård is a farm on a great estate and they have created a considerable number of buildings and spaces for retreats here. This Christian centre aims to be a place where people of all ages, regardless of family or church background, can come and experience the forgiving and healing presence of God. The facilities are excellent for individuals, small and large groups, conferences, youth groups and, of course, for the retreats that Lia Gård run themselves. They will warmly welcome you even if all you want is a refuge for quiet and relaxation. **Highly Recommended.**

PORTUGAL

MONCHIQUE

Quinta Pintados Tel: +351 282 955 320
Apartado 31 Email: retreat@pintados.co.uk
Monchique Website: www.pintados.co.uk
8550-909 Algarve
Portugal

Open spirituality – Arts – Healing

Situated in the peaceful and beautiful Serra de Monchique in the western Algarve, Quinta Pintados is a renovated traditional Algarve farmhouse. Based in seven acres of mountainside, its vegetable and fruit terraces are farmed organically – helping with these extensive gardens can be part of your retreat. It is run by Reiki master Keith Beasley, who can provide a wide range of workshops or consultations during your stay, to both help you on your particular path by providing tools and insights and to give you the chance to just chill out in the extensive grounds or walk the surroundings mountains. At Pintados, they offer support, inspiration and encouragement for the whole person. Retreats are wide ranging and can include art and craft retreats, drop-in retreats for those on holiday elsewhere in the Algarve, family retreats specifically for one-parent or one-child families, gardening and prayer retreats, healing retreats, healing therapy retreats using Reiki, Angel, Law of Attraction work and other approaches, insight retreats, journalling retreats (including mentoring for artists and writers), meditation retreats, eco-spirituality retreats, private retreats, weekend retreats and working retreats.

SÃO BRÁS DE ALPORTEL

The Samara Foundation Email: info@tonysamara.org
Apartado 293 Website: www.tonysamara.org
8150-909 São Brás de Alportel
Portugal

Mind Body Spirit – Open spirituality

The Samara Foundation is headed by Tony Samara and he explains that the underlying theme of his programmes is to open people's minds and hearts to others so that we can understand the depth of a person, the uniqueness of a person and with that complex understanding be there for that person rather than trying to change the world. The Samara Foundation events are held not just in its homebase of Portugal but in other countries. Information is available in a number of languages from English and Portuguese to Dutch, Italian, Spanish and Japanese. Retreats take place in the Netherlands, Slovenia, Croatia and in Portugal itself.

ROMANIA

BOROD / BEZNEA

Casa Delureni
Transylvanian Guest House
and Retreat Centre
Beznea
Romania

Tel: +40 259 315664
Mobile: +40 740 538956

UK contact details:
Canon Pat Robson
Mill Cottage, Mill Lane
Grampound
Cornwall TR2 4RU
England

Tel: 01726 844457
Mobile: 07867 577416
Email: intercelt@aol.com
Website: www.casadelureni.com

Christian – Anglican – Ecumenical – Open spirituality

Everyone is welcome here. There are six en suite twins in the guest house, as well as four chalets, each with twin en suite and divan bed. Casa Delureni can accommodate group conferences, courses or planned retreats. Myers-Briggs psychological testing and courses can be arranged to suit your needs. They run their own excellent restaurant. Special Activities include camping, fishing, walking, painting, bird watching, wild flowers, reflexology, massage, aromatherapy, Reiki healing, and yoga. Volunteer charitable work is also possible. Currently, most courses are about £350 and if you attend as a non-participant but share the accommodation the cost is about £250. This cost includes a one-day excursion in the mountains. B&B rates are about £30 per night; for two or more sharing is about £20 per night; a packed lunch is £3 and dinner at the restaurant is £12. The travel arrangements are complex so you need to check these out carefully when you book and then recheck that you have made the correct travel plan to Romania and that the connections are set up from the arrival point in the country to the final destination of Casa Delureni. Bookings are taken by letter, telephone or email to Canon Pat Robson, as above. **Highly Recommended.**

BUCHAREST

Asociatia Fecioara Maria a Milostivirii In Romania (The Association of Our Lady of Mercy in Romania) Str. Popa Nicolae nr.6 Bl.23, Sc.B, Et.1, Apt.23 Sector 2 Bucuresti Romania

Tel: +40 212 401297
Email: afmromania@gmail.com
Website: www.ourladyofmercy.ro

Christian – Roman Catholic – Ecumenical

The Association of Our Lady of Mercy in Romania tries to respond to the needs of marginalised senior citizens and families. The institute is one of three strands of the Mercy Family in Great Britain. The mission began in October 2000 when Sister Rose Carmel arrived in Bucharest from Leeds. She came in blind faith as she had no clear concept of her mission at the time. After settling down in Bucharest, she felt that the plight of old people and of poor families who kept their children and struggled to educate them were, for her, the priority needs. Today, association groups in Bucharest are run as clubs, open to senior citizens with small pensions, and are known as St Brendan's Boat. The association presently has 16 volunteers and, in addition to providing food and meals to these clubs, they support about 20 families with children. While this association neither runs retreats nor receives visitors for accommodation, they are listed by the *Good Retreat Guide* as a place where you might wish, if the spirit so moves you, to make what we might call a Compassion of the Heart Retreat. You stay locally in a modest B&B or with a family – or perhaps in the Franciscan Convent in Bucharest – and you do a week's volunteer work. It is indeed satisfaction for the soul.

'When we go on retreat, we have the opportunity to leave behind out worldly responsibilities and daily habits; we let go a little and that letting go is similar to the process of letting go when we die. We let go in order to enter into our spiritual self more fully'
– Anna Howard

SWITZERLAND

MONTREAUX

Clinique La Prairie
1815 Clarens-Montreaux
Switzerland

Tel: +41 (0)21 989 3311
Fax: +41 (0)21 989 3333
Email: info@laprairie.ch
Website: www.laprairie.ch

Spa

With Alpine air and views and Lake Geneva in your sight, this famous and modern spa and medical clinic continues to keep its brilliant reputation with traditional and innovative treatments. The clinic's rejuvenation programme has been long enjoyed by celebrities and politicians as well as ordinary folk. The spa packages currently start from £240 and the clinical medical care has various rates. Whatever you think a top-class spa holiday should be, then La Prairie should meet your expectations.

VITZNAU

Stiftung Felsentor Meditationszentrum
Romiti / Rigi
Vitznau CH – 6354
Switzerland

Tel: +41 (0)41 397 1776
Fax: +41 (0)41 397 1778
Email: info@felsentor.ch
Website: www.felsentor.ch

Buddhist (Zen tradition) – Inter-faith

Felsentor is wonderfully located on Mount Rigi, high above Lake Lucerne and surrounded by pastures and forests with views of the upper Alps. The Felsentor Foundation was created in 1999 with the intention of establishing a place for retreats. Today, it is run by a resident community, who have found their core practice in Zen Buddhist but have drawn inspiration and guidance from the meditative and contemplative traditions of all religions. In addition to offering a programme of workshops and retreats, they are establishing a centre for animal rights with an animal sanctuary. However, do not assume you can bring your pet because, rather oddly, pets of any kind are not allowed here. During the summer months, they run a small vegetarian restaurant and cultivate a large vegetable and flower garden. Felsentor offers a wide range of opportunities for people to acquire and deepen their skills in meditation and body awareness in a lovely situation. The main guest house has all modern facilities and is very much a large Swiss mountain place, while the meditation hall is simple in an oriental manner. The environment at Felsentor and the community lifestyle help to increase awareness of self and the world around you.

TURKEY

An treasure house of art and culture, Turkey straddles two worlds and gives us a taste of both – the familiar European and the magnificent Middle East. Retreats here have been slow to develop. With such a vast offering of remarkable architecture and famous places to visit, a good climate, and fabulous food, Turkey is likely to soon be on a par with Greece for yoga and holistic holidays and retreats.

FETHIYE

Huzur Vadisi
Göcek
Fethiye
Turkey

Email: huzvad@aol.com
Website: www.huzurvadisi.com

Yoga – Holistic

Huzur Vadisi has been going for almost 20 years now as a venue for yoga holidays in the pine-forested mountains of Turkey's amazing Turquoise Coast. The centre is built around a traditional farmstead with a natural-stone swimming pool and a spacious yoga studio. Accommodation is in comfortably appointed yurts, which are scattered among the olive groves. A variety of retreats, holidays and teacher-training courses are available from May to October. Turkish cuisine is recognised as one of the great cuisines of the world and this is reflected in the food served at Huzur Vadisi. Prices include accommodation based on two sharing, all meals and the course/workshop. Currently, there is a single supplement charge of £150. Flights and transfers are not included. Visit the website for full and up-to-date details. Massage and therapies are priced according to length of session and type of treatment, beginning at around £30. **Highly Recommended.**

Huzur Vadisi / Bikram Yoga Holidays	Tel: 0207 692 6900
Bikram Yoga (North)	Email: kam@bikramyoga.co.uk
173–175 Queens Crescent	Website: www.bikramyoga.co.uk
London NW5 4DS	
England	

Yoga – Bikram yoga

In addition to Huzur Vadisi's own programme, **Bikram Yoga Holidays** hold retreats there too, led by founder Michele Pernetta. Along with yoga teaching and practice, massage and cranial osteopathy is available. Currently, they offer two week-long yoga retreats, with up to 25 places on each. A typical schedule includes daily Bikram classes, a trip to a hammam and to Fetiyhe and a boat trip. Bikram Yoga Holidays also organise retreats in Spain, where you can have all creature comforts or you can get closer to nature and unwind in a tipi. The retreats in Spain are at the **Holistic Health Retreat Centre, Pizarra, Malaga**. Privacy, peace and vegetarian food as well as yoga and meditation by qualified teachers are on offer at both retreats.

'Like water that can clearly mirror the sky and the trees only so long as its surface is undisturbed, the mind can only reflect the true image of the Self when it is tranquil and wholly relaxed'
– Indra Devi

AFRICA

Except in countries where religious or political reasons forbid them, you are likely to find a Catholic or Protestant Mission centre wherever you go in this vast continent. It may be a convent, monastery, mission out-reach group, church, school, orphanage, hospital or preventive medicine facility. Many of these places either have guest houses or can offer you temporary accommodation. In many of the former British colonies, you will probably find religious, yoga, and Mind Body Spirit retreat centres that offer the kind of programmes offered in Europe.

EGYPT

Baraka-Gardens Mountain and Desert Garden Retreats
El Freish – Garden of Mohammed Abu Aluan
St Katherine, Sinai
Egypt

Fax: +20 2 (0)69 347 0042
Email: info@baraka-gardens.com
Website: www.baraka-gardens.com

Eco-spirituality – Bedouin – Islamic

Baraka-Gardens Mountain and Desert Garden Retreats was founded by the local sheikhs of the Jabaleya Bedouin tribe and Zoltan Matrahazi, who spends much of the year living with the Jabaleya. Operations are arranged through the Mountain Tours Office (Maktab Rahalat Gabaleya), a tourist company run by the sheikhs since 1987. The aim of the initiative is to bring work to garden owners and to encourage people to further the upkeep of their gardens, while at the same time providing quiet retreats for those who want to experience the slow pace of life of the Bedouin and the silence and magic of the mountains and the desert. Apart from bringing direct benefit to garden owners through visitors, Baraka-Gardens helps to restore and improve gardens so more people can earn a living from what they know and love most: the mountains and the desert. Operating in the mountains requires a lot of planning and hard work – camels, fresh supplies and more, plus the fact that the owner of the garden has to labour all year just to ensure his garden is up to scratch. For retreats, Baraka-Gardens provides firewood, cooking equipment and utensils, a trained and certified guide acting as your host and present at all times, camels to carry luggage, equipments and supplies, an assistant guide to bring daily supplies and finally, when you happily sink into it, comfortable accommodation with clean bedding and mosquito net. All you need to bring is your personal belongings, good walking shoes, hat, insect repellent and sunscreen. The nature walks and hikes are of different difficulty levels for either an afternoon or a full day. Exact charges are difficult to give as it depends on many factors – how many people are in a group, which garden you choose, how long you stay in one place, how much you bring with you, what services you need or don't need, and so on. Prices can range between 20€ and 70€ per day per person, depending on number of people and the programme. Please contact them for an exact price. Included in any case are food, drinking water, non-alcoholic beverages, herbal teas, tea, coffee, fresh Bedouin breads baked daily and organic fruit, vegetables and herbs according to season. Not included are your flights, visa and travel insurance. **Highly Recommended.**

Faith Retreats – Cairo	Tel: 01993 851519
Partnership House	Fax: 01993 851514
Cote	Email: info@faithretreats.com
Oxfordshire OX182EG	Website: www.faithretreats.com
England	

Christian – Ecumenical

Faith Retreats is all about discovering a new depth and breadth of Christian faith. They offer a new and exciting retreat to the ancient land of Eygpt with the aim of discovering a people who really 'live' by their faith, who so totally trust in the Lord that they truly do not live with the fears we encounter so often in our daily lives in Europe. Such encounters frequently cloud our insights and even our relationship with God. Faith Retreats is a bold new venture – and a much needed one in the retreat field. We say this simply because many of the British-led retreats abroad do not involve themselves with local people in any way but just receive their services. Here the involvement is different and serves a spiritual purpose. Currently, the 10-day retreat is £349 per person, which includes everything except air transport to Cairo. This seems to us to be remarkable value for such an exceptional spiritual adventure.

KENYA

Fatuma's Tower
PO Box 323 – 80500
Lamu
Kenya

Tel: +254 (0)42 4632213
Email: gillies@africaonline.co.ke
Website: www.fatumastower.com

Open spirituality – Yoga – Mind Body Spirit

Fatuma's Tower is a renovated eighteenth-century Arab house in an enchanting and secluded fishing village on the island of Lamu – even the
name rings romantic and invitingly in the ear. The tower is named after Fatuma Abu Bakar, a Swahili noblewoman who lived in this ancient
sanctuary until the end of the nineteenth century. After her death, the
house fell into ruins until it was carefully restored beginning in 1998
by English yoga teacher Gilles Turle, who has lived in Kenya for over 40
years. He and his wife welcome everyone for a few nights or weeks as
individuals or as groups – and it is not necessary to be into yoga. Gillies
leads daily yoga practice at Fatuma's Tower and UK-based Ashtanga
Vinyasa yoga teacher Liz Lark (**www.lizlark.com**) leads yoga retreats
here once or twice a year. The historic tower house has five double
bedrooms and a large yoga hall and library, as well as a ground-floor
family apartment with three double rooms. In the gardens, the Garden
Cottage has two double rooms, both with bathrooms. There is a small
plunge pool, and therapy rooms, in the gardens. All rooms have solar-
powered hot water, fans and mosquito nets. Current room charges are:
double occupancy 95€; single occupancy 70€; single room with shared
bathroom 50€. **Highly Recommended.**

'The mind is the Buddha himself'
– Ma-tsu

Shaanti Holistic Health Retreat
Diani Beach
Kenya

Email: info@shaantihhr.com
Website: www.shaantihhr.com

Mind Body Spirit – Yoga – Meditation – Holistic

Whether you want to watch the sun set with a glass of wine, take a sunrise yoga session, lie back for an Ayurvedic massage or just walk on the beach, Shaanti Holistic Health Retreat offers a delightful boutique beachside hotel, designed to let you take your own path to relaxation and reflection. All accommodation comprises en suite sea-front bedrooms. A swimming pool, massage rooms, restaurant, yoga and meditation classes, a yoga terrace and, of course, the beach are all available. For morning yoga classes, they provide blocks, belts and comfortable yoga mats. Vegetarian food – with personalised menus – is offered with the guidance of their resident nutritionist. It is a great holistic holiday place to revitalize yourself.

To book, please contact:

Nairobi Office
PO Box 42200
Nairobi
00100 Kenya

Tel: +254 (0)20 4440662 / +254 (0)20 4440663
Fax: +254 (0)20 4440665

Shaanti Retreat – Diani Office
PO Box 80
Ukunda
Kenya

Tel: +254 (0)40 3202064 /
+254 (0)40 3202921
Fax: +254 (0)40 3202236

Shaanti Holistic Health Retreat
(UK/Europe agents)
Wellbeing Escapes
3 Lonsdale Road
London NW6 6RA
England

Tel: 0207 6446120
Email: peter@wellbeingescapes.co.uk
Website: www.wellbeingescapes.co.uk

MOROCCO

In:Spa Retreats – Morocco   Tel: 0208 9680501
Studio 8   Website: www.inspa-retreats.com
160 Barlby Road
London W10 6BD
England

Yoga – Mind Body Spirit – Holistic

In:Spa Retreats holds holistic well-being retreats on the Moroccan coast (an hour south of Agadir) at a lovely country villa situated in 15 acres of walled garden. There are 10 guest rooms, two swimming pools and yoga on offer. There are also a number of therapies available, including massage, nutritional advice, personal trainers and an abundance of clean air with some morning walks and hiking to get your mind, body and spirit going. The scenery is beautiful and in the background are the Atlas Mountains. If swimming doesn't appeal, try the tennis courts. If you have not yet been to Morocco, it is a marvellous place – polite people, palaces made of sand, radiant dawns and sunsets, and tajines, couscous and other traditional dishes to delight you. When your personal trainer is not watching, try some Kab el Ghazal (Moroccan almond cookies) with your tea. With powdered sugar on them, of course!

Pure Blue Water: Surf Morocco   Tel: 01326 316363
PO Box 360   Fax: 01326 317606
Falmouth   Email: enquiries@purebluewater.com
Cornwall TR11 3WY   Website: purebluewater.com
England

Yoga – Holistic Surfing

Although the predominant focus of the Pure Blue Water holidays is surfing, they also offer twice-daily yoga classes at their north Moroccan villa. The classes here are designed for keen surfers who want to increase stamina, get themselves into a faster reaction time, learn how to maintain a calmer mind, increase their lung capacity and get even more mobility and flexibility from their body. That is what yoga can do and in this retreat you learn to achieve it in a marvellous seaside villa that once belonged to an assistant to the king. The sand is on the doorstep and the surf a few steps away. With six bedrooms, good food, luxury comfort, maid service, a limit of 12 guests and all the surfing you want, you will know you are on a special retreat.

SOUTH AFRICA

Ekukhanyeni Christian Retreat   Tel: +27 (0)13 7552479 /
and Guest House   +27 (0)82 9239569
Ekukhanyeni Farm   Email: info@ekukhanyeni.co.za
Brondal, National Road R37   Website: www.ekukhanyeni.co.za
Nelspruit – Lydenburg
South Africa

Postal address:
Ekukhanyeni Christian Retreat and Guest House
PO Box 13067
Nelspruit
1200 South Africa

Christian

Ekukhanyeni, which means 'place of light', is based at the foot of an impressive mountain among trees and forests. The guest house consists of nine twins and one large double, all en suite. In addition, there are youth camp dormitories and meeting rooms for group conferences. The dormitories are rustic in design but have full facility accommodation for school, sports and church camps. In addition to spiritual retreats, Ekukhanyeni welcomes church groups, family reunions, small wedding parties and individual guests who are simply looking for some time away and to relax and rest. Located just 45 kilometres from the Kruger National Park and 25 kilometres from the Lowveld Botanical Gardens, you have plenty of opportunities to explore some amazingly beautiful places. Rates for B&B and full board are available; visit the website for details. English, Afrikaans and German are spoken here. One guest's testimonial reads: 'Thank you for the wonderful hospitality, kindness, good cooking and the fabulous break.' And that sums up how many of the guests feel about Ekukhanyeni!

Emoyeni Retreat Centre
PO Box 190
Mooinooi
0325 South Africa

Tel: +27 (0)14 5743662
Email: retreat@emoyeni.org.za
Website: www.emoyeni-retreat.com

Buddhist

Emoyeni Retreat Centre is situated on the northern slopes of the Magaliesberg mountains about 100 kilometres north west of Johannesburg. *Emoyeni* is a Zulu name meaning 'place of the spirit'. The centre is broadly based on Buddhist principles and meditation techniques. Their approach includes the practice of mindfulness and an attitude of non-harm towards all living beings. In accordance with these principles, Emoyeni Retreat Centre sets an example for a lifestyle of simplicity. Accommodation and other facilities are simple and basic, with the emphasis on functionality rather than luxury in order to encourage introspection and inquiry. In addition to presenting retreats on Buddhist meditation and philosophy, Emoyeni offers a wide range of workshops that encourage the extension of awareness into compatible disciplines such as ecology, psychology, art, Tai Chi and yoga. There is accommodation for 14 guests and six resident members. There is also a meditation hall. All the food is lacto-vegetarian. Everyone is welcome to this peaceful place. **Highly Recommended.**

Emseni Retreat House
Emseni Methodist Church
Plot 61, Road 59, Benoni
South Africa

Tel: +27 (0)82 3349244
Email: lyn@nfmc.org.za
Website: www.emsenimc.co.za

Christian – Methodist – Open to all

All those who lead the planned retreats here are members of the Emseni Retreat Ministry. The special activities include pastoral care and counselling, Ignatian Spirituality, prayer guidance and Benedictine study experience. Everyone is welcome, whether a person of faith or not. The church and facilities are modern and comfortable. On offer are individual retreats from one to eight days, as well as group and pilgrimage retreats. Costs vary for each retreat. Please see the planned retreats on their online programme for more details. For individual or group stays, it is best to discuss when booking. Pilgrimage groups can use the retreat house as a base during their tour.

Hebron Christian Retreat
32 Sterkfontein Caves Road
Kromdraai, Krugersdorp
South Africa

Tel: +27 (0)73 7681460
Fax: +27 (0)88 011 9570258
Email: info@hebrononline.co.za /
reservations@hebrononline.co.za
Website: hebrononline.co.za

Postal Address:
Hebron Christian Retreat
PO Box 7037
Krugersdorp North
1741 South Africa

Christian – Open to All

Hebron Christian Retreat is situated in a beautiful valley within the Cradle of Humankind World Heritage Site and offers a place and space for Christian retreats and conferences. The vision here was to make a place where God's people would be healed, restored, rested and equipped in respect of their personal lives, their relationships with God and others, especially those close to them, and their professional lives at their workplaces and businesses. Accommodation is provided in the Old House, with 10 bedrooms, all en suite. The rooms have home-style furnishings and are comfortable and nicely decorated. All facilities have air-conditioning with double glass doors leading on to a verandah or directly on to the lawns. The rates include breakfast. Dinner is available by prior arrangement. Five-day and weekend stays are available, fully catered. Some limited self-catering is possible. There are two other facilities available for groups and conferences.

Mdumbi Backpackers
Thani Village, Monhosi A/A 5099
Ngqeleni Mthatha
South Africa

Tel: +27 (0)47 5750437
Fax: +27 (0)47 5750437
Email: mdumbi@mdumbi.co.za
Website: www.mdumbi.co.za

Eco-spirituality – Christian – Open to all

Here is an ultimate surfers' retreat – a laid-back, rustic and relaxing getaway for all eco-friendly travellers. Near Coffee Bay on a truly wild coast, Mdumbi Backpackers, which is on the grounds of the United Reform Church, is a community-driven incentive that works to promote broad-based community involvement in sustainable eco-tourism. This region is the homeland of the Xhosa-speaking people and their distinguished traditions and culture, which, thankfully, are still alive today. Here you can hike, snorkel and fish. As to the beach and surfing, it is epic. The communication in rural Transkei is not that reliable yet so please leave good details if nobody answers when you telephone – they will ring back. Don't rely on emails for booking enquiries without confirming details with them directly before you travel.

Saint Hilda's House,
PO Box 1272
Manzini, Swaziland
South Africa

Tel/Fax: +27 (0)268 5053323
Email: jdean@africaonline.co.sz

Christian – Anglican

Founded as an educational order, the Sisters of the Order of the Holy Paraclete have diversified their work in the UK to include overseas development work in addition to their established hospitality, retreats and spiritual direction, hospital chaplaincy, inner-city involvement, preaching and mission. The Mother House is at St Hilda's Priory near Whitby. Overseas, the Order's long-standing commitment to Africa has been extended in new developments, such as raising awareness of Aids and providing a home for abused girls in Swaziland, as well as fostering vocations to religious life in Ghana and South Africa with several new houses recently opening. Here at this South African priory you may find it is possible to stay for a short private retreat with the community.

Solitude Retreat Centre
Farm 33, Petrus Stroom
Dargle, Midlands
KwaZulu-Natal
South Africa

Tel (mobile): +27 (0)82 4651514
Fax: +27 (0)86 6159004
Email: bestill@solitude.org.za
Website: www.solitude.org.za

Postal Address:
Solitude Retreat Centre
PO Box 69
Dargle 3265
South Africa

Christian – Open spirituality

Solitude Retreat Centre is situated in a peaceful part of the KwaZulu-Natal Midlands. There are panoramic views of the valley and good walking to nearby forests. They offer four self-catering cottages for individual and group retreats, small conferences and workshops, family gatherings and simple restful breaks. Pets are welcome, free of charge. Ask for current rates when you enquire about booking. The focus here is on prayer, meditation and relating to nature, which in this case is bountiful and all around you.

UGANDA

Kabubbu Resort and Conference Centre
Manyangwa, Gayaza–Kiragi Rd
Kampala
Uganda

Christian

The Kabubbu Resort and Conference Centre is a charitable effort of the Quicken Trust in the UK, who have evolved a mission in Kabubbu to help these Uganda peoples to a better life. Uganda is one of the poorest places in Africa and the epicentre of the world's Aids epidemic. The Trust's mission is to partner with those who are in poverty and special need through no fault of their own. The aim is to assist them in their self-determination to provide themselves with a better future. From this has arisen the Quicken Trust's vision for their work, which is to provide research, resources and practical skills to assist the people – by whatever means achievable – to enable them to free themselves from the injustice of poverty imposed by others.

Accommodation at the centre is in traditional thatched round houses. They are semi-detached, making 10 units for two people each, to receive a total of 20 visitors. Each unit is fully serviced with rainwater collected from the roofs of the primary school and other buildings – now there is an idea to take back home if your local authority allows it! Kabubbu have completed dormitory accommodation for larger volunteer groups, such as school parties. This includes two en suite rooms for teachers/leaders. The accommodation is divided so that girls and boys are in separate sections. Dining is in a thatched open-sided restaurant with barbeque and bar area. Professional cooking of local and international food is served, with a speciality in Indian dishes.

Kabubbu is a terrific place to come on retreat and, recalling the words of St Paul, to back up your Christian faith with some on-the-spot action. It is also a good place for a company to bring a group for volunteer team-building projects. When we extend our hearts and hands in this way, we most often come away having received much more than we gave – and with this usually comes more insight into ourselves and our own lives. **Highly Recommended.**

Local contact details:

Kabubbu Resort and Conference Centre   Tel: +256 (0)77 2582704
PO Box 31955   Email: kabubbutourism@yahoo.com
Kampala
Uganda

UK contact details:
The Quicken Trust   Email: visitbubbu@quickentrust.com
PO Box 113   Website: www.quickentrust.com
Hailsham
East Sussex BN27 4US
England

AUSTRALIA

Today Australia is a multi-racial and multi-cultural nation with its own special culture. It still incorporates the original Australian settlers' hardiness and deep affection for the great outdoors while developing into a stimulating modern society with extensive international influences and aspects. Many of these influences are Asian, which helps account for the rapid growth of Buddhism in Australia. This factor, and the growth of Buddhist practice among the general public, has meant that funding for Buddhist monasteries and retreat centres has quickly become readily available. In addition, Australia, like most of the Western world, has developed a widespread interest in meditation for spiritual or health reasons and almost all Buddhist centres offer such training. There are a great number of Christian retreat centres, some new and many of long standing, all of which offer some personal retreat accommodation or a retreat and event programme. Many churches, as in Britain and America, offer group retreats and prayer and study groups. Usually it is possible to join these groups for a short time if you are a visitor to a city or area.

BOWRAL

Hartzer Park Retreat and Conference Centre
Eridge Park Rd
PO Box 116
Bowral NSW 2576
Australia

Tel: +61 (0)2 4861 3223
Fax: +61 (0)2 4862 1872
Email: hartzprk@bigpond.net.au
Website: www.hartzerpark.org.au

Christian – Roman Catholic

Personal retreats, spiritual direction and weeks of guided prayer are all on offer here and open to everyone. There is a chapel, gardens, library, art room, labyrinth and, best of all, a warm welcome from this Community of the Daughters of Our Lady of the Sacred Heart. Hartzer Park offers a variety of accommodation from single and twin rooms to two self-contained units and a separate house, which is suitable for those on an extended retreat. All the food is home-prepared and there is full board available.

DOUGLAS PARK

Saint Mary's Towers Retreat Centre
415 Douglas Park Drive
Douglas Park NSW 2569
Australia

Tel: +61 (0)2 4630 0233
Fax: +61 (0)2 4630 9364
Email: towersretreat@bigpond.com
Website: www.towersretreat.abundance.org.au

Christian – Roman Catholic

Set in 500 hectares of pleasant bush and pasture land, St Mary's Towers tries to cultivate a place of contemplative silence and warm hospitality. There are planned retreats and on the spiritual-help aspect St Mary's offers the Eucharist and the Sacrament of Reconciliation in addition to spiritual direction and daily prayers and services. Complete silence is observed during the retreat. The tariffs at this centre are lower than most comparable services in Australia. The suggested retreat rate is all inclusive and covers your accommodation, meals, retreat programme and spiritual director, starting from $85 for one day. Meals are professionally prepared and served in a modern dining room. The rooms are well equipped, clean and very comfortable. There are also conference rooms and facilities for groups. Please note that all written enquiries should be addressed to the Administrator at PO Box 19a rather than 415 Douglas Park Drive.

EAST KURRAJOG

Drogmi Retreat Centre
1224B Comleroy Road
East Kurrajong NSW 2758
Australia

Tel: +61 (0)2 4576 0083
Email: info@drogmi.org
Website: www.drogmi.org

Buddhist – Sakya School of Tibetan Buddhism

A 40-acre retreat centre close to Sydney, the Drogmi Retreat Centre is high up in the Wollemi National Park, in a silent, calm setting where the scenery is very beautiful. Khenpo Ngawang Dhamchoe is the founder of this centre. Appointed as spiritual director by His Holiness the 41st Sakya Trizin, Khenpo has been a monk for over 35 years. He is highly respected in Australia and internationally for his profound knowledge and the clarity of his inspirational teachings. He is also the most highly qualified Sakya Lama living in Australia. There are various teaching and meditation practice retreats led by him or by other respected teachers. Please direct all written enquiries to: PO Box 388, Strathfield, NSW 2135.

MANGROVE CREEK

Satyananda Yoga Mangrove Retreat Centre
300 Mangrove Creek Road
Mangrove Creek NSW 2250
Australia

Tel: +61 (0)2 4377 1171
Email: mangrove@satyananda.net
Website: www.satyananda.net

Hindu – Yoga – Satyananda yoga

Satyananda yoga is an internationally renowned system of yoga that is firmly grounded in tradition and adapted to suit the needs of contemporary living. It includes Hatha, Raja, Karma, Jnana, Mantra and Bhakti yogas as well as other branches and presents them in a unified method. Residential retreats, including personal yoga retreats, are on offer in a planned programme. The retreat centre offers a yoga studio, library, dining and kitchen rooms. There is disabled access to two bedrooms. Camping sites are available, but note that the sites are unpowered. Vegetarian and organic food is served here. **Highly Recommended.**

MOUNT WILSON

Self-Realization Meditation Healing Centre
Balangara
11–15 Farrer Road West
Mount Wilson NSW 2786
Australia

Tel: +61 (0)2 4756 2042
Fax: +61 (0)2 4756 2044
Email: info@selfrealizationcentres.org.au
Website: www.selfrealizationcentres.org.au

Open spirituality

Nestled between the World Heritage-listed Blue Mountains National Park and the Wollemi National Park, the Self-Realization Meditation Healing (SRMH) Centre is close to the village of Mount Wilson. Situated on 25 acres surrounded by rainforest and with its own gardens, the centre offers professionally qualified teachers and therapists and receives ongoing training through the worldwide SRMH Centre organisation, founded by Mata Yogananda Mahasaya Dharma. Meditation is taught either on a one-to-one basis or in a small group. There is a programme of courses and events. In addition the centre offers a number of therapies, including progressive method counselling, personal healing, couples counselling, individual or group meditation, animal healing, one-to-one yoga and Hatha yoga classes.

NEW NORCIA

Benedictine Community of	Tel: +61 (0)8 9654 8018
New Norcia	Fax: +61 (0)8 9654 8097
New Norcia WA 6509	Email: norciawa@newnorcia.wa.edu.au
Australia	Website: newnorcia.wa.edu.au

Monastery Guest House and	Tel: +61 (0)8 9654 8002
St Ildephonsus' Cottage	Fax: +61 (0)8 9654 8097
Benedictine Community	Email: guesthouse@newnorcia.wa.edu.au
of New Norcia	Website: newnorcia.wa.edu.au
New Norcia WA 6509	
Australia	

Christian – Roman Catholic – Benedictine

New Norcia has been home to a community of Benedictine Monks since the first Spanish missionaries arrived in 1846 and to this day the community operates all the buildings and attractions. It is an extraordinary phenomenon, harking back to pre-Reformation days when monasteries were the centre not just for religion but for learning, art and health – and were usually the biggest property owners as well. So when the community says that wherever you eat in town, their aim is for you to experience warm monastic hospitality, they can actually deliver it. This includes your accommodation as well. Abbey ale and wines are served at their New Norcia Hotel. Snacks and drinks are readily available at their New Norcia Roadhouse. Then there is their Monastery Guest House, the Old Convent, a cottage, colleges and camping. At their colleges they provide events, courses, catering and accommodation for school and adult groups of between 30 and 500 people. Want a picnic lunch? Let them pack one of their gourmet picnic-boxes – for just you or 50 people – and you can reserve a dining space to go with it. If all this sounds like you will be visiting some modern consumerist town, you could not be more wrong. New Norcia is a Victorian Colonial-era place, full of graceful highly stylised buildings with many delightful architectural features. While true that it is distant from big cities and lively development towns, New Norcia with its Benedictine community has a remote, yesterday kind of charm – an interesting, popular and decidedly good place to go on retreat. **Highly Recommended.**

SERPENTINE

Bodhinyana Buddhist Monastery
216 Kingsbury Drive
Serpentine WA 6125
Australia

Tel: +61 (0)8 9525 2420
Fax: +61 (0)8 9525 3420
Website: www.bodhinyana.org.au

Buddhist (Theravada Thai tradition)

Operated by the Buddhist Society of Western Australia, Bodhinyana Buddhist Monastery is set in over 240 acres of land where the monks live in a scattered development of huts. The monastery provides an ideal environment of solitude and simplicity, which is excellent for the monks who dedicate their lives to the practice and cultivation of virtue, meditation and wisdom.

Jhana Grove Retreat Centre
283 Kingsbury Drive
Serpentine WA 6125
Australia

Tel: +61(0)8 9525 3314
Website: www.jhanagrove.org.au

Buddhist (Theravada Thai tradition)

Jhana Grove Retreat Centre is a new and modern retreat complex, located just one kilometre from **Bodhinyana Buddhist Monastery** (see above) and designed especially for meditation retreats in the Buddhist tradition. It must rank at the moment as one of the best purpose-built centres of this kind in the world. Meditation is well known to relieve the stresses of modern life, enhancing health and even assisting in the healing of a number of diseases, mainly by its positive effect on the auto-immune system. Meditation is also known to the Buddhist world as the essential path to inner peace and eventual enlightenment. It is for these reasons that the Buddhist Society of Western Australia decided to build and operate this large meditation centre. Though it is close to the Bodhinyana Buddhist Monastery, Jhana Grove is located on a secluded piece of land surrounded by natural forest. The facilities are first-rate, including those for the disabled. The former premier of Western Australia, Dr Geoff Gallop, is the patron of the Centre. **Highly Recommended.**

SYDNEY

Vijayaloka Buddhist Retreat Centre
7 Howard Road
Minto Heights NSW 2566
Australia

For bookings:

Sydney Buddhist Centre	Tel: +61 (0)2 9519 0440
PO Box 574	Email: info@sydneybuddhistcentre.org.au
Newtown NSW 2042	Website: www.sydneybuddhistcentre.org.au
Australia	

Buddhist – Friends of the Western Buddhist Order (FWBO)

The **Sydney Buddhist Centre** offer retreats for complete newcomers and those with more experience. **Vijayaloka** is its retreat centre, located about one hour from the heart of Sydney. There are various meditation retreats, and different styles of retreat, which include introductory, family and study retreats. It provides simple shared accommodation for approximately 40 people in a bush setting on the Georges River. Vijayaloka is available for hire by groups wishing to run activities that are in keeping with a Buddhist retreat atmosphere. It will appeal to those looking for simple, inexpensive accommodation. Groups can either self-cater, or catering can be provided. The facilities include: a large kitchen, two shower/toilet blocks, each with three toilets and three showers. A large building houses the kitchen, a dining area and a sitting room that can be rearranged to suit various purposes. A large room at the end of the western dormitory wing can be used for such activities as meditation, yoga and study. There is no disabled access at present. All retreat bookings are made through the Sydney Buddhist Centre. And remember, mates, if you want to walk in the bush, bring suitable shoes.

TULLERA

Bodhi Tree Forest Monastery   Tel: +61 (02) 6628 2426
and Retreat Centre   Email: webmaster@buddhanet.net
78 Bentley Road   Website: www.buddhanet.net/bodhi-tree
Tullera NSW 2480
Australia

Buddhist (Theravada tradition) – Vipassana meditation

Everyone is welcome at the Bodhi Tree Forest Monastery and Retreat Centre, which was founded in 2005 by an Australian monk who had spent many years studying in Burma and Sri Lanka. The monastery holds weekend, 10-day and longer teaching retreats for the local, national and international community. They have attracted many visitors from Brisbane, a large city two and a half hours' north, to their weekend programmes – Australia, a vast country, has no Theravada Buddhist meditation centres north of Sydney. The monastery is developing three hermitage areas, situated separately in a wooded valley. Venerable Pannyavaro, the founder of the community, pioneered a Buddhist presence on the Internet as webmaster of **www.buddhanet.net** – one of the most outstanding resources for information on Buddhism and Buddhist places and events.

VARROVILLE

Mount Carmel Retreat Centre   Tel: +61 (0)2 9603 1269
Mount Carmel Priory   Fax: +61 (0)2 9603 1007
247 St Andrews Road   Email: retreats@carmelite.com
Varroville NSW 2566   Website: www.carmelite.com
Australia

Christian – Roman Catholic

The friars warmly welcome everyone at their simple but comfortable retreat centre, where they hope your stay will be personally rewarding and as prayerful as possible. The community is both contemplative and apostolic, so it is peaceful and a good place for prayer and reflection. There is plenty to do here – lots of wildlife to observe, walking and hiking, nature in abundance, and cows and horses in the fields. You can join the friars in their church and prayer services. There is a planned retreat programme at the centre. At present there are three communities of friars in the Australian region: this one at **Mount Carmel Priory** in Varroville, Sydney; **Infant Jesus Priory** in Morley, Perth; and **St Ives Priory** in the Diocese of Broken Bay. All of these communities are responsible for the care of their local parishes.

'Never ask your friends for anything that is not right, and never do anything for them yourself unless it is right. But then do it without even waiting to be asked. Always be ready to help; never hang back'
– Cicero, on friendship

ASIA

CHINA

Religion in China has been characterised by pluralism since the beginning of its ancient and distinguished history. Confucianism, Taoism, Buddhism, tribal and clan religions make up this multi-faceted spirituality. In recent years, there has been a huge government-backed programme to rebuild Buddhist and Taoist temples. Today many of these places have thriving monastic communities or resident religious caretakers and are in some of the most beautiful places in China. Many ordinary Chinese people stay in temples to work and study. Such guests are warmly welcomed either to pay to stay or to agree to work in return for food and board. While it is always a courtesy to contact a temple before arriving, if you do arrive unannounced you will not be turned away; their open hospitality for everyone is famous. Finding monasteries and temples in China is more difficult than in Japan and South Korea because, for example, there is a better setup in the latter two countries for tourists to experience life in a temple. This is due to the fact that these countries experienced an earlier and greater volume of tourism from the West. Now, with a massive increase in popularity, China is catching up. Bear in mind that if you stay in these places, you will find the accommodation basic – probably dormitories – but adequate and suitable for the kind of retreat you are making. Walking, or travelling by bike, air and train are the usual ways to get about in China and, if you are trying to find a train, a good place to start is **www. chinahighlights.com/china-trains**

'Stop talking, stop thinking, and there is
nothing you will not understand'
Seng-ts'an Sosan

BEIJING

DaWangLu Studio
Soho New Town
Tower A, 5th Floor, Suite 501
Beijing
China

ShunYi Studio	Tel: + 86 (0)10 8589 6474
Le Lemon Lake Club House	Tel: + 86 (0)10 5900 3192
Shunyi	Email: sherrirao@yahoo.com.cn
Beijing	Website: www.int.fine-yoga.com
China	

Yoga – Ashtanga yoga foundations

Fine Yoga was the earliest training base for traditional Ashtanga yoga in China. The founder Sherri Rao was the first mainland Chinese to train directly with the late master of Ashtanga yoga, Sri Krishna Pattabhi Jois. The organisation teaches a range of traditional and popular internationally recognised yoga styles and has three studios in Beijing: Soho New Town in Chaoyang; and Le Lemon Lake Club House and Grand Hills Club House, both of which are in Shunyi. Yoga instruction is available for Ashtanga yoga, flow yoga, Hatha yoga, hot yoga, kids' yoga, and pre-natal yoga. There is a regular programme of instruction at all levels with modern yoga facilities.

HEBEI

Bailin Temple	Tel: +86 (0)311 8494 2447 /
23 East Shita Road	+86 (0)311 8492 7167
Zhao County 051530	Fax: +86 (0)311 8492 5691
Hebei Province	
China	

Buddhist – Zen

Bailin Temple Monastery is about 250 kilometres from Beijing and the monks there receive guests with warm hospitality. A few speak English and there are usually some visiting Chinese students who speak English as well. Living with them in the community, you join in their daily schedule. This starts with sitting meditation at 05:00, which is about the same time as the first prayers of the Divine Office in a Christian monastery. Bailin Temple was first built around the third century AD and its name means the 'Temple of Cypress Woods'. Many ordinary Chinese people stayed in the temple to work and study, either paying to stay or working in return for their food and lodging. The Zen's Way of Life summer camp retreat is held every July for young people to develop understanding of Dharma. During this seven-day retreat, every participant does morning and night meditation and prayer, listens to Dharma teachings and takes part in discussions. **Highly Recommended.**

HONG KONG

Honeyville Canossian Retreat House   Tel: +852 (0)2817 8660
57 Mount Davis Road   Email: honeyvil@netvigator.com
Pok Fu Lam   Website: home.netvigator.com/~honeyvil/
Hong Kong
China

Christian – Roman Catholic

Overlooking Victoria Harbour, Honeyville Canossian Retreat House is run by the Canossian Sisters. There is a chapel, library and two prayer rooms and the accommodation rates are inexpensive by Hong Kong standards. There is disabled access, and a fully equipped conference room, which takes up to 100 people, completes the modern facilities on offer here. The retreat house is very popular with both local and visiting Catholics so you need to make your reservations well in advance. Everyone is welcomed by the Canossian Sisters, who, in addition to offering hospitality, have a special ministry with visually impaired girls.

'The battle of the spiritual man is always with himself'
– Richard Rohr, OFM

YANGSHUO

Yangshuo Mountain Retreat   Tel: +86 (0)773 8777 091
Wang Gong Shan Jiao   Fax: +86 (0)773 8777 092
Feng Lou Cun Wei   Email: reception@
Gao Tian, Yangshuo   yangshuomountainretreat.com /
Guangxi   reservations@yangshuomountainretreat.com
China   Website: yangshuomountainretreat.com

Non-religious – Open spirituality

Situated at the foot of truly remarkable limestone peaks and on the grassy banks of the Dragon River, the Yangshuo Mountain Retreat is a green eco-friendly countryside hotel that promotes sustainable tourism in China through its business practices. This includes helping to conserve Yangshuo culture by only employing locals from neighbouring villages. It is also involved in supporting charities, particularly the China–US Medical Foundation, which was founded by the owner of the hotel. Yangshuo Mountain Retreat offers a peaceful and different getaway from city and career life. In their restaurant, they feature Yangshuo cuisine along with some Western dishes and they grow most of their own vegetables. From the hotel, it is a 30-minute hike to spectacular Moon Hill and the Copper Gate Mountain – one of the best Yangshuo rock-climbing crags. Great mountain biking is also possible around here. On offer are 29 rooms with accommodation for 54 guests – all bedrooms have river or mountain views. A stay here, with some tough biking and rock climbing, will prepare you in physical shape and mental alertness for a meditation retreat at a Zen temple monastery. On the hand, if you simply want a quiet retreat, some space for peace, or to get away for a few days from homogenised international hotel life, then Yangshuo Mountain Retreat is good for that too.

INDIA

Even though yoga is practised around the world now, when anyone thinks of the word *yoga*, they think of India, which has been the central core of yogic practice for thousands of years. It is difficult to say whether one yoga retreat is better than the other in India, for the benchmark of excellence is more in the teaching than in the facilities. But in India, you find both some of the most experienced teachers in the world and some of the most luxurious facilities available anywhere, ranging from former palaces to modern spa hotels. In addition, there are ashrams where you may practise under a particular yoga master. The hospitality, the service, the scenery and the yoga in India can be outstanding. No matter where you live in Western Europe, you will be able to find either teachers or agencies specialising in yoga retreats and courses in India. These retreat journeys are usually led by certified yoga teachers so that you feel well supported in visiting a new country and culture.

Nuture Life Centre Retreats Tel: 0797 4813890 (UK)
India and Britain Programmes Email: enq@nurturelifecentre.com
Website: www.nurturelifecentre.com

Yoga – Mind Body Spirit

These retreats, which are held in both India and Britain, are offered in a variety of yogic, Mind Body Spirit, and traditional themes and practices – including Hatha yoga, Pranayama, Kriyas with Mudras, Chakra balancing, silent meditation, hiking – and on personal development using coaching and self-discovery tools. Masseurs, nutritionists, and tantra, chanting, Reiki and other therapists are often invited to add to the experience on the retreat. The aim of these retreats is to expand your awareness and connection to your inner core of being so that harmony of self develops and you feel at peace. It is an opening of the heart process. The retreats are run by Shira Bassi, who is a certified Hatha yoga instructor. Notably, 10% of all proceeds is donated to the Shakti Anand Orphanage Trust: **www.shaktianandorphanage.com**

GOA

Panchavatti Tel: +91 (0)98 22580632
Corjuem Island Email: info@islaingoa.com
Aldona, Bardez Website: www.islaingoa.com
Goa 403508
India

Yoga

This is a stunning place, overlooking the Mapusa River on the island of Corjuem. The owner Loulou Van Damme, from Belgium, offers daily practice in Satyananda yoga in a lovely house set in a marvellous location on the island. You can do your yoga, then relax in the pool and have some great Western-style food. With a music room, a garden, views, a library of interesting books and bikes to ride, who needs the usual Goa tourist beach crowd? Baby-sitting is available if you are bringing an infant – but you need to check with Loulou when you book. Rates vary according to the time of year but they start from about £111. All meals and soft drinks are included in the price.

Satsanga Retreat	Tel: +91 (0)832 2472823
No. C/93 Naika Vado	Email: info@satsangaretreat.com
Verla Canca, Bardez	Website: www.satsangaretreat.com
Goa 403510	
India	

Yoga – Open spirituality

Family-run Satsanga Retreat is situated in a small village and offers yoga retreats, yoga teacher training and yoga holidays taught by teachers from around the world. Although they run a planned programme of retreats and courses, they welcome individual guests throughout the season. When there is no retreat scheduled, a daily morning yoga class is held. The centre features vegetarian meals, massage treatments, swimming pool and a tropical garden, along with comfortable accommodation.

KERALA

Mundax Homestay Retreat	Tel: +91 (0)94 47550804
Plappallil	Email: mathew@mundax.com
Kuttikkanam PO	Website: www.mundax.com
Thekkady, Idukki District	
Kerala	
India	

Open spirituality

Mundax Homestay Retreat, situated in a beautiful valley, offers a large en suite guestroom with its own lounge and reading room. Meals are all provided and you join the host for them. He is a qualified yoga teacher, having completed his yoga teacher training at Yoga Vidya Gurukul and offers introductory and intermediate yoga sessions. You can combine your stay as a restful retreat holiday with learning yoga and meditation. There are lots of activities to choose from including trekking, a Jeep safari, boat cruises, an elephant ride, a spice garden visit, and tea and herb factory visits. They can arrange Ayurvedic body massage and Panchakarma (purification) packages for guests at a nearby Ayurvedic health centre. The nearest airport is Kochi International Airport, about 125 kilometres away. The nearest train station is at Kottayam, about 75 kilometres away. Mundax Homestay Retreat can organise a taxi pick-up for you from either the airport or the train station. In addition to this accommodation, they also offer a self-catering two-bedroom cottage set in several acres of coffee plantations and just five minutes' walk from the main house.

Tulasidalam School of Yoga Pada
Thelliyoor PO
Pathanamthitta
Kerala 689544
India

Tel: +91 (0)469 2662190
Email: mail@india-yoga.com
Website: www.india-yoga.com

Hindu – Yoga

The Tulasidalam School of Yoga Pada was founded by Shri Raman Pillai some 70 years ago to offer facilities for deep yoga studies. The classes are given in the traditional Gurukula samprthaya, where the student stays with the guide for the duration of study, gaining the experience of yoga not just in asanas but in all the steps of yoga. The small village of Thelliyoor is peacefully situated in lush green surroundings and silence. All the modern amenities are within easy reach here. The meditation course is for ten days based on the yoga traditions. In the course you are guided through the Chakra meditation/Om meditation and the Natya yoga (dance) meditation, and you receive therapy on personal levels. The course is designed mainly to help the retreatants reach higher levels of meditation and is perhaps even more beneficial for those who have completed yoga teacher training courses. Accommodation is shared on these courses and the food provided is Kerala vegetarian dishes. During the course, participants are required to avoid non-vegetarian food, narcotics, alcohol and cigarettes. The donation for the meditation retreat is currently 500€ per person, which includes accommodation and food for 12 days and the course fees. To register, first request a booking form and meditation details by email. **Highly Recommended.**

Yoga and Ayurveda Retreats   Tel: 07704 873430 (UK)
Hotel Sea Breeze   Email: pam@bodybalancefunction.co.uk
Kovalam   Website: www.bodybalancefunction.co.uk
Kerala
India

Open spirituality – Yoga – Ayurveda

People born and raised in Kerala often call it paradise. It is an exceptionally lovely part of India and, indeed, the world. Yoga and Ayurveda retreats are essentially healing retreats with yoga and Ayurvedic therapies with qualified yoga teachers and are supervised by an Ayurvedic doctor. The therapies on offer are: Abhyanga (full body massage); Vishesha Shari (a deeply relaxing and harmonious massage, which strengthens skin and tissue as well as the lymphatic and immune systems); Pancha Karma (five special therapies to correct the essential balance of the body); Pizichil (massage with warm medicated oil); Pinda Sweda (warm oil and herb massage); Mukha Abhyanga (oil and cream facial massage, which relaxes facial nerves); Shirodhara (steady streaming of warm, fragrant oil). Your treatment will depend upon your initial consultation with the Ayurvedic doctor, which will include an in-depth assessment of your health, medical history, diet and lifestyle. Hatha yoga classes are held in the morning and are suitable for all levels and abilities. The yoga is led by an experienced British Wheel of Yoga teacher. **Highly Recommended.**

TAMIL NADU

Saccidananda Ashram	Tel: +91(0)432 322260
Shantivanam, Thannirpalli PO	Fax: +91 (0)432 322280
639107 Kulittalai–Trichy District	Email:
Tamil Nadu	brothermartin111@hotmail.com
India	Website: www.bedegriffiths.com

Christian – Roman Catholic

This one of the most famous Roman Catholic monastic communities to be founded since the Second World War. It was the vision of English Benedictine monk Bede Griffiths. He taught, wrote, promoted and lived concepts arising from Inter-Religious Dialogue, particularly between East and West. Through his writings and teachings, and most especially through the example of his own lifestyle, Bede Griffiths has touched the lives of many thousands of people around the world. His message continues to be challenging. Saccidananda Ashram is a very popular place of retreat and pilgrimage, and deservedly so. From time to time, Brother Martin of the community visits Britain to give retreats, which are very popular. **Highly Recommended.**

Sri Vast Ashram	Tel: +91 (0)413 2622592 /
Old Auroville Road	+91 (0)413 2622285
Kuilapalayam Post	Email: info@srivast.org
605101 Auroville	Website: www.srivast.org
Tamil Nadu	
India	

Sri Vast International Foundation	Tel: +46 (0)35 51126
Bokelund	
Skäpparp 436	
31040 Harplinge	
Sweden	

Hindu – Open spirituality

Sri Vast Ashram is situated in a lush green area, only some 20 minutes' walk from the ocean on the east coast of the state of Tamil Nadu, which borders Kerala. When on retreat here, you usually can visit famous Pondicherry and the Shiva Pyramid. The foundation, the community in Sweden and Sri Vast Ashram are led by the widely respected and followed Guru Guruji Sri Vast. On the retreat, the aim is an inner journey to rediscover a pure and nature life for yourself, which connects your inner being with a harmonious interaction with all that surrounds you – be it human or nature. This rediscovery can result in profound positive personal changes. If you are not going on a specific retreat but coming for an individual one, it is recommended you stay for a minimum of three days. The accommodation facilities vary upon availability from single, double and dormitory, of which many have their own bathroom facilities. All ashram buildings are constructed in ecological harmony to the south Indian tropical climate and offer a serene and relaxing atmosphere.

UTTARANCHAL

Ananda Spa	Tel: +91 (0)137 8227500
The Palace Estate	Fax: +91 (0)137 8227550
Narendra Nagar	Email: sales@anandaspa.com
Tehri-Garhwal	Website: www.anandaspa.com
249175 Uttaranchal	
India	

Ayurveda – Yoga – Vedanta

Here is one of those places that is often called 'ultimate' – a world-class spa, set in the magic of India and once a palace of the Maharaja of Tehri-Garhwal, now with every facility you can imagine to get you detoxed, de-stressed and restored for a rejuvenated mind, body and spirit. The programme here is based on Ayurveda, yoga and Vedanta traditions, combined with modern therapies – a sort of best of old and new thinking as it were. The huge spa at 24,000 square feet offers over 79 body and beauty treatments, integrating the traditional with contemporary Western spa approaches. There are 24 treatment rooms and European systems of holistic health, a team of qualified nutritionists, Ayurvedic physicians and spa therapists. The therapies and activities programme is individually designed with health goals to meet your needs. A well-equipped gym, golf, walks, moonlight exercises, guided meditation, professional entertainment and an outdoor lap pool are available too. Harmony of surroundings and self are the keynotes at Ananda.

INDONESIA

Indonesia consists of 17,508 islands, with small villages and grand cities in about 6,000 of them. The island that most calls up romantic images of easy living, tropical flowers, white sand beaches and lush mountains is Bali. It has a tropical climate with just two seasons: you get wet or you stay dry in a temperature that stays more or less constant at about 28°C, which means it can be fairly humid. (Think New Orleans, if you are American.) Bali's main produce are rice, copra, spices, coffee and a wide range of vegetables. The majority of the people are Hindu but with a special Balinese slant on their religion. With its long history of popular tourism, English is widely spoken. There are a number of holistic retreats, spas, and a range of yoga, Pilates and other types of courses available in Bali. We list just a few such places out of a wide selection. You will find that a number of British and French yoga teachers offer individual retreats in Bali and in other Indonesian places, such as Java.

BALI

Aziza Healing Adventures: Bali Retreats   Tel: +1 (0)416 6960086
59 Crewe Ave   Fax: +1 (0)416 6960087
Toronto   Email: info@aziza.ca
Ontario M4C 1A1   Website: www.aziza.ca
Canada

Open spirituality – Non-denominational

Aziza Healing Adventures organise Bliss Wellness Journey and Balance Wellness Journey retreats at selected resorts in Bali and elsewhere, with the aim of placing you in a situation where you can relax and explore your inner being for healing and a better understanding of self. The resort location in Bali has been chosen because of its exceptional natural beauty, quality of accommodations and the diversity of activities available to enable participants to enjoy their surroundings to the fullest. Personal growth programmes are balanced with activities that include spa, yoga, forest walks, journal writing, cultural tours, labyrinth meditations, creative explorations and social time. Resorts used vary in size from intimate groups of eight to groups of 30-plus. Private and shared rooms are usually both available.

Bali Botanica Day Spa Tel: +62 (0)361 976739
Jl Sanggingan Email: info@balibotanica.com
Ubud Website: www.balibotanica.com
Gianyar, Bali
Indonesia

Spa – Holistic

Bali Botanica Day Spa in Ubud was recently acclaimed as one of Bali's top 10 spas. They offer a wide variety of treatment on a non-residential basis. Many guests have found their special day at Botanica well worthwhile, with refreshing results to body, mind and spirit – and excellent value for money as well. The package includes four treatments and a juice and spa lunch. If you stay locally for a yoga course, this is a healthy and fun day out.

Bali Mountain Retreat Centre Tel: +62 (0)828 3602645 (mobile)
Mount Batukaru Email: info@balimountainretreat.com
Tabanan, Bali 82162 Website: www.balimountainretreat.com
Indonesia

Eco-spirituality – Holistic – Yoga

The kind of retreat you want to take at this place is a private one for relaxing while learning about Balinese culture and exploring the marvellous surrounding nature, which includes rice fields, tropical forests, temples, local crafts and music, coffee plantations, and much more. The flora and fauna of the area is wonderful – butterflies and more that you never have seen before except in picture books. The mountain air is revitalising and the accommodation is a blend of traditional Balinese with modern Asian amenities. On offer are cycling tours, guided walks and a number of interesting day trips and special events, as well as yoga. For the curious, we suggest their offer of a Vanilla Walk, and for those not easily embarrassed, some lessons in belly dancing. If you wonder what this has to do with spirituality, then discover that when you relax, let go and join in with other people's way of life, the resulting insight and happiness frees not just the mind but the soul.

Desa Seni
Jalan Kayu Putih #13
Pantai Berawa, Canggu
Bali 80361
Indonesia

Tel: +62 (0)361 8446392
Email: info@desaseni.com
Website: www.desaseni.com

Mind Body Spirit – Yoga – Holistic

Desa Seni is an eco-friendly village resort, which provides an experience of Indonesia through its culture. Yoga, art, organic farming and detox programmes are all on offer here. The accommodation is in antique wooden houses, which have been restored and refurbished to modern standard. These range from one-bedroom village houses up to deluxe two-bedroom ones with kitchens. All room rates include breakfast and transportation to and from the airport. They grow their own organic produce and have a restaurant next to the swimming pool. As well as the number of detox and revitalising packages available, Desa Seni offers open-air yoga in a studio overlooking their gardens. All yoga retreats and group programmes are led by experienced teachers.

Sarinbuana Eco-Lodge
Mount Batukara
Desa Sarinbuana, Wanagiri
Tabanan, Bali 80543
Indonesia

Tel: +62 (0)361 7435198
Email: info@baliecolodge.com
Website: www.baliecolodge.com

Eco-spirituality – Yoga – Mind Body Spirit

Sarinbuana Eco-Lodge is located high up on the slopes of Mount Batukaru, with spectacular views of southern Bali. Just 10 minutes' away is Bali's largest protected rainforest. The lodge is a perfect retreat for nature lovers, bird watchers, families on get-away holidays, walkers, mountain climbers, small retreat groups, and those who would like to do some workshops or courses combined with an exciting adventure in the kind of tropical scenery they do not get back home. Some of the workshops available here are: yoga; traditional medicine and Balinese healing plants; Balinese massage instruction; Balinese calligraphy;

Balinese wood carving; music. There is also an extensive teaching programme on permaculture methods. Accommodation is in individual Balinese wooden bungalows, set in lush green surroundings with all modern conveniences. There is an open-air dining room that looks out to tropical forests and which serves traditional Balinese food using produce from their own organic and forest gardens. Vegetarian, gluten-free and vegan meals are available, as well as a children's menu. Note that email is the most effective form of communication as the phone line is unreliable.

Zen Resort Bali
PO Box 18, Desa Ume Anyar
Seririt
Singaraja, Bali
Indonesia

Tel/Fax: +62 (0)362 93578
Email: contact@zenresortbali.com
Website: www.zenresortbali.com

Yoga – Open spirituality

The focus here is on meditation, yoga, Ayurvedic treatment, and Balinese spa and massage, with the goal of healing for harmony and well-being of mind, body and spirit. The Ayurvedic therapists are from India and each programme is designed for the individual guest. Zen Resort Bali is a small place set above the sea, surrounded by a beach on one side, and on the others by vineyards and rice terraces. There are walks, music, chants, sunbeds and hammocks to soothe your way to some rejuvenation. They do B&B and offer quiet single and double rooms.

'When you want to shout: "Give me space!", when you feel squeezed, rattled, crowded and pressured, go into your Inner Self. Find there peace, calm, a new awareness, perhaps God. Learn to live in this world and not to let the outside world live too much in you'
– Stafford Whiteaker

Zen Bali Retreat and Spa
Jalan Suweta
Banjar Sambahan Ubud
Gianyar, Bali
Indonesia

Tel: +62 (0)361 972685
Email: info@kumarasakti.com
Website: www.zenbali.com

Yoga – Holistic – Spa

Zen Bali Retreat is located in the hills of Ubud, a place where many artists and writers have found space and peace. Zen Bali offers well-appointed rooms, two swimming pools, a large open pavilion overlooking a river, dining room, gardens and views of rice fields, and a spa whose treatments include Ayurvedic Chakra Dhara Massage. For the sake of ensuring quietness for guests, children under 14 years of age are restricted from the resort and there are no televisions in the rooms. Organic vegetarian meals are provided by professional chefs and all dietary requirements are catered for. There is a full programme of yoga retreats, plus a wide range of spa treatments and speciality retreats, such as a combined yoga and Pilates package. The teachers are mainly European and all are well qualified.

JAPAN

With their charm, good manners and keen hospitality, the Japanese make their country a lovely place for a retreat. On top of that, their traditional food is remarkably delicious, even without their famous sushi. Staying at a temple is a good choice for your retreat in Japan. The lodging at temples is called *shukubo* and anyone can stay regardless of his or her religion. In temples, you can join in their Zen meditation and often join the monks for their once-a-day vegetarian meal. Staying at a temple is not necessarily cheap, but the experience is well worth it. Temples in Japan are Buddhist and shrines are Shinto. At least 50 temples receive guests. **Koyasan Shukubo Temple Lodging Cooperative** can help you make a reservation (Tel: +81 (0)736 562616. Website: www.shukubo.jp). Another informative website is **templelodging.com**

Soto Zen is one of the main Zen traditions in Buddhism in Japan. Here is a list of some Soto Zen Buddhist temples that currently open to foreigners visiting Japan. The name of the city, town or place is first, then the name of the temple.

Aichi: **Aichi Senmon Ni-sodo Shoboji**, **Chokoji**, **Rinsenji** and **Sokichiji**
Akita: **Kokenji**
Aomori: **Judoji** and **Kounji**
Chiba: **Nihonji**
Ehime: **Zuioji**
Fukui: **Daihonzan Eiheiji**, **Hokyoji** and **Tenryuji**
Gifu: **Enchoji** and **Shosoji**
Gunma: **Kinryuji** and **Unmonji**
Hiroshima: **Doshinji**
Hyogo: **Antaiji**
Ishikawa: **Daijoji**
Iwate: **Dokeiji**, **Shoboji**
Kagoshima/Okinawa: **Fukushoji**
Kanagawa: **Daihonzan Sojiji**
Kochi/Kagawa: **Hoshion-shoja**
Mie: **Kannonji**, **Koutaiji** and **Teiganji**
Miyagi: **Daimanji**
Miyazaki: **Jigenji**
Nagasaki: **Kotaiji**
Nara: **Nan'yoji**
Niigata: **Hokoji**, **Kogenji**, **Ryusen-in** and **Toryuji**
Okayama: **Toshoji**
Saitama: **Shogakuji**, **Shugenji** and **Shuko-in**
Shimane: **Tokoji**
Shizuoka: **Rinso-in**, **Sanmyoji**, **Seikenji**, **Senkoji**, **Soseiji** and **Zuiunji**
Tochigi: **Daioji**, **Joshinji** and **Kentokuji**
Tokyo: **Daihonzan Eiheiji Betsuin Chokokuji**, **Kichijoji**, **Kirigayaji** and **Kounji**
Tottori: **Daigaku-in**
Yamagata: **Gyokusenji** and **Senzoji**
Yamaguchi: **Kotakuji** and **Zenshoji**

FUKUI

Seiro-zan Tenryu-ji
(Temple of the Heavenly Dragon)
Kasuga 1-64
Matsuoka-cho, Yoshida-gun
Fukui-ken 910-1133
Japan

Tel/Fax: +81 (0)776 610471
Email: kaz@allweneedislove.org
Website: www.tenryuji.org

Buddhist – Soto Zen

Tenryu-ji temple was first built in 1653, then in 1867 fell on hard times and became uninhabited. Starting in 1979, a monks hall was built for Zen practice and the temple was re-inhabited by monks. In the temple garden, there is a stone inscribed with a poem by Matsuo Basho (1644–1694) the great master of haiku poetry who wrote one of the greatest classics in world literature, *The Narrow Road to Oku*. It is one of the most inspiring spirituality and travel books. Basho stayed at Tenryu-ji and, reluctant to leave, he left behind a poem to say so: 'I scribbled something/Planning to tear up my fan/but parting was sad.' Everyone is welcome at the temple for a short or long stay, regardless of gender, age, nationality or religion. **Highly Recommended.**

KAWAUCHI

Monastery of St Clare
715, 3 Chome, Kawauchi
Kiry-ushi
Gumma-ken 376-0041
Japan

Tel/Fax: +81 (0)27 7659100
Website: www.poorclare.org/japan

Christian – Roman Catholic – Poor Clares

This is one of a dozen Poor Clare communities in Japan. Like most Poor Clare Houses, the sisters live an enclosed life and usually receive only women as guests. Normally, they have only one or two guest rooms. If you stay with the Poor Clares, the intention of your private retreat should be one of prayer, silence, solitude and simplicity. We suggest you always write the community rather than telephone so you can explain why you particularly wish to stay with them. The Monastery of

St Clare at Kawauchi is a community of 13 sisters. All are Japanese except the Abbess. There is a Catholic liturgical hymnal used throughout Japan, as well as a musical setting for the Liturgy of the Hours. These are supplemented here with Latin and English hymns, guitar songs and older traditional hymns. In Japan, material poverty is limited so to undertake a vow of poverty has special implications. This factor is an agent in speeding up the religious discovery that true poverty is interior poverty – one of the most difficult spiritual practices undertaken by a Christian who lives in a developed consumerist country.

OHSUMI

Ohsumi Health and Wellness Retreat
Ohsumi
Kagoshima
Kyushu
Japan

Email:
info@ohsumi-retreat.org
Website: www.ohsumi-retreat.org

Open spirituality – Holistic

Ohsumi is an area within the Kagoshima prefecture, which is located in the southern tip of Kyushu Island in Japan. This region is little known by foreign tourists but is appreciated nationally by the Japanese for its beautiful landscape, various agricultural products, excellent spas, rich history and distinctive local culture, language and traditions. The Ohsumi Health and Wellness Retreat is run by Ohsumi Renaissance Association (ORA), founded and headed by Osamu (Sam) Aridome, and is a product of his long search for his mission in life. Sam offers a retreat and holistic holiday programme that includes cultural and art visits, the chance for a more intimate knowledge of local people and customs, and the experience of spas and other healing facilities. Visit the website for full details and explanations of what is on offer.

'Love is the essence of the deepest meditation'
– William Johnston, SJ

NEW ZEALAND

New Zealand has a variety of health retreats, yoga retreats, and meditation centres as well as Buddhist, Christian and eco-spirituality retreats. In such a beautiful country, which has already suffered from the effects of climate change, many places have holistic, ecological and nature themes. There are well established Christian retreat places, Buddhist and meditation centres.

COLVILLE

Mahamudra Centre
RD4, Main Road
Colville, Coromandel
New Zealand

Tel: +64 (0)7 8666851
Email: retreat@mahamudra.org.nz
Website: www.mahamudra.org.nz

Buddhist (Mahayana tradition)

You don't have to be Buddhist to visit and enjoy Mahamudra in its lovely setting. It is a Tibetan Buddhist Meditation Centre, established in 1981 under the guidance of two Tibetan lamas: Lama Thubten Yeshe and Lama Zopa Rinpoche. Mahamudra is a member of the Foundation for the Preservation of the Mahayana Tradition (FPMT), an international organisation with over 150 centres, hospices and projects worldwide. Peace, tranquillity and simplicity are the hallmarks of this centre, which offers teachings in the Buddhist way of life and the practice of meditations and devotions in the Mahayana tradition. Other centres of this foundation, plus other Buddhist centres, are listed below.

Other FPMT centres in New Zealand:

Amitabha Hospice Service, Auckland – www.amitabhahospice.org

Chandrakiriti Tibetan Buddhist Meditation Centre, Nelson – www.chandrakirti.co.nz

Dorje Chang Institute, Auckland – www.dci.org.nz

Other Buddhist centres in New Zealand:

Trashi Gomang Centre, Auckland – www.trashigomang.org.nz

Jam Tse Dhargyey Ling Centre, Whangarei – www.mandala.org.nz

COROMANDEL

Mana Retreat Centre
R.D. I
Coromandel
New Zealand

Tel: +64 (0)7 8668972
Fax: +64 (0)7 8668214
Email: be@manaretreat.com
Website: www.manaretreat.com

Yoga – Mind Body Spirit – Open spirituality

Mana is a retreat sanctuary nestled in the bush-covered hills of the Coromandel ranges. It was established for the exploration and awakening of consciousness, the unfolding of our creative and healing potential and realisation of our essential unity. Mana offers courses in many fields – voice and movement exploration, bodywork, meditation, yoga, men's and women's courses and a wide variety of programmes in the creative and healing arts. Positive personal transformation, increased creativity and wellness are the aims of all these courses and events.

THAMES

Sudarshanaloka Retreat Centre
PO Box 538
Thames 3500
New Zealand

Tel: +64 (0)7 8685341
Email: sudarshanaloka@xtra.co.nz
Website: www.sudarshanaloka.org/
sudarshanaloka.html

Buddhist – Friends of the Western Buddhist Order (FWBO)

Sudarshanaloka is a full-facility, multi-purpose retreat complex high in the Coromandel hills, overlooking Tikapa Moana. With capacity for up to 50 residents, including a limited disability suite, a library and devotional spaces, this progressively developing project provides a new Buddhist retreat facility for New Zealand and visitors interested in Buddhist practice. The centre is available for other community groups and associations to run seminars and retreats. As to the centre's situation and mission, the name implies it all, for *Sudarshanaloka* means 'land of beautiful vision'. **Highly Recommended.**

Carmelite Missionaries Center   Tel: +63 (0)46 4831003
of Spirituality   Fax: +63 (0)46 4835090
Kabangaan Road   Email: cmcs_booking@yahoo.com
Iruhin West   Website: www.cmcenterofspirituality.blogspot.com
Tagaytay City 4120
Philippines

Christian – Roman Catholic

The Carmelite Missionaries Center of Spirituality (CMCS) is a retreat and conference centre for spirituality. It is located in Iruhin West, which has a quiet atmosphere. CMCS offers a place of encounter with God and a sense of renewal. It is surrounded by a serene environment of natural beauty where one may seek clarity of spirit and renewal without distraction in a planned programme or for a time spent alone in quiet and prayer. The CMCS has other houses, including one in Kenya and other places in Africa. Clergy, religious and lay people all use this Iruhin West retreat. Everyone is welcome.

'All mystics seem to arrive at the same final vision of the reality of life, which is its universal unity – the absolute oneness of all Creation. What such men and women have to tell us makes for sacred listening'
– Stafford Whiteaker

SRI LANKA

Sri Lanka today still boasts a veritable treasure house of art and culture, beaches, cities, temples, magnificent traditional dancing and music, and wonderful processions of elephants. It is all-enchanting; little wonder that Marco Polo fell under its spell. With some 70% of the population being Buddhists, the remainder is almost equally divided between Muslims, Hindus and Christians.

BOOSA

The White House
Villa de Zoysa
Boossa
Galle District 80270
Sri Lanka

Tel: +94 (0)91 2267123
Email: info@villadezoysa.com
Website: www.villadezoysa.com

Yoga – Meditation – Buddhist influences

This is a large white colonial-type villa, built in 1927 and surrounded by its large gardens where frangipana and coconut palm trees grow in profusion. The property has been retained in the de Zoysa family ever since it was built and is unique in south Sri Lanka. Original antiques, art and crafts collections, polished hardwood beams and open courtyards and terraces present an inviting holiday environment. On offer are yoga and meditation for a maximum of 12 guests at any one time.

'Pure love has no motive, it has nothing to gain'
– Swami Vivekananda

EMBOGAMA

Ulpotha Village
Yoga and Ayurveda Centre
Embogama
Kurunegala District 60718
Sri Lanka

Tel: 0208 1233603 (UK)
Email: info@ulpotha.com
Website: www.ulpotha.com

Postal Address:
Ulpotha
36 Galle Face Court 2
Galle Road
Colombo 3
Sri Lanka

Yoga – Ayurveda – Holistic holiday

Voted one of the top 10 retreats and spas in the world by *Vogue* magazine and nominated by Virgin Holidays Responsible Tourism Awards
for Best for Conservation of Cultural Heritage, Ulpotha is a village in
its own private world with an eco-spirituality vision that influences all
it offers to its guests. To benefit fully from Ulpotha you should plan to
stay a full two weeks and try to arrange your dates to coincide with a
particular yoga teacher that you favour. All stays here begin and end on
Sundays and prices do not include travel costs. Yoga classes are usually
held in the early morning and late afternoon. All levels of experience
can be accommodated. The costs of staying are currently about £775
per person per week and in peak season the rates rise to about £900.
There is a single supplement charge and another rate for Ayurveda
treatments. For the majority of the year, when guests are absent from
Ulpotha, the village reverts back to a holistic, traditional agrarian-
based lifestyle, concentrating on farming, environmental, social and
cultural activities. Ulpotha village's farming methods, vision and their
work with rice varieties has been remarkable in terms of environment
and ecology. **Highly Recommended.**

POLWATTE

St Margaret's Convent
157 St Michael's Road
Polwatte
Colombo 3
Sri Lanka

Christian – Anglican

The Sisters of St Margaret are an Episcopal religious order of women. They run a retreat house, a children's home (mainly for those orphaned in the ongoing civil strife), a hostel for young women, a home for elderly people, and are involved in parish work and church embroidery. Women are welcome. Please write to them if you would like to stay for a personal retreat.

THAILAND

Amazing value for money, marvellous sites and cultural treasures, delicious food, and the friendly and hospitable people of Thailand, have all long been discovered by those from the West. The country is filled with tourists all year round and the choice of holidays, from yoga to gay-friendly to luxury resorts, is huge. But many still do not take advantage of retreating to one of Thailand's temples. Most Europeans just book something through a travel agent or a yoga centre or teacher, where all details and travel are covered in the best no-problem modern way of life. Yet, Thailand is the home of the Thai Forest Buddhist tradition, which has grown so rapidly in the West in terms of its monasteries and retreat centres for Buddhist teaching, study and practice. So it is worthwhile directly contacting a Thai Buddhist temple and going there to enjoy the hospitality and retreats they offer. If you are an international business traveller, Thailand is a good place to begin a new approach to your journey by staying in a monastic setting rather than yet another frankly boring if comfortable international hotel. Even if all you do at the temple is relax and rest for a couple of days, it is real break for mind, body and spirit – leaving the laptop and mobile in your suitcase. Even in the rush and thrust of global capitalism, you can still maintain some sense of inner peace and perspective in a stay that is perhaps not so market and money orientated. If you already meditate, a retreat like this can offer a deepening of your practice. If you are a tourist to Thailand, the events, journeys, adventures and discoveries are practically limitless and these too may change your perspective and bring you new awareness if you look, listen and open a compassionate heart. Try the swing and sway of a tropical forest exploration on top of an elephant.

CHAIYA

International Dhamma Hermitage Email: khun.reinhard@gmail.com
Wat Suan Mokkh Website: www.suanmokkh-idh.org
Chaiya
Surat Thani Province
Thailand

Buddhist (Theravada tradition)

Since 1989, when the Suan Mokkh International Dhamma Hermitage was founded, some 20,000 people from all over the world and many walks of life have participated in the monthly meditation retreats here, varying in age from 17 to 70 years. These 10-day silent meditation retreats are only for very serious participants. Each retreat starts on the first day of the month. Instructions are in English. Registration has to be in person on the last day of the previous month; those who arrive a day early, to better ensure being offered a place, can stay free at Suan Mokkh overnight. Do not arrive later than early afternoon on registration day. They will not accept people for less than 10 days. Besides learning and practising how to meditate, participants will get an introduction to some other aspects of the Buddha's teaching, including the Four Noble Truths, which include the Noble Eightfold Path. Before registration you will be provided with comprehensive information about what to expect. There is a pre-registration informal but compulsory personal interview with a member of staff. At this meeting you will be able to clarify any questions you may have. The centre makes it very clear: when you have been through the interview and understand what is going to happen, you should leave if you are not certain that you want to participate fully in a serious and committed manner. Suan Mokkh's library and its spiritual theatre are well known in Thai Buddhist circles. No advance bookings are possible. There are no facilities for postal, telephone or email bookings. **Highly Recommended.**

KATHU

Karuna Meditation Centre
Nakatani Village
6/30 Moo 6 Kamala
Kathu, Phuket 83150
Thailand

Tel: +66 (0)8 2803 0153 (mobile)
Email: info@meditate-thailand.com
Website: www.meditate-thailand.com

Buddhist – Non-sectarian – Holistic

Karuna Meditation Centre is one of the foremost Buddhist meditation and holistic health centres in Thailand. It is much recommended in European media. A non-sectarian Buddhist place, it operates on the principle of noble silence, which is conducive to calming and settling the mind. This fosters the development of insight. Dharma talks, yoga instruction and bi-weekly meditation interviews are when discussion and group sharing takes place. Accessible for the beaches and sea and not far from the centre of things, Karuna offers good facilities, therapies, courses and vegetarian food. **Highly Recommended.**

KHLONG LUANG

The Middle Way Meditation Retreat
The Middle Way Bangkok Office
40 Moo 8 Klong Soang
Khlong Luang, Pathum Thani 12120
Thailand

Tel: +66 (0)8 5695 1660 /
+66 (0)8 2333 3082 (mobile)
Email: info@medidationthai.org
Website:
www.meditationthai.org

Buddhist (Theravada tradition) – Dhammakaya meditation technique

Dhammakaya meditation is designed to provide balanced mind and body relaxation. The Middle Way Meditation Retreat offers a sanctuary for meditation in a situation of beautiful hills and green scenery with planned seven-day retreats. They offer a English-language meditation course almost every month.

KOH PHANGAN

Monte Vista Retreat Center   Tel: +66 (0)77 238951
162/1 Nai Wok Beach Moo 1   Email: montevistathailand@yahoo.com
Koh Phangan   Website: www.montevistathailand.com
Surat Thani 84280
Thailand

Mind Body Spirit – Yoga

Here is a safe haven in a tranquil, pleasant situation where you can detox, get some various therapies and generally relax and renew mind, body and spirit. There are daily morning yoga sessions in a group and evening meditations. Monte Vista is located five minutes' walk from the beach for swimming, surfing and just playing about. Other activities, include hiking in the jungle, movies, diving, wakeboarding, kayaking, snorkelling or watching an authentic Muay Thai Boxing Match. The centre offers a number of therapies and treatments including oil massage, aromatherapy massage, Ayurvedic massage and head massage, Reiki, Thai foot massage, yoga Nidra, colonic treatment, dietary consultation, Mandala painting, biomat treatment and a Create Your Own Yoga Retreat. A guest package usually includes three meals per day, lodging, one daily treatment, daily yoga and daily meditation. A good slogan for a retreat at Monte Vista would be 'Finding Harmony'.

KOH SAMUI

Health Oasis Resort   Tel: +66 (0)77 420124
26/4 Moo 6   Fax: +66 (0)77 420125
Maenam, Koh Samui   Email: contactus@healthoasisresort.com
Surat Thani 84330   Website: www.healthoasisresort.com
Thailand

Holistic Health – Spa

Health Oasis Resort is a well-established detox and healing spa, right on the beachfront of the tropical island of Koh Samui on the south-east coast of Thailand. It is the only licensed traditional medicine hospital in Koh Samui and one of a few such facilities in Thailand. Health Oasis has two traditional medicine doctors on its staff and offers Thai traditional herbs and certified training in Thai traditional massage. Detox, supervised fasting, hydrotherapy, naturopathy, iridology, aura light readings, personal counselling, yoga, meditation, hypnotherapy, Reiki, and Swedish and Thai massage are all on offer. Standard and deluxe rooms and a three-bedroom house are available, all in a traditional Thai presentation. It also has a vegetarian restaurant. **Highly Recommended.**

NON TONG

Lisu Hill Tribe Experience.
Non Tong
Near Soppong (Pangmapha)
Maehongson Province
Thailand

Tel: +66 (0)8 9998 4886 (mobile)
Email: homestay@lisuhilltribe.com
Website: www.lisuhilltribe.com

Shamanism – Animism with Buddhism and Christianity –
Vipassana meditation

American holistic health therapist Albert Schmaedick and his wife Susanan, who is a member of the Lisu mountain people, set up this retreat a few years ago. Its aim is to help save the Lisu people's way of life and their traditional ways of healing. The Lisu traditionally follow the Animist spirituality path, which is similar to Native American spirituality and other aboriginal tribal cultures. Today, many Lisu have become Buddhist or Christian. The concept of this retreat is that you live with a Lisu family in a traditional bamboo or teak house and experience their lifestyle and village life – working, eating and playing their way. You can experience healing methods and wild edible cuisine, and there are courses and workshops in traditional handicrafts, natural healing, dancing and more taught by the Hill Tribe people themselves. Consultations with the local shamans are possible but must be arranged in advance.

THALANG

(V)

Phuket International Academy
(PIA): Mind Centre
115/15 Moo 7 Thepkasattri Road
Thepkasattri, Thalang
Phuket 83110
Thailand

Tel: +66 (0)76 336000
Fax: +66 (0)76 336081
Email:
info@phuketinternationalacademy.com
Email for retreat applications:
ksnow@sbinstitute.com (Put 'Phuket' in the Subject line)
Website: www.phuketinternationalacademy.com

Meditation – Mind Body Spirit – Buddhist traditions

Could this be one of the world's most exciting new developments in meditation retreats and training and the scientific investigation of meditation itself? Klaus Hebben, a German businessman and philanthropist as well as a sincere Buddhist practitioner, with Dr Alan Wallace of the **Santa Barbara Institute for Consciousness Studies** in California, is building a mind-training centre in Phuket, where long-term retreats, say of 80 days, can be held on a regular basis under Wallace's supervision. The meditation centre will be part of a larger complex, which includes a state-of-the-art school for children aged 3–18 and a world-class athletic training centre, where Olympic-level candidates can do winter training. Dr Wallace began leading eight-week retreats there in 2010.

The founders sum up what they are trying to do here as follows: 'The Phuket Mind Research and Development Academy offers a wide range of training to enhance the cognitive and emotional faculties of its participants. The foundation of such training is focused on the development of attention skills, which are needed for all meaningful human endeavours. Methods are also taught for cultivating mindfulness, empathy, compassion and emotional balance in order to fully unveil the inner resources of the human mind.'

The 40-room academy has a spacious meeting hall and dining facility, as well as a state-of-the-art cognitive scientific research laboratory. Here the effects of such mental training is investigated by leading scientists from around the world, and their insights, both pedagogical and physical, enhance the education provided in PIA Day School and in the PIA Sports, Arts and Wellness Centre, while also enriching the training offered in PIA Mind Centre itself.

The Phuket International Academy complex occupies a valley in the north east of Phuket Island, which is off the south-west coast of Thailand. Given that Dr Wallace has a distinguished reputation as a monk, scholar, teacher and researcher – and his articles about meditation and his work are known and respected worldwide – we suspect that his retreats will be fully booked at least a year in advance. We hope this is so and that the founding vision of these two Buddhist practitioners will be fully realised in the years to come to the benefit of all of us.

'Elected silence, sing to me
And beat upon my whorled ear,
Pipe me to pastures still and be
The music that I care to hear'
– Gerald Manley Hopkins

YOGA CENTRES

Yoga is a practice that involves the body, the mind and the spirit. It is a spiritual tradition that is thousands of years old. Many people practise yoga to keep fit, but yoga is much more than that – it can calm you and help both physical and emotional healing. There are many local yoga classes as well as clubs and groups throughout Britain and across Europe. Most of these do not own a meeting centre of their own, so they meet in various venues from halls to community and local leisure centres and modern health and fitness clubs. Educational authorities now commonly include yoga classes in their adult and evening education programmes. The following is a selection of places around Britain and Ireland where you can find yoga courses and classes. Check out retreat places we have listed under other countries, such as Greece, since many places in such sunny climates offer yoga. The integration of yoga and the re-establishment of meditation as tools in the Christian spiritual journey has taken a long time, but it has now arrived with both being widely offered in traditionally religious retreat places.

BRITAIN

The **British Wheel of Yoga** (BWY) is the information centre for yoga in Britain. It has a nationwide network of teachers and representatives, who are available to help you at a local level.

British Wheel of Yoga (Central Office)
25 Jermyn Street
Sleaford
Lincolnshire NG34 7RU
England

Tel: 01529 306851
Fax: 01529 303233
Email: office@bwy.org.uk
Website: www.bwy.org.uk

ENGLAND

•••

LONDON

Always at the heart of things, London has classes and courses in special yoga centres, dance studios, gyms, alternative therapy centres, health associations, church halls and private homes. The available classes and places is almost without limit.

Affinity Yoga (throughout London). Tel: 0208 9653380. Email: info@ affinityyoga.com. Website: www.affinityyoga.com

Anja Yoga, SW16. Contact: Anja Lange. Tel: 07963 820702. Email: info@ yogaembodied.com. Website: www.yogaembodied.com

The Chi Kri School of Yoga, Harrow, Middlesex. Contact: Neil Patel. Tel: 0208 4277755; Mobile: 07956 608899. Email: neil@chikri.com. Website: www.chikri.com

Ealing Yoga, W5. Contact: Angela Bradbury. Mobile: 07717 221756. Email: info@ealingyoga.co.uk. Website: www.ealingyoga.co.uk

Himalayan Institute of Yoga Science and Philosophy. Tel/Fax: 0208 5678889. Email: enquiries@himalayaninstitute.org.uk. Website: www. himalayaninstitute.org.uk

Life Centre, W8. Tel: 0207 2214602. Email: info@thelifecentre.com. Website: www.thelifecentre.org

London School of Yoga, NW11. Contact: Melissa Freedman. Mobile: 07737 921129. Email: melissafreedman@hotmail.co.uk. Website: www. londonschoolofyoga.com

The Loving Heart Centre, NW6. Email: love@lovingheartcentre.net. Website: www.lovingheartcentre.net

Iyengar Yoga Institute Maida Vale, W9. Tel: 0207 6243080. Email: office@iyi.org.uk. Website: www.iyi.org.uk

Satyananda Yoga Centre, SW12. Tel: 0208 6734869. Email: enquiries@ syclondon.com. Website: www.syclondon.com

School of Yoga, Westminster and Croydon. Tel: 0208 6573258. Email: more_info@schoolofyoga.co.uk. Website: www.schoolofyoga.co.uk

GO-Yoga: West London Yoga Shala, W12. Mobile: 07803 032463. Email: amandagoyoga@live.co.uk. Website: www.go-yoga.co.uk

Yoga for the Mind (numerous locations in London). Mobile: 07988 821323. Email: email@yogaforthemind.info. Website: www.yogaforthemind.info

BERKSHIRE

Berks Yoga Teacher's Circle. Contact: Sylvia Smith. Tel: 01344 772298. Email: sylviasmith@qiyoga.co.uk

BRISTOL AND NORTH SOMERSET

Centre for Yoga Studies, Bristol. Mobile: 07768 278728. Email: info@yogastudies.org. Website: www.yogastudies.org

Yogaliving, Bath. Contact: Derek Thorne. Tel: 01761 470819. Email: admin@yogaliving.co.uk. Website: www.yogaliving.co.uk

BUCKINGHAMSHIRE

North Buckinghamshire Yoga Association. Contact: Carol Smith. Tel: 01908 643171. Email: yoginicarol@talktalk.net

CAMBRIDGESHIRE

Cambridge Yoga and Fitness. Contact: Liz Smith. Tel: 01223 811936. Website: www.cambridgeyogaandfitness.org

CHESHIRE

Cheshire Yoga Teachers' Association. Contact: Christine Royle. Tel: 01619 738319. Website: www.cyta.org.uk

CORNWALL

Newquay Bowen Clinic and Yoga Studio, Cornwall. Contact: Pam Luker. Tel: 01637 870548. Email: pamullola@btinternet.com. Website: www.newquaybowenclinic.co.uk

DURHAM

Darlington Yoga Group. Contact: June Hirst. Email: june@jhirst. orangehome.co.uk. Website: www.dyg.org.uk

DERBYSHIRE

Derbyshire Yoga Teachers' Association, Chesterfield. Contact: Chris Jolly. Tel: 0115 9329431.

DEVON

Devon School of Yoga, Sidmouth. Tel/Fax: 01392 420573. Email: info@ devonyoga.com. Website: www.devonyoga.com

Devon Yoga Teachers' Federation. Contact: Barbara Cooper. Tel: 01752 794605. Email: barbarac0@blueyonder.co.uk.

Yogi Ma Lakshmi, Exeter. Contact: Yogi Ma Lakshmi. Mobile: 07971 686889. Email: saleeslight@btinternet.com. Website: www.saleeslight.com

ESSEX

Iyengar Yoga Centre for Essex, Chelmsford. Email: info@iyce.com. Website: www.iyce.com

Satyananda Yoga Centre, Colchester. Contact: Swami Yoga Prakash. Tel: 01206 823383.

School for Living Yoga, Loughton. Tel: 0208 5024270. Website: www. yogauk.com/links/organisations

HAMPSHIRE

Karuna Yoga School, Southampton. Contact: Paul Riddy. Tel: 0238 0773987. Website: www.karunayoga.co.uk

Satchidananda Wholistic Trust, Alton. Contact: Swami Satchidananda Ma. Tel: 01420 562027. Email: info@swtrust.org. Website: www.swtrust. org

Sukha Yoga Club, Basingstoke. Contact: Jane Roberson. Tel: 01256 762891. Website: www.janerobersonyoga.co.uk

KENT

Mid-Kent Yoga School (Iyengar Yoga), West Malling. Contact: Lin Craddock. Tel: 01622 820190. Email: lin@iyengar-yoga.co.uk. Website: www.iyengar-yoga.co.uk

Viniyoga in Kent, Deal. Contact: Jennifer Bentley. Mobile: 07947 636576. Website: www.jenniferbentley.co.uk

LANCASHIRE

Oswaldtwistle Yoga Group. Contact: Julie Hill. Tel: 01254 396182. Email: jyhill56@hotmail.com. Website: www.pendlelife.co.uk/roundabout/ opencms/directory/health/yogawithjulie

LEICESTERSHIRE

Keythorpe Yoga, Yoga Retreats. Contact: Sarah Cawkwell. Tel: 0116 2593748. Website: www.keythorpeyoga.co.uk

Leicestershire Yoga Circle, Judgemeadow Community College. Contact: Janine Wilson. Tel: 0116 2433512. Email: jay.pawpies@tiscali.co.uk.

LIVERPOOL AND MERSEYSIDE

Ashtanga Yoga, Liverpool. Contact: Helen Aldred. Mobile: 07861 242773. Email: yoga@planetholistics.co.uk. Website: www.planetholistics.co.uk

British Wheel of Yoga – Hatha Yoga. Contact: Justine Aldersey-Williams. Mobile: 07005 801124. Email: justine@yogawirral.co.uk. Website: www.yogawirral.co.uk

Liverpool Wellbeing and Yoga Centre. Tel: 0151 7099169. Email: info@liverpoolwellbeing.com. Website: www.liverpoolwellbeing.com/centre

Merseyside Yoga Association. Contact: Janet Irlam. Tel: 01516 526343. Website: www.yogauk.com/links/organisations.htm

MANCHESTER

Manchester and District Instutute of Iyengar Yoga. Contact: Janice Yates. Tel: 0161 3390748. Email: janice.yates@sky.com. Website: www.mdiiy.org.uk

NORFOLK

Bliss Yoga, Norwich. Contact: Jessica McKenna. Email: Jessica@blissyoganorwich.co.uk. Website: www.blissyoganorwich.co.uk

Norfolk Yoga Group. Contact: Hilary Norman. Tel/Fax: 01953 885122. Email: Hilary@norfolkyoga.co.uk. Website: www.norfolkyoga.co.uk/classes.php

Yoga for Wellbeing, Norwich. Contact: Caroline Horrocks. Mobile: 0775 4116410. Email: info@yoga4wellbeing.com. Website: www.yoga4wellbeing.com

OXFORDSHIRE

Ruth White Yoga Centre, Oxfordshire. Contact: Ruth White. Tel: 01993 831032; Fax: 01993 831400. Email: info@ruthwhiteyoga.com. Website: www.ruthwhiteyoga.com

SOMERSET

Self-Realization Meditation Healing Centre, Queen Camel. Tel: 01935 850266. Email: info@selfrealizationcentres.org. Website: www.selfrealizationcentres.org

SUFFOLK

Radha House, Pakefield. Contact: Jayne Boys. Tel: 01502 513859. Email: radha.bg@lineone.net. Website: radha.org/wordpress-mu/jamesward76

SUSSEX

Bihar School of Yoga, Worthing. Tel: 01903 820525. Email: enquiries@yogaworthing.com. Website: www.yogaworthing.com

Patanjali Yoga Centre and Ashram, Battle. Contact: Sri Indar Nath. Tel: 01424 870538. Website: www.patanjali-centre.org.uk

Pure Yoga Bliss, Hove. Contact: Gina Leung. Mobile: 07972 789554. Email: pureyogabliss@gmail.com. Website: www.pureyogabliss.com

YORKSHIRE

Ashtanga Power Yoga, York. Contact: Rob Leadley. Tel: 01904 632104. Email: cityyoga@yahoo.com. Website: www.yogayork.com

Raja Yoga (Seven Spiritual Laws of Yoga), Haworth and Keighley, West Yorkshire. Contact: Sheila Murray. Tel: 01535 648761. Email: Sheila@sheilamurray.co.uk. Website: www.sheilamurray.co.uk

WEST MIDLANDS

Birmingham and District Institute of Iyengar Yoga. Contact: Jayne Orton. Tel: 0121 6082229. Email: info@iyengaryoga.uk.com. Website: www.iyengaryoga.uk.com

Parkdale Yoga Centre, Wolverhampton. Contact: Pete Yates or Anna Ingham. Tel: 01902 424048. Email: info@heartyoga.co.uk. Website: www.heartyoga.co.uk

Satyananda Yoga Centre, Birmingham. Tel: 0845 4582967.
Email: mail@sycbirmingham.com. Website: www.sycbirmingham.com

WILTSHIRE

The European Shiatsu School (residential courses), Shaw. Tel:
01323 430025. Website: www.shiatsu.net

WINCHESTER

Yogamania Namaste, Winchester, Hants. Contact: Samantha Lee. Tel:
01962 761853; Mobile: 07884 384399. Email: yogamaniac@hotmail.com.
Website: homepages.tesco.net/supersoulfighter/yogamania.htm

WALES

Abergavenny Natural Therapy Centre. Tel: 01873 858391.
Website: www.thebestof.co.uk/local/abergavenny/business-guide/feature/
abergavenny-natural-therapy-centre/40510

Mandala Yoga Ashram, Llandeilo. Tel/Fax: 01558 685358. Email:
email@mandalayoga.freeserve.co.uk. Website: www.mandalayoga.net

SCOTLAND

Dhanakosa Buddhist Retreat and Yoga Centre, Scotland. Tel: 01877
384213. Email: info@dhanakosa.com. Website: www.dhanakosa.com

Glasgow Yoga Centre, Glasgow. Tel: 0141 4295170. Email: info@
yoginirmalendu.com. Website: www.yoginirmalendu.com

Personal Session Yoga, Glasgow. Contact: Simone Moir. Tel: 0141
5524420. Email: simoneyoga@myoneonone.com. Website: www.
myoneonone.com

IRELAND

An Sanctoir, Cork. Tel: +353 (0)28 37155. Email: ansanctoir@gmail.com. Website: www.ansanctoir.ie

East Clare Yoga Centre, County Clare. Contact: Susanne. Tel: +353 (0)61 640923. Email: info@eastclareyoga.com. Website: www. eastclareyoga.com

Viniyoga Ireland, Dublin. Contact: Hanne Gillespie. Tel: +353 (0)1 2889012. Email: hanneg@eircom.net. Website: www.yoga-ireland.com/classes/dsouth.htm

Yoga Fellowship of Northern Ireland, Rathfriland. Contact: Jane Wright. Tel: 028 91889219. Email: info@yfni.co.uk. Website: www.yfni.co.uk

A SPIRITUAL NOTEBOOK

CONTEMPLATIVE DIALOGUE WITH RELIGION AND SCIENCE

Elizabeth West

The modern age demands new thinking to make Christianity meaningful to modern scientific people. Views of God and the universe have changed radically through the discoveries of science. The vastness of the cosmos as we now understand it makes adherence to a very anthropomorphic view of God difficult. This is an area where I think the Eastern religions, and Buddhism in particular, can help. The Buddhist view of the cosmos is even bigger than that of science and is cyclical in nature. There are many practices within Buddhism that do not demand any type of belief system, but rather help us to explore the nature of reality in order to recognize the hidden assumptions we have that may prevent us from opening to the true nature of that reality. Contemplative practice is a major tool for such spiritual exploration.

These days there is a growing urgent awareness of the need for humanity to change if we are to survive on the planet. Many believe, and I am one of them, that the only hope humanity has of changing quickly enough is through a renaissance in such contemplative practice. There is certainly a new interest in it within the Christian tradition – a tradition very much neglected since the time of the reformation. Everywhere we see new editions of the writings of mystics who experienced the fruits of contemplation. However there is another dimension that is equally important, and that is what we in the West can learn from the East.

This is just the tip of the iceberg in terms of where this dialogue can lead us. Modern science – in particular quantum theory – points to a non-dual universe, as do Eastern religions. There are hints of it in Christianity, but it has not been well developed. It is another vast area to be explored in depth in dialogue.

Elizabeth West, a former Christian nun who has close links with the Bede Griffiths Sangha in India, the World Community for Christian Meditation, and the Awakened Heart Sangha, formed the Buddhist Christian Network in 1999. The Network publishes a newsletter and holds seminars and workshops. www.buddhist-christian.org

SILENCE AND SOLITUDE: EARLY AND LATE

Paul A. & Karen Karper Fredette

How many of us can remember looking for a hidden place when we were children? A place where no one would look for us, where we could be alone? For some of us, it didn't have to be far away. A place beneath the front porch or a shady spot between the hedge and the house would do. What mattered was that no one else knew of it and that we could sneak off to our hidey-hole whenever we wished. We didn't need to stay there for long; it was enough to know our special place was there whenever we felt overwhelmed by people or noise or too much activity swirling around us.

As a very small child, I would hide under the hydrangea bushes that grew along the edge of the yard. There, in my quiet place, I would dream or play with an imaginary friend or talk with the God who my mother said, always hears us. Gradually my secret place became less of a place to play and more consciously a place to pray. I needed such a solitary spot and would look for one whenever we moved to another house. I believe this need contained the seeds that, in later life, sprouted and grew into my hermit vocation.

Not everyone is called to be a hermit but I believe we all need a certain degree of solitude – a time and place where we can be alone, where we can be ourselves and where we can listen with more attention to the inner dialogue with the Divine that is always murmuring beneath the surface of our active, problem-solving mind. For some individuals, the need to be alone is satisfied with occasional times spent apart from the members of our household – a weekend retreat at set intervals or a yearly vacation that allows us to be still and contemplate the beauty of a lakeside vista or stretch our eyes upward to mountain heights.

Most of us will realize that our private place requires not only solitude but also silence. Noise can be as invasive to our inner world as the 'chatty Kathy' who too frequently knocks at our kitchen door or rings our phone just when we had hoped for some needed quiet time. Until we learn that we have not only a need but a *right* to personal times of refreshment and renewal, we will (to our own detriment) allow the unwanted caller to take away what little solitude we had carved out of our day. It requires a special strength of character to turn off our cell phone or inform the surprise guest that we are not available at this time. We are not being selfish; we are becoming self-saving.

Before long, we may realize that the solitude we have carved into our daily routine and the silence that opens our inner senses to the Divine whisper is the best part of our day. At this point, some of us may recognize we are being called to a special vocation, that of a hermit. We may find ways to live our eremitical calling hidden in the everyday hum of the city. Or we will have to take more drastic steps to guarantee the solitude and silence we crave. Some of us will find a place off the beaten track where our very obscurity will become a gift to the world. Through us the sweet grace of the Holy will flow in quiet streams to many thirsting souls.

Paul A. & Karen Karper Fredette *minister to hermits worldwide through their quarterly newsletter,* Raven's Bread, *and are the authors of* Consider the Ravens, On Contemporary Hermit Life, *iUniverse, USA 2008.*

RETREATS FOR GAY MEN AND LESBIAN WOMEN
Urs Mattmann

Special retreats for Lesbian, Gay, Bisexual and Trans-sexual people offer the opportunity to help such men and women to discover where they are on their journey as spiritual beings in this world. There can be opportunities to discover sexual orientation as a source of strength and to connect with and re-discover their potential as people who are loved and capable of loving others, with a contribution to make to the world. It is a secure space in which to talk about religious feelings and experiences.

While Christian spirituality is universal, it is also incarnated into specific and diverse life situations. For example, in Advent we can remember that Christ was born in the midst of outcasts of his time, yet the angels announced his birth and wise men came to visit him. As gay men and women of faith, we too experience that the religions of our time do not necessarily want us in their midst, yet we find our place, trust our journey and are blessed.

In the past decades, a large worldwide Gay and Lesbian movement has evolved. This progress toward the integration of homosexuality as an acceptable social and human reality is an evolutionary step of justice and compassion, just as were the abolition of slavery and the liberation of women. Yet important questions about the spirituality of gay people have not yet been raised, which is not surprising given the homophobic context of much religion. Gays and lesbians, of course, often go to traditional spiritual retreats, yet they can hardly expect that gay spiritual concerns will be addressed. In my experience, the majority of retreat teachers and leaders, while not making obvious homophobic remarks, still all too often make the assumption that everybody in the retreat group is heterosexual.

It is therefore important that there are retreats for Gay and Lesbian people just as there are specific ones today for women only, or for men or people in the Third Age or people with special issues such as bereavement or long-term disability.

In a gay retreat a person is free to ask questions like: *What is the deeper spiritual meaning of being gay and what are its gifts? Is there a special calling for Gay people? How do we deal with wounds from encounters with homophobic religious people and institutions? How can Gay people create inclusive religious language or spiritually-informed gay sexual ethics?* It's about having space and listening to God in a spiritual setting relevant to gays and lesbians.

Just as at other retreats, retreats for LGB people can offer group discussions, lectures, guided visualisations and meditations, contemplation and bodywork, chakra work and rituals, liturgies and worship services. Such retreats are now available in Christian, Buddhist and non-denominational programmes.

Urs Mattmann *was for many years a member of an ecumenical European Christian Church Order. He is a social worker and Psychosynthesis counsellor with a background in Christian spirituality and meditation and is the author of* Coming In: Gays and Lesbians Reclaiming the Spiritual Journey, *published by the Iona Community's Wild Goose Publications. Email: umattmann@btinternet.com*

LIVING IN COMMUNITY

Anna Howard

Communities vary enormously in size, in intention and in structure. Some have a spiritual focus, others an ecological one. Some are self-sufficient, others rely on the financial independence of each person or family living there. What they seem to have in common is a collective intention to live and practise a way of life that deviates from the cultural norm. Very often the desire to live in, or set up, community comes from a disillusionment with society and a longing to live with others in more creative, sustainable, nourishing and fulfilling ways. Increasingly there is a recognition that if we are to survive and thrive as human beings on Earth, we need to cooperate and co-create with each other, and living in community offers a very real opportunity to do this.

The Abbey in Sutton Courtney is one such community. We live and work together as a mixed lay community, supported by a body of volunteers and a Council of Trustees. Each one of us is very different and it is those differences that make community life at best rich, inspiring and meaningful and at worst full of conflict and potential atrophy. There is a commitment here to work with the 'shadow', to face conflict, to support creativity and individual wellbeing, to encourage spiritual growth, to offer our time and work in service to others. We don't have a single spiritual tradition or path that we all follow. This has advantages and disadvantages, but it is the shared commitment to the core values of compassion, tolerance, honesty and enquiry that permeates our community life and generates an atmosphere of 'lived spirituality'. It is also the sense of humour needed and often generated by the awareness of how often we fail that lifts the spirit more than any fulfillment of spiritual ideals!

For the outsider looking in, community life – whether it is a lay or monastic one – often takes on a kind of mystique; dreams of Utopia flourish in those that visit for a few hours or days. But stay a little longer and the dream soon gives way to the reality of rubbing up against our wounds, dark sides and egos. The reality of living in community can be as painful as any other way of life. Yet, with the right tools and a sincere intention, many of the pitfalls that sabotage our longed-for peace and happiness can be worked through in transformative ways.

Anna Howard *was educated at Oxford University and has been a student of Tibetan Buddhism for 13 years, included two years at Kagyu Samye Ling Tibetan Monastery. She is currently a member of the Abbey community.*

GLOSSARY

Alexander Technique: Gentle manipulation that guides the body into a more natural posture and relaxed state, bringing awareness of how to do the same by yourself.

Aromatherapy: A holistic treatment that helps many conditions. Essential oils are selected for each person's needs and gently massaged into the skin, which absolves it into the body.

Ayurveda: An ancient Indian system of medicine that uses the principles of nature to help promote and maintain health by keeping the individual in equilibrium with nature. Ayurvedic treatments aim to cleanse and heal mind, body and spirit.

Bahá'í: This religion's key beliefs are in one God, the unity of mankind, independent investigation of truth, the common foundation of all religions, the harmony of science and religion, equality of opportunity for men and women, elimination of all prejudices, universal education, abolition of the extremes of poverty and wealth, establishment of world peace, and the concept of progressive revelation.

Buddhism, Buddha: Buddhism has no personal deity. It makes no claim to have a divinely inspired book and it has no central organising authority. The teachings of Buddhism are an inheritance from Siddhartha Gautama's own search for truth. He was believed to be *enlightened*, that is to be a Buddha. Thus the emphasis for Buddhists is on a tradition of teachings. While they begin by learning about these teachings, in the end each individual must discover their own experience of truth and what it has taught them. The *Noble Eightfold Path* in Buddhist teachings is concerned with wisdom, morality, concentration and meditation. Central to Buddhism is meditation, of which there are various methods.

Catholic Church: There are some 22 Catholic Churches in a federation under the Bishop of Rome, the Pope. These Catholic Churches are different in their implementation of the same religion in terms of their spirituality, advanced theology, liturgical services, liturgical calendar, saints, rules, regulations, customs, history and languages. In theological terms, *all* Catholics accept the definitions, creeds and canon laws of the first seven Ecumenical Councils, which form the basis of the books that we know today as *The New Testament*.

Charismatic retreat: Christian healing retreat that may involve praying in tongues and prophecy.

Choir: A body of singers assisting at Divine Office. Lay singers are usually the choir at church services, but the choir in a monastery usually consists of the religious members of that community.

Christianity, Christian life: The common focus of Christianity is on the person of Jesus of Nazareth. He is seen as the criterion by which all of life is to be evaluated. The universal significance of Jesus is always asserted. The name *Christians* was originally given to early followers of Jesus who believed him to be the *Christ* or Messiah. Christ's role is seen as that of redeemer of all humanity.

Community: In the Christian sense, a group of people who live together under a common rule, usually but not always with obedience to one person, who worship together and whose lives are devoted to seeking God. Buddhist communities live the same way but the goal is different. It is traditional for communities to be of either men or women, but this is not always so. There are lay people who also live together with much the same purpose or based on various spiritual visions and ideas.

Compline: The last prayer at night in the Catholic and Anglican liturgy.

Contemplative: A person devoted to religious meditation, who gives seeking God as the primary purpose and aim of his or her life.

Contemplative prayer: Contemplative prayer is silent and based not on knowing *about* God, but on knowing God.

Counselling: A form of helping people with various personal or relationship problems through understanding, and empathic and uncritical listening. This approach is combined with helping the person to clarify the problem and decide what action to take.

Cursillo: A renewal weekend retreat for Christians to try to experience their religion from new perspectives.

De Mello retreats: Anthony de Mello SJ was a popular spiritual guide who wrote a number of books of methods and practices for increasing prayer, meditation and deepening the inner self through various exercises and stories for reflection.

Dharma: Dharma is the intrinsic property of something, the thing that holds it together, that which sustains it. Thus it is the essential, final character of something, including a person. For example, the dharma of water is its wetness. Used in both Hindu and Buddhist traditions to represent the truth or spiritual teachings.

Directed retreat: A 6- to 8-day retreat consisting of silent prayer and deep inner reflection, including a daily meeting with a spiritual director. An Ignatian retreat is usually a directed one.

Divine Office, Canonical Hours, Liturgy of the Hours, Offices: All these terms are used to describe the official daily prayer cycle of the Catholic Church, which is an adaptation of the liturgy of the Jewish synagogue that has evolved over the centuries. The *hours* consist of seven or eight periods of prayer, which may be chanted, sung or spoken together in a group or individually. These are called Virgils, Lauds, Terce, Sext, None, Vespers and Compline. A version is used by the Anglican Church, usually referred to as Morning Prayer and Evensong. The liturgy is built around psalms, songs and words from scripture. The Divine Office provides the daily prayer structure for monastic life.

Druidry: This is considered by many to be the native spirituality of ancient Britain. Based on the relationship between the individual and the spirits of nature, it has evolved from a magical pagan religion into a modern ethical concept and practice of living in a sacred manner.

Eco-spirituality: A spirituality based on relating our inner self and the way we live to Earth, the natural world and all other creatures. Through realising our connection to Earth, we may deepen the universality of our spirituality. Eco-spirituality is mirrored in Celtic spirituality.

Ecumenical, Ecumenical Movement: The movement in the Christian Church towards the visible union of all believers in Christ. This aspiration for unity is an old one and widely popular today. A retreat house or retreat programme that is *ecumenical* is open to all of Christian faith no matter to which church they belong.

Enclosure: The practice of taking religious vows and remaining within a religious house without excursions into the outside world. Enclosed communities are sexually segregated. Today some communities are semi-enclosed; that is, the members leave the convent or monastery only rarely and for specific necessary purposes, such as visits to the dentist.

Enneagram: The Enneagram is a method intended to help you see yourself in the mirror of your mind, especially seeing images of your personality that have become distorted by your basic attitudes to yourself. The Enneagram is reputed to have originated in Afghanistan some 200 years ago or perhaps in the early years of Christian influence in Persia. It then moved to the Indian subcontinent where it remained an oral tradition known to Sufi masters. Representing a journey into self, the purpose of the Enneagram is self-enlightenment. According to this system, there are nine types of human personality. These each have a basic compulsion to behave in a certain way and this behaviour is maintained through a defence mechanism that avoids any change. For example, there are personality types who avoid at all cost anger or failure or weakness or conflict. The Enneagram technique leads to self-criticism which, in turn, leads to self-discovery. From there, a person may gain a freedom from the negative aspects of self and thus open the way to deeper faith. Advocates of this spiritual exercise believe its careful study results in a new self-understanding and provides practical guidelines for healing.

Eucharist: The word means 'thanksgiving' and is the term applied to the central act of Christian worship, instituted by Christ who *gave thanks*, and because the service is the supreme act of Christian thanksgiving to God. Other names used are *Holy Communion*, *The Lord's Supper* and the *Mass*. Bread and wine are used in an act of sacred consecration and prayer to form the service of thanksgiving.

Evangelical: Evangelicals are Christians who try to live according to the Christian scriptures viewed as the supreme authority for Christian life. They feel strongly called upon to help bring others into the Christian Church by means of evangelism (meaning 'good news') by sharing what Christians believe God has done in and through Jesus Christ.

Fellowship of Contemplative Prayer: An association of individuals and groups who follow the way of prayer taught by the founder, Robert Coulson, which is called *The Prayer of Stillness.* Groups and retreats are largely self-run. There are various publications available and retreats offered around the country. For details, contact: Fellowship of Contemplative Prayer, 202 Ralph Road, Solihull, West Midlands B90 3LE, England (Tel/Fax: 0121 7456522).

Forms of address in religions: The Pope and the Dalai Lama are addressed as *His Holiness.* In Islam, when using the word *Allah,* whether spoken or written, the correct phrase is: 'Allah, most gracious, most merciful.' If you speak of Muhammad, the correct phrase is: 'Muhammad, peace be upon him.' When speaking of Jesus Christ, it is acceptable to refer to him as *Jesus, Jesus Christ, Christ, Lord Jesus* or *the Christ.* You can refer to a monk as *Brother* even if he should turn out to be a priest with the title of *Father.* Nuns are called *Sister.* A Christian religious superior of a monastery is called according to the status of his or her monastery. For example if it is an abbey, he is called *Abbot* or *Father Abbot* and she is *Abbess* or *Mother Abbess.* The superior of a priory is known as *Prior* and *Father Prior* or *Prioress* and *Mother Prioress.* Religious superiors of less grand establishments are simply called

Father, Father Superior or *Brother* and women superiors are addressed as *Mother Superior.* These titles will serve you in most religious retreat houses. When you hear any variation, change accordingly to match the common usage of the place.

Guided retreat: A retreat that is guided from time to time by a spiritual director, but not on a daily basis as for a directed retreat (see above).

Hajj: The Hajj is a pilgrimage to the Kaaba (see below) made by millions of Muslims each year. It is performed to commemorate the struggles of Abraham, Ismail and Hagar in submitting their wills to God.

Hermitage Retreats, Poustinia, Poustinia Experience: *Poustinia* is a Russian word meaning 'hermitage'. These were originally little isolated huts, located deep in the forests of Russia. What they offered were total silence, solitude and the uninterrupted time to seek God. Today there are a few of these in Britain and Ireland, usually in the form of a self-catering cottage or a small caravan parked outside a monastery in a field.

Hinduism, Hindus: The Hindu tradition allows the use of various symbols, names, terms and images that may help people to discover the divine. Within the religion, there are both those who believe in one God and for whom there is a distinction between God and the world, and those who believe that God is simultaneously both one and many. A number of central values are shared by most Hindus, although in practice they may differ in interpretation. These key ideals and values include respect for parents and elders, reverence for teachers, regard for guests, vegetarianism, non-violence, tolerance of other races and religions, the sanctity of marriage, the discouragement of all pre-marital and extra-marital sexual relationships, the sacredness of the cow, and an appreciation of the equality and sanctity of all living beings.

Icon: A painting or enamel that represents a saint or other sacred person. Icon painting retreats use the painting of the icon as a structure and centring for prayer. Making one is called 'icon writing'.

Inter-denominational: Common to several religious denominations.

Inter-faith: Common to several different religions. An inter-faith retreat would be one held with members of two or more faiths.

Ignatian Exercises, Saint Ignatius of Loyola: St Ignatius (1491–1556) was founder of the Society of Jesuits. He wrote *Spiritual Exercises,* which has remained one of the great Christian spirituality practices for deepening faith and inner awareness of God. Ignatian retreats are usually 8, 10 or 30 days or 3 months in duration and have recently regained much of their former popularity. A spiritual director is assigned to guide you through it. There is much solitude and silence so that time and space is given over to meditation and reflection.

Islam, Muslim: Islam is monotheistic and Allah, most gracious, most merciful, is all-merciful, all-powerful and all-present. He controls and sustains the universe and, although humans may choose which path of life to follow, all eventually return to God, to whom they are accountable. Islam rests on seven basic beliefs: the oneness of God, the books revealed by God, belief in the prophets, the angels, a Day of Judgement, life after death, and that all power belongs to God alone. The word *Muslim* means 'anyone or anything that submits itself to the will of God'. Followers of Islam number over 1.5 billion worldwide. Along with Judaism and Christianity, it is considered to be one of the three Abrahamic traditions; that is, all descend from Abraham (see the Old Testament). Islam is one of the fastest growing religions in the world. It is a complete way of living that governs all facets of life: moral, spiritual, social, political, economical and intellectual. Muslims believe in and acknowledge all the prophets of old, from Adam to Jesus.

Kaaba: In their five daily prayers, Muslims face the Kaaba in Mecca, Saudi Arabia. It is a cube-shaped stone structure that was originally built by Prophet Adam and later rebuilt by Prophet Abraham. Muslims believe that the Kaaba was the first house of worship on Earth dedicated to the worship of one god. Muslims do not worship the Kaaba, but it serves as a central focal point for Muslims around the world, unifying them in worship and symbolizing their common belief, spiritual focus and direction.

Laity, lay man or lay woman: Members of the Christian Church who do not belong to the clergy.

Lectio divina: An ancient Christian tradition going back to the early Church. It is a slow meditative reading, usually of Holy Scripture, which results in a state of inner prayer and contemplation. Part of the daily devotional practices of Christian monasteries, it is being carried out today by an increasing number of lay people. Some monasteries now offer *Lectio divina* retreats.

Listening: In the spiritual sense and in personal retreat guidance, to truly listen to another person is to hear at a deep level what the other person is actually saying from her or his heart – not just the words but what they signify for that person. It springs both from religious concepts of listening to the Word of God – in other words a way of hearing with the heart – and from many of the contemporary techniques of psychotherapy where listening plays a key role.

Masculine spirituality: Men's ritual retreats renew the positive aspect of masculinity by bringing men together to live in harmony for a few days of retreat in which they open themselves to each other about deep feelings – how it is to be a man and how they feel about spiritual issues and the more profound questions of living. These are aspects of men's lives that they usually do not openly discuss.

Massage: Massage counteracts stress by bringing about deep relaxation of the body and person. As the muscles relax, breathing improves and circulation strengthens. It helps restore harmony and balance to the mind and body. It also strengthens the body itself.

Meditation: In Christian meditation, the term denotes mental prayer. Its method is the devout reflection on a chosen, often biblical, theme to deepen spiritual insight. In Buddhist and Hindu practice, meditation is a way towards personal development by directly working on the mind to transform it. Although there are hundreds of approaches to meditation, these divide into two main streams of practice. One is to calm and refresh the mind, relax the body and relieve psychological tensions so a deeply contented state is achieved. The other aims at developing wisdom in the context of self, others and the nature of all things. Breathing techniques are often part of the meditation method.

Melkite: The Melkite Greek Catholic Church and the Roman Latin Catholic Church are the same religion. For more information go to the website for the Melkite Greek Catholic Church Information Center: www.mliles.com/melkite (email: mliles@mliles.com).

Monks, nuns, religious: Monks are men and nuns (or sisters) are women who have vowed to live a life together in a community of one gender, devoted to seeking God or enlightenment. They may be Christian, for example, and may make promises of poverty, chastity and obedience. Buddhism also has monks and nuns who live in communities, as does Hinduism.

Myers-Briggs retreats: Isabel Myers-Briggs spent 40 years investigating personality types, building upon the research into personality done by Carl Jung. She set out eight qualities or characteristics found in each person. Myers-Briggs believed there were 16 personality types, all of which are either introverted or extroverted, and either perceiving or judging. By discovering which Myers-Briggs personality type you are, you select the form of spirituality that best suits you. The idea is that some personalities respond better and more easily to one form of spirituality than another.

Non-religious: Belonging to no established religion or faith. This does not mean you are an atheist.

Non-retreatant: A description often used by those running retreat houses and used in this guide. It refers to a person who is staying at a retreat centre for rest and relaxation during a short, quiet holiday and is not planning to attempt anything of a spiritual nature. Many places do not want visitors who only desire a holiday and this is understandable. Other places actively encourage this type of guest.

Order: Monks, nuns and religious belong to Orders that dictate the type of life they lead. Among the best known Orders in Western Christianity are: the Society of Jesus, noted for teaching and missionary work; the Benedictines, with an emphasis on prayer, work and study of scripture and holy books; the Dominicans, who are known for intellectual study; the Carmelites, who lead a life centred on silent prayer and meditation; and the Franciscans, who follow the rule of St Francis of Assisi.

Pilgrim, pilgrimage: Journeys to holy places motivated by personal devotion, with the aim of obtaining supernatural help or as an act of penance or thanksgiving. Lourdes has acquired world fame as a place of pilgrimage (see France section). Pilgrims are those who are in the process of a pilgrimage.

Preached retreat: A group retreat in which a speaker or facilitator gives talks each day, usually on a particular theme with scripture as its core.

Private retreat: A retreat period of solitude and usually much silence without guidance or direction from anyone.

Reflexology: This ancient healing therapy originated in China centuries ago. It is a form of compression massage of the feet and hands in which energy pathways in the body are activated, benefiting self-healing and inducing a feeling of well-being. It is also used to treat specific areas of complaint or blocked energy.

Refectory: Monastery dining room.

Reiki: An Asian healing technique in which an energy transfer occurs between the therapist and the patient by the laying on of hands. This may promote healing, a sense of well-bring and the reduction of stress.

Sacrament: A sacrament is an outward and visible sign of an inward and spiritual grace given to Christians by Christ. In Christian theology, the term has wide variations. Three sacraments – Baptism, Confirmation and Orders – are held to be non-repeatable. The Eucharist (see entry above) is a sacrament.

Sacred sites: Since prehistoric times sacred sites have exerted a mysterious attraction to pilgrims from every region and religion. Such places are still believed by billions of people to offer the power of healing and spiritual awareness. They are places like the Grotto of Lourdes in France, Stonehenge or Glastonbury Tor in Great Britain and the Ganges River in India.

St Benedict, the Rule of St Benedict: St Benedict (480–543) is considered the founder of Western Monasticism. Religious life as he conceived it is essentially social. He developed rules for successful monastic living, known as the *Rule of St Benedict* or sometimes by the title of the *Household of God.* His instructions are entirely occupied with regulating the life of a community of men or women who have chosen to live, work, pray and eat together. It is a moderate and reasonable balance of ordinary human needs and feelings. The Rule is widely used in Catholic religious communities. Today, it has become increasingly popular among lay Catholics as a guide to daily living.

St Teresa of Avila: St Teresa of Avila (1515–82) wrote *The Interior Castle* in order to lead individuals from the beginnings of spiritual growth to the heights of mysticism. The steps she describes in this work constitute Teresian spirituality. These steps are viewed as mansions, and we progress in our spiritual pilgrimage from one to the next. The seven mansions are those of self-knowledge, detachment, humility and aridity, affective prayer, the beginning of our union with God, the mystical experience or the prayer of quiet, and, finally, the last mansion of peaceful union with God. Teresian spirituality is, at once, both logical and mystical.

Scripture, Holy Scripture: The sacred writings of the Old and New Testament, together known as the Bible.

Shamanism, Shaman: One of the religions in which all the good and evil of life is thought to be brought about by spirits that can be influenced only by Shamans. Shamanic religions include those of the North American Natives and people of the Ural region in Siberia. A Shaman is a priest or medicine-man, a *master of ecstasy* in touch with the realm of experience or reality that exists outside the limited, narrow state of our normal waking consciousness. By performing certain acts and rituals, a Shaman is able to influence good and evil spirits and change consciousness to bring about a greater state of wholeness. It is widely used for the discovery of the inner person and for healing. Shamanism, particularly that of Native Americans, has greatly increased its popularity in the West, especially in Great Britain and France (see Eagle's Wing Centre for Contemporary Shamanism in the London section). Programmes of many Mind Body Spirit places often include courses and workshops with shamanic themes or practices, such as sweat lodges, chanting, drumming, dancing.

Shiatsu: This is a powerful Japanese healing therapy. *Shiatsu* means 'finger pressure' and when it is applied on specific areas, blocked energies are released with increased circulation and general flexibility resulting.

Sufism: Sufism is a commitment to the practical and accessible aspects of Islam but emphasises the inner or mystical aspects of the faith. The members of Sufi Orders may use various aids for their spiritual development, including meditation, chanting or ritual dancing.

Swedenborg: The New Jerusalem Church was based on the theological writings of Emanuel Swedenborg (1688–1772). His works had an immense impact upon the shaping of the world as we know it today, especially through poets and artists. People who follow these beliefs are called Swedenborgians and they claim a world membership of around 50,000.

Tai Chi (chuan): Ancient Chinese method to achieve meditation through movement in a series of flowing, extremely graceful, slow and gentle movements or exercises intended to quiet the inner self, the mind and the body. The movements also actively exercises most of the muscles of the body. They can be done by people of any age.

Vipassana meditation: Insight meditation, originating in south-east Asia and now popular in Europe, practised to attain mindfulness and understanding of the nature of self and others. It assumes that kindness, compassion and generosity of spirit may be cultivated by a person.

Virgin Mary, the Blessed Virgin Mary, Mary: The mother of Jesus Christ. In the Bible, Mary figures prominently in the stories of Jesus' birth. Belief in Mary's intercessions through direct prayer to her is probably a very old Christian belief dating from the third to early fourth centuries. While there are others in the world, the most famous shrines to Mary are at Lourdes (see France section) and Fatima, where there were apparitions of her. Mary's presence in the New Testament stories is marked by her obedience to God and her humility.

Yoga: Yoga is one of the six main schools of Hinduism. Yoga philosophy regards both spirit and matter as real and traces the whole of the physical universe to a single source. In modern practice, especially in the West, some elements of yoga are emphasised more than others. The calm and deliberate movements in yoga can lend themselves to deep relaxation and a peaceful harmony between mind and body. Yoga in its various systems is now a global spiritual practice.

Zen: A transliteration of the Sanskrit word *Dhyana*, meaning 'meditation'.

WIN a weekend retreat at Croydon Hall in Somerset

Set within Exmoor National Park, Croydon Hall is a holistic training venue that is a haven of peace and quiet to which to retreat. We are offering you and a guest the chance to win a weekend retreat, where you can take some time out from your busy world to recharge your batteries and re-connect with yourself.

As well as two nights B&B, you will be able to enjoy a three-hour pass to the Hall's spa facilities where you can soak your tired muscles in the jacuzzi, relax in the steam room or use the Swedish sauna to get rid of those toxins. You can also stretch your legs in the six acres of grounds and enjoy walks in the surrounding countryside. Or if you are seeking a little bit of stillness, you will be able to participate in the group evening meditations. To view Croydon Hall's website please visit www.croydonhall.co.uk

To enter the competition all you need to do is answer the following question and email your answer to competitions@hayhouse.co.uk with *The Good Retreat Guide* in the subject header. Closing date for entries is 31st August 2010.

Q. Who is the author of *The Good Retreat Guide*?

Terms and Conditions

The competition prize is for one winner and a guest to enjoy two-nights bed and breakfast at Croydon Hall. Accommodation will be either a double or twin-bedded room, depending on request and availability. The winner and their guest will have access to the spa facilities for a three-hour maximum period once over the weekend. The prize also includes unlimited access to the outdoor pool (available March–November) and participation in the group meditations throughout the weekend. Any extras – including any treatments, telephone use, bar bills or meals – are to be paid for by the winner. This prize cannot be exchanged for cash and cannot be used against any other retreats that Croydon Hall runs or any workshops that are run by third party organisers at the Hall. By entering the competition you will automatically join the Hay House and Croydon Hall mailing lists. No multiple entries allowed. All entrants must be aged 18 or over. All entries must be received by 31st August 2010; the competition winner will be informed by 10th September 2010. Prize must be claimed within six months of the winner being notified.

NOTES

NOTES

NOTES

NOTES

NOTES

NOTES

NOTES

NOTES

NOTES

JOIN THE HAY HOUSE FAMILY

As the leading self-help, mind, body and spirit publisher in the UK, we'd like to welcome you to our family so that you can enjoy all the benefits our website has to offer.

 EXTRACTS from a selection of your favourite author titles

 COMPETITIONS, PRIZES & SPECIAL OFFERS Win extracts, money off, downloads and so much more

 LISTEN to a range of radio interviews and our latest audio publications

 CELEBRATE YOUR BIRTHDAY An inspiring gift will be sent your way

 LATEST NEWS Keep up with the latest news from and about our authors

 ATTEND OUR AUTHOR EVENTS Be the first to hear about our author events

 iPHONE APPS Download your favourite app for your iPhone

 HAY HOUSE INFORMATION Ask us anything, all enquiries answered

join us online at **www.hayhouse.co.uk**

 292B Kensal Road, London W10 5BE
T: 020 8962 1230 E: info@hayhouse.co.uk

We hope you enjoyed this Hay House book.
If you would like to receive a free catalogue featuring additional
Hay House books and products, or if you would like information
about the Hay Foundation, please contact:

Hay House UK Ltd
292B Kensal Road • London W10 5BE
Tel: (44) 20 8962 1230; Fax: (44) 20 8962 1239
www.hayhouse.co.uk

***

Published and distributed in the United States of America by:
Hay House, Inc. • PO Box 5100 • Carlsbad, CA 92018-5100
Tel: (1) 760 431 7695 or (1) 800 654 5126;
Fax: (1) 760 431 6948 or (1) 800 650 5115
www.hayhouse.com

***

Published and distributed in Australia by:
Hay House Australia Ltd • 18/36 Ralph Street • Alexandria, NSW 2015
Tel: (61) 2 9669 4299, Fax: (61) 2 9669 4144
www.hayhouse.com.au

***

Published and distributed in the Republic of South Africa by:
Hay House SA (Pty) Ltd • PO Box 990 • Witkoppen 2068
Tel/Fax: (27) 11 467 8904
www.hayhouse.co.za

***

Published and distributed in India by:
Hay House Publishers India • Muskaan Complex • Plot No.3
B-2• Vasant Kunj • New Delhi - 110 070
Tel: (91) 11 41761620; Fax: (91) 11 41761630
www.hayhouse.co.in

***

Distributed in Canada by:
Raincoast • 9050 Shaughnessy St • Vancouver, BC V6P 6E5
Tel: (1) 604 323 7100
Fax: (1) 604 323 2600

***

Sign up via the Hay House UK website to receive the Hay House
online newsletter and stay informed about what's going on with your
favourite authors. You'll receive bimonthly announcements
about discounts and offers, special events, product highlights,
free excerpts, giveaways, and more!
www.hayhouse.co.uk